# Borland Turbo Assembler Reference

# Debugging and Profiling

## Turbo Debugger and Profiler Command Line Reference

## Supporting Utilities Reference

## TOOLHELP.DLL and STRESS.DLL Function Reference

# Help Compiler Reference

## New Features in Version 3.1 Help Compiler

## Help Compiler Project Reference

THE WAITE GROUP®

# BORLAND C++
# DEVELOPER'S BIBLE

MARK PETERSON

WAITE GROUP
PRESS™

Corte Madera, California

AA3 6217

**Editorial Director**  *Scott Calamar*
**Development Editor**  *Mitchell Waite*
**Content Editor**  *Harry Henderson*
**Design and Production**  *Barbara Gelfand*
**Illustrations**  *Frances Hasegawa*
**Cover Design**  *Kathy Locke; Locke & Veach*
**Production Manager**  *Julianne Ososke*

Waite Group Press is distributed to bookstores and book wholesalers by Publishers Group West, Box 8843, Emeryville, CA 94662, 1-800-788-3123 (in California 1-510-658-3453).

Printed in the United States of America

92 93 94 95 • 10 9 8 7 6 5 4 3 2 1

Library of Congress Cataloging in Publication Data

Peterson, Mark (Mark C.)
    Borland C++ developer's Bible / Mark Peterson.
        p. cm.
    Includes index.
    ISBN: 1-878739-16-6: $29.95
    1. C++ (Computer program language) 2. Turbo C++ (Computer program)
I. Title.
QA76.73.C15P49  1992
005.26'2--dc20

                                                        92-22012
                                                         CIP

# PREFACE

About a month after I started using BC++ version 2.0, I became curious about an item in the system menu called GREP. What exactly did GREP do and how could I use it to help develop applications? I finally found the documentation for GREP in a text file of the DOC directory that was created by the BC++ INSTALL utility. Much to my surprise, this DOC directory also included a wealth of information on other useful utilities, many of which I didn't previously know existed.

As I worked with the text files, I found that they were rather hard to use as a reference. One reason is that they are organized as tutorials. This is a good arrangement for learning about the utility, but it isn't much help in day-to-day usage. Secondly, I found it very cumbersome loading the text files into an editor window any time I needed to look up a command switch or syntax for one of the utilities. Printing the text files helped a little, but because I don't keep the most tidy desk in the world, they kept getting lost in the chaos of other paperwork. "What I need," I thought, "is a book that documents all these utilities." However, none of the books I could find on BC++ make any mention at all of the BC++ utilities.

Well, if no one else was going to write the book I wanted, I decided I might as well write it myself. I didn't think too many people would be interested in a book on just the BC++ utilities, so I thumbed through the BC++ manuals looking for ideas on other topics I could cover. I soon realized that while Borland does an excellent job of presenting the compiler options, they do not cover them to any depth. How many people actually knew what these compiler options were actually doing to their applications? Without this information, it is difficult to determine when an option should be used and when it should be avoided.

I've written this book with the intention of providing hard copy documentation on the BC++ utilities. I've also treated the main applications, such as compiler, linker, debugger, and profiler, as another form of utility and provided in-depth documentation on each of the command line options. For those of you C and C++ programmers who also know assembly language, I've included an entire chapter on writing inline assembly language in C and C++ applications. In that chapter, I've included documentation on how to include 80386 specific inline assembly language instructions. The last chapter of this book is a complete Windows application and Dynamic Link Library for generating high-speed fractals. It is written in a combination of both C++ and 80386 specific inline assembly language.

Mark C. Peterson

*To my wife, Lisa,*
*and my daughter, Samantha*

# ACKNOWLEDGMENTS

Mitchell Waite and Scott Calamar helped guide the overall direction of this book. Harry Henderson did a fabulous job of reviewing the initial draft and provided me with many useful suggestions. I'd like to thank the people at Borland for their help and technical expertise: Chopin Yen, Nan Borreson, Jeff Stock, Phil Rose, David Intersimeone, and the many others who helped with the technical review of this book. I'd also like to thank Tim Wegner for his help in starting this book, Bert Tyler for introducing me to the usefulness of fixed-point mathematics, and Chris J. Lusby Taylor for his suggested changes to my sine/cosine algorithm.

Dear Reader:

A lot more goes into writing a C or C++ program than procedural logic and proper syntax. The major manufacturers of computer languages and environments, as they are called today, provide a barrage of tools and utilities to build, text, and optimize your programs. The Borland C++ Application Framework package, for example, provides an entire professional development system of C and C++ compilers with a vast number of options to make programs run faster and more efficiently. There are assemblers to deal with machine code, there are linkers to turn object code into executables, and there are critical debugger programs to get the program running when the syntax is incorrect. The Borland package also contains the IDE interface, development systems for DOS and Windows, a library of custom objects, and much more.

The book you are holding in your hands, I think, fills a gaping void in the programmer's library. Unlike the Bibles that we have produced that cover the *syntax* of each C library function, the *Borland C++ Developer's Bible* documents in exacting detail the *tools* and *utility* programs that make up the Borland C and C++ environment. In the book you'll find information that goes well beyond Borland's own documentation, covering the MAKE utility, the Linker, the Turbo Assembler, the Debugger and Profiler, the Help Compiler, the Resource Utility, Object Windows, and even Borland Windows Custom Controls. The book demonstrates how to use these tools with concise, practical examples, and ties them all together in a fun and interesting fractal-generating program.

WAITE GROUP
PRESS™

We are also proud that this book completely details undocumented features added to Version 3.1 of Borland C++. Almost one hundred pages were added before going to press to completely cover the Help compiler's new macro library, the TOOLHELP and STRESS Windows debugging support libraries, Borland Windows Custom Controls (BWCC), the new compiler options for 386 code generation, object data calling, and much more!

 A catalog of our titles can be obtained by filling out our reader response card, found in this book. Thanks again for considering the purchase of this title. If you care to tell me anything you like (or don't like) about the book, please use our Reader Satisfaction Report Card, or write me direct in care of Waite Group Press. I can also be contacted on CompuServe as 75146,3515.

Sincerely,

*Mitchell Waite*

Mitchell Waite

# ABOUT THE AUTHOR

Mark Peterson is coauthor of the recent best-seller, *Fractal Creations*, which is based on the internationally popular program called *Fractint*. Mark wrote the majority of the math in *Fractint* using hand coded assembler routines. Some of these routines are described in Mark's article written for *Tech Specialist* ("Warp Speed Transcendentals," Oct. 1990). He is also the originator of the algorithm for the self-optimizing binary tree called a Precedence Tree, which is described in the article he wrote for *Dr. Dobbs Journal* ("Setting Precedence," Sept. 1989). Mark is the owner of *The Yankee Programmer*, a computer consulting company that specializes in writing high performance algorithms and applications.

# INTRODUCTION

*The Waite Group's Borland C++ Developer's Bible* is divided into ten chapters. Each chapter focuses on one aspect of developing an application. The first section of each chapter is a tutorial that provides an overview of the chapter and provides you with a general idea of how to use the utilities covered in the chapter. Following the tutorial section is a reference section which details the command line options for the utility or the internal syntax for utilities such as those providedwith the Resource Compiler or Help Compiler.

## Chapter 1  The IDE and Supporting Utilities

This chapter covers the command line options BC++ IDE, how to use GREP, and also how to create and load custom editor macros using TEMC. It also covers THELP, UNZIP, and FCONVERT.

## Chapter 2  The Borland C++ Compiler Reference

This chapter covers all the compiler options available with the Borland C++ compiler, how you control them from the command line, and the menus for either the DOS and Windows IDE or from within the source code. This chapter also includes a discussion of how each option affects the code generated for your application.

## Chapter 3  Projects and Transfers

This chapter covers the IDE's project manager, how to write transfer items, and how to use transfer items as source code translators. The reference section documents the transfer macros. This chapter also covers the PRJ2MAK, PRJCFG, PRJCVNT, and TRANCOPY utilities.

## Chapter 4  Borland C++ Make Reference

This chapter covers the protected mode MAKE utility and its real mode counterpart, MAKER. The tutorial provides an in-depth discussion on how to write .MAK files for building an application. The reference section covers both the command line options and the directives you can use in the .MAK file.

## Chapter 5  Borland C++ Linker Reference

This chapter covers how to perform manual linking with TLINK for both DOS and Windows applications, TLINK's command line options, and the IMPLIB and TLIB utilities. It also includes a reference section on the module definition file (.DEF) statements.

## Chapter 6  Borland Turbo Assembler Reference

The first part of this chapter covers how to write inline assembly language instructions to manipulate data in C and C++ applications, how to enable the 80386 and 80387 instruction sets, and how to use TASM to compile the inline assembly instructions. The latter portion of this chapter is a reference section on the command line options for TASM.

## Chapter 7  Borland Turbo Debugger/Profiler Reference

This chapter covers the requirements, features, and advantages of each of the debugger and profiler utilities and their associated command line parameters. The supporting utilities that aid in debugging and profiling an application are also discussed, including their command line parameters and any applicable error messages. These include EMSTEST, TD286INS, TDDEV, TDINST, TDMAP, TDMEM, TDNMI, TDREMOTE, TDRF, TDSTRIP, TDWINST, TDUMP, TFINST, TFREMOTE, WINSIGHT, WREMOTE, and WRSETUP.

## Chapter 8  Help Compiler Reference

This chapter covers how to create help files for Windows application. The reference section covers the help compiler syntax. This chapter also documents portions of the Rich Text Format (RTF) for text files as it applies to the Help Compiler.

## Chapter 9  Resource Utility Reference

This chapter is a detailed reference to the RC and WORKSHOP utilities and the BWCC custom control library. This chapter also covers the creation of custom controls that can be used by the WORKSHOP resource editor.

## Chapter 10  Fractal DLL and Application

In this chapter we will design and develop a full-fledged Windows application and Dynamic Link Library that draws a variety of fractals. It is written in a combination of C++ and 80386 specific inline assembly language. This chapter also includes a fixed point and custom floating-point C++ math library, which you should find useful in other applications.

# CONTENTS

# EXTENDED CONTENTS

## Chapter 2  Borland C++ Compiler Reference 49

## Chapter 3  Projects and Transfers  237

# Chapter 5  Borland C++ Linker Reference 325

## Chapter 6  Borland Turbo Assembler Reference   389

## Chapter 7  Borland Turbo Debugger/Profiler Reference  429

## Chapter 8  Help Compiler Reference 569

## Chapter 9  Resource Utility Reference 655

## Chapter 10  Fractal DLL and Application     747

# THE IDE AND SUPPORTING UTILITIES

# 1

The Integrated Developer's Environment (IDE) is an editor, compiler, linker, project manager, and debugger all in one. In it, you can create, compile, and debug almost all your DOS applications without ever leaving the IDE. This greatly speeds application development, especially during the debugging stage, when you are constantly testing, modifying, and recompiling your source code. Also included with the Borland C++ (BC++) compiler package are several utilities that work with the IDE to help you develop your source code. These include TEMC for compiling IDE macros and assigning them to keystokes, and GREP for searching text files for specific strings. BC++ also includes a memory-resident help application, called THELP, which provides access to the IDE's help files if you choose to use an external text editor. If during the course of development you find you need a file that you did not load onto the hard disk during installation, you can use the UNZIP utility to extract the file from the distribution disks. Windows programmers sometimes need to convert DOS text files (also refered to as OEM text files) into the standard ANSI text files used in Windows. BC++ includes the FCONVERT utility for translating DOS text files to ANSI text files and vice versa.

This chapter covers the command line options BC++ IDE, how to use GREP, and also how to create and load custom editor macros using TEMC. It also covers THELP, UNZIP, and FCONVERT.

## THE BORLAND C++ INTEGRATED DEVELOPER'S ENVIRONMENT

The IDE centers around a fully functional text editor. The text editor in the IDE goes beyond merely allowing you to enter text. You block text selections by arrowing through the text while holding down the (Shift) key, you copy or cut blocks of text to the clipboard by using either (Ctrl)-(Ins) or (Shift)-(Del), respectively, and you paste text from the clipboard to the text editor by pressing (Shift)-(Ins). Some keystrokes are different depending on whether you've selected the [CUA] (Common User Access) convention or the [Alternate] convention in the [Options][Environment][Preferences] menu. The CUA convention is the industry standard for keystroke assignment utilized by most Windows applications. The Alternate convention is the keystroke assignment used in Turbo C++

3

and BC++ Version 2.0. Many of these keystrokes are shortcuts to menu item selections, whereas others perform actions that have no menu item. Table 1-1 lists the keystokes and their actions. Note that you can reassign most of these keystokes by editing and recompiling the DEFAULT.TEM macro script as described later in this chapter.

| CUA | ALTERNATE | MENU | DESCRIPTION |
|---|---|---|---|
| | `Ctrl`-`F3` | Debug \| Call stack | Display the function call stack |
| | `Ctrl`-`F4` | Debug \| Evaluate/Modify | Evaluate an expression |
| | `Ctrl`-`F5` | | Resize or reposition the active window |
| | `F2` | File \| Save | Save the active editor window |
| | `F3` | File \| Open | Open a text file |
| | `F4` | Run \| Go to cursor | Execute the application to the line of source code located at the cursor's position |
| | `F5` | Window \| Zoom | Resize the currently active window to cover the entire screen |
| `Alt`-`1` | `Alt`-`1` | | Activate window #1 |
| `Alt`-`2` | `Alt`-`2` | | Activate window #2 |
| `Alt`-`3` | `Alt`-`3` | | Activate window #3 |
| `Alt`-`4` | `Alt`-`4` | | Activate window #4 |
| `Alt`-`5` | `Alt`-`5` | | Activate window #5 |
| `Alt`-`6` | `Alt`-`6` | | Activate window #6 |
| `Alt`-`7` | `Alt`-`7` | | Activate window #7 |
| `Alt`-`8` | `Alt`-`8` | | Activate window #8 |
| `Alt`-`9` | `Alt`-`9` | | Activate window #9 |
| `Alt`-`BS` | `Alt`-`BS` | Edit \| Undo | "Undo" the previous editor action |
| `Alt`-`F1` | `Alt`-`F1` | Help \| Previous topic | Display the previous help topic |
| `Alt`-`F4` | `Alt`-`X` | File \| Exit | Exit the IDE |
| `Alt`-`F5` | `Alt`-`F4` | Debug \| Inspect | Display the inspector window |
| `Alt`-`F7` | `Alt`-`F7` | Search \| Previous error | Highlight the previous compiler error |
| `Alt`-`F8` | `Alt`-`F8` | Search \| Next error | Highlight the next compiler error |
| `Alt`-`F9` | `Alt`-`F9` | Compile \| Compile | Compile the currently active editor window |
| `Alt`-`0` | `Alt`-`0` | Window \| List | Display the list of open windows |
| `Alt`-`Shift`-`BS` | `Alt`-`Shift`-`BS` | Edit \| Redo | "Undo" the previous "Undo" (i.e., Redo) |
| `Ctrl`-`Del` | `Ctrl`-`Del` | Edit \| Clear | Delete the selected block of text |

| Ctrl-Ins | Ctrl-Ins | Edit | Copy | Copy the selected block of text to the clipboard |
|---|---|---|---|
| Ctrl-F1 | Ctrl-F1 | Help | Topic search | Context sensitive help |
| Ctrl-F2 | Ctrl-F2 | Run | Program reset | Restart the application |
| Ctrl-F4 | Alt-F3 | Window | Close | Close the currently active window |
| Ctrl-F5 | Ctrl-F7 | Debug | Add watch | Add a watch expression |
| Ctrl-F6 | F6 | Window | Next | Activate the next window in the window list |
| Ctrl-F9 | Ctrl-F9 | Run | Run | Run the application |
| F1 | F1 | Help | Display the help screen |
| F1-F1 | F1-F1 | Help | Help on Help | Display the Help on Help screen |
| F3 | Ctrl-L | Search | Search Again | Repeat last search |
| F5 | Ctrl-F8 | Debug | Toggle Break-Point | Set or clear a breakpoint |
| F7 | F7 | Run | Trace into | Trace into a function call |
| F8 | F8 | Run | Step over | Step over a function call |
| F9 | F9 | Compile | Make | Recompile any changed source code files and link |
| F10 | F10 | | Highlight the menu bar |
| Shift-Del | Shift-Del | Edit | Cut | Copy the selected block of text to the clipboard and delete |
| Shift-F1 | Shift-F1 | Help | Index | Display the help index |
| Shift-F5 | Alt-F5 | Window | User screen | Display the application's output screen |
| Shift-Ins | Shift-Ins | Edit | Paste | Insert the contents of the clipboard into the text |

**Table 1-1 IDE Editor keystrokes**

You execute the IDE for BC++ by running BC.EXE. BC uses the following command line syntax:

```
bc [options] [project/source[source][. . .]]
```

BC always loads three different files when it executes: a configuration (.TC) file, a desktop (.DSK) file, and a project (.PRJ) file. The .TC file contains information on editor settings, the keyboard macros, auto save flags, and mouse settings. The .PRJ file contains the compiler and liner settings, the directory paths, the files compiled by the project, and translator information for compiling assembly language and resource files. The .DSK file contains information on open windows in the IDE, history lists, watches, breakpoints, and the contents of the IDE's clipboard.

If you execute BC without any command line options, BC will load the project (.PRJ) file located in the current directory. If there is no project file in the current directory, there is more than one .PRJ file, or you list source files on the command line instead of project files, then BC will load the default project file called TCDEF.DPR and the default desktop file called TCDEF.DSK. Any changes you make to the IDE settings when no project is open are saved to these default files. The IDE also uses the settings in the default files when creating a new project.

BC will load a specific project file if you list it on the command line using the .PRJ file extension. For example, the following command line loads the MYAPP.PRJ project:

```
bc myapp.prj
```

BC will automatically load the associate desktop file called MYAPP.DSK or create one if it does not exist.

BC also automatically loads the configuration file called TCCONFIG.TC located in the current directory. If BC cannot find the configuration file in the current directory, then it will look for the file in the same directory as BC.EXE. The arrangement allows you to have different macro sets for different projects by placing custom configuration files in the same directory as your project and starting BC from your project directory. See the TEMC utility described later in this chapter for more information on defining macros and keystroke assignments.

## Turbo C++ (TC++) for Windows

Also included with BC++ Version 3.0 is Turbo C++ for Windows (TCW). It is important to remember that TCW is a Windows version of TC++ and not a Windows version of BC++. Not all the applications you can create using BC++ are compatible with TCW. For example, TCW will only compile Windows applications and Windows Dynamic Link Libraries. It does not support any of the new optimization features found in BC++. It does not support transfer items, which means you are restricted to the 8088 and 80286 instruction set for inline assembly language and also cannot use .ASM files in your project list. It does not support the compilation of resource script files and instead relies on you to manually create the binary resource file using either Resource Workshop or calling RC (the Resource Compiler) from DOS. This book assumes for the most part that you are using BC++ to create your Windows applications instead of TCW. However, this book does list the elements of BC++ that correspond to elements of TCW where applicable.

Note that object code (.OBJ) files containing C++ code compiled using BC++ Version 3.0 are *not* compatible by default with those compiled using TCW (or earlier versions of BC++ for that matter). BC++ compiles C++ code using advanced coding techniques that are incompatible with the older techniques used in TCW. You use the -Vo option on the BCC command line to enable all the BC++ backward compatibility options. If you compile your code in the BC++ IDE, enable all the options listed in the "Options" section of the [Options][Compiler][Advanced C++ Options] menu and select the [Same size as 'this' pointer] option to maintain compatibility with TC++ and TCW.

## Borland C++ for Windows

BC++ Version 3.1 includes a Windows hosted version of the IDE called Borland C++ for Windows, or BCW. This compiler is fully compatible with the DOS compiler and does not require setting any of the backward compatibility options. It also contains an integrated resource compiler which is capable of compiling resource script files as well as binding binary resource files to the executables built using BCW. However, as with TCW, BCW will only compile Windows applications and Dynamic Link Libaries and does not support transfer items. One other restriction is that the resulting applications and DLLs will only run on a machine with an 80286 or better.

## BC Command Line Options Reference

The following is a list of command line options used by BC. Of the following command line options, TCW and BCW only support the /b and /m options.

You can list as many options as you like on the command line. Following a command line option with a '-' disables the option, whereas you enable an option by placing a '+' character after the option. BC assumes a '+' character if you do not specifically use the '-' symbol.

Note that the command line options are not case sensitive. Also, you must precede the option with a '/' character.

---

## /b                                                                      Build Project

---

### Purpose
You use the /b option to build a project file automatically and then exit the IDE.

### Default
/b–

Enter the IDE in the interactive mode.

### Usage
BC /b MYAPP.PRJ

Rebuild MYAPP.PRJ and exit.

### Description
The /b option allows you to build project files without having to select the [Compile][Build] menu item in the IDE. The IDE rebuilds all the target files in the project list even if they are not out of date. The IDE then exits to DOS and prints the contents of the "Message" window to the standard output. This feature allows you to rebuild several projects by executing a single batch (.BAT) file and to capture any errors to a file using DOS redirection.

This option is identical to the /m option, except that it rebuilds all the source files.

### See Also

/m                                Make Project
Chapter 7: b (Profilers)          Batch Mode Profiling

## /d                                                    Dual Monitor Display Mode

### Purpose

You use the /d option if you have two monitors on your system and you want the IDE displayed on the secondary monitor.

### Default

/d–

> Display the IDE on the primary monitor.

### Usage

BC /d

> Display the IDE on the secondary monitor.

### Description

If your system is equipped with two monitors, such as a monochrome and a color monitor, you can use the /d option to display the IDE on the secondary monitor and use the primary monitor exclusively for your application. This is especially useful in graphics programming when you need to debug a section of code which accesses the video hardware registers. It is also convenient for normal programming, as it allows you to continuously view the output of your program on the primary monitor while stepping through the source code on the secondary monitor.

There are a few things you should not do when operating in the dual monitor mode:

- Do not change monitors using the MODE command while in the IDE's DOS shell.
- Do not access the video ports for the secondary monitor.
- Do not run an application that utilizes the secondary monitor.

Note that the /d option is ignored if the IDE does not detect two monitors on your system.

### See Also

/l                                LCD Display Mode
Chapter 7: do, dp, ds             Local Display Mode

## /e[=Pages]                                           Swap with Expanded Memory

### Purpose

You use the /e option to instruct the IDE to reserve all expanded memory for use by the IDE if necessary. The 'Pages' parameter specifies the number of EMS pages to be reserved.

## Default

/e

Reserve all available expanded memory for use by the IDE.

## Usage

BC /e–

Do not use expanded memory.

BC /e=4

Reserve only four pages (64K) of expanded memory for use by the IDE.

## Description

The IDE uses expanded memory during compilation to make more room for large applications by swapping portions of main memory with expanded memory. The /e option, which is enabled by default, reserves all available expanded memory for use by the IDE. If your application also needs to use expanded memory, you should limit the amount of expanded memory reserved by the IDE by using the /e=*Pages* option, or simply instructing the IDE not to use any expanded memory with the /e- option.

Note that if your application uses expanded memory but your system only has extended memory, you can use the -f*Segment* option for the standalone debuggers to emulate expanded memory for your application using your system's extended memory.

## See Also

| | |
|---|---|
| /r*Drive* | Set Swap Drive |
| /r | Set Swap Drive |
| /x[=*kBytes*] | Extended Memory Allocation |
| Chapter 2: Qe, Qx | Expanded and Extended Memory Usage |
| Chapter 7: -f*Segment* | EMS Emulation |
| Chapter 7: y*kBytes*, ye*Pages* | Overlay Pool Size |


## /h, /?                                  Display the BC Help Screen

## Purpose

The /h and /? options display the help screen for BC.

## Default

None.

## Usage

BC /h

Display the help screen for the IDE.

BC /?

Same as above.

## Description

The /h and /? options display the following help screen:

```
Borland C++ Version 3.0  Copyright (c) 1990, 1991 Borland International
Syntax:  BC [option [option...]] [srcname|projname [srcname...]]

srcname   is any ASCII file (default extension assumed)
projname  is a project file (must have .PRJ extension)
option    is any of the following: (/x- = turn option x off):
/b                batch mode build project then exit
/d                dual monitor mode with BC++ on the other monitor
/e[=n]          * use n pages of expanded memory for swapping
/h                displays this help
/l                LCD/B&W colors for screen
/m                batch mode make project then exit
/p                restore palette on EGA after swap
/rx               use alternate disk 'x' for swap file
/s              * allow maximum swapping (thrashing)
/x[=n]            use n KB for the code and data memory pool
                * means enabled by default
```

# /l

**LCD Display Mode**

## Purpose

You use the /l option to specify suitable colors if you are running BC on an LCD screen.

## Default

/l–

Display the IDE using normal colors.

## Usage

BC /l

Display the IDE using colors suitable for an LCD display.

## Description

The default colors for the IDE do not display well on the LCD screen used by most portable and laptop computers. The /l option displays the IDE using colors more suitable for LCD screens.

## See Also

/d     Dual Monitor Display Mode

# /m                                                                    Make Project

## Purpose
You use the /m option when you want to make a project automatically and then exit the IDE.

## Default
`/m-`
> Enter the IDE in the interactive mode.

## Usage
`BC /m MYAPP.PRJ`
> Rebuild MYAPP.PRJ and exit.

## Description
The /m option allows you to make a project file without having to select the [Compile][Make] menu item. The IDE rebuilds all target files if the associated source file was modified since the last build. The IDE exits to DOS and prints the contents of the "Message" window to the standard output. This feature allows you to rebuild several projects by executing a single batch (.BAT) file and to capture any errors to a file using DOS redirection.

   This option is identical to the /b option, except that it only rebuilds the files which have changed since the last build.

## See Also
| | |
|---|---|
| /b | Build Project |
| Chapter 7: b (Profilers) | Batch Mode Profiling |

# /p                                                                  Preserve Palette

## Purpose
You use the /p option to preserve the video palette registers if your application modifies the display colors. This keeps your application from interfering with the IDE display and vice versa.

## Default
`/p-`
> Do not preserve the video palette registers.

## Usage

BC /p

> Preserve the original video palette registers.

## Description

You use the /p option if your application modifies the display palette. This option saves the colors of the video display registers and restores them to the original state when the screen is swapped to the IDE display or you exit the IDE. The /p option also restores the display colors set by your application when the IDE display is inactive.

## See Also

Chapter 7:  vp     Preserve Video Palette

# /rDrive                                              Set Swap Drive

## Purpose

You use the /r option to set the swap drive used by the IDE to a specific disk drive.

## Default

/r-

> Use the drive containing BC.EXE as the swap disk.

## Usage

BC -re

> Use the E: drive as the swap disk.

## Description

The IDE swaps memory to the disk during compilation if it runs out of main memory and expanded memory. You use the -r*Drive* option to instruct the IDE to use a disk on the one containing BC.EXE, such as a RAM disk. For example, if BC.EXE is located on the C: drive, then the IDE will use the C: drive as the swap disk. However, if you have a RAM disk as, say, the E: drive, you should use the -re option to instruct the IDE to use E: instead of C:.

## See Also

/e[=*Pages*]     Swap with Expanded Memory
/x[=*kBytes*]    Extended Memory Allocation

## /s                                        Use Overlay Space

### Purpose
You use the /s option to make more room for internal memory tables at the expense of overlay space. This option is obsolete in BC++ Version 3.0.

### Description
The old real mode IDE in BC++ Version 2.0 used overlays. The /s option, which was on by default, sometimes crowded out the memory space used for overlay swapping and resulted in "disk thrashing," or extensive use of the disk drive. Disabling the /s option corrected the thrashing problem. BC++ Versions 3.0 and 3.1, however, only operate in the protected mode and do not use overlays.

## /x[=*kBytes*]                          Extended Memory Allocation

### Purpose
You use the /x[=*kBytes*] option to specify how much memory the IDE is allowed to use. The *kBytes* parameter specifies the number of kilobytes to reserve for use by the IDE.

### Default
/x
    Use all available extended memory.

### Usage
BC /x=1500
    Use only 1.5MB of extended memory for the IDE.

### Description
The IDE normally reserves all available extended memory for its own use, leaving none for the application. You use the /x option to limit the amount of extended memory reserved by the IDE so as to leave some available for your application.

### See Also
| | |
|---|---|
| /e[=*Pages*] | Swap with Expanded Memory |
| /r*Drive* | Set Swap Drive |
| Chapter 2:  Qe, Qx | Expanded and Extended Memory Usage |
| Chapter 7:  y*kBytes*, ye*Pages* | Overlay Pool Size |

## The IDE Editor Macro Compiler Reference

The IDE uses macros assigned to specific keystrokes to implement many of the functions in the IDE. These macro definitions and keystroke assignments are stored in a configuration file used by the IDE called TCCONFIG.TC. The TEMC utility is a compiler that either modifies or creates this configuration file, which can be used by either the DOS IDE (BC.EXE) or the Windows IDE (TCW.EXE). The following is the syntax for the TEMC utility:

```
temc [-c][-u] script[.TEM] config[.TC]
```

TEMC will read the *script* file and either modify or create the *config* file. All the old macro definitions are discarded if you use the -c option. TEMC normally modifies the alternate character set, i.e., the macro set in use when the [Options][Environment][Preferences] [Alternate] menu option is set. The -u option modifies the macro set in use with the [CUA] (Common User Access) menu item selection in the [Options][Environment][Preferences] menu.

The BC++ compiler package installs five script files in the \BORLANDC\DOC directory. They are as follows:

| File | Usage |
| --- | --- |
| BRIEF.TEM | Contains macros for emulating the Brief programmer's editor. |
| CMACROS.TEM | Contains macros useful when writing C or C++ applications. See the CMACROS reference later in this section. |
| DEFAULTS.TEM | Contains the default macros used by the IDE. Modifying this file enables you to change the default macro definitions and key assignments. |
| DOSEDIT.TEM | Contains the macros for emulating the MS-DOS 5.0 EDIT.EXE text editor. |
| EPSILON.TEM | Contains the macros for emulating the Epsilon programmer's editor. |

## Macro Definitions and Comments

The script files contain three types of entries: comments, macro definitions, and key assignments. Comments in the macro script use the same /* and */ character delimiters as normal C and C++ comments. Macro definitions use the following syntax:

```
MACRO name
    command;
    [command;]
    . . .
END;
```

The *name* parameter is the name you assign the macro definition. The *command* parameter is the name of a previously defined macro. This can either be a macro defini-

14

tion in another part of the script or one of the predefined macros listed in either Table 1-2 or Table 1-3. Table 1-2 lists the predefined macros that perform their tasks without leaving the editor window. Table 1-3 lists the predefined macros that either leave the editor window temporarily or exit the current editor window entirely. Note that macro names compiled by TEMC are not case sensitive.

The following example creates a macro definition for placing a copyright notice:

```
/* Copyright macro definition */
MACRO Copyright
   InsertText("/*  Copyright (C) 1991, Mark C. Peterson.\n");
   InsertText("    All rights reserved.\n");
   InsertText("*/\n\n");
end;
```

| MACRO | ACTION |
|---|---|
| BackspaceDelete | Destructive backspace that deletes the character passed over. |
| BottomOfScreen | Move to the bottom of the screen. |
| CenterFixScreenPos | Adjust the screen, if necessary, to keep the cursor visible. Place the cursor as close to the center of the screen as possible if an adjustment is performed. |
| CopyBlock | Copy the selected text and mark the new location for the selected text. |
| CursorCharLeft | Move the cursor one character to the left, skipping over tab characters, or move to the end of the previous line. |
| CursorCharRight | Move the cursor one character to the right, skipping over tab characters, or move to the beginning of the next line. |
| CursorDown | Move the cursor down one screen row. |
| CursorLeft | Move the cursor one column to the left on the screen. |
| CursorRight | Move the cursor one column to the right on the screen. |
| CursorSwitchedLeft | Same as CursorLeft except this macro responds to the through cursor tab option. |
| CursorSwitchedRight | Same as CursorRight except this macro responds to the through cursor tab option. |
| CursorUp | Move the cursor up one screen row. |
| DeleteBlock | Delete the selected block of text. |
| DeleteChar | Delete the character under the cursor. |
| DeleteLine | Delete the line of text at the cursor. |
| DeleteToEOL | Delete the text from the cursor to the end of the line. |
| DeleteWord | Delete the text from the cursor location to the beginning of the next word. |
| EndCursor | Move the cursor to the end of the text file. |

*Table 1-2 (continued)*

| MACRO | ACTION |
|---|---|
| ExtendBlockBeg | Begin marking a block of text. |
| ExtendBlockEnd | Complete marking a block of text. |
| FixCursorPos | Place the cursor in a valid text column. |
| FixScreenPos | Place the cursor in a valid text location by adjusting the screen display. |
| FullPaintScreen | Redraw the entire screen. |
| HideBlock | Do not highlight blocked text. |
| HighlightBlock | Highlight blocked text. |
| HomeCursor | Move the cursor to the beginning of the text file. |
| IndentBlock | Indent the selected block of text. |
| InsertText | Insert a string literal into the text. |
| LeftOfLine | Move the cursor to the beginning of the line. |
| LiteralChar | Inserts a character literal into the text. |
| MarBufModified | Marks the text file as modified. |
| MarkBufUnModified | Marks the text file as unmodified. |
| MatchPairBackward | Search backward for the matching (') or (") character if one is located under the cursor and place the cursor at the matching location. |
| MatchPairForward | Search forward for the (') or (") character if one is located under the cursor and place the cursor at the matching location. |
| MoveBlock | Cut the selected block of text. |
| MoveToBlockBeg | Move the cursor to the beginning of the selected block of text. |
| MoveToBlockEnd | Move the cursor to the end of the selected block of text. |
| MoveTo Mark | Move the cursor to the 'n' location set by the SetMark(n) macro where 'n' is a decimal digit from 0–9. |
| MoveToPrevPos | Move the cursor to the position set by the SetPrevPos macro. |
| MoveToTempPos | Move the cursor to the position set by the SegTempPos macro. This macro is intended for internal use by the IDE. |
| NullCmd | Executes a NULL keystroke. You assign this macro to a keystroke you want to disable. |
| OutdentBlock | Unindents the selected block of text. |
| PageDown | Move the cursor down the number of lines in the window. |
| PageScreenDown | Scroll the screen down the number of lines in the window. |
| PageScreenUp | Scroll the screen up the number of lines in the window. |
| PageUp | Move the cursor up the number of lines in the window. |

| | |
|---|---|
| PaintScreen | Redraw the modified portions of the screen. |
| ReDo | Perform a Redo operation. (See the UnDo macro.) |
| RightOfLine | Move the cursor to the end of the line of text. |
| RightOfWord | Move the cursor to the beginning of the next word. |
| ScrollScreenDown | Scroll the screen down one line. |
| ScrollScreenUp | Scroll the screen up one line. |
| SetAutoIndent | Enable Auto Indenting. |
| SetAutoOutdent | Enable unindents via backspaces. |
| SetBlockBeg | Set the cursor location at the beginning of a block of text. |
| SetBlockEnd | Set the cursor location at the end of a block of text. |
| SetCursorThrough TabMode | Enable the through tabs option. |
| SetInsertMode | Enable the text insert mode. |
| SetMark | Mark the cursor location for later use by the MoveToMark(n) macro where 'n' is a digit between 0–9. |
| SetOptimalFillMode | Enable the optimal fill mode. |
| SetPrevPos | Save the cursor location for later use by the MoveToPrevPos macro or the SwapPrevPos macro. |
| SetTabbingMode | Enables the use of real tab characters. |
| SetTempPos | Save the cursor location for later use by the MoveToTempPos macro. This macro is intended for internal use by the IDE. |
| SmartRefreshScreen | Redraws the modified portions of the screen. |
| SmartTab | Insert either a real tab character or the appropriate number of spaces depending on the editor options settings. |
| SwapPrevPos | Exchange the current location of the cursor with the position saved with the SetPrevPos macro. |
| ToggleAutoIndent | Toggle the Auto Indent option state. |
| ToggleAutoOutdent | Toggle the Backspace Unindents option state. |
| ToggleCursorThrough TabMode | Toggles the Cursor Through Tabs option state. |
| ToggleHideBlock | Toggle the internal flag governing the highlighting of selected blocks of text. |
| ToggleInsert | Toggle the Insert/Overwrite option state. |
| ToggleOptimalFillMode | Toggle the Optimal Fill option state. |
| ToggleTabbingMode | Toggle the Use Tab Character option state. |
| TopOfScreen | Move the cursor to the top of the display window. |
| UnDo | UnDo the previous operation. (See the ReDo macro.) |

*Table 1-2 (continued)*

| MACRO | ACTION |
|---|---|
| WordLeft | Move the cursor to the start of the previous word. Move the cursor to the end of the previous line if the word is at the beginning of a line. |
| WordRight | Move the cursor to the beginning of the next word. Move the cursor to the beginning of the next line if the word is at the end of a line. |

**Table 1-2 Predefined macros that do not exit the editor**

| MACRO | ACTION |
|---|---|
| AddWatch | Select the [Debug][Watches] [Add Watch] menu item. |
| ChangeDirectory | Select the [File][Change Dir] menu item. |
| ChangeModeFlags | Restore mode flags, such as Insert/Overwrite and Auto Indent, to their menu item settings. |
| ClipCopy | Copy the selected block of text to the clipboard. |
| ClipCut | Cut the selected block of text to the clipboard. |
| ClipPaste | Insert the contents of the clipboard at the cursor location. |
| ClipShow | Display the contents of the clipboard. |
| CloseWindow | Close the current editor window. |
| CompileFile | Select the [Compile][Compile] menu item. |
| CompileMenu | Pull down the [Compile] menu. |
| CompilerOptions | Pull down the [Options][Compiler] menu. |
| DebugMenu | Pull down the [Debug] menu. |
| EditMenu | Pull down the [Edit] menu. |
| FileMenu | Pull down the [File] menu. |
| GetFindString | Open the [Search][Find] menu. |
| GotoWindow1 | Activate window #1. |
| GotoWindow2 | Activate window #2. |
| GotoWindow3 | Activate window #3. |
| GotoWindow4 | Activate window #4. |
| GotoWindow5 | Activate window #5. |
| GotoWindow6 | Activate window #6. |
| GotoWindow7 | Activate window #7. |
| GotoWindow8 | Activate window #8. |
| GotoWindow9 | Activate window #9. |

| | |
|---|---|
| Help | Open the Help window. |
| HelpMenu | Pull down the [**H**elp] menu. |
| HelpIndex | Open the [**H**elp][**I**ndex] window. |
| Inspect | Open the [**D**ebug][**I**nspect] window. |
| LastHelp | Display the previous Help window. |
| MakeProject | Select the [**C**ompile][**M**ake] menu item. |
| Menu | Highlight the menu bar. |
| Modify | Select the [**D**ebug][**E**valuate/Modify] menu. |
| NextError | Select the [**S**earch][**N**ext error] menu item. |
| NextWindow | Activate the next window in the IDE. |
| OpenFile | Select the [**F**ile][**O**pen] menu item. |
| OptionsMenu | Pull down the [**O**ptions] menu. |
| PrevError | Select the [**S**earch][**P**revious error] menu item. |
| PrintBlock | Print the selected block of text. |
| ProjectMenu | Pull down the [**P**roject] menu. |
| Quit | Exit the IDE. |
| ReadBlock | Open a dialog box to read a file into the editor window. |
| RepeatSearch | Select the [**S**earch][**S**earch again] menu item. |
| Replace | Select the [**S**earch][**R**eplace] menu item. |
| Reset Program | Select the [**R**un][**P**rogram reset] menu item. |
| RunMenu | Pull down the [**R**un] menu. |
| RunToHere | Select the [**R**un][**G**o to cursor] menu item. |
| SaveFile | Select the [**F**ile][**S**ave] menu item. |
| SaveFileAs | Select the [**F**ile][**Sa**ve as] menu item. |
| SearchMenu | Pull down the [**S**earch] menu. |
| Step | Select the [**R**un][**S**tep over] menu item. |
| SystemMenu | Pull down the system menu. |
| ToggleBreakpoint | Toggle the break point status of the source code line located at the cursor. |
| Trace | Select the [**R**un][**T**race into] menu item. |
| Transfer0 | Select transfer item #0. |
| Transfer1 | Select transfer item #1. |
| Transfer2 | Select transfer item #2. |
| Transfer3 | Select transfer item #3. |
| Transfer4 | Select transfer item #4. |

*Table 1-3 (continued)*

| | |
|---|---|
| Transfer5 | Select transfer item #5. |
| Transfer6 | Select transfer item #6. |
| Transfer7 | Select transfer item #7. |
| Transfer8 | Select transfer item #8. |
| Transfer9 | Select transfer item #9. |
| ViewCallStack | Select the [**D**ebug][**C**all stack] menu item. |
| ViewUserScreen | Select the [**W**indow][**O**utput] menu item. |
| WindowCascade | Select the [**W**indow][**C**ascade] menu item. |
| WindowList | Select the [**W**indow][**L**ist all] menu item. |
| WindowMenu | Pull down the [**W**indow] menu. |
| WindowTile | Select the [**W**indow][**T**ile] menu item. |
| WordHelp | Select the [**H**elp][**T**opic] search menu item. |
| WriteBlock | Open dialog box to write the selected block of text to a file. |
| ZoomWindow | Select the [**W**indow][**Z**oom] menu item. |

**Table 1-3 Predefined macros that exit the editor window**

## Macro Keystrokes Assignments

Macros are assigned to keystrokes using the following syntax:

```
keystroke : macro;
```

Table 1-4 lists the names for the 'keystroke' parameter, and 'name' is the name of the macro. For example, the 'Copyright' macro is assigned to the (Alt)-(Shift)-(C) keystroke by placing the following in the .TEM file:

```
Alt-Shift-c : Copyright;
```

You can also assign keystrokes directly to a series of macro commands without assigning the macro a name using the following syntax:

```
keystroke : BEGIN
   command;
   [command;]
   . . .
END;
```

For example, the copyright notice macro is assigned directly to the (Alt)-(Shift)-(C) key as follows:

```
Alt-Shift-c : BEGIN
   InsertText("/*  Copyright (C) 1992, Mark C. Peterson.\n");
   InsertText("    All rights reserved.\n");
```

```
        InsertText("*/\n\n");
    END;
```

The macro compiler also allows you to assign a series of keystrokes to a macro using the '+' character. For example, you use the following to invoke the 'Copyright' macro when you press (Ctrl)-(k) and then the (c) key:

```
Ctrl-k + c : Copyright;
```

The spaces before and after the '+' character are optional.

Note that the macro compiler distinguishes between upper- and lowercase keystrokes. The above macro definition will only work for lowercase. You instruct the macro compiler to accept either upper- or lowercase keystrokes by placing the '@' character immediately before the letter. For example, the following assignment allows the use of either (c) or (C) following the (Ctrl)-(k) keystroke:

```
Ctrl-k + @c : Copyright;
```

Placing a '^' character before a keystroke is the same as using the '@' character except that the macro compiler will also allow the (Ctrl) key to be held down, during the keystroke. For example, the following assignment allows the use of (c), (C), or (Ctrl)-(c) following the (Ctrl)-(k) keystroke:

```
Ctrl-k + ^c : Copyright:
```

Note that you cannot use the '@' and '^' keystroke modifiers on the initial keystroke on an assignment, but only in the second, third, or other subsequent keystrokes in a series of keystrokes.

| KEYSTROKE NAME | COMMENT | KEYSTROKE NAME | COMMENT | KEYSTROKE NAME | COMMENT |
|---|---|---|---|---|---|
| BkSp | Backspace | Home | Home key | Return | Return key |
| Del | Delete | Ins | Insert | RgAr | Right arrow |
| DnAr | Down arrow | LfAr | Left arrow | Space | Spacebar |
| F1–F10 | Function keys | PgDn | Page down | Star | Gray '*' key on keypad |
| End | End key | PgUp | Page up | Tab | Tab key |
| Enter | Return key | Plus | Gray '+' key on keypad | UpAr | Up arrow |
| Esc | Escape | PrtSc | Print Screen | Minus | Gray '-' key on keypad |

**Table 1-4 Keystroke names for special keys**

# The CMACROS.TEM File

The CMACROS.TEM file contains several definitions for inserting text into the editor window which is useful when writing C and C++ applications. You add the macro definitions to your current configuration file as follows:

```
temc \borlandc\doc\cmacros \borlandc\tcconfig
```
*for Alternate command set*
```
temc -u \borlandc\doc\cmacros \borlandc\tcconfig
```
*for CUA command set*

The following reference section lists the added macro definitions. The keystroke for activating the macro is listed to the right of the heading. The '_' symbol in the "Inserted Text" section shows the location of the cursor following the execution of the macro.

# MainCIO <Alt-I>

## Purpose
Place the outline of the main() function of a C application that uses the STDIO.H header file.

## Inserted Text
```
#include <stdio.h>

int main(void)
{
    _
   return 0;
}
```

# MainCPPIO <Alt-N>

## Purpose
Place the outline of the main() function of a C++ application that uses the IOSTREAM.H header file.

## Inserted Text
```
#include <iostream.h>

int main(void)
{
    _
   return 0;
}
```

# MakeComment <Alt-K>

## Purpose
Add a set of comment bars.

**Inserted Text**

```
/
***********************************************************

‾***********************************************************/
```

# MakeFunctText                                          <Alt-T>

### Purpose

Create a function description section out of a function prototype. Place the cursor immediately to the right of the prototype before executing the macro. The *prototype* parameter in the inserted text section shows the resulting location of the original prototype.

```
/*****************************************************
Function: prototype

Description:
*****************************************************/

‾
```

# MakeMain                                               <Alt-M>

### Purpose

Place the outline of the main() function of a C or C++ application.

### Inserted Text

```
int main(void)
{
    ‾return 0;
}
```

# MakeStub                                               <Alt-Z>

### Purpose

Create a function definition stub out of a function name. Place the cursor immediately to the right of the prototype before executing the macro.

### Inserted Text

```
void FunctionName( void )
{
        printf("This is\n");
}_
```

## GREP Reference

The GREP utility is a powerful application that will locate the lines of text containing a specific string from a list of text files. The GREP utility is derived from a UNIX utility of the same name. The acronym 'GREP' stands for "Global Regular Expression Print."

You normally use GREP to search for text from the IDE. The IDE reformats the output of GREP for use in the IDE's message window for finding and editing specific strings in your source code. This section covers how to use GREP as a standalone application; however, you can use virtually all the features of GREP in the IDE as you would if you were executing GREP from a DOS command line.

GREP uses the following command line syntax:

```
grep [options] ["]string["] [files . . .]
```

## File Lists

The *files* parameter instructs GREP as to which files to search for the given *string*. For example, you instruct GREP to search only one file as follows:

```
grep hello myfile.txt
```

The above command line executes GREP and instructs it to search MYFILE.TXT and print every line of text containing the expression "hello." You instruct GREP to search multiple files using either wildcards in the filename, such as *.C, or by listing more than one file. For example, the following command line instructs GREP to look for "hello" in MYFILE.TXT and all files with a .C extension in the current directory:

```
grep hello myfile.txt *.c
```

Note that the *files* parameter is optional. If you do not specify any files on the command line, GREP will search the text in the standard input. This feature is useful for constructing pipe and redirection statements.

## String Expressions

You can write the *string* parameter either with or without full quotations. Single word strings do not require enclosing quotations. However, you must enclose multiple word expressions, i.e., string expressions containing spaces, within full quotations. Otherwise, GREP will confuse words in the *string* with filenames in the *files* parameter. For example, the following command line instructs GREP to look for the expression "int x" in MYCODE.C:

```
grep "int x" mycode.c
```

Without the enclosing quotations, GREP would interpret the word "x" in the string as a search file in the *files* parameter.

## Special Characters

GREP interprets the search string as a "regular expression." This means there are several characters that have special meaning to GREP. The following reference lists each special character and provides an example search using the following text file:

**grep\test.c**
```
#include <stdio.h>

int a1;
int a2;
int a12;
int a13;
int a111112;
int a32;
int a321;
int a132;

int SayHello(void)
{
    return(printf("Hello, World!\n"));
}

void main()
{
    SayHello();
}
```

Note that you can disable GREP's regular expression usage by disabling the -r command line option. GREP will then interpret all characters as literals.

## ^                                        Match if at Beginning of Line

Placing the '^' symbol at the start of a string expression instructs GREP to only consider the string in the text as matching if it is located at the beginning of the line. For example, the following execution of GREP searches for the string "void" at the beginning of a line:

```
grep ^void *.c
```

GREP then prints:

```
File TEST.C:
void main()
```

Note that GREP does not print the line "int SayHello(void)" since the "void" string is not at the beginning of a line.

## $                                           Match if at End of Line

Placing the '$' symbol at the end of a string expression instructs GREP to only consider the string expression in the text as matching if it is located at the end of a line. For example, the following execution of GREP searches for the string ")" at the end of a line:

```
grep )$ *.c
```

GREP then prints:

```
File TEST.C:
int SayHello(void)
void main()
```

Note that GREP does not match the following lines even though the ")" string is located at the end of the line:

```
return(printf("Hello, World!\n"));
SayHello();
```

### ■ Match Any Character

The '.' character in a string expression is equivalent to the '?' wildcard character for DOS filenames. GREP will accept any character in the same relative position as the '.' character as matching. For example, the following execution of GREP searches for three-character strings that start with 'a' and end with '2':

```
grep a.2 *.c
```

GREP prints:

```
File TEST.C:
int a12;
int a32;
int a321;
```

Note that GREP does not print any of the integer declarations in which the second character following 'a' is not a '2'. Also note that GREP matches the line containing 'a321', because the first three characters of the term, 'a32', match the search parameter. See the 'w' command line option for whole word searches.

### * Match Zero or More Duplicate Characters

The "*" special character does not operate in the same way as the '*' wildcard character does in DOS. Placing a '*' after a character in a string expression instructs GREP to consider text as matching if it contains zero or more occurrences of that character. For example, the following execution of GREP searches for strings that start with 'a', end with '2', and have zero or more '1' characters in between:

```
grep a1*2 *.c
```

GREP prints:

```
File TEST.C:
int a2;
int a12;
int a111112;
```

**+**  **Match One or More Duplicate Characters**

Placing the '+' after a character in a string expression instructs GREP to consider text as matching if it contains one or more occurrences of that character as opposed to zero or more for the '*' character. For example, the following execution of GREP searches for strings that start with 'a', end with '2', and have one or more '1' characters in between:

```
grep a1+2 *.c
```

GREP prints:

```
File TEST.C:
int a12;
int a111112;
```

Note that the 'a2' string is not matched because it does not have at least one '1' character between the 'a' and the '2'.

## *[character set]*  **Character Set Matching**

The *[character set]* expression in a string is treated by GREP as a single character. GREP considers the text as matching if the character in the same relative position as *[character set]* is one of the characters listed in the set. For example, the following instructs GREP to search for strings that start with "a1" and have either 1, 2, or 3 as the third character:

```
grep a1[123] *.c
```

This produces the following result from GREP:

```
File TEST.C:
int a12;
int a13;
int a111112;
int a132;
```

You can also list portions of the character set as a range of characters using the " symbol. For example, the following command line is operationally identical to the previous example, but instead specifies a range of characters between '1' and '3':

```
grep a1[1-3] *.c
```

GREP also supports exclusive character searches using the '^' character at the beginning of the *[character set]* expression. The '^' character in *[character set]* means "not one of the following characters." For example, the following searches for integer declaration strings starting with 'a' but which do not have a '1' as the second character:

```
grep "int a[^1]"*.c
```

This produces the following result:

```
File TEST.C:
int a2;
int a32;
int a321;
```

27

## \                                                          Character Literal

You use the ' \ ' character in a string expression to specify a literal character rather than one of the special characters or a command line formatting character such as a space, tab, or one of the enclosing quotes. For example, the following instructs GREP to search for strings containing a double quotation mark:

```
grep \" *.c
```

### GREP Command Line Options
The following reference section lists the command line options for GREP. You can list the options on the command line separately, with each option preceded by a '-' character and followed by a space such as the following:

```
grep -r -i -l "string" *.c
```

Or you can list the options as a group with only one leading '-' symbol. For example, the following command line is identical to the command line above:

```
grep -ril "string" *.c
```

Options are disabled by placing a '-' after the option. For example, the following command line disables the -r option:

```
grep -r- "string" *.c
```

Note that the examples in this section use the same text file as the "Special characters" section.

## -c                                                                  Print

### Purpose
You use the -c option to print a count of the number of matching lines of text instead of the text lines themselves.

### Default
```
-c-
```
Print the matching line of text.

### Description
GREP normally prints the filename followed by the lines of text that match the string expression. The -c option prints the filename followed by the count for the number of lines containing the string.

## Example

Print the count of lines containing the "int" string at the start of a line:

```
grep -c "^int" *.c
```

GREP prints the following output:

```
File TEST.C:
9 lines match
```

# -d                                                    Search All Subdirectories

## Purpose

The -d option is used to expand the search to files in the subdirectories of any explicitly listed search directories.

## Default

```
-d-
```

    Search only the current directory or the directory specified in the pathname.

## Description

GREP will normally limit its search to files either in the current directory or to any directory explicitly listed as part of the pathname. The -d option instructs GREP to search all subdirectories of an explicitly listed search directory. Note that GREP will not automatically search the subdirectories of the current directory. You must explicitly list the current directory as part of the pathname to have GREP search the subdirectories of the current directory.

## Example

Search for the files in this chapter source and the Chapter 5 source that use the string "Hello, World!":

```
grep -dl "Hello, World!" .\*.c ..\ch5\*.c
```

    The -l option instructs GREP to only print the filenames containing a match rather than actually printing the lines of text. The above command line produces the following output:

```
File .\GREP\TEST.C:
File ..\CH5\EXAMP1\HELLO.C:
File ..\CH5\RESPFILE\HELLO.C:
File ..\CH5\E\HELLO.C:
File ..\CH5\L\HELLO.C:
File ..\CH5\M\HELLO.C:
File ..\CH5\T\HELLO.C:
File ..\CH5\COMPRESS\HELLO.C:
```

## -i                                                                    Ignore Case

### Purpose
You use the -i option to perform a string search without regard to case sensitivity.

### Default
```
-i-
```
Perform a case sensitive string search.

### Description
GREP normally discriminates between upper- and lowercase letters as it performs a string search. You use the -i option when you need to perform a string search without regard to the case of the letters.

### Example
Search for the string "hello" using the -i option:

```
grep -i hello *.c
```

GREP ignores the case difference between "hello" and "Hello" and prints the following matching lines of text:

```
File TEST.C:
/* Print the "Hello, World!" statement */
int SayHello(void)
    return(printf("Hello, World!\n"));
    SayHello();
```

## -l                                                                List Filenames Only

### Purpose
The -l option prints only files containing the search string and not the actual lines of text that match.

### Default
```
-l-
```
Print the filename and matching line of text.

### Description
The -l option instructs GREP to only list the filename when it finds a match and then move on to the next file. This produces the fastest possible search, making it useful for narrowing down a large list of possible search files.

## Example

Search in this chapter's source directory and the Chapter 5 source directory for files that use the string "Hello, World!":

```
grep -dl "Hello, World!" .\*.c ..\ch5\*.c
```

The -d option instructs GREP to search the subdirectories. The above command line produces the following output:

```
File .\GREP\TEST.C:
File ..\CH5\EXAMP1\HELLO.C:
File ..\CH5\RESPFILE\HELLO.C:
File ..\CH5\E\HELLO.C:
File ..\CH5\L\HELLO.C:
File ..\CH5\M\HELLO.C:
File ..\CH5\T\HELLO.C:
File ..\CH5\COMPRESS\HELLO.C:
```

## -n                                                                    Print Line Numbers

## Purpose

You use the -n option to instruct GREP to print the line numbers associated with each printed line of matching text.

## Default

```
-n-
```

Print the line of text without any line numbers.

## Description

GREP normally only prints the line of text containing the matching string. Using the -n option instructs GREP to also print the line number associated with the text.

## Example

Print the lines of text containing the "a1" string and the associated line numbers using the -n option:

```
grep -n a1 *.c
```

GREP prints the following output:

```
File TEST.C:
4       int a1;
6       int a12;
7       int a13;
8       int a111112;
11      int a132;
```

## -o                          Print the Filename with Each Line of Text

### Purpose
The -o option prints each matching line of text preceded by the filename, making it easier to implement UNIX-style piping.

### Default
–o–

    Print only the line of text containing the matching string.

### Description
UNIX style command line piping is easier to implement if each line is preceded by the associated filename. The -o option for GREP prints the filename first each time it prints a matching line of text.

### Example
Print the lines of text containing the string "a1" preceded by the associated filename:

```
grep –o a1 *.c
```

GREP prints the following output:

```
TEST.C  int a1;
TEST.C  int a12;
TEST.C  int a13;
TEST.C  int a111112;
TEST.C  int a132;
```

## -r                                Enable Regular Expression Usage

### Purpose
The -r option instructs GREP to regard text containing the '^', '.', '*', '$', '\ ', '+', and [*character set*] expressions as regular expressions requiring special search handling.

### Default
–r

    Interpret the special characters as part of a regular expression.

### Description
A "regular expression" is one in which GREP interprets certain characters as special search directives. See the "Special characters" section earlier in this chapter for details of each character. Disabling this option instructs GREP to treat all characters in the search string as literal characters having no special meaning.

### Example
Search for the '*' character by disabling the -r option:

```
grep -r- "*" *.c
```

GREP normally interprets the '*' character as a special search directive and will generate an error message with the above usage when regular expression was not disabled. With the -r option disabled, however, GREP generates the following output:

```
File TEST.C:
/* Dummy variables */
/* Print the "Hello, World!" statement */
```

---

**-u**                                                          **Update Default Options**

---

### Purpose
You use the -u option to modify the default settings for the command line options.

### Default
N/A

### Description
Using the -u option instructs GREP to write the listed option settings as the default options. GREP will prompt you for instruction as to which copy of GREP.COM to modify, as follows:

```
Enter output name for new program file [C:\BORLANDC\BINB\GREP.COM]:
```

GREP displays the pathname for the copy processing the -u option as the default copy to modify. You simply press (Enter) to modify that copy or enter a pathname for a different copy. GREP will create a new copy of itself if the file does not already exist.

You view the current default settings for GREP by entering the following:

```
grep ?
```

GREP will then generate the following output:

```
Turbo GREP Version 3.0 Copyright (c) 1991 Borland International
Syntax:    GREP [-rlcnvidzuwo] searchstring file[s]

Options are one or more option characters preceeded by "-", and option-
ally followed by "+" (turn option on), or "-" (turn it off). The default
is "+".
        -r+  Regular expression search    -l-  File names only
        -c-  match Count only             -n-  Line numbers
        -v-  Non-matching lines only      -i-  Ignore case
        -d-  Search subdirectories        -z-  Verbose
        -u-  Update default options       -w-  Word search
        -o-  UNIX output format           Default set: [0-9A-Z_]
```

A regular expression is one or more occurrences of: One or more characters optionally enclosed in quotes. The following symbols are treated
specially:

| | | | |
|---|---|---|---|
| ^ | start of line | $ | nd of line |
| . | any character | \ | quote next character |
| * | match zero or more | + | match one or more |

[aeiou0-9]   match a, e, i, o, u, and 0 thru 9
[^aeiou0-9]  match anything but a, e, i, o, u, and 0 thru 9

## Example

Set the -r option as disabled by default:

```
grep -r- -u
```

## -V                                                    Print Nonmatching Lines

## Purpose

You use the -v option when you want to view the lines of text that do not match the
search string.

## Default

-v-

Print the lines of text that match the search string.

## Description

The -v option instructs GREP to print the text lines that do not contain a match rather
than the text lines that do contain a match to the search string.

## Example

Print the lines of text that do not contain the '{', '}', or ';' characters:

```
grep -v [{};] *.c
```

GREP generates the following output:

```
File TEST.C:
#include <stdio.h>

/* Dummy variables */

/* Print the "Hello, World!" statement */
int SayHello(void)

void main()
```

# -w[*set*]    Word Search

## Purpose

You use the -w option to search for complete words rather than partial strings. The '[set]' parameter permits you to specify alternative characters to be considered as part of a word.

## Default

-w-
>   Search for partial words.

-w[a-zA-Z0-9_]  *for -w option without the [set] parameter*
>   Treat alphanumeric characters and an underscore as legal word characters.

## Description

The -w option instructs GREP to look for the search string as a complete word. It uses the '[set]' parameter as the definition of which characters are considered word characters. For example, the -w option without the [set] parameter uses normal C and C++ identifier characters as word characters. This ensures characters such as ';', '(', and ')' are not treated as part of the word.

## Example

Search for the usage of the "a1" string as a complete word:

```
grep -w a1 *.c
```

The above command line generates the following output:

```
File TEST.C:
int a1;
```

# -Z    Verbose Listing

## Purpose

You use the -z option to include line numbers with the matching lines of text and also give a count of the matching lines.

## Default

-z-
>   Print only the lines of text containing the matching string.

### Description

GREP normally only prints the line of text containing the matching string. Using the -z option instructs GREP to also print the line number associated with the text and a summary count of the matching number of lines.

### Example

Search for the usage of the "a1" string using a verbose listing:

```
grep -z a1 *.c
```

The above command line generates the following output:

```
File TEST.C:
4   int a 1;
6   int a 12;
7   int a 13;
8   int a 111112;
11  int a 132;
5 lines match
```

# THE THELP UTILITY REFERENCE

The THELP.EXE utility is a memory-resident application you use outside the IDE to access the help files available in BC++. It is particularly useful when you develop your applications in an external editor and want to access the help files used by the BC++ IDE. THELP uses the following command line syntax:

```
thelp [options]
```

Once executed, you call up the help file display by pressing the number '5' key on the keypad with the "Num Lock" off. You can assign other "hot keys" using the K command line option. You maneuver through the help file display using the arrow and tab keys. Table 1-5 lists the keystrokes and their actions.

| | |
|---|---|
| Shift Arrow | Mark a block of text for pasting using Ctrl P. |
| Home | Move to the beginning of a line. |
| End | Move to the end of a line. |
| Tab | Move to the next keyword field. |
| Shift Tab | Move to the previous keyword field. |
| PgUp | Move to the previous screen. |
| PgDn | Move to the next screen. |
| Enter | Displays the selected keyword field. |
| Esc | Exit the help session. |

| | |
|---|---|
| (F1) | Displays the table of contents for the help file. |
| (Shift)-(F1) | Displays the index for the help file. |
| (Alt)-(F) | Select a new help file. |
| (Ctrl)-(P) | Paste a block of text selected using the (Shift)-(Arrow) keys into the system keyboard buffer. |

**Table 1-5 THELP Keystrokes**

The following is a list of command line options for the THELP utility. You should place commonly used command line options in a text file called THELP.CFG. The THELP utility reads the contents of the THELP.CFG file as if they were entered on the command line. Note that options explicitly listed on the command line will override the options listed in the THELP.CFG file.

## /C*ElementAttribute*                    Set Display Color

### Description

The /C*ElementAttribute* command line option sets the color for different elements of the THELP display screen. The 'Element' parameter of the option corresponds to one of the display elements listed in Table 1-6. The even numbered elements are for color systems and the odd numbered elements are for monochrome displays.

| ELEMENT | COLOR | MONOCHROME |
|---|---|---|
| Border | 0 | 1 |
| Normal text | 2 | 3 |
| Keyword text | 4 | 5 |
| Selected keyword text | 6 | 7 |
| Example text | 8 | 9 |
| Blocked text | A | B |

**Table 1-6 Display elements corresponding to the 'Element' parameter**

The 'Attribute' parameter is a two-digit code that corresponds to the colors listed in Table 1-7. The first digit is the background color and the second digit is the foreground color. Background colors '8' through 'F' are the same as background colors '0' through '7,' except the foreground color is blinking.

| COLOR | DIGIT | COLOR | DIGIT |
|-------|-------|-------|-------|
| Black | 0 | Dark-gray | 8 |
| Blue | 1 | Light-blue | 9 |
| Green | 2 | Light-green | A |
| Cyan | 3 | Light-cyan | B |
| Red | 4 | Light-red | C |
| Magenta | 5 | Violet | D |
| Brown | 6 | Yellow | E |
| Gray | 7 | White | F |

**Table 1-7 Colors associated with different attributes on a color system**

Table 1-8 lists the text attributes associated with a specific 'Attribute' parameter on a monochrome system.

| CODE | ATTRIBUTE | CODE | ATTRIBUTE |
|------|-----------|------|-----------|
| 01 | Normal-intensity underlined text | 87 | Normal-intensity blinking text |
| 07 | Normal-intensity text | 89 | High-intensity underlined blinking text |
| 09 | High-intensity underlined text | F0 | Reverse background blinking text |
| 0F | High-intensity text | FF | High-intensity blinking text |
| 70 | Reverse background text | | |

**Table 1-8 Monochrome display attributes**

### Example
The default text attributes display both normal text and keyword text in the same way when you run THELP on a monochrome system. Load THELP with the color attribute of keywords displayed as high-intensity text:

```
thelp /C50F
```

## /Ffilename                                                   Help File

### Description
There are three help files shipped with the BC++ package that THELP is able to run. These include:

TCHELP.TCH          Help file for the IDE, C, C++, and Windows API.
TVCHELP.TCH         Help file for Turbo Vision.
OWLHELP.TCH         Help file for Object Windows.

THELP loads the TCHELP.TCH file if you do not use the /F*filename* option. You can also use (Alt)-(F) to change the help file in the middle of a help session. You can list up to eight different help files on the command line and switch between them using (Alt)-(F). Note that you must use full pathnames for all help files that are located in a directory other than the current directory.

### Example
Load THELP with the help file for Object Windows:

```
thelp /f\BORLANDC\BIN\OWLHELP.TCH
```

## /H, /?                                              Display the Help Screen

### Description
The /H, /?, and ? command line options display the following help screen:

```
Turbo Help Version 3.0 Copyright (c) 1991 Borland International

Usage: THELP [options]

/C#xx    Select color: #=color number, xx=hex color value
/Fname   Full pathname of help file
/H,/?    Display this help screen
/Kxxyy   Hotkey: xx=shift state, yy=scan code
/U       Remove Thelp from memory
/Wx,y,w,h   Set the window size (Ex:/W0,0,80,25)
```

### Example
Display the help screen for THELP:

```
thelp /?
```

## /K*keycode*                                                  Set Hot Key

### Description
THELP loads as a memory-resident utility that you activate by pressing the '5' key on the number pad. You use the /K*keycode* option to set a "hot key" other than the '5' key to execute THELP. The 'keycode' parameter is a four-digit code. The first two digits specify the (Shift), (Ctrl), and (Alt) keypress status, and the second two digits specify the

scan code for the key. Table 1-9 lists the possible keypress status codes and Table 1-10 lists the scan codes.

| KEYPRESS STATUS | CODE |
|---|---|
| (Right Shift) | 01 |
| (Left Shift) | 02 |
| (Right Shift)(Left Shift) | 03 |
| (Ctrl) | 04 |
| (Ctrl)(Right Shift) | 05 |
| (Ctrl)(Left Shift) | 06 |
| (Ctrl)(Left Shift)(Right Shift) | 07 |
| (Alt) | 08 |
| (Alt)(Right Shift) | 09 |
| (Alt)(Left Shift) | 0A |
| (Alt)(Right Shift)(Left Shift) | 0B |
| (Alt)(Ctrl) | 0C |
| (Alt)(Ctrl)(Right Shift) | 0D |
| (Alt)(Ctrl)(Left Shift) | 0E |
| (Alt)(Ctrl)(Left Shift)(Right Shift) | 0F |

**Table 1-9 Keypress status codes**

| KEY | SCAN CODE | KEY | SCAN CODE |
|---|---|---|---|
| A | 1E | 0 | 0B |
| B | 30 | 1 | 02 |
| C | 2E | 2 | 03 |
| D | 20 | 3 | 04 |
| E | 12 | 4 | 05 |
| F | 21 | 5 | 06 |
| G | 22 | 6 | 07 |
| H | 23 | 7 | 08 |
| I | 17 | 8 | 09 |
| J | 24 | 9 | 0A |
| K | 25 | F1 | 3B |
| L | 26 | F2 | 3C |

| SCAN KEY | CODE | SCAN KEY | CODE |
|----------|------|----------|------|
| M | 32 | F3 | 3D |
| N | 31 | F4 | 3E |
| O | 18 | F5 | 3F |
| P | 19 | F6 | 40 |
| Q | 10 | F7 | 41 |
| R | 13 | F8 | 42 |
| S | 1F | F9 | 43 |
| T | 14 | F10 | 44 |
| U | 16 | F11 | 57 |
| V | 2F | F12 | 58 |
| W | 11 | | |
| X | 2D | | |
| Y | 15 | | |
| Z | 2C | | |

**Table 1-10 Key scan codes**

### Example

Load THELP with (Alt)-(F1) as the "hot key":

```
thelp /k083B
```

The digits '08' represent (Alt) and the '3b' digits represent (F1).

## /U                                    Remove THELP from Memory

### Description

The /U command line option removes THELP from memory. You use the /U option when you need more memory. If you want to change a command line option, you use the /U option to remove THELP from memory and reload THELP again using the desired command line options. Note that any TSR applications loaded after THELP must be removed before using this option.

### Example

Remove THELP from memory:

```
thelp /u
```

## /Wx,y,w,h                                    Set Display Dimensions

### Description

The /W command line option specifies the dimensions of the THELP display. The 'x' and 'y' parameters set the column and row for the upper left-hand corner of the display. The 'w' and 'h' parameters set the width and height of the display.

### Example

Load THELP with the display set to cover the entire screen:

```
thelp /w0,0,80,25
```

# UNZIP REFERENCE

The installation processes uses the UNZIP utility to decompress the files stored on the distribution disks. This utility is a modified version of the shareware PKUNZIP, which is licensed for use by Borland International. The modifications include a different copyright message and help screen; however, the utility is functionally identical to PKUNZIP.

The syntax for UNZIP is as follows:

```
unzip [options] zipfile [destination] [files.../@filelist]
```

The 'zipfile' parameter is the filename for the .ZIP file. You can use wildcards such as '*' or '?' with the 'zipfile' parameter.

The 'destination' parameter is the directory path where UNZIP should place the extracted files. UNZIP will place the files in the current directory if you do not specify a destination.

The 'files' parameter is a list of files UNZIP should extract from 'zipfile.' You can list any number of files and also use wildcards. Alternatively, you can also create a text file containing the list of filenames and use '@filename,' where 'filename' is the name of the text file containing the list.

You would normally use the UNZIP utility with the FILELIST.DOC text file to manually extract files from the distribution disk. FILELIST.DOC contains a listing of the BC++ files listed by disk number and .ZIP file. For example, FILELIST.DOC lists the files for the CURSOR application example as located on distribution disk #3 in the file CURSOR.ZIP. To extract the files for the CURSOR application, you'd create the directory where you'd like the files, such as C:\CURSOR, put disk #3 in drive A:, and enter the following:

```
unzip a:cursor.zip c:\cursor
```

This will extract all the files in CURSOR.ZIP into the C:\CURSOR directory. You could also enter the following to extract only the C++ source code files:

```
unzip a:cursor.zip c:\cursor *.cpp
```

You can also use more than one file to extract as well as list specific files. For example, the following will extract the CURSOR.CPP file and also all the .H files:

```
unzip a:cursor.zip c:\cursor cursor.cpp *.h
```

The following is a list of the command line options for UNZIP:

| | |
|---|---|
| -c[m] | Print the extracted file to the screen. The 'm' option uses pauses after listing one page of text. |
| -d | Automatically create any directories stored in the .ZIP file. None of the files in the BC++ distribution disks contain stored directories. |
| -o | Overwrite existing files with the same name and extension. |
| -p[a/b/c][1/2/3] | Extract the files to the printer in either (a) Asc, (b) Binary, or (c) to a COM port. The '1', '2', and '3' parameters specify the port number. |
| -q | Use ANSI comments. This option does not apply to BC++ distribution disks. |
| -t | Tests the integrity of the .ZIP file. |
| -v[b/c/d/e/n/p/s/r] | Lists the files stored in a .ZIP file. The listing is either (b) brief or sorted by either (c) CRC data, (d) date/time, (e) extension, (n) name, (p) percentage, (s) size, or (r) in reverse order. |

## FCONVERT REFERENCE

OEM text is the DOS character set shown in Table 1-11. ANSI text is the character set normally used in Windows and is shown in Table 1-12.

As you can see by comparing the two tables, there is not a one-to-one correlation between the OEM and ANSI character sets. The FCONVERT utility is a Windows application that converts ANSI text files to OEM text files or OEM text files to ANSI text files. Figure 1-1 shows the main window for FCONVERT.

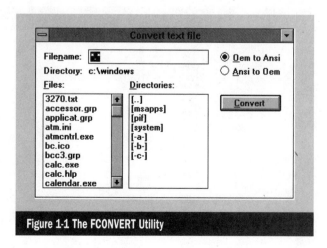

Figure 1-1 The FCONVERT Utility

| Dec | Chr | Dec | Chr | Dec | Chr | Dec | Chr | Dec | Chr | Dec | Chr | Dec | Chr | Dec | Chr |
|---|---|---|---|---|---|---|---|---|---|---|---|---|---|---|---|
| 000 |  | 032 |  | 064 | @ | 096 | ` | 128 | Ç | 160 | á | 192 | └ | 224 | α |
| 001 | ☺ | 033 | ! | 065 | A | 097 | a | 129 | ü | 161 | í | 193 | ┴ | 225 | β |
| 002 | ☻ | 034 | " | 066 | B | 098 | b | 130 | é | 162 | ó | 194 | ┬ | 226 | Γ |
| 003 | ♥ | 035 | # | 067 | C | 099 | c | 131 | â | 163 | ú | 195 | ├ | 227 | π |
| 004 | ♦ | 036 | $ | 068 | D | 100 | d | 132 | ä | 164 | ñ | 196 | ─ | 228 | Σ |
| 005 | ♣ | 037 | % | 069 | E | 101 | e | 133 | à | 165 | Ñ | 197 | ┼ | 229 | σ |
| 006 | ♠ | 038 | & | 070 | F | 102 | f | 134 | å | 166 | ª | 198 | ╞ | 230 | µ |
| 007 | • | 039 | ' | 071 | G | 103 | g | 135 | ç | 167 | º | 199 | ╟ | 231 | τ |
| 008 | ◘ | 040 | ( | 072 | H | 104 | h | 136 | ê | 168 | ¿ | 200 | ╚ | 232 | Φ |
| 009 | ○ | 041 | ) | 073 | I | 105 | i | 137 | ë | 169 | ⌐ | 201 | ╔ | 233 | Θ |
| 010 | ◙ | 042 | * | 074 | J | 106 | j | 138 | è | 170 | ¬ | 202 | ╩ | 234 | Ω |
| 011 | ♂ | 043 | + | 075 | K | 107 | k | 139 | ï | 171 | ½ | 203 | ╦ | 235 | δ |
| 012 | ♀ | 044 | , | 076 | L | 108 | l | 140 | î | 172 | ¼ | 204 | ╠ | 236 | ∞ |
| 013 | ♪ | 045 | - | 077 | M | 109 | m | 141 | ì | 173 | ¡ | 205 | ═ | 237 | φ |
| 014 | ♫ | 046 | . | 078 | N | 110 | n | 142 | Ä | 174 | « | 206 | ╬ | 238 | ε |
| 015 | ¤ | 047 | / | 079 | O | 111 | o | 143 | Å | 175 | » | 207 | ╧ | 239 | ∩ |
| 016 | ► | 048 | 0 | 080 | P | 112 | p | 144 | É | 176 | ░ | 208 | ╨ | 240 | ≡ |
| 017 | ◄ | 049 | 1 | 081 | Q | 113 | q | 145 | æ | 177 | ▒ | 209 | ╤ | 241 | ± |
| 018 | ↕ | 050 | 2 | 082 | R | 114 | r | 146 | Æ | 178 | ▓ | 210 | ╥ | 242 | ≥ |
| 019 | ‼ | 051 | 3 | 083 | S | 115 | s | 147 | ô | 179 | │ | 211 | ╙ | 243 | ≤ |
| 020 | ¶ | 052 | 4 | 084 | T | 116 | t | 148 | ö | 180 | ┤ | 212 | ╘ | 244 | ⌠ |
| 021 | § | 053 | 5 | 085 | U | 117 | u | 149 | ò | 181 | ╡ | 213 | ╒ | 245 | ⌡ |
| 022 | ▬ | 054 | 6 | 086 | V | 118 | v | 150 | û | 182 | ╢ | 214 | ╓ | 246 | ÷ |
| 023 | ↨ | 055 | 7 | 087 | W | 119 | w | 151 | ù | 183 | ╖ | 215 | ╫ | 247 | ≈ |
| 024 | ↑ | 056 | 8 | 088 | X | 120 | x | 152 | ÿ | 184 | ╕ | 216 | ╪ | 248 | ° |
| 025 | ↓ | 057 | 9 | 089 | Y | 121 | y | 153 | Ö | 185 | ╣ | 217 | ┘ | 249 | • |
| 026 | → | 058 | : | 090 | Z | 122 | z | 154 | Ü | 186 | ║ | 218 | ┌ | 250 | · |
| 027 | ← | 059 | ; | 091 | [ | 123 | { | 155 | ¢ | 187 | ╗ | 219 | █ | 251 | √ |
| 028 | ∟ | 060 | < | 092 | \ | 124 | ¦ | 156 | £ | 188 | ╝ | 220 | ▄ | 252 | η |
| 029 | ↔ | 061 | = | 093 | ] | 125 | } | 157 | ¥ | 189 | ╜ | 221 | ▌ | 253 | ² |
| 030 | ▲ | 062 | > | 094 | ^ | 126 | ~ | 158 | ₧ | 190 | ╛ | 222 | ▐ | 254 | ■ |
| 031 | ▼ | 063 | ? | 095 | _ | 127 | █ | 159 | ƒ | 191 | ┐ | 223 | ▀ | 255 |  |

**Table 1-11 OEM text is the standard DOS character set**

| Dec | Chr | Dec | Chr | Dec | Chr | Dec | Chr | Dec | Chr | Dec | Chr | Dec | Chr | Dec | Chr |
|---|---|---|---|---|---|---|---|---|---|---|---|---|---|---|---|
| 000 | • | 032 |  | 064 | @ | 096 | ` | 128 | • | 160 |  | 192 | À | 224 | à |
| 001 | • | 033 | ! | 065 | A | 097 | a | 129 | • | 161 | ¡ | 193 | Á | 225 | á |
| 002 | • | 034 | " | 066 | B | 098 | b | 130 | ‚ | 162 | ¢ | 194 | Â | 226 | â |
| 003 | • | 035 | # | 067 | C | 099 | c | 131 | ƒ | 163 | £ | 195 | Ã | 227 | ã |
| 004 | • | 036 | $ | 068 | D | 100 | d | 132 | „ | 164 | ¤ | 196 | Ä | 228 | ä |
| 005 | • | 037 | % | 069 | E | 101 | e | 133 | … | 165 | ¥ | 197 | Å | 229 | å |
| 006 | • | 038 | & | 070 | F | 102 | f | 134 | † | 166 | ¦ | 198 | Æ | 230 | æ |
| 007 | • | 039 | ' | 071 | G | 103 | g | 135 | ‡ | 167 | § | 199 | Ç | 231 | ÿ |
| 008 | • | 040 | ( | 072 | H | 104 | h | 136 | ˆ | 168 | ¨ | 200 | è | 232 | è |
| 009 | • | 041 | ) | 073 | I | 105 | i | 137 | ‰ | 169 | © | 201 | É | 233 | é |
| 010 | • | 042 | * | 074 | J | 106 | j | 138 | ˇ | 170 | ª | 202 | ê | 234 | ê |
| 011 | • | 043 | + | 075 | K | 107 | k | 139 | ‹ | 171 | « | 203 | ë | 235 | ë |
| 012 | • | 044 | , | 076 | L | 108 | l | 140 | Œ | 172 | ¬ | 204 | ì | 236 | ì |
| 013 | • | 045 | - | 077 | M | 109 | m | 141 | • | 173 | - | 205 | í | 237 | í |
| 014 | • | 046 | . | 078 | N | 110 | n | 142 | • | 174 | ® | 206 | î | 238 | î |
| 015 | • | 047 | / | 079 | O | 111 | o | 143 | • | 175 | ¯ | 207 | ï | 239 | ï |
| 016 | • | 048 | 0 | 080 | P | 112 | p | 144 | • | 176 | ° | 208 | – | 240 |  |
| 017 | • | 049 | 1 | 081 | Q | 113 | q | 145 | ' | 177 | ± | 209 | Ñ | 241 | ñ |

| | | | | | | | |
|---|---|---|---|---|---|---|---|
| 018 • | 050 2 | 082 R | 114 r | 146 ' | 178 ² | 210 ò | 242 ò |
| 019 • | 051 3 | 083 S | 115 s | 147 " | 179 ³ | 211 ó | 243 ó |
| 020 • | 052 4 | 084 T | 116 t | 148 " | 180 ´ | 212 ô | 244 ô |
| 021 • | 053 5 | 085 U | 117 u | 149 • | 181 μ | 213 õ | 245 õ |
| 022 • | 054 6 | 086 V | 118 v | 150 - | 182 ¶ | 214 Ö | 246 ö |
| 023 • | 055 7 | 087 W | 119 w | 151 – | 183 • | 215 ◊ | 247 ó |
| 024 • | 056 8 | 088 X | 120 x | 152 ~ | 184 , | 216 Ø | 248 Ø |
| 025 • | 057 9 | 089 Y | 121 y | 153 ™ | 185 ¹ | 217 ù | 249 ù |
| 026 • | 058 : | 090 Z | 122 z | 154 ˜ | 186 º | 218 ú | 250 ú |
| 027 • | 059 ; | 091 [ | 123 { | 155 . | 187 » | 219 û | 251 û |
| 028 • | 060 < | 092 \ | 124 \| | 156 œ | 188 ¼ | 220 ü | 252 ü |
| 029 • | 061 = | 093 ] | 125 } | 157 • | 189 ½ | 221 Y | 253 y |
| 030 • | 062 > | 094 ^ | 126 ~ | 158 • | 190 ¾ | 222 ß | 254 ß |
| 031 • | 063 ? | 095 _ | 127 • | 159 Ÿ | 191 ¿ | 223 ß | 255 ÿ |

**Table 1-12 ANSI text is the character set normally used in Windows**

Table 1-13 shows the resulting character set when FCONVERT converts the OEM character set to an ANSI character set. Table 1-14 shows the character set when FCONVERT converts the ANSI character set to the OEM character set.

| | | | | | | | |
|---|---|---|---|---|---|---|---|
| 000 | 032 | 064 @ | 096 ' | 128 Ç | 160 á | 192 + | 224 _ |
| 001 • | 033 ! | 065 A | 097 a | 129 ü | 161 í | 193 - | 225 ß |
| 002 • | 034 " | 066 B | 098 b | 130 é | 162 ó | 194 - | 226 _ |
| 003 • | 035 # | 067 C | 099 c | 131 â | 163 ú | 195 + | 227 ¶ |
| 004 • | 036 $ | 068 D | 100 d | 132 ä | 164 ñ | 196 - | 228 _ |
| 005 • | 037 % | 069 E | 101 e | 133 à | 165 Ñ | 197 + | 229 _ |
| 006 • | 038 & | 070 F | 102 f | 134 å | 166 ª | 198 \| | 230 μ |
| 007 • | 039 ' | 071 G | 103 g | 135 ç | 167 º | 199 \| | 231 _ |
| 008 • | 040 ( | 072 H | 104 h | 136 ê | 168 ¿ | 200 + | 232 _ |
| 009 | 041 ) | 073 I | 105 i | 137 ë | 169 _ | 201 + | 233 _ |
| 010 | 042 * | 074 J | 106 j | 138 è | 170 ¬ | 202 - | 234 _ |
| 011 | 043 + | 075 K | 107 k | 139 ï | 171 ½ | 203 - | 235 _ |
| 012 | 044 , | 076 L | 108 l | 140 î | 172 ¼ | 204 \| | 236 _ |
| 013 | 045 - | 077 M | 109 m | 141 ì | 173 \| | 205 - | 237 _ |
| 014 | 046 . | 078 N | 110 n | 142 Ä | 174 « | 206 + | 238 _ |
| 015 ¤ | 047 / | 079 O | 111 o | 143 Å | 175 » | 207 - | 239 _ |
| 016 • | 048 0 | 080 P | 112 p | 144 É | 176 _ | 208 - | 240 _ |
| 017 • | 049 1 | 081 Q | 113 q | 145 æ | 177 _ | 209 - | 241 ± |
| 018 • | 050 2 | 082 R | 114 r | 146 Æ | 178 _ | 210 - | 242 _ |
| 019 • | 051 3 | 083 S | 115 s | 147 ô | 179 \| | 211 + | 243 _ |
| 020 ¶ | 052 4 | 084 T | 116 t | 148 ö | 180 \| | 212 + | 244 _ |
| 021 § | 053 5 | 085 U | 117 u | 149 ò | 181 \| | 213 + | 245 _ |
| 022 • | 054 6 | 086 V | 118 v | 150 û | 182 \| | 214 + | 246 _ |
| 023 • | 055 7 | 087 W | 119 w | 151 ù | 183 + | 215 + | 247 _ |
| 024 • | 056 8 | 088 X | 120 x | 152 ÿ | 184 + | 216 + | 248 • |
| 025 • | 057 9 | 089 Y | 121 y | 153 Ö | 185 \| | 217 + | 249 • |
| 026 • | 058 : | 090 Z | 122 z | 154 ü | 186 \| | 218 + | 250 • |
| 027 • | 059 ; | 091 [ | 123 { | 155 ¢ | 187 + | 219 + | 251 _ |
| 028 • | 060 < | 092 \ | 124 \| | 156 £ | 188 + | 220 _ | 252 n |
| 029 • | 061 = | 093 ] | 125 } | 157 ¥ | 189 + | 221 \| | 253 ² |
| 030 - | 062 > | 094 ^ | 126 ~ | 158 p | 190 + | 222 _ | 254 ˉ |
| 031 | 063 ? | 095 _ | 127 • | 159 f | 191 + | 223 _ | 255 _ |

**Table 1-13 Character set resulting when OEM is converted to ANSI with FCONVERT**

| | | | | | | | | | | | | | | | |
|---|---|---|---|---|---|---|---|---|---|---|---|---|---|---|---|
| 000 | | 032 | | 064 | @ | 096 | ` | 128 | Ç | 160 | | 192 | A | 224 | à |
| 001 | ☺ | 033 | ! | 065 | A | 097 | a | 129 | ü | 161 | í | 193 | A | 225 | â |
| 002 | ☻ | 034 | " | 066 | B | 098 | b | 130 | é | 162 | ¢ | 194 | A | 226 | â |
| 003 | ♥ | 035 | # | 067 | C | 099 | c | 131 | â | 163 | £ | 195 | A | 227 | a |
| 004 | ♦ | 036 | $ | 068 | D | 100 | d | 132 | ä | 164 | ¤ | 196 | Ä | 228 | ä |
| 005 | ♣ | 037 | % | 069 | E | 101 | e | 133 | à | 165 | ¥ | 197 | Å | 229 | â |
| 006 | ♠ | 038 | & | 070 | F | 102 | f | 134 | å | 166 | ▌ | 198 | Æ | 230 | æ |
| 007 | • | 039 | ' | 071 | G | 103 | g | 135 | ç | 167 | § | 199 | Ç | 231 | ç |
| 008 | ◘ | 040 | ( | 072 | H | 104 | h | 136 | ê | 168 | " | 200 | E | 232 | è |
| 009 | ○ | 041 | ) | 073 | I | 105 | i | 137 | ë | 169 | c | 201 | É | 233 | é |
| 010 | ■ | 042 | * | 074 | J | 106 | j | 138 | è | 170 | a | 202 | E | 234 | ê |
| 011 | ♂ | 043 | + | 075 | K | 107 | k | 139 | ï | 171 | « | 203 | E | 235 | ë |
| 012 | ♀ | 044 | , | 076 | L | 108 | l | 140 | î | 172 | ¬ | 204 | I | 236 | ì |
| 013 | ♪ | 045 | - | 077 | M | 109 | m | 141 | ì | 173 | - | 205 | I | 237 | í |
| 014 | ♫ | 046 | . | 078 | N | 110 | n | 142 | Ä | 174 | r | 206 | I | 238 | î |
| 015 | ¤ | 047 | / | 079 | O | 111 | o | 143 | Å | 175 | _ | 207 | I | 239 | ï |
| 016 | ► | 048 | 0 | 080 | P | 112 | p | 144 | É | 176 | ° | 208 | D | 240 | d |
| 017 | ◄ | 049 | 1 | 081 | Q | 113 | q | 145 | æ | 177 | ± | 209 | Ñ | 241 | ñ |
| 018 | ↕ | 050 | 2 | 082 | R | 114 | r | 146 | Æ | 178 | 2 | 210 | O | 242 | ò |
| 019 | ‼ | 051 | 3 | 083 | S | 115 | s | 147 | ô | 179 | 3 | 211 | O | 243 | ó |
| 020 | ¶ | 052 | 4 | 084 | T | 116 | t | 148 | ö | 180 | ' | 212 | O | 244 | o |
| 021 | § | 053 | 5 | 085 | U | 117 | u | 149 | ò | 181 | µ | 213 | O | 245 | o |
| 022 | ▬ | 054 | 6 | 086 | V | 118 | v | 150 | û | 182 | ¶ | 214 | Ö | 246 | ö |
| 023 | ↨ | 055 | 7 | 087 | W | 119 | w | 151 | ù | 183 | • | 215 | L | 247 | 1 |
| 024 | ↑ | 056 | 8 | 088 | X | 120 | x | 152 | ÿ | 184 | , | 216 | O | 248 | ° |
| 025 | ↓ | 057 | 9 | 089 | Y | 121 | y | 153 | Ö | 185 | 1 | 217 | U | 249 | ù |
| 026 | → | 058 | : | 090 | Z | 122 | z | 154 | Ü | 186 | o | 218 | U | 250 | ú |
| 027 | ← | 059 | ; | 091 | [ | 123 | { | 155 | ¢ | 187 | » | 219 | U | 251 | û |
| 028 | ∟ | 060 | < | 092 | \ | 124 | ¦ | 156 | £ | 188 | ¼ | 220 | Ü | 252 | ü |
| 029 | ↔ | 061 | = | 093 | ] | 125 | } | 157 | ¥ | 189 | ½ | 221 | Y | 253 | y |
| 030 | ▲ | 062 | > | 094 | ^ | 126 | ~ | 158 | P₸ | 190 | _ | 222 | _ | 254 | _ |
| 031 | ▼ | 063 | ? | 095 | _ | 127 | ■ | 159 | ƒ | 191 | ¿ | 223 | β | 255 | ÿ |

**Table 1-14 Character set resulting when ANSI is converted to OEM with FCONVERT**

# BORLAND C++
# COMPILER
# REFERENCE

# 2

The compilers in the Borland C++ package have a set of general default options that will compile most simple applications. For more complex applications, such as large DOS programs or Windows applications, you will need to alter the default behavior of the compiler. You may, for example, have an application that is too large for compilation using the default small memory model. Or you may wish to compile an application to a .COM file. Compiling Windows applications or Dynamic Link Libraries requires different compiler options than the default settings. You may also wish to enhance the performance or reduce the size of your application. Selection of memory models and target applications as well as code optimization can all be done by enabling or disabling certain compiler options.

This chapter covers all the compiler options available with the Borland C++ compiler, how you control them from the command line, from the menus for either the BC++ or TCW IDE, or from within the source code. This chapter also includes a discussion of how each option affects the code generated for your application. Each option includes an example application demonstrating how to use the option.

The reference section lists the compiler options alphabetically by their command line letters. You can use almost every command line option in the IDE either directly as a menu or dialog box option, indirectly as a local option to a project file, or as a #pragma directive within the source code. The reference section also discusses the equivalent IDE menu option or #pragma directive, if applicable.

## THE COMMAND LINE COMPILER OPTIONS

Borland C++ Version 3.0/3.1 comes with only one command line compiler, called BCC. Unlike Version 2.0, which had a command line compiler that operated in both the real and the protected modes, BCC in Version 3.0/3.1 will only operate in the protected mode. This means you will need a machine with an 80286 microprocessor (or better) and at least 3 Megabytes of extended memory. This allows the compiler to utilize a DOS extender to operate in the protected mode and utilize all your computer's memory as if it were normal DOS memory. This greatly increases compilation speed by eliminating the need to swap portions of memory into and out of extended or expanded memory when compiling large source files. The disadvantage is that it takes longer to load a protected mode compiler than the old, real-mode BCC. This means it may take longer to compile small source files.

BCC uses the following syntax:

```
BCC [option [option . . .]]  filename[.C][.CPP][.ASM][.OBJ][.LIB]
filename[.C][.CPP][.ASM][.OBJ][.LIB] . . .
```

You can list as many options as you like provided you precede each option with the '-' symbol. In general, listing an option on the command line enables the feature, whereas listing the option with the '-' symbol disables the option. For example, consider the following:

```
BCC -C -ff- SOURCE.C
```

Listing the -C option on the command line enables nested comments. The '-' character following the -ff disables the fast floating-point option during the compilation of SOURCE.C.

After the command line options, you list the component source files for your application, including any precompiled object code files, library files, or assembly language files. The command line compiler defaults to compiling any file with a .C extension as a C source file and files with a .CPP extension, or no extension at all, as a C++ source file. You modify this default behavior using the -P*ext* option. The compiler passes assembly language files to an external assembler for compilation and passes library and any precompiled object files directly to the linker. Table 2-1 summarizes the filename extension and the corresponding actions taken by the compiler.

| EXTENSION | FILE TYPE | COMPILER ACTIONS |
|-----------|-----------|------------------|
| .ASM | Assembly Language | Passed to external assembler |
| .C | C Source Code | Compiled by the command line compiler |
| .CPP | C++ Source Code | Compiled by the command line compiler |
| .LIB | Library File | Passed to TLINK |
| .OBJ | Object Code | Passed to TLINK |

**Table 2-1 Filename extensions and the command line compiler**

After either the command line compiler or the external assembler compiles the source code, the compiler then calls Turbo Linker (TLINK) to create the executable file. The compiler passes TLINK the compiled .OBJ files, the other .OBJ files listed on the command line, and any .LIB files. The compiler passes other parameters to the linker, such as the memory model, executable filename, case sensitivity, etc., depending on the compiler options used.

# COMPILER OPTIONS AND THE IDE MENU

Almost every command line option has an equivalent feature in the DOS and Windows IDE. For example, the -mm compiler option compiles the source code using the medium memory model. You specify this option in the IDE by marking the [Medium] item in the [Options][Compiler][Code Generation] menu. The boldfaced command line letters correspond to the highlighted letters in the IDE. The reference section of this chapter lists the IDE menu equivalent for each command line option. Table 2-2 lists the command line compiler options by their IDE menu option equivalent.

### [Options][Compiler][Code generation...]

| Model | | Options | |
|---|---|---|---|
| Tiny | -mt | Treat enums as ints | -b |
| Small | -ms | Word alignment | -a |
| Medium | -mm | Duplicate strings merged | -d |
| Compact | -mc | Unsigned characters | -K |
| Large | -ml | Pre-compiled headers | -H |
| Huge | -mh | Generate assembler source | -S |
| | | Compile via assembler | -B |

| Assume SS equals DS | |
|---|---|
| Default for memory model | -mx |
| Never | -mx! |
| Always | -Fs |

| Defines | -Dmacro |
|---|---|

### [Options][Compiler][Advanced code generation...]

| Floating-Point | | Options | |
|---|---|---|---|
| None | -f- | Generate underbars | -u |
| Emulation | -f | Line numbers debug info | -y |
| 8087 | -f87 | Debug info in OBJs | -v |
| 80287 | -f287 | Browser info into OBJs | -R |
| | | Fast floating point | -ff |
| Instruction Set | | Fast huge pointers | -h |
| 8088/8086 | -1- | Generate COMDEFs | -Fc |
| 80186 | -1 | Automatic far data | -Ff |
| 80286 | -2 | | |
| 80386 | -3 | | |
| | | Far Data Threshold | -Ff=size |

*Table 2-2 (continued)*

| [**O**ptions][**C**ompiler][**E**ntry/Exit Code...] | | |
|---|---|---|
| **Prolog/Epilog Code Generation** | | |
| DOS **s**tandard | | (Default) |
| DOS **o**verlay | | -Y |
| Windows **a**ll functions exportable | -W | |
| Windows **e**xplicit functions exported | -WE | |
| Windows **sm**art callbacks | | -WS |
| Windows **D**LL all functions exportable | -WD | |
| Windows DLL **ex**plicit functions exported | -WDE | |

| Calling Convention | Stack Options | | |
|---|---|---|---|
| **C** | -p- | Standard stack **f**rame | -k |
| **P**ascal | -p | Test stack **o**verflow | -N |
| **R**egister | -pr | | |

| [**O**ptions][**C**ompiler][C++ Options...] | | | |
|---|---|---|---|
| Use C++ Compiler | C++ Virtual Tables | | |
| CPP e**x**tension | -P- | **S**mart | -V |
| **C**++ always | -P | **L**ocal | -Vs |
| | | **E**xternal | -V0 |
| Template Generation | **P**ublic | -V1 | |
| **Sm**art | -Tg | | |
| **E**xternal | -Tdx | | |
| **G**lobal | -Tgd | | |
| Options | | | |
| **O**ut-of-line inline functions | -vi- | | |
| **F**ar virtual tables | -Vf | | |

| [**O**ptions][**C**ompiler][Advanced C++ options...] | |
|---|---|
| C++ Member Pointers | |
| Support **a**ll cases | -Vmv |
| Support **m**ultiple inheritance | -Vmm |
| Support **s**ingle inheritance | -Vms |
| Smallest for **c**lass | -Vmd |

Virtual base object pointers

    Always **n**ear                                 -Vb-

    **D**efault for memory model   -Vb

Options

    'deep' **v**irtual bases     -Vv

    True '**pa**scal' member functions             -Vp

    **H**onor precision of member pointers      -Vmp

    **C**onstructor displacements  -Vc

Pass class values via **r**eference  -Va

    Vta**b**le pointer follows data members       -Vt

**[O**ptions]**[C**ompiler]**[O**ptimizations...]

| Optimizations | | Register Variables | |
|---|---|---|---|
| **G**lobal register allocation | -Oe | **N**one | -r- |
| Invariant code motion | -Om | Register key**w**ord | -rd |
| Induction **v**ariables | -Ov | **A**utomatic | -r |
| **L**oop optimization | -Ol | | |
| Su**p**ress redundant loads | -Z | Common Subexpressions | |
| **C**opy propagation | -Op | No **o**ptimization | -Od |
| Assu**m**e no pointer aliasing | -Oa | Optimize local**l**y | -Ol |
| Dead code elimination | -Ob | Optimize glo**b**ally | -Og |
| **J**ump optimization | -O | | |
| Inline int**r**insic functions | -Oi | Optimize for | |
| **St**andard stack frame | -k | Size | -Os |
| Object data calling | -po | Sp**e**ed | -Ot |

**D**efault  -Od       **F**astest Code  -O2     **S**mallest Code    -O1

**[O**ptions]**[C**ompiler]**[S**ource...]

| Keywords | | Source Options | |
|---|---|---|---|
| **B**orland C++ | -AT | Nested comments | -C |
| **A**NSI | -A | | |
| **U**NIX V | -AU | **I**dentifier Length | -i*n* |
| Kernighan and **R**itchie | -AK | | |

*Table 2-2 (continued)*

**[O**ptions**][C**ompiler**][M**essages**][D**isplay...**]**

Display Warnings

| | | | |
|---|---|---|---|
| **A**ll | -w | **E**rror: Stop After | -j*n* |
| **S**elected | -w*xxx* | **W**arnings: Stop After | -g*n* |
| **N**one | -w- | | |

**[O**ptions**][C**ompiler**][M**essages**][P**ortability...**]**

| | |
|---|---|
| **N**on-portable pointer conversion | -wrpt |
| Non-portable pointer **c**omparison | -wcpt |
| Constant out of **r**ange in comparison | -wrng |
| Constant is **l**ong | -wcln |
| Conversion may lose **s**ignificant digits | -wsig |
| **M**ixing pointers to signed and unsigned char | -wucp |

**[O**ptions**][C**ompiler**][M**essages**][A**nsi violations...**]**

| | |
|---|---|
| **V**oid functions may not return a value | -wvoi |
| **B**oth return and return of a value used | -wret |
| **S**uspicious pointer conversion | -wsus |
| **U**ndefined structure 'ident' | -wstu |
| **R**edefinition of 'ident' is not identical | -wdup |
| **H**exadecimal value more than three digits | -wbig |
| Bit **f**ields must be signed or unsigned int | -wbbf |
| 'ident' declared as both e**x**ternal and static | -wext |
| **D**eclare 'ident' prior to use in prototype | -wdpu |
| Division by **z**ero | -wzdi |
| **I**nitializing 'ident' with 'ident' | -weas |
| Initialization is only **p**artially bracketed | -wpin |

**[O**ptions**][C**ompiler**][M**essages**][C**++ warnings...**]**

| | |
|---|---|
| **B**ase initialization without a class name is obsolete | -wobi |
| Functions containing 'ident' are not e**x**panded inline | -winl |
| Temporary used to **i**nitialize 'ident' | -wlin |

54

| | |
|---|---|
| **T**emporary used for parameter 'ident' | -wlvc |
| The constant **m**ember 'ident' is not initialized | -wnci |
| This **s**tyle of function definition is now obsolete | -wofp |
| **U**se of 'overload' is now unnecessary and obsolete | -wovl |
| Assi**g**ning 'type' to 'enumeration' | -wbei |
| 'function1' **h**ides virtual function 'function2' | -whid |
| **N**on-const function 'ident' called for const object | -wncf |
| Base **c**lass 'ident' is inaccessible because also in 'ident' | -wibc |
| **O**verloaded prefix operator used as a postfix operator | -wpre |
| Array size of '**d**elete' ignored | -wdsz |
| Use **q**ualified name to access nested type 'ident' | -wnst |

[**O**ptions][**C**ompiler][**M**essages][**F**requent errors...]

| | |
|---|---|
| **F**unction should return a value | -wrvl |
| **U**nreachable code | -wrch |
| **C**ode has no effect | -weff |
| **P**ossible use of 'ident' before definition | -wdef |
| '**i**dent' is assigned a value which is never used | -waus |
| Parameter 'ident' is **n**ever used | -wpar |
| Possibly incorrect **a**ssignment | -wpia |

[**O**ptions][**C**ompiler][**M**essages][**L**ess frequent errors...]

| | |
|---|---|
| **S**uperfluous & with function | -wamp |
| **A**mbiguous operators need parentheses | -wamb |
| Structure passed by **v**alue | -wstv |
| **N**o declaration for function 'ident' | -wnod |
| Call to function with no **p**rototype | -wpro |
| Restarting **c**ompile using assembly | -wasc |
| **U**nknown assembler instruction | -wasm |
| **Il**l formed pragma | -will |
| Co**n**dition is always (true/false) | -wccc |
| **A**rray variable 'ident' is near | -wias |
| '**i**dent' declared but never used | -wuse |

*Table 2-2 (continued)*

| | [**O**ptions][**C**ompiler][**N**ames...] | | |
|---|---|---|---|
| Code **S**egment | -zC*name* | **B**BS Segment | -zD*name* |
| Code **G**roup | -zP*name* | BBS **G**roup | -zG*name* |
| Code **C**lass | -zA*name* | BBS Class | -zB*name* |
| **D**ata Segment | -zR*name* | Far Data Segme**n**t | -zE*name* |
| Data Group | -zS*name* | Far Data Grou**p** | -zH*name* |
| Data Class | -zT*name* | **F**ar Data Class | -zF*name* |

**Table 2-2 Command line compiler options listed by their IDE menu option equivalent**

# LOCAL PROJECT OPTIONS

IDE menu selections act globally on all the source files in your project. You can, however, customize the compiler options for individual files in the project. You do this by entering one or more of the compiler options listed in Table 2-2 as a local option to a project file. For example, if you want one particular source file compiled using the 80286 instruction set, word aligned data, default to unsigned characters and disable fast floating-point, you highlight that particular file in the project window, press (Ctrl)-(O) to bring up the local options menu, and enter the following in the [Command Line Options] box:

```
-2 -a -K -ff-
```

The options you list in the [Command Line Options] box of a file's local options menu will override the global menu options. You cannot use all the compiler options as a local option to a project file. You can use any compiler option listed in the reference section marked as "Local Option" as a local command line option to a project file. Also, not all command line options have an equivalent option in the IDE menu. You must use some options, such as the -Hu option, as a local command line option to a project file. Table 2-3 lists the options you can use as local options but which have no equivalent IDE menu option.

| | |
|---|---|
| -Fm | Use Fc, Ff, Fs Options |
| -Hu | Use, but do not Create, a Pre-Compiled Header |
| -H=*filename* | Save Pre-Compiled Headers in *filename* |
| -o*filename* | Object Code Filename |
| -T*xxx* | Pass *xxx* Options to the External Assembler |
| -U*tag* | #undef *tag* |

**Table 2-3 Local command line options with no equivalent IDE menu option**

# #PRAGMA OPTION DIRECTIVES

While local project options provide control over the compiler's operation for individual source files, the #pragma option directives provide even finer control over the compiler options within the source code. For example, consider the following:

```
#pragma option -h

void Fast(void)
{. . .

#pragma option -h-
void Slow(void)
{. . .

#pragma option -h.
void Default(void)
{
```

The '#pragma option -h' directive enabled the fast huge pointer calculation option for the Fast() function, which was disabled by the '#pragma option -h-' directive for the Slow() function. The '#pragma option -h.' directive returned the option to the state it was in at the very beginning of the source file.

Some #pragma options, because of the effect they have on the compiler, are only effective if you place them at the very beginning of the source file before you use any C or C++ instructions or any preprocessor directives involving macros starting with two leading underscores, such as __SMALL__. Other #pragma option directives can appear later in the source code provided they are between functions. Still others can appear anywhere. Any restrictions on the placement of the #pragma option directive associated with the compiler option are stated in the "Usage" section of the reference listing.

Some command line compiler options have no direct #pragma option directive, but instead use another equivalent instruction in the source file. For example, you do not use the -B compiler option directly as a '#pragma option -B' directive. Instead you would use the '#pragma inline' directive that accomplishes the same thing. The reference section lists any #pragma aliases. The '#pragma' column in the heading is blank if there is no #pragma directive corresponding to the compiler option.

# COMPILING FOR SPEED

The fractal program and math library included with the book are written for speed. There is only so much optimization, however, that can be performed on a source code level without resorting entirely to assembly language. We can, however, enlist the aid of the compiler by enabling or disabling the following compiler options to improve the performance of our application:

-a    This option instructs the compiler to align data to start on an even address boundary. The microprocessor can access memory more quickly if the address is on an even boundary.

-d      This option will merge any duplicate strings in the application, making the application smaller. While this will not improve the speed, it will not slow us down either.

-ff     This option instructs the compiler to ignore any float typecasting. Typecasting a double to a float does two things: it reduces the accuracy and slows down the application. We can do without either of these features.

-h      Our application does not utilize huge pointers, but if it did, we would definitely want to enable this option!

-ms    The small memory model provides the fastest access to both code and data. It also has the added benefit of generating smaller executable code than all the other memory models except tiny.

-N-    The -N option inserts extra code at the start of each function that checks for a stack overflow condition. The process involves a considerable amount of extra code and slows down an application. This option should be disabled unless you are debugging.

-O2    The -O2 option enables all the remaining compiler options that increase the application's execution speed.

# THE PREPROCESSOR UTILITY

The preprocessor utility, CPP.EXE, performs a single pass of your source code and generates a text file containing the expansion of any #include files and macro usage. For example, consider the following application:

**cpp\test.c**

```
#define MACRO x

void main(void)
{
    int MACRO = 0;

    printf("The MACRO equals %d\n", MACRO);
}
```

You execute CPP just as you would the command line compiler, BCC, using the same options as for a normal compilation. CPP will ignore any options which do not apply. For example, you execute CPP for the above file as follows:

```
cpp test.c
```

You can list as many files as necessary. If you do not specify an extension, CPP will assume a .CPP file extension. Note that the CPP treats all files as .C files.

The following is the output from the CPP utility:

**cpp\test.i**
```
    test.c 1:
    test.c 2:
    test.c 3: void main(void)
    test.c 4: {
    test.c 5: int x = 0;
    test.c 6:
    test.c 7: printf("The MACRO equals %d\n", x);
    test.c 8: }
    test.c 9:
    test.c 10:
```

# COMPILER OPTIONS REFERENCE

The following reference section contains all the command line options that are available for BCC. Each command line option contains the following compatibility heading:

- C
- C++
- CPP
- TC++
- TCW/BCW
- BC 2.0
- BC 3.0/3.1
- BCC
- Local
- #pragma

Table 2-4 lists each heading and its meaning.

| HEADING | COMMENTS |
|---------|----------|
| C | Option applies to source code written in C. |
| C++ | Option applies to source code written in C++. |
| CPP | The CPP.EXE preprocessor utility utilizes this option. Options which are not marked indicate that CPP ignores the option. |
| TC++ | Option is used by TC++ Version 2.0. |
| TCW/BCW | There is a menu item in TC++ and BC++ for Windows which corresponds to this command line option. |
| BC 2.0 | This option is available in BC++ Version 2.0. |
| BC 3.0 | This option is available in BC++ Version 3.0 and 3.1. |
| Local | You can use this option as a local option to a project file. |
| #pragma | You can use this option in a #pragma directive. |

**Table 2-4 Compatibility headings**

# @filename

**Response File**

| | | | | |
|---|---|---|---|---|
| ■ C | ■ C++ | CPP | ■ TC++ | TCW/BCW |
| ■ BC 2.0 | ■ BC 3.0/3.1 | BCC | Local | #pragma |

## Purpose

The @*filename* option expands the text contained within *filename* as if it were typed in on the command line. This allows, for example, the use of files that direct the compiler to use different memory models, set the location of include and library files, etc.

## IDE Option

N/A

## Usage

```
BCC @C:\PROJECT.OPT SOURCE.C
```

## Description

The @*filename* option provides macro expansion of text on the command line. The text file specified by the pathname can contain anything you normally place on the compiler's command line. Generally this would be any group of command line options you plan to use globally with many different source code files.

As shown in the example below, you can also use more than one @*filename* on the command line. For example, you could have general options in one file and a list of warning message options in another file. Note that while any number of @*filename* files may be listed on the command line, you cannot place any @*filename* arguments within another @*filename* text file, i.e., recursive command line expansion is not supported.

## See Also

+*filename*    Alternate configuration file

## Example

This example uses two files that contain a list of options, PROJECT.OPT and WARNING.LST, that will be used to compile the file TEST.C:

**pfile\test.c**
```
    #include <stdio.h>

    void main(void)
    {
       printf("This is a test");
    }
```

The file PROJECT.OPT contains the options to compile TEST.C in the tiny memory model, uses 80286 code, informs the compiler the code contains no floating-point, and specifies the location of include and library files:

**pfile\project.opt**

| | |
|---|---|
| −mt | *Use the tiny memory model* |
| −2 | *Use 80286 instructions* |
| −f− | *Do not link the floating point library* |
| −IC:\BORLANDC\INCLUDE | *Location of include files* |
| −LC:\BORLANDC\LIB | *Location of library files* |

The WARNING.LST file contains a list of warning message options:

**pfile\warning.lst**

| | |
|---|---|
| −wamb | *Warn about ambiguous operators* |
| −wamp | *Warn about superfluous ampersands* |
| −wasm | *Warn if restarting with assembler* |
| −wdef | *Warn if a function is used before definition* |

To compile the file from the DOS command line or from within a MAKE file using the two option files, you enter the following:

```
BCC @project.opt @warning.lst test.c
```

The BCC compiler will then expand the PROJECT.OPT and WARNING.LST files and interpret the command line as if the following were entered:

```
BCC −mt −2 −f− −IC:\BORLANDC\INCLUDE −LC:\BORLANDC\LIB −wamb −wamp −
wasm −wdef test.c
```

# +*filename*                          Alternate Configuration File

| | | | | |
|---|---|---|---|---|
| ▪ C | ▪ C++ | CPP | TC++ | TCW/BCW |
| ▪ BC 2.0 | ▪ BC 3.0/3.1 | ▪ BCC | Local | #pragma |

## Purpose
The +*filename* option tells the compiler to use an alternate configuration file. The compiler will then use the default compiler options contained in the file.

## IDE Option
Configuration files are used by the command line compiler only. Project files (.PRJ) are the IDE equivalent of a configuration file (.CFG). Use PRJCFG to convert .CFG files to .PRJ files or vice versa.

## Default
BCC +TURBOC.CFG SOURCE.C

Use the configuration file called TURBOC.CFG located in the current or compiler directory.

## Usage
BCC +MYDEF.CFG TEST.C

Use the configuration file called MYDEF.CFG in the current directory.

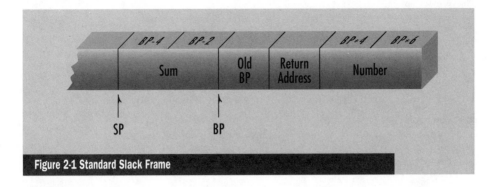

**Figure 2-1 Standard Slack Frame**

## Description

A configuration file (.CFG) is a text file containing a list of command line options. Like the *@filename* option, the command line options listed in the *+filename* file can be either separated by spaces or listed on different lines.

Note that you may not include *@filename* macro expansion files or source files within a configuration file. Only command line options can be listed in the *+filename* file.

## See Also

| | |
|---|---|
| *@filename* | Response File |
| Chapter 3: PRJCFG | Utility |

## Example

Write a configuration text file and compile the following source code using the *+filename* option:

**plusfile\test.c**

```
#include <stdio.h>

void main(void)
{
    printf("This is a test");
}
```

**plusfile\test.cfg**

| | |
|---|---|
| -mt | *Use the tiny memory model* |
| -2 | *Use 80286 instructions* |
| -f- | *Do not link the floating point library* |
| -IC:\BORLANDC\INCLUDE | *Location of include files* |
| -LC:\BORLANDC\LIB | *Location of library files* |
| -wamb | *Warn about ambiguous operators* |
| -wamp | *Warn about superfluous ampersands* |
| -wasm | *Warn if restarting with assembler* |
| -wdef | *Warn if a function is used before definition* |

## 1, 2, 3                                          Microprocessor Instruction Set

| | | | | |
|---|---|---|---|---|
| ▪ C | ▪ C++ | CPP | ▪ TC++ | ❶ TCW/BCW |
| ▪ BC 2.0 | ❶ BC 3.0/3.1 | ▪ BCC | ▪ Local | ▪ #pragma |

❶ Only BCW and BC++ version 3.1

### Purpose

The -1 compiler option generates source code that uses the 80186 extended instructions and 80286 real-mode instructions. The -2 compiler option generates code that uses the 80286 protected-mode instruction set. Using these options creates smaller and faster executable code; however, the resulting executable code will not run on a machine that uses the 8086 processor, such as an IBM PC or XT class machine. The -3 option instructs the compiler to generate 80386 specific instructions and enables the use of the extended pseudo registers.

### IDE Option

Options I Compiler I Advanced code generation I 8088/8086   *for -1-*   (DOS only)
Options I Compiler I Advanced code generation I 80186      *for -1*    (DOS only)
Options I Compiler I Advanced code generation I 80286      *for -2*
Options I Compiler I Advanced code generation I 80286      *for -3*

### Default

```
-1-     (for the DOS compiler)
```
    Generate 8086 instructions.

```
-2      (for TCW and BCW)
```
    Generate 80286 instructions.

### Usage

```
BCC -1 SOURCE.C
```
    Generate code using the 80186 and real-mode instruction set.

```
#pragma option -1
```
    Same as above. This option must appear before any C or C++ instruction.

```
BCC -2 SOURCE.C
```
    Generate code using 80286 protected-mode instructions.

```
#pragma option -2
```
    Same as above. Must appear before any C or C++ instruction.

```
BCC -3 SOURCE.C
```
    Generate code using 80386 protected mode instructions.

```
#pragma option -3
```
Same as above. This option must appear before any C or C++ instruction.

## Description

Compiling your applications using the 80186 and 80286 instruction set produces smaller and faster executable code, especially if your application performs a significant number of function calls. This is mainly because the 80186 and 80286 instruction set contains the ENTER and LEAVE instructions that set and restore the function's stack frame. C and C++ functions use a stack frame to allow access to the variables passed to the function using the Base Pointer (BP) register and also provide stack space for local variables.

Setting the stack frame for a function using 8086 instructions is normally accomplished as follows:

```
;
;      long RecursiveAddition(long Number)
;

_RecursiveAddition  proc      near
        push  bp          Save old base pointer
        mov   bp,sp        Set new base pointer
        sub   sp,4         Make room for the local variable, Sum
```

The above code sets the stack frame for the RecursiveAddition function used in the example application listed below. First the old base pointer is saved onto the stack, then the current stack pointer is used as the new base pointer and 4 bytes are subtracted from the stack pointer to set aside space on the stack for the local variable, Sum. With the stack frame set in this way, the passed parameter, Number, can be accessed using an address of [bp+4], and the local variable, Sum, can be accessed using [bp-4]. Before the function returns, the stack frame is restored to its previous state as follows:

```
        mov   sp,bp        Remove the local variable space
        pop   bp           Restore the old BP value
        ret                Return from the function call
```

The local variable, Sum, is removed from the stack by setting the stack pointer with the value of the BP register. The old base pointer is then popped back into the BP register off the stack and a normal function return executed. The RET instruction pops the return address off the stack and the calling function removes the Number variable by incrementing the stack pointer by four.

Using 80186 and 80286 instructions allows the stack frame to be set using a single ENTER instruction and to be restored using the LEAVE instruction. As shown in the example application, this saves 10 bytes of code and increases the execution speed by 35%.

If you know your application will only be running on a machine with an 80386SX or better microporcessor, you should use the -3 option to generate 80386 specific instructions. Enabling the 80386 instruction set allows the compiler to use the 32-bit extended registers of the 80386SX/DX and 80486SX/DX microprocessors. For example, the compiler normally generates the following code to multiply two type long integers:

```
;
;   c = a * b;
```

```
;
    mov     cx,word ptr [bp-2]
    mov     bx,word ptr [bp-4]
    mov     dx,word ptr [bp-6]
    mov     ax,word ptr [bp-8]
    call    near ptr N_LXMUL@
    mov     word ptr [bp-10],dx
    mov     word ptr [bp-12],ax
```

The above assembly language loads four 16-bit registers with the 'a' and 'b' variables and calls the N_LXMUL@ function to perform the 32-bit multiplication. The function returns the 32-bit result in the DX:AX registers. However, if you enable the 80386 instruction, the compiler will generate the following code:

```
;
;   c = a * b;
;
    mov     eax,dword ptr [bp-4]
    imul    eax,dword ptr [bp-8]
    mov     dword ptr [bp-12],eax
```

Here, the compiler first loads the 'a' variable into the eax register. It then multiplies by the 'b' register and stores the result in the EAX register in a single instruction. Using the 80386 extended registers produces faster and smaller code.

The -3 option also enables the following extended register and segment register pseudo variables:

```
_EAX,       _EBX      _ECX      _EDX
_EDI        _ESI      _FS       _GS
```

One use for the extended register pseudo variables is for model independent dereferencing of pointers. For example, consider the following function:

```
#pragma inline
#pragma option -3

void Mul32bit(unsigned long *a, unsigned long *b)
{
    long Ans;

    _EAX = *a
    _EDX = *b;
    asm {
        mul  edx
        shrd eax, edx, 16
        mov  Ans, eax
    }
    printf("Ans = %lx\n", Ans);
}
```

In the above function the compiler dereferences the two 'a' and 'b' pointers and loads them into the EAX and EDX registers for use by the inline assembly language block. If you were to dereference the two pointers manually in the assembly language block, you would have to determine whether they were near or far pointers. and write the appropriate code for each possibility. The compiler does this for you automatically when you use the pseudo variables.

Note that TCW and BCW will only generate code for machines with an 80286 or better microprocessor. TCW only supports the -2 option. BCW supports the -2 and the -3 options.

## See Also
Assembly language instructions ENTER and LEAVE.

| | |
|---|---|
| ff | Use Fast Floating Point |
| f, f87, f287 | Floating Point Instruction Type |
| G | Compile in Favor of Speed |
| h | Use Fast huge Pointer Calculations |
| p | Use the Pascal or Fastcall Calling Convention |

## Example
Write an example application that performs many function calls by recursively adding the numbers 1 through 500 and compile the application with and without the -1 command line option. When the following example is compiled with the -1 command line option, the resulting executable code is 10 bytes smaller and runs 35% faster:

**80186\test.c**

```
#pragma option -1

#include <stdio.h>

long Limit;

long RecursiveAddition(long Number)
{
    long Sum;

    if(Number < Limit)
        Sum = RecursiveAddition(Number + 1);
    else
        Sum = 0;
    return(Sum + Number);
}

void main(void)
{
    long Sum;

    Limit = 500;
    Sum = RecursiveAddition(0);
    printf("Sum = %ld\n", Sum);
}
```

# A, AK, AT, AU                                          Language Keywords

---

| | | | | |
|---|---|---|---|---|
| ■ C | ❶ C++ | ■ CPP | ■ TC++ | ■ TCW/BCW |
| ■ BC 2.0 | ■ BC 3.0/3.1 | ■ BCC | ■ Local | #pragma |

❶   Only the -AT and -AU options will compile C++ source code.

## Purpose

The -A, -AK, and -AU options restrict the allowable keywords and syntax you can use in your application. You normally use one of these options to keep your code compatible with other compilers. The -AT option, which has the same effect as disabling the -A option, enables the use of all BC++ keywords.

## IDE Option

| | |
|---|---|
| Options \| Compiler \| Source \| Borland C++ | -AT or -A- |
| Options \| Compiler \| Source \| ANSI | -A |
| Options \| Compiler \| Source \| UNIX V | -AU |
| Options \| Compiler \| Source \| Kernighan and Ritchie | -AK |

## Default

`-A-, -AT`

Use all Borland C++ keywords.

## Usage

`BCC -AT SOURCE.C`

Allow the use of all Borland C++ keywords and modern C and C++ syntax. (default)

`BCC -A- SOURCE.C`

Same as above.

`BCC -AU SOURCE.C`

Restrict source code to UNIX V compatible keywords and syntax for C and C++.

`BCC -A SOURCE.C`

Compile using ANSI compatible keywords.

`BCC -AK SOURCE.C`

Compile using K & R compatible keywords.

## Description

You use the -A, -AU, or -AK option to emulate an ANSI, UNIX V, or K & R compatible compiler, respectively. The default option, -AT, allows all Borland C++ keywords and syntax. The -A- option is identical to the -AT option. Table 2-5 shows the keywords available for each of the different compilers.

| COMPILER OPTION | | | | | | KEYWORDS | | | |
|---|---|---|---|---|---|---|---|---|---|
| **K & R** | -AK | auto | break | case | char | continue | default | do | double else |
| | | enum | extern | float | for | goto | if | int | long |
| | | return | short | sizeof | static | struct | switch | typedef | union |
| | | while | | | | | | | |
| **ANSI** | -A | auto | break | case | char | const | continue | default | do |
| | | double | else | enum | extern | float | for | goto | if int |
| | | long | register | return | short | signed | sizeof | static | struct |
| | | -switch | typedef | union | unsigned void | volatile | while | | |

*Table 2-5 (continued)*

| UNIX V | -AU | auto | break | case | catch | char | class | const | continue | |
|---|---|---|---|---|---|---|---|---|---|---|
| | | default | delete | do | double | else | enum | extern | float | for |
| | | friend | goto | if | inline | int | long | operator | private | |
| | | protected | public | register | return | short | signed | sizeof | static1 | |
| | | struct | switch | template | this | typedef | union | unsigned | virtual | |
| | | void | volatile | while | | | | | | |

| Borland | -AT | _AH | _AL | asm | _AX | auto | _BH | _BL | break | _BX |
|---|---|---|---|---|---|---|---|---|---|---|
| | | case | catch | _cdecl | cdecl | _CH | char | _CL | class | |
| | | const | continue_cs | | _CX | default | delete | _DH | _DI | |
| | | _DL | do | double | _DS | _ds | _DX | else | enum | _ES |
| | | _es | _export | extern | _far | far | _FLAGS | float | for | |
| | | friend | goto | huge | if | inline | int | interrupt | _loads | long |
| | | _near | near | operator | _pascal | pascal | private | protected | public | |
| | | register | return | _saveregs_seg | | short | _SI | signed | sizeof | _SP |
| | | _SS | _ss | static | struct | switch template | | this | typedef | |
| | | union | unsigned | virtual | void | volatile while | | | | |

**Table 2-5 Table of keywords**

Additionally, if ANSI compatibility is selected, i.e., the -A option, then the __STDC__ macro is defined as the constant 1.

If you choose to use either the K & R or UNIX V compatibility options, you will not be able to use the include files supplied with the Borland C++ package. These files will only work with either Borland C++ or ANSI compatibility.

The Borland C++ *Programmer's Guide* incorrectly documents this option as being usable from a #pragma directive.

### See Also

| | |
|---|---|
| C | Allow Nested Comments |
| K | Default to signed/unsigned Characters |
| i*n* | Use *n* Significant Characters for Tags |
| p | Use the Pascal or Fastcall Calling Convention |
| u | Precede Tags with an Underscore |

### Example

Write an ANSI compatible application that counts from one to ten.

**a\ansi.c**

```
#include <s

void main(void)
{
   unsigned n;

   for (n = 1; n <= 10; n++)
      printf("Count: %d\n", n);
}
```

The above application can be compiled with checking for only ANSI compatible keywords by entering the following from the DOS command line:

```
bcc -A ansi.c
```

## a                                                        Byte/Word Alignment

- C
- BC 2.0
- C++
- BC 3.0/3.1
- CPP
- BCC
- TC++
- Local
- TCW/BCW
- #pragma

### Purpose
The -a option forces the compiler to align integer-sized or larger objects on a word boundary. Using the -a option creates applications that can access data more quickly, but usually requires more data space.

### IDE Option
Options | Compiler | Code | Word Alignment

### Default
```
-a-
```
No alignment (compact data).

### Usage
```
BCC -a SOURCE.C
```
Aligns all data 2 bytes or larger on an even address.

```
#pragma option -a
```
Same as above. This statement must appear between functions or object declarations to be effective.

### Description
The 80x86 family of microprocessors used in IBM compatible machines can access data more quickly if the data is located on an even address. The -a option ensures that all data objects 2 bytes in size or larger start on an even address. An even starting address is also referred to as starting on a word boundary. Depending on the arrangement of your application data and the number of times a data access is performed, this option may or may not produce a noticeable speed increase or an increase in size.

### See Also
| | |
|---|---|
| 1, 2, 3 | Microprocessor Instruction Set |
| b | Word Sized enums |
| d | Merge Duplicate String Literals |
| ff | Use Fast Floating Point |
| G | Compile in Favor of Speed |

h    Use Fast huge Pointer Calculation
O    Enable Jump Optimizations
Z    Assume No Indirect Assignments

## Example

Write an application that performs many accesses to two integers. One integer will start on an odd address and the other on an even address, such as the following:

**align\word.c**

```c
#include <stdio.h>

/* The FirstInt and SecondInt variables are on odd addresses */
char FirstChar;
int FirstInt;
int SecondInt;

/* Force word alignment */
   #pragma option -a

/* The ThirdInt variable is on an even address because
   of the -a option */
int ThirdInt;

void main(void)
{
    register int n;

    /* Print the different addresses */
    printf("FirstInt:    %p\n", &FirstInt);
    printf("SecondInt:   %p\n", &SecondInt);
    printf("ThirdInt:    %p\n", &ThirdInt);

/* Access an odd aligned integer 10,000 times */
    for(n = 0; n < 10000; n++)
        SecondInt = (int)n;

/* Access an even aligned integer 10,000 times */
    for(n = 0; n < 10000; n++)
        ThirdInt = (int)n;
}
```

The FirstInt and SecondInt both start on an odd address. The ThirdInt would also start on an odd address if it were not for the #pragma option -a directive. The following printout from the application shows the addresses for each integer:

**word\output**

```
FirstInt:    032C
SecondInt:   032E
ThirdInt:    0328
```

The first for() loop accesses the odd addressed integer, SecontInt, 10,000 times. The second for() loop accesses the even addressed integer, ThirdInt, 10,000 times. Running the executable code in Turbo Profiler and setting the timing on both for loops shows the loop with the even-addressed integer operates 79% faster than the loop with the integer starting on an odd address.

## B                                           Use an External Assembler instead of BASM

| ▪ C | ▪ C++ | CPP | ▪ TC++ | ▪ TCW/BCW |
| ▪ BC 2.0 | ▪ BC 3.0/3.1 | ▪ BCC | ▪ Local | ❶ #pragma |

❶ Use #pragma inline

### Purpose
The -B option tells the compiler your source code contains inline assembly language instructions which cannot be compiled by the Built-in Assembler (BASM). The -B option causes the compiler to compile the source code to a temporary .ASM file and pass it to the external assembler.

### IDE Option
Option | Compiler | Code Generation | Compile via Assembler

### Default
—B—
Compile directly to .OBJ file using BASM to compile inline assembly language.

### Usage
BCC —B SOURCE.C
Compile to .ASM file and pass to an external assembler.

#pragma inline
Same as above; compiler will restart the compile at the point where the #pragma inline instruction is placed.

### Description
Normally the compiler uses the more restrictive Built-in Assembler (BASM) to compile inline assembly language. BASM will compile the same assembly language instructions as the Turbo Assembler (TASM) except for macros, 80386, 80387, or 80486 microprocessor instructions, and the Ideal mode syntax. See Chapter 8 for more details on the differences between TASM and BASM. The -B option, or the #pragma inline equivalent, must be used to compile inline assembly language instructions that cannot be handled by the Built-in Assembler. The -B option causes the compiler to first generate an assembly language listing of the source code and then pass it to an external assembler. The default external assembler is the Turbo Assembler (TASM). Use the -E*filename* command line option to specify a different assembler or edit the TASM transfer item if you are using the IDE.

### See Also
Chapter 8     Inline Assembler Reference
E*filename*   External Assembler

## Example

Write an application using 80386 instructions to copy a long integer. The following application will not compile without the #pragma inline instruction. Without this instruction, the BASM compiler will generate four error messages.

**asm\inline.c**
```
#pragma inline

#include <stdio.h>

void main(void)
{
    Long Source = 0x12345678, Dest;

    asm {
    .386
        mov eax, Source     /* Load the 4-byte number */
        mov Dest, eax       /* Save it in Dest */
    .8086
    }
    printf("Dest = 0x%lx\n", Dest);
}
```

## b                                                    Use Word Sized enums

- C           - C++          CPP           TC++          - TCW/BCW
- BC 2.0      - BC 3.0/3.1   - BCC         - Local       - #pragma

### Purpose

The -b option causes the Borland C++ compiler to generate integer-sized enumerations. This maintains compatibility with Turbo C 2.0. Turning the -b option off with -b- causes the compiler to treat enumerations as characters whenever possible.

### IDE Option

Option | Compiler | Code Generation | Treat enums as ints

### Default

-b

Treat enumerations as integers.

### Usage

BCC -b- SOURCE.C

Treat enumerations as characters whenever possible.

#pragma option -b-

Same as above.

### Description

Whenever enumerations are used in an application, such as an assignment or a comparison, they occupy space in the application. Disabling word-sized enumerations produces smaller executable files.

## See Also

| | |
|---|---|
| a | Byte/Word Alignment |
| d | Merge Duplicate String Literals |
| G | Compile in Favor of Speed |

## Example

Write an application using byte-sized enumerations and compile with and without the word-sized enumeration option. The following application uses word-sized enumerations to process keystrokes. Compiling this file with word-sized enumerations using the -b option creates an executable code that is 2 bytes larger than the code produced by compiling with the option disabled.

**b\enum.c**

```c
#include <conio.h>

    #pragma option -b-

    enum { ESCAPE = 27, RETURN = '\r', LINE_FEED = '\n' };

void main(void)
{
    int Done = 0;

    while(!Done)                        /* Loop until Done != 0 */
    {
        char c;

        /* Grab a keyboard character */
        c = getch();
        if(c == ESCAPE)                 /* Is it an escape? */
                Done = 1;               /* Setup to exit */
        if(c == RETURN)                 /* Is it a return? */
            putch(LINE_FEED);
        if(!Done)                       /* Print it */
            putch(c);
    }
}
```

# C                                                    Allow Nested Comments

| | | | | |
|---|---|---|---|---|
| ▪ C | ▪ C++ | ▪ CPP | ▪ TC++ | ▪ TCW/BCW |
| ▪ BC 2.0 | ▪ BC 3.0/3.1 | ▪ BCC | ▪ Local | ▪ #pragma |

## Purpose

The -C option allows you to include comment token pairs, /* ... */, within other comment tokens.

## IDE Option

Option I Compiler I Source I Nested Comments

## Default

-C-

Nested comments are not allowed.

## Usage

```
BCC -C SOURCE.C
```
Allow nested comments.

```
#pragma option -C
```
Same as above.

## Description

Some programmers temporarily remove sections of code from their source file by enclosing them within a pair of comment tokens. If the deleted code section also contains comments, then those comments are considered *nested* within the outer comment tokens. For example, consider the following:

```
/* This section of code is deleted
   for(n = 0; n < 60000; n++);  /* Delay Loop */
/
```

The "Delay Loop" comment is nested with the comments used to delete the code section. Normally the compiler ignores all the code after the first /* comment token until it finds a */ token which, in the above code, is the "Delay Loop" comment. The compiler will then generate an error when it encounters the second */ comment token on the next line. The -C option tells the compiler to look for pairs of comment tokens thereby allowing comments to be nested.

Use of this option is not recommended for ANSI compatible source code. The ANSI standard does not allow nested comments. Instead of commenting out source code, the programmer is expected to delete a section of code using preprocessor directives. For example, the delay loop could be removed from the source code as follows:

```
#ifdef DELAY
    for(n = 0; n < 60000; n++);  /* Delay Loop */
#endif
```

Unless the DELAY macro is defined, the delay loop code will not be compiled into the executable code. This form of code deletion has the added benefit of allowing code sections to be compiled or removed by either defining or not defining certain macros. With the above format, the delay loop can be compiled back into the executable code by using the -D option to define the macro DELAY.

## See Also

Dtag, Dtag=string     #define tag string

## Example

Write an application that contains nested comments. The following application normally counts from 1 to 10 using a delay loop to produce a slight delay between counts. This delay loop has been commented out. If the -C option were not used, the compiler would generate an error on the second */ token.

**nested_c\nested.c**

```
#include <stdio.h>

#pragma option -C

void main(void)
{
   unsigned int n, count;

   for(count = 0; count < 10; count++)
   {
   /* This section of code is deleted.
      for(n = 0; n < 60000; n++); /* Delay Loop */
   */
   printf("Count = %d\n", count);
   }
}
```

| **c** | | | | **Compile Only** |
|---|---|---|---|---|
| ▪ C | ▪ C++ | CPP | ▪ TC++ | ▪ TCW/BCW |
| ▪ BC 2.0 | ▪ BC 3.0/3.1 | ▪ BCC | Local | #pragma |

### Purpose
The -c option instructs the compiler to only compile the source code and not call the Turbo Linker (TLINK) to create the executable file.

### IDE Option
Options | Make | Link (Break Make On . . .)

### Default
-c-

Call TLINK after compiling to create the executable file.

### Usage
BCC -c SOURCE.C

Compile to an .OBJ file only.

### Description
The -c option is used only as a command line option from DOS or in a MAKE file to prevent the command line compiler from calling TLINK after compiling the source code. This enables you to compile many different source code modules using separate calls to BCC and then link them all with a single call to the linker.

You can compile a file in the currently active editor window without linking by using the [Compile][Compile to OBJ] menu option. Individual source modules can be excluded from the linking by checking the [Exclude from link] box under on the local options menu.

**See Also**

S                          Compile to .ASM file

Chapter 6: TLINK

**Example**

Write a simple "Hello, C" application, compile to an .OBJ file using the -c option, and call TLINK separately:

**c\hello.c**
```
#include <stdio.h>
void main(void)
{
    printf("Hello, C!\n"); /* Print "Hello, C!" */
}
```

You would enter the following from the DOS command line to compile the above file :

```
bcc -c hello.c
```

This would compile the HELLO.C file to a small memory model .OBJ file. You would enter this from DOS to create an executable file:

```
tlink c0s hello, hello,, cs
```

The C0S file is the small memory model startup file and CS is the small memory model library file.


# Dtag, Dtag=string                                    #define tag string

- C          - C++          - CPP          - TC++          - TCW/BCW
- BC 2.0     - BC 3.0/3.1   - BCC          - Local          ❶ #pragma

❶ You use a #define directive in the source files rather than any #pragma directive.

**Purpose**

The -D*tag* option defines a macro string that will override any macro definitions in the source file that have the same name.

**IDE Option**

Options | Compile | Code Generation | Defines

**Default**

(none)

**Usage**

```
BCC -DDELAY SOURCE.C
```
Define a NULL string macro called DELAY.

```
BCC -DTITLE="Count" SOURCE.C
```
Define a "MY_APP" string macro called TITLE.

```
BCC -DDELAY -DTITLE="Count" SOURCE.C
```
Define both the DELAY and TITLE macros.

```
BCC -DDELAY;TITLE="Count" SOURCE.C
```
Same as above.

### Description

The -D*tag* option is used to define string macros that may or may not be in the source files. A NULL string is used if there is no string specified. If a string is specified using the -D*tag*=*string* option, the string cannot contain any spaces. Spaces can be included in the IDE's [Define] box. If there is a macro in the source file with the same name, the -D*tag* macro definition will be used in lieu of the definition in the source file. More than one macro definition can be defined from both the command line and from the IDE. In the IDE, you separate each definition with semicolons. You simply include another -D option for declaring more than one macro definition from the command line or separate the definitions with semicolons. The -D*tag* option may also be used as a local option in individual project files.

### See Also

@*filename*                           Response File
Chapter 6: D*symbol*, D*symbol*=*string*     Macro String Definition

### Example

Write an application using macros to control the inclusion or deletion of a code section and to define the application's title. The following source code will count from 1 to 10. You either include or exclude the delay loop by either defining or not defining a DELAY macro. The application's title is specified by the TITLE macro:

**define\count.c**
```
#include <stdio.h>

void main(void)
{
    unsigned int n, count;

    printf(TITLE "\n");              /* Print the title */
    for(count = 0; count < 10; count++)
    {
#ifdef DELAY
        for(n = 0; n < 60000; n++);  /* Delay Loop */
#endif
        printf("Count = %d\n", count);
    }
}
```

The above file is compiled to include the delay loop and use "Count" for the title by entering the following from the DOS command line:

```
bcc -DDELAY -DTITLE="Count" count.c
```

## d                               Merge Duplicate Strings Literals

- C
- C++
- CPP
- TC++
- TCW/BCW
- BC 2.0
- BC 3.0/3.1
- BCC
- Local
- #pragma

### Purpose
The -d option instructs the compiler to merge identical string literals and store them as a single string literal. This creates smaller executable files.

### IDE Option
Options | Compiler | Code Generation | Duplicate strings merged

### Default
-d-

    Duplicate string literals are not merged.

### Usage
BCC -d SOURCE.C

    Merge duplicate string literals.

#pragma option -d

    Same as above.

### Description
The -d option instructs the compiler not to store any duplicate string literals. For example, if the -d option is enabled and you define the string literal "String" in one section of the code and again in another portion, only the first string literal will actually be stored. The address of the first occurrence for the literal will be used in lieu of storing a duplicate string.

### See Also
| | |
|---|---|
| a | Byte/Word Alignment |
| b | Word Sized enums |
| G | Compile in Favor of Speed |

### Example
Write an application using four identical string literals using the #pragma option -d statement for two of the four.

merge\strlit.c
```
i#include <stdio.h>

/* Disable the string literal merge option */
#pragma option -d-

char *Str1 = "String";
char *Str2 = "String";

/* Enable the option to merge string literals */
#pragma option -d
```

78

```
char *Str3 = "String";
char *Str4 = "String";

void main(void)
{
    /* Print the two strings and their addresses */
    printf("Str1 = %s, address = %p\n", Str1, Str1);
    printf("Str2 = %s, address = %p\n", Str2, Str2);
    printf("Str3 = %s, address = %p\n", Str3, Str3);
    printf("Str4 = %s, address = %p\n", Str4, Str4);
}
```

The first two identical string literals in the following application are compiled without merging. The last two are compiled with the -d option enabled. After the -d option was enabled, the compiler used the address of the first identical string literal it found rather than storing a new string literal as shown by the following output from the application:

```
Str1 = String, address = 00B2       Unique string
Str2 = String, address = 00B9       Unique string
Str3 = String, address = 00B2       Same as Str1
Str4 = String, address = 00B2       Same as Str1
```

# Efilename                                                    External Assembler

| ▪ C | ▪ C++ | CPP | ▪ TC++ | TCW/BCW |
|---|---|---|---|---|
| ▪ BC 2.0 | ▪ BC 3.0/3.1 | ▪ BCC | Local | #pragma |

## Purpose
The E*filename* option allows you to specify a specific assembler for the compiler to call rather than the Turbo Assembler (TASM) to process inline assembly language instructions or compile other .ASM files.

## IDE Option
You can instruct the IDE to use a different assembler by editing the Turbo Assembler transfer item. This is not recommend, however, as other assemblers do not interface well with the IDE.

## Default
`-Etasm.exe`

Use TASM to process inline assembly language and .ASM files.

## Usage
`BCC -Emasm.exe SOURCE.ASM`

Use MASM to compile the SOURCE.AMS assembly language file.

`BCC -B -Emasm.exe SOURCE.C`

Use MASM to compile the .ASM file generated by the -B option.

### Description

The compiler normally uses TASM if an external assembler is required for compilation. The -E*filename* option enables you to tell the compiler to use a different assembler. Note that the .EXE file extension must be included in the *filename*.

### See Also

| | |
|---|---|
| B | Use TASM instead of BASM |
| S | Compile to an .ASM File |
| T*xxx* | Pass *xxx* Options to the Assembler |

### Example

Write an application containing inline assembly language and use the Microsoft Assembler as the external assembler.

**asm\inline.c**

```
#pragma inline

#include <stdio.h>

void main(void)
{
    long Source = 0x12345678, Dest;

    asm {
    .386
        mov eax, Source      /* Load the 4-byte number */
        mov Dest, eax        /* Save it in Dest        */
    .8086
    }
    printf("Dest = 0x%lx\n", Dest);
}
```

The above code can be compiled with the Microsoft Assembler as the external assembler by entering the following from the DOS command line:

```
bcc -B -Emasm.exe inline.c
```

The -B option forces the compiler to use an external assembler instead of the Built-in Assembler. The -Emasm.exe tells the compiler to use MASM instead of TASM.

## e*filename*                                         Executable Filename

| | | | | |
|---|---|---|---|---|
| ■ C | ■ C++ | CPP | ■ TC++ | TCW/BCW |
| ■ BC 2.0 | ■ BC 3.0/3.1 | ■ BCC | Local | #pragma |

### Purpose

The -e*filename* option instructs the compiler to name the executable file as *filename*.EXE rather than the default name.

### IDE Option

N/A

**Default**

The name of the executable file defaults to the name of the first source (.C, .CPP, or .ASM) or object (.OBJ) file passed to the command line compiler.

**Usage**

`BCC -eNEW_NAME SOURCE.C`

Creates an executable file called NEW_NAME.EXE.

**Description**

The actual naming of the executable file is controlled by the Turbo Linker (TLINK). TLINK has a command line syntax as follows:

`TLINK objfiles, exename, mapname, libraries, deffile`

The exename is the name of the executable file created by TLINK. When the IDE or the command line compiler calls TLINK, it passes TLINK the name it should use for the executable file. The -e*filename* option lets you specify the name passed to TLINK for the command line compiler. This option has no effect if the command line compiler is not used to call TLINK.

The name of the executable file defaults to the project filename if you are using the IDE project manager. When you compile single source file applications in the IDE that are not associated with a project, then the name of the executable file is the same as the source filename. To rename the executable file from the IDE you have to change the project filename if you are using a project file, or the source filename for applications without a project.

**See Also**

| | |
|---|---|
| c | Compile Only |
| o*filename* | Object Code Filename |
| S | Assembler Listing |

**Example**

Compile the HELLO.C source file application below and rename the executable file to HI.EXE using the -e*filename* option:

**c\hello.c**
```
#include <stdio.h>

void main(void)
{
    printf("Hello, C!\n"); /* Print "Hello, C!" */
}
```

You would enter the following from the DOS command line to compile the above file and rename the executable:

```
bcc -ehi hello.c
```

The -ehi option causes TLINK to name the executable HI.EXE.

# Fc                                                        Generate COMDEFs

- C          - C++           CPP           TC++          - TCW/BCW
- BC 2.0     - BC 3.0/3.1  - BCC          - Local         #pragma

## Purpose
The -Fc option instructs the compiler to generate communal variable definitions for any declared, but undefined, global variables that are not either static or external.

## IDE Option
Options | Compiler | Advanced code generation | Generate COMDEFs

## Default
−Fc−

Generate a normal uninitialized variable in the associated module for any undefined global variable.

## Usage
BCC −Fc SOURCE.C

Generate a communal variable shared by all modules for any undefined global variable.

## Description
There is a difference between a variable *declaration* and a variable *definition*. A variable declaration simply declares a variable without initializing it as follows:

```
int VarInt;
```

A variable definition declares the variable and defines its initial value, such as the following:

```
int VarInt = 0;
```

This allows you to declare your variable in one location in the source file and actually define the variable in another. The following is perfectly acceptable in C or C++:

```
int VarInt;
int VarInt = 0;
```

The first line declares the VarInt variable and the second is the actual definition. If the compiler reaches the end of the source file and doesn't find a definition for the variable, it automatically creates an uninitialized variable definition.

When the -Fc option is enabled, however, the compiler will not generate an uninitialized variable when it reaches the end of the source file. Instead, it will create a *communal* variable definition in the object file for later resolution by the linker. The Turbo Linker resolves communal variables by only creating one instance of the variable that is shared by all the source modules. Communal variables are very similar to external variable declaration except that none of the source files needs to contain the definition.

The compiler will use an initialization value in a source file if it finds one. The linker will generate an error, however, if it finds more than one definition for a communal variable. If none of the modules has a definition for the variable, such as in the example application below, then the linker creates a single uninitialized definition.

## See Also

| Ff, Ff=*size* | Automatic Far Variables |
| Fm | Use Fc, Ff, Fs Options |
| Fs | Assume SS equals DS at Run Time |

## Example

Write an application using communal variables in the header file. The application below uses one header file, COMDEF.H, that is shared between two source modules, MAIN.C and SET.C.

**comdef\comdef.h**

```
#include <stdio.h>

/* GlobalInt is declared here, but it is not actually defined
   in any module */
int GlobalInt;

void SetGlobalTo2(void);
```

**comdef\main.c**

```
#include "comdef.h"

void main(void)
{
    /* Set the value of GlobalInt to 1 and print */
    GlobalInt = 1;
    printf("MAIN GlobalInt = %d\n", GlobalInt);

    /* Set the value of GlobalInt to 2 in the SET module and print */
    SetGlobalTo2();

    /* See if the value changed here in the MAIN module */
    printf("MAIN GlobalInt = %d\n", GlobalInt);
}
```

**comdef\set.c**

```
#include "comdef.h"

void SetGlobalTo2(void)
{
    /* Print the initial value, then Set to 2 and print again */
    printf("SET  GlobalInt = %d\n", GlobalInt);
    GlobalInt = 2;
    printf("SET  GlobalInt = %d\n", GlobalInt);
}
```

The application is compiled using communal variables as follows:

```
bcc -Fc main.c set.c
```

Compiling the above source code with the communal variable option disabled, i.e., without the -Fc option, will generate an error during the link stage. This is because the 'GlobalInt' variable is declared in a header file that is used by two different modules. Without the communal variable option, the compiler creates an uninitialized definition for 'GlobalInt' in both the MAIN and SET modules. TLINK sees two variable definitions with the same name, 'GlobalInt', and generates an error. With the -Fc option enabled, however, only one instance of 'GlobalInt' is created. This single instance of 'GlobalInt' is shared by both the MAIN and SET modules as shown by the following output from the application:

```
MAIN GlobalInt = 1
SET  GlobalInt = 1
SET  GlobalInt = 2
MAIN GlobalInt = 2
```

# Ff, Ff=*size*                                    Automatic Far Variables

- C            ■ C++          CPP          TC++          ■ TCW/BCW
- BC 2.0       ■ BC 3.0/3.1  ■ BCC        ■ Local        #pragma

## Purpose
The -Ff option tells the compiler to automatically place any global variables larger than the threshold in a far data segment. The -Ff=*size* option specifies the threshold used by the -Ff option.

## IDE Option
Options | Compiler | Advanced code generation | Automatic far data
Options | Compiler | Advanced code generation | Far Data Threshold

## Default
-Ff-
    Data will only be placed in a far data segment if it is explicitly declared as far.

-Ff=32767
    Automatic far data threshold set to 32767 bytes.

## Usage
BCC -Ff=1024 SOURCE.C
    Any data item larger than 1024 bytes will be placed in its own far data segment unless explicitly declared as near.

## Description
The -Ff and -Ff=*size* options are very useful when more space is needed in a module's data segment than 64K. Using the two options causes the compiler to automatically place any global data item that is larger than the threshold specified by the -Ff=*size* option into its own far data segment.

Note that the compiler ignores the -Ff option for small, medium, and tiny memory model applications. You can, however, still use the 'far' keyword to manually place data in a far segment in small and medium memory model applications.

**See Also**

| | |
|---|---|
| Fc | Generate COMDEFs |
| Fm | Use Fc, Ff, Fs Options |
| Fs | Assume SS equals DS at Run time |

**Example**

Write a large memory model application with more than 64K of data and compile using a far data threshold of 20K. The following application uses 80K of data:

**far_data\ff.c**

```
#include <stdio.h>

/* These first two arrays are smaller than the threshold,
   of 20K, so they will be placed in this module's
   data segment */
char Small[10000];
char Large[19999];

/* These are larger than the threshold so they will each have
   their own data segment */
char Larger[20000];
char Largest[30000];

void main(void)
{
    /* Print the data segment for this module */
    printf("Data Segment = 0x%X\n", _DS);

    /* Print the addresses of each array as a far pointer */
    printf("Small   = %Fp\n", (void far *)Small);
    printf("Large   = %Fp\n", (void far *)Large);
    printf("Larger  = %Fp\n", (void far *)Larger);
    printf("Largest = %Fp\n", (void far *)Largest);
}
```

When the above application is compiled in any memory model except huge without using automatic far data, the compiler will generate the following error message:

```
Error ff.c 23: Too much global data defined in file
```

This error message is telling you the data space for the file is more than 64K. However, compiling the application as follows:

```
bcc -ml -Ff=20000 ff.c
```

will cause the compiler to put the Larger and Largest arrays, which have a size greater than or equal to the threshold of 20K, into their own data segments. The Small and Large arrays are both in the module's data segment, as shown by the application's output:

```
Data Segment = 0x3270
Small   = 3270:519D
Large   = 3270:037E
Larger  = 263B:0000
Largest = 2B1D:0000
```

# Fm

## Use Fc, Ff, Fs Options

| | | | | |
|---|---|---|---|---|
| ■ C | ■ C++ | CPP | TC++ | ■ TCW/BCW |
| ■ BC 2.0 | ■ BC 3.0/3.1 | ■ BCC | Local | #pragma |

## Purpose
The -Fm option tells the compiler to use the -Fc, -Ff, and -Fs options to ensure compatibility with source code ported from other operating systems.

## IDE Option
N/A

## Default
```
-Fm-
```
The -Fc, -Ff, and -Fs options are disabled.

## Usage
```
BCC -Fm SOURCE.C
```
The -Fc, -Ff, and -Fs options are enabled.

## Description
The -Fm option is very useful for porting code from other operating systems that do not have segmented addressing. The -Fm option simulates this situation by using communal variables, and automatic far data and placing the stack segment inside the data segment.

Note that the compiler ignores the -Ff option for small, medium, and tiny memory model applications. You can, however, still use the 'far' keyword to manually place data in a far segment in small and medium memory model applications.

## See Also
| | |
|---|---|
| Fc | Generate COMDEFs |
| Ff, Ff=*size* | Automatic Far Variables |
| Fs | Assume SS equals DS at Run time |

## Example
See the examples for the -Fc, -Ff, and -Fs options.

# fs

## Assume SS Equals DS at Run Time

| | | | | |
|---|---|---|---|---|
| ■ C | ■ C++ | CPP | TC++ | ■ TCW/BCW |
| ■ BC 2.0 | ■ BC 3.0/3.1 | ■ BCC | Local | #pragma |

## Purpose
The -Fs option instructs the compiler to create an application in which the data segment is assumed equal to the stack segment at run time.

**IDE Option**
Options | Compiler | Code Generation | Always

**Default**
-Fs-
The stack and data segments are assumed to be the default for the memory model.

**Usage**
BCC -Fs SOURCE.C
The stack and data segments are assumed to be equal regardless of the memory model.

**Description**
The -Fs option is useful for porting code from other operating environments where the stack segment is the same as the data segment. When this option is enabled, the compiler will instruct the Turbo Linker (TLINK) to use the alternate startup module appropriate for the memory model. The alternate startup module will be linked into DOS applications. This will place the stack in the data segment at run time.

Note: This option is ignored for Windows applications, Dynamic Link Libraries, and huge memory model applications.

**See Also**

| | |
|---|---|
| Fc | Generate COMDEFs |
| Ff, Ff=*size* | Automatic Far Variables |
| Fm | Use Fc, Ff, Fs Options |
| mc | Use the Compact Memory Model |
| mh | Use the Huge Memory Model |
| ml | Use the Large Memory Model |
| mm, mm! | Use the Medium Memory Model |
| ms, ms! | Use the Small Memory Model |
| mt, mt! | Use the Tiny Memory Model |

**Example**
Write an application that prints the value of the data and stack segments, and compile for the large memory model using the -Fs option.

always\main.c
```
#include "always.h"

void main(void)
{
    /* Print the Data and Stack segments for the MAIN module */
    printf("MAIN Data Segment  = 0x%X\n", _DS);
    printf("MAIN Stack Segment = 0x%X\n", _SS);

    /* Print the Data and Stack Segments for the OTHER module */
    PrintDS_SS();
}
```

**always \ other.c**

```
#include "always.h"

void PrintDS_SS(void)
{
    printf("OTHER Data Segment  = 0x%X\n", _DS);
    printf("OTHER Stack Segment = 0x%X\n", _SS);
}
```

The above application is compiled in the large memory model using the -Fs option as follows:

```
bcc -ml -Fs -ealways main.c other.c
```

The -ml option specifies the large memory model and -e always names the executable file as ALWAYS.EXE.

The stack segment is normally not equal to the data segment in the large memory model. However, compiling a large memory model application with the -Fs options links a startup module that places the stack within the data segment, as shown by the output from the above application:

```
MAIN Data Segment    = 0x2639
MAIN Stack Segmentq  = 0x2639
OTHER Data Segmentq  = 0x2639
OTHER Stack Segmentq = 0x2639
```

The data segment is equal to the stack segment in both the MAIN and the OTHER source modules.

# f, f87, f287                                      Floating Point Instruction Type

| ▪ C | ▪ C++ | CPP | ▪ TC++ | ❶ TCW/BCW |
|-----|-------|-----|--------|-----------|
| ▪ BC 2.0 | ▪ BC 3.0/3.1 | ▪ BCC | Local | #pragma |

❶ You can only use emulated floating point or inline 80287 code in TCW and BCW.

## Purpose
The -f, -f87, and -f287 options control the type of floating point instructions generated by the compiler. The -f option instructs the compiler to generate emulated floating-point. The -f87 and -f287 options instruct the compiler to generate 8087 or 80287 inline floating point instructions, respectively.

## IDE Option
Options | Compiler | Advanced Code Generation | None     *-f*
Options | Compiler | Advanced Code Generation | Emulate *-f*
Options | Compiler | Advanced Code Generation | 8087     *-f87, DOS BC++ only*
Options | Compiler | Advanced Code Generation | 80287     *-f287*

## Default

–f

Link the emulated floating point library if the application contains floating-point operations.

## Usage

BCC –f– SOURCE.C

Generate a link error if the application contains any emulated floating-point.

BCC –f87 SOURCE.C

Generate inline 8087 instructions.

BCC –F287 SOURCE.C

Generate inline 80287 instructions.

## Description

All floating-point operations in C and C++ are compiled into either actual or emulated coprocessor instructions. These instructions are executed at run time by either a coprocessor installed in the machine or by a set of library functions that emulate the operation of the coprocessor. The -f option compiles emulated floating-point instructions into the application. This option also links the MATH*x*.LIB library, which contains the coprocessor emulation functions. If the machine running the application has a coprocessor, then these emulated instructions are written to replace the emulated code with inline coprocessor instructions as the emulated instructions are executed. This means that if the machine is equipped with a floating-point coprocessor, the code will operate much more quickly after the first execution of a code section.

With the -f87 and -f287 options, the compiler generates the same emulated code as the -f option. At link time, however, the linker replaces the emulated instruction code with inline coprocessor instructions and does not link the emulation functions from the MATH*x*.LIB library. Because the emulated instructions do not have to be replaced with coprocessor instructions at run time, the application operates slightly faster on machines equipped with floating-point coprocessors, but will lock up on machines without a coprocessor. The absence of the emulated floating-point functions from the MATH*x*.LIB also reduces the size of the application by 10K.

The -f287 option instruction saves a slight amount of space and time over the -f87 option whenever a comparison is made involving floating-point numbers. Consider the following section of C code:

```
double Ans;

if(Ans < 4.0)
    Ans = 4.0;
```

On an assembly language level, the comparison between Ans and 4.0 is made using the FCOMP instruction. This instruction sets or clears status flags within the coprocessor. These status flags are made readable by the microprocessor using the FSTSW coprocessor instruction. The 8087 coprocessor will only support the FSTSW instruction that stores the status flags in memory. These status flags are then retrieved from memory by the microprocessor and a branch instruction either executes or bypasses the Ans = 4.0 expression. The 80287, on the other hand, will store the flags directly into the microprocessor's AX register. Because the flags do not have to be retrieved from memory, fewer instructions are needed, thereby saving a slight amount of code size and processing time. This is the only difference between the -f87 and -f287 options. You should note that applications compiled with the -f287 option will lock up machines that are not equipped with an 80287 coprocessor.

In any case, the compiler will not link the emulated floating-point library if your application does not contain floating-point. The only advantage to disabling floating-point using the -f- options arises when you want to know if your source code contains any floating-point instructions. Disabling the -f option forces the compiler not to link the floating-point library. The linker will then generate an error if your application does contain floating-point.

Note that the Borland C++ *Programmer's Guide* states this option may be used in a #pragma. This is not correct, as these options must act through the linker on the application as a whole. Individual files cannot be compiled using the -f87 and -f287 options while others are compiled with emulated floating-point.

### See Also

| | |
|---|---|
| 1, 2, 3 | Microprocessor Instruction Set |
| G | Compile in Favor of Speed |
| O | Enable Jump Optimizations |
| Chapter 6: E, R | Emulated/Real Floating Point Instructions |

### Example

Write an application that counts from 1 to 10,000 using floating-point instructions and compile with the -f, -f87, and -f287 options:

**f\fltpt.c**

```
#include <stdio.h>

void main(void)
{
    double n, Limit = 10000.0;

    /* Count from 1 to 10,000 using floating point */
    for(n = 0.0; n < Limit; n = n + 1.0);
}
```

The above code is compiled into different applications using the -f, -f87, and -f287 options as follows:

```
bcc   -v   -f287   -ew287 fltpt.c
bcc   -v   -f87    -ew87  fltpt.c
bcc   -v   -f      -eno87 fltpt.c
```

The -v option embeds debugging information for use by the Turbo Profiler (TPROF). The -ew287, -ew87, and -eno87 options name the resulting applications W287.EXE, W87.EXE, and NO87.EXE. Table 2-6 lists the size and performance of each application.

| APPLICATION | SIZE (BYTES) | TIME (SECONDS) |
|-------------|--------------|----------------|
| NO87.EXE | 23,678 | 3.2735 |
| W87.EXE | 13,426 | 0.2504 |
| W287.EXE | 13,410 | 0.2477 |

**Table 2-6 Performance of the for( ) loop**

Note that the N087 application was tested with the "87" environmental variable set to "N" so as to force the application to use emulated floating-point. The speed is identical to the W87 application if the application is allowed to use an onboard coprocessor.

# ff                                                           Use Fast Floating-Point

- C          - C++        CPP        - TC++       ❶ TCW/BCW
- BC 2.0     - BC 3.0/3.1  - BCC      - Local      - #pragma

❶ BCW only

## Purpose
The -ff option allows the compiler to generate faster and more accurate floating-point code by treating all floating-point operations as type *long double*.

## IDE Option
Options | Compiler | Advanced Code Generation | Fast floating-point

## Default
`-ff`
> Enable fast floating-point evaluation.

## Usage
`BCC -ff- SOURCE.C`
> Adhere to type float typecasting.

`#pragma option -ff-`
> Same as above; this option must appear between functions and variable declarations.

`#pragma option -ff`
> Enable fast floating-point evaluation; this option must appear between functions and variable declarations.

## Description

Floating-point operations on DOS machines are always calculated using type *long double*. Type *float* and integer numbers are first loaded into the coprocessor stack (or emulated coprocessor stack for emulated floating-point) and converted to type *long double*. Any subsequent math operations are then performed with *long double* precision. Because of this, some code expressions require the compiler to truncate the accuracy of a number in order to adhere to normal C semantics. Consider the following expression:

```
double One = 1.0, Two = 2.0, Three = 3.0;
(float)(One / Three) + Two;
```

The result of the expression (One / Three) is a type double; however, the expression is explicitly typecast to a type float. Normal C semantics require the compiler to truncate the result to the precision of a type float. This is done by temporarily storing the result of the expression as a type float and then reloading it again as a long double. The truncated result is then added to the variable Two. With fast floating-point enabled, the typecast on the (One / Three) expression is ignored, enabling the compiler to avoid truncating the result of (One / Three) and to simply add it to the variable Two. Thus full floating-point accuracy is maintained. This produces smaller, faster, and more accurate code.

Note that there has been a problem with the compiler since the first release of Borland C, in which fast floating-point cannot be turned off if the variables involved are type *float* instead of type *double*. For example, if the variables One and Two were declared as type *float* rather than type *double*, fast floating-point could not be defeated and the entire expression would be evaluated as type *long double* with no intermediate type *float* result.

## See Also

h          Use Fast huge Pointer Calculation

## Example

Write an application that evaluates an expression using both fast floating-point and normal floating-point:

**ff\fastf.c**

```
#include <stdio.h>

/* Define three type double variables */
double One = 1.0, Two = 2.0, Three = 3.0;

/* Enable fast floating point */
#pragma option -ff

double FastFloat(void)
{
    double Ans;

    Ans = (float)(One / Three) + Two;
    return(Ans);
}

/* Disable fast floating point */
#pragma option -ff-
```

```
double NormFloat(void)
{
   double Ans;

   Ans = (float)(One / Three) + Two;
   return(Ans);
}

void main(void)
{
   double Diff;

   /* Calculate the difference in accuracy between fast floating
   point and normal floating point */
   Diff = FastFloat() - NormFloat();

   /* Print the difference */
   printf("Difference = %g\n", Diff);
   }
```

FastFloat() and NormFloat() are identical functions in the above application. The FastFloat() function is compiled with the fast floating-point option enabled, whereas the NormFloat() function is compiled with the option disabled. The difference between the results of the two functions is calculated in the main() function and printed:

```
Difference = -9.93411e-09
```

The difference between the two functions lies in the way the expression (One / Three) is evaluated. This expression is evaluated as a *float* in the NormFloat() function and as a *long double* in the FastFloat() function.

## gn                                                            Stop Compiling After *n* Warnings

- C          - C++         - CPP         - TC++        - TCW/BCW
- BC 2.0     - BC 3.0/3.1  - BCC         - Local       - #pragma

### Purpose
The -g*n* option instructs the compiler to stop compiling after generating *n* warning messages.

### IDE Option
Options | Compiler | Messages | Display | Warnings: stop after

### Default
−g100
   Stop compiling after 100 warning messages.

### Usage
BCC −g30 SOURCE.C
   Stop compiling after 30 warning messages.

```
#pragma option -g30
```
Same as above.

## Description
The -g*n* option lets you specify the number of warning messages the compiler should tolerate before suspending compilation. The compiler generates a nonfatal error when the limit to the number of allowable warning messages is reached and stops compilation. The value of *n* can be any number between 0 and 255. A value of zero instructs the compiler to tolerate all warning messages and continue compiling to the end of the source code or to the limit of the acceptable number of error messages. If you instruct the project manager to only break on fatal errors or at link time, the compiler will cease compilation of the current file when the warning limit is reached and start compiling the next file in the project. Note that disabling the warning message display option in the IDE defeats this option even if the #pragma option -g*n* statement is included in the source code. Disabling the warning message displays with the command line compiler option -w-, however, it will not defeat the #pragma form of this option.

## See Also
| | |
|---|---|
| j*n* | Stop after *n* Errors |
| N | Error on Stack Overflows |
| w | Display Warnings |
| w*xxx* | Individual Warning Messages |

## Example
Write an application that generates at least four warning messages and use the -g*n* option to stop compiling after three warnings:

**gn\test.c**
```
/* Instruct the compiler to stop after three warning messages */
#pragma option -g3

/* Enable the "Call to function with no prototype" and the
   "Possible use of identifier before definition" warnings */
#pragma warn +pro
#pragma warn +def

void main(void)
{
   /* Declare two variables, but do not initialize */
   int One, Two;

   /* Call a function twice without a prototype */
   BogusFunct(One);
   BogusFunct(Two);
}
```

The above application would generate at least four warnings messages if it were not for the -g3 option in the #pragma statement. The compiler stops on line 16 after generating three warning messages:

```
Borland C++ Version 2.0 Copyright (c) 1991 Borland International
test.c:
Warning test.c 15: Call to function 'BogusFunct' with no prototype in
function main
Warning test.c 15: Possible use of 'One' before definition in function
main
Warning test.c 16: Call to function 'BogusFunct' with no prototype in
function main
Error test.c 16: Too many error or warning messages in function main
*** 1 errors in Compile ***

    Available memory 296416
```

# H, Hu                                                   Precompiled Headers

| ▪ C | ▪ C++ | CPP | TC++ | ▪ TCW/BCW |
|-----|-------|-----|------|-----------|
| ▪ BC 2.0 | ▪ BC 3.0/3.1 | ▪ BCC | ▪ Local | #pragma |

## Purpose

The -H option instructs the compiler to compile the header files used by the source code into a symbolic information (.SYM) file. If the -H option is enabled and the .SYM file already exists, then the compiler will use the precompiled header information in the .SYM file, thereby saving compilation time. The -Hu option instructs the compiler to use any information in the .SYM file if it is already there, but not to store any new precompiled information.

## IDE Option

Options | Compiler | Code Generation | Precompiled headers

## Default

-H-

Do no store or use precompiled information in a .SYM file.

## Usage

BCC -H SOURCE.C

Store precompiled header information in a .SYM file or use it if it already exists.

BCC -Hu SOURCE.C

Use information in a .SYM file, but do not store any new information.

## Description

The -H option can save you a considerable amount of time when compiling applications, especially Windows applications which use the large WINDOWS.H header file. With this option enabled, the compiler will store the compiled information contained in the WINDOWS.H file in a .SYM file. The next time the source file is compiled, the compiler will check to see if anything has changed since the information in the .SYM file was generated. If everything is identical, the compiler will use this precompiled information rather than spend time compiling the information a second time. Table 2-7 lists the conditions that must be met for the compiler to use the .SYM file. The compiler will also use the precompiled header information in other source files provided the conditions listed in Table 2-7 are met.

---

**For the compiler to use the .SYM file, the following conditions must be met when compared against the last compilation:**

❏ have identical include files including the same time/date stamp and indirect headers

❏ have include files listed in the same order

❏ be the same language (either C or C++)

❏ have identical macro definitions

❏ have identical compiler options as follows:

| | |
|---|---|
| -m*x* | (memory model including SS != DS) |
| -u | (leading underscores on externals) |
| -i*n* | (significant characters for tags) |
| -W*x* | (target application) |
| -p | (Pascal calling convention) |
| -pr | (Fastcall calling convention) |
| -b | (treatment of enums as integers) |
| -K | (Default to either signed or unsigned characters) |
| -V*x* | (virtual table control) |

**Table 2-7 Conditions for using precompiled header information**

---

### See Also
H=*filename*  Save Precompiled Header Information in *filename*

### Example
Write a Windows application that uses precompiled headers and compare the times required to compile the application. The Windows application below creates a single application window in the center of the screen and displays the text "Hello, Windows!":

**header\test.c**
```
#include <windows.h>

char AppTitle[] = "Hello, Windows!";

/* Define the application window's message processing function */
long FAR PASCAL WndProc(HWND hWnd, unsigned msg, WORD wParam,
                        LONG lParam)
{
   RECT rect;
```

```
    PAINTSTRUCT ps;
    HDC hDC;

    switch(msg)
    {
    /* Paint the window */
    case WM_PAINT:
        hDC = BeginPaint(hWnd, &ps);

        /* Display the application title in the center of
            the window */
        GetClientRect(hWnd, &rect);
        DrawText(hDC, AppTitle, sizeof(AppTitle) - 1, &rect,
                DT_SINGLELINE | DT_VCENTER | DT_CENTER);

        EndPaint(hWnd, &ps);
        break;

    /* Time to quit! */
    case WM_DESTROY:
        PostQuitMessage(0);
        break;

    /* All other messages go here. */
    Default:
            return(DefWindowProc(hWnd, msg, wParam, lParam));
    }
    return(0);
}


int PASCAL WinMain(HANDLE hInstance, HANDLE hPrevInstance,
                LPSTR lpCmdLine, int nCmdShow)
{
    int xDim, yDim;
    HWND hWnd;
    MSG msg;

    /* Register the application window class */
    if(!hPrevInstance)
    {
        WNDCLASS wc;

        wc.style            = CS_HREDRAW | CS_VREDRAW;
        wc.lpfnWndProc      = WndProc;
        wc.cbClsExtra       = 0;
        wc.cbWndExtra       = 0;
        wc.hInstance        = hInstance;
        wc.hIcon            = LoadIcon(NULL, IDI_HAND);
        wc.hCursor          = LoadCursor(NULL, IDC_ARROW);
        wc.hbrBackground    = GetStockObject(WHITE_BRUSH);
        wc.lpszMenuName     = NULL;
        wc.lpszClassName    = AppTitle;

      if(!RegisterClass(&wc))
        return(FALSE);
    }

    /* Get the screen dimensions */
    xDim = GetSystemMetrics(SM_CXSCREEN);
    yDim = GetSystemMetrics(SM_CYSCREEN);
```

```
hWnd = CreateWindow(AppTitle, AppTitle, WS_OVERLAPPEDWINDOW,
        xDim / 4, yDim / 4, xDim / 2, yDim / 2,
        NULL, NULL, hInstance, NULL);

if(hWnd == NULL)
  return(FALSE);

/* Display the window */
ShowWindow(hWnd, nCmdShow);

/* Enter the message loop */
while(GetMessage(&msg, 0, 0, 0))
{
  TranslateMessage(&msg);
  DispatchMessage(&msg);
}

/* Exit the application */
return(0);
}
```

You would enter the following to compile this application from the DOS command line using precompiled headers:

```
bcc -H -H=test.sym -WS test.c
rc test.exe
```

The -H option tells the compiler to use precompiled headers. The -H=test.sym tells the compiler to use the TEST.SYM file to store the precompiled symbolic information. The -WS option designates a Windows target application that uses smart callbacks. The second line calls Microsoft's Resource Compiler, which is the final step needed to create a Windows 3.0 compatible application. The compiler creates the .OBJ file five times faster when it uses the precompiled header information.

## H=*filename*                          Save Precompiled Headers in *filename*

- C
- BC 2.0
- C++
- BC 3.0/3.1
- CPP
- BCC
- TC++
- Local
- TCW/BCW
- #pragma

### Purpose
The -H=*filename* option designates the file the compiler is to use for saving or retrieving precompiled header information.

### IDE Option
In the IDE, the project name with a .SYM extension is used to store precompiled header information. Use the #pragma hdrfile directive in the source code to change the default.

### Default
```
-H=TCDEF.SYM
```
Use the TCDEF.SYM file in the compiler directory.

## Usage

```
BCC -H -H=SOURCE.SYM SOURCE.C
```
Use or store precompiled header information in the SOURCE.SYM file.

```
#pragma hdrfile "SOURCE.SYM"
```
Same as above; this must appear before any #include statements.

## Description
Precompiled header information can be placed in any file of your choosing by using the -H=*filename* option. Overall, however, it is better to use the TCDEF.SYM file to save disk space.

## See Also
H, Hu          Precompiled Headers

## Example
See the example listed in the -H option.

---

# h                                        Use Fast huge Pointer Calculation

---

| ▪ C | ▪ C++ | CPP | TC++ | TCW/BCW |
|---|---|---|---|---|
| ▪ BC 2.0 | ▪ BC 3.0/3.1 | ▪ BCC | ▪ Local | ▪ #pragma |

## Purpose
The -h option instructs the compiler not to modify a huge pointer's segment unless the offset is beyond the 64K boundary. This can speed up programs that heavily access huge data.

## IDE Option
Options | Compiler | Advanced code generation | Fast huge pointers

## Default
```
-h-
```
Normalize all huge pointers.

## Usage
```
BCC -h SOURCE.C
```
Only normalize a huge pointer address if the resulting offset is beyond 0xFFFF.

```
#pragma option -h
```
Same as above; this must appear between functions and declarations to be effective.

```
#pragma option -h-
```
Normalize all huge pointers; this must appear between functions and declarations to be effective.

## Description

A huge pointer is really a specialized form of a far pointer. Far pointers are a 32-bit value in which the higher 16 bits represent the segment location and the lower 16 bits are the offset from the location of the segment to a physical location in memory. One *segment* represents a 16-byte block of memory. To convert a far pointer to an absolute location in memory, you multiply the segment by 16 (or $2^4$) and add the offset as follows:

```
unsigned Segment   = FarPtr >> 16;
unsigned Offset    = FarPtr & 0xFFFF;
long AbsAddr       = (Segment << 4) + Offset;
```

Many different segment:offset combinations can point to the same absolute location in memory. For example, the far pointer 2632:1338 points to the same location as 2765:0008. Both far pointers have an absolute address of 0x27658 in physical memory. The second far pointer is a *normalized* location of the first far pointer. In a normalized address, the segment is adjusted to place the offset value as low as possible. Normalizing a far pointer is done by computing the absolute address as shown above, and then converting back to a far pointer as follows:

```
unsigned Segment = AbsAddr >> 4;
unsigned Offset  = AbsAddr & 0xF;
void far *FarPtr = (Segment << 16) | Offset;
```

Huge pointers are exactly the same as far pointers except that this normalization calculation is performed any time there is any arithmetic on the pointer. This keeps the offset portion of the pointer as low as possible, which helps prevent exceeding the 16-bit range of the offset. The drawback is that the normalization calculation is very time consuming and not always necessary. The -h option enables fast huge pointer calculation in which the pointer value is only normalized if the result of the arithmetic exceeds the 16-bit range of the offset. For example, if a huge pointer has a value of 3654:0004 and an offset of 0x99 is added, a normalized huge pointer would have a value of 365D:000D. With fast huge pointer arithmetic, however, the resulting value is 3654:009D, i.e., the offset is simply added and the result is not normalized. If a logical comparison is made of these two values, however, the compiler will correctly interpret the values as identical, as shown in the example below.

The problem associated with not normalizing huge pointers is that errors can result when accessing structure fields. For example, if indexing a huge array of structures results in an offset just below the offset's 16-bit range, then accessing one of the fields in the structure could result in a segment wrap-around and overwrite other areas of memory. Therefore, fast huge pointer calculations should be used with caution.

## See Also

ff          Use Fast Floating Point

## Example

Write an application which uses both normalized huge pointers and fast pointers:

**h\hugeptr.c**

```
#include <stdio.h>
#include <alloc.h>

char huge *HugePtr;
unsigned long ArraySize = 0x11000L;

#pragma option -h-

/* Return a huge pointer with the fast option disabled */
char huge *NormPtr(unsigned long n)
{
    return(&HugePtr[n]);
}

/* Use this as a reference to gauge the speed of data access
   via a huge pointer */
void Slow(void)
{
    unsigned long n;

    for(n = 0; n < ArraySize; n++)
        HugePtr[n] = 0;
}

#pragma option -h

/* Return a huge pointer with the fast pointer option enabled */
char huge *FastPtr(unsigned long n)
{
    return(&HugePtr[n]);
}

/* Use this function to see how much faster data access is
   with the fast pointer option enabled */
void Fast(void)
{
    unsigned long n;

    for(n = 0; n < ArraySize; n++)
        HugePtr[n] = 0;
}

void main(void)
{
    /* Allocate the huge character array */
    HugePtr = (char huge *)farmalloc(ArraySize);

    /* Only proceed if there was enough memory */
    if(HugePtr != NULL)
    {
        /* Print the address of HugePtr */
        printf("\nHugePtr = %Fp\n", HugePtr);

        /* Print the normalized and fast address for HugePtr[0x99]
           and HugePtr[0x10099] */
```

```
printf("Normalized HugePtr[0x99]    = %Fp\n", NormPtr(0x99));
printf("Fast HugePtr[0x99]          = %Fp\n", FastPtr(0x99));
printf("Normalized HugePtr[0x10099] = %Fp\n", NormPtr(0x10099L));
printf("Fast HugePtr[0x10099]       = %Fp\n", FastPtr(0x10099L));

/* We still have fast huge pointer arithmetic enabled, does it
   interfere with huge pointer comparison? */
if(NormPtr(0x99) == FastPtr(0x99))
    printf("Huge pointers are normalized for comparisons\n");
else
    printf("Whoops!  Huge pointers are not normalized\n");

/* Flag these in the Turbo Profiler to gauge the speed */
Slow();
Fast();
}
}
```

The NormPtr() function computes the address of an index to HugePtr using normalized huge pointers. The FastPtr() function is identical to NormPtr() except that it uses fast huge pointer arithmetic. The result from these functions is printed for index values of 0x99 and 0x10099. These results are also compared in a logical if() statement to ensure that the compiler is properly handling logical comparisons. The following is the output from the application:

```
HugePtr = 3654:0004
Normalized HugePtr[0x99]    . = 365D:000D
      Fast HugePtr[0x99]      = 3654:009D
Normalized HugePtr[0x10099] = 465D:000D
      Fast HugePtr[0x10099]   = 4654:009D
Huge pointers are normalized for comparisons
```

The last two functions, Slow() and Fast(), access the HugePtr array 0x11000 times using normalized arithmetic and fast arithmetic. The Turbo Profiler shows the Fast() function operating almost five times faster than the Slow() function.

## I*path*                                    Set Include Files Directory

- C
- C++
- CPP
- TC++
- TCW/BCW
- BC 2.0
- BC 3.0/3.1
- BCC
- Local
- #pragma

### Purpose
The -I*path* option specifies the directory location where the compiler should look for include files.

### IDE Option
Options | Directories | Include Directories

### Default
`-I.`

Look for include files in the current directory.

## Usage

```
BCC -IC:\BORLANDC\INCLUDE SOURCE.C
```
Look for include files in the c:\borlandc\include directory.

```
BCC -IC:\BORLANDC\INCLUDE;.. SOURCE.C
```
Look for include files in the c:\borlandc\include and parent directories.

```
BCC -IC:\BORLANDC\INCLUDE -I.. SOURCE.C
```
Same as above.

## Description

Header files, sometimes referred to as *include* files, are usually not located in the same directory as the source code. The -I*path* option tells the compiler where to look for the include files listed in an #include *<filename>* statement specified in the source files or if it cannot find the file listed in an #include "*filename*" statement in the current directory. More than one directory path can be listed with the -I*path* option and in the IDE "Include Directories" box provided, the directory paths are separated by semicolons. The command line compiler also supports more than one -I*path* option listed on the command line. Directories are searched in the listed order.

## See Also

| | |
|---|---|
| L | Set the Location of Library Files |
| Chapter 5: L*path* | Set Library Seach Path |
| Chapter 6: I*path* | Set Include Path |
| Chapter 7: sd*Path* | Source Code Directory |
| Chapter 7: sd*Directory* | Source Code Directory |

## Example

Write an application that uses an include file located in the parent directory:

**include\main.c**
```
    #include <test.h>

    void main(void)
    {
        PrintStr("This is a test.\n");
    }
```

**include\test.c**
```
    #include <stdio.h>
    #include <test.h>

    void PrintStr(char *Str)
    { printf(Str);
    }
```

**test.h**
```
    void PrintStr(char*);
```

Both the MAIN and TEST modules in the above application use an include file located in the parent directory and an include file, STDIO.H, located in the \BOR-

LANDC\INCLUDE directory. The application is compiled by specifying an include file search path as follows:

```
bcc -I\borlandc\include;.. test.c main.c
```

This instructs the compiler to first look in the \borlandc\include file of the current disk drive and, if it does not find the include file there, to search the parent directory of the current directory.

## *in*                                                      Use *n* Significant Characters for Tags

- C
- BC 2.0
- C++
- BC 3.0/3.1
- CPP
- BCC
- TC++
- Local
- TCW/BCW
- #pragma

### Purpose
The -i*n* option tells the compiler to use *n* significant characters when matching an identifier or tags to functions or variables. You normally use this option when porting code that relies on a specific identifier length.

### IDE Option
Options | Compiler | Source | Identifier Length

### Default
−i32

Recognize 32 significant characters for an identifier.

### Usage
BCC −i8 SOURCE.C

Use only the first 8 characters of an identifier.

#pragma option −i8

Same as above; must be placed before any C directive to be effective.

### Description
The ANSI standard for C states that the maximum allowable number of significant characters is 32. Some earlier compilers, however, only recognized the first 8 characters of an identifier. If you are porting code from one of these compilers, you can use the -i*n* option to tell the compiler to only use the first 8 characters of an identifier. This means, for example, that the following declarations would refer to the same variable if the -i8 option were used:

```
int VariableOne;
int VariableTwo;
```

Because the compiler will only use the first 8 characters of the two identifiers, both declarations are effectively the following:

```
int Variable;
int Variable;
```

The value of *n* in the -i*n* option and the IDE equivalent can be anywhere from 1 to 32.

C++ is supposed to support unlimited identifier lengths. This option should have no effect on C++ source code; however, this is not the case with the current release. Identifier lengths in C++ source code are limited to the value specified by the -i*n* option, which defaults to 32. This means the maximum identifier length in C++ source code is also limited to 32 characters.

## See Also

| | |
|---|---|
| A, AT, AK, AU | Language Keywords |
| Fc | Generate COMDEFs |
| Ff | Automatic *far* Variables |
| Fm | Use Fc, Ff, Fs Options |
| Fs | Assume SS equals DS |
| Chapter 6: MV *number* | Set Maximum Symbol Length |

## Example

Write an application using an identifier length of 8 characters.

**in\test.c**

```
/* Set the identifier length to 8 */
#pragma option -i8

#include <stdio.h>

/* Declare VariableOne and VariableTwo */
int VariableOne;
int VariableTwo;

void main(void)
{
   /* Try setting them to different values */
   VariableOne = 1;
   VariableTwo = 2;

   /* Print the value of each */
   printf("VariableOne = %d\n", VariableOne);
   printf("VariableTwo = %d\n", VariableTwo);

   /* Print their addresses */
   printf("VariableOne: %Fp\n", (void far *)&VariableOne);
   printf("VariableTwo: %Fp\n", (void far *)&VariableTwo);
}
```

Because the first 8 characters of VariableOne and VariableTwo are identical, the compiler treats each of them as one variable called "Variable." This is shown by the following output from the application:

```
VariableOne = 2
VariableTwo = 2
VariableOne: 25E7:033E
VariableTwo: 25E7:033E
```

Both VariableOne and VariableTwo have the same value and the same address.

# Jg, Jgd, Jgx                                        Template Generation

| C | ■ C++ | CPP | TC++ | ❶ TCW/BCW |
|---|-------|-----|------|-----------|
| BC 2.0 | ■ BC 3.0/3.1 | ■ BCC | ■ Local | ■ #pragma |

❶ BCW only.

## Purpose

You use the -Jgd and -Jgx options to control the placement of template functions gener-ated by the compiler. You use the -Jg option to instruct the compiler to control the placement of template function code.

## IDE Option

Options | Compiler | C++ Options | Smart       *for -Jg*
Options | Compiler | C++ Options | Global      *for -Jgd*
Options | Compiler | C++ Options | External    *for -Jgx*

## Default

`-Jg`

The compiler will automatically determine the placement of template function code.

## Usage

`BCC -Jgx EXTERNAL.C -Jgd MAIN.C`

Generate external template function references in EXTERNAL.C and generate code for all function templates used in MAIN.C. Note that all template functions used in EXTERNAL.C must also be used in MAIN.C.

`#pragma option -Jg`

The compiler will automatically determine the placement of template function code. The directive must appear between function definitions.

`#pragma option -Jgd`

Generate function code for all template functions without regard to duplication. The directive must appear between function definitions.

`#pragma option -Jgx`

Assume the code for a template function is located in a different module. The di-rective must appear between function definitions.

## Description

The compiler normally generates the code for template functions or member functions of a template class when the template is actually used in a module. Because of this, the compiler could generate the same function in different modules of your source code. For example, consider the following template definition for the Max() function:

```
template <class T> T Max(T x, T y)
{
    return((x > y) ? x : y);
}
```

The compiler does not generate any code for the template definition itself, because it does not know whether 'T' is a type 'int', a type 'double', or some other data type until the template is actually used. If your application uses the function to compare two type 'doubles', then the compiler will generate the code corresponding to the following function definition:

```
double Max(double x, double y)
{
    return((x > y) ? x : y);
}
```

If you use the template in two different modules, then the compiler will generate the above function code in each module. The -Jg option, which is enabled by default, tolerates these multiple template function definitions and instructs TLINK to remove duplicate template function code during the linking. The -Jgd option is similar to the -Jg option in that it tolerates multiple template function definitions; however, TLINK will not remove duplicates, but will instead issue a warning message. The -Jgx option, on the other hand, instructs the compiler not to generate any code for template functions and instead references them as external functions which are resolved by TLINK.

If you want the template function code placed in a particular module, but you do not want duplicate functions, you can use a combination of the -Jgx and -Jgd options to control where the compiler places the template function code. For example, when the compiler encounters a use of the Max() function template and you've enabled the -Jgx option, the compiler assumes the code for the function template is located in another module and generates an external reference. You then use the template function in the module where you would like the code located and compile with the -Jgd option enabled. TLINK will then link the external reference in the first module to the function code in the second module.

## See Also

V, Vs, V0, V1     C++ Virtual Table Options

## Example

Write an application using the Max() template function in two different modules called TEST.CPP and MAIN.CPP. Place the template function code in MAIN.CPP using a combination of the -Jgx and -Jgd options as #pragma directives:

**jg\test.h**

```
#ifndef TEST_H
#define TEST_H

#include <iostream.h>

// Define the Max() template function
template <class T> T Max(T x, T y)
{
    return((x > y) ? x : y);
}
```

```
    void OtherMax();

    #endif
```

**jg\test.cpp**
```
    #include "test.h"

    // Generate an external reference for the Max() function
    #pragma option -Jgx
    void OtherMax()
    {
       double a = 2.0, b = 3.0;

       cout << Max(a, b) << "\n";
    }
```

**jg\main.cpp**
```
    #include "test.h"

    // Generate code for the Max() function in this module
    #pragma option -Jgd
    void main(void)
    {
       double a = 1.0, b = 2.0;

       cout << Max(a, b) << "\n";
       OtherMax();
    }
```

# j*n*                                                        Stop after *n* Errors

- C
- BC 2.0
- C++
- BC 3.0/3.1
- CPP
- BCC
- TC++
- Local
- TCW/BCW
- #pragma

## Purpose
The -j*n* option instructs the compiler to stop compiling after generating *n* error messages.

## IDE Option
Options | Compiler | Messages | Display | Errors: Stop After

## Default
-j25
>    Stop compilation after generating 25 error messages.

## Usage
BCC -j10 SOURCE.C
>    Stop compilation after generating 10 error messages.

```
#pragma option -j10
```
    Same as above.

## Description

You can enter any number between 0 and 255 as the value for $n$ in the -j$n$ option and the compiler will stop compilation after generating $n$ nonfatal error messages. The compiler will always cease compilation if a fatal error is generated. Specifying a 0 for the value of $n$ instructs the compiler to cease compilation only if an error is generated at the end of the file.

## See Also

g$n$          Stop Compiling after $n$ Warnings

## Example

Write an application with at least four errors and instruct the compiler to cease compilation after generating two errors using the -j2 option:

**jn\test.c**
```
    #pragma option -j2

    #include <stdio.h>

    void main(void)
    {
      /* These variables were never declared and should generate
         four errors. The compiler stops after generating
         two messages. */
      One   = 1;
      Two   = 2;
      Three = 3;
      Ans = One + Two + Three;

      printf("Ans = %d", Ans);
    }
```

None of the four variables, One, Two, Three, or Ans, were ever defined or declared in the above application. The compiler would normally generate four error messages, but because of the #pragma option j2 directive, the compiler stops after generating two error messages and generates the final "Too many errors . . ." message.

```
    Borland C++ Version 2.0 Copyright (c) 1991 Borland International
    test.c:
    Error test.c 10: Undefined symbol 'One' in function main
    Error test.c 11: Undefined symbol 'Two' in function main
    Error test.c 11: Too many errors or warning messages in function main
    *** 3 errors in Compile ***

        Available memory 275712
```

# K                                    Default to signed/unsigned Characters

- C            ▪ C++         CPP         ▪ TC++         ▪ TCW/BCW
- BC 2.0       ▪ BC 3.0/3.1  ▪ BCC       ▪ Local        ▪ #pragma

## Purpose
The -K option instructs the compiler to default to unsigned character types whenever the *char* keyword is used without a *signed* or *unsigned* modifier.

## IDE Option
Options | Compiler | Code Generation | Unsigned characters

## Default
```
-K-
```
Default to signed characters.

## Usage
```
BCC -K SOURCE.C
```
Default to unsigned characters.

```
#pragma option -K
```
Same as above.

## Description
Before the ANSI standard was adopted, there were some compilers that treated a type *char* as signed, whereas other compilers treated them as unsigned. The -K option allows you to port code from these older compilers that treated the *char* data type as an *unsigned char.*

## See Also
| | |
|---|---|
| A, AK, AT, AU | Language Keywords |
| Fc | Generate COMDEFs |
| Ff, Ff=*size* | Automatic Far Variables |
| Fm | Use Fc, Ff, Fs Options |

## Example
Write an application that defaults to both signed and unsigned characters using the #pragma option -K directive:

**k\test.c**
```
#include <stdio.h>

/* Default to unsigned characters */
#pragma option -K

/* Declare a type char with all the bits turned on */
char KEnabled = 0xff;
```

```
/* Default to signed characters */
#pragma option -K-

/* Declare another type char with all the bits turned on */
char KDisabled = 0xff;

void main(void)
{
  int n;

  /* Assign each character type to an integer and print */
  n = KEnabled;
  printf("KEnabled  = %d\n", n);
  n = KDisabled;
  printf("KDisabled = %d\n", n);
}
```

The above application creates two type *char* variables called KEnabled and KDisabled. The KEnabled variable is declared with the compiler directed to default to unsigned characters, whereas the KDisabled variable defaults to a signed character. Both variables are initialized with all 8 bits turned to one, using 0xFF. The application uses the two variables as an assignment to a signed integer and the result from the assignment is printed as follows:

```
KEnabled  = 255
KDisabled = -1
```

Because the KEnabled variable defaulted to an unsigned character, the compiler converts it to 255, whereas the signed KDisabled variable is converted to -1.

# k                                                    Use a Standard Stack Frame

| | | | | |
|---|---|---|---|---|
| ▪ C | ▪ C++ | CPP | ▪ TC++ | ▪ TCW/BCW |
| ▪ BC 2.0 | ▪ BC 3.0/3.1 | ▪ BCC | ▪ Local | ▪ #pragma |

## Purpose
The -k option instructs the compiler to generate the code to create a standard stack frame even if a stack frame is not required by the function.

## IDE Option
Options | Compiler | Entry/Exit Code | Standard stack frame

## Default
-k

Generate a standard stack frame for all functions.

## Usage
```
BCC -k- SOURCE.C
```

Only generate a stack frame when required.

```
#pragma option -k-
```
Same as above; must appear between functions and declarations to be effective.

## Description

The compiler generates code to create a stack frame so that the local variables and passed parameters are accessible to the code within a function. If a function is not passed any parameters and does not have any local variables, then no stack frame is required. Debugging applications, however, need to create a stack frame for all functions to trace back through the called subroutines. For example, all called functions must have a standard stack frame for the Turbo Debugger "Stack" window to function properly. This is why the compiler defaults to generating a stack frame for all functions. Disabling this option creates smaller applications and generates faster code.

## See Also

| | |
|---|---|
| 1, 2, 3 | Microprocessor Instruction Set |
| a | Byte/Word Alignment |
| ff | Use Fast Floating Point |
| h | Use Fast huge Calculations |
| p | Use Pascal or Fastcall Calling Convention |

## Example

Write an application that contains a function that does not require a stack frame. Compile the application with and without the -k option and compare the size and speed:

**std_stk\test.c**

```
    int Sum;

    /* Because this function is not passed any parameters and does not
       have any local variables, it does not need a stack frame. */
    void IncSum(void)
    {
       Sum++;
    }

    void main(void)
    {
       unsigned n;

       for(n = 0; n < 60000; n++)
           IncSum();
    }
```

The above application can be compiled into an STD.EXE and NON_STD.EXE application with and without standard stack frames, respectively, as follows:

```
    bcc -v -k  -estd      test.c
    bcc -v -k- -enon_std  test.c
```

The -v option places debugging information into the application, which allows it to run in the Turbo Profiler. The -estd and -enon_std options name the executable files

STD.EXE and NON_STD.EXE. The NON_STD application is compiled without standard stack frames. The NON_STD application is 16 bytes smaller than STD and operates 7% faster.

# L*path*                                                        Set the Location of Library Files

| | | | | |
|---|---|---|---|---|
| ▪ C | ▪ C++ | CPP | ▪ TC++ | ▪ TCW/BCW |
| ▪ BC 2.0 | ▪ BC 3.0/3.1 | ▪ BCC | Local | #pragma |

## Purpose
The -L*path* option passes information to the linker regarding the directory location of library files.

## IDE Option
Options | Directories | Library files

## Default
```
-L
```
Look for library files in the current directory.

## Usage
```
BCC -L\BORLANDC\LIB SOURCE.C
```
Look for library files in the \BORLANDC\LIB directory of the current drive.

## Description
The linker needs to know where to find the library files it will use to link the application. The -L*path* option allows you to specify that location via the IDE or the command line compiler. This option is usually used in the TURBOC.CFG file created by the BC++ installation utility. The -L*path* option is functionally identical to the -L*path* option for the Turbo Linker.

## See Also
| | |
|---|---|
| I*path* | Set Include Files Directory |
| Chapter 5: L*path* | Set Library Seach Path |
| Chapter 6: I*path* | Set Include Path |
| Chapter 7: ds*Path* | Source Code Directory |
| Chapter 7: t*Path* | Startup Directory |

## Example
Write a "Hello, C!" application and compile using the -L*path* option to explicitly declare the location of library files:

**lib\hello.c**

```
#include <stdio.h>

void main(void)
{
    printf("Hello, C!");
}
```

The above application can be compiled using the -L*path* option as follows:

```
bcc -L\borlandc\lib hello.c
```

## lx                                          Pass an Option to the Linker

| | | | | |
|---|---|---|---|---|
| ▪ C | ▪ C++ | CPP | ▪ TC++ | TCW/BCW |
| ▪ BC 2.0 | ▪ BC 3.0/3.1 | ▪ BCC | Local | #pragma |

### Purpose
The -l*x* command line option will pass the linker option *x* to the Turbo Linker.

### IDE Option
N/A

### Default
None

### Usage
```
BCC -lt SOURCE.C
```
Inform the linker that the target application is a .COM file.

```
BCC -v -l-v SOURCE.C
```
Compile with debug information in the .OBJ file, but not the .EXE file.

### Description
The command line compiler will normally call the Turbo Linker if there are no errors encountered during compilation. The -l*x* option allows you to pass the linker any options you would normally pass to TLINK if you were to call it separately. You can use more than one -l*x* option on the command line.

### See Also
| | |
|---|---|
| e*filename* | Executable Filename |
| M | Create a .MAP File |

## Example

Compile the "Hello, C!" application in the -L*path* example to a .COM file using the -lt option. This is accomplished by entering the following on the command line:

```
bcc -mt -lt hello.c
```

The - mt option compiles the application using the tiny memory model and the -lt option tells the linker that the target application is a .COM file.

# M                                                      Create a .MAP file

| | | | | |
|---|---|---|---|---|
| ▪ C | ▪ C++ | CPP | ▪ TC++ | ▪ TCW/BCW |
| ▪ BC 2.0 | ▪ BC 3.0/3.1 | ▪ BCC | Local | #pragma |

## Purpose

The -M option instructs the compiler to map the executable file by creating a listing of the segments and addresses as well as a list of public symbols and their addresses.

## IDE Option

Options | Linker | Off          *for -M-*
Options | Linker | Segments     *for -M -l-m*
Options | Linker | Publics      *for -M*
Options | Linker | Detailed     *for -M -ls*

## Default

−M−

Do not create a .MAP file.

## Usage

BCC −M SOURCE.C

Create a .MAP file with segments and publics.

BCC −M −l−m SOURCE.C

Create a .MAP file with segments using only the -l linker option and the -M map option.

BCC −M −ls SOURCE.C

Create a detailed .MAP file using the -l linker option and the -M map option.

## Description

Mapping the executable file is very useful for tracking down linking error. For example, if you have an application that is unable to link with a function call you have in one source module with a function definition in another module, you can create a .MAP file of both to see how the compiler is constructing your function names. This lets you check the name mangling performed in C++, the number of significant characters used, case sensitivity, etc.

See Chapter 5 for a detailed discussion of the contents of mapped executable files.

## See Also

| | |
|---|---|
| e*filename* | Executable Filename |
| l*x* | Pass an Option to the Linker |
| Chapter 6: L, LA | Generate a List File |

## Example

Write an application with two modules that contains an unresolved function call. Also map the executable file to show the discrepancy.

**map\main.c**
```
void main(void)
{
    int Result;

    /* Call the pascal function FunctCall() */
    Result = FunctCall();
}
```

**map\test.c**
```
/* Set the pascal calling convention */
#pragma option -p

int FunctCall(void)
{
    return(1);
}
```

The call to the FunctCall() function in main() is made using the normal C calling convention, whereas the *pascal* calling convention is used in the definition of FunctCall. The normal C calling convention uses case sensitivity and uses a leading underscore for all public symbols. The *pascal* calling convention, on the other hand, is case insensitive and does not use leading underscores. The problem is easy to see when the application is compiled with a mapped executable file as follows:

```
bcc -M test.c main.c
```

The executable file is mapped during the link stage, which contains the name and address of all the public symbols as well as any errors encountered. The definition for the FuncCall function is listed as:

```
0000:0239    FUNCTCALL
```

The error for the unresolved function call is listed as:

```
Error: Undefined symbol _FunctCall in module main.c
```

The linker is unable to resolve a function call to _FunctCall because the definition for the function is labeled FUNCTCALL.

## mc                                    Use the Compact Memory Model

- C
- C++
- CPP
- TC++
- TCW/BCW
- BC 2.0
- BC 3.0/3.1
- BCC
- Local
- #pragma

### Purpose
The -mc option instructs the compiler to use the compact memory model while compiling the source code.

### IDE Option
Options | Compiler | Code Generation | Compact

### Default
```
-ms
```
Use the small memory model.

### Usage
```
BCC -mc SOURCE.C
```
Compile using the compact memory model.

```
#pragma option -mc
```
Same as above; must appear before the first C or C++ declaration.

### Description
The compact memory model is normally used for applications that have a large amount of data but a relatively small amount of code. While this memory model can be used for Windows applications, it is not recommended. Because this memory model uses far pointers for data, all the data in the Windows application must be located in fixed data segments. This creates logjams in memory that make dynamic memory allocation difficult. The small or medium memory model is recommended if you are programming for Windows. If your Windows application requires more than 64K, you can either dynamically allocate the memory at run time or place your initial data in a resource file.

The compact memory model has four basic areas: code space, initial data space, stack space, and dynamic data space (see Figure 2-2).

## Code Space

As with the small memory model, all the applications functions in the compact memory model are located in a single code segment. An application's function code can occupy up to 64K of memory. All functions are assumed to be *near* functions unless you supply

117

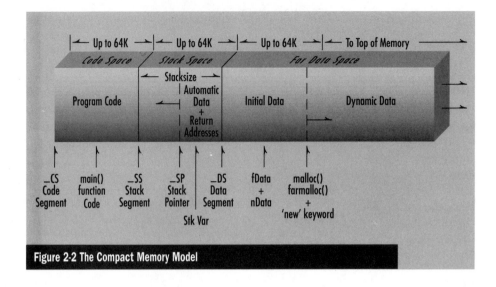

**Figure 2-2 The Compact Memory Model**

an explicit *far* keyword. Far functions will still be located in the same code space as the near functions, but they will be compiled with a far return that enables them to be called by functions located outside of the application's code space. More room can be created in the default code segment by placing far functions in separate segments using the #pragma option -z directive.

Near pointers to functions default to a type _cs near pointer. When a type _cs near pointer is converted to a far pointer, the 16-bit pointer value is used as the low word of the far pointer and the Code Segment (CS) register is used as the high word.

## Initial Data

Compact memory model applications have one initial data segment that can be up to 64K in size. All the initial data in the compact memory model application defaults to this segment unless an explicit *far* keyword is used. Each *far* variable is given its own segment. Variables can be forced into the same segment by using the #pragma option -z directive.

The -Ff and -Ff=*size* options can be used in the compact memory model to automatically give variables with a size greater than or equal to *size* their own data segment, thus leaving more room in the initial data segment.

## Stack Space

An application that uses the compact memory model has a separate segment for the stack space. This allows the stack to grow to as large as 64K. Like all memory models, the Stack Pointer (SP) register starts at the high end of the stack and moves downward in memory as functions are called and local data within the functions are allocated. The size of the stack area in Windows applications can be set using the STACKSIZE declaration in the application's .DEF file.

Note that the stack space can be placed in the same data segment as the initial data by using the -Fs option. This option will cause the linker to load the compatibility startup code, which will place the stack within the data segment. The total size for both the stack space and the initial data would then be restricted to 64K. This option only applies to DOS applications.

## Dynamic Data Space

The memory area following the stack segment at the end of memory is used for dynamic memory allocation in DOS programs. Calls to the malloc() in DOS programs return far pointers from this memory area as does the 'new' keyword in C++. The 'new' keyword in Windows applications allocates global memory.

## Data Pointers

Because the compact memory model uses data located in several different segments, the compiler defaults to 32-bit far pointers for all pointers to data. This increases the size of your application and, because 32-bit far pointers are used instead of 16-bit near pointers, data intensive applications run more slowly than memory models that default to near pointers. Your application can save space and increase the execution speed by explicitly using near pointers. Care must be taken, however, to ensure the near pointer is of the proper type. For example, consider the following two functions:

**mc\ss.c**

```
    typedef struct
    {
        long x, y;
    }   POINT;

    /* Define a function using the default pointers */
    void FarAddPoints(POINT *One, POINT *Two, POINT *Ans)
    {
       Ans->x = One->x + Two->x;
       Ans->y = One->y + Two->y;
    }

    /* Define a function using stack near pointers */
    void NearAddPoints(POINT _ss *One, POINT _ss *Two, POINT _ss *Ans)
    {
       Ans->x = One->x + Two->x;
       Ans->y = One->y + Two->y;
    }

    void main(void)
    {
       unsigned n;
```

```
/* Declare these variables on the stack */
POINT One, Two, Ans;
One.y = One.x = 1;
Two.y = Two.x = 2;

/* Check the speed of the default pointers */
for(n = 0; n < 60000L; n++)
   FarAddPoints(&One, &Two, &Ans);

/* Check the speed using the near stack pointers */
for(n = 0; n < 60000L; n++)
   NearAddPoints(&One, &Two, &Ans);
}
```

Both the NearAddPoints() and FarAddPoints() functions are functionally identical, except the NearAddPoints() adds the two points using type _ss pointers, whereas FarAddPoints() adds them using the default far pointer. The type _ss pointer is a 16-bit near pointer referenced to the stack segment. Using type _ss pointers instead of the default far pointers causes the compiler to generate smaller and more efficient code. The NearAddPoints() function in the above code operates 10% faster than the FarAdd-Points() function and is also 3 bytes smaller. The disadvantage to using specialized near pointer types, such as the type _ss pointer above, is that the data must be located in a specific segment. In the above code, the data was located on the stack segment. If the data were located in either the initial data segment or a far segment or were dynamically allocated, the FarAddPoints() function would have still operated properly, whereas the NearAddPoints() function would have caused a memory overwrite.

## Compact Model Link Files

Applications compiled with the compact memory model must be linked with compatible startup and library files. If you are compiling the source code in the compact memory model and then calling TLINK separately, you must link your application using the startup and library files listed in Table 2-8 that are appropriate for the target application.

|  | DOS APPLICATION | WINDOWS APPLICATION | WINDOWS DLL |
|---|---|---|---|
| **Regular Startup** | COC.OBJ | COWC.OBJ | CODC.OBJ |
| **Compatibility Startup** | COFC.OBJ | n/a | n/a |
| **Math Library** | MATHC.LIB | MATHWC.LIB | MATHWC.LIB |
| **Windows RT Library** | n/a | CWC.LIB | CWC.LIB |
| **Run-time Library** | CC.LIB | CC.LIB | CC.LIB |

Table 2-8 Object code and library files for the compact memory model

## See Also

| | |
|---|---|
| mh | Use the Huge Memory Model |
| ml | Use the Large Memory Model |
| mm | Use the Medium Memory Model |
| ms | Use the Small Memory Model |
| mt | Use the Tiny Memory Model |

## Example

Write an application using the huge memory model and print the locations of code, initial data, data on the stack, and dynamic data, as well as the Code Segment, Data Segment, and Stack Segment registers.

mc\Example.c

```
#include <malloc.h>
#include <stdio.h>

char    nData[] = "This is near data";
char far fData[] = "This is far data";

void main(void)
{
  int StkVar;
  char     *nBuff;        /* Near data pointer */
  char far *fBuff;        /* Far data pointer */

  nBuff = malloc(40);     /* From near data space */
  fBuff = farmalloc(40);  /* From far data space */

  printf("Code Segment            %X\n", _CS);
  printf("main():                 %Fp\n", (void far *)main);
  printf("fData:                  %Fp\n", (void far *)fData);
  printf("\n");
  printf("Data Segment            %X\n", _DS);
  printf("nData:                  %Fp\n", (void far *)nData);
  printf("\n");
  printf("Stack Segment           %X\n", _SS);
  printf("StkVar:                 %Fp\n", (void far *)&StkVar);
  printf("nBuff pointer:          %Fp\n", (void far *)&nBuff);
  printf("fBuff pointer:          %Fp\n", (void far *)&fBuff);
  printf("\n");
  printf("malloc() returned:      %Fp\n", (void far *)nBuff);
  printf("farmalloc() returned:   %Fp\n", (void far *)fBuff);
}
```

The above application is compiled using the compact memory model as follows:

```
bcc -mc Example.c
```

Executing the application produces the following output:

mc\output

```
Code Segment        24B8
main():             24B8:0210
fData:              263D:0000
```

```
Data Segment              263F
nData:                    263F:0092

Stack Segment             268B
StkVar:                   268B:1000
nBuff pointer:            268B:0FFC
fBuff pointer:            268B:0FF8

malloc() returned:        27CE:0004
farmalloc() returned:     27D1:0004
```

As indicated by the application's output, the main function code is located in the code segment. The data for the nData string is located in the data segment, whereas the data for the fData string is located in a separate far segment. The three stack variables, StkVar, nBuff, and fBuff, are all located in the stack segment. Both malloc() and farmalloc() returned allocated data from a unique segment.

If the above application were compiled using the -Fs option, the output would look as follows:

```
Code Segment              24B8
main():                   24B8:020C
fData:                    263D:0000

Data Segment              263F
nData:                    263F:01A2

Stack Segment             263F
StkVar:                   263F:15C0
nBuff pointer:            263F:15BC
fBuff pointer:            263F:15B8

malloc() returned:        27DE:0004
farmalloc() returned:     27E1:0004
```

Here the stack space is located within the data segment and both DS and SS registers are equal.

## mh                                          Use the Huge Memory Model

- C
- BC 2.0
- C++
- BC 3.0/3.1
- CPP
- BCC
- TC++
- Local
- TCW/BCW
- #pragma

### Purpose
The -mh option instructs the compiler to use the huge memory model while compiling the source code.

### IDE Option
Options | Compiler | Code Generation | Huge

## Default

`—mh`

Use the huge memory model.

## Usage

`BCC —mh SOURCE.C`

Use the huge memory model.

`#pragma option —mh`

Same as above; must appear before the first C or C++ declaration.

## Description

The huge memory model is normally used for applications that require both a large amount of code and an extremely large amount of initial data. Whereas this memory model can be used for DOS applications, it cannot be used for Windows applications or Windows Dynamic Link Libraries. The compiler and linker will not prevent you from creating a Windows application or DLL using the huge memory model; however, the resulting application will not run in the Windows environment.

The huge memory model uses many different segments for both code and data. These segments can be grouped into four basic areas: code space, initial data space, the stack space, and dynamic data space (see Figure 2-3).

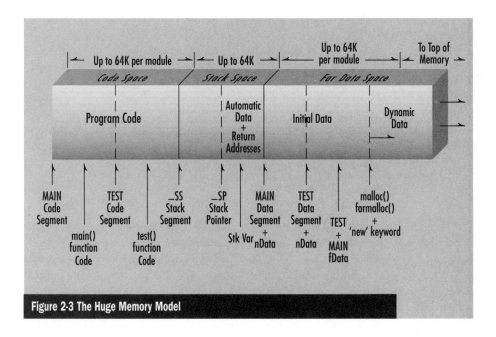

**Figure 2-3 The Huge Memory Model**

## Code Space

Each module in a huge application has a separate code segment for all the functions within the module. This allows applications to have up to 1 Meg of code provided any one module does not exceed 64K. If you have more than 64K of code in a module, you should either split the module into two different modules or place specific functions into another segment using the #pragma option -z directive.

All functions in the huge memory model default to type *far_loadds* functions. This means the compiler generates code that will load the Data Segment (DS) register with the segment address for the module's initial data at the beginning of each function call. The compiler also generates code to return from the function by restoring the DS register to its original value and executing a far return instruction. This involves a significant amount of processing overhead for frequently called functions. Consider the following application code:

```
long Sum;

/* Define a near function */
static void near FastFnct(long Number)
{
  Sum += Number;
}

/* Define an identical default function */
void SlowFnct(long Number)
{
  Sum += Number;
}

void main(void)
{
   unsigned n;

   /* Initialize the value of 'Sum' */
   Sum = 0;

   /* Test the speed of the default function */
   for(n = 0; n < 60000; n++)
       SlowFnct(n);

   /* Test the speed of the faster near function */
   for(n = 0; n < 60000; n++)
       FastFnct(n);
}
```

Both the Fast() and Slow() functions use identical code, but the Fast() function is declared as near, whereas the Slow() function defaults to a *far_loadds* function. As a near function, Fast() operates 20% faster than the Slow() function. The speed increase would be even more dramatic if the compiler did not perform a redundant load of the DS register at the beginning of the Fast() function. Hopefully future versions of the compiler will streamline the compiling of near functions in huge memory by removing this redundant load. Note that because the function is declared as *near* it cannot be called from any other module.

If your huge memory model application contains C++ source code, then the virtual function tables for each object class will be placed in the related code space module. Virtual tables are normally placed somewhere in the data space unless you use the -Vf option (Far C++ virtual tables).

## The Stack and Dynamic Data Space

An application that uses the huge memory model has a separate segment for the stack space. This allows the stack to grow to as large as 64K. Note that even though there is a compatibility startup file for the huge memory model, COFH.OBJ, that is supposed to place the stack segment in the same location as the data segment when you use the -Fs option, this file is identical to the normal startup file, COH.OBJ. As such, the -Fs option is ineffective for the huge memory model.

The memory area following the application to the end of memory is used for dynamic memory allocation in DOS applications. Calls to both the malloc() and farmalloc() functions and the 'new' keyword in C++ return far pointers to this memory area.

## Pointers

Because the huge memory model uses data located in many different segments, the compiler defaults to 32-bit far pointers for both code and data. Note that the huge memory model uses normal *far* pointers and not *huge* pointers. If you are using memory objects larger than 64K, you will still have to explicitly declare their pointers as *huge*.

Far pointers to data increase the size of your application. Also, because the compiler passes 32-bit pointers to functions, these functions operate more slowly than if they used 16-bit near pointers. Your application can save code space and execution time by explicitly using specialized near pointers, such as type _ss and _ds. Care must be taken, however, to ensure the near pointer type corresponds to the data. See the compact memory model description for an example of using specialized near pointers.

## Huge Memory Model Link Files

Applications compiled with the huge memory model must be linked with compatible startup and library files. If you are using the IDE or the command line compiler, then the proper files will be linked automatically. You should use the files listed in Table 2-9 if you are calling TLINK separately.

| | DOS APPLICATION | WINDOWS APPLICATION | WINDOWS DLL |
|---|---|---|---|
| **Regular Startup** | COH.OBJ | n/a | n/a |
| **Compatibility Startup** | COFH.OBJ | n/a | n/a |
| **Math Library** | MATHH.LIB | n/a | n/a |
| **Windows RTibrary** | n/a | n/a | n/a |
| **Run-time Library** | CH.LIB | n/a | n/a |

**Table 2-9 Huge memory model link files**

## See Also

| | |
|---|---|
| mc | Use the Compact Memory Model |
| ml | Use the Large Memory Model |
| mm, mm! | Use the Medium Memory Model |
| ms, ms! | Use the Small Memory Model |
| mt, mt! | Use the Tiny Memory Model |

## Example

Write an application using the huge memory model and print the locations of code, initial data, data on the stack, and dynamic data, as well as the Code Segment, Data Segment, and Stack Segment registers.

**mh\test.c**

```c
#include <malloc.h>
#include <stdio.h>

static char     nData[] = "This is near data";
static char far fData[] = "This is far data";

void test(void)
{
  int StkVar;
  char      *nBuff;       /* Near data pointer */
  char far  *fBuff;       /* Far data pointer */

  nBuff = malloc(40);     /* From near data space */
  fBuff = farmalloc(40);  /* From far data space */

  printf("TEST Code Segment          %X\n", _CS);
  printf("TEST test():               %Fp\n", (void far *)test);
  printf("TEST fData:                %Fp\n", (void far *)fData);
  printf("\n");
  printf("TEST Data Segment          %X\n", _DS);
  printf("TEST nData:                %Fp\n", (void far *)nData);
  printf("\n");
  printf("TEST Stack Segment         %X\n", _SS);
  printf("TEST StkVar:               %Fp\n", (void far *)&StkVar);
  printf("TEST nBuff pointer:        %Fp\n", (void far *)&nBuff);
  printf("TEST fBuff pointer:        %Fp\n", (void far *)&fBuff);
  printf("\n");
  printf("TEST malloc() returned:    %Fp\n", (void far *)nBuff);
  printf("TEST farmalloc() returned: %Fp\n", (void far *)fBuff);
}
```

**mh\main.c**

```c
#include <malloc.h>
#include <stdio.h>

static char     nData[] = "This is near data";
static char far fData[] = "This is far data";

/* Declare a prototype to the test() function */
void test(void);
```

```
void main(void)
{
    int StkVar;
    char     *nBuff;        /* Near data pointer */
    char far *fBuff;        /* Far data pointer */

    nBuff = malloc(40);     /* From near data space */
    fBuff = farmalloc(40);  /* From far data space */

    printf("MAIN Code Segment         %X\n", _CS);
    printf("MAIN main():              %Fp\n", (void far *)main);
    printf("MAIN fData:               %Fp\n", (void far *)fData);
    printf("\n");
    printf("MAIN Data Segment         %X\n", _DS);
    printf("MAIN nData:               %Fp\n", (void far *)nData);
    printf("\n");
    printf("MAIN Stack Segment        %X\n", _SS);
    printf("MAIN StkVar:              %Fp\n", (void far *)&StkVar);
    printf("MAIN nBuff pointer:       %Fp\n", (void far *)&nBuff);
    printf("MAIN fBuff pointer:       %Fp\n", (void far *)&fBuff);
    printf("\n");
    printf("MAIN malloc() returned:   %Fp\n", (void far *)nBuff);
    printf("MAIN farmalloc() returned: %Fp\n", (void far *)fBuff);
    printf("\n");
    test();
}
```

The above application is compiled using the huge memory model by entering the following:

```
bcc -mh test.c main.c
```

As shown by the following output, both the TEST and MAIN modules are given unique segments for the data and code while they both share the same stack segment.

```
MAIN Code Segment            2331
MAIN main():                 2331:0002
MAIN fData:                  2376:0000

MAIN Data Segment            235D
MAIN nData:                  235D:0002

MAIN Stack Segment           23B3
MAIN StkVar:                 23B3:0FFE
MAIN nBuff pointer:          23B3:0FFA
MAIN fBuff pointer:          23B3:0FF6

MAIN malloc() returned:      24F6:0004
MAIN farmalloc() returned:   24F9:0004

TEST Code Segment            231F
TEST test():                 231F:000A
TEST fData:                  235C:0000

TEST Data Segment            2344
TEST nData:                  2344:0000

TEST Stack Segment           23B3
```

```
TEST StkVar:              23B3:0FEC
TEST nBuff pointer:       23B3:0FE8
TEST fBuff pointer:       23B3:0FE4

TEST malloc() returned:   24FC:0004
TEST farmalloc() returned: 24FF:0004
```

The application uses two initial data variables, one near called nData and the other called fData, as well as three stack variables called StkVar, nBuff, and fBuff. Keep in mind that the data space for nBuff and fBuff that holds the pointer values is physically located on the stack even though what the pointer is referencing many be located elsewhere in memory. The location of each of the variables, the main and test functions, and the data space allocated by malloc and farmalloc are printed as far variables in both the MAIN and TEST modules.

# ml                                          Use the Large Memory Model

- C           - C++          - CPP          - TC++         - TCW/BCW
- BC 2.0      - BC 3.0/3.1   - BCC          - Local        - #pragma

## Purpose
The -ml option instructs the compiler to use the large memory model for compiling an application.

## IDE Option
Options | Compiler | Code Generation | Large

## Default
```
-ml
```
Use the large memory model.

## Usage
```
BCC -ml SOURCE.C
```
Use the large memory model.

```
#pragma option -ml
```
Same as above; must appear before the first C or C++ declaration.

## Description
The large memory model is normally used for applications that use a large amount of code and data. Although this memory model can be used for Windows applications, it is not recommended. All the data in the application must be located in fixed data segments to be usable by the default far pointers. Fixed data segments in Windows create log jams in the memory that are difficult for Windows to maneuver around. The small or medium memory model is recommended if you are programming for Windows. If

your Windows application requires more than 64K, you can either dynamically allocate the memory at run time or place your initial data in a resource file.

The large memory model has four basic areas: code space, initial data space, stack space, and dynamic data space (see Figure 2-4). Each module in a large memory model application has a separate code segment for the functions within the module. This allows the application to have up to 1 Meg of code provided any one module does not contain more than 64K of code. This restriction is relatively easy to accommodate by either splitting large modules into two smaller modules or placing specific functions in another segment using the #pragma option -z directive.

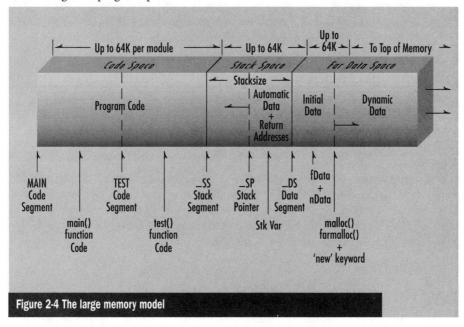

**Figure 2-4 The large memory model**

All functions in the large memory model default to type far pointers. The compiler generates code to perform a far function call and to return from the function by executing a far return. This involves a significant amount of processing overhead for frequently called functions. This overhead can be eliminated by using the *near* keyword on functions only used locally within a module. See the huge memory model for an example of an application using near functions.

The initial data, stack space, dynamic memory allocation, and data pointers for the large memory model are identical to those for the compact memory model.

## Large Model Link Files

Applications compiled with the large memory model must be linked with compatible startup and library files. If you are compiling the source code in the large memory model and then calling TLINK separately, you must link your application using the startup and library files listed in Table 2-10 that are appropriate for the target application.

| | DOS APPLICATION | WINDOWS APPLICATION | WINDOWS DLL |
|---|---|---|---|
| **Regular Startup** | COL.OBJ | COWL.OBJ | CODL.OBJ |
| **Compatibility Startup** | COFL.OBJ | n/a | n/a |
| **Math Library** | MATHL.LIB | MATHWL.LIB | MATHWL.LIB |
| **Windows RT Library** | n/a | CWL.LIB | CWL.LIB |
| **Run-time Library** | CL.LIB | CL.LIB | CL.LIB |

**Table 2-10 Object code and library files for the large memory model**

### See Also

| | |
|---|---|
| mc | Use the Compact Memory Model |
| mh | Use the Huge Memory Model |
| mm, mm! | Use the Medium Memory Model |
| ms, ms! | Use the Small Memory Model |
| mt, mt! | Use the Tiny Memory Model |

### Example

Write an application using the huge memory model and print the locations of code, initial data, data on the stack, and dynamic data, as well as the Code Segment, Data Segment, and Stack Segment registers. The example application code for the large memory model is identical to that for the huge memory model. You enter the following to compile the application using the large memory model:

```
bcc -ml test.c main.c
```

When compiled for the large memory model, the application has the following output:

```
MAIN Code Segment           2317
MAIN main():                2317:0001
MAIN fData:                 232C:0000

MAIN Data Segment           232E
MAIN nData:                 232E:0212

MAIN Stack Segment          2399
MAIN StkVar:                2399:0FFE
MAIN nBuff pointer:         2399:0FFA
MAIN fBuff pointer:         2399:0FF6

MAIN malloc() returned:     24DC:0004
MAIN farmalloc() returned:  24DF:0004

TEST Code Segment           2306
TEST test():                2306:0000
TEST fData:                 232A:0000

TEST Data Segment           232E
TEST nData:                 232E:0092
```

```
TEST Stack Segment          2399
TEST StkVar:                2399:0FEE
TEST nBuff pointer:         2399:0FEA
TEST fBuff pointer:         2399:0FE6

TEST malloc() returned:     24E2:0004
TEST farmalloc() returned:  24E5:0004
```

The application uses two initial data variables, one a near called nData and the other a far called fData, as well as three stack variables called StkVar, nBuff, and fBuff. Keep in mind that the data space for nBuff and fBuff that holds the pointer values is physically located on the stack even though what the pointer is referencing may be located elsewhere in memory. The location of each of the variables, the main and test functions, and the data space allocated by malloc and farmalloc are printed as far variables in both the MAIN and TEST modules.

The code in the TEST and MAIN functions are each given unique segments as indicated by the test() and main() function addresses. Note that the Data Segment (DS) register is set to the location of the initial data. The stack, however, is located in a different segment. Both the malloc() and farmalloc() functions return data from unique data segments.

## mm, mm!                                Use the Medium Memory Model

- C          ▪ C++          ▪ CPP          ▪ TC++          ▪ TCW/BCW
- BC 2.0     ▪ BC 3.0/3.1   ▪ BCC          ▪ Local         ▪ #pragma

### Purpose
The -mm option instructs the compiler to use the medium memory model. The -mm! option also tells the compiler to use the medium memory model, but to assume that the Data Segment (DS) register will not be the same as the Stack Segment (SS) register at run time.

### IDE Option
Options | Compiler | Code Generation | Medium          *for mm*
Options | Compiler | Code Generation | Medium | Never          *for mm!*

### Default
−mm
   Use the medium memory model.

### Usage
BCC −mm SOURCE.C
   Use the medium memory model.

#pragma option −mm
   Same as above; must appear before the first C or C++ declaration.

```
BCC -mm! SOURCE.C
```
Same as above except assume DS !=SS at run time.

```
#pragma option -mm!
```
Same as above; must appear before the first C or C++ declaration.

### Description

The medium memory model is normally used for applications that have a large amount of code but a relatively small amount of data. This memory model, as well as the small memory model, are recommended for Windows applications and Windows Dynamic Link Libraries. The medium memory model has three basic areas: code space, near data space, and far data space (see Figure 2-5).

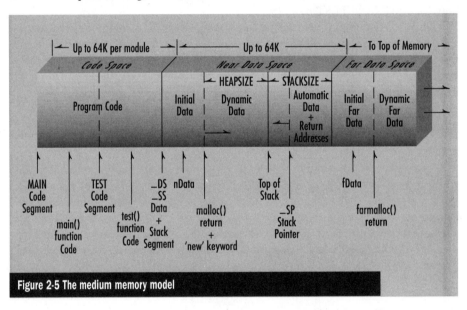

**Figure 2-5 The medium memory model**

    Each module in an application using the medium memory model has a separate code segment. All the functions within a given module will be located within the same code segment. This arrangement allows your application to have up to 1 Meg of code provided any one of the modules does not exceed 64K. This restriction is relatively easy to accommodate by either splitting large modules into two smaller modules or placing specific functions in another segment using the #pragma option -z directive.

    All functions in the medium memory model default to type far pointers. The compiler generates code to perform a far function call and to return from the function by executing a far return. This involves a significant amount of processing overhead for frequently called functions. This overhead can be eliminated by using the *near* keyword for functions only used locally within a module. See the huge memory model for an example of an application using near functions.

The near data space, far data space, and data pointers for the medium memory model are identical to those for the small memory model. See the small memory model for a discussion about assuming that the DS register will not equal the SS register at run time.

## Medium Model Link Files

Applications compiled with the medium memory model must be linked with compatible startup and library files. If you are compiling the source code in the medium memory model and then calling TLINK separately, you must link your application using the startup and library files listed in Table 2-11 that are appropriate for the target application.

| | DOS APPLICATION | WINDOWS APPLICATION | WINDOWS DLL |
|---|---|---|---|
| Regular Startup | COM.OBJ | COWM.OBJ | CODM.OBJ |
| Compatibility Startup | COFM.OBJ | n/a | n/a |
| Math Library | MATHM.LIB | MATHWM.LIB | MATHWM.LIB |
| Windows RT Library | n/a | CWM.LIB | CWM.LIB |
| Run-time Library | CM.LIB | CM.LIB | CM.LIB |

Table 2-11 Object code and library files for the medium memory model

### See Also

| mc | Use the Compact Memory Model |
|---|---|
| mh | Use the Huge Memory Model |
| ml | Use the Large Memory Model |
| ms, ms! | Use the Small Memory Model |
| mt, mt! | Use the Tiny Memory Model |

### Example

Write an application using the huge memory model and print the locations of code, initial data, data on the stack, and dynamic data, as well as the Code Segment, Data Segment, and Stack Segment registers. The example application code for a large memory model is identical to that for the huge memory model. You enter the following to compile the application using the medium memory model:

```
bcc -mm test.c main.c
```

When compiled for the medium memory model, the application has the following output:

```
MAIN Code Segment        2652
MAIN main():             2652:0006
MAIN fData:              2665:0000

MAIN Data Segment        2667
MAIN nData:              2667:022A
```

```
MAIN Stack Segment         2667
MAIN StkVar:               2667:FFF2
MAIN nBuff pointer:        2667:FFF0
MAIN fBuff pointer:        2667:FFEC

MAIN malloc() returned:    2667:0A8C
MAIN farmalloc() returned: 3667:0004

TEST Code Segment          2642
TEST test():               2642:000E
TEST fData:                2663:0000

TEST Data Segment          2667
TEST nData:                2667:00AA

TEST Stack Segment         2667
TEST StkVar:               2667:FFE4
TEST nBuff pointer:        2667:FFE2
TEST fBuff pointer:        2667:FFDE

TEST malloc() returned:    2667:0AB8
TEST farmalloc() returned: 366A:0004
```

The application uses two initial data variables, one a near called nData and the other a far called fData, as well as three stack variables called StkVar, nBuff, and fBuff. Keep in mind that the data space for nBuff and fBuff that holds the pointer values is physically located on the stack even though what the pointer is referencing may be located elsewhere in memory. The location of each of the variables, the main and test functions, and the data space allocated by malloc and farmalloc are printed as far variables in both the MAIN and TEST modules.

As shown by the addresses for the test() and main() functions, the codes in the TEST and MAIN modules were each assigned unique code segments. All the initial data, the stack, and dynamic memory allocation using the malloc() function used the same data segment.

# ms, ms!                                      Use the Small Memory Model

- C
- C++
- CPP
- TC++
- TCW/BCW
- BC 2.0
- BC 3.0/3.1
- BCC
- Local
- #pragma

## Purpose
The -ms option tells the compiler to use the small memory model when compiling the source code. The -ms! option tells the compiler to use the small memory model and to assume that the Data Segment (DS) register will not be the same value as the Stack Segment (SS) register at run time.

## IDE Option
Options | Compiler | Code Generation | Small                    *for ms*
Options | Compiler | Code Generation | Small | Never            *for ms!*

## Usage

```
BCC -ms SOURCE.C
```

Command line options compile the small memory model assuming that SS is equal to DS.

```
BCC -ms! SOURCE.C
```

Same as above except the SS register is assumed to be different than the DS register at run time.

```
#pragma option -ms
```

Stating a memory model in a pragma is only effective if it appears before the first C or C++ declaration.

```
#pragma option -ms!
```

Same as above; the '!' is ignored for #pragmas.

## Description

The small memory model has three basic memory areas: code space, near data space, and far data space (see Figure 2-6).

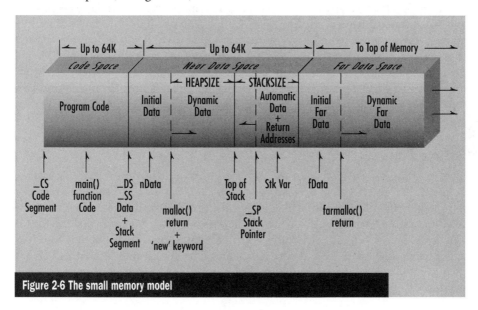

**Figure 2-6 The small memory model**

# Code Space

All the application's functions in a small memory model are located in a single code space segment. This code space can occupy up to 64K of memory. All functions are assumed to be *near* functions unless you supply an explicit *far* keyword as follows:

```
void far Function(void)
```

```
{ . . .
```

Far functions will still be located in the same code space as the near functions, but they are compiled such that they can be called by functions located outside of the application's code space. Near pointers to functions default to a type _cs near pointer. When type _cs near pointers are converted to far pointers, the 16-bit pointer value is used as the low word of the far pointer and the value in the Code Segment (CS) register is used as the high word.

## Near and Far Data

Small memory model applications have one near data space segment that can be up to 64K in size. The near data space contains the application's initial data, local heap, and application stack. The application's initial near data is physically located in the lower portion of the application's near data space.

All data in a small memory model defaults to near data unless an explicit *far* keyword is used as follows:

```
int far v1, far v2;
```

Each *far* variable is given its own segment. This means every *far* variable declaration will use at least 16 bytes of memory. For example, the two integer variables above, v1 and v2, would normally use 2 bytes of memory for a total of 4 bytes. However, because they are declared as *far*, they each take up 16 bytes of memory for a total of 32 bytes. Data objects larger than 16 bytes are the next higher multiple of 16 bytes in size. For example, a far character array that is 17 bytes in size will use 32 bytes of memory. This means that applications that use extensive explicit far data declarations for small data objects are likely to waste a considerable amount of space.

## Stack Space

The application's stack occupies the top portion of near memory space. The Stack Pointer (SP) register starts at the high end of the stack area and moves down in memory as functions are called and local data within the function is allocated. The size of the stack area can be set using the STACKSIZE declaration in the application's .DEF file for Windows applications. The size of the stack is adjusted as needed at run time for DOS applications, but not for Windows applications. The top of the stack area (TOS) is physically located at the lower end of the stack area. Lowering the SP register to a value below the TOS results in a stack overflow.

## Local and Far Heap

The area of memory between the initial near data and the TOS, which is sometimes called the *local heap*, is used for dynamic memory allocation. The initial size of this area is set by the HEAPSIZE declaration in the application's .DEF file for Windows applications. In both DOS and Windows applications, the size of the heap is adjusted as needed at run time; however, the size of the local heap, stack, and initial near data can never be larger than 64K.

When a small memory model application calls either the malloc or calloc function or a C++ application uses the 'new' keyword, memory is allocated from the local heap. As more dynamic memory is allocated, the malloc and calloc functions return successively higher locations in the near data space. Memory can be allocated from the far data space using the farmalloc function. As with all far data, each allocation is given its own unique memory segment, which means each allocation has a memory size that is the next higher multiple of 16 bytes. These functions all return a NULL pointer when the size of the requested memory is larger than the available free space.

## Near Data Pointers When SS Will Equal DS

All near data pointers in a small memory model are type _ds near pointers, including variables allocated on the stack. Type _ds near pointers are converted to far pointers by using the 16-bit value of the near pointer as the low word of the far pointer and the value in the Data Segment (DS) register as the high word. Except for certain specific instances, such as with DOS memory-resident applications or Windows Dynamic Link Libraries (DLL), the Stack Segment (SS) register will always be the same as the DS register in this memory model. This allows near pointers to data allocated on the stack area to be treated as type _ds near pointers.

## Assuming SS Will Not Equal DS

If you are writing an application that will operate using another application's stack, such as a DOS memory-resident program or a Windows DLL, you need to tell the compiler not to assume the DS register will be equal to the SS register at run time. When this assumption is no longer made, the compiler will default to type _ss near pointers for stack data rather than type _ds near pointers. Memory overwrites can occur if pointers to stack data are treated as type _ds near pointers and the SS register is not equal to the DS register at run time. Consider the following Windows DLL code, which passes two near pointers to the CopyStrings function and converts them to far pointers for the call to lstrcpy:

**ms\ds_not_s\Example.c**

```
#pragma option -ms

#include <windows.h>

char nData[] = "Pointer offset from the DS register";

/* With no _ds or _ss specifier, the compiler assumes both To and From
   are type _ds near pointers */
void CopyStrings(char *To, char *From)
{
   lstrcpy(To, From); /* To call the far string copy function the
                         compiler converts both near pointers
                         to far pointers using the DS register */
}

void far Fnct(void)
{
   char Automatic[80];
```

```
    CopyStrings(Automatic, nData);  /* Pass the function two near
                                       pointers */
}
```

Both the nData and Automatic strings are passed to the StringCopy function as near pointers. Within the StringCopy function they are converted to far pointers and passed to the Windows lstrcpy function. The near pointer for the nData is an offset from the DS register and the Automatic near pointer is an offset from the SS register. In a normal Windows application, the DS register is equal to the SS register at run time so both pointers can be considered type _ds near pointers without creating any problems. Remember, though, that DLLs don't have their own stack and instead use the calling application's stack. This means the SS register will not be the same as the DS register at run time. This would result in a memory overwrite, because the To pointer points to a location in the calling application's stack which is not located in the DLL's near data space, and the compiler has generated code which assumes that it is in the DLL's near data space. Telling the compiler not to assume that DS is equal to SS causes all pointers to stack data to default to type _ss near pointers. Because the CopyStrings function is expecting two type _ds near pointers and the call to CopyStrings passes a type _ss near pointer, the compiler flags the problem with a "Suspicious pointer conversion" warning. The problem can be corrected by using explicit type _ss near pointer declarations as follows:

**ms\ds_not_s\examp2.c**

```
#pragma option -ms!

#include <windows.h>

char nData[] = "Pointer offset from the DS register";

/* The To and From near pointers are explicitly declared as type _ss and
   type _ds near pointers for proper far pointer conversion. */
void CopyStrings(char _ss *To, char _ds *From)
{
    lstrcpy(To, From);  /* To call the far string copy function the
                           compiler now converts the two near pointers
                           to far pointers using the SS register for
                           the To pointer and the DS register for the
                           from pointer. */
}

void far Fnct(void)
{
    char Automatic[80];

    CopyStrings(Automatic, nData);  /* Pass the function two near
                                       pointers */
}
```

Now the far pointers are converted properly using the DS register for the From pointer and the SS register for the To pointer. As you can see, the ms! option does not generate code that is any different than that generated by the ms option, but only causes the compiler to default to type _ss near pointers for stack data rather than type _ds pointers. This applies to both the -mt! (tiny) and -mm! (medium) memory model options.

## Small Model Link Files

Applications compiled with the small memory model must be linked with startup and library files that are compatible with the model. If you are using the IDE or BCC command line to both compile and link your source code, these two compilers will automatically use the startup and library files listed in Table 2-12 below when the small memory model is used.

| | DOS APPLICATION | WINDOWS APPLICATION | WINDOWS DLL |
|---|---|---|---|
| Regular Startup | C0S.OBJ | C0WS.OBJ | C0DS.OBJ |
| Compatibility Startup | C0FS.OBJ | n/a | n/a |
| Math Library | MATHS.LIB | MATHWS.LIB | MATHWS.LIB |
| Windows RT Library | n/a | CWS.LIB | CWS.LIB |
| Run-time Library | CS.LIB | CS.LIB | CS.LIB |

Table 2-12 Object code and library files for the small memory model

### See Also

mc          Use the Compact Memory Model
mh          Use the Huge Memory Model
ml          Use the Large Memory Model
mm, mm!     Use the Medium Memory Model
mt, mt!     Use the Tiny Memory Model

### Example

Write an application that uses two initial data variables, one a near called nData and the other a far called fData. Define three stack variables called StkVar, nBuff, and fBuff. Keep in mind that the data space for nBuff and fBuff that holds the pointer values is physically located on the stack even though what the pointer is referencing many be located elsewhere in memory. Print the location of each of the variables, the main function, and the data space allocated by malloc and farmalloc as far variables. The following is a typical output from the application when compiled with the small memory model:

```
ms\output
    main():              24B8:0239
    fData:               2647:0000
    nData:               2649:00AA
    StkVar:              2649:FFF4
    nBuff pointer:       2649:FFF2
    fBuff pointer:       2649:FFEE
    malloc() returned:   2649:0836
    farmalloc() returned: 3649:0004
```

The high word of the far pointer is the segment and the low word is the offset. The code space is located in segment address 24B8 and the near data space in segment address 2649. The far data space is any free area of memory that is not either of these two segments.

Figure 2-6 shows the physical layout of the small memory model as it relates to the example application below. The main function code is located in the code space. The data for the nData strings is located at the bottom of the near data space, whereas the data for the fData string is located in the far data space. Physically, the segment for the fData variable is actually located between the code space and the near data space, as indicated by the 2647 segment address, which is immediately before the near data segment address of 2649. However, Figure 2-6 shows all the far space as one contiguous memory area for clarity. The three local variables in the main() function, the StkVar integer and the nBuff and fBuff pointers, are located on the application's stack near the top of the near data space, as indicated by the 2649 segment address and the high offsets, such as FFEE. The malloc() function allocates memory out of the near data space, as shown by the 2649 segment address. The farmalloc() function allocates memory out of the far data space, which is located above the application, as indicated by the 3649 segment address. Again, the memory area allocated by the farmalloc() could be physically located anywhere in memory and not necessarily immediately following the application. Any free area of memory that is not a part of the code space or near data space is considered far data space.

**ms\Example.c**

```
#include <malloc.h>
#include <stdio.h>

char     nData[] = "This is near data";
char far fData[] = "This is far data";

void main(void)
{
    int StkVar;
    char     *nBuff;        /* Near data pointer */
    char far *fBuff;        /* Far data pointer */

    nBuff = malloc(40);     /* From near data space */
    fBuff = farmalloc(40); /* From far data space */

    printf("main():             %Fp\n", (void far *)main);
    printf("fData:              %Fp\n", (void far *)fData);
    printf("nData:              %Fp\n", (void far *)nData);
    printf("StkVar:             %Fp\n", (void far *)&StkVar);
    printf("nBuff pointer:      %Fp\n", (void far *)&nBuff);
    printf("fBuff pointer:      %Fp\n", (void far *)&fBuff);
    printf("malloc() returned:  %Fp\n", (void far *)nBuff);
    printf("farmalloc() returned: %Fp\n", (void far *)fBuff);
}
```

# mt, mt!                            Use the Tiny Memory Model

- C       ■ C++       ■ CPP       ■ TC++       TCW/BCW
- BC 2.0     ■ BC 3.0/3.1    ■ BCC       ■ Local       ■ #pragma

## Purpose

The -mt option instructs the compiler to use the tiny memory model. The -mt! option tells the compiler to use the tiny memory model and to assume that the Data Segment (DS) register will not be the same value as the Stack Segment (SS) register at run time.

## IDE Option

Options I Compiler I Code Generation I Tiny             *for -mt*
Options I Compiler I Code Generation I Tiny I Never     *for -mt!*

## Default

```
-mt
```
Use the tiny memory model.

## Usage

```
BCC -mt SOURCE.C
```
Use the tiny memory model.

```
#pragma option -mt
```
Same as above; must appear before the first C or C++ declaration.

```
BCC -mt! SOURCE.C
```
Same as above except assume DS !=SS at run time.

```
#pragma option -mt!
```
Same as above; must appear before the first C or C++ declaration.

## Description

The tiny memory model is normally used for small applications totaling less than 64K. Note that this memory model is not suitable for Windows applications. The compiler and linker will not prevent you from creating a Windows application or Dynamic Link Library using the tiny memory model; however, the resulting application will not run in the Windows environment.

An application compiled using the tiny memory model consists of only near space and far space, as shown in Figure 2-7.

All the application's code, the initial data, and the stack are located in the near space. Dynamic memory allocations using the malloc() function or the "new" keyword also come from the near space. Dynamic memory allocated by calls to farmalloc(), however, come from the far space.

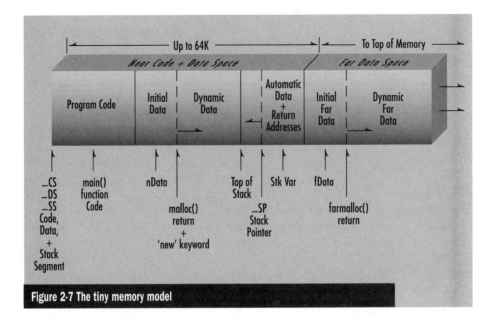

**Figure 2-7 The tiny memory model**

The tiny memory model is the only memory model that can be used to create .COM executable files. Note that you need to add the -lt option to the command line to compile an application to a .COM file as shown in the example application below. Also note that .COM files cannot be created directly from the IDE.

## Tiny Model Link Files

Applications compiled with the tiny memory model must be linked with startup and library files that are compatible with the model. If you are using the IDE or BCC command line to both compile and link your source code, these two compilers will automatically use the startup and library files listed in Table 2-13 below when the tiny memory model is used.

| | DOS APPLICATION | WINDOWS APPLICATION | WINDOWS DLL |
|---|---|---|---|
| Regular Startup | COT.OBJ | n/a | n/a |
| Compatibility Startup | COFT.OBJ | n/a | n/a |
| Math Library | MATHS.LIB | n/a | n/a |
| Windows RT Library | n/a | n/a | n/a |
| Run-time Library | CS.LIB | n/a | n/a |

**Table 2-13 Object code and library files for the tiny memory model**

## See Also

| | |
|---|---|
| mc | Use the Compact Memory Model |
| mh | Use the Huge Memory Model |
| ml | Use the Large Memory Model |
| mm, mm! | Use the Medium Memory Model |
| ms, ms! | Use the Small Memory Model |

## Example

Write an application using the tiny memory model and print the locations of the code, initial data, data on the stack, and dynamic data, as well as the Code Segment, Data Segment, and Stack Segment registers. The example application code for the tiny memory model is identical to that for the compact memory model (see that entry for the listing). You enter the following to compile the application to a file using the tiny memory model:

```
bcc -mt Example.c
```

When compiled for the tiny memory model, the application has the following output:

```
Code Segment        24B8
main():             24B8:0311
fData:              2658:0000

Data Segment        24B8
nData:              24B8:1AB2

Stack Segment       24B8
StkVar:             24B8:FFF4
nBuff pointer:      24B8:FFF2
fBuff pointer:      24B8:FFEE

malloc() returned: 24B8:2296
farmalloc() returned:      34B8:0004
```

As shown above by the addresses for the main() function, nData, and StkVar, almost everything is located in the same segment. Dynamic memory allocation also comes from the near space, as shown by the address returned by the malloc() function. Only the far data variable, fData, and the memory allocated by the farmalloc() function reside in the far space.

An application cannot contain any far data if you'd like to compile it to a .COM file. You can, however, dynamically allocate far memory at run time using the farmalloc() function. For example, the following application is identical to the previous application except that it does not contain any initial far data:

**mt\tiny_com.c**
```
    #include <malloc.h>
    #include <stdio.h>

    char    nData[] = "This is near data";
```

```
void main(void)
{
    int StkVar;
    char     *nBuff;        /* Near data pointer */
    char far *fBuff;        /* Far data pointer */

    nBuff = malloc(40);     /* From near data space */
    fBuff = farmalloc(40);  /* From far data space */

    printf("Code Segment          %X\n", _CS);
    printf("main():               %Fp\n", (void far *)main);
    printf("\n");
    printf("Data Segment          %X\n", _DS);
    printf("nData:                %Fp\n", (void far *)nData);
    printf("\n");
    printf("Stack Segment         %X\n", _SS);
    printf("StkVar:               %Fp\n", (void far *)&StkVar);
    printf("nBuff pointer:        %Fp\n", (void far *)&nBuff);
    printf("fBuff pointer:        %Fp\n", (void far *)&fBuff);
    printf("\n");
    printf("malloc() returned:    %Fp\n", (void far *)nBuff);
    printf("farmalloc() returned: %Fp\n", (void far *)fBuff);
}
```

As shown by the following output from the .COM application above, everything is located in the same segment except for the memory address returned by the farmalloc() function:

```
Code Segment          24A8
main():               24A8:0311

Data Segment          24A8
nData:                24A8:1A82

Stack Segment         24A8
StkVar:               24A8:FFF4
nBuff pointer:        24A8:FFF2
fBuff pointer:        24A8:FFEE

malloc() returned:    24A8:224A
farmalloc() returned: 34A8:0004
```

# N                                                    Error on Stack Overflows

- C          ▪ C++         CPP      ▪ TC++      ▪ TCW/BCW
- BC 2.0     ▪ BC 3.0/3.1  ▪ BCC    ▪ Local     ▪ #pragma

## Purpose
The -N option tells the compiler to generate code that checks for a stack overflow condition when entering a function.

## IDE Option
Options | Entry/Exit code | Test stack overflow

## Default

–N–

Do not check for stack overflows.

## Usage

BCC –N SOURCE.C

Check for stack overflows at run time.

#pragma option –N

Same as above; must appear between functions and declarations.

## Description

When stack overflow checking is enabled using the -N option, the compiler generates at the start of every function an instruction that compares the value of the Stack Pointer (SP) register to a global variable called __brklvl. The __brklvl value is initially sent to the top of the initial data in memory models where the stack is located in the same segment as near data. As memory is allocated using the malloc() function or the C++ "new" keyword, the value in this variable increases. Function calls and automatic variables within a function take up space on the stack and lower the value in the SP register. If the SP register falls below the value of __brklvl, indicating a stack overflow condition exists, then the application is aborted and a "Stack overflow!" message is printed to the screen.

Because of the extra processing overhead and code space taken up by this option, it is only recommend for use during debugging.

## See Also

| | |
|---|---|
| v | Compile with Debug Information |
| vi | Compile Out-of-Line Inline C++ functions |

## Example

Write an application that overflows the stack and periodically print the available stack space.

**n\test.c**
```
#include <stdio.h>
#include <alloc.h>

/* Enable stack checking */
#pragma option –N

/* Declare the integer BC++ uses to check the stack */
extern unsigned __brklvl;

/* Write an unlimited recursive function to overflow the stack */
    char *UnlimitedRecursion(char *PassedBuff)
{
    /* Declare a 3,000-byte buffer space to quickly eat up the stack */
    char Buffer[3000];

    /* Keep track of our available stack space */
    printf("Free stack space = %u\n", _SP – __brklvl);
```

```
    /* Perform a recursive function call */
    UnlimitedRecursion(Buffer);
    return(PassedBuff);
}

void main(void)
{
    /* Start by taking a large chunk of the stack */
    char Buff[50000];

    /* Overflow the stack */
    UnlimitedRecursion(Buff);
}
```

The main() function removes 50K from the stack to get things moving and each recursive iteration of the UnlimitedRecursion() function removes another 3+K. The amount of available stack space is calculated in each iteration by subtracting __brklvl from the SP register. The output from the application is as follows:

```
Free stack space = 11158
Free stack space = 8152
Free stack space = 5146
Free stack space = 2140
Stack overflow!
```

# n*path*                                                    Set Output Directory to *path*

- C
- BC 2.0
- C++
- BC 3.0/3.1
- CPP
- BCC
- TC++
- Local
- TCW/BCW
- #pragma

## Purpose
The -n*path* option specifies the directory location for the compiler to store the compiled .OBJ, .ASM, .COM, or .EXE files.

## IDE Option
Options | Directories | Output Directory

## Default
```
-n.
```
Save compiled output in the current directory.

## Usage
```
BCC -n\OUTPUT SOURCE.C
```
Save compiled output in the \OUTPUT directory.

## Description
The output of the compiler can be directed to any directory location using the -n*path* option. This option is useful if you compile source code from many different directories into one common directory.

## See Also

| | |
|---|---|
| I*path* | Set Include Files Directory |
| L*path* | Set the Location of Library Files |

## Example

Compile the "Hello, C!" application used in the example application for the -L*path* option and send the output to the \PDG\CH2\OUTPUT directory. This is accomplished by entering the following from the \PDG\CH2\LIB directory:

```
bcc -n..\output hello.c
```

The above stores HELLO.OBJ and HELLO.EXE in the \PDG\CH2\OUTPUT directory.

# O                                               Enable Jump Optimizations

- C
- BC 2.0
- C++
- BC 3.0/3.1
- CPP
- BCC
- TC++
- Local
- TCW/BCW
- #pragma

## Purpose

The -O option instructs the compiler to optimize jumps in the compiled source code and remove any unreachable code. You should use this option whenever you perform an optimization compilation.

## IDE Option

Options | Compiler | Optimizations | Jump optimizations

## Default

```
-o-
```
Optimizations disabled.

## Usage

```
BCC -O SOURCE.C
```
Optimizations enabled.

## Description

The Borland C++ compiler takes some shortcuts when it compiles source code that enables it to compile your code as fast as possible. The result is that some redundant jump instructions are left in the object code. By enabling the -O option, you are telling the compiler to take more time and remove the redundancies. Doing so creates smaller and faster applications. You should note that the redundant jumps make it easier to step through the code in the Turbo Debugger. Without them, the program flow tends to jump around. You may want to leave this option disabled if you are debugging your code and then enable the option for the production version of the application.

**See Also**

| | |
|---|---|
| 1,2 | Microprocessor Instruction Set |
| a | Byte/Word Alignment |
| ff | Fast floating-point |
| k | Use a Standard Stack Frame |
| N | Error on Stack Overflows |
| r, rd | Use Automatic Register Variables |
| Z | Assume No Indirect Assignments |

**Example**

Write an application with a function that contains redundant jumps and compile with and without jump optimizations enabled.

**o\test.c**

```
/* Enable optimizations */
#pragma option -O

int Fast(int Parameter)
{
   if(Parameter != 0)
   {
    Parameter--;
    return(Fast(Parameter));
   }
   return(0);
}

#pragma option -O-

int Slow(int Parameter)
{
   if(Parameter != 0)
   {
    Parameter--;
    return(Fast(Parameter));
   }
   return(0);
}

void main(void)
{
   Fast(3000);
   Slow(3000);
}
```

The Fast() function is compiled with the jump optimizations enabled and the Slow() function with the option disabled. The Fast() function operates 25% faster than the Slow() function.

## o*filename*                                    Object Code Filename

- C
- BC 2.0
- C++
- BC 3.0/3.1
- CPP
- BCC
- TC++
- Local
- TCW/BCW
- #pragma

### Purpose
The -o*filename* option is used to rename the object code file created by the compiler.

### IDE Option
N/A

### Default
The default is to use the same filename as the source code with an .OBJ extension.

### Usage
```
BCC -oNEW_NAME SOURCE.C
```
Save the compiled object code as NEW_NAME.OBJ.

### Description
You can name the object code file anything you choose using the -o*filename* option. You can also use this option to specify a different directory location for the object code file. For example, if you use the option as -o\BORLANDC\LIB\NEW_NAME, then the NEW_NAME.OBJ file will be stored in the \BORLANDC\LIB directory. The compiler will pass TLINK the correct filename for linking. Note that the executable filename will still be the same as the source filename or the name specified with the -e*filename* option.

### See Also
e*filename*            Executable Filename
P, P*ext*              C/C++ Source Code File Extensions

### Example
Compile the "Hello, C!" application used in the example application for the -L*path* option and rename the object code file to NEW_NAME.OBJ. This is done by entering the following:

```
bcc -onew_name hello.c
```

## Oa                                              Assume No Pointer Aliasing

- C          ■ C++        CPP         TC++        ❶ TCW/BCW
  BC 2.0     ■ BC 3.0/3.1  ■ BCC      ■ Local     ■ #pragma
❶ BCW only.

### Purpose
The -Oa option instructs the compiler to disregard any pointer aliasing while generating optimized code. This option should be used with caution.

### IDE Option
Options | Compiler | Optimizations | Assume no pointer aliasing

### Default
-O-a
    Discard information on common subexpression and copy propagation when calling functions involving pointers.

### Usage
BCC -O2 -Oa SOURCE.C
    Assume no pointer aliasing while optimizing SOURCE.C.

#pragma option -Oa
    Same as above. The directive must appear between function definitions.

#pragma option -O-a
    Assume pointers are aliases. The directive must appear between function definitions.

### Description
The compiler can perform a number of optimizations if it is sure data is not modified via pointer aliases. The -Oa option tells the pointer not to worry about this situation and to optimize without regard to pointer aliases. This can create problems, however, if your code *does* contain aliases, as shown in the example section below.
    Note that the -Oa option is not an optimization in itself, but instead enables other optimization options to generate more efficient code. Because of the possible introduction of bugs, the -Oa option is not enabled by either the -O1 or the -O2 option.

### See Also
Od, O1, O2, Ox     Enable/Disable Groups of Optimizations

### Example
Write an application demonstrating a bug introduced by the -Oa option. Control the enabling and disabling of the -Oa option using #pragma directives:

oa\test.c
```
#include <stdio.h>
```

```
/* Enable all speed optimizations */
#pragma option -O2

void ModifyData(int *xPtr)
{
    *xPtr += 1;
}

/* Assume no pointer aliasing */
#pragma option -Oa
int BuggyFunction(void)
{
    int y = 1;

    ModifyData(&y);
    return(y);
}

/* Assume pointers are aliases */
#pragma option -O-a
int GoodFunction(void)
{
    int y = 1;

    ModifyData(&y);
    return(y);
}

void main(void)
{
    printf("GoodFunction() = %d\n", GoodFunction());
    printf("BuggyFunction()= %d\n", BuggyFunction());
}
```

The ModifyData() function increments the integer parameter passed via a pointer, which is not a problem with the -Oa option disabled as shown with the GoodFunction() function. However, the BuggyFunction() is compiled with the assumption that no pointers are aliases, which means the compiler assumes the 'y' variable is not modified by the ModifyData() function and returns the value of '1' without using the stack variable, 'y', thereby saving execution time. However, since ModifyData() does modify the 'y' variable, the use of the -Oa option introduces a bug into the application as shown by the following output:

```
GoodFunction()  = 2
BuggyFunction() = 1
```

## Ob                                              Dead Code Elimination

- C            ■ C++         CPP          TC++        ❶ TCW/BCW
  BC 2.0       ■ BC 3.0/3.1  ■ BCC        ■ Local      ■ #pragma
❶ BCW only.

### Purpose
The -Ob option eliminates dead code storage. You should use this optimization option whenever you also use the -Oe option for global register allocation and live range testing.

## IDE Option

Options | Compiler | Optimizations | Dead code elimination

## Default

```
-Od
```
Compile without any optimizations.

## Usage

```
BCC -Ob SOURCE.C
```
Eliminate any unnecessary code in SOURCE.C.

```
#pragma option -Ob
```
Same as above. The directive must appear between function definitions.

```
#pragma option -O-b
```
Disable dead code elimination optimization. The directive must appear between function definitions.

## Description

The -Ob option instructs the compiler to remove any code it determines to be unnecessary. However, for the compiler to determine which sections of code are unnecessary, the -Oe option must be enabled, instructing the compiler to test the live range for variables. For example, consider the following function:

```
/* Enable live range testing */
#pragma option -Oe

/* Enable the elimination of dead code */
#pragma option -Ob
int ElimDeadCode(void)
{
    int a, b, c;

    a = b = c = 1.0;
    b = c + a;
    return(a);
}
```

In this function, only the value of the variable 'a' is returned. With the -Oe option enabled, the compiler is able to determine that the storage and addition operation involving the 'b' and 'c' variables accomplishes nothing. The -Ob option gives the compiler permission to remove the unnecessary code, as shown in the following assembly code generated for the ElimDeadCode() function:

```
_ElimDeadCode  proc  near
        push    bp
        mov     bp,sp
        sub     sp,2
    ;
    ;   {
    ;       int a, b, c;
```

```
;
;       a = b = c = 1.0;
;
        mov   ax,1
        mov   word ptr [bp-2],ax
;
;       b = c + a;
;
;
;       return(a);
;
        mov   ax,word ptr [bp-2]
        jmp   short @1@58
@1@58:
;
;   }
;
        mov   sp,bp
        pop   bp
        ret
_ElimDeadCode endp
```

The compiler ignores the storage and addition operation involving the 'b' and 'c' variables and only stores and returns the value of 1 in the 'a' variable. Without the -Ob option (and also the -Oe option, which enables the -Ob option to operate), the unnecessary code would be left in the function, taking up space and slowing down the execution.

## See Also

Od, O1, O2, Ox      Enable/Disable Groups of Optimizations
Oe      Global Register Allocation and Live Range Testing

## Example

Write an application using the -Oe and -Ob options to eliminate useless code from a function. See the Description section above for a discussion of the code eliminated from the ElimDeadCode() function.

### ob\test.c

```c
#include <stdio.h>

/* Enable live range testing */
#pragma option -Oe

/* Enable the elimination of dead code */
#pragma option -Ob
int ElimDeadCode(void)
{
    int a, b, c;

    a = b = c = 1.0;
    b = c + a;
    return(a);
}

/* Disable the elimination of dead code */
#pragma option -O-b
```

```
int LeaveDeadCode(void)
{
  int a, b, c;

  a = b = c = 1.0;
  b = c + a;
   return(a);
}

void main(void)
{
  ElimDeadCode();
  LeaveDeadCode();
}
```

# Oc, Og                     Local/Global Common Subexpression Elimination

- C            ■ C++          CPP           TC++        ❶ TCW/BCW
  BC 2.0       ■ BC 3.0/3.1  ■ BCC         ■ Local      ■ #pragma

❶ BCW only.

## Purpose
The -Oc and -Og optimization options instruct the compiler to create additional temporary variables as necessary to eliminate recalculating the same expressions. The -Oc option limits its scope to local blocks of code. The -Og option eliminates common subexpressions throughout the entire function block. You would normally use the -Og optimization option. You use the -Oc option if the -Og creates too many temporaries and is overloading the stack.

## IDE Option
Options I Compiler I Optimizations I No optimization       *for -O-c-g*
Options I Compiler I Optimizations I Optimize locally       *for -Oc*
Options I Compiler I Optimizations I Optimize globally       *for -Og*

## Default
−Od
    Compile without any optimizations.

## Usage
BCC −Og SOURCE.C
    Compile SOURCE.C and eliminate common subexpressions globally throughout a function.

#pragma option −Og
    Same as above. The directive must appear between function definitions.

```
BCC -Oc SOURCE.C
```
Compile SOURCE.C and eliminate common subexpressions locally within code blocks.

```
#pragma option -Oc
```
Same as above. The directive must appear between function definitions.

```
#pragma option -O-c-g
```
Do not eliminate common subexpressions. The directive must appear between function definitions.

## Description

The -Og and -Oc options look for instances in your functions in which you are recalculating the same expression. For example, the code used in the example section below calculates the expression "a + c / b" three different times when it actually only needs to be calculated once. The -Og option looks for these redundant calculations and instead of generating code to recalculate the expression, it stores the result from the first calculation and generates code to reuse the stored value. The difference between the -Og option and the -Oc option is that -Og looks for common subexpressions throughout the whole function, whereas the -Oc option looks for common subexpressions only within code blocks. As shown in the example section below, the compiler forgets that it already calculated the expression "a + c / b" once it enters the code block after the 'if' statement when the -Oc option is enabled.

Note that enabling the -Op option automatically enables the -Og option. By the same token, enabling the -Oc option will disable both the -Og and the -Op option.

## See Also

Od, O1, O2, Ox      Enable/Disable Groups of Optimizations
Op      Copy Propagation

## Example

Write an application demonstrating a common subexpression elimination on a local and global level using #pragma directives. Compare the relative speeds. The Global(), Local(), and Default() functions in the following application each use the expression "a + c / b" three times. The default() function is compiled without common subexpression elimination and it calculates the expression three times. The Local() function is compiled using the -Oc option and as such, it calculates the expression once for the assignment to 'y' and reuses the result for the 'if' statement. But because the assignment to 'x' is in code block, it recalculates the expression a second time. The -Og option is used to compile the Global() function. In this function, the expression "a + c / b" is calculated once for the assignment to 'y' and the result reused for the 'if' statement and the assignment to 'x.'

**og\test.c**
```
int a = 2, b = 4, c = 6, x, y;
```

155

```
/* Enable global subexpression elimination */
#pragma option -Og
void Global(void)
{
    unsigned n;

    for(n = 0; n < 10000; n++)
    {
      y = a + c / b;
      if(a + c / b)
      {
        x = a + c / b;
      }
    }
}

/* Enable local subexpression elimination */
#pragma option -Oc
void Local(void)
{
    unsigned n;

    for(n = 0; n < 10000; n++)
    {
        y = a + c / b;
        if(a + c / b)
        {
            x = a + c / b;
        }
    }
}

/* Disable subexpression elimination */
#pragma option -O-c-g
void Default(void)
{
    unsigned n;

    for(n = 0; n < 10000; n++)
    {
        y = a + c / b;
        if(a + c / b)
        {
            x = a + c / b;
        }
    }
}

void main(void)
{
    Global();
    Local();
    Default();
}
```

The Local() function operates 17% faster than the default() function. The Global() function operates twice as fast as the default() function and 70% faster than the Local() function. Also, the code for both the Local() and the Global() functions is significantly smaller than the code for the default() function.

# Od, O1, O2, Ox          Enable/Disable Groups of Optimizations

- C          ■ C++          CPP          TC++          ❶ TCW/BCW
  BC 2.0     ■ BC 3.0/3.1   ■ BCC        ■ Local       ■ #pragma

❶ BCW only.

## Purpose
The -Od option disables all optimizations, whereas the -O1 option enables optimization for generating the smallest code, and the -O2 option enables optimizations for generating the fastest code. The -Ox option is the same as the -O2 option and is included for compatibility with Microsoft C.

## IDE Option
Options | Compiler | Optimizations | Fastest Code     *for -O2 and -Ox*
Options | Compiler | Optimizations | Smallest Code    *for -O1*
Options | Compiler | Optimizations | Default          *for -Od*

## Default
−Od
    Compile with all optimization options disabled.

## Usage
BCC −O1 SOURCE.C
    Compile SOURCE.C with all the size optimization options enabled.

#pragma option −O1
    Same as above. The directive must appear between function definitions.

BCC −O2 SOURCE.C
    Compile SOURCE.C with all the speed optimization options enabled.

#pragma option −O2
    Same as above. The directive must appear between function definitions.

#pragma option −O2
    Compile with all optimizations disabled. The directive must appear between function definitions.

## Description
You should normally compile your source code using the default -Od option while you are still developing and debugging your source code for a number of reasons. First, the compilation speed is much faster with optimizations disabled. The compiler will typically take three or four times longer to compile the same source code with the optimiza-

tions enabled, depending on the complexity of the source. Second, many of the optimizations will eliminate sections of your source code and alter the program flow, which will make it difficult to trace through using a debugger. Finally, some optimizations, such as the -Oa optimization for assuming no aliases, can introduce bugs into your source code that are hard to track down.

Once the source is developed and debugged, you should use either the -O1 or the -O2 option to compile for either code size or speed, respectively. The -O1 option enables the following optimizations:

| | |
|---|---|
| -O | Optimize jumps |
| -Ob | Dead code elimination |
| -Oe | Global register allocation |
| -Os | Optimize in favor of size |
| -k- | Use a nonstandard stack frame |
| -Z | Suppress redundant register loads |

The -O2 option enables the following optimizations:

| | |
|---|---|
| -O | Optimize jumps |
| -Ob | Dead code elimination |
| -Oe | Global register allocation |
| -Og | Eliminate common subexpressions in an entire function |
| -Oi | Intrinsic inline functions |
| -Ol | Invariant code motion |
| -Op | Copy propagation |
| -Ot | Optimize in favor of speed |
| -Ov | Induction variables |
| -k- | Use a nonstandard stack frame |
| -Z | Suppress redundant register loads |

### See Also

| | |
|---|---|
| Oa | Assume No Pointer Aliasing |
| Ob | Dead Code Elimination |
| Oc, Og | Local/Global Common0 Subexpression Elimination |
| Oe | Global Register Allocation and Live Range Testing |
| Oi | Inline Intrinsic Functions |
| Ol | Loop Compaction |
| Om | Invariant Code Optimization |
| Op | Copy Propagation |
| Ov | Loop Induction Optimization |

| pr | Enable Fastcall Calling Convention |
| Z | Register Usage Optimization |

## Example

Write an application and compile using the -Od, -O1, and -O2 options:

**od\test.c**
```c
/* Declare a global long */
long Sum;

/* Add a number to Sum */
void AddNum(int n)
{
    Sum += n;
}

/* Generate code without optimizations */
#pragma option -Od

void default(void)
{
    unsigned n;

    Sum = 0;
    for(n = 0; n < 60000; n++)
        AddNum(n);
}

/* Generate code slanted towards speed */
#pragma option -O2

void Speed(void)
{
    unsigned n;

    Sum = 0;
    for(n = 0; n < 60000; n++)
        AddNum(n);
}

/* Generate code slanted towards size */
#pragma option -O1

void Size(void)
{
    unsigned n;

    Sum = 0;
    for(n = 0; n < 60000; n++)
        AddNum(n);
}

void main(void)
{
```

```
/* Execute both functions for evaluation in the Turbo Profiler */
Default();
Speed();
Size();
}
```

The default() function is compiled without optimizations, whereas the Speed() and Size() functions are compiled using -O2 and -O1, respectively. The resulting code for the Size() function is 1 byte smaller than both the Speed() and Default() functions. The

Size() function operated 8% slower than the default() function. The Speed() function operated 4% faster than Default(). Of course, the speed and size differences for other applications will vary depending on the code.

## Oe                                   Global Register Allocation and Live Range Testing

| ■ C | ■ C++ | CPP | TC++ | ❶ TCW/BCW |
| BC 2.0 | ■ BC 3.0/3.1 | ■ BCC | ■ Local | ■ #pragma |

❶ BCW only

### Purpose
The -Oe option instructs the compiler to globally evaluate register variable usage. The -Oe option also provides information from the results of its live-range testing that enables the -Ob option to operate correctly.

### IDE Option
Options | Compiler | Optimizations | Global register allocation

### Default
-Od

Compile without any optimizations.

### Usage
BCC -Oe SOURCE.C

Evaluate functions globally for register allocation and enable live-range testing.

#pragma option -Oe

Same as above. The directive must appear between function definitions.

#pragma option -O-e

Disable global register allocation optimization and live-range testing. The directive must appear between function definitions.

### Description
The -Oe option gives the compiler permission to spend as much time as it needs evaluating your code to find the optimal usage for register variables. As part of this evalua-

tion, it stores information on the lifetime and use of different variables. This information is in turn used by other optimization options, such as the -Ob option. In general, you should use the -Oe option whenever you perform optimizations.

**See Also**

| Od, O1, O2, Ox | Enable/Disable Groups of Optimizations |
| Ob | Dead Code Elimination |

**Example**

See the example for the -Ob option.

# Oi                                          Inline Intrinsic Functions

| ■ C | ■ C++ | CPP | TC++ | ❶ TCW/BCW |
| BC 2.0 | ■ BC 3.0/3.1 | ■ BCC | ■ Local | ■ #pragma |

❶ BCW only.

**Purpose**

You use the -Oi optimization to have BC++ place the code for several standard C function calls inline rather than performing a library function call. This optimizes the execution speed for the application, but also increases the application's file size.

**IDE Option**

Options | Compiler | Optimizations | Inline intrinsic functions

**Default**

```
-Od
```
Compile without any optimizations.

**Usage**

```
BCC -Oi SOURCE.C
```
Enable inline generation for all intrinsic functions while compiling SOURCE.C.

```
#pragma option -Oi
```
Same as above. The directive must appear between function definitions.

```
#pragma option -O-i
```
Disable inline generation of all intrinsic functions. The directive must appear between function definitions.

```
#pragma intrinsic FnctName
```
Enable inline generation for only the 'FnctName' intrinsic functions. The 'FnctName' parameter must be one of the functions listed in Table 2-14.

```
#pragma intrinsic -FnctName
```
Disable inline generation for the 'FnctName' intrinsic functions. The 'FnctName' parameter must be one of the functions listed in Table 2-14.

## Description

Function calls are an expensive commodity in terms of execution time. Each parameter for the function call must be pushed onto the stack at a cost of 2 to 5 clock cycles per parameter. The 'call' and subsequent 'ret' processor instructions involved in a function call cost 40 to 60 clock cycles. If the automatic register variables option, -r, is enabled, then the compiler will use code to save and restore the SI and DI registers at a cost of another 8 to 20 clock cycles. In total, a function call will cost your application a minimum of 44 clock cycles each time it executes. This is very expensive when compared to a function such as rotl(), which only takes a few clock cycles to execute when the code is generated inline.

The -Oi option instructs the compiler not to generate function calls for 19 different functions, called *intrinsic* functions, and instead to place the function code directly in the application. This is known as *function inlining* because the functions are placed inline with the program flowpath rather than through a function call. For example, consider the following instruction:

```
Length += strlen(Str);
```

The compiler generates the following code to perform a normal function call to the strlen() function:

```
mov ax,offset DGROUP:_Str
push    ax
call    near ptr _strlen
pop cx
add word ptr [bp-4],ax
adc word ptr [bp-2],0
```

However, when the -Oi option is enabled, the compiler generates the following code:

```
mov di,offset DGROUP:_Str
push    ds
pop es
xor ax,ax
mov cx,65535
repnz    scasb
not cx
dec cx
add word ptr [bp-4],cx
adc word ptr [bp-2],0
```

This is basically the same function code as that located in the C library, but instead of calling the strlen() function, the compiler places the function code directly into the application. As shown in the example section below, this increases the speed at the expense of application size.

Table 2-14 lists the library functions that are generated inline with the -Oi option enabled. You can also control the inline generation of individual intrinsic functions using the "#pragma intrinsic" directive for any function listed in Table 2-14.

| | | |
|---|---|---|
| memchr | memcmp | memcpy |
| stpcpy | strcat | strchr |
| strcmp | strcpy | strlen |
| strncat | strncmp | strncpy |
| strnset | strrchr | fabs |

**Table 2-14 List of inline intrinsic functions enabled by the -Oi option**

You must include the header file containing the intrinsic function for the -Oi option to operate correctly!

Note that the __BCOPT__ macro is always defined in BC++ and undefined when you use TCW/BCW. This means the _rotl(), _rotr(), and alloca() functions are always generated inline when you compile your source code in BC++ and you use the associated header files, but generated out-of-line when you compile using TCW/BCW.

### See Also

| | |
|---|---|
| Od, O1, O2, Ox | Enable/Disable Groups of Optimizations |
| Ol | Loop Compaction |

### Example

Write an application using inline and out-of-line intrinsic functions and compare the relative speeds. In the application below, the compiler generates the strlen() function inline in the Fast() function and performs a function call to strlen() in the Slow() function. The Fast() function operates 71% faster than the Slow() function. The Fast() function is also a few bytes larger than the Slow() function.

**oi\test.c**

```
#include <string.h>

char Str[] = "test";

/* Enable generation of inline intrisic functions */
#pragma option -Oi
long Fast(void)
{
    unsigned n;
    long Length = 0;

    for(n = 0; n < 10000; n++)
        Length += strlen(Str);
    return(Length);
}
```

```
/* Use function calls for intrinsic functions */
#pragma option -O-i
long Slow(void)
{
    unsigned n;
    long Length = 0;

    for(n = 0; n < 10000; n++)
        Length += strlen(Str);
    return(Length);
}

void main(void)
{
    Fast();
    Slow();
}
```

# Ol

**Loop Compaction**

| | | | | |
|---|---|---|---|---|
| ■ C | ■ C++ | CPP | TC++ | ❶ TCW/BCW |
| BC 2.0 | ■ BC 3.0/3.1 | ■ BCC | ■ Local | ■ #pragma |

❶ BCW only.

## Purpose

The -Ol option instructs the compiler to use 80x86 processor string instructions to replace certain code expressions in a loop.

## IDE Option

Options I Compiler I Optimizations I Loop optimization

## Default

−0d

Compile without any optimizations.

## Usage

BCC −Ol SOURCE.C

Enable loop compaction optimizations while compiling SOURCE.C.

#pragma option −Ol

Same as above. The directive must appear between function definitions.

#pragma option −O−l

Disable loop compaction optimizations. The directive must appear between function definitions.

## Description

The -Ol optimization option operates in similar fashion to the -Oi option, which places inline code for intrinsic functions. With the -Ol option enabled, the compiler examines the source code involving loop constructs and looks for opportunities to replace the code with intrinsic 80x86 instructions. For example, consider the following loop structure:

```
char a[100];

for(n = 0; n < 100; n++)
    a[n] = 0;
```

With the -Ol option enabled, the compiler evaluates the above loop, determines that the expression 'a[n] = 0' is the equivalent of a strset() function, and replaces it with intrinsic inline code for the strset() function.

Note that it is generally more efficient to use intrinsic functions with the -Oi option enabled. This is because the compiler will only perform loop compaction for 'char' and 'int' data types and not for types 'long.' Also, it does not perform loop compaction for code involving movement of data from one location to another. For example, consider the following:

```
int a[100], b[100];

for(n = 0; n < 100; n++)
    a[n] = b[n];
```

The loop compaction optimization ignores an opportunity to use intrinsic inline function code and instead compiles the above as it is written, i.e., by loading each element of 'b' into a register and moving it to 'a.' A more efficient method is to write the code as follows and enable the -Oi option:

```
int a[100], b[100];

memcpy((char*)a, (char*)b, sizeof(a));
```

With the -Oi optimization enabled, the compiler replaces the memcpy() function with an inline intrinsic function code utilizing the 'rep movsw' assembly language instruction.

### See Also

Od, O1, O2, Ox          Enable/Disable Groups of Optimizations
Oi                      Inline Intrinsic Functions

### Example

Write an application containing two identical loop functions. Compile one function with loop optimizations enabled and the other with optimizations disabled and compare the relative speeds. In the following application, the Fast() function operates over six times faster than the Slow() function.

**ol\test.c**
```
int d1[1000];

/* Enable loop optimization */
#pragma option -Ol
void Fast(void)
{
```

```
    unsigned n;

    for(n = 0; n < 1000; n++)
        d1[n] = 10;
}

/* Disable loop optimization */
#pragma option -O-l
void Slow(void)
{
    unsigned n;

    for(n = 0; n < 1000; n++)
        d1[n] = 10;
}

void main(void)
{
    Fast();
    Slow();
}
```

# Om                                    Invariant Code Optimization

- C          ■ C++          CPP          TC++          ❶ TCW/BCW
  BC 2.0     ■ BC 3.0/3.1  ■ BCC        ■ Local       ■ #pragma

❶ BCW only.

## Purpose
The -Om option instructs the compiler to look for calculations in a loop which do not change during the iteration of the loop and to move the invariant code out of the loop, thereby increasing execution speed.

## IDE Option
Options | Compiler | Optimizations | Invariant code motion

## Default
-Od
     Compile without any optimizations.

## Usage
BCC -Om SOURCE.C
     Enable invariant code motion optimizations while compiling SOURCE.C.

#pragma option -Om
     Same as above. The directive must appear between function definitions.

#pragma option -O-m
     Disable invariant code motion optimizations. The directive must appear between function definitions.

## Description

You probably have on occasion inadvertently placed calculation code in a loop which does not change as the loop iterates. The loop function will, of course, operate more efficiently if the calculation is performed once outside the loop and only the result is used in the loop. The -Om option instructs the compiler to look for these situations and move the code outside of the loop for you. For example, consider the following loop:

```
for(n = 0; n < 1000; n++)
    d1[n] = a + b + c;
```

A literal interpretation of the above code instructs the compiler to calculate the expression 'a + b + c' 1,000 times. Since the value of 'a + b + c' does not change with each iteration, it is much more efficient to calculate the value outside of the loop and use the result. With the -Om option enabled, the compiler will compile the above loop as if you had written it as follows:

```
temp = a + b + c;
for(n = 0; n < 1000; n++)
    d1[n] = temp;
```

## See Also

Od, O1, O2, Ox        Enable/Disable Groups of Optimizations

## Example

Write an application containing invariant code in a loop and compare the relative speed increase when compiled using the -Om optimization option. In the following code, the calculation for the expression 'a + b + c' is moved out of the loop. This enables the Fast() function to operate over six times faster than the Slow() function with only a few bytes increase in code size.

om\test.c
```
    int d1[1000];

    /* Enable invariant code motion optimization */
    #pragma option -Om
    void Fast(int a, int b, int c)
    {
      unsigned n;

      for(n = 0; n < 1000; n++)
          d1[n] = a + b + c;
    }

    /* Disable invariant code motion optimization */
    #pragma option -O-m
    void Slow(int a, int b, int c)
    {
      unsigned n;

      for(n = 0; n < 1000; n++)
          d1[n] = a + b + c;
    }
```

```
void main(void)
{
    Fast(1, 2, 3);
    Slow(1, 2, 3);
}
```

## Op                                                   Copy Propagation

- C          ▪ C++          CPP          TC++          ❶ TCW/BCW
  BC 2.0     ▪ BC 3.0/3.1   ▪ BCC        ▪ Local        ▪ #pragma

❶ BCW only.

### Purpose

The -Op option instructs the compiler to remember the value assigned to variables and to reuse the value when you use that variable again rather than looking up the value again in memory. This option works best if the register allocation option, -r, is enabled.

### IDE Option

Options | Compiler | Optimizations | Copy propagation

### Default

−Od

Compile without any optimizations.

### Usage

BCC −Op SOURCE.C

Enable copy propagation optimizations while compiling SOURCE.C.

#pragma option −Op

Same as above. The directive must appear between function definitions.

#pragma option −O−p

Disable copy propagation optimizations. The directive must appear between function definitions.

### Description

With the -Op option enabled, the compiler keeps track of the values assigned to variables and reuses those values rather than reloading the value from memory. For example, consider the following code:

```
a = x;
b = a;
c = b;
```

It is much faster to store the value of 'x' directly in both 'b' and 'c' rather than moving the contents of 'a' into 'b' and 'c'. For example, the compiler loads the value of 'x' into the DX register and generates the following code with the -Op option enabled:

```
;           a = x;
;
    mov     dx,word ptr [bp+4]
    mov     word ptr DGROUP:_a,dx
;
;           b = a;
;
    mov     word ptr DGROUP:_b,dx
;
;           c = b;
;
    mov     word ptr DGROUP:_c,dx
```

On the other hand, without the -Op option enabled, or if the -r option for automatic register variables is disabled, the compiler will generate the following less efficient code:

```
;           a = x;
;
    mov     ax,word ptr [bp+4]
    mov     word ptr DGROUP:_a,ax
;
;           b = a;
;
    mov     ax,word ptr DGROUP:_a
    mov     word ptr DGROUP:_b,ax
;
;           c = b;
;
    mov     ax,word ptr DGROUP:_b
    mov     word ptr DGROUP:_c,ax
```

Here the compiler loads the value of 'x' and 'a' into the AX register and manually moves the data to the 'b' and 'c' variables. The above code is not only costly in terms of speed, but also in terms of the size of the application.

Note that the compiler will not retain the value resulting from some calculated expressions. For example, in the following code, the compiler will not retain the value for the temporary variable created to calculate the expression '(x * 2) + 1', but instead reloads the value of 'a' for assignment to 'b':

```
a = (x * 2) + 1;
b = a;
```

Also note that enabling the -Op option automatically enables the -Og option. By the same token, enabling the -Oc option will disable both the -Og and the -Op options.

### See Also

| | |
|---|---|
| Od, O1, O2, Ox | Enable/Disable Groups of Optimizations |
| Oc, Og | Local/Global Common Subexpression Elimination |
| r, rd | Use Automatic Register Variables |
| po | Localize Object members |

### Example

Write an application to test the speed increase of the -Op copy propagation optimization. In the following code, the Fast() function operates 39% faster than the Slow()

function because it uses the value stored in the processor register for the assignments of 'b' and 'c.' The Slow() function, on the other hand, looks up the value of 'a' in memory for the assignments to 'b' and 'c' because the -Op option is disabled.

**op\test.c**

```
int a, b, c;

#pragma option -Op
void Fast(int x)
{
    unsigned n;

    for(n = 0; n < 1000; n++)
    {
        a = x;
        b = a;
        c = b;
    }
}

#pragma option -O-p
void Slow(int x)
{
    unsigned n;

    for(n = 0; n < 1000; n++)
    {
        a = x;
        b = a;
        c = b;
    }
}

void main(void)
{
    Fast(1);
    Slow(1);
}
```

# Os, Ot                                   Compile in Favor of Speed or Time

| | | | | |
|---|---|---|---|---|
| ▪ C | ▪ C++ | CPP | ▪ TC++ | ▪ TCW/BCW |
| ▪ BC 2.0 | ▪ BC 3.0/3.1 | ▪ BCC | ▪ Local | ▪ #pragma |

## Purpose
The -Os option is used to tell the compiler to favor execution speed over size in code generation. The -Ot option optimizes for size at the expense of an application's execution speed.

## IDE Option
Options | Compiler | Optimizations | Size          *for -Os*
Options | Compiler | Optimizations | Speed         *for -Ot*

## Default

```
-Os
```
Optimize for size.

## Usage

```
BCC -Ot SOURCE.C
```
Optimize for speed.

```
#pragma options -Ot
```
Same as above; must be used between functions and declarations.

```
#pragma options -Os
```
Optimize for size; must be used between functions and declarations.

## Description

Although Borland C++ is geared mainly towards high-speed compiling, it can slant the generated code slightly to favor either execution speed or application size. The difference in application size when compiling an application for speed is very small, with the resulting application size averaging roughly 1 to 2% larger.

## See Also

| | |
|---|---|
| O | Enable Jump Optimizations |
| P | Use Pascal or Fastcall Calling Convention |

## Example

Write an application with a pair of identical functions. Compile one function for speed and the other for size and test their performance in the Turbo Profiler:

**g\test.c**
```
/* Declare a global long */
long Sum;

/* Add a number to Sum */
void AddNum(int n)
{
    Sum += n;
}

/* Generate code slanted towards speed */
#pragma option -Ot

void Speed(void)
{
    unsigned n;

    Sum = 0;
    for(n = 0; n < 60000; n++)
        AddNum(n);
}
```

```
/* Generate code slanted towards size */
#pragma option -Os

void Size(void)
{
    unsigned n;

    Sum = 0;
    for(n = 0; n < 60000; n++)
        AddNum(n);
}

void main(void)
{
    /* Execute both functions for evaluation in the Turbo Profiler */
    Speed();
    Size();
}
```

The above application contains two identical functions, called Speed() and Size(), which sum the numbers 0 through 60,000. Speed() is compiled for speed and Size() is compiled for size. Comparing the two functions in the Turbo Profiler shows that the Speed() function runs 9% faster than the Size() function, but is 1 byte larger.

# Ov                                    Loop Induction Optimization

| | | | | |
|---|---|---|---|---|
| ■ C | ■ C++ | CPP | TC++ | ❶ TCW/BCW |
| BC 2.0 | ■ BC 3.0/3.1 | ■ BCC | ■ Local | ■ #pragma |

❶ BCW only.

## Purpose
The -Ov option instructs the compiler to precalculate indexes to variable arrays and increment the index in the loop rather than recalculate an offset with each iteration.

## IDE Option
Options | Compiler | Optimizations | Induction variables

## Default
-Od
    Compile without any optimizations.

## Usage
BCC -Ov SOURCE.C
    Enable induction variable optimizations while compiling SOURCE.C.

#pragma option -Ov
    Same as above. The directive must appear between function definitions.

```
#pragma option -O-v
```
Disable induction variable optimizations. The directive must appear between function definitions.

## Description
When you use an Arrray with an index, the compiler generates code that calculates the element of the array as follows:

```
ArrayPtr + (Index * Size)
```

where 'ArrayPtr' is the base address for the array and 'Size' is the size of each element in the array. If you index an array in a loop, then the compiler generates code to multiply the index times the size of each element to determine the address for the element. For example, consider the following code:

```
for(n = 0; n < 1000; n++)
    Array[n].x = n;
```

If each element in 'Array' is 7 bytes long, then the compiler normally generates code to calculate 'Array + (n * 7)' when evaluating Array[n]. With the -Ov option enabled, however, the compiler generates code as if you had written the following instead:

```
for(temp = Array, n = 0; n < 1000; temp++, n++)
    *temp = n;
```

With this coding, the address of 'temp' is incremented by 7 with each iteration thereby eliminating the need to perform 1,000 multiplication instructions.

You should note that if each element in 'Array' is 1 or 2 bytes in length, such as when you are working with a type 'char' or 'int,' then the code generated with the -Ov option enabled is slightly slower than it is with it disabled. This is because the normal method for calculating the offset with these element sizes is slightly faster then calculating the offsets incrementally.

## See Also
Od, O1, O2, Ox     Enable/Disable Groups of Optimizations
Ol                 Loop Compaction

## Example
Write an application which tests the speed advantage of using the -Ov option. In the following application, the -Ov option is enabled for the Fast() function and disabled for the Slow() function. With the -Ov option enabled, the compiler generates code to calculate the address for the expression 'Array[n]' incrementally in the Fast() function, which enables it to operate 34% faster than the Slow() function.

**ov\test.c**
```
struct MY_STRUCT
{
    char Str[5];
    int x;
};
```

```
struct MY_STRUCT Array[1000];

/* Enable the -Ov option */
#pragma option -Ov
void Fast(void)
{
    unsigned n;

    for(n = 0; n < 1000; n++)
        Array[n].x = n;
}

/* Disable the -Ov option */
#pragma option -O-v
void Slow(void)
{
    unsigned n;

    for(n = 0; n < 1000; n++)
        Array[n].x = n;
}

void main(void)
{
    Fast();
    Slow();
}
```

Note that if the elements in 'Array' were integers rather than forming an odd-sized structure, the Slow() function would actually operate slightly faster than the Fast() function.

# P, P*ext*                       C/C++ Source Code File Extensions

| | | | | |
|---|---|---|---|---|
| ■ C | ■ C++ | ❶ CPP | ■ TC++ | ■ TCW/BCW |
| ■ BC 2.0 | ■ BC 3.0/3.1 | ■ BCC | Local | #pragma |

❶ The -P option for CPP instructs it to include source line information. This option is on by default. Use the -P- option to supress the inclusion of source information. The -P*ext* option does not apply to CPP and is ignored.

## Purpose

The -P option instructs the compiler to treat all source files as C++ source code regardless of the file extension. The -P*ext* is the same as the -P option except that it also specifies the file extension to append to any files listed without an extension.

## IDE Option

Options | Compiler | C++ Options | CPP extensions only     *for -P-*
Options | Compiler | C++ Options | C++ always              *for -P*
Options | Environment | Editor | Default extension        *for ext*

## Default
−P−

Compile CPP extensions only as C++ source code.

## Usage
```
BCC -P SOURCE.C
```
Compile as a C++ source file.

```
BCC -PSRC SOURCE
```
Compiles file SOURCE.SRC as a C++ source file.

```
BCC -P-SRC SOURCE
```
Compiles file SOURCE.SRC as a normal C source file.

## Description
The compiler normally expects C++ source code to have a .CPP file extension. Not all programmers, however, save their C++ source code using this extension. The -P option allows you to tell the compiler to treat all source code as C++ source code.

If you are using the command line compiler, you can change the default file extensions the compiler adds to any files listed without an extension. Normally the compiler appends a .CPP extension to any files listed without an extension. For example, the compiler would assume you are referring to the file SOURCE.CPP in the following command line:

```
bcc source
```

The compiler would then look for the file SOURCE.CPP and generate an error if it could not find the file. You can change the extension the compiler appends by placing the new one after the -P option.

If you program mainly in C instead of C++, you may wish to have the compiler default to adding a .C extension and compile the source code as a normal C application. The best way to accomplish this is to add the -P-C option to your TURBOC.CFG file. Then the compiler would execute the above command line by looking for the file SOURCE.C and compiling it as a normal C application.

Note that this option can also be used as a local option to a project file. This allows you to specify a C or C++ compile for individual files in a project.

## See Also
*efilename*          Executable Filename
*ofilename*          Object Code Filename

## Example
Write a TURBOC.CFG file that defaults to compiling normal C code and appends a .C file extension.

```
-IC:\BORLANDC\INCLUDE
-LC:\BORLANDC\LIB
-P-C
```

The compiler will use the above as default settings for the command line compiler if the file is called TURBOC.CFG and placed in the same directory as the compiler. The -I and -L options specify the directory locations of the include and library files. With the above defaults, the "Hello, C!" application can be compiled by entering the following:

```
bcc hello
```

## p, pr                                    Use the Pascal or Fastcall Calling Convention

| ■ C | ■ C++ | ❶ CPP | ❷ TC++ | ❷ TCW/BCW |
|-----|-------|-------|--------|-----------|
| ❷ BC 2.0 | ■ BC 3.0/3.1 | ■ BCC | ■ Local | ■ #pragma |

❶   The -p option only.

❷   The -pr option is only available in BC++ Version 3.0/3.1.

### Purpose
The -p option is used to instruct the compiler to default to the Pascal calling convention. You normally use this option when you are writing utilities in C or C++ to run in Pascal applications. You use the -pr option to enable the _fastcall calling convention for passing parameters via register variables rather than on the stack.

### IDE Option
Options | Compiler | Entry/Exit Code | C          *for -p-*
Options | Compiler | Entry/Exit Code | Pascal     *for -p*
Options | Compiler | Entry/Exit Code | Register   *for -pr*

### Default
```
-p-
```
Use the C calling convention.

### Usage
```
BCC -p SOURCE.C
```
Use the Pascal calling convention.

```
#pragma option -p
```
Same as above; must appear between functions and variable declarations.

### Description
When parameters are passed to a called function, they are placed on the stack. They have to be removed from the stack after the function returns. The C and Pascal calling conventions use two different techniques to clean the passed parameters off the stack. The C convention assumes that the function being called knows little about the number of

parameters passed and generates code to clean up the stack with each function call. The advantage of this technique is that more parameters can be placed on the stack than the function expects. This enables functions that accept a variable number of parameters, such as printf(), to operate properly. This calling convention is also more tolerant of programming errors in which there is a mismatch between the number of parameters passed to a function and the number of parameters expected. The disadvantage is that if the application performs 20 calls to the function, then the code for cleaning the stack has to be placed in 20 different locations.

## Pascal Calling Convention

With the Pascal calling convention, it is the function receiving the parameters that cleans up the stack. The advantage of this technique is that there is only one set of code to clean off the stack parameters. The second advantage is that the parameters can be cleaned off the stack at the same time the function return is executed. This is a much faster method than the C calling convention. The disadvantage of this approach is that the function performing the call must pass the number of parameters expected by the function—no more and no less. If there is a mismatch, then the application will crash. It is important that your application utilize prototypes if you decide to use the Pascal calling convention. When your application uses prototypes, the compiler will flag any mismatch between the prototype, the function call, and the function definition.

The Pascal calling convention also passes parameters on the stack in an order that is reversed from that of the C calling convention. In C, the last arguments are pushed onto the stack first before the function call is made. This places the arguments in ascending order in memory. The Pascal calling convention pushes the parameters onto the stack in the order in which they are listed in the function call. The arguments are then in a descending order in memory.

Finally, the Pascal calling convention names functions differently than the C convention. C functions are case sensitive and always have a leading underscore. Pascal functions are case insensitive and have no leading underscore.

The Pascal calling convention can be specified on individual functions by using the *pascal* keyword. Likewise, if you are using the -p option, you can specify individual functions as using the C calling convention by declaring the function as *cdecl*.

Note that all Windows API functions use the Pascal calling convention. However, the language libraries for Windows applications still use the C calling convention.

## Fastcall Calling Convention

The Fastcall calling convention is new to BC++. Instead of defaulting to *pascal* or *cdecl* functions, which use the stack for passing parameters, functions instead default to type *_fastcall* functions. Functions with the type *_fastcall* keyword pass as many parameters as possible via microprocessor registers rather than on the stack. In theory this means the parameters passed in a function do not need to be pushed onto the stack before calling the function or to be removed from the stack after the function call returns, which should reduce execution time and code size. However, in actual applications, use of the _fastcall_ calling convention will probably result in slower execution speeds, as it reduces the ability of the compiler to use automatic variables efficiently and also requires additional storage for the register parameter as a local variable, as shown in the Example section below. Borland included the Fastcall calling convention to maintain compatibility with Microsoft C source code. You should avoid using it in normal programming.

Table 2-15 lists the registers used for parameter passing. Note that there are no guarantees as to which parameters are placed in what registers.

| DATA TYPE | REGISTERS |
| --- | --- |
| Signed and unsigned characters | AL, DL, BL |
| Signed and unsigned integers | AX, DX, BX |
| Signed and unsigned longs | DX:AX |
| Near pointers | AX, DX, BX |

Far pointers, unions, structures, and floating-point numbers are passed on the stack.

**Table 2-15 Registers used by the Fastcall calling convention**

Like functions with the _pascal_ and _cdecl_ keywords, functions using the _fastcall_ keyword use a different naming convention. Type _fastcall_ functions are case sensitive and are preceded by an "@" symbol instead of a leading underscore.

**See Also**

u                              Precede Tags with an Underscore

**Example**

Write an application that uses two identical functions using the Pascal, Fastcall, and normal C calling conventions.

p\test.c
```
/* Enable the Pascal calling convention */
#pragma option -p

long Sum;

/* This function now defaults to the Pascal calling convention */
void Pascal(long Number)
{
    Sum += Number;
}

/* Because this function uses the _fastcall keyword, it uses the
   Fastcall calling convention. */
void _fastcall Fastcall(long Number)
{
```

```
      Sum += Number;
}

/* This function is identical to the previous function, except we are
using the C calling convention as declared by the cdecl keyword. */
void cdecl Normal(long Number)
{
      Sum += Number;
}

void cdecl main(void)
{
      unsigned n;

      /* Call each function 60,000 times */
      for(n = 0; n < 60000; n++)
          Pascal(n);

      for(n = 0; n < 60000; n++)
          Fastcall(n);

      for(n = 0; n < 60000; n++)
          Normal(n);
}
```

The Pascal() function uses the Pascal calling convention, whereas the identical Normal() and Fastcall() functions use the normal C and Fastcall calling conventions, respectively. The Pascal() function operates 15% faster than the Normal() function,

The Fastcall() function, however, showed only a very slight half-percent increase in speed over the Normal() function. This is largely due to the compiler creating a local variable to retain the contents of 'Number' and then using the local variable rather than the register. When the same code is compiled using the -O2 option to enable all speed optimizations, the Fastcall() function actually runs 10% *slower* than the Normal() function. This was because the Normal() function did not require the creation of a stack frame (see the -k option), whereas Fastcall() did require a stack frame to support the storage of the local parameter.

## po                                                    Localize Object Members

| C | ■ C++ | CPP | TC++ | ❶ TCW/BCW |
|---|-------|-----|------|-----------|
| BC 2.0 | ❶ BC 3.0/3.1 | ■ BCC | ■ Local | ■ #pragma |

❶ Only BCW and BC++ version 3.1

### Purpose

The -po option instructs the compiler to leave the *this* pointer for an object in the SI register for near data models and the DS:SI register pair for far data models. This localizes the object members which results in smaller and faster code.

## IDE Option
Options | Compiler | Optimizations | Object data calling

## Default
-po-
> Use normal code generation

## Usage
```
BCC -po SOURCE.C
```
> Use the object data calling code generation.

```
#pragma option -po
```
> Same as above, must appear between functions and variable declarations

## Description
The code normally generated by the compiler for accessing data members effectively translates into a dereferencing of the *this* pointer for the object. For example, consider the following function for the SLOW object from the example application:

```
void SLOW::Sum(long x)
{
  while(xñ)
    a += b;
}
```

The compiler generates the following assembly language code for the function:

```
;
;           a += b;
;
 les bx,dword ptr [bp+6]
 mov ax,word ptr es:[bx+6]
 mov dx,word ptr es:[bx+4]
 les bx,dword ptr [bp+6]
 add word ptr es:[bx],dx
 adc word ptr es:[bx+2],ax
```

The above assembly language code would look as follows when written in straight C:

```
this->a += this->b;
```

The -po option uses a more efficient method for accessing data members by first localizing the object data and then calling the member function. The compiler accomplishes this by loading the SI register with the *this* pointer before calling the member function rather than pushing the pointer onto the stack. The compiler loads the DS:SI register pair in far data models. For example, consider the assembly language code generated for the FAST object from the example application:

```
;
;           a += b;
;
 mov ax,word ptr [si+6]
 mov dx,word ptr [si+4]
```

```
add word ptr [si],dx
adc word ptr [si+2],ax
```

The above code executes almost twice as fast as the similar SLOW member function. The speed increase is even more dramatic in applications operating with Windows in the standard or enhanced mode. The LES instruction required to load the *this* pointer takes 7 clock cycles to execute on an 80386 when executed in DOS. However, when an application runs in Windows standard or enhanced mode, the microprocessor must check to ensure the selector loaded into the ES register is valid. This increases the execution time for the LES instruction more than three-fold to 22 clock cycles. The -po option virtually eliminates the need for executing an LES instruction within member functions.

## See Also

Op                         Copy Propagation

## Example

Write an application to compare the speed of an object class compiled with and without the -po compiler option:

**po\test.cpp**

```
#include <stdio.h>

#pragma option -po
struct FAST
{
  long a, b;
  void Sum(long x);
  FAST() { a = 0; b = 1; }
};

#pragma option -po-
struct SLOW
{
  long a, b;
  void Sum(long x);
  SLOW() { a = 0; b = 1; }
};

void FAST::Sum(long x)
{
  while(xñ)
    a += b;
}

void SLOW::Sum(long x)
{
  while(xñ)
    a += b;
}

void main(void)
{
  FAST Fast;
  SLOW Slow;

  Fast.Sum(10000L);
  Slow.Sum(10000L);
}
```

The FAST object class is compiled using the -po option to localize its data members. This enables the Sum() member function to operate twice as fast as the Sum() function for the SLOW object.

## Qe, Qx — Expanded and Extended Memory Usage

| | | | | |
|---|---|---|---|---|
| ▪ C | ▪ C++ | CPP | ▪ TC++ | TCW/BCW |
| ▪ BC 2.0 | ▪ BC 3.0/3.1 | ▪ BCC | Local | #pragma |

### Purpose
The -Qe and -Qx options are used to tell the command line compiler how much expanded or extended memory it can use while compiling.

### IDE Option
N/A

### Default
−Qe
> Use all available expanded memory.

−Qx
> Use all available extended memory.

### Usage
`BCC −Qe− SOURCE.C`
> Do not use any expanded memory.

`BCC −Qe=10 SOURCE.C`
> Use ten 16K pages of expanded memory.

`BCC −Qx=100 SOURCE.C`
> Use only 100K of extended memory.

### Description
The compiler uses all available extended memory in the flat memory model. You should use the -Qx option if your application also uses extended memory. The -Qx option will limit the amount of extended memory used by BCC. It will also utilize all expanded memory if it is available unless you specifically tell it not to by using the -Qe- option.

### See Also
| | |
|---|---|
| B | Use an External Assembler Instead of BASM |
| H | Precompiled Header |
| Chapter 1: /e[=*Pages*] | Swap with Expanded Memory |
| Chapter 1: /x[=*kBytes*] | Extended Memory Allocation |

## Example

Because the compiler only uses expanded or extended memory for very large and complex source modules, no example application is included with this option.

## r, rd                                                  Use Automatic Register Variables

- C          ■ C++          CPP          ■ TC++          ■ TCW/BCW
- BC 2.0     ■ BC 3.0/3.1   ■ BCC        ■ Local         ■ #pragma

## Purpose

The -r option instructs the compiler to automatically use register variables whenever possible. The -rd option tells the compiler to only use register variables for declarations that contain the *register* keyword.

## IDE Option

Options | Compiler | Optimizations | None              *for -r-*
Options | Compiler | Optimizations | Register keyword   *for -rd*
Options | Compiler | Optimizations | Automatic          *for -r*

## Default

−r
    Automatically use register variables.

## Usage

BCC −r− SOURCE.C
    Do not use register variables.

BCC −rd SOURCE.C
    Use declared register variables only.

## Description

Register variables are local integer variables that are stored in processor registers rather than on the stack. The microprocessor can access register variables much more quickly from registers than it can from the stack.

    With the -r option enabled (the default), every function that uses the SI and DI registers preserves their contents by pushing them onto the stack and restoring them before returning. Disabling the use of register variables with the -r- option tells the compiler that it is free to use the SI and DI registers without having to preserve their contents. This could create problems if you have one section of code with the -r option enabled and you call a function with the option disabled, as the called function could overwrite the register variable stored in the SI or DI register. You should be very cautious about mixing code with the register variable option enabled with code having the option disabled within the same application.

The -rd option instructs the compiler to use register variables only if they are declared. This option is included for backward compatibility with previous compiler versions.

Note that the compiler sometimes uses the AX, BX, CX, and DX processor registers to store register variables. This can cause problems for certain inline assembly language codes. See Chapter 6 for details.

### See Also

| | |
|---|---|
| Od, O1, O2, Ox | Enable/Disable Groups of Optimizations |
| Op | Copy Propagation |
| Z | Register Usage Optimization |

### Example

Write an application with identical functions in which one is compiled with automatic register variables and the other with the option disabled.

**r\test.c**

```
/* Enable register optimizations */
#pragma option -r

/* This automatically creates a register variable for 'n' */
void Fast(void)
{
   unsigned n;

   for(n = 0; n < 60000; n++);
}

/* Disable register optimizations */
#pragma option -r-

/* The compiler uses a stack variable for 'n' */
void Slow(void)
{
   unsigned n;

   for(n = 0; n < 60000; n++);
}

void main(void)
{
   /* Test the speed of the two functions */
   Fast();
   Slow();
}
```

Both the Fast() and Slow() functions count from 0 to 60,000. The Fast() is compiled with automatic register variables so the compiler stores the 'n' variable in the SI register. The Slow() function is compiled with register variables disabled so the compiler stores the 'n' variable on the stack. The use of register variables enables the Fast() function to operate 230% faster than the Slow() function on an 80386 machine. The speed increase would be even more dramatic on an XT class machine.

# S

**Compile to an .ASM File**

---

| | | | | |
|---|---|---|---|---|
| ■ C | ■ C++ | CPP | ■ TC++ | TCW/BCW |
| ■ BC 2.0 | ■ BC 3.0/3.1 | ■ BCC | ■ Local | #pragma |

## Purpose
The -S option compiles the source code to an assembly language file (.ASM) instead of an object code file (.OBJ).

## IDE Option
Options I Compiler I Code generation I Source

## Default
–S–
> Generate an .OBJ file.

## Usage
`BCC -S SOURCE.C`
> Generate an .ASM file.

## Description
This option compiles the source code to an .ASM file rather than an .OBJ file. The resulting file uses the same base pathname as the source code file and an .ASM extension. The resulting file contains the original C or C++ source code intermixed with the actual assembly and can be compiled to an .OBJ file using the Turbo Assembler.

Producing .ASM files from C or C++ source code is very useful as it allows you to see exactly how the compiler is compiling your source code. Knowing the code the compiler generates allows you to adjust your programming techniques to produce tighter and more efficient object code.

## See Also
| | |
|---|---|
| B | Use TASM Instead of BASM |
| E*filename* | External Assembler |
| M | Create a .MAP File |
| CPP preprocessor utility | TLINK |

## Example
This example shows the compiled assembly language output of the following source code:

**s\example.c**
```
void main(void)
{
    int a = 1;
    int b = 2;
    int c;

    c = a + b;
}
```

185

Compiling the source code with the following command line produces the .ASM file listed below:

```
BCC -S -Ic:\borlandc\include Example.c
```

**s\example.asm**
```
        ifndef   ??version
?debug macro
        endm
publicdll macro             name
            public   name
            endm
$comm   macro     name,dist,size,count
        comm      dist name:BYTE:count*size
        endm
        else
$comm   macro     name,dist,size,count
        comm      dist name[size]:BYTE:count
        endm
        endif
        ?debug   S "Example.c"
        ?debug   C E9786BD916096578616D706C652E63
_TEXT   segment byte public 'CODE'
_TEXT   ends
DGROUP  group    _DATA,_BSS
        assume   cs:_TEXT,ds:DGROUP
_DATA   segment word public 'DATA'
d@      label    byte
d@w     label    word
_DATA   ends
_BSS    segment word public 'BSS'
b@      label    byte
b@w     label    word
_BSS    ends
_TEXT   segment byte public 'CODE'
    ;
    ;   void main(void)
    ;
        assume   cs:_TEXT
_main   proc     near
        push     bp
        mov      bp,sp
        sub      sp,6
    ;
    ;   {
    ;     int a = 1;
    ;
        mov      word ptr [bp-2],1
    ;
    ;     int b = 2;
    ;
        mov      word ptr [bp-4],2
    ;
    ;     int c;
    ;
    ;     c = a + b;
    ;
        mov      ax,word ptr [bp-2]
        add      ax,word ptr [bp-4]
```

```
        mov        word ptr [bp-6],ax
;
;       }
;
        mov        sp,bp
        pop        bp
        ret
_main   endp
        ?debug     C E9
_TEXT   ends
_DATA   segment word public 'DATA'
s@      label      byte
_DATA   ends
_TEXT   segment byte public 'CODE'
_TEXT   ends
        public     _main
        end

_
```

## T*xxx*                              Pass *xxx* Options to the Assembler

▪ C          ▪ C++         CPP          ▪ TC++          TCW/BCW
▪ BC 2.0     ▪ BC 3.0/3.1  ▪ BCC        ▪ Local         #pragma

### Purpose
The -T*xxx* option is used to pass a command line string to the external assembler.

### IDE Option
Used only as a local option or by editing the command line parameters of the Turbo Assembler transfer.

### Default
See the Description.

### Usage
```
BCC -T/DMY_MACRO SOURCE.ASM
```
Pass the parameter /DMY_MACRO to the external assembler.

```
BCC -T- SOURCE.ASM
```
Do not pass default or any other previously defined options to the external assembler.

### Description
The compiler passes the external assembler the default set of parameters listed in Table 2-16, depending on the model and language options in effect. You can have the compiler send additional options using the -T*xxx* option. For example, consider the following command line parameters:

```
bcc -ml -f87 -TDMY_MACRO source.asm
```

The above will cause the compiler to call the external assembler as follows:

```
tasm.exe source/D__LARGE__ /D__CDECL__ /r/ml /DMY_MACRO ,source ;
```

The -T- instructs the compiler not to pass any previously defined parameters. For example:

```
bcc -ml -f87 -T/DMY_MACRO -T- source.asm
```

This time any previously defined parameters were disabled using the -T-. This removes the previous /DMY_MACRO parameter.

| OPTION | PARAMETER |
|--------|-----------|
| -mc | /D__COMPACT__ |
| -mh | /D__HUGE__ |
| -ml | /D__LARGE__ |
| -mm | /D__MEDIUM__ |
| -ms | /D__SMALL__ |
| -mt | /D__TINY__ |
| -p | /D__PASCAL__ |
| -p- | /D__CDECL__ |
| -f | /e |
| -f87 | /r |
| -f287 | /r |
| (all) | /ml |

Table 2-16 Default parameters sent to the external assembler

## See Also

B                          Use an External Assembler instead of BASM
E*filename*                External Assembler

## Example
Write an application to capture the parameters sent to the external assembler.

**t\test.c**
```c
#include <stdio.h>

int main(int Num, char *Arg[])
{
    unsigned n;
    FILE *File;

    /* Open a file call "param" */
    File = fopen("param", "wt+");

    /* Check to make sure we opened the file */
    if(File != 0)
    {
```

```
        /* Send the command line parameters to the file */
        for(n = 0; n < Num; n++)
            fprintf(File, "%s ", Arg[n]);
    }

    fclose(File);

    /* Return an error to prevent linking */
    return(-1);
}
```

The above application will send any command line parameters it receives to a file called PARAM. To see which parameters the compiler is sending the assembler for the -v and -p options, you can enter the following:

```
bcc -v -p -TDMY_MACRO -Etest.exe source.asm
```

The -Etest.exe option instructs the compiler to use TEST.EXE as the external assembler. TEST.EXE will send the following to the PARAM file:

```
test.exe source/D__SMALL__ /D__PASCAL__ /e/zi/ml /DMY_MACRO ,source ;
```

# U*tag*                                                            #undef *tag*

| ■ C | ■ C++ | ■ CPP | ■ TC++ | TCW/BCW |
| ■ BC 2.0 | ■ BC 3.0/3.1 | ■ BCC | ■ Local | ❶ #pragma |

❶   Use #undef *tag*.

## Purpose
The -U*tag* option instructs the compiler to undefine any previous definition of *tag* in the command line.

## IDE Option
N/A

## Default
None

## Usage
```
BCC -DMACRO -UMACRO SOURCE.C
```
Undefine the previous definition of MACRO.

## Description
The -U*tag* option is normally used in MAKE files or as a local option in a project file to undefine any macro definition global to the entire project.

## See Also
Dtag, Dtag=string     #define tag string

## Example

Write an application utilizing a macro, and compile using the -D option to define the macro and the -U option to undefine the macro.

**undef\count.c**

```
#include <stdio.h>

void main(void)
{
    unsigned int n, count;

    for(count = 0; count < 10; count++)
    {
#ifdef DELAY
        for(n = 0; n < 60000; n++);  /* Delay Loop */
#endif
        printf("Count = %d\n", count);
    }
}
```

The above code counts from 0 to 9 with a momentary delay between numbers if the DELAY macro is defined. Enter the following to demonstrate the operation of the -U option:

```
bcc -DDELAY -UDELAY count.c
```

The above command line will first define the DELAY macro and then undefine it. The resulting application then counts without any delays.

| u | | | | Precede Tags with an Underscore |
|---|---|---|---|---|

- C
- BC 2.0
- C++
- BC 3.0/3.1
- CPP
- BCC
- TC++
- Local
- TCW/BCW
- #pragma

## Purpose

The -u option tells the compiler to automatically precede global type *cdecl* functions and variables with a leading underscore. You use this option when interfacing with library code containing functions without a leading underscore.

## IDE Option

Options | Compiler | Advanced code generation | Generate underbars

## Default

-u

Precede global *cdecl* functions and variables with an underbar.

## Usage

```
BCC -u- SOURCE.C
```

Do not use a preceding underbar.

```
#pragma option -u-
```

Same as above; must appear before any C or C++ identifiers.

## Description

C and C++ functions and variables are type *cdecl*. The compiler distinguishes the difference between these types of variables and type *pascal* variables by automatically adding a leading underbar (sometimes called an underscore) to the beginning of each global identifier via the -u option. Disabling this option instructs the compiler not to add the leading underbar. Note if you disable this option, you will have to manually add a leading underbar to library function identifiers.

This option has no effect on type *pascal* identifiers.

## See Also

p                           Use the Pascal or Fastcall Calling Convention

## Example

Write an application with the -u option disabled.

**u\main.c**

```
/* Ensure the underbar option is disabled */
#pragma option -u-

char *String(void)
{
    return("This function name has no leading underbar.\n");
}

/* The main() function must be defined with a leading underbar */
void _main(void)
{
    char *Str;

   /* The String() function does not need a leading underbar */
   Str = String();

   /* The printf() library function call does need a leading underbar
    */ _printf(Str);
}
```

Both the main() function and the printf() library function must be written with a leading underbar with the -u option disabled in the above application.

# V, Vs, V0, V1                                    C++ Virtual Table Options

|   C    | ■ C++        | CPP   | ■ TC++  | ■ TCW/BCW |
|--------|--------------|-------|---------|-----------|
| ■ BC 2.0 | ■ BC 3.0/3.1 | ■ BCC | ■ Local | #pragma   |

## Purpose

The -V, -Vs, -V0, and -V1 options are used to tell the compiler how to handle the function tables required by C++ virtual functions. The -V option creates only one virtual function table for each object class. The -Vs option generates a function table in each module that contains an object with virtual functions. The -V0 option is used in conjunction with the -V1 option to specify which module should contain the virtual function table.

## IDE Option

Options | Compiler | C++ Options | Smart         *for -V*
Options | Compiler | C++ Options | Local           *for -Vs*
Options | Compiler | C++ Options | External     *for -V0*
Options | Compiler | C++ Options | Public        *for -V1*

## Default

```
-V
```
Generate one virtual table per object class.

## Usage

```
BCC -Vs SOURCE.C
```
Generate a virtual table in each module that uses a virtual function.

```
BCC -V1 SOURCE.C
```
Generate a virtual table only in the SOURCE module.

```
BCC -V0 SOURCE.C
```
Look for a virtual table outside of the SOURCE module.

## Description

Virtual functions allow a base class object to call different versions of the same function defined in various derived classes. The compiler implements this C++ feature by creating a *virtual function table* of function pointers. These pointers reference the functions defined in the appropriate derived classes.

These options are also used by the compiler to resolve inline function definitions that cannot be expanded inline. For example, the following code cannot be expanded inline:

```
inline Wait(void)
{
    unsigned n;

    // Count to 10,000
    for(n = 0; n < 10000; n++);
}
```

Even though the function is defined using the *inline* keyword, the compiler cannot expand the function inline because it contains an automatic variable, *n*. Rather than generating an error, however, the compiler instead issues a warning and creates a normal function definition. Where this function is located and the number of copies generated by the function depend on which virtual function option is used. The -V option only creates one copy of the function. The -Vs option creates one copy of the function in each module where it is used. The -V1 and -V0 options can be used together to specify which module should contain the function as described below for virtual functions.

The compiler defaults to using the -V option, known as *Smart* virtual tables. This option creates the most compact and efficient executable files. Rather than compiling the virtual table directly into the .OBJ file, the table is instead created by the Turbo

Linker. To implement this feature, the compiler creates an .OBJ file containing a temporary segment called *virtual* in each module that uses virtual functions. This virtual segment contains the information needed by the Turbo Linker to adequately link the virtual function calls to the virtual function table created by TLINK. The temporary virtual segment is discarded by TLINK and not included in the executable file. The disadvantage of using this feature is that the resulting .OBJ files can only be linked by TLINK Version 2.0 or later. If you are creating .OBJ files that are destined to be linked by TLINK, then this option is a better choice.

The -Vs option, known as the *Local* virtual table option, creates virtual tables in each module. This option creates standard .OBJ files that can be utilized by other linkers. Many virtual tables will be duplicated between modules in large applications compiled using the local virtual table option. This produces a larger executable file.

Unlike the local virtual table option, which places virtual tables in every module, the -V1 option is used in conjunction with the -V0 option to manually place global virtual tables in specific modules. The -V1 option is called the *Public* virtual table option and it tells the compiler to generate any virtual tables it needs in the target module just as it would with the local virtual table option. The -V1 option, however, also declares the generated tables as *public,* making them globally visible to the rest of the application. Other modules in the application can then be compiled using the -V0 option, known as the *External* virtual table option. The -V0 option tells the compiler to declare any virtual tables it needs as *extern,* meaning their location is outside of the target module and should be resolved by the linker. The combination of the -V1 and -V0 options provides you with the most control over the location of virtual tables and also produces .OBJ files that are usable by other linkers. The disadvantage is the resulting executable files are always larger than applications compiled using the -Vs option.

Note that if you use the External IDE menu option, one of the modules in your project containing the virtual functions must be compiled with a virtual table. This is done by using -V1 as a local option to designate which module should contain the table. You would use the Public IDE Option if the virtual table is located within one of your applications library modules or you are linking an .OBJ file that contains the virtual table.

**See Also**

| | |
|---|---|
| Jg, Jgd, Jgx | Template Generation |
| Vf | Generate Far C++ Virtual Tables |

**Example**

Write an application that uses virtual functions and compile using the smart and local options and a combination of the public and external virtual table options.

**vx\list.h**

```
#ifndef LIST_H
#define LIST_H

#ifndef __IOSTREAM_H
  #include <iostream.h>
#endif
```

```
struct LIST
{
   unsigned NumItems;

   LIST()
   {
      NumItems = 0;
   }
   virtual void PrintItem(ostream&, unsigned) = 0;
};

ostream& operator<<(ostream& stream, LIST& list);

struct STR_LIST : LIST
{
   char **Str;

   ~STR_LIST();
   STR_LIST& operator<<(char*);
   void PrintItem(ostream&, unsigned);
};

struct DOUBLE_LIST : LIST
{
   double *Num;

   ~DOUBLE_LIST();
   DOUBLE_LIST& operator<<(double);
   void PrintItem(ostream&, unsigned);
};

#endif
```

**vx\list.cpp**

```
#include "list.h"

ostream& operator<<(ostream& stream, LIST& list)
{
   for(unsigned n = 0; n < list.NumItems; n++)
   {
     list.PrintItem(stream, n);
     stream << "\n";
   }
   return(stream);
}

STR_LIST::~STR_LIST()
{
   if(NumItems != 0)
      delete Str;
}

STR_LIST& STR_LIST::operator<<(char* NewStr)
{
   char **NewList = new char*[NumItems + 1];
   if(NumItems != 0)
   {
      memcpy(NewList, Str, NumItems * sizeof(char*));
      delete Str;
```

```
   }
   Str = NewList;
   Str[NumItems++] = NewStr;
   return(*this);
}

void STR_LIST::PrintItem(ostream& stream, unsigned item)
{
   if(item < NumItems)
      stream << Str[item];
}

DOUBLE_LIST::~DOUBLE_LIST()
{
   if(NumItems != 0)
      delete Num;
}

DOUBLE_LIST& DOUBLE_LIST::operator<<(double NewNum)
{
   double *NewList = new double[NumItems + 1];
   if(NumItems != 0)
   {
      memcpy(NewList, Num, NumItems * sizeof(double));
      delete Num;
   }
   Num = NewList;
   Num[NumItems++] = NewNum;
   return(*this);
}

void DOUBLE_LIST::PrintItem(ostream& stream, unsigned item)
{
   if(item < NumItems)
      stream << Num[item];
}
```

**vx\main.cpp**

```
#include "list.h"

void SecondList(void);

void FirstList(void)
{
   STR_LIST Strings;
   DOUBLE_LIST Doubles;

   Strings << "One"
           << "Two"
           << "Three";

   Doubles << 1.0
           << 2.0
           << 3.0;

   cout << Strings;
   cout << Doubles;
}
```

```
void main(void)
{
  FirstList();
  SecondList();
}
```

**vx \ test.cpp**
```
#include "list.h"

void SecondList(void)
{
    STR_LIST Strings;
    DOUBLE_LIST Doubles;

    Strings << "Four"
         << "Five"
         << "Six";

    Doubles << 4.0
         << 5.0
         << 6.0;

    cout << Strings;
    cout << Doubles;
}
```

The above application creates and prints two lists of strings and two lists of doubles. The strings are printed using the PrintItem() virtual function. Both the STR_LIST and DOUBLE_LIST object classes define their own unique PrintItem() function, which is called via the equivalent virtual function declared in the LIST base class. The application is compiled using the different virtual table options as follows:

**vx \ compile.bat**
```
bcc -V  -eSmart    test.cpp main.cpp list.cpp
bcc -Vs -eLocal    test.cpp main.cpp list.cpp
bcc -V1 -c list.cpp
bcc -V0 -eExternal test.cpp main.cpp list.obj
```

# Va, Vb, Vc, Vo, Vp, Vt, Vv    C++ Backward Compatibility Options

| C | ■ C++ | CPP | TC++ | ❷ TCW/BCW |
|---|-------|-----|------|-----------|
| BC 2.0 | ■ BC 3.0/3.1 | ■ BCC | ❶ Local | ❶ #pragma |

❶  The -Va, -Vp, -Vt, and -Vv options only.

❷  BCW only.

## Purpose
The -Va, -Vb, -Vc, -Vp, -Vt, and -Vv options instruct the compiler to generate object code files compatible with TC++, TCW, and BC++ Version 2.0. You use the -Va to return references using a temporary variable instead of directly onto the stack. The -Vb option instructs the compiler to store the same size pointers for virtual base classes as the

"this" pointer. The -Vc option tells the compiler to use hidden members and code for virtual base class pointers. The -Vp option places the 'this' pointer as the last parameter of a function call. The -Vt option places virtual tables before nonstatic data members. The -Vv option enables pointers to virtual base class members. You should normally only use the -Vo option, which enables all of the above options, whenever you need to maintain compatibility with TC++, TCW, or BC++ Version 2.0.

## IDE Option

| | |
|---|---|
| Options I Compiler I Advanced C++ Options I Always near | *for -Vb-* |
| Options I Compiler I Advanced C++ Options I Same size as 'this' pointer | *for -Vb* |
| Options I Compiler I Advanced C++ Options I 'deep' virtual bases | *for -Vv* |
| Options I Compiler I Advanced C++ Options I True 'pascal' pointers | *for -Vp* |
| Options I Compiler I Advanced C++ Options I Disable constructor displacements | *for -Vc* |
| Options I Compiler I Advanced C++ Options I Pass class values via reference | *for -Va* |
| Options I Compiler I Advanced C++ Options I Vtable pointer follows data members | *for -Vt* |

## Default

−Va−

Pass objects directly onto the stack.

−Vb−

Compile virtual base class pointers as near pointers.

−Vc−

Use hidden members and code for accessing some virtual base classes.

−Vp−

Place the 'this' pointer as the last parameter on all function calls.

−Vt−

Place the virtual table before any nonstatic data members.

−Vv−

Enable pointers to virtual base class members.

## Usage

BCC −Va SOURCE.CPP

Pass objects via a reference to a temporary.

#pragma option −Va

Same as above. The directive must appear before the object class declaration or definition.

#pragma option −Va−

Pass objects directly onto the stack. The directive must appear before the object class declaration or definition.

BCC −Vb SOURCE.C

Compile virtual base class pointers as if they were the same size as the 'this' pointer.

`BCC -Vc SOURCE.C`

Do not add hidden members or code to implement accessing virtual base class members via a pointer.

`#pragma option -Vc`

Same as above. The directive must appear before the object class declaration or definition.

`#pragma option -Vc-`

Use hidden members and code for accessing some virtual base classes. The directive must appear before the object class declaration or definition.

`BCC -Vp SOURCE.C`

Place the 'this' pointer as the first parameter of type Pascal function calls.

`#pragma option -Vp`

Same as above. The directive must appear before the object class declaration or definition.

`#pragma option -Vp-`

Place the 'this' pointer as the last parameter on all function calls. The directive must appear before the object class declaration or definition.

`BCC -Vt SOURCE.C`

Place virtual function tables after nonstatic data members.

`#pragma option -Vt`

Same as above. The directive must appear before the object class declaration or definition.

`#pragma option -Vt-`

Place virtual function tables before nonstatic data members. The directive must appear before the object class declaration or definition.

`BCC -Vo SOURCE.C`

Generate object code for SOURCE.C that is compatible with TC++, TCW, and BC++ Version 2.0.

## Description

C++ source code compiled using BC++ Version 3.0/3.1 by default is incompatible with object code compiled using TC++, TCW, and BC++ 2.0. BC++ 3.0/3.1 compiles C++ code differently in a number of ways from the methods used in the other compilers. These differences will cause your resulting applications to crash if you mix .OBJ files from BC++ Version 3.0/3.1 and with .OBJ files created from the other compilers. You can use the -Va, -Vb, -Vc, -Vp, -Vt, and -Vp options to individually control the new C++ compiling features, however, you would normally only use the -Vo option. The -Vo option enables all the backward compatibility switches and causes BC++ to generate object code that is compatible with TC++, TCW, and BC++ Version 2.0.

The following describe each of individual backward compatibility options.

# Va    Passing Objects Via a Reference

BC++ 3.0/3.1 passes objects directly onto the stack, whereas the other compilers use a less efficient method of creating a temporary object and passing a reference address to the temporary. Functions compiled using BC++ 3.0/3.1 expect to be passed a copy of the entire object, whereas functions compiled by the other compilers expect to receive a pointer to a temporary object. For example, consider the following code:

```
#pragma option -Va
struct SLOW
{
    int x;

    // Constructor
    SLOW() { x = 0; }
};

// Pass FAST objects directly onto the stack
#pragma option -Va-
struct FAST
{
    int x;

    // Constructor
    FAST() { x = 0; }
};

int Slow(SLOW a)
{
    return(a.x);
}

int Fast(FAST a)
{
    return(a.x);
}
```

The SLOW object is compiled using the -Va option to pass objects via a reference to a temporary. The FAST object is compiled with the -Va option disabled and passes objects directly on the stack. The following is the assembly language code for the Fast() and Slow() functions:

```
;         Fast(FastObj);
;
 sub sp,2
 mov ax,word ptr [bp-2]
 mov word ptr [bp-10],ax
 call     near ptr @Fast$q4FAST
 . . .

;         Slow(SlowObj);
;
 mov ax,word ptr [bp-4]
 mov word ptr [bp-6],ax
 lea ax,word ptr [bp-6]
 push     ax
```

```
call    near ptr @Slow$q4SLOW
. . .
```

As shown in the above code, the Fast() function, which uses the BC++ 3.0/3.1 method for passing objects, places a copy of the object directly onto the stack. The Slow() function passes an object using the method compatible with the other compilers and instead creates a temporary object and passes the Slow() function a reference to the object. Obviously, if you use BC++ 3.0/3.1 to call a function in a library compiled using one of the other compilers, the function will not operate correctly because it is expecting a reference to a temporary rather than an entire copy of an object.

## Vb    Virtual Base Pointer Size

Because a virtual base class for an object is always located in the same module as the derived class, Borland chose to compile virtual base class pointers as 16-bit near pointers to save space when an object is located in far memory. Note, however, that the code generated by the compiler is slightly slower when used for accessing objects using the near pointer than it is when using the default far pointer. The -Vb option has no effect if the 'this' pointer is a 16-bit near pointer.

## Vc    Disable Constructor Displacements

The compiler may sometimes need to add additional hidden data members to derived classes when the construct for the derived class calls an overridden virtual function while executing a constructor or destructor. The -Vc option instructs the compiler not to add these hidden members. This means that some virtual functions called during execution of a constructor or destructor may not operate as expected with this option enabled.

## Vp    True Pascal Function Calls

TC++, TCW, and BC++ Version 2.0 place the 'this' pointer for pascal functions as the first argument when calling a *pascal* function, whereas BC++ defaults to placing the 'this' pointer as the last parameter for all function calls. The -Vp option instructs BC++ to use the calling convention compatible with the other compilers.

Placing the 'this' pointer after all function parameters results in slightly faster code. For example, consider the following application:

```
#pragma option -Vp
struct SLOW
{
    int x;

    int pascal operator+=(int);
};

int pascal SLOW::operator+=(int a)
{
    x += a;
    return(x);
}
```

```
#pragma option -Vp-
struct FAST
{
    int x;

    int pascal operator+=(int);
};
int pascal FAST::operator+=(int a)
{
    x += a;
    return(x);
}
void main(void)
{
    FAST Fast;
    SLOW Slow;

    Fast.x = 0;
    Slow.x = 0;
    for(unsigned n = 0; n < 10000; n++)
        Fast += 1;

    for(n = 0; n < 10000; n++)
        Slow += 1;
}
```

The -Vp option in the #pragma directive for the SLOW object class instructs the compiler to place the 'this' pointer for *pascal* functions as the first parameter, disabling the -Vp option for the FAST object class. Comparing identical loops utilizing FAST and SLOW objects shows that the call to the *pascal* operator +=() function for the FAST object class operates 11% faster than the same function for SLOW objects.

# Vt    Virtual Tables Following Nonstatic Data Members

BC++ places virtual function tables before an object's nonstatic data members. This enables the compiler to generate faster and smaller code because the 'this' pointer references the function table pointer directly. TC++, TCW, and BC++ Version 2.0 place function tables after nonstatic data members, which sometimes increases the size of the application slightly and results in slower execution speeds.

# -Vv    Disable Deep Virtual Pointers

BC++ Version 3.0/3.1 allows you to declare pointers to virtual base class members. To implement this feature, the compiler must store additional pointers to these base classes, which makes the layout for class objects different than it is in previous versions. The -Vv option instructs the compiler to use the same class layout as the earlier version of BC++.

### See Also
Vmp                     Member Pointer Precision

### Example
See the examples used in the Description section.

# Vf                                              Generate Far C++ Virtual Tables

| C | ■ C++ | CPP | TC++ | ■ TCW/BCW |
|---|-------|-----|------|-----------|
| ■ BC 2.0 | ■ BC 3.0/3.1 | ■ BCC | ■ Local | ❶ #pragma |

❶ Use the *huge* or *_export* keyword modifiers for the applicable class definition.

## Purpose
The -Vf option is used in combination with the -V, -Vs, -V1, or -V0 options to create a far (32-bit) virtual table and place it in the code segment.

## IDE Option
Options I Compiler I C++ Options I Far virtual tables

## Default
−Vf−

Generate a virtual function table using default sized function pointers and place the table in the data segment.

## Usage
BCC −Vf −V SOURCE.C

Generate smart far virtual tables.

BCC −Vf −Vs SOURCE.C

Generate local far virtual tables.

BCC −Vf −V1 SOURCE.C

Generate public far virtual tables.

BCC −Vf −V0 SOURCE.C

Generate external far virtual tables.

## Description
The compiler normally creates a virtual table using the same type of function pointers as called for by the memory model. That is, near function pointers are used for virtual tables created in the tiny, small, and compact memory models, whereas far pointers are used for the medium, large, and huge memory model applications. These tables are then placed in one of the application's data segments. The -Vf option creates far virtual tables. These tables always contain far function pointers that are 32 bits in length. The tables themselves are located in one of the code segments instead of in a data segment.

The -Vf option is equivalent to defining all the classes in the target module using either the *huge* or *_export* keyword. As an example using the LIST class, compiling with the -Vf option is equivalent to defining the LIST class as follows:

```
struct huge LIST
{
    . . .
```

The -Vf option is useful for creating more room in a data segment by moving the virtual tables to the code segment. Another use for this option is to allow the Windows applications to call virtual functions within a Dynamic Link Library. A Windows application cannot call function pointers located in a DLL's data segment, but it can call the virtual function directly if the virtual table is located in the DLL's code segment.

The disadvantage to using the -Vf option is that all object classes that the pointers reference to objects are all far pointers. This slows down the operation of the application and increases the size of the executable file. As a general rule, it is better to define the individual classes as *huge* rather than all the classes in a target module using the -Vf option.

### See Also

| | |
|---|---|
| V, Vs, V0, V1 | C++ Virtual Table Options |
| WD, WDE | Compile for a Windows Dynamic Link Library |

### Example

Compile the previous application using the smart and local options and a combination of the public and external far virtual table options. This is accomplished by compiling the application as follows:

**vf\compile.bat**
```
bcc -Vf -V  -eSmart   test.cpp main.cpp list.cpp
bcc -Vf -Vs -eLocal   test.cpp main.cpp list.cpp
bcc -Vf -V1 -c list.cpp
bcc -Vf -V0 -eExternal test.cpp main.cpp list.obj
```

The resulting executable files, SMART.EXE, LOCAL.EXE, and EXTERNAL.EXE, all have their object classes defined as *huge*. The resulting applications are larger than they are without the far virtual tables and do not operate as fast.

# Vmd, Vmm, Vms, Vmv                  C++ Member Pointer

| C | ▪ C++ | CPP | TC++ | ❶ TCW/BCW |
|---|---|---|---|---|
| BC 2.0 | ▪ BC 3.0/3.1 | ▪ BCC | ▪ Local | ▪ #pragma |

❶ BCW only.

### Purpose

The -Vmd, -Vmm, -Vms, and -Vmv options control the precision used by the compiler to store member pointers. The -Vmv option is the most general and least efficient method that covers all cases. You should use either -Vms option if your code does not contain pointers which reference members in virtual base classes or to some members of some base classes of classes using multiple inheritance. The -Vmm option is functionally identical to the -Vms except that it allows pointers to members of any base class except virtual base classes. The -Vmd option instructs the compiler to store member pointers which can point to any member of a class provided the class is fully defined.

## IDE Option

Options | Compiler | Advanced C++ Options | Support all cases _for -Vmv_
Options | Compiler | Advanced C++ Options | Support multiple inheritance _for -Vmm_
Options | Compiler | Advanced C++ Options | Support single inheritance _for -Vms_
Options | Compiler | Advanced C++ Options | Smallest for class _for -Vmd_

## Default

−Vmv

Store member pointers in a format that can be used in all cases.

## Usage

BCC −Vmd SOURCE.C

Store member pointers in a format that can be used to point to any member in the class provided the class is fully defined.

#pragma option −Vmd

Same as above. The directive must appear before the object class declaration or definition.

BCC −Vmm SOURCE.C

Store member pointers in a format that can be used with multiple inheritance.

#pragma option −Vmm

Same as above. The directive must appear before the object class declaration or definition.

BCC −Vms SOURCE.C

Store member pointers in a format that can be used with single inheritance and most multiple inheritance classes.

#pragma option −Vms

Same as above. The directive must appear before the object class declaration or definition.

## Description

Member pointers are pointers that reference specific data types in an object class. For example, consider the following application code:

**vm\examp.cpp**

```cpp
#include <iostream.h>

struct OBJECT
{
    int a, b, c;
};

// Declare a member pointer to an integer in OBJECT
int OBJECT::*Ptr;

void PrintPtr(OBJECT& x)
{
    // Print the member pointed to by 'Ptr'
    cout << x.*Ptr << "\n";
}
```

```
void main(void)
{
    OBJECT x;

    x.a = 1;
    x.b = 2;
    x.c = 3;

    // Point to member 'a'
    Ptr = &OBJECT::a;
    PrintPtr(x);

    // Point to member 'b'
    Ptr = &OBJECT::b;
    PrintPtr(x);

    // Point to member 'c'
    Ptr = &OBJECT::c;
    PrintPtr(x);
}
```

The 'Ptr' variable in the above code is a pointer to an integer member of the OBJECT class. Ideally, all the compiler needs to store in 'Ptr' is the offset to the data member. When the above source code uses the pointer with the 'x.*Ptr' expression, the compiler dereferences 'Ptr' by adding the value stored in 'Ptr' to the 'this' pointer for object 'x'. Although this method of member pointer storage works in the simple case above, it does not always work in more complicated cases in which member pointers can point to members in virtual base classes and in certain instances involving multiple inheritance.

The -Vmv option instructs the compiler to store member pointers in a format that will work in all cases. However, this option creates less efficient code, which both increases the size of your application and slows the execution speed, as shown in the example section.

The best option for storage of member pointers is the -Vmd. This option instructs the compiler to use the most efficient storage method for member pointers. You can only use this option efficiently, however, if the object class is fully defined when the compiler encounters the member pointer declaration. For example, consider the following code:

```
struct OBJECT
{
    int a, b, c;
    int OBJECT::*Ptr;

    void Increment();
};
```

'Ptr' in the above OBJECT class points to a member in the OBJECT class. Because the OBJECT class is not fully defined when the compiler encounters the 'Ptr' declaration, the compiler is forced to use the more general storage method normally used with the -Vmv option. The compiler issues the following warning message when you compile code using the -Vmd option, and it is forced to use the -Vmv option:

```
Maximum precision used for member pointer type 'int OBJECT::*'
```

In these situations, you should use the -Vms or -Vmm option. These options are identical, except that the -Vms option will not allow you to point to some members involving classes of base classes. Neither of these options allows you to point to members of a virtual base class. For example, the 'Ptr' member of the FAST object in the example section below cannot point to the 'x' member of the virtual base class A, whereas the 'Ptr' in the SLOW object class can point as it is compiled using the more general -Vmv option.

### See Also
Va, Vb, Vc, Vo, Vp, Vt, Vv   C++ Backward Compatibility Options

### Example
Write an application which demonstrates the efficiency of using the -Vms option as opposed to the more general -Vmv option. In the example below, the -Vms option is declared using a #pragma directive for the FAST class, whereas the -Vmv option is used for the SLOW class. The resulting FAST::Increment() function operates over five times faster than the SLOW::Increment() function. Note, however, that since the code declares the FAST object with the -Vms option in effect, the 'Ptr' member pointer cannot be used to point to the 'x' member in the A virtual base class. Attempting to compile the statements commented out will result in an error message. The 'Ptr' member pointer in the SLOW object class does not have this restriction and can point to the 'x' member in the A virtual base class.

**vm\test.cpp**

```cpp
#include <iostream.h>

struct A
{
    int x;
};

struct B : virtual A
{
    int y;
};

#pragma option -Vms
struct FAST : virtual A, B
{
    int FAST::*Ptr;

    void Increment();
};

void FAST::Increment()
{
    for(unsigned n = 0; n < 10000; n++)
        (this->*Ptr)++;
}

#pragma option -Vmv
struct SLOW : virtual A, B
{
    int SLOW::*Ptr;

    void Increment();
};

void SLOW::Increment()
{
    for (unsigned n = 0; n < 10000; n++)
```

```
        (this->*Ptr)++;
}
void main(void)
{
    FAST Fast;
    SLOW Slow;

    Slow.x = Fast.x = 0;
    Slow.y = Fast.y = 0;
```

```
/* Because 'Fast' is a FAST object that was defined using
   -Vms member pointer storage, attempting to compile the
   statement below will generate an error. This is because
   'x' is a data member of a virtual base class.

   Fast.Ptr = &FAST::x;
   Fast.Increment();
*/
```

```
    Fast.Ptr = &FAST::y;
    Fast.Increment();

    Slow.Ptr = &SLOW::x;
    Slow.Increment();
    Slow.Ptr = &SLOW::y;
    Slow.Increment();
}
```

## V, Vi                                           Compile with Debug Information

| ❶ C | ■ C++ | CPP | ■ TC++ | ■ TCW/BCW |
|-----|-------|-----|--------|-----------|
| ■ BC 2.0 | ■ BC 3.0/3.1 | ■ BCC | ■ Local | ■ #pragma |

❶  The -v option only. The -vi option applies to C++ source code.

### Purpose
The -v option tells the compiler to include debugging information readable in the object code
(.OBJ) and executable (.EXE) files for use by the Turbo Debuggers for DOS and Windows.
The -vi option tells the compiler not to generate a callable function for inline functions.

### IDE Option
Options I Compiler I Advanced I Debug info in OBJs                *for -v*
Options I Compiler I C++ Options I Out-of-line inline functions *for -vi*
Project I Local options I Exclude debug information             *for -v- on indi-*
                                                                *vidual files*

### Default
−v−

  Do not include debug information.

−vi−

  Do not expand functions inline if the -v option is used.

## Usage

```
BCC -v SOURCE.C
```
Include debug information in the .OBJ file and do not expand C++ inline functions.

```
#pragma option -v
```
Same as above; the directive must appear before any C or C++ statements.

```
BCC -v -vi SOURCE.C
```
Include debug information in the .OBJ file and expand inline functions.

```
#pragma option -vi
```
Same as above; the directive must appear before any C or C++ statements.

## Description

The compiler will place symbolic information into the generated .OBJ file that can be used by the Turbo Debugger and IDE debugger if the target modules are compiled using the -v option. This information includes things like the source file and line numbers associated with code sections as well as variable names, types, and locations. This enables the debugger to display the source code associated with a section of code as it is executed, set break points, and monitor the contents of local and global variables. You always have the option of removing this debug information later using the TDSTRIP utility.

Note that if the -v option is used on the command line to both compile and link an application, the compiler will automatically call TLINK using the -v option to include the symbolic information in the executable file. In the IDE, either the Standalone or On item must be selected in the [Options][Debugger] menu to include the debug information in the executable file.

The compiler will normally create actual functions for all C++ functions if the -v option is used even if they are declared as *inline*. This enables the Turbo Debugger to step through the inline functions. Compiling modules using the -vi option tells the compiler to expand inline functions whenever possible rather than creating real functions suitable for the debugger.

It is generally a good idea to turn off all optimizations whenever you are compiling with debug information. Because the optimizations will rearrange and eliminate certain sections of code, stepping through an application can be difficult.

## See Also

| | |
|---|---|
| y | Compile Line Number Information |
| Chapter 6: ZD, ZI, ZN | Debugging Information Options |
| Chapter 7: | Borland Turbo Debugger Reference |
| Chapter 7: TDSTRIP Utility | |

## Example

Write an application using inline functions and compile with debug information both while expanding functions inline and without inline expansion.

**v\fixed.h**
```
struct FIXED
{
```

```
    long Num;

    // Define the default constructor
    FIXED() { }

    // Define a constructor initialized with a long
    FIXED(long Number)
    {
      // Assume an FIXED created with a long is already formatted
      Num = Number;
    }
    FIXED operator+(FIXED &a)
    {
      return(a.Num + Num);
    }
};

extern FIXED One, Two, Three, Four;

void FirstAdd();
void SecondAdd();
```

**v\first.cpp**

```
    // Ensure inline expansion is disabled for debug files
    #pragma option -vi-

    #include "fixed.h"

    void FirstAdd()
    {
      /* The debugger will step into the FIXED::operator+() function
         because the function is not expanded inline */
      Three = One + Two;
    }
```

**v\second.cpp**

```
    // Turn on inline expansion and add two FIXED objects
    #pragma option -vi

    #include "fixed.h"

    void SecondAdd()
    {
      /* The debugger steps over the FIXED::operator+() function
         because it is expanded inline */
      Four = Two + Two;
    }
```

**v\test.cpp**

```
    #include "fixed.h"

    FIXED One(1L << 16), Two(2L << 16), Three, Four;

    void main(void)
    {
      FirstAdd();
      SecondAdd();
    }
```

The above application uses a FIXED object class similar to the one used in the fractal program described in Chapter 10. An inline function is used for addition. The

209

debugger will step into the inline addition function within the FirstAdd() function because it was compiled with the -vi option disabled. The module containing the SecondAdd() function is compiled with inline expansion with the -vi option enabled. Because the inline function is not expanded out-of-line, the debugger steps over rather than into the addition.

## W, WE, WS                      Compile for a Windows Application

- C
- BC 2.0
- C++
- BC 3.0/3.1
- CPP
- BCC
- TC++
- Local
- TCW/BCW
- #pragma

### Purpose
The -W, -WE, and -WS options tell the compiler that the target application is to run in the Windows environment. The -W option creates an .OBJ file with all the functions treated as if they will be called by the Windows environment. The -WE option only treats functions defined with the _export keyword as callable from Windows. The -WS option, called *smart callbacks*, is the most efficient of the three because it does not require the use of exports for functions called by Windows.

### IDE Option
Options | Compiler | Entry/Exit Code | Windows all functions exportable    *for -W*
Options | Compiler | Entry/Exit Code | Windows explicit functions exported   *for -WE*
Options | Compiler | Entry/Exit Code | Windows smart callbacks           *for -WS*

### Default
None. BCC defaults to compiling a DOS application.

### Usage
`BCC -W SOURCE.C`
Compile a Windows application with all functions exportable.

`#pragma option -W`
Same as above. The directive must appear before any C or C++ keywords.

`BCC -WE SOURCE.C`
Compile a Windows application in which only functions defined with the _export keyword are exportable.

`#pragma option -WE`
Same as above. The directive must appear before any C or C++ keywords.

`BCC-WS SOURCE.C`
Callback functions do not need to be exported.

`#pragma option -WS`
Same as above. The directive must appear before any C or C++ keywords.

**Description**

The -W, -WE, and -WS options all tell the compiler that the target application is a Windows executable file. The command line compiler will automatically inform the Turbo Linker of the target application. TLINK will then link the appropriate library modules to create the Windows executable file. Note that the Resource Compiler (RC) is not called automatically. RC must be called manually after the executable file is created. These options also define the _WINDOWS macro during compilation.

The differences among the three Windows executable options arise in the manner in which they handle callback functions. Many features in Windows require your application to supply Windows with a function that will be called periodically by Windows to process some type of information, such as dialog window messages or font enumerations. These functions called by Windows are known as callback functions. Executing a callback function requires some preparation on the part of the programmer. A method must be used for setting the proper value Data Segment (DS) register when the callback function is executed which will make the data in the application accessible from the callback function. This is known as *data binding*. In DOS applications the data binding, or setting the DS register to the proper value, is accomplished on startup. The value of the DS registers is then modified as required during program execution. Keeping track of the location of data in a DOS application is relatively simple when compared to Windows applications because the data in DOS is fixed in one physical location within the machine after startup. In Windows, however, the applications data can be shuffled to different locations in memory whenever Windows is given control of the computer. As such, the data binding has to occur each time a callback function is executed.

Using the -WS option, called smart callbacks, is the fastest and most convenient way to perform data binding for callback functions. This option relies on the Stack Segment (SS) being the same as the Data Segment (DS), as with the small and medium memory models, and the fact that Windows always sets the value of the SS register before executing a callback function. When the -WS option is enabled, the compiler generates a prolog code section (the prolog is a section of code that is executed before the main body of the function) that moves the value of the SS register to the DS register for all *far* functions in the target module. This data binding method eliminates the need to use Windows' MakeProcInstance() function or to export any callback functions as required by the -W and -WE options described below. Instead, a call to a function which requires a callback function, such as DialogBox(), is performed directly as follows:

```
int FAR PASCAL CallBackFnct(HWND hDlg, unsigned msg, WORD wParam,
        LONG lParam);
. . .

DialogBox(hThisInstance, "ABOUT_DLG", hWnd, CallBackFnct);
```

Note that this option will only work if the application is compiled using either the small or the medium memory model.

The -W and -WE options require a more traditional data binding method typical of most Windows applications compiled using Microsoft C. This method involves *exporting* the function to Windows and then calling the MakeProcInstance() function at run time to create an intermediate function known as a *thunk*. Functions are exported

211

to Windows by either listing them in the EXPORT section of the Module Definition file (.DEF) or defining the function using the _export keyword. Exported functions are used to create a table in the executable's header section that associates the function with a particular data segment. The MakeProcInstance() function is then called at run time to create a thunk for the function. A function pointer to the thunk is then passed to Windows for use as the callback function. For example, the following uses MakeProcInstance() to create and use a thunk for a dialog box callback procedure:

```
FARPROC thunk;

thunk = MakeProcInstance(CallBackFnct, hThisInstance);
DialogBox(hThisInstance, "ABOUT_DLG", hWnd, thunk);
FreeProcInstance(thunk);
```

As shown, the MakeProcInstance() function is used to create the thunk. The thunk is then passed to the DialogBox() function in place of a pointer to CallBackFnct(). When Windows executes the thunk, the code created by MakeProcInstance will perform the data binding and then execute an indirect function call to CallBackFnct().

Both the -W and the -WE options require the above data binding method for callback functions. The difference between them is that the -W option generates code that is compatible with the thunk for all functions, whereas the -WE option only generates compatible code for functions defined using the _export keyword. The -WE option is more efficient than the -W option, but neither is as efficient as the -WS option.

## See Also

WD, WDE          Compile for a Windows Dynamic Link Library
Chapter 5:          Module Definition File EXPORTS statement

## Example

Write a Windows application using smart callbacks, then rewrite the application using exports. Compile the application using exports with both the -W and -WE options. The source code below creates a simple "Hello, Windows!" application that also contains a menu and an "About" dialog box.

The HELLO.H file is an include file that is used by both the BC++ compiler (BCC) and the resource compiler (RC). The RC_INVOKED macro is checked to separate the C specific instructions from the definitions common to both BCC and RC.

**wx\hello.h**
```
#include <windows.h>

/* Because the resource compiler defines the RC_INVOKED macro,
   it will skip this next section. Most C and C++ header information
   causes errors in the resource compiler.
*/
#ifndef RC_INVOKED
  /* Global variable */
  extern HANDLE hThisInstance;

  /* Prototypes */
  int FAR PASCAL CallBackFnct(HWND hDlg, unsigned msg, WORD wParam,
                LONG lParam);
```

```
     void AboutHello(HWND hWnd);
#endif

/* Define the menu item macros */
#define IDM_ABOUT 1000
#define IDM_EXIT  2000
#define ID_OK     3000
```

HELLO.C contains the main body of the application. This source code is common to all three applications. Note that the _export keyword in the CallBackFnct() function is not required for the application compiled using the -WS option, which compiles using smart callbacks, or the -W option, which compiles all functions as exportable. If, however, the _export keyword is not used with the -W option, the CallBackFnct() would have to be listed in the EXPORTS section of the module definition (.DEF) file.

**wx\hello.c**
```
#include "hello.h"

char AppTitle[] = "Hello, Windows!";
HANDLE hThisInstance;

/*We know not all the variables are used, so we may as well disable
   the warning message. */
#pragma warn -par

/* Define the application window's message processing function */
long FAR PASCAL WndProc(HWND hWnd, unsigned msg, WORD wParam,
                        LONG lParam)
{
   RECT rect;
   PAINTSTRUCT ps;
   HDC hDC;

   switch(msg)
   {
      /* Is it a menu command? */
      case WM_COMMAND:
          switch(wParam)
          {
             case IDM_ABOUT:
                 /* Display the 'About Hello' dialog box */
                 AboutHello(hWnd);
                 break;
             case IDM_EXIT:
                 /* Leave the application by destroying the main
                 window */
                 DestroyWindow(hWnd);
                 break;
          {
          break;

      /* Paint the window */
      case WM_PAINT:
          hDC = BeginPaint(hWnd, &ps);

          /* Display the application title in the center of
             the window */
          GetClientRect(hWnd, &rect);
```

```
            DrawText(hDC, AppTitle, sizeof(AppTitle) - 1, &rect,
                     DT_SINGLELINE | DT_VCENTER | DT_CENTER);

            EndPaint(hWnd, &ps);
            break;

      /* Time to quit! */
      case WM_DESTROY:
            PostQuitMessage(0);
            break;

      /* All other messages go here. */
      Default:
            return(DefWindowProc(hWnd, msg, wParam, lParam));
   }
   return(0);
}

int FAR PASCAL _export CallBackFnct(HWND hDlg, unsigned msg,
                                    WORD wParam, LONG lParam)
{
   switch(msg)
   {
      HWND hButton;

      case WM_INITDIALOG:
            /* The is a work-around for the DEFPUSHBUTTON bug which
               sets the initial focus to the "OK" button. No
               initialization code should not be necessary. */
            hButton = GetDlgItem(hDlg, ID_OK);
            SetFocus(hButton);
            break;

      case WM_COMMAND:
            /* Because the pushbutton is the only possible command,
               then it must have been pushed. Time to close the
               dialog box. */
            EndDialog(hDlg, 0);
            break;

      Default:
            return(0);
   }
   return(1);
}

int PASCAL WinMain(HANDLE hInstance, HANDLE hPrevInstance,
                   LPSTR lpCmdLine, int nCmdShow)
{
   int xDim, yDim;
   HWND hWnd;
   MSG msg;

   /* Make the instance handle globally available */
   hThisInstance = hInstance;

   /* Register the application window class */
   if(!hPrevInstance)
```

```
{
    WNDCLASS wc;

    wc.style            = CS_HREDRAW | CS_VREDRAW;
    wc.lpfnWndProc      = WndProc;
    wc.cbClsExtra       = 0;
    wc.cbWndExtra       = 0;
    wc.hInstance        = hInstance;
    wc.hIcon            = LoadIcon(NULL, IDI_HAND);
    wc.hCursor          = LoadCursor(NULL, IDC_ARROW);
    wc.hbrBackground    = GetStockObject(WHITE_BRUSH);
    wc.lpszMenuName     = "MainMenu";
    wc.lpszClassName    = AppTitle;

  if(!RegisterClass(&wc))
    return(FALSE);
}

/* Get the screen dimensions */
xDim = GetSystemMetrics(SM_CXSCREEN);
yDim = GetSystemMetrics(SM_CYSCREEN);

hWnd = CreateWindow(AppTitle, AppTitle, WS_OVERLAPPEDWINDOW,
        xDim / 4, yDim / 4, xDim / 2, yDim / 2,
        NULL, NULL, hInstance, NULL);

if(hWnd == NULL)
  return(FALSE);

/* Display the window */
ShowWindow(hWnd, nCmdShow);

/* Enter the message loop */
while(GetMessage(&msg, 0, 0, 0))
{
  TranslateMessage(&msg);
  DispatchMessage(&msg);
}

/* Exit the application */
return(0);
}
```

The ABOUT.DLG file defines the "About . . ." dialog box. It is included in the compilation of the HELLO.RC file by the resource compiler.

**wx\about.dlg**

```
ABOUT_DLG DIALOG
  DISCARDABLE LOADONCALL PURE MOVEABLE
  0, 0, 107, 64
STYLE WS_POPUP | WS_CAPTION | WS_SYSMENU | 0x80L
CAPTION "About . . ."
BEGIN
  DEFPUSHBUTTON "OK",                   ID_OK, 37, 45, 32, 12
  CTEXT         "Hello, Windows!",      102,  19, 10, 69, 12
  CTEXT         "by Mark Peterson, 1991" 103,  10, 24, 87, 13
END
```

215

The HELLO.RC file is compiled by the resource compiler. It contains the menu resource and dialog box resource. The dialog box resource is defined in ABOUT.DLG.

**wx\hello.rc**
```
#include "hello.h"
#include "about.dlg"

MainMenu MENU
{
  MENUITEM "E&xit",   IDM_EXIT
  MENUITEM "&About",  IDM_ABOUT
}
```

The above files are common to all three example applications. The ABOUT.C file is used for the smart callbacks example using the -WS option (SMART.EXE) and the ABOUT_EX.C file shows how exports are used with the -W and -WE options (ALL.EXE and EXPORT.EXE).

**wx\about.c**
```
#include "hello.h"

void AboutHello(HWND hWnd)
{
    DialogBox(hThisInstance, "ABOUT_DLG", hWnd, CallBackFnct);
}
```

**wx\about_ex.c**
```
#include "hello.h"

void AboutHello(HWND hWnd)
{
    FARPROC thunk;

    thunk = MakeProcInstance(CallBackFnct, hThisInstance);
    DialogBox(hThisInstance, "ABOUT_DLG", hWnd, thunk);
    FreeProcInstance(thunk);
}
```

The three applications, SMART.EXE, ALL.EXE, and EXPORT.EXE, are compiled as follows:

**wx\compile.bat**
```
rc -r -iC:\BORLANDC\INCLUDE hello.rc
bcc -eSmart  -WS hello.c about.c
rc hello.res smart.exe
bcc -eAll    -W hello.c about_ex.c
rc hello.res all.exe
bcc -eExport -WE hello.c about_ex.c
rc hello.res export.exe
```

The first call to RC invokes the resource compiler, which creates the binary resource file, HELLO.RES, that is used in the remaining calls to RC. The SMART.EXE application is compiled using smart callbacks, ALL.EXE is compiled using all functions exportable, and EXPORT.EXE is compiled using only functions with the _export keyword as exportable.

# WD, WDE                                   **Compile for a Windows Dynamic Link Library**

- C           ■ C++           CPP            TC++          ■ TCW/BCW
- BC 2.0      ■ BC 3.0/3.1   ■ BCC          ■ Local        ■ #pragma

## Purpose
The -WD and -WDE options tell the compiler that the target application is a Windows Dynamic Link Library (DLL). The -WD option tells the compiler to generate code so that all functions in the target module can be called from outside the DLL, i.e., they are all exportable. The -WDE option instructs the compiler to only generate exportable code for functions defined using the _export keyword.

## IDE Option
Options | Compiler | Entry/Exit Code | Windows DLL all functions exportable      *for -WD*
Options | Compiler | Entry/Exit Code | Windows DLL explicit functions exported   *for -WDE*

## Default
None. BCC defaults to compiling a DOS application.

## Usage
```
BCC -WD SOURCE.C
```
Compile a Windows DLL with all functions exportable.

```
#pragma option -WD
```
Same as above. The directive must appear before any C or C++ keywords.

```
BCC -WE SOURCE.C
```
Compile a Windows DLL in which only functions defined with the _export keyword are exportable.

```
#pragma option -WDE
```
Same as above. The directive must appear before any C or C++ keywords.

## Description
The -WD and -WDE options tell the compiler to compile the application as a Windows Dynamic Link Library, or DLL. If the command line compiler is used to create the DLL executable file, then it will pass TLINK the -twd option, instructing TLINK to create a DLL.

The difference between the -WD and the -WDE options is the way in which functions are designated for exporting; that is, which functions can be called by other applications provided they are listed in the import library. The -WD option compiles the target module so that all functions within the module can be exported. The -WDE options compile only those functions defined with the _export keyword as exportable.

Chapter 10 contains information on creating a DLL in C++. See the -W, -WE, -WS options for information on the relationship between exporting functions and data binding.

## See Also

W, WE, WS         Compile for a Windows Application
Chapter 5:           Module Definition File EXPORTS statement

## Example

See Chapter 10 for an example of the -WDE option.

---

## W                                                          Display Warnings

- C
- BC 2.0
- C++
- BC 3.0/3.1
- CPP
- BCC
- TC++
- Local
- TCW/BCW
- #pragma

## Purpose

The -W option enables the display of compiler warning messages.

## IDE Option

Options I Compiler I Messages I Display I All       *for* -w
Options I Compiler I Messages I Display I Selected       *for* -w*xxx*
Options I Compiler I Messages I Display I None       *for* -w-

## Default

-w
     Display selected compiler warning messages.

## Usage

```
BCC -w- SOURCE.C
```
     Disable display of all warning messages.

```
#pragma option -w-
```
     Same as above.

## Description

The -w option is used to control the display of compiler warning messages. If the -w-
option is used to disable all warning messages, individual warning messages can be enabled using the -w*xxx* option on the command line or with the #pragma warning directive within the source code.

## See Also

w*xxx*              Individual Warnings
Chapter 5: d        Duplicate Symbols Warning
Chapter 6: W      Warning Message Control

## Example

Write an application using the -w- option to inhibit the display of warning messages. The
following application uses the printf() function, but does not compile the STDIO.H include

file. This generates the warning message "Call to function 'printf' with no prototype in function Function." The #pragma option -w- directive disables all warning messages, so no warning message is generated for the printf() function usage in main().

**w\test.c**
```
/* Enable the "No prototype" warning messages */
#pragma warn +pro

void Function(void)
{
  /* This function call will generate a warning message */
  printf("This function call has no prototype.\n");
}

/* Disable all warning messages */
#pragma option -w-

void main(void)
{
  /* All warnings have been disabled, so no messages are generated
     for this function call */
  printf("This function call also has no prototype.\n");
}
```

## *WXXX*                                          Individual Warnings

- C
- BC 2.0
- C++
- BC 3.0/3.1
- CPP
- BCC
- TC++
- Local
- TCW/BCW
- #pragma

### Purpose
The -w*xxx* option is used to enable or disable specific warning messages.

### IDE Option
Options | Compiler | Messages | Portability...

| | | |
|---|---|---|
| + | Nonportable pointer conversion | -wrpt |
| + | Nonportable pointer comparison | -wcpt |
| + | Constant out of range in comparison | -wrng |
| | Constant is long | -wcln |
| | Conversion may lose significant digits | -wsig |
| | Mixing pointers to signed and unsigned char | -wucp |

Options | Compiler | Messages | Ansi violations...

| | | |
|---|---|---|
| + | Void functions may not return a value | -wvoi |
| + | Both return and return of a value used | -wret |
| + | Suspicious pointer conversion | -wsus |
| + | Undefined structure 'ident' | -wstu |
| + | Redefinition of 'ident' is not identical | -wdup |
| + | Hexadecimal value more than three digits | -wbig |
| | Bit fields must be signed or unsigned int | -wbbf |
| + | 'ident' declared as both external and static | -wext |

| | | |
|---|---|---|
| + | Declare 'ident' prior to use in prototype | -wdpu |
| + | Division by zero | -wzdi |
| + | Initializing 'ident' with 'ident' | -wbei |
| | Initialization is only partially bracketed | -wpin |

Options | Compiler | Messages | C++ warnings...

| | | |
|---|---|---|
| + | Base initialization without a class name is obsolete | -wobi |
| + | Functions containing 'ident' are not expanded inline | -winl |
| + | Temporary used to initialize 'ident' | -wlin |
| + | Temporary used for parameter 'ident' | -wlvc |
| + | The constant member 'ident' is not initialized | -wnci |
| + | This style of function definition is now obsolete | -wofp |
| + | Use of 'overload' is now unnecessary and obsolete | -wovl |
| + | Assigning 'type' to 'enumeration' | -weas |
| + | 'function1' hides virtual function 'function2' | -whid |
| + | Nonconst function 'ident' called for const object | -wncf |
| + | Base class 'ident' is inaccessible because also in 'ident' | -wibc |
| | Overloaded prefix operator used as a postfix operator | -wpre |
| + | Array size of 'delete' ignored | -wdsz |
| + | Use qualified name to access nested type 'ident' | -wnst |

Options | Compiler | Messages | Frequent errors...

| | | |
|---|---|---|
| + | Function should return a value | -wrvl |
| + | Unreachable code | -wrch |
| + | Code has no effect | -weff |
| | Possible use of 'ident' before definition | -wdef |
| + | 'ident' is assigned a value which is never used | -waus |
| + | Parameter 'ident' is never used | -wpar |
| + | Possibly incorrect assignment | -wpia |

Options | Compiler | Messages | Less frequent errors...

| | | |
|---|---|---|
| | Superfluous & with function | -wamp |
| | Ambiguous operators need parentheses | -wamb |
| | Structure passed by value | -wstv |
| | No declaration for function 'ident' | -wnod |
| | Call to function with no prototype | -wpro |
| + | Restarting compile using assembly | -wasc |
| | Unknown assembler instruction | -wasm |
| + | Ill formed pragma | -will |
| + | Condition is always (true/false) | -wccc |
| + | Array variable 'ident' is near | -wias |
| | 'ident' declared but never used | -wuse |

## Default

The IDE options above with a + symbol are the default warning messages.

## Usage

```
BCC —Wxxx SOURCE.C
```

Enable warning message *xxx*.

```
#pragma option -wxxx
```
Same as above.

```
#pragma warn +xxx
```
Same as above.

```
BCC -w-xxx SOURCE.C
```
Disable warning message *xxx*.

```
#pragma option -w-xxx
```
Same as above.

```
#pragma warn -xxx
```
Same as above.

```
#pragma warn .xxx
```
Restore enabled/disabled state of the warning message display as it was at the beginning of the source code.

## Description

The -w*xxx* option allows you to enable or disable specific warning messages either from the command line or in the source code. Specific compiler warning messages can be enabled or disabled from within the source code using either the #pragma option -w*xxx* or the #pragma warn *xxx* directive. The #pragma directives override the prior state of warning messages enabled or disabled earlier in the source code, from the command line, or from the IDE menu.

## See Also

| | |
|---|---|
| w | Display Warnings |
| Chapter 5: d | Duplicate Symbols Warning |
| Chapter 6: W | Warning Message Control |

## Example

Write an application which enables and disables a compiler warning message using the #pragma warn *xxx* directive. The following source code uses the printf() function but does not include the STDIO.H header file which contains the prototype. With the warning message enabled using the #pragma warn +pro directive, the message "Call to function 'printf' with no prototype in function Function" is displayed. The compiler warning is disabled using the #pragma warn -pro directive, thereby suppressing the display of the message in a later usage of the printf() function.

**wxxx\test.c**
```
/* Enable the "No prototype" warning messages */
#pragma warn +pro

void Function(void)
{
```

221

```
    /* This function call will generate a warning message */
    printf("This function call has no prototype.\n");
}

/* Disable all warning messages */
#pragma warn -pro

void main(void)
{
    /* The 'pro' compiler warning has been disabled, so no message is
        generated for this function call */
    printf("This function call also has no prototype.\n");
}
```

## X                                    Disable Autodependency Output

- C              - C++            CPP        - TC++         - TCW/BCW
- BC 2.0         - BC 3.0/3.1  - BCC         - Local        - #pragma

### Purpose
The -X option tells the compiler not to include autodependency information in the .OBJ file. You use this option to reduce the size of .OBJ files that will be placed in a library.

### IDE Option
None

### Default
-X-
  Include autodependency information in the .OBJ file.

### Usage
BCC -X SOURCE.C
  Do not include autodependency information in the SOURCE.OBJ file.

### Description
The compiler normally includes information in the compiled .OBJ file on the header files used in the module along with the data/time stamp of each include file. This information is used by both the IDE and the MAKE utility to perform autodependency checking. The IDE and MAKE utility will use this information to rebuild a module automatically if one of the header files used in the earlier compilation has a later date/time stamp than the one recorded in the .OBJ file. This autodependency information is not always necessary in an .OBJ file, such as when an .OBJ file is to be part of a library file. The -X option can be used to tell the compiler not to include autodependency information in the .OBJ file and thereby save on disk space.

### See Also
v, vi                    Compile with Debug Information
Chapter 6: Q             Suppress Autodependency and Copyright Information

## Example

Write an application that uses include files and compile with and without autodependency information using the -X option.

**x\test.c**
```
#include <stdio.h>

void main(void)
{
   printf("To C or to CPP, that is the question. . .");
}
```

The following compiles the above application to a WITH.OBJ file that contains the header information and a WITHOUT.OBJ file that does not contain the header file information.

```
bcc -c -oWith.obj       test.c
bcc -c -oWithout.obj -X test.c
```

The WITH.OBJ compiles to 413 bytes, whereas the WITHOUT.OBJ file compiles to 276 bytes.

# Y, Yo                                            Overlay the Compiled Files

- C
- BC 2.0
- C++
- BC 3.0/3.1
- CPP
- BCC
- TC++
- Local
- TCW/BCW
- #pragma

## Purpose

The -Y option enables BC++'s overlay manager. The -Yo option is used to designate which modules should be placed in the overlay. You use overlays to increase the size of applications that will run in limited DOS memory.

## IDE Option

Options | Compiler | Entry/Exit Code | DOS overly   *for -Y*
Project | Local options | Overlay this module   *for -Yo*

## Default

None. BCC defaults to compiling a DOS application.

## Usage

```
BCC -Y SOURCE.C -Yo OVERLAY.C
```
Compile an overlaid application with the SOURCE module as the base and the OVERLAY module as the overlay.

## Description

You can write applications that are larger than a machine's available DOS memory space by using overlays. An application that uses overlays consists of at least one or more base modules and one or more overlay modules. All the modules in an application that uses overlays must be compiled with the -Y option. Those modules that are not one of the base modules, i.e., an overlay module, are compiled using the -Yo option. If you use a separate call to TLINK, you will need to execute TLINK using the -o option to create the overlaid executable.

Application overlays are managed by the Virtual Run-time Object-Oriented Memory Manager (VROOMM). When a function is called or data is accessed in one of the overlaid modules, the VROMM checks to see if it is already loaded into memory and, if not, it loads the segment containing the data or function. If there is not enough room in memory, then VROOMM discards segments by writing them to expanded or extended memory, if available, or to the disk. Segments are discarded until there is enough room in memory to load the overlay segment.

## Restrictions

An application that uses overlays should always use far function definitions. For this reason, the compiler only supports overlays if the application is compiled in the medium, large, or huge memory model. If you need to use some near functions in the application, you must ensure no functions in an overlay are called before the application returns from the near function call.

You should not overlay modules that contain time critical routines. It takes time for VROOMM to swap overlay segments in and out of memory and load other segments from the disk. The execution time of routines in the overlay will vary depending on the amount of available memory. You should also avoid placing interrupt routines in an overlay module, as this could cause a reentering of DOS that will crash the machine.

Note that overlays cannot be used in Windows applications. Windows applications use a different type of overlay mechanism that is controlled by the Windows operating system. For more information on how Windows overlays applications, see the Description of the Module Definition File (.DEF) in Chapter 5.

## Controlling Memory Usage

BC++ provides a global variable and two functions for controlling how VROOMM manages overlay memory usage.:

```
extern unsigned _ovrbuffer;
extern int far _OvrInitEms(unsigned emsHandle, unsigned emsFirst,
                           unsigned emsPages);
extern int far _OvrInitExt(unsigned long extStart,
                           unsigned long extLength);
```

The _ovrbuffer variable controls the size of the overlay buffer. The default size is twice the size of the largest overlay segment.

The _OvrInitEms() function initializes expanded memory. The emsHandle parameter should be a legal EMS handle. If the _OvrInitEms() function is called with the emsHandle set to 0, the function will check for expanded memory and allocate enough memory to load all the overlays minus the value of _ovrbuffer. The emsFirst and emsPages designate the first page of usable EMS memory and the number of pages available to VROOMM, respectively. The function returns 0 if successful.

The -OvrInitExt() function initializes extended memory. Setting the extStart parameter to 0 causes the function to check for extended memory on the system and, if found, allocates the amount of memory needed to load all the overlays minus the value of _ovrbuffer. If the machine running your application does not have an extended memory manager, you should set the value of extStart to the starting address of usable extended memory. The extLength parameter is used to specify the maximum amount of extended memory VROOMM should use for overlays. Setting this value to 0 tells VROOMM that it can use all available extended memory after the extStart address or, if extStart is 0, all the extended memory it needs or can allocate. The _OvrInitExt() function returns 0 if it is successful.

### See Also
Chapter 6: O, OP      Generate TLINK/Phar Lap Overlay Code

### Example
Write an application that uses overlays, the _ovrbuffer variable, and the _OvrInitEms(), and _OvrInitExt() functions. The following application sets the minimum size of the overlay to 2024 bytes and then checks to see if expanded or extended memory is available.

**overlay\base.c**

```
#include <stdio.h>

/* DOS.H contains the _ovrbuffer external declaration and the
   prototypes for ovrInitEms() and ovrInitExt() functions */

#include <dos.h>

/* Prototype for the function in the OVERLAY.C module */
void PrintSomething(void);

void main(void)
{
    /* Set the size of the overlay buffer */
    _ovrbuffer = 2048;

    /* See if there is any expanded memory available */
    printf("The size of the overlay buffer is %d bytes.\n", _ovrbuffer);
    if(_OvrInitEms(0, 0, 0))
        printf("No expanded memory available for VROOMM.\n");
    else
        printf("Expanded memory initialized for overlay Usage.\n");

    /* See if there is any extended memory available */
    if(_OvrInitExt(0, 0))
        printf("No extended memory available for VROOMM.\n");
    else
        printf("Extended memory initialized for overlay Usage.\n");

    /* Call a function located in the overlay */
    PrintSomething();
}
```

**overlay\overlay.c**

```
#include <stdio.h>

void PrintSomething(void)
{
    printf("This function is located in an overlay.\n");
}
```

The above application is compiled from the DOS command line as follows:

```
bcc -Y -mm base.c -Yo overlay.c
```

The -Y parameter compiles the application with VROOMM. The -mm parameter specifies the medium memory model. All the target files listed after the -Yo parameter are placed in the overlay, whereas all the files before the -Yo parameter are placed in the base application. For the above application, the only OVERLAY module is placed in the overlay.

## y                                          Compile Line Number Information

- C
- BC 2.0
- C++
- BC 3.0/3.1
- CPP
- BCC
- TC++
- Local
- TCW/BCW
- #pragma

## Purpose
The -y option compiles the source filename and line numbers associated with each line of code into the .OBJ file.

## IDE Option
Options | Compiler | Advanced code generation | Line numbers debug info

## Default
-y-
  Do not include line number information in .OBJ files.

## Usage
```
BCC -y SOURCE.C
```
  Compile with line number information in the .OBJ file.

```
#pragma option -y
```
  Same as above. This is only effective if declared between function definitions or object declarations.

## Description
The -y option is from the earlier days of TC before Borland released the Turbo Debugger and implementation of the -v option. This option was used to provide generic information to other debugging applications such as Microsoft's CodeView. The -y option only compiles the source filename and the line number associated with each section of code,

which enables the debugger to step through the execution of an application but set watches or break points. The -v option must be used if you are debugging with the Turbo Debugger.

## See Also

| | |
|---|---|
| v, vi | Compile with Debug Information |
| Chapter 6: ZD, ZI, ZN | Debugging Information Options |

## Example

Write a simple application and compile using the -y option. Link the application for use in Microsoft's CodeView.

**y\test.c**

```
#include <stdio.h>

void main(void)
{
   unsigned Count;

   printf("Counting from one to ten.\n");
   for(Count = 0; Count < 10; Count++)
      printf("Count = %d\n", Count);
}
```

**y\test.lnk**

```
/CO /NOD /NOE c:\borlandc\lib\cOs.obj +
test.obj
test.exe
NUL
c:\borlandc\lib\cs.lib
```

The following example is an example of linking the object file using Microsoft's LINK.EXE application. Note that while you may step through the source code of the executable file in CodeView, you cannot set a watch on the Count variable.

```
link @test.lnk;
```

# Z                                                          Register Usage Optimization

- C
- BC 2.0
- C++
- BC 3.0/3.1
- CPP
- BCC
- TC++
- Local
- TCW/BCW
- #pragma

## Purpose

The -Z option instructs the compiler to suppress redundant register loads.

## IDE Option

Options I Compiler I Optimizations I Optimize register Usage

## Default

```
-Z-
```

## Usage

```
BCC -Z SOURCE.C
```
Optimize register usage in SOURCE.C.

```
#pragma option -Z
```
Same as above. This directive is only effective when used between function declarations.

## Description

In many instances, the compiler will load the same register value a number of times. For example, consider the following code:

```
struct MYSTRUCT
{
  int x;
  struct MYSTRUCT *Next;
};
void Funct(struct MYSTRUCT *a)
{
  if(a->Next->x > 10)
    a->Next->x = 0;
}
```

The compiler places the value of 'a' into the 'si' register at the start of the function and generates the remaining code as follows:

```
;
;         if(a->Next->x > 10)
;
        mov  bx,word ptr [si+2]        calculate the address for 'x'
        cmp  word ptr [bx],10
        jle  short @1@86
;
;             a->Next->x = 0;
;
        mov  bx,word ptr [si+2]        calculate the address for 'x'
        mov  word ptr [bx],0
@1@86:
;
;    }
```

The compiler generates code to dereference the expression 'a->Next->x' by placing the address for 'x' into the BX register. It does this a second time it encounters another 'a->Next->x' expression even though the value from the first calculation is still in the BX register. The -Z option instructs the compiler to suppress the redundant register load and use the value in the BX register rather than recalculating. For example, with the -Z option enabled, the compiler instead generates the following code:

```
;
;         if(a->Next->x > 10)
;
```

```
        mov  bx,word ptr [si+2]          calculate the address for 'x'
        cmp  word ptr [bx],10
        jle  short @1@86
    ;
    ;           a->Next->x = 0;
    ;
        mov  word ptr [bx],0
@1@86:
    ;
    ;       }
```

This results in both faster and smaller code. For this reason, both the -O1 and the -O2 options automatically enable the -Z option.

## See Also

Od, O1, O2, Ox        Enable/Disable Groups of Optimizations

## Example

Write an application that demonstrates the relative speed gain achieved by using the -Z option:

**z\test.c**
```c
struct MYSTRUCT
{
    int x;

    struct MYSTRUCT *Next;
};

#pragma option -Z
void Fast(struct MYSTRUCT *a)
{
    unsigned n;

    for(n = 0; n < 10000; n++)
        if(a->Next->x > 0)
            a->Next->x++;
}

#pragma option -Z-
void Slow(struct MYSTRUCT *a)
{
    unsigned n;

    for(n = 0; n < 10000; n++)
        if(a->Next->x > 0)
            a->Next->x++;
}

void main(void)
{
    struct MYSTRUCT a;

    a.x = 0;
    a.Next = &a;

    Fast(&a);
    Slow(&a);
}
```

The Fast() function is compiled with the -Z option enabled, whereas the -Z option is disabled for compilation of the Slow() function. The Fast() function operates 28% faster and is 2 bytes smaller than the Slow() function.

## *zXname*                                                   Rename Segment

- C
- BC 2.0
- C++
- BC 3.0/3.1
- CPP
- BCC
- TC++
- Local
- TCW/BCW
- #pragma

### Purpose
The -*zXname* option enables you to control the naming of segments, groups, and classes for where your applications code, data, and far data are placed. You use this option when you need code or data placed or grouped into specific segments.

### IDE Option
| | |
|---|---|
| Options I Compiler I Names I Code Segment | -z*Cname* |
| Options I Compiler I Names I Code Group | -z*Pname* |
| Options I Compiler I Names I Code Class | -z*Aname* |
| Options I Compiler I Names I Data Segment | -z*Rname* |
| Options I Compiler I Names I Data Grouft | -z*Sname* |
| Options I Compiler I Names I Data Class | -z*Tname* |
| Options I Compiler I Names I BBS Segment | -z*Dname* |
| Options I Compiler I Names I BBS Group | -z*Gname* |
| Options I Compiler I Names I BBS Class | -z*Bname* |
| Options I Compiler I Names I Far Data Segment | -z*Ename* |
| Options I Compiler I Names I Far Data Group | -z*Hname* |
| Options I Compiler I Names I Far Data Class | -z*Fname* |

### Default
The *filename* in the following tables denotes the name of the target module. The *objname* denotes the name of the far object.

### CODE

| Model | Segment | Group | Class |
|---|---|---|---|
| Tiny | -zC_TEXT | -zPDGROUP | -zACODE |
| Small | -zC_TEXT | (none) | -zACODE |
| Medium | -zC*filename*_TEXT | (none) | -zACODE |
| Compact | -zC_TEXT | (none) | -zACODE |
| Large | -zC*filename*_TEXT | (none) | -zACODE |
| Huge | -zC*filename*_TEXT | (none) | -zACODE |

## INITIALIZED DATA

| Model | Segment | Group | Class |
|---|---|---|---|
| Tiny | -zR_DATA | DGROUP | -zTDATA |
| Small | -zR_DATA | DGROUP | -zTDATA |
| Medium | -zR_DATA | DGROUP | -zTDATA |
| Compact | -zR*filename*_DATA | DGROUP | -zTDATA |
| Large | -zR*filename*_DATA | DGROUP | -zTDATA |
| Huge | -zR*filename*_DATA | (none) | -zTDATA |

## UNINITIALIZED DATA

| Model | Segment | Group | Class |
|---|---|---|---|
| Tiny | _BBS | DGROUP | -zBBBS |
| Small | _BBS | DGROUP | -zBBBS |
| Medium | _BBS | DGROUP | -zBBBS |
| Compact | *filename*_BBS | DGROUP | -zBBBS |
| Large | *filename*_BBS | DGROUP | -zBBBS |
| Huge | *filename*_BBS | (none) | -zBBBS |

## FAR DATA

| Model | Segment | Group | Class |
|---|---|---|---|
| All | -zE*objname*_FAR | (none) | -zFFAR_DATA |

## Usage

`BCC −z`*Xname* `SOURCE.C`

Rename the segment name associated with *X* to *name*.

`#pragma option −z`*Xname*

Same as above. The directive must appear between function definitions and object declarations to be effective.

`#pragma option −z`*X**

Restore the segment name associated with *X* to the name it was at the beginning of the source module.

`BCC −z`*X**name* `SOURCE.C`

Rename the segment name to the default name followed by *name*.

`#pragma option −z`*X**name*

Same as above. The directive must appear between function definitions and object declarations to be effective.

231

## Description

The compiler generates four types, or classes, of segments: CODE, DATA, BBS, and FAR_DATA. Program code is placed in the CODE segment. Data that is initialized to some value at the beginning of program execution is placed in the DATA segment. Data which does not need to be initialized is placed in the BBS segment. Far data is placed in the FAR_DATA segment. All the segments that are of the same class are physically placed next to each other in memory. For example, all the code in an application is in the CODE segment class. This means all the code segments in an application will be placed in one contiguous block of memory. You can create your own classes for the compiler to use with the -zA*name*, -zT*name*, -zB*name*, and -zF*name* for code, initialized data, uninitialized data, and far data. Note that the name of code segment classes used in Windows applications must end with the letters 'CODE.'

The compiler places code and the different types of data into specific 64K segments depending on the memory model. For example, all the code in an application compiled using the small memory model is placed in a segment called _TEXT. Because the size of a segment is limited to 64K and all the code in a small memory model application is placed in the _TEXT segment, all the code in a small memory application is placed in the same 64K segment. Placing all the code in the same segment ensures that all functions can be compiled using near code pointers. In a medium memory model application, the code is placed in the segment called *filename*_TEXT, where *filename* is the name of the module. This method of naming code segments allows your application as much program code as it needs provided the code in no one module exceeds 64K. You can write code in one module and have it placed in the same code as another module by renaming the code segment. For example, suppose you had a medium memory model application with a SOURCE and a MAIN module and the MAIN module contained the following code:

```
#pragma option -zCSOURCE_TEXT
void MainFunct(void)
{
  . . .
```

The #pragma option -zCSOURCE_TEXT directive renames the code segment for MainFunct() to SOURCE_TEXT. This places the code for MainFunct() into the same segment as the code in the SOURCE module. -zC*name*, -zR*name*, -zD*name*, and -zE*name* rename the segments for code, intialized data, uninitialized data, and far data, respectively.

Different segment classes can also be grouped into the same physical segment in memory. The best example of this is the segment groupings used to create the tiny memory model. All the segment classes, except FAR_DATA, are in a group called DGROUP. This means that the code, initialized data, and uninitialized data are all placed within the same 64K segment. The segment groupings used to create the small memory model place the DATA, BBS, and STACK segment classes all within the DGROUP grouping, thereby placing all three within the same 64K segment. This ensures near data pointers can be used to point to all three types of data. Only a few segment classes are associated with a segment grouping for the different memory models. Most segments are not associated with a group. You can place different segment classes within the same group in your source code to create your own custom memory models.

For example, the following will create a memory model in which the code segment is placed in the same segment as the initialized and uninitialized data, but the stack and dynamic data are in different segments:

```
BCC -mc -zPDGROUP SOURCE.C
```

The -mc option compiles the source code using the compact memory model. This memory model groups the initialized and uninitialized data segments into the DGROUP grouping. (See the -mc option reference listing for a figure on the default segments for the compact memory model.) The -zPDGROUP option places the code segment within the DGROUP.

You should use caution when renaming segments. The compiler is designed to handle six standard memory models: tiny, small, medium, compact, large, and huge. Renaming segments using the -z*Xname* option creates custom momory models that may or may not coincide with the pointer types. For example, consider following:

```
#pragma option -zCMY_SEGMENT
#include <stdio.h>

void far MyFunction(void)
{
   printf("This won't work!");
}
```

The above places the code for MyFunction() in a unique segment called MY_SEGMENT. If the above were compiled in a small memory model application, then the function call to printf() would default to a near function call. However, the function code for MyFunction() is located in MY_SEGMENT, whereas the code for printf() is located in the _TEXT segment.

### See Also

| | |
|---|---|
| mc | Use the Compact Memory Model |
| mh | Use the Huge Memory Model |
| ml | Use the Large Memory Model |
| mm | Use the Medium Memory Model |
| ms | Use the Small Memory Model |
| mt | Use the Tiny Memory Model |
| Chapter 5: P, P=*size* | Pack Code Segments |
| Chapter 6: A | Order Segments Alphabetically |
| Chapter 6: S | Order Segments Sequentially |

### Example

Write a small memory model application using the -zC*name* option to place a function in a different segment than the _TEXT segment.

**zx\test.h**
```
/* Declare a prototype to a function in a different segment */
unsigned far MyFunction(void);
```

**zx\main.c**

```
#include <stdio.h>
#include "test.h"

void main(void)
```

# PROJECTS
# AND
# TRANSFERS

# 3

When you write source code in an editor window and compile, the IDE will call the integrated compiler to create the object code file, and then call TLINK to create the executable file. This process works fine for small applications, but if your application requires that the source code be spread out among several different files, you will need to create a project and use the IDE's Project Manager to build the application.

There are many advantages to using projects. The primary advantage is that a project keeps a list of file dependencies for you and is much easier to use than manually recompiling changed files using the command line compiler or using the MAKE utility (see Chapter 4 for details on the MAKE utility). Another advantage is a project keeps one set of compiler options from affecting an application compiled with a different set of compiler options. Each project file contains information on the compiler option settings so that changes in the compiler options for one project do not affect any other project. For example, you can designate one project, called SMALL to compile using the small memory model and another project, called COMPACT using the compact memory model. Each time you load either the SMALL, or COMPACT project, the IDE will automatically set the correct memory model.

Each project also has an associated desktop file. This file keeps track of the screen layout and cursor location for the editor windows. If you have the [Options][Environment][Preferences][Desktop] menu item selected, then each time you load a project, the screen will be laid out exactly as you last left it down to the correct location of the cursor.

Also, if the IDE is started and there is only one project file in the current directory, the IDE will automatically load that project and the associated desktop. Loading a project then becomes as easy as changing to the proper directory and simply typing BC.

## CREATING A SIMPLE PROJECT

The most simple project you could create would contain one source code module compiled as a DOS application, such as the following HELLO.C application:

```
#include <stdio.h>

void main(void)
{
   printf("Hello, World!\n");
}
```

To create a project for HELLO.C which you'd use to build the HELLO.EXE application, you first select the [Project][Open] menu item, enter HELLO in the [Load Project File] menu item, and press return. The IDE will then either load the HELLO.PRJ if it already exists in the current directory, or, if it does not, the IDE will create HELLO.PRJ. The IDE will also display at the bottom of the screen the Project window containing the list of files in the project. For newly created projects, this file list will be empty. To add a file to the list, you either select [Project][Add item] or press the (Insert) key. This will bring up the "Add Item to Project List" menu. You can then either choose from the list of files or enter HELLO.C and press return.

To build the HELLO project, you select either [Compile][Make] or [Compile][Build], just as you would if you were not using a project. The Project Manager will use the IDE's integrated compiler along with the global options selected in the IDE menu to compile the HELLO.C source code. After the HELLO.OBJ file is created, the Project Manager then calls TLINK to create the HELLO.EXE executable file.

## MORE COMPLEX PROJECTS

Your projects can contain as many files as you need. Besides adding .C files to a project, you can also add .ASM, .CPP, .DEF, .LIB, .OBJ, .RC, and .RES files. The Project Manager will build the application correctly by properly handling each file in the project list. To do this, the Project Manager may need to call on other compilers besides the Integrated Compiler. That is, the Project Manager must transfer control of the build process to the source code *translator* that is appropriate for the source file. A translator is an application that translates a source file into another type of file. For example, the IDE translates your C and C++ code into object code using the integrated compiler. It also calls an external application to translate assembly language source files to object code using Borland's Turbo Assembler (TASM) and resource script files to binary resource script using Microsoft's Resource Compiler (RC). The IDE calls these translators by executing a *transfer item,* which will call either TASM or RC to compile the source code.

The Project Manager automatically selects one of the IDE's predefined source code translators for many project files based on the extension of the filename. For example, if the file has an .ASM extension, the Project Manager selects the TASM translator. Some files you add to a project, such as object code files with an .OBJ extension, do not need to be passed to a translator and are instead simply passed to TLINK during the linking stage. Table 3-1 lists the filename extensions and the corresponding translator selected by the Project Manager.

| ADDED FILE | CONTENTS | OUTPUT FILE | TRANSLATOR |
| --- | --- | --- | --- |
| filename.ASM | Assembly Language Source | filename.OBJ | TASM |
| filename.C | C Language Source | filename.OBJ | IDE Compiler |
| filename.CPP | C++ Language Source | filename.OBJ | IDE Compiler |
| filename.DEF | Module Definition File | filename.DEF | (none, passed to TLINK) |
| filename.LIB | Library File | filename.LIB | (none, passed to TLINK) |

| *filename*.OBJ | Object Code | *filename*.OBJ | (none, passed to TLINK) |
| *filename*.RC | Resource Script | *filename*.RES | Resource Compiler (prelink) |
| *filename*.RES | Binary Resource File | *filename*.RES | Resource Compiler (postlink) |

**Table 3-1 The translator assigned by the Project Manager for a given file extension**

## LOCAL OPTIONS

In the DOS IDE, you can change the translator or output filename assigned by the Project Manager, or tell the IDE to use different compiler options when the Project Manager compiles a certain file. This is done by modifying the local options associated with a file in the project list. Highlight the file in the Project window for which you'd like to modify the local options and either select the [Project][Local options] menu or press (Ctrl)-(O). This will display the "Override Options" menu, as shown in Figure 3-1.

Note that the IDE in Turbo C++ for Windows (TCW) does not support local options for files in the project list. Borland C++ for Windows (BCW) does support local compiler options.

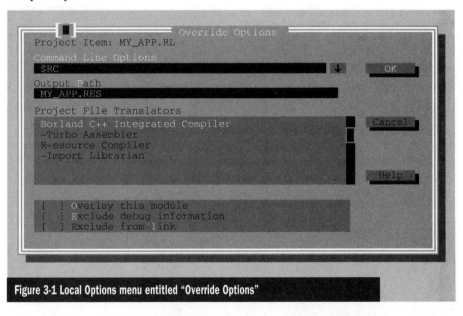

**Figure 3-1 Local Options menu entitled "Override Options"**

Normally the IDE will use the compiler options you set in the global menu. If you enter a compiler option in the [Command Line Options] menu box of the Local options menu, these options will override any global options for just that one file. For example, you could enter -h and -ff- in the [Command Line Options] menu box and the integrated compiler will use fast huge pointers and disable fast floating-point regardless of the settings in the [Options][Compiler][Code Generation] menu. See Chapter 2 for a complete listing of the available command line options.

You may also enter transfer macros into the [Command Line Options] menu box. A transfer macro either expands to a character string or instructs the compiler to perform some type of action. See the Transfer Macro Reference at the end this chapter for a complete listing of transfer macros.

The [Output path] menu box contains the filename the Project Manager expects to be the result from the translator. The contents of this box serve two purposes. One purpose is to allow the Project Manager to check on the time/date stamp of the file on the disk to see if it is out of date with the file in the project list and rebuild the file if necessary. The filename in this menu box is also used to expand the $OUTNAME macro. This macro in turn controls the filename passed to the translator as the expected output filename.

The [Overlay this module] and the [Exclude debug information] options are the equivalent of the -y and -v- command line compiler options, respectively. These options are described in Chapter 2. Selecting the [Exclude from link] menu item instructs the Project Manager not to pass the name in the [Output path] menu box to the linker. The Project Manager automatically checks this item for .RC and .RES files.

## DEFINING YOUR OWN TRANSLATORS

The [Project File Translators] menu allows you to specify the translator the Project Manager should use to compile the source code. The IDE comes with four predefined translators: Borland C++ Integrated Compiler, Turbo Assembler, Resource Compiler,

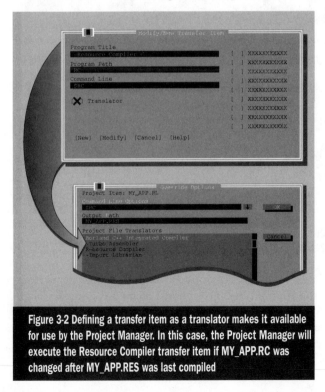

Figure 3-2 Defining a transfer item as a translator makes it available for use by the Project Manager. In this case, the Project Manager will execute the Resource Compiler transfer item if MY_APP.RC was changed after MY_APP.RES was last compiled

and the Import Librarian. You can select one of these predefined translators or you can define other transfer item translators and assign them to a file in the project list using the Local options menu. You do this by first defining a new transfer item using the [Options][Transfer] menu and ensuring the [Translator] menu item is selected as shown in Figure 3-2 for the Resource Compiler transfer item definition.

Note that since the IDE in both Turbo C++ for Windows (TCW) and Borland C++ for Windows (BCW) do not support transfer items, they cannot support user-defined translators.

Not all transfer items are translators. If the [Translator] menu item is not selected, then the transfer item is only available for manual use from the IDE's [System] menu. Nontranslator transfer items, such as GREP, access utilities supplied with the BC++ compiler package. For example, the GREP transfer item accesses the GREP.EXE utility.

The following is a list of the predefined translator and nontranslator transfer items and their definitions. Note that the '~' symbol in the title causes the following letter to be highlighted in the [System] menu.

## Translators

Turbo Assembler:
```
Program Title
 ~Turbo Assembler

Program Path
 TASM

Command Line
 /MX /ZI /O $TASM
```

Resource Compiler:
```
Program Title
 R~esource Compiler

Program Path
 RC

Command Line
 $RC
```

Import Librarian:
```
Program Title
 ~Import Librarian

Program Path
 IMPLIB

Command Line
 $IMPLIB
```

## Nontranslators

GREP:
```
Program Title
 ~GREP
```

```
    Program Path
     GREP

    Command Line
     -n+ $MEM(64) $NOSWAP $PROMPT $CAP MSG(GREP2MSG)void *.c $SAVE PROMPT
```

Turbo Debugger:
```
    Program Title
     Turbo ~Debugger

    Program Path
     td

    Command Line
     $EXENAME
```

Turbo Profiler:
```
    Program Title
     Turbo ~Profiler

    Program Path
     tprof

    Command Line
     $EXENAME
```

# CONTROLLING THE PROJECT MANAGER

Normally the Project Manager executes all the translators for the files in the project list and, if there are no errors, calls the linker to create the executable file. There may be times when you'd like the Project Manager to stop when it encounters an error or warning so that the problem can be corrected before the build process continues. This is done in the [Options][Make] menu. Here you select either [Warnings], [Errors], [Fatal Errors], or [All sources processed]. The [Warnings] selection instructs the Project Manager to stop the build process if it encounters a warning message. With the [Errors] selection, the Project Manager will continue the build process even if there are warnings but will stop the build if an error is encountered. The [Fatal Errors] setting, which is the default, will only stop the build process for a fatal error, such as an inability to open a file in the project list. Selecting the [All sources processd] item will process all files in the project list.

# AUTODEPENDENCIES

All the BC++ compilers create object code files, which contain information on the include files used to build them (see the -X option in Chapter 2). If the [Check auto-dependencies] menu item is checked in the [Options][Make] menu, then the Project Manager will use this information to see if one of the include files has changed since the object file was compiled. If autodependencies are not enabled, then the Project Manager will not check on the include files and will only compile the files in the project list that are newer than the object code file.

You can view filenames stored in the object code files that the Project Manager will use for autodependency checking by selecting the [Project][Include files] for a file in the project list. The following is a list of include files used by an application that used the #include <fstream.h> directive. Note that the filenames for all the #include directives used in the FSTREAM.H file are also stored.

```
Include files         Location
    FSTREAM.H         ..\BORLANDC\INCLUDE
    IOSTREAM.H        ..\BORLANDC\INCLUDE
    MEM.H             ..\BORLANDC\INCLUDE
    _DEFS.H           ..\BORLANDC\INCLUDE
    _NULL.H           ..\BORLANDC\INCLUDE
```

You can load any of the files listed in the [Project][Include] window into an editor window by highlighting the desired file and pressing (Enter). You can only use the [Project] [Include] menu item on files that have been successfully compiled into .OBJ files with autodependency information (see the -X option in Chapter 2).

## DEFAULT LIBRARIES

The Project Manager uses the default libraries appropriate for the selected memory model. Tables 3-2 and 3-3 list the default libraries for each memory model.

|  | TINY | SMALL | COMPACT |
|---|---|---|---|
| Reg. DOS Startup | C0T.OBJ | C0S.OBJ | C0C.OBJ |
| Compatibility DOS Startup | C0FT.OBJ | C0FS.OBJ | C0FC.OBJ |
| Windows .EXE Startup | N/A | C0WS.OBJ | C0WC.OBJ |
| Windows .DLL Startup | N/A | C0DS.OBJ | C0DC.OBJ |
| Floating-point Library | MATHS.LIB | MATHS.LIB | MATHC.LIB |
| Run-time Library | CS.LIB | CS.LIB | CC.LIB |
| Windows Run-time Library | N/A | CWINS.LIB | CWINC.LIB |

Table 3-2 Default libraries for the tiny, small, and compact memory models

|  | MEDIUM | LARGE | HUGE |
|---|---|---|---|
| Reg. DOS Startup | C0M.OBJ | C0L.OBJ | C0H.OBJ |
| Compatibility DOS Startup | C0FM.OBJ | C0FL.OBJ | C0FH.OBJ |
| Windows .EXE Startup | C0WM.OBJ | C0WL.OBJ | N/A |
| Windows .DLL Startup | C0DM.OBJ | C0DL.OBJ | N/A |
| Floating-point Library | MATHM.LIB | MATHL.LIB | MATHC.LIB |
| Run-time Library | CM.LIB | CL.LIB | CC.LIB |
| Windows Run-time Library | CWINM.LIB | CWINL.LIB | N/A |

Table 3-3 Default libraries for the medium, large, and huge memory models

You can override the use of these files by listing your own library files in the project list. To override the startup file, you should have your startup file as the first file in the project list. The name of this file must have the name C0x?????.OBJ, where the 'x' is the letter corresponding to the memory model. For example, to use a startup file for the large memory model, you could name the file C0LMINE.OBJ. To override one of the standard libraries, you need to name the file Cx?????.LIB, where again 'x' corresponds to the memory model. Note that if you are overriding the standard library that the Project Manager will not link the floating-point emulation library. If you are overriding the standard library, you must explicitly list one of the MATHx.LIB files in the project list if you would like it to be linked with your application.

# PROJECT NOTES

You can keep a list of notes about a project using the Project Notes window. You display this window by selecting the [Window][Project Notes] menu item. This is a good place to keep notes on revision history, bug reports, or other information related to the project. The contents of the Project Notes window are automatically saved with the project file.

# TRANSFER MACRO REFERENCE

The following is a detailed reference listing of the transfer macros. You use these macros in either a transfer item or on the command line of the local options for a project file. Each transfer macro is listed in alphabetical order and includes a detailed description, cross-reference, and example. On the righthand side of each macro heading is the macro type. There are three different types of macros: Instruction, State, and Filename. An Instruction macro, such as $CAP EDIT, instructs the IDE to perform some type of action. A State macro, such as $COL, expands to a character string and reflects a particular state of the IDE. For example, the $COL macro expands the column position of the cursor in the editor. The filename macros either extract information out of a full pathname, such as the drive or directory, or expand to a full pathname, such as the name of the project file.

## $CAP EDIT                                                        Instruction

### Description
The $CAP EDIT macro instructs the IDE to capture any text sent to the DOS standard output by a Transfer Item application so that you can edit the text in an IDE window. The IDE creates a temporary file and uses the DOS redirection facility to send the output to the temporary file. After the Transfer Item terminates and control returns to the IDE, the IDE opens a new window that contains the contents of the temporary file.

This capture process will only work if the Transfer Item uses the standard output recognized by DOS. Text output sent directly to the screen will not be captured.

### See Also
$CAP MSG(*filter*)

### Example

Write a Transfer Item that will execute a DOS command and capture the output to an IDE window. We then define the Transfer Item as follows:

```
Program Title
 Capture DOS ~Output

Program Path
 COMMAND

Command Line
 /c $NOSWAP $CAP EDIT $PROMPT
```

The /c command line parameter instructs the COMMAND shell to exit after completing the command. The $PROMPT item instructs the IDE to prompt you for additional command line parameters. You can then enter something such as "dir \ borlandc\examples\*.cpp /w" to load all the example filenames supplied with BC++ into the Transfer Output window. The IDE would then execute the DOS command and load the following:

```
C:\PDG\CH3 >dir \borlandc\examples\*.cpp /w

 Volume in drive C is PETERSON
 Volume Serial Number is 172C-516E
  Directory of C:\BORLANDC\EXAMPLES

  DEF2.CPP     LIST2.CPP    VCIRC.CPP    VPOINT.CPP   BITMAP.CPP
  DLLDEMO.CPP  DLLSHELL.CPP TODODLGS.CPP TODOLIST.CPP TODOWIN.CPP
  WHELLO.CPP
    11 file(s)   62263 bytes
                 3401728 bytes free
```

You can then cut and paste the text in the window or save the entire window as a new file using the [File][Save As] IDE menu item.

# $CAP MSG(*filter*)                                                    Instruction

### Description

The $CAP MSG(*filter*) transfer macro is used in four of the IDE's predefined Transfer Items:

```
GREP                 uses $CAP MSG(GREP2MSG.EXE)
IMPLIB               uses $CAP MSG(IMPL2MSG.EXE)
Resource Compiler    uses $CAP MSG(RC2MSG.EXE)
TASM                 uses $CAP MSG(TASM2MSG.EXE)
```

These four transfer filters convert the output from GREP, IMPLIB, TASM, and RC into a format that is compatible with the IDE's Message window. Borland includes the source code to these four filters in the BORLANDC \ EXAMPLES directory as the following files: GREP2MSG.C, IMPL2MSG.C, RC2MSG.C, and TASM2MSG.C.

### See Also
$CAP EDIT

## Example

Write a transfer item which loads all lines of source code that contain the word under the cursor into the message window. The GREP transfer item is a very useful programming tool. The drawback is that any word you'd like GREP to locate must be typed into the IDE's prompt box. We can, however, write a modified GREP transfer item such that the item will isolate the word under the cursor and pass it to GREP. This new transfer item requires using the following application called GREPWORD:

**grepword.cpp**

```cpp
#include <fstream.h>
#include <stdlib.h>
#include <ctype.h>
#include <process.h>

int isnum(char *Str)
{
    if(atoi(Str) == 0)
    {
      if(Str[0] != '0')
        return(0);
    }
    return(1);
}

int main(int NumArg, char *ArgStr[])
{
    cout << "\nGREPWORD Application\n";
    cout << "by Mark Peterson, 1991\n\n";

    // Check for valid arguments
    if((NumArg < 4) || !isnum(ArgStr[1]) || !isnum(ArgStr[2]))
    {
      cerr << "This application is intended for use as an ";
      cerr << "IDE Transfer Item\n";
      exit(-1);
    }

    // Open the file for input
    ifstream File(ArgStr[3]);
    if(!File)
    {
      cerr << "Unable to open file '" << ArgStr[3];
      cerr << "' for input.\n";
      exit(-1);
    }

    char LineStr[201], WordStr[201];
    unsigned Line = atoi(ArgStr[2]);

    // Count down to the appropriate line number
    while(Line--)
    {
      File.getline(LineStr, sizeof(LineStr));
      unsigned Count = File.gcount();
      if(Count == (sizeof(LineStr) -1))
      {
```

```
            cerr << "File " << ArgStr[3] << " has a line containing ";
            cerr << "more than 200 characters\n";
            exit(-1);
        }
    }

    // Extract the word from LineStr
    unsigned Col = atoi(ArgStr[1]);
    unsigned StartOfWord = 0, LookingForWord = 1;
    for(unsigned n = 0; n < Col; n++)
    {
        if(LookingForWord)
        {
            if(isalnum(LineStr[n]))
            {
                StartOfWord = n;
                LookingForWord = 0;
            }
        }
        else
        {
            if(!isalnum(LineStr[n]))
                LookingForWord = 1;
        }
    }

    n = StartOfWord;
    while(isalnum(LineStr[n]))
    {
        WordStr[n - StartOfWord] = LineStr[n];
        n++;
    }
    WordStr[n - StartOfWord] = 0;

    spawnlp(P_OVERLAY, "GREP", "GREP", "-n+", WordStr, ArgStr[4], 0L);
}
```

The GREPWORD application uses the following syntax:

```
GREPWORD Column Row File Filelist
```

GREPWORD uses the Column and Row parameters supplied by the IDE via the transfer item to locate a specific word in File. It then executes GREP and passes it the word identified by the Column and Row parameters. The transfer item must then be written to capture the output of GREP and convert it to a format compatible with the Message window as follows:

```
Program Title
 GREP ~Word

Program Path
 GREPWORD

Command Line
 $NOSWAP $SAVE ALL $COL $LINE $EDNAME *$EXT($EDNAME)
 $CAP MSG(GREP2MSG)
```

247

In the Command Line above, the $NOSWAP macro prevents the user screen from being displayed. The $SAVE ALL saves all modified editor files to the disk so that GREPWORD and GREP may use them. The $COL and $LINE macros expand to the cursor location within the currently active editor window. The $EDNAME expands to the name of the currently active editor window. The $EXT macro expands the file extension of the editor window filename. The $CAP MSG(GREP2MSG) macro captures the output of GREP and converts it for use by the Message window using the GREP2MSG.EXE application.

# $COL                                                        State

### Description
The $COL macro expands to the cursor's column number location in the current editor file. This is useful if you are writing a transfer item that needs to locate a word or character in the current editor file. The $COL macro expands to zero if the current window is not an editor file, such as the project window.

### See Also
$LINE, $EDNAME

### Example
Write a transfer item using the $COL state macro. The following is the transfer item used in the $CAP MSG(*filter*) macro:

```
Program Title
 GREP ~Word

Program Path
 GREPWORD

Command Line
 $NOSWAP $SAVE ALL $COL $LINE $EDNAME *$EXT($EDNAME)
 $CAP MSG(GREP2MSG)
```

# $CONFIG                                                     State

### Description
The $CONFIG macro expands to the name of the IDE's current configuration file. This allows a transfer item to modify the IDE's configuration file. When this macro is used, the IDE will save the current configuration file, execute the transfer item, and then reload the configuration file after the transfer item has terminated.

**See Also**
$PRJNAME

**Example**
Write a transfer item which compiles a new set of keyboard macros and adds them to the current configuration file using TEMC:

```
Program Title
 Compile ~Macros

Program Path
 TEMC

Command Line
 $EDNAME $CONFIG
```

The above transfer item will execute TEMC, which will compile the macros defined in the active editor window and add to the current configuration file.


# $DEF                                                                    State

---

**Description**
The $DEF macro expands to the definitions listed in the [Options][Compiler][Code generation][Defines] menu item. You use the transfer item macro to pass project translators any macro definitions defined globally throughout the project.

**See Also**
$INC, $LIB

**Example**
Modify the Resource Compiler transfer item to pass RC the macro definitions defined in the [Options][Compiler][Code generation][Defines] menu item. The default transfer for the RC is as follows:

```
Program Title
 R~esource Compiler

Program Path
 RC

Command Line
 $RC
```

You modify the RC transfer item to use the IDE menu definitions by changing the Command Line above to the following:

```
-d$DEF $RC
```

## $DEP(*list*) Instruction

### Description

This macro allows you to instruct the Project Manager to recompile the target module if one of the files in *list* has changed since the target module was last built. The files in *list* can be separated by a space, comma, or semicolon.

This transfer macro only applies to translators and is normally used as a local option for a project file. Any explicit dependencies listed in $DEP() are checked after the Project Manager has looked for any autodependencies. Note that the Project Manager automatically tracks dependencies associated with the include files for C or C++ source code, but not those for resource script or assembly language source files.

### See Also

Autodependencies

### Example

Write the local options associated with an .RC such that the IDE's Project Manager will rebuild the file if one of the component files listed in the .RC file changes. The WFRACTAL.RC file in Chapter 10 includes references to the following files: ABOUT.DLG, ATPOINT.CUR, WFRACTAL.ICO, and WFRACTAL.H. If one of these files changes, then WFRACTAL.RC needs to be rebuilt. You instruct the IDE's Project Manager to do this by writing a [Project][Local Options]{Command Line} menu item for WFRACTAL.RC as follows:

```
$SAVE ALL $DEP(ABOUT.DLG, ATPOINT.CUR, WFRACTAL.ICO, WFRACTAL.H)
```

The $SAVE ALL macro saves all modified editor files before compiling. This ensures both ABOUT.DLG and WFRACTAL.H are saved to the disk before they are used by the Resource Compiler.

## $DIR(*pathname*) Filename

### Description

The $DIR(*pathname*) macro extracts the directory portion of *pathname*, i.e., the macro $DIR(C:\SUB_DIR\NAME.EXT) expands to SUB_DIR. This is normally used to construct a full pathname from another pathname. For example, the $IMPLIB macro uses the following to construct the pathname for the .LIB file:

```
$DRIVE($EXENAME)$DIR($EXENAME)$NAME($EXENAME).LIB
```

The $EXENAME expands the full pathname for the target application. If the full pathname for the target application were C:\SUB_DIR\NAME.EXE, then the above would expand to C:\SUB_DIR\NAME.LIB.

**See Also**
$DRIVE(), $EXT(), $NAME()

**Example**
Write a macro that extracts a pathname for a library file using the $DIR macro:

```
$DRIVE($EXENAME)$DIR($EXENAME)$NAME($EXENAME).LIB
```

# $DRIVE(*pathname*)                          Filename

**Description**
The $DRIVE() macro extracts the drive portion of the pathname. This is normally used to construct a new pathname from some other pathname.

**See Also**
$DIR(), $EXT(), $NAME()

**Example**
Write a macro that extracts a pathname for a library file using the $DRIVE macro:

```
$DRIVE($EXENAME)$DIR($EXENAME)$NAME($EXENAME).LIB
```

# $EDNAME                                     Filename

The $EDNAME macro expands to the full pathname of the currently active editor file or, if the macro is executed by the Project Manager, it expands to the name of the project file being compiled; otherwise the macro expands to a NULL string. This macro would normally be used to create a transfer item that needs to read or modify the file in the currently active editor window or for translators.

**See Also**
$EXENAME, $OUTNAME, $PRJNAME

**Example**
Write a transfer item using the $EDNAME state macro. The following is the transfer item used in the $CAP MSG(*filter*) macro:

```
Program Title
 GREP ~Word

Program Path
 GREPWORD
```

```
Command Line
  $NOSWAP $SAVE ALL $COL $LINE $EDNAME *$EXT($EDNAME)
  $CAP MSG(GREP2MSG)
```

# $ERRCOL, $ERRLINE, $ERRNAME                       State

### Description
The IDE Message window contains information on the column, row, and filename associated with each line. The $ERRCOL, $ERRLINE, and $ERRNAME macros expand to the information associated with the highlighted line if the Message window is currently active. This would normally be used to write a transfer item that needs to manipulate specific errors sent to the Message window.

   Note that the [Options][Environment][Preferences][Save Old Messages] menu item must be selected or the messages in the Message window will be erased before the transfer item executes.

### See Also
$COL, $LINE, $EDNAME

### Example
Write a transfer item that captures the column, line, and filename associated with an error in the Message window into the Transfer Output window. This is done using the $CAP EDIT macro as follows:

```
Program Title
  Capture Error Info

Program Path
  COMMAND

Command Line
  /c echo $ERRCOL $ERRLINE $ERRNAME $CAP EDIT
```

# $EXENAME                                         Filename

The $EXENAME macro expands to the full pathname for the target application. The target application is usually the project name with an .EXE extension. If there is no project open, then the macro uses the current editor file as the basis for the pathname. If the target application is a DLL, i.e., the Windows DLL option is selected in the [Options][Linker] IDE menu, then the $EXENAME macro uses the .DLL extension instead of the .EXE extension.

### See Also
$EDNAME, $OUTNAME, $PRJNAME

**Example**

Write a macro that extracts a pathname for a library file using the $EXENAME macro:

```
$DRIVE($EXENAME)$DIR($EXENAME)$NAME($EXENAME).LIB
```

# $EXT(*pathname*)            Filename

## Description

The $EXT(*pathname*) macro extracts the extension portion of the pathname including the leading period. For example, the macro $EXT(C: \ SUB_DIR\FILE.EXT) expands to .EXT. This macro is normally used to construct a pathname for the transfer item based on an existing pathname.

## See Also

$DIR(), $DRIVE(), $NAME()

## Example

Write a transfer item that loads a directory listing of all the files with the same extension as the currently active editor file into the transfer output window:

```
Program Title
 Files by E~xt

Program Path
 COMMAND

Command Line
 /c $NOSWAP $CAP EDIT dir *$EXT($EDNAME)
```

The $NOSWAP macro instructs the compiler not to swap to the user screen while executing the macro. The $CAP EDIT macro captures the output of the DOS 'dir' command. The *$EXT($EDNAME) macro expands to the extension of the file in the currently active editor window.

# $IMPLIB            Instruction

## Description

The $IMPLIB macro is intended for use with the Import Library transfer item. The macro expands to one of the following depending on the setting in the [Options][MAKE][Generate Import Library] menu:

```
$NOSWAP $CAP MSG(IMPL2MSG) $DRIVE($EXENAME)$DIR($EXENAME)$NAME($EXENAME).LIB $EXENAME
$NOSWAP $CAP MSG(IMPL2MSG) $DRIVE($EXENAME)$DIR($EXENAME)$NAME($EXENAME).LIB filename.DEF
```

The $NOSWAP macro tells the IDE not to swap the display to the user's screen. The $CAP MSG(IMPL2MSG) macro tells the IDE to capture the output and convert it to a format compatible with the Message window using the IMPL2MSG.EXE application. The $DRIVE($EXENAME)$DIR($EXENAME)$NAME($EXENAME).LIB expression constructs a .LIB filename based on the target executable filename. The last $EXENAME passes TLIB the full pathname of the target executable.

If the [Options][MAKE][Generate Import Library] menu is set to Use DEF File Exports, then when the macro expands it will use the .DEF file listed in the project.

### See Also
$RC, $TASM

### Example
See the predefined Import Library transfer item.

## $INC                                                                   State

### Description
The $INC macro expands to the contents of the [Options][Directories][Include] menu item. You normally use this macro in a transfer item translator to pass the location of include files to the translator.

### See Also
$LIB

### Example
Modify the TASM transfer item to pass the location of include files to TASM:

```
Program Title
~Turbo Assembler

Program Path
TASM

Command Line
$SAVE CUR /MX /ZI /O /I$INC $TASM
```

The /I$INC expands to pass TASM the location of include files listed in the [Options][Directories][Include] menu item.

# $LIB

**State**

## Description
The $LIB macro expands to the contents of the [Options][Directories][Libraries] menu item. This macro would normally be used to define a transfer item that executes a linker other than TLINK. This macro could also be used to specify a directory location used by a library manager.

## See Also
$INC

## Example
Write a transfer item that creates/updates an import library in the default library directory:

```
Program Title
 Update ~MY_LIB

Program Path
 IMPLIB

Command Line
 $NOSWAP $CAP MSG(IMPL2MSG) $LIB\MY_LIB $EXENAME
```

# $LINE

**State**

## Description
The $LINE macro expands to the line number of the cursor's location in the currently active editor window. The macro expands to zero if no editor file is active.

## See Also
$COL, $ERRLINE

## Example
Write a transfer item using the $COL state macro. The following is the transfer item used in the $CAP MSG(*filter*) macro:

```
Program Title
 GREP ~Word

Program Path
 GREPWORD
```

```
Command Line
 $NOSWAP $SAVE ALL  $COL $LINE $EDNAME *$EXT($EDNAME)
 $CAP MSG(GREP2MSG)
```

# $MEM(kb)                                    Instruction

The IDE needs to set aside a portion of memory for use by a transfer item before the transfer item is executed. The $MEM(kb) macro tells the IDE how much memory is required by the transfer item in kilobytes. For example, the macro $MEM(64) tells the IDE to set aside 64K of memory. The IDE will then set aside that much memory or as much as it can, whichever is less. If a macro is executed that does not contain a $MEM(kb) macro, then the IDE sets aside as much memory as it can.

Note that the IDE uses a considerable amount of memory during debugging while stepping through a program. To regain this memory, press (Ctrl)-(F2).

This macro is ineffective when used on an 80386 machine or better. On these machines, the IDE will always set aside 640K or as much memory as it can.

## See Also
$NOSWAP, $PROMPT

## Example
Write a transfer item with the $MEM(64) that executes the DOS 5.0 MEM command and capture the output:

```
Program Title
 Check $MEM(64)

Program Path
 COMMAND

Command Line
 /c mem $NOSWAP $CAP EDIT $MEM(64)
```

# $NAME(*filename*)                              Filename

## Description
The $NAME(*filename*) macro extracts the base portion of the filename. For example, the macro $NAME(C:\SUB_DIR\FILE.EXT) expands to FILE.

## See Also
$DIR(), $DRIVE(), $EXT()

**Example**

Write a macro that extracts a pathname for a library file using the $DIR macro:

```
$DRIVE($EXENAME)$DIR($EXENAME)$NAME($EXENAME).LIB
```

## $NOSWAP                                                          Instruction

### Description

The IDE will normally display the user screen when executing a transfer item. The $NOSWAP macro instructs the IDE to display a small popup box to indicate which transfer item is running rather than swapping to the user screen. You would normally use this macro whenever the output of the transfer item is captured with either the $CAP EDIT or the $CAP MSG(*filter*) macro.

### See Also

$MEM(), $PROMPT

### Example

Write a transfer item using the $NO SWAP macro. The following is the transfer item used in the $CAP MSG(*filter*) macro:

```
Program Title
  GREP ~Word

Program Path
  GREPWORD

Command Line
  $NOSWAP $SAVE ALL  $COL $LINE $EDNAME *$EXT($EDNAME)
  $CAP MSG(GREP2MSG)
```

## $OUTNAME                                                          Filename

### Example

The $OUTNAME macro expands to the full pathname for the currently active editor window. If the macro is executed by the Project Manager as part of a translator, the macro expands to the Output Path for the file being compiled. For example, the $OUTNAME macro, when used with the WFRACTAL.CPP file as the active window, expands to:

```
C:\PDG\CH10\WFRACTAL\WFRACTAL.OBJ
```

Any changes in either the [Project][Local Options][Output Path] or the [Options][Directories][Output] will also modify the expansion of the $OUTNAME macro. The $OUTNAME macro expands to a NULL string if the currently active window is not an editor window.

### See Also
$EDNAME, $EXENAME, $PRJNAME

### Example
Write a transfer item translator that updates a library with the .OBJ file associated with the currently active editor window:

```
Program Title
 Update Project Library

Program Path
 TLIB

Command Line
 $DRIVE($EXENAME)$DIR($EXENAME)$NAME($EXENAME).LIB -+$OUTNAME
```

## $PRJNAME                                              Filename

### Description
The $PRJNAME expands to the name of the currently active project file. It expands to a NULL string if no project file is open.

### See Also
$EDNAME, $EXENAME, $OUTNAME

### Example
Write a macro which extracts a pathname for a library file using the $PRJNAME macro:

```
$DRIVE($PRJNAME)$DIR($PRJNAME)$NAME($PRJNAME).LIB
```

## $PROMPT                                               Instruction

### Description
The $PROMPT macro instructs the IDE to prompt you for parameters to add to the command line of the transfer item before it is executed. You can then either enter the additional parameters manually or press the down arrow key and select/modify a previous command for that transfer item. Note that the entire command line is expanded regardless of the position of the $PROMPT macro within the command line.

### See Also
$NOSWAP, $MEM(kb)

**Example**

Write a transfer item to execute any DOS command using the $PROMPT macro:

```
Program Title
DOS Command

Program Path
COMMAND

Command Line
/c $PROMPT
```

## $RC                                                              Instruction

**Description**

The $RC macro is intended to be used with the predefined Resource Compiler transfer item. It expands in one of two ways depending on whether the expansion is associated with the local option of a project file or is executed by the IDE Project Manager to bind a .RES file to the target executable. If the $RC file macro is used in the [Project][Local Options][Command Line Options] menu item box, then the macro expands as follows:

```
$SAVE CUR $NOSWAP $CAP MSG(RC2MSG) -R -I$INC -FO $OUTNAME $EDNAME
```

The $SAVE CUR macro saves the file being compiled. The $NOSWAP prevents the user screen from being displayed. The $CAP MSG(RC2MSG) captures the output of the resource compiler and converts it to a format compatible with the Message window using the RC2MSG.EXE application. The -R command instructs the Resource Compiler to only create, but not bind, the .RES file. The -I$INC macro tells the resource compiler the location of the include files. The -FO $OUTNAME parameter instructs the Resource Compiler to name the resulting binary resource file the filename listed in the [Project][Local Options][Output Path] menu item. The $EDNAME passes the Resource Compiler the name of the file being compiled.

If the macro is executed by the Project Manager after the executable file has been created, then the macro expands as the following:

```
$NOSWAP $CAP MSG(RC2MSG) ResourceName $EXENAME
```

If there is a file in the project list with an .RES extension, then this filename is used for the ResourceName. If there is no file with an .RES extension, but there is a file with an .RC extension, then the ResourceName will be the filename expanded by the $OUTNAME for the .RC file. If there is no file with an .RES or .RC extension, then ResourceName expands to a NULL string, which causes the Resource Compiler to convert the .EXE file to one compatible with Windows 3.0.

**See Also**
$IMPLIB, $TASM

**Example**

Modify the Resource Compiler transfer macro to save all modified files before executing:

```
Program Title
 R~esource Compiler

Program Path
 RC

Command Line
 $SAVE ALL $RC
```

# $SAVE ALL                                             Instruction

The $SAVE ALL macro instructs the IDE to save to the disk any files that have changed before executing the transfer item. The files are saved without prompting. This macro is equivalent to selecting the [Files][Save All] menu item in the IDE. You would normally use this macro if the transfer item needs to use a file that may have been edited in an editor window that is not automatically checked by the Project Manager's autodependency checking. For example, the Project Manager cannot check for autodependencies associated with .RC files and therefore does not know which files need to be saved. This means that if you modify an include file used by a resource file and build the application without saving the .H file to the disk, the Resource Compiler will use the old .H file instead of the new one.

**See Also**

$SAVE CUR, $SAVE PROMPT

**Example**

Modify the Resource Compiler transfer macro to save all modified files before executing:

```
Program Title
 R~esource Compiler

Program Path
 RC

Command Line
 $SAVE ALL $RC
```

# $SAVE CUR                                             Instruction

**Description**

The $SAVE CUR macro saves the currently active editor window before executing the transfer item. The file is saved without prompting. If the macro is executed by the

Project Manager, then the IDE saves the file being compiled. A transfer item normally uses this macro if it either uses or modifies editor files, such as the GREP transfer item. A translator transfer item can also use this macro to save the file being compiled so that any modifications made in an editor window are updated to the disk file used by the translator.

**See Also**
$SAVE ALL, $SAVE PROMPT

**Example**
Rewrite the GREP transfer item to save the currently active editor window:

```
Program Title
 ~GREP

Program Path
 GREP

Command Line
 $SAVE CUR —n+ $MEM(64) $NOSWAP $PROMPT $CAP MSG(GREP2MSG)void *.c
```

# $SAVE PROMPT                                                    Instruction

---

The $SAVE PROMPT macro instructs the IDE to prompt you to save all modified files in the editor windows. For example, if you execute a transfer item containing the $SAVE PROMPT macro or the Project Manager calls a translator that contains the macro, and the file MYFILE.CPP in one of the editor windows has been changed, the IDE will display the following:

```
WARNING:
  MYFILE.CPP
  not saved.  Save?
```

**See Also**
$SAVE ALL, $SAVE CUR

**Example**
One flaw in the GREP transfer item definition is that it does not save any of the files in the editor windows before executing the transfer. This can sometimes cause GREP to be out of synch with the files in the editor windows. Rewrite the GREP transfer item to prompt you to save all files:

```
Program Title
 ~GREP

Program Path
 GREP
```

```
Command Line
$SAVE PROMPT —n+ $MEM(64) $NOSWAP $PROMPT $CAP MSG(GREP2MSG)void *.c
```

## $TASM                                                    Instruction

### Description

The $TASM macro is intended for use with the Turbo Assembler. The macro expands as follows:

```
$NOSWAP $SAVE CUR $CAP MSG(TASM2MSG) $EDNAME $OUTNAME
```

The $NOSWAP macro instructs the IDE not to display the user screen while executing TASM. The $SAVE CURR tells the IDE to first save the currently active editor window, or, if the transfer item was executed by the Project Manager, to save the file being compiled. The $CAP MSG(TASM2MSG) macro instructs the IDE to capture the output of TASM and convert it to a format compatible with the Message window using the TASM2MSG.EXE application. The $EDNAME macro expands the filename for the current editor file or file being compiled. The $OUTNAME macro expands to the associated .OBJ file filename.

### Example

Modify the TASM transfer item to pass the location of include files to TASM using the $TASM macro:

```
Program Title
~Turbo Assembler

Program Path
TASM

Command Line
$SAVE CUR /MX /ZI /O /I$INC $TASM
```

The /I$INC expands to pass TASM the location of include files listed in the [Options][Directories][Include] menu item.

## $WRITEMSG(*filename*)                                     Instruction

### Description

The WRITEMSG(*filename*) macro copies the contents of the Message window to *filename*. This macro would normally be used to pass the contents of the Message window to a transfer item.

Note that the [Options][Environment][Preferences][Save Old Messages] menu item must be selected or the messages in the Message window will be erased before the transfer item executes.

### See Also
$CAP MSG(), $ERRCOL, $ERRLINE, $ERRNAME

### Example
You use the $WRITEMSG() macro to send the contents of the Message window to any legal DOS file or device. Write a transfer item using $WRITEMSG to send the contents of the Message window to the printer:

```
Program Path
 Print Message Window

Program Path
 COMMAND

Command Line
 /C $NOSWAP $WRITEMSG(PRN)
```

## Project Utility Reference
The BC++ compiler package comes with several utilities to help manage your project. These utilities are normally located in the \ BORLANDC \ BIN directory.

# PRJ2MAK

### Purpose
The PRJ2MAK utility will convert a project file (.PRJ) to a make file (.MAK). The .MAK file can then be used with Borland's MAKE.EXE utility.

### Syntax
```
PRJ2MAK prjfile[.PRJ] [makefile.MAK] [cfgfile.CFG]
```

If you execute the PRJ2MAK utility with only a filename without an extension, such as MYAPP, then the utility will attempt to convert a file called MYAPP.PRJ to MYAPP.MAK and use the configuration file MYAPP.CFG if it can be found. If you execute PRJ2MAK with the .PRJ and .MAK text/file explicitly listed on the command line, but not the .CFG file, then the utility will look for a .CFG with the same base name as the .PRJ file.

### Description
There are times when you may want to compile an application without using the IDE or you may just wish to see a text output of the build process. The PRJ2MAK utility converts a project file to a readable .MAK text file that can be used with Borland's MAKE.EXE utility.

The make file created by PRJ2MAK uses virtually all the information contained in the .PRJ file: compiler options, linker options, libraries, the include and library paths, etc. Most of this information will be placed in a temporary .CFG file when MAKE builds the .MAK file.

You should note that the PRJ2MAK utility does not always create a .MAK file that corresponds 100% with the original .PRJ file. For example, the warning message options created for the .CFG file are typically incorrect. Also it translates the $DEP() macro into a format that is incompatible with the MAKE utility.

## See Also
Chapter 4 on the MAKE utility.

## Example
Create a simple project file and convert it to a make file. The following make file was created from the HELLO.C application in Chapter 2.

```
prj2mak hello
```

The PRJ2MAK utility reads the information in the HELLO.PRJ file and creates the following file called HELLO.MAK

```
.AUTODEPEND

#  *Translator Definitions*
CC = bcc +HELLO.CFG
TASM = TASM
TLIB = tlib
TLINK = tlink
LIBPATH = C:\BORLANDC\LIB
INCLUDEPATH = C:\BORLANDC\INCLUDE


#  *Implicit Rules*
.c.obj:
  $(CC) -c {$< }

.cpp.obj:
  $(CC) -c {$< }

#  *List Macros*


EXE_dependencies = \
 hello.obj

#  *Explicit Rules*
hello.exe: hello.cfg $(EXE_dependencies)
  $(TLINK) /v/x/c/P-/L$(LIBPATH) @&&|
c0s.obj+
hello.obj
hello
    # no map file
graphics.lib+
emu.lib+
maths.lib+
cs.lib
|
```

```
# *Individual File Dependencies*
hello.obj: hello.cfg hello.c

# *Compiler Configuration File*
hello.cfg: hello.mak
  copy &&|
-v
-r-
-d
-vi
-H=HELLO.SYM
-w-ret
-w-nci
-w-inl
-w-par
-w-cpt
-w-dup
-w-pia
-w-ill
-w-sus
-w-ext
-w-ias
-w-ibc
-w-pre
-w-nst
-I$(INCLUDEPATH)
-L$(LIBPATH)
| hello.cfg
```

# PRJCFG

### Purpose
The PRJCFG utility converts project files to configuration files or vice versa.

### Syntax
`PRJCFG prjfile.PRJ cfgfile.CFG`
　　Creates CFGFILE.CFG from PRJFILE.PRJ.

`PRJCFG cfgfile.CFG prjfile.PRJ`
　　Creates PRJFILE.PRJ from CFGFILE.CFG.

`PRJCFG filename`
　　Creates the configuration file called FILENAME.CFG from the project file FILENAME.PRJ.

### Description
A configuration file can be used by the command line compiler by means of the +*filename* option (see Chapter 2). The PRJCFG utility extracts the compiler options from the project file and writes them to a text configuration file readable by the com-

mand line compiler. Note that the configuration file only includes compiler options and not the include or library paths.

When PRJCFG is used to create a project file from a configuration file, the .PRJ file created will contain the compiler options listed in the .CFG file. The .PRJ file will be created with an empty project list.

Note that the utility will overwrite any existing .PRJ or .CFG file.

### See Also
+*filename* in Chapter 2

### Example
Create a configuration file for HELLO.C from the HELLO.PRJ project in Chapter 2. This is done by entering:

```
prjcfg hello
```

The following is the resulting HELLO.CFG file:

```
-j0
-v
-d
-V
-vi
-wamb
-wnod
```

# PRJCVNT

### Purpose
The PRJCVT utility converts Turbo C++ project files to Borland C++ project files.

### Syntax
```
PRJCNVT turboc[.PRJ][.TC] bc[.PRJ]
```
Converts either TURBOC.PRJ or TURBOC.TC to BC.PRJ. If there is no extension, then PRJCNVT looks for a .TC file and, if it does not find one, then it looks for a .PRJ file. If an output name is not specified or the base name of the Turbo C project file is the same as the Borland C++ project file, then the PRJCNVT utility will first rename the old file with a .BAK extension.

### Description
If you use a .CFG file as the input, then PRJCNVT will combine the compiler options in the .CFG file with the dependencies in the .PRJ file when it creates the Borland C++ compatible .PRJ file. There must be a corresponding project defined in the current directory if you are using a .CFG file.

Note that if a .PRJ or TC file is used, then this utility does not copy the compiler options. In this case it would only copy the dependencies in the Turbo C project file to the project list in the Borland C++ project file.

### Example

Convert a Turbo C project file called MYPROJ.PRJ to a Borland C++ project file. This is done by entering the following:

```
prjcnvt myproj
```

# TRANCOPY

### Purpose

The TRANCOPY utility copies transfer items in one project file to another project file.

### Syntax

```
TRANCOPY [-r] source[.PRJ] dest[.PRJ]
```

Copy all the transfer items in SOURCE.PRJ to DEST.PRJ. Replace the entire set of transfer items in DEST.PRJ with the SOURCE.PRJ items if the -r option is used.

### Description

The IDE keeps track of defined transfer items for each individual project and when no project is open. If a transfer item is defined when no project is open, then the new transfer item will be present anytime no project file is open. However, if a transfer item is defined while a project file is open, then the item is local to that particular project and cannot be used once the project is closed or another project is opened. This utility provides a handy means for moving transfer items from project to project.

### See Also

Translator and Nontranslator transfer items

### Example

Copy the transfer items defined in the WFRACTAL.PRJ to the FRACTDLL.PRJ. This is done by entering the following:

```
trancopy wfractal fractdll
```

# BORLAND C++
# MAKE
# REFERENCE

# 4

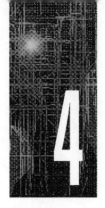

Although the IDE's Project Manager is a very useful tool, it cannot handle all situations. For example, you may prefer a different text editor than the IDE and you may not want to call up BC every time you need to build the application. You may want to update an object code library as part of the build process or you could be building an application that requires some type of postlink process other than invoking the Resource Compiler. Each of these situations is best handled by using Borland's protected mode MAKE utility or the real-mode MAKER utility.

Note that both the MAKE and MAKER utilities are functionally identical except that the MAKER utility supports a few extra command line options and directives for controlling swapping the utility to the disk. This chapter normally refers to the MAKE utility; however, all the features in MAKE are also supported by MAKER.

## EXPLICIT RULES

The MAKE utility (and the real-mode MAKER utility) operates by reading a text file containing a list of rules governing the build process for the application. The most simple rule you can write is called an *explicit rule*. With an explicit rule you define what target files are dependent on specific source files and what to do if one of the dependent files has changed since the target file was created. A list of explicit rules has the following format:

```
target_filename : [source_filename [source_filename] . . . ]
  [Command]
  [Command]
  [Command]
  . . .

target_filename : [source_filename [source_filename] . . . ]
  [Command]
  . . .
```

The MAKE utility will expect the definition of an explicit rule to start on the first character of the line and the dependent source files to be separated from the target file by a colon. The list of commands following the target/dependent filenames are the commands executed by the MAKE utility if one of the source files is newer than the target file. Each command in the list must be indented by at least one space or tab character. This enables the MAKE utility to differentiate between the command list and the next rule definition.

The target and dependent file list portion of a rule can be up to 4096 characters long. The MAKE utility supports the use of the ' \' character to split both rule definitions and commands over several lines. For example, you could list each dependent file on a separate line as follows:

```
# Place each dependent file on a separate line.
target.obj : source1.c \
             source2.c \
             source3.c \
             source4.c \
             source5.c
```

Note that the ' \' character must be the last nonwhitespace character on the line.

The '#' is used in .MAK files to add comments. Comments can be placed anywhere in the .MAK file so long as they do not follow a line continuation character. In general, it is best to place comments on separate lines.

## COMMAND LINE FORMAT

The MAKE utility itself uses the following command line format:

```
make [option list] [target [target] . . .]
```

When you execute the MAKE utility, it first looks for a file called BUILTINS.MAK in the current directory. If MAKE cannot find a file by that name in the current directory, it reads the default BUILTINS.MAK file in the directory containing the MAKE utility, usually \ BORLANDC \ BIN. The default BUILTINS.MAK file contains several macro definitions and rule definitions (see the -p option for a listing of the rule and macro definitions). After reading BUILTINS.MAK, MAKE then looks for either MAKEFILE or MAKEFILE.MAK in the current directory. (You can specify a different filename for your .MAK file if you like by using the -f*filename* option.) The MAKE utility will then read the list of rules in the .MAK file and build each of the targets listed on the command line. Note that both the option list and target list are optional. If you do not specify any targets on the command line, the MAKE utility will build the target file for the first rule definition; otherwise, it will build the target files in the order listed on the command line.

## EXAMPLE .MAK FILE

The following is a simple .MAK file using explicit rules to build the "Hello, MAKE!" application:

**hello\ source.c**

```
#include <stdio.h>

void main(void)
{
    printf("Hello, MAKE!\n");
}
```

272

**hello\makefile.mak**

```
# .MAK file to build the "Hello, MAKE!" application

target.exe : target.obj
   bcc target.obj

target.obj : source.c
   bcc -c -otarget source.c
```

Both the TARGET.OBJ and the TARGET.EXE files are built by entering the following at the DOS prompt:

```
make target.obj target.exe
```

The MAKE utility reads MAKEFILE.MAK and locates the rule governing the build of the TARGET.OBJ file. Because there is no TARGET.OBJ file, the MAKE utility executes the 'bcc -c -otarget source.c' command. MAKE then looks for the rule governing the build of TARGET.EXE and again, because TARGET.EXE does not exist, it executes the command list for the TARGET.EXE rule. Both the TARGET.OBJ file and the TARGET.EXE file are stored on the disk and each is stamped with the current date and time by DOS.

If you were to attempt to build the TARGET.OBJ a second time by executing 'make target.obj,' the MAKE utility would again read MAKEFILE.MAK and find the rule governing the build process of TARGET.OBJ, but this time there is already a TARGET.OBJ file stored on the disk. MAKE then checks the time/date stamp for TARGET.OBJ against that of SOURCE.C. Because the TARGET.OBJ file has a later time/date stamp than SOURCE.C, the MAKE utility assumes that TARGET.OBJ is up-to-date and does not execute the command list, as shown in Figure 4-1.

Suppose sometime after the first build of TARGET.OBJ you make a modification to SOURCE.C. When the text editor you were using saves the file to the disk, DOS will stamp the file with the current date and time. Now if you were to again execute the 'make target.obj' command, the MAKE utility would again compare the time/date

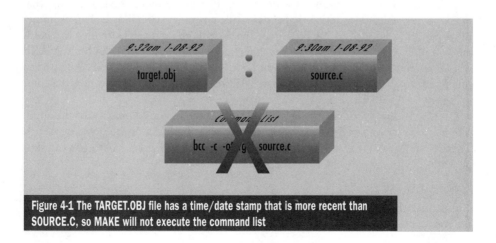

Figure 4-1 The TARGET.OBJ file has a time/date stamp that is more recent than SOURCE.C, so MAKE will not execute the command list

stamps and see that the SOURCE.C file has been changed since the last time TARGET.OBJ was built. Because the target file is out-of-date with respect to the source file, MAKE would execute the command list for the TARGET.OBJ rule and rebuild TARGET.OBJ as shown in Figure 4-2.

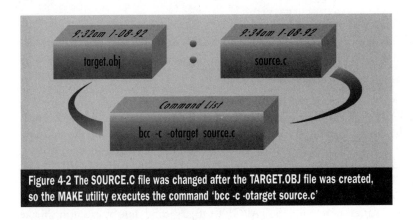

Figure 4-2 The SOURCE.C file was changed after the TARGET.OBJ file was created, so the MAKE utility executes the command 'bcc -c -otarget source.c'

## LINKED DEPENDENCIES

The MAKE utility also supports linked dependencies. This means that MAKE will also treat the dependent files of any target you build as target files themselves if the .MAK file contains a rule governing its build. As shown in Figure 4-3, MAKE will always build all dependent target files before building the original target.

Consider the .MAK file for the "Hello, MAKE!" application. Suppose you change SOURCE.C again and then enter the following:

```
make target.exe
```

The MAKE utility examines the dependent files for TARGET.EXE and notes that the dependent file TARGET.OBJ also has a rule governing its build. It then examines the dependent files for TARGET.OBJ and, because there are no rules defined for building SOURCE.C, and SOURCE.C was changed since TARGET.OBJ was built, MAKE will execute the command list to rebuild TARGET.OBJ. Now TARGET.OBJ has a time/date stamp that is more recent than TARGET.EXE, so MAKE executes the command list for TARGET.EXE.

It is generally a good idea to list the rule governing the build process for the application itself first followed by the rules governing the building of the dependent files. Then, if the .MAK file is called either MAKEFILE or MAKEFILE.MAK, you can simply enter the following to build the application:

```
make
```

Because the first rule listed in MAKEFILE.MAK is for the build of TARGET.EXE, the above is the command line equivalent of entering 'make target.exe.'

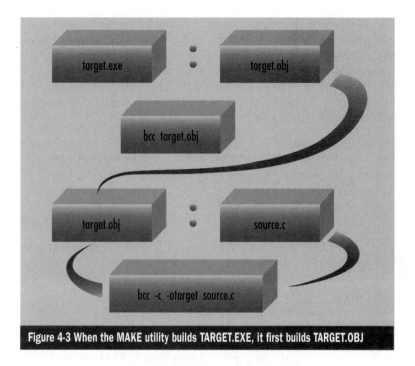

**Figure 4-3 When the MAKE utility builds TARGET.EXE, it first builds TARGET.OBJ**

# MACROS

The MAKE utility supports macro definitions and expansions. Macros can be defined either on the command line using the -D*symbol* option or within the .MAK file text. Details on the usage of the -D*symbol* command line option are in the command line reference section towards the end of this chapter.

## Defining a Macro

A macro is defined in the .MAK file text using the following syntax:

```
macro_name = symbol
```

The start of the macro_name in the definition must be the first character in a line without any leading spaces or tabs. The macro_name itself also cannot contain any spaces or tabs.

## Macro Expansion

Unlike macro expansions in C and C++, in which you instruct the compiler to expand a macro by using the macro_name, the MAKE utility expects the following syntax to indicate a macro expansion:

```
$(macro_name)
```

The name of the macro must be preceded by the '$' character and enclosed within parentheses for the macro to be expanded. If the macro_name is undefined, then MAKE expands the macro to a NULL string. If the undefined macro is used as an argument to a conditional directive, the undefined macro is expanded to a numerical zero.

As an example of macro definition usage, the following .MAK file defines a WARNINGS macro, which consists of a list of command line warning message options, and passes the macro to BCC:

**macro1\makefile.mak**

```
# .MAK file to build the "Hello, MAKE!" application

# Define the WARNINGS macro
WARNINGS = \
    -wbbf \
    -weas \
    -wamb \
    -wsig

target.exe : target.obj
   bcc target.obj

target.obj : source.c
   bcc -c -otarget $(WARNINGS) source.c
```

MAKE expands the command line for the TARGET.OBJ rule to the following

```
bcc -c -otarget -wbbf -weas -wamb -wsig source.c
```

Macro expansions can be used virtually anywhere in the .MAK file text. The only restriction is that a macro expansion cannot be used as part of the name for another macro definition. A macro can, however, be used as part of the definition of another macro. Macros can also be used to designate target and dependent files. The following example uses macro expansions to define the target and source file as part of the explicit rule definition:

**macro2\makefile.mak**

```
# .MAK file to build the "Hello, MAKE!" application

# Define the SOURCE and TARGET macros
SOURCE = source
TARGET = my_app

# Define the WARNINGS macro
WARNINGS = \
    -wbbf \
    -weas \
    -wamb \
    -wsig

$(TARGET).exe : $(TARGET).obj
   bcc $(TARGET).obj

$(TARGET).obj : $(SOURCE).c
   bcc -c -o$(TARGET) $(WARNINGS) $(SOURCE).c
```

In the above .MAK file, we've defined the TARGET macro as 'my_app' and the SOURCE macro as 'source.' Using macros instead of explicit names enables you to write generic .MAK files that can be used to build other applications by simply changing the filenames for the SOURCE and TARGET macros.

## Predefined Macro Names

The MAKE utility has five predefined macros:

```
__MSDOS__ = 1
__MAKE__  = 0x0360
MAKE      = filename
MAKEFLAGS = flags
MAKEDIR   = directory
```

The __MSDOS__ macro is always defined as the number '1'. The __MAKE__ macro is always defined as the version number of the MAKE utility in hexadecimal format. The MAKE macro is the name of the MAKE utility, usually either MAKE for the protected mode version or MAKER for the real-mode version. The MAKEFLAGS macro contains the command line options used to invoke MAKE. For example, the MAKEFILE macro is defined as "KNsr" for the following execution of MAKE:

```
make -r -s -N -K
```

The MAKEDIR macro is defined as the current directory.

The MAKE utility also uses all environmental variables as macro definitions. For example, entering the following on the DOS command line creates an environment variable called DEBUG and sets it equal to one:

```
set DEBUG=1
```

The MAKE utility will then create a macro definition for the above environmental variable as one of the predefined macros called DEBUG, which will expand to the string "1."

## Definition Test Macro

The MAKE utility also supports a macro that is used to test for the definition of a macro. The definition test macro uses the following syntax:

```
$d(macro_name)
```

This macro expands to a numerical one if the macro_name is defined as zero or if the macro_name is undefined.

The definition test macro is normally used as an argument in the !if() conditional directive. For example, you can use a command line macro definition to control the memory model used during compilation as follows:

```
# If not, is the MEDIUM memory model defined?
!if($d(MEDIUM))
MODEL = -mm
```

```
!else
MODEL = -ms
!endif
```

The $d() in the above tests for the definition of the MEDIUM macro. If the macro is defined, the MODEL macro is defined as the medium memory model command line option. Otherwise, MODEL is defined as the small memory model.

## Pathname Macros for Explicit Rules

The MAKE utility also has eight special macros that expand to different portions of the target file's full pathname. Table 4-1 lists the macro expansions for explicit rules.

| MACRO | EXPANSION |
|-------|-----------|
| $< | Full target pathname including the extension (same as $@) |
| $@ | Target filename with full path (same as $<) |
| $* | Full target pathname without the extension |
| $: | Target drive and directory path only |
| $. | Target filename only (no drive or directory) |
| $& | Target filename without the extension (no drive or directory) |
| $** | All dependent files |
| $? | All out-of-date dependent files |

**Table 4-1 Pathname macro expansions when used in explicit rules**

For example, consider the following .MAK file:

**macro3\makefile.mak**
```
..\macro3\test.obj : test.c test.h
    type &&!
    The full target pathname: - - - - - - - - - - - $<
    The full target pathname: - - - - - - - - - - - $@
    The target pathname (no file extension):- - - $*
    The target drive and directory path:- - - - - $:
    The target filename (no drive or directory):- $.
    The target filename without extension:- - - - $&
    All dependent files:- - - - - - - - - - - - - $**
    All out-of-date dependent files:- - - - - - -$?
    !
```

If TEST.C is newer than TEST.OBJ and TEST.OBJ is newer than TEST.H, then the above .MAK file produces the following temporary file:

```
The full target pathname: - - - - - - - - - - - - - - - ..\macro3\test.obj
The full target pathname: - - - - - - - - - - - - - - - ..\macro3\test.obj
The target pathname (no file extension):- - - - - -..\macro3\test
The target drive and directory path:- - - - - - - -..\macro3\
```

```
The target filename (no drive or directory):- - test.obj
The target filename without extension:- - - - - test
All dependent files:- - - - - - - - - - - - - - test.c test.h
All out-of-date dependent files:- - - - - - - - test.c
```

## Macro Modifiers

Many times you will only need the drive, directory, or just the base name of the target file. The MAKE utility supports four different *macro modifiers,* which extract portions of the name out of a pathname macro. For example, the D macro modifier extracts the drive and directory from a pathname. Consider the following rule:

```
..\macro4\target.obj : test.c test.h
    echo $(<D)
```

The $(<D) macro expands to the following:

```
..\macro4\
```

Table 4-2 lists the pathname macro modifiers. All of these modifiers are equivalent to an existing pathname macro. They are supported by MAKE so as to provide compatibility with Mircosoft's NMAKE utility (see the -N option).

| MODIFIER | DESCRIPTION |
|----------|-------------|
| D | Extract the drive and directory |
| F | Extract the base filename and extension |
| B | Extract only the base name |
| R | Extrat the drive, directory, and base name (no extension) |

**Table 4-2 Pathname macro modifiers**

# IMPLICIT RULES

Implicit rule definitions operate in the same manner as explicit rules except that you do not have to explicitly state the command list. You also do not have to state the dependent files in some cases. An implicit rule definition uses the following syntax:

```
.xxx.yyy:
    [Command]
    [Command]
    . . .
```

where 'xxx' is the extension for the source file and 'yyy' is the extension for the target file. As with the explicit rule definitions, there does not have to be a command list for the rule.

Implicit rules by themselves do nothing. However, if MAKE finds an explicit rule with no command list and there is an implicit rule that matches the file extensions for the target and source files, then MAKE uses the command list defined in the matching implicit rule to build the target. For example, consider the following .MAK file:

**imp1\makefile.mak**

```
.c.obj:
    bcc -c $<

.asm.obj:
    bcc -c $<

test.exe : test.obj main.obj assembly.obj
    bcc test.obj main.obj assembly.obj

test.obj : test.c

main.obj : main.c

assembly.obj : assembly.asm
```

In the above .MAK file, the explicit rules governing the build of TEST.OBJ and MAIN.OBJ have no command list. Because there is an implicit rule governing the build of .OBJ files based on .C source files, MAKE uses the command list for the .c.obj: implicit rule to build these two targets. This means the above .MAK file will execute as if it were written using the following explicit rules:

```
test.exe : test.obj main.obj assembly.obj
    bcc test.obj main.obj assembly.obj

test.obj : test.c
    bcc -c $*.c

main.obj : main.c
    bcc -c $*.c

assembly.obj : assembly.asm
    bcc -c $*.asm
```

The .MAK file would look like the following after the pathname macros are expanded:

```
test.exe : test.obj main.obj assembly.obj
    bcc test.obj main.obj assembly.obj

test.obj : test.c
    bcc -c test.c

main.obj : main.c
    bcc -c main.c

assembly.obj : assembly.asm
    bcc -c assembly.asm
```

## Pathname Macros for Implicit Rules

Note that the $< macro expands differently in an implicit rule than it does in an explicit rule. In an explicit rule, the $< macro expands to the full pathname for the target file. However, the $< macro expands to the pathname for the dependent file in an implicit rule. Other pathname macros also expand differently when you use them in an implicit rule. Table 4-3 lists the pathname macro expansions when you use them in an implicit rule.

| MACRO | EXPANSION |
|-------|-----------|
| $< | Full pathname for the dependent file (same as $** and $?) |
| $@ | Target pathname |
| $* | Full dependent pathname without the extension |
| $: | Dependent drive and directory path |
| $. | Dependent filename (no drive or directory) |
| $& | Dependent filename without extension (no drive or directory) |
| $** | Full pathname for the dependent file (same as $< and $?) |
| $? | Full pathname for the dependent file (same as $< and $**) |

**Table 4-3 Pathname macro expansions when used with implicit rules**

For example, consider the following .MAK file:

**macro4\makefile.mak**
```
.c.obj:
  type &&!
  The full dependent pathname: - - - - - - - - - - $<
  The full target pathname:- - - - - - - - - - - - $@
  The dependent pathname (no file extension):- - - $*
  The dependent drive and directory path:- - - - $:
  The dependent filename (no drive or directory):-$.
  The dependent filename without extension:- - - - $&
  The full dependent pathname: - - - - - - - - - - $**
  The full dependent pathname: - - - - - - - - - - $?
!

..\macro3\test.obj : test.c test.h
```

The above .MAK file produces the following temporary file:

```
The full dependent pathname: - - - - - - - - - - - ..\macro3\test.c
The full target pathname:- - - - - - - - - - - - - ..\macro3\test.obj
The dependent pathname (no file extension):- - - ..\macro3\test
The dependent drive and directory path:- - - - - ..\macro3\
The dependent filename (no drive or directory):-test.c
The dependent filename without extension:- - - - test
The full dependent pathname: - - - - - - - - - -   ..\macro3\test.c
The full dependent pathname: - - - - - - - - - -   ..\macro3\test.c
```

## Implied Dependencies Using Implicit Rules

The MAKE utility will also look for implicit rules governing the build of dependent files if there is no dependent file list. For example, consider the following:

**imp2\makefile.mak**
```
.c.obj:
  bcc -c $<

.asm.obj:
  bcc -c $<
```

281

```
test.exe : test.obj main.obj assembly.obj
    bcc test.obj main.obj assembly.obj

test.obj :

main.obj :

assembly.obj :
```

In this .MAK file, none of the source files are listed for the TEST.OBJ, MAIN.OBJ, or ASSEMBLY.OBJ targets. In this case, the MAKE utility looks for files in the current directory that match one of the implicit rules. For example, when MAKE sees that the TEST.OBJ target has no source file listed, it looks for a match to the .c.obj: implicit rule by looking in the current directory for TEST.C. Because the file exists, MAKE uses it to build TEST.OBJ. When MAKE attempts to build ASSEMBLY.OBJ, there is no ASSEMBLY.C file to match the .c.obj: implicit rule, so it attempts to find a match to the .asm.obj: implicit rule. Because ASSEMBLY.ASM is in the current directory, MAKE uses the .asm.obj rule and the assembly language file to build ASSEMBLY.OBJ.

Note that any include files used by the source files that change can be made to trigger a rebuild of the target if the .autodepend directive is included at the beginning of the .MAK file text or if the -a command line option is used when invoking MAKE.

MAKE will also use an implicit rule to build dependent files even if no target file is listed in the .MAK file text. In the following example .MAK file, the TEST.OBJ, MAIN.OBJ, and TARGET.OBJ target files are only listed as dependent files of TEST.EXE:

**imp3\makefile.mak**
```
    #enable autodependency checking
    .autodepend

.c.obj:
    bcc -c $<

.asm.obj:
    bcc -c $<

test.exe : test.obj main.obj assembly.obj
    bcc test.obj main.obj assembly.obj
```

The MAKE utility matches the implicit rules for each of TEST.EXE's dependent files just as if they were listed as separate targets.

## BATCH PROCESSING SOURCE FILES

The Borland C++ command line compiler, BCC.EXE, can compile more than one source file in a single call. This feature saves a considerable amount of time by eliminating the need to load the command line compiler for each separate source file. The MAKE utility has a batch processing feature that allows you to send more than one source file with a single call to an application such as BCC. Batch processing uses the following syntax:

```
command { batch file } . . .
```

As the MAKE utility builds target files it will combine all the batch files which have the same command and only execute the command once. Consider the following:

**batch1\makefile.mak**
```
test.exe : test.obj main.obj assembly.obj
  bcc test.obj main.obj assembly.obj

test.obj : test.c
  bcc -c { test.c }

main.obj : main.c
  bcc -c { main.c }

assembly.obj : assembly.asm
  bcc -c { assembly.asm }
```

Because all the .OBJ targets have the same 'bcc -c' command before the { *batch file* } expression, MAKE combines the three commands into the single following command:

```
bcc -c test.c main.c assembly.asm
```

This reduces the number of times BCC is loaded from four to two (once to compile and again to link), thus making the build process much faster.

The use of batch processing works especially well with implicit rules. For example, the following .MAK file is equivalent to the previous example, only it uses implicit rules:

**batch2\makefile.mak**
```
#enable autodependency checking
.autodepend

.c.obj:
  bcc -c { $< }

.asm.obj:
  bcc -c { $< }

test.exe : test.obj main.obj assembly.obj
  bcc test.obj main.obj assembly.obj
```

The above implicit rules place the { } brackets around the $< dependent pathname macro. This causes MAKE to generate a single statement controlling compilation of the source code followed by the linking of TEST.EXE as follows:

```
bcc -c test.c main.c assembly.asm
bcc test.obj main.obj assembly.obj
```

The first statement is the result of the implicit rule and the batch processing called for by the { } brackets. The second statement is the explicit rule listed for the TEST.EXE target.

# THE TOUCH UTILITY

The TOUCH.EXE utility that comes with the BC++ package is designed to help you use the MAKE utility more efficiently. TOUCH changes the time/date stamp of a file to the current time and date. This enables you to force the rebuild of targets by changing the time/date stamp of one of the dependent files.

The following is the syntax for TOUCH:

```
touch filename [filename . . .]
```

Any number of filenames can be listed on the command line. You may also use DOS wildcard characters such as * and ?. There are no option settings for the TOUCH utility.

As an example of how to use TOUCH, consider the following .MAK file:

```
test.exe : test.obj main.obj assembly.obj
    bcc test.obj main.obj assembly.obj

test.obj : test.c
    bcc -c test.c

main.obj : main.c
    bcc -c main.c

assembly.obj : assembly.asm
    bcc -c assembly.asm
```

Suppose you wanted debug information for MAIN.C but not the other two source files. Change the .MAK file to add the -v option to the MAIN.OBJ rule as follows:

```
test.exe : test.obj main.obj assembly.obj
    bcc -v test.obj main.obj assembly.obj

test.obj : test.c
    bcc -c test.c

main.obj : main.c
    bcc -c -v main.c

assembly.obj : assembly.asm
    bcc -c assembly.asm
```

If you've already built the TEST.EXE file, you could use the -B option to tell MAKE to rebuild, but this would unnecessarily rebuild the TEST.OBJ and ASSEMBLY.OBJ targets. A better method would be to use TOUCH to make MAIN.C more recent than TEST.EXE as follows:

```
touch main.c
```

The TOUCH utility would then stamp the MAIN.C file with the current time and date, thereby ensuring MAKE will see it as more recent than TEST.EXE. Because TEST.C and ASSEMBLY.ASM still have their original time/date stamps, MAKE will only rebuild MAIN.OBJ and TEST.EXE.

## COMMAND LINE OPTIONS

Many aspects of the build process can be controlled using command line arguments to the MAKE utility. These arguments enable you to specify the input file MAKE should use, the search path for include files, and many directive-related items, such as autodependency exit status checking. Some of the options, such as the macro definition and include path options, require you to use a character string with the option. These options would be entered as follows:

```
make -xstring
```

The options that do not use strings can be either enabled or disabled from the command line as follows:

```
make -x -y-
```

In the above, the 'x' option is enabled and, because the 'y' option is followed by '-', it is disabled.

The following section is a detailed reference to each of the command line options for the MAKE utility. Note that the Default section shows the default setting of the MAKE utility as shipped. You can change the default setting for any nonstring option using the -W option.

Command line options are case sensitive.

## a                                                    Autodependency Checking

▪ MAKE        ▪ MAKER

### Purpose
The -a command line option instructs the MAKE utility to enable autodependency checking. Typically, you use this option to ensure an automatic rebuild of source files when you've changed a dependent include file.

### Default
```
-a-
```
Disable autodependency checking while building targets in MAKEFILE.MAK.

### Usage
```
make -a
```
Enable autodependency while building targets in MAKEFILE.MAK.

### Description
BC++ will normally compile include file information into the object code (.OBJ) file. This information is accessible by both the MAKE utility and the IDE's Project Manager. The -a option is used to either enable or disable the checking of this information while evaluating an implicit or explicit rule. When MAKE evaluates a rule and autodependency checking is enabled, MAKE will examine the time/date stamps for all the filenames stored in the target .OBJ file and compare them with time/date stamp for the .OBJ itself. If one of the include files used to build the .OBJ file is newer than the target .OBJ file, then MAKE will execute the command regardless of the time/date stamp for the source file.

Note that autodependency checking only applies if the target file is an .OBJ file. Also, any .autodepend or .noautodepend directives in the .MAK file will override the command line option.

### See Also

| | |
|---|---|
| .autodepend, .noautodepend | Autodependency Checking |
| B | Build All Targets |
| Chapter 2: X | Disable Autodependency Output |

### Example

Write an application and a .MAK file that uses the autodependency checking command line option. The following source file, TEST.C, uses TEST.H as an include file:

**a\test.c**
```
#include "test.h"
#include <stdio.h>

void main(void)
{
    printf("The NUMBER macro is defined as:  %d\n", NUMBER);
}
```

**a\test.h**
```
#define NUMBER 8
```

The application is built using the following:

**a\makefile.mak**
```
test.obj : test.c
    bcc test.c
```

Because the TEST.H file is not listed as a dependent file in the explicit rule 'test.obj : test.c', the MAKE utility will not normally check the time/date stamp for TEST.H to see if it is newer than TEST.OBJ. Executing MAKE with the following command line will enable autodependency checking and force a rebuild of TEST.OBJ if there was any change to TEST.H:

```
make -a
```

# B                                          Build All Targets

- MAKE   - MAKER

### Purpose

Build all target files regardless of dependency time/date stamps. This option would normally be used if some compiler option in the .MAK file were changed and the entire application needed to be rebuilt.

## Default

–B–

Only build a target file if the time/date stamp of one of the dependency files is newer than the time/date stamp of the target file.

## Usage

`make –B`

Build all target files.

## Description

Normally a target file is only built if one of the dependent files listed in the implicit or explicit rule is newer than the target. The MAKE utility checks for this condition by comparing the time/date stamp for all the listed dependencies against the time/date stamp of the target. Sometimes, however, the entire application needs to be rebuilt even if none of the source files has changed, such as when the application is recompiled using a different memory model. The -B option tells the MAKE utility to treat all targets as if they were out-of-date and execute the command associated with the rule.

## See Also

| | |
|---|---|
| .autodepend, .noautodepend | Autodependency Checking |
| a | Autodependency Checking |
| Chapter 2: X | Disable Autodependency Output |

## Example

Write a .MAK file that will compile the application in the previous example using the different memory models. Build using the small memory model and then rebuild using the medium memory model.

**b\makefile.mak**

```
# Was the MODEL macro define on the command line?
!if(!$d(MODEL))
  # Nope, print an error message and abort
  !error The MODEL macro is undefined
!endif

test.obj : test.c
  #The $(MODEL) expands to the character string MODEL was defined
  # as on the command line.
  bcc –$(MODEL) test.c
```

The above .MAK file will build the TEST application using the memory model specified on the command line. For example, to compile the application using the small memory model you would execute the MAKE utility as follows:

```
make –DMODEL=ms
```

The -DMODEL=ms command line option defines the MODEL macro as 'ms.' This causes the -$(MODEL) parameter to expand as '-ms' and compile the TEST application using the small memory model.

You would enter the following to compile the TEST application using the medium memory model:

```
make -DMODEL=mm
```

However, if you have already compiled the TEST application using the small memory model, then the MAKE utility will do nothing, as none of the dependent files for TEST.OBJ have changed. In this case, you would use the -B command line option to force the MAKE utility to rebuild TEST as follows even though none of the dependent files has changed:

```
make -DMODEL=mm -B
```

## *Dsymbol, symbol=string*                                    **Macro Definition**

- MAKE    - MAKER

### Purpose
The -D*symbol* and -D*symbol=string* command line options are used to define macros for expansion within the .MAK file. Macro definitions are normally used to control the build process or set compiler command line options.

### Default
None

### Usage
```
make -DMY_MACRO
```
Define MY_MACRO macro as a NULL string.

```
make -DMACRO=MyString
```
Define MY_MACRO macro as 'MyString.'

### Description
Macros are extremely useful in controlling the build process. For example, you could write a .MAK file that tests to see if the DEBUG macro is defined and alter the build process to compile with debug information as follows:

**d\makefile.mak**
```
!if $d(DEBUG)
D_MACRO = -v -vi
!endif

test.obj : test.c
   bcc $(D_MACRO) test.cpp
```

If the DEBUG macro is defined on the command line using the -D option, such as '-DDEBUG', then the D_MACRO is defined as '-v -vi'. Otherwise, the D_MACRO is undefined and expands to a NULL string.

### See Also
U*macro*       Undefined Macro
$(*macro*)     Execute/Expand Macro

### Example
See the description above and the example used with the -B option.

## d*directory*                     **Swap Directory**

MAKE     ■  MAKER

### Purpose
You use the -d*directory* option to tell MAKER which directory to use when it creates a swap file. This enables you to specify a faster drive, such as a RAM disk. This option is ignored by the protected mode MAKE utility.

### Default
-d..\
    Place the swap file in the current directory.

### Usage
-dc:\temp\
    Place the swap file in the TEMP directory on the C: drive.

-de:\
    Place the swap file in the root directory on the E: drive.

### Description
You use the -d*directory* option with either the -S command line option or the .swap directive, which instructs MAKER to save itself to the disk while executing DOS commands. This frees more conventional memory for use by the DOS command. When MAKER swaps to the disk, it creates a file called SWAP000.$$$, which it normally places in the current directory. You'd use the -d*directory* option if your current driver were full or to specify a directory on a faster disk drive such as a RAM disk.

### See Also
S                Swap MAKE Out of Memory
.swap, .noswap    Swap MAKE Out of Memory Directives

## Example

Write a .MAK file that executes a directory listing showing the location of the temporary file and execute MAKER using the -S and -d*directory* options:

**ddir\makefile.mak**
```
     ALWAYS:
          dir \temp
```

You enter the following to place the swap file in the \TEMP directory:

```
     maker -S -d\temp\
```

---

**e**                                                    **Do Not Override Environmental Variable**

---

- MAKE    - MAKER

## Purpose

You use the -e option to instruct MAKE not to redefine any of the predefined macros
created from an environmental variable.

## Default

```
-e
```
Redefine any predefined macros created from environmental variables as required.

## Usage

```
make -e
```
Do not redefine any predefined macros created from environmental variables.

## Description

MAKE will normally redefine any macro definitions that have the same name as a previous macro definition, including those created from environmental variables. The -e
option instructs MAKE to ignore any redefinition of macros that correspond to environmental variables.

## See Also

r              Ignore BUILTINS.MAK

## Example

Create an environemental variable called DEBUG and show that any attempted redefinition is supressed by the -e option. The following .MAK file attempts to define the
DEBUG macro as "12345" and prints an error message showing whether the redefinition was successful or not successful:

**e\makefile.mak**
```
     DEBUG = 12345
```

```
!if($(DEBUG) == 12345)
!error The debug macro was redefined
!else
!error The debug macro was not redefined
```

If you execute MAKE using the -e option, it will print the following error message showing that the -e option suppressed the redefinition of the DEBUG macro:

```
MAKE Version 3.6  Copyright (c) 1991 Borland International
Fatal makefile.mak 7: Error directive: The debug macro was not rede
fined
```

## f*filename*                                     Use *filename* as the Input File to MAKE

■ MAKE        ■ MAKER

### Purpose
The -f*filename* option instructs MAKE to use *filename* as the input file. This option would normally be used to execute a .MAK file that has a name other than MAKEFILE.MAK or MAKEFILE.

### Default
```
-fmakefile.mak
```

### Usage
```
make -fmy_file.mak
```
   Use MY_FILE.MAK as the input file.

### Description
The MAKE utility needs an input file that defines the rules for building an application. Normally MAKE will look for a file called MAKEFILE.MAK in the current directory. The -f*filename* allows you to use .MAK files with a different name or files that are located in a different directory. Note that the *filename* parameter does not need to have a .MAK extension.

### See Also
I*directory*     Designate a Default Directory for !include

### Example
Write a .MAK file called TEST.MAK and use it as the input file for the MAKE utility. One of the .MAK files from the previous examples can be copied to TEST.MAK and then used as an input file for MAKE as follows:

```
copy makefile.mak test.mak
make -ftest.mak
```

# i

- MAKE   - MAKER

## Purpose
The -i option instructs the MAKE utility to ignore the exit status of an application executed by an implicit or explicit rule. This allows the build process to continue even if an application, such as the BCC compiler, generates an error or warning messages.

## Default
-i-

Abort the build process if an application returns a nonzero exit status.

## Usage
-i

Ignore an application's exit status.

## Description
Every application you run in the DOS environment, including BCC and TLINK, returns an integer to DOS upon exiting. This integer value indicates the status of the process, known as the exit status. For example, if BCC or TLINK compiles or links without any warnings or errors, then it returns a 0 as an exit status. If it generates an error, then it returns a nonzero value. The more severe the error, the higher the value of the exit status.

By default, the MAKE utility examines the exit status of any application executed by an implicit or explicit rule and, if it is nonzero, then MAKE aborts the build process and prints an error message.

## See Also
-, .ignore, .noignore    Set/Ignore Exit Status Prefix and Directives

## Example
Write a .MAK file that builds an application using multiple targets in which one of the target files generates an error. Tell the MAKE utility to ignore errors and attempt to build all targets:

**i\test1.c**

```
#include "bogus.h"
#include <stdio.h>

void main(void)
{
    printf("Hello from test1.\n");
}

i\test2.c
```

```
#include <stdio.h>

void main(void)
{
    printf("Hello from test2.\n");
}
```

**i\makefile.mak**

```
test1.exe : test1.c
    bcc test1.c

test2.exe : test2.c
    bcc test2.c
```

Both TEST1.C and TEST2.C are identical, except TEST1.C contains a call to a nonexistent include file called BOGUS.H. The MAKE utility will attempt to build the TEST1.EXE target, note the nonzero exit status from the compiler, and abort the build process. By entering the following, however, the MAKE utility will ignore the exit status from the compiler and build the TEST2.EXE target.

```
make -i test1.exe test2.exe
```

# K                                              Keep All Temporary Files

- MAKE    - MAKER

## Purpose
The -K option tells the MAKE utility not to delete any temporary files created by the << or the && redirection operators. This option would normally be used to debug a .MAK file.

## Default
```
-K-
```
   Delete all temporary files created by MAKE during the build process.

## Usage
```
make -K
```
   Do not delete any temporary files created by MAKE.

## Description
The << and && operators in a .MAK file create temporary files that can then be used as part of the build process. Normally the MAKE utility deletes these files just before the utility terminates. The -K option tells MAKE not to delete these files. If your .MAK file is not performing correctly, you can build using the -K option and then examine the temporary files created by MAKE to determine if the contents of the file are as expected.

## See Also
*name << delimiter, name && delimiter*          Redirection to a Temporary File

### Example

Write a .MAK file using the && redirection operator. Build the .MAK file using the -K option to examine the contents of the temporary file created by MAKE:

```
k\makefile.mak
     ALWAYS :
       type &&!
     This text was stored in a temporary file called MAKE0000.$$$
     !
```

Because the target ALWAYS does not exist and will never be built, the 'type' command will always be executed. The && operator creates a temporary file that contains the text delimited by the '!' characters. The name of the temporary file is then passed to the 'type' command.

You would enter the following to retain the temporary file created by MAKE:

```
make -K
```

## Idirectory                              Designate a Default Directory for !include

- MAKE        ■ MAKER

### Purpose

The -I*directory* directive instructs the MAKE utility to also look for include files in the *directory* specified.

### Default

```
-I-
```
Look for include files in the current directory only.

### Usage

```
make -IC:\INCLUDE\MAKE
```
Look for include files in the current directory and in C:\INCLUDE\MAKE.

### Description

When the MAKE utility encounters an !include directive, it will look for the include file in the current directory. This -I*directory* option allows you to specify the search path MAKE should use when looking for include files.

### See Also

| | |
|---|---|
| !include | Include Makefile |
| *.path.ext* | File Search Path |

### Example

Write a .MAK file that uses an include file located in a different directory. Call MAKE.EXE using the -I option to specify the include path:

**include\test.c**
```
#include "test.h"
#include <stdio.h>

void main(void)
{
    printf("The NUMBER macro is defined as:  %d\n", NUMBER);
}
```

**c:\include\make\debug.inc**
```
!if $d(DEBUG)
D_MACRO = -v -vi
!endif
```

**include\makefile.mak**
```
!include <DEBUG.INC>

test.obj : test.c
   bcc $(DEBUG) test.c
```

The MAKEFILE.MAK file uses the DEBUG.INC file as part of the build process. With this file located in the C:\INCLUDE\MAKE directory, the MAKE utility should be executed as follows:

```
make -IC:\INCLUDE\MAKE
```

## m                                    Display Time/Date Stamp

■ MAKE    ■ MAKER

### Purpose

You use the -m option to have MAKE print the time/date stamp for the target and dependent files.

### Default

```
-m-
```
Do not print the time/date stamp for the target and dependent files.

### Usage

```
make -m
```
Print the time/date stamp for dependent files.

## Description

You may wish to view the time/date stamp for your application's source and object code files as MAKE builds your application. The -m option instructs MAKE to print the time and date stamps for all dependent and target files even if the target file is up to date.

## See Also

n          Do Not Execute Commands

## Example

Execute MAKE using the -m option.

**m\makefile.mak**

```
test.exe : test.c test.h
  bcc test.c
```

MAKE prints the following while processing the above .MAK file with the -m option enabled:

```
test.exe         does not exist
   test.c        Thu Oct 03 13:58:07 1991

   test.h        Thu Oct 03 14:01:26 1991
```

Note that the TEST.C and TEST.H dependent files are indented with respect to the target file, TEST.EXE.

# N                    Set NMAKE Compatibility

■ MAKE     ■ MAKER

## Purpose

You use the -N option if you are using a .MAK file written to operate under Microsoft's NMAKE utility.

## Default

−N−

Use normal MAKE syntax rules.

## Usage

MAKE −N

Build the .MAK file using NMAKE syntax rules.

## Description

Microsoft's NMAKE utility is similar to Borland's MAKE and MAKER utilities, except for the following differences:

- The $$ symbol expands to a '$' literal character, whereas a single '$' character is ignored.

- NMAKE uses the '^' symbol as a line continuation character instead of a '\'.

- If the '^' character is followed by a nonspecial character, the '^' character is ignored.

- NMAKE uses the !ifdef and !ifndef directives instead of $d() to test for a macro definition.

- The pathname macro $: and macro modifier 'D' do not end in a trailing backspace.

- Implicit rules are evaluated from the bottom up rather than the top down if MAKE cannot find an extension listed in the .suffixes directive.

- The $* pathname macro expands to the target filename in both the explicit and the implicit rules instead of just the explicit rule.

## See Also
.suffixes    Specify Implicit Rule Usage Precedence

## Example
Execute MAKE with the -N option enabled. The $d() macro in the following .MAK file is ignored when the -N option is enabled:

**nmake\makefile.mak**
```
    !if $d(DEBUG)
    D_MACRO = -v -vi
    !endif

    test.obj : test.c
      bcc $(D_MACRO) test.c
```

## n                                          Do Not Execute Commands

- MAKE      - MAKER

## Purpose
The -n option instructs the MAKE utility to print, but not execute, the commands in the command list associated with the build process. This option is very useful when debugging complex .MAK files.

## Default
```
-n-
```
    Execute and print the command list for a build process.

## Usage
```
make -n
```
    Print, but do not execute, the command list for a build process.

## Description

As .MAK files become more complex, it becomes highly probable they will not always work as expected and need to be debugged. The -n option provides the ability to execute a .MAK file without having any of the associated commands for a build process actually executed. As a rule, MAKE calls COMMAND.COM to execute commands in the command list; however, with the -n option enabled, MAKE only prints the commands without calling COMMAND.COM. As MAKE pretends to build targets, it acts as though the target is actually built. For example, consider the following .MAK file:

**n\makefile.mak**

```
# .MAK file to build the "Hello, MAKE!" application

target.exe : target.obj
   bcc target.obj

target.obj : source.c
   bcc -c -otarget source.c
```

If, while using the -n option, MAKE pretends to build the TARGET.OBJ file, it will also pretend to build the TARGET.EXE file even though the TARGET.OBJ file does not actually exist.

## See Also

| | |
|---|---|
| K | Keep All Temporary Files |
| m | Display Time/Date Stamp |
| p | Print Macro and Rule Definitions |

## Example

Execute the .MAK file in the description section using the -n option. MAKE will produce the following output:

**n\output.**

```
MAKE Version 3.6  Copyright (c) 1991 Borland International

Available memory 532032 bytes

        bcc -c -otarget source.c
        bcc target.obj
```

## p                                                     Print Macro and Rule Definitions

■ MAKE        ■ MAKER

## Purpose

You use the -p option to instruct MAKE to print the macro and rule definitions before building a .MAK file.

## Default

-p-

Do not print macro and rule definitions.

## Usage

```
make -p
```
Print macro and rule definitions before building the .MAK file.

## Description

Sometimes MAKE does not build .MAK files in exactly the way you may expect. This could be due to a macro or rule definition in the BUILTINS.MAK file or one of the predefined macros definitions. The -p option prints all the macro and ruled definitions, which is useful when you need to debug a .MAK file.

## See Also

| | |
|---|---|
| K | Keep All Temporary Files |
| m | Display Time/Date Stamp |
| n | Do Not Execute Commands |

## Example

Execute MAKE with the -p option enabled for the following .MAK file:

**p\makefile.mak**
```
.c.obj:
    bcc -c $<

.asm.obj:
    bcc -c $<

test.exe : test.obj main.obj assembly.obj
    bcc test.obj main.obj assembly.obj

test.obj : test.c

main.obj : main.c

assembly.obj : assembly.asm
```

MAKE will produce the following output, which prints all the macro definitions and implicit and explicit rules for the above .MAK file:

```
Macros:
    MAKEFLAGS = p
         MAKE = MAKE
       PASCAL = TPC
         RC   = RC
     __MSDOS__ = 1
     __MAKE__  = 0x0360
      MAKEDIR = C:\BORLANDC\BIN
           AS = TASM
           CC = BCC
Implicit Rules:
    .asm.obj:
        commands:   bcc -c $<
    .c.obj:
        commands:   bcc -c $<
    .cpp.obj:
        commands:   $(CC) $(CFLAGS) /c $&.cpp
    .c.exe:
```

```
        commands:    $(CC) $(CFLAGS) $&.c
     .pas.exe:
        commands:    $(PASCAL) $(PFLAGS) $&.pas
     .rc.res:
        commands:    $(RC) $(RFLAGS) /r $&
Targets:
   test.exe:
      flags:
      dependants: test.obj main.obj assembly.obj
      commands:    bcc test.obj main.obj assembly.obj
   test.obj:
      flags:
      dependants:  test.c
      commands:
   main.obj:
      flags:
      dependants:  main.c
      commands:
   assembly.obj:
      flags:
      dependants:  assembly.asm
      commands:
```

Note that many of the implicit rules and macro definitions in the example are in the default BUILTINS.MAK file located in the \BORLANDC\BIN directory. Also note that any environmental variables defined on your system will be listed as a macro definition.

# q                                                  Return Up-to-Date Status

- MAKE    - MAKER

## Purpose
The -q option is listed by the -h option as returning an up-to-date status of a target file and is intended for use with batch (.BAT) files. This option, however, is not operational.

# r                                                       Ignore BUILTINS.MAK

- MAKE    - MAKER

## Purpose
You use the -r option when you want MAKE to ignore any rule or macro definitions in the BUILTINS.MAK file.

## Default
-r-

Read the contents of BUILTINS.MAK before building a .MAK file.

## Usage

```
make -r
```
Ignore the contents of BUILTINS.MAK while building a .MAK file.

## Description

MAKE will normally read the contents of any file called BUILTINS.MAK before building a .MAK file. The -r option tells MAKE not to read BUILTINS.MAK, thereby ignoring its contents.

## See Also

e          Do Not Override Environmental Variable

## Example

Execute the following .MAK file using the -p option to print the macro and rule definitions with the -r option enabled:

**r\makefile.mak**

```
.c.obj:
   bcc -c $<
.asm.obj:
   bcc -c $<

test.exe : test.obj main.obj assembly.obj
   bcc test.obj main.obj assembly.obj

test.obj : test.c
main.obj : main.c

assembly.obj : assembly.asm
```

Normally, MAKE will use the contents of the default BUILTINS.MAK located in the \BORLANDC\BIN directory, which contains several implicit rules and macro definitions (see the -p option for a complete listing). With the -r option enabled, MAKE prints the following, which lists only the predefined macros and the previous implicit rule defnitions:

**Macros:**

```
MAKEFLAGS  = pr
     MAKE  = MAKE
  __MSDOS__ = 1
   __MAKE__ = 0x0360
  MAKEDIR   = C:\BORLANDC\BIN
```

**Implicit Rules:**

```
.c.obj:
    commands:  bcc -c $<
.asm.obj:
    commands:  bcc -c $<
```

**Targets:**

```
test.exe:
    flags:
```

```
      dependants: test.obj main.obj assembly.obj
      commands:   bcc test.obj main.obj assembly.obj
test.obj:
      flags:
      dependants: test.c
      commands:
main.obj:
      flags:
      dependants: main.c
      commands:
assembly.obj:
      flags:
      dependants: assembly.asm
      commands:
```

# S
**Swap MAKE Out of Memory**

MAKE ▪ MAKER

## Purpose
The -S option instructs the MAKE utility to remove itself from memory while executing a command. This leaves more room in memory for command execution.

## Default
-s-

Leave MAKE resident in memory while executing commands.

## Usage
make -S

Remove MAKE from memory while executing commands.

## Description
Some commands will require a large amount of memory to operate. The -S option instructs the MAKE utility to temporarily remove itself from memory while the commands are executed. MAKE will be reloaded for the disk after the execution of each command to continue processing the .MAK file. This leaves more memory available for the executed commands, but because MAKE needs to be reloaded after each execution, the -S option always increases the time needed to build an application.

## See Also
d*directory*            Swap Directory
.swap, .noswap     Swap MAKE Out of Memory Directive

## Example
Write a .MAK file that calls the DOS 'mem' command and execute with and without the -S option:

**swap\makefile.mak**
```
ALWAYS :
    mem
```

Using the -S command frees an additional 89K of memory, but the .MAK file also takes twice as long to execute. Note that because the ALWAYS: target does not exist, the 'mem' rule is always executed.

## S                                                                    Silent Mode

■ MAKE     ■ MAKER

### Purpose
The -s option, known as the silent mode, instructs the MAKE utility not to print commands as they are executed.

### Default
```
-s-
```
Print each command as it is executed.

### Usage
```
-s
```
Use the silent mode while executing commands.

### Description
Some people prefer not to have the screen cluttered with command execution messages. The -s option suppresses the printing of commands before they are executed. Note that the -s option does not suppress the printing of applications called by the build rule. For example, BCC still prints the warning and error messages regardless of the -s option. Use the >NUL redirection command to suppress these messages.

### See Also
.silent, .nosilent   Silent Mode Directive
@ *command*          Silent Mode Prefix

### Example
Execute the following .MAK file using the -s option.

**s\makefile.mak**
```
# .MAK file to build the "Hello, MAKE!" application

target.exe : target.obj
    bcc target.obj >NUL

target.obj : source.c
    bcc -c -otarget source.c >NUL
```

When the above .MAK file is executed using the -s option, it produces the following output:

**s\output.c**

```
MAKE Version 3.6  Copyright (c) 1991 Borland International
Available memory 532032 bytes
```

# Umacro                                                    Undefined Macro

- MAKE       - MAKER

## Purpose
The -U*macro* option undefines a previous command line macro definition.

## Default
None

## Usage
```
make -DMY_MACRO=str -UMY_MACRO
```
Undefines the MY_MACRO definition.

## Description
You use the -U*macro* option to undefine a macro previously defined on the command line. This option is very rarely used. Note that the -U*macro* option has no effect on macros defined within the .MAK file text.

## See Also
| | |
|---|---|
| D*symbol, symbol=string* | Macro Definition |
| !undef | Undefined Macro Directive |

## Example
See the Usage section.

# W, ?, h                                          Write/Display Default Options

- MAKE       - MAKER

## Purpose
The -W option instructs the MAKE utility to save the currently used nonstring command line options as the default options. The -? and -h options display the command line options and their current default settings.

## Default

```
-W-
```
Only use the current command line options for this build process.

## Usage

```
make -a -W
```
Enable autodependency checking as the default command line option.

```
make -?
```
Display the command line options and their current default settings.

```
make -h
```
Same as above.

## Description

If you find yourself frequently using the same command line options, you may want to make these default options. The -W option will write the current command line options to MAKE.EXE, thereby enabling them as the defaults. Table 4-4 lists the options that can have their default settings altered.

| | |
|---|---|
| a | Autodependency Checking |
| B | Build All Targets |
| e | Do Not Override Environmental Variables |
| K | Keep All Temporary Files |
| N | Set NMAKE Compatibility |
| p | Display Macro and Rule Definitions |
| q | Return Up-to-Date Status |
| r | Ignore Rule Definitions in BUILTINS.MAK |
| s | Silent Mode |
| S | Swap MAKE Out of Memory |

**Table 4-4 Options written to MAKE.EXE by the -W option**

You can check to see the current default settings for MAKE by using the -? or the -h command line option. As shown in the following output, all options are disabled by default:

**w\output**
```
MAKE Version 3.6 Copyright (c) 1991 Borland International
Syntax: MAKE [options ...] target[s]

-B               Builds all targets regardless of dependency dates
-Dsymbol         Defines symbol
-Dsymbol=string  Defines symbol to string
```

```
-Idirectory     Names an include directory
-K              Keeps (does not erase) temporary files created by MAKE
-S              Swaps MAKE out of memory to execute commands
-W              Writes all nonstring options back to the .EXE file
-Usymbol        Undefined symbol
-ffilename      Uses filename as the MAKEFILE
-a              Performs autodependency checks for include files
-i              Ignores errors returned by commands
-n              Prints commands but does not do them
-s              Silent, does not print commands before doing them
-? or -h        Prints this message
```

```
   Options marked with '+' are on by default.
   To turn off a default option, follow it by a '-',
      for example: -a-
```

Those command line options which are enabled by default will have a '+' following the command line option letter. For example, if autodependency checking is enabled by default, the -? option will display the command line option as follows:

```
-a+       Performs autodependency checks for include files
```

Note that when one of the -W, -?, or -h options is used, MAKE will not process any .MAK files. Also note that any command line options written after the -W option will not be written as a default. For example, in the following command line, -e command line options are enabled by default, but not the -K options, because it appears after the -W command line option:

```
make -e -W -K
```

## See Also

Chapter 7:  w (Virtual Debugger/Profiler)    Write Options

## Example

Enable autodependency checking and silent mode operation as the defaults for MAKE:

```
make -a -s -W
```

When the above is executed, MAKE will prompt with the following:

```
MAKE Version 3.6  Copyright (c) 1991 Borland International

Write options to C:\BORLANDC\BIN\MAKE.EXE? ( Y/N ) [N]:
```

Entering a 'y' will modify the copy of MAKE in the C:\BORLANDC\BIN directory. The MAKE utility will prompt you for a different directory and filename if you enter an 'n.' Note that MAKE will not create a new MAKE.EXE file if it does not already exist.

# PREFIXES, OPERATORS, AND DIRECTIVES

Command line options are not the only method of controlling aspects of the MAKE utility. Many of the command line options have alternative directives that can be placed in the text of the .MAK file. The operation of MAKE can also be controlled by using various command prefixes and operators.

The following is a detailed reference listing of the directives and operators prefixes that can be used in the .MAK file text. Note that directives must start on a new line and cannot have any leading whitespaces or tabs. Prefixes and temporary file operators can only be used in the command list portion of a rule definition. Tokens can be used anywhere in the .MAK file.

Keep in mind that the MAKE utility processes .MAK files as a whole rather than interpreting each individual line. For this reason, if you use conflicting directives, such as .ignore and .noignore, in the same .MAK file, then MAKE will use the last directive in the file. For example, in the following .MAK file, MAKE encounters the .noignore directive after the .ignore directive, and therefore does not ignore the exit status:

```
.ignore
test.exe : test.obj main.obj assembly.obj
   bcc test.obj main.obj assembly.obj

test.obj : test.c
   bcc -c test.c

main.obj : main.c
   bcc -c main.c

.noignore
assembly.obj : assembly.asm
   bcc -c assembly.asm
```

# #                                                          Comment Token

▪ MAKE     ▪ MAKER

## Purpose
The # token introduces a comment into the .MAK file text. This enables you to add text to a .MAK file which the MAKE utility will not try to interpret as a rule definition or command.

## Syntax
`#text<new-line>`
   The text from the # token and to the end of the line is ignored by the MAKE utility.

## Description
Adding comments to your .MAK file helps to make them more readable. It also provides a way of maintaining a history of development work within the body of the .MAK file.

Comments may not be extended beyond one line. Each new line of comment text must begin with a # character.

Note that comments may not be added after a line continuation token, '\'. The line continuation token must be the last character on the line. However, comments may be placed within temporary files. The MAKE utility strips all comments from temporary files before writing them to the disk.

## See Also

| | |
|---|---|
| \ | Line Continuation Token |
| << | Input Redirection from a Temporary File |
| && | Create a Temporary File |

## Example

Write a .MAK file that contains comments:

**comment\makefile.mak**

```
# This is a comment

target.exe : target.obj       # Explicit rule for TARGET.EXE
    bcc target.obj            # Link TARGET.EXE using BCC

target.obj : source.c         # Explicit rule for TARGET.OBJ
    bcc -c -otarget source.c  # Compile TARGET.OBJ using BCC
```

## @, .silent, .nosilent · Silent Command Prefix and Directives

- MAKE
- MAKER

## Purpose

The @ prefix instructs the MAKE utility not to print the following command before it is executed. The .nosilent and .silent directives tell the MAKE utility to enable or disabled silent mode operation, respectively, i.e., to print or not to print commands as they are executed.

## Syntax

`@command`

Dot not print the 'command' before executing.

`.silent`

Enable silent mode operation for the remaining commands. The directive must start at the beginning of a line.

`.nosilent`

Disable silent mode operation for the remaining commands. The directive must start at the beginning of a line.

## Description

Sometimes you may not want the screen cluttered with command execution messages from the MAKE utility. Unlike the -s option, which suppresses the printing of all commands, the @ prefix only suppresses the printing of a single command. You can use the .silent and .nosilent directives to suppress printing of groups of commands.

Note that disabling silent mode operation by using the -s- option has no effect on the @ prefix or the .silent directive. By the same token, the @ prefix will override a .nosilent directive.

Also note that either the .silent directive or the .nosilent directive can be used in a .MAK file, but not both. The MAKE utility scans the entire .MAK file before processing and uses the last occurrence of either .silent or .nosilent. Use the @ prefix to customize the MAKE utility's printing of commands.

### See Also

s               Silent Mode Command Line Option

### Example

Write a .MAK file using the @ prefix as well as the .nosilent directives:

**silent\makefile.mak**
```
# Disable silent mode operation using the .nosilent directive
.nosilent

# Use the @ prefix to specify the silent mode while
#    building TEST.EXE
test.exe : test.obj main.obj assembly.obj
    @bcc test.obj main.obj assembly.obj

test.obj :  test.c
    bcc -c test.c

main.obj : main.c
    bcc -c main.c

assembly.obj : assembly.asm
    bcc -c assembly.asm
```

## -, .ignore, .noignore     Set/Ignore Exit Status Prefix and Directives

■ MAKE          ■ MAKER

### Purpose

The '-' prefix and the .ignore and .noignore directives tell the MAKE utility to ignore the exit status of the executed command and continue the build process. If the '-' prefix is followed by a number, then the build process is aborted only if the exit status level exceeds the value of the given number.

### Syntax

*−command*

Execute 'command' and continue the build process regardless of the value of the exit status from 'command'.

`-number command`

Execute 'command' and abort the build process if the exit status level exceeds the value of 'number'.

`.ignore`

Do not check the exit status of commands. The directive must start at the beginning of a line.

`.noignore`

Check the exit status of commands and abort the build process if the value is nonzero. The directive must start at the beginning of a line.

## Description

Every application you run in DOS returns an integer value indicating the exit status of the application. The value of the exit status is normally zero if the application operated correctly or nonzero if there was an error. The more severe the error, the higher the value of the exit status. Note that the BCC command line compiler only returns a nonzero exit status for errors and not warning messages.

The MAKE utility normally examines the value of the exit status returned by an application executed from the command list of a rule. The build process is terminated and the target file deleted if the exit status is nonzero. The .ignore directive instructs the MAKE utility not to check the exit status of commands and to continue the build process. The .noignore directive does the opposite and instructs MAKE to check on the exit status and abort the build if it is nonzero. Both these directives override the -i command line option setting.

The '-' prefix to a command instructs MAKE to ignore the exit status of that command only. If the '-' prefix is followed by a number, then MAKE will compare the exit status to the value of the number and only continue the build process if the value is equal to or less than the given number. Otherwise, the build process is aborted and the target deleted. The '-' prefix overrides the -i command line option as well as the .ignore and .noignore directives.

Note that either the .ignore directive or the .noignore directive can be used in a .MAK file but not both. The MAKE utility scans the entire .MAK file before processing and uses the last occurrence of either .ignore or .noignore. The .ignore directive also overrides all '-' prefixes.

## See Also

i           Ignore Exit Status Option

## Example

Write a .MAK file that will continue the build process when one of the commands returns a nonzero exit status:

**ignore\makefile.mak**

```
        # Disable exit status checking
        # .ignore
```

```
test.exe : test.obj main.obj assembly.obj
    bcc test.obj main.obj assembly.obj

test.obj : test.c
    bcc -c test.c

main.obj : main.c
    bcc -c main.c

assembly.obj : assembly.asm
    bcc -c assembly.asm
```

## <<  Input Redirection from a Temporary File Operator

■ MAKE    ■ MAKER

### Purpose
The << operator tells the MAKE utility to construct a temporary file and redirect that file as input to a command.

### Syntax
*command* <<*delimiter*
    *text*
*delimiter*
    Create a temporary file containing the 'text' between the two delimiters and redirect this file as input to 'command.' There can be no spaces between the first character delimiter and the << operator. The terminating delimiter must be the first character in a new line.

### Description
Some applications you use in a command list may not accept command line parameters. Instead, they may operate through interactive keyboard responses. The << operator allows you to create a temporary file containing the appropriate responses for the command and redirect the file as the standard input to the application. The temporary file is named MAKE????.$$$, where ???? is a four-digit number. The first temporary file is named MAKE0000.$$$, the second MAKE0001.$$$, and so on.

The delimiter character used with the << redirection operator can be any character except the comment token, #, and the line continuation token, \. Note that any macros within the delimited text are expanded before they are written to the temporary file. Any comments are stripped from the delimited text.

### See Also
&&     Create a Temporary File Operator
K      Save Temporary Files Option

## Example

Write a .MAK file that uses the DOS linker to create an executable file. Pass the parameters to the linker using the interactive mode via the << redirection operator.

**red_temp\makefile.mak**

```
# .MAK file to build the "Hello, MAKE!" application

target.exe : target.obj
    link <<!
    \borlandc\lib\c0s.obj +
    target.obj
    target.exe
    NUL.MAP
    \borlandc\lib\cs.lib
!

target.obj : source.c
    bcc -c -otarget source.c
```

## &&            Create a Temporary File Operator

- MAKE    ■ MAKER

## Purpose

The && operator will create a temporary file. This temporary file is normally used to create a response file for BCC as the .MAK file is executed.

## Syntax

*<<delimiter*

    *text*

*delimiter*

Create a temporary file containing the 'text' between the two delimiters and expand the && operator to the name of the temporary file.. There can be no spaces between the first character delimiter and the && operator. The terminating delimiter must be the first character in a new line.

## Description

The MAKE utility uses COMMAND.COM to execute commands in a command list. Because of this, the number of arguments for a command is limited to a standard DOS command line, i.e., 127 characters. Some applications, such as BCC.EXE, have provisions for passing command line options via a response file, thus bypassing the DOS imposed limit. For example, BCC allows the use of the *@filename* parameter, which instructs the compiler to read 'filename' as if the commands were typed on the command line. The && operator instructs MAKE to generate a temporary file that can then be used as a response file.

The delimiter character used with the && operator can be any character except the comment token, #, and the line continuation token, \. Note that any macros within the delimited text are expanded before they are written to the temporary file. Any comments are stripped from the delimited text.

### See Also

| | |
|---|---|
| K | Save Temporary Files Option |
| << | Input Redirection from a Temporary File |
| Chapter 2: | @*filename* |

### Example

Write a .MAK file that enables all the compiler warning messages using a temporary response file created by MAKE.

**temp\makefile.mak**

```
test.exe : test.obj
    bcc test.obj

test.obj : test.c
    bcc @&&|
    -wrpt # Nonportable pointer conversion
    -wcpt # Nonportable pointer comparison
    -wrng # Constant out of range in comparison
    -wcln # Constant is long
    -wsig # Conversion may lose significant digits
    -wucp # Mixing pointers to signed and unsigned char
    -wvoi # Void functions may not return a value
    -wret # Both return and return of a value used
    -wsus # Suspicious pointer conversion
    -wstu # Undefined structure 'ident'
    -wdup # Redefinition of 'ident' is not identical
    -wbig # Hexadecimal value more than three digits
    -wbbf # Bit fields must be signed or unsigned int
    -wext # 'ident' declared as both external and static
    -wdpu # Declare 'ident' prior to use in prototype
    -wzdi # Division by zero
    -wpin # Initialization is only partially bracketed
    -wobi # Base initialization without a class name is obsolete
    -winl # Functions containing 'ident' are not expanded inline
    -wlin # Temporary used to initialize 'ident'
    -wlvc # Temporary used for parameter 'ident'
    -wnci # The constant member 'ident' is not initialized
    -wofp # This style of function definition is now obsolete
    -wovl # Use of 'overload' is now unnecessary and obsolete
    -weas # Assigning 'type' to 'enumeration'
    -whid # 'function1' hides virtual function 'function2'
    -wncf # Nonconst function 'ident' called for const object
    -wrvl # Function should return a value
    -wrch # Unreachable code
    -weff # Code has no effect
    -wdef # Possible use of 'ident' before definition
    -waus # 'ident' is assigned a value which is never used
```

```
      -wpar  # Parameter 'ident' is never used
      -wpia  # Possibly incorrect assignment
      -wamp  # Superfluous & with function
      -wamb  # Ambiguous operators need parentheses
      -wstv  # Structure passed by value
      -wnod  # No declaration for function 'ident'
      -wpro  # Call to function with no prototype
      -wasc  # Restarting compile using assembly
      -wasm  # Unknown assembler instruction
      -will  # Ill formed pragma
      -wuse  # 'ident' declared but never used
  | test.c
```

In the above .MAK file, the command line warning options for BCC are stripped of comments and saved in a temporary file called MAKE0000.$$$. The && operator then expands to the MAKE0000.$$$ filename creating the following command:

```
    bcc @MAKE0000.$$$ test.c
```

The MAKE0000.$$$ file is normally deleted before MAKE terminates unless the -K command line option is used.

## .autodepend, .noautodepend    Autodependency Checking Directives

- MAKE    - MAKER

### Purpose
The .autodepend and .noautodepend directives control the status of autodependency checking within the .MAK file text.

### Syntax
`.autodepend`
    Enable autodependency checking

`.noautodepend`
    Disable autodependency checking

### Description
The MAKE utility and the IDE's Project Manager both have access to information compiled into the .OBJ files regarding the include files used to compile the source. The .autodepend directive enables the checking of this information when evaluating an implicit or explicit rule. This means MAKE will examine the time/date stamps for all the include filenames used to compile to an .OBJ file and compare them to the time/date stamp of the target .OBJ file itself. If one or more of the include files have changed since the last time the .OBJ file was built, then MAKE will rebuild the .OBJ target.

The .noautodepend directive tells the MAKE utility not to check the .OBJ files for dependencies. This means that any include files used to build the .OBJ file will need to be stated explicitly in the rule definition.

Note that the .autodepend and .noautodepend directives override the -a command line option. Also note that either the .autodepend or the .noautodepend directive can be used in a .MAK file, but not both. The MAKE utility scans the entire .MAK file before processing and uses the last occurrence of either .autodepend or .noautodepend.

### See Also
a                    Autodependency Checking Option
Chapter 2: X    Disable Autodependency Output

### Example
Write a .MAK file that ensures autodependency checking is enabled regardless of the status of the -a command line option.

**autodep\makefile.mak**
```
# Ensure autodependency is enabled
.autodepend

test.exe : test.obj main.obj
   bcc test.obj main.obj

test.obj : test.c
   bcc -c test.c

main.obj : main.c
   bcc -c main.c
```

# !error                                        Print Error and Abort Directive

▪ MAKE        ▪ MAKER

### Purpose
The !error directive instructs the MAKE utility to print an error message and abort the build process. The !error directive is normally used within the body of a conditional directive.

### Syntax
!error *text*
   Print 'text' as an error and abort the build process.

### Description
It may be desirable to abort the build process under certain conditions, such as when a command line macro definition is required by the build process. The !error directive will both abort the build process and print the associated error message.

### See Also
!if, !elif, !else, !endif    Conditional Expression

## Example

Write a .MAK file that will compile an application only if the small or medium memory model is specified as a command line macro.

**error\makefile.mak**

```
# Is the SMALL memory model defined?
!if($d(SMALL))
MODEL = -ms

# If not, is the MEDIUM memory model defined?
!elif($d(MEDIUM))
MODEL = -mm

# If neither the SMALL or MEDIUM macro is defined, then print
#   an error message.
!else
!error Need to define either the SMALL or MEDIUM command line macro.
!endif

test.exe : test.obj
    bcc $(MODEL) test.obj

test.obj : test.c
    bcc $(MODEL) test.c
```

If neither the SMALL nor the MEDIUM macro is defined on the MAKE command line, then MAKE executes the !error directive by printing the error message "Need to define either the SMALL or MEDIUM command line macro" and aborting the build process.

# !if, !ifdef, !ifndef, !elif, !else, !endif   Conditional Expression Directives

- MAKE    - MAKER

## Purpose

The !if, !ifdef, !ifndef, !elif, !else, and !endif directives are used to control the build process of the .MAK file. These directives are used in the same manner as their #if, #ifdef, #ifndef, #elif, #else, and #endif preprocessor directive counterparts in C and C++.

## Syntax

```
!if(first_exp)
Body_One
!elif(second_exp)
Body_Two
!else
Body_Three
!endif
```

If the numerical value of *first_exp* is nonzero, then *Body_One* is processed, or else if *second_exp* is nonzero, then *Body_Two* is processed. If both *first_exp* and *second_exp* are zero, then *Body_Three* is processed.

`!ifdef` *macro*

tests if the definition of *macro* is defined and either processes the following statement if the macro is defined or skips over the statements to an !else, !elif, or !endif directive if it isn't.

`!ifndef` *macro*

tests if the definition of *macro* is not defined and either processes the following statement if it isn't or skips over the statements to an !else, !elif, or !endif directive if the macro is defined.

## Description

Conditional expression !if allows you to use command line macros and macros defined in the .MAK file text to control the build process. The !if and !elif directives will first expand any macros, attempt to convert the macros and any explicit character strings to a 32-bit signed numerical value, and then evaluate the expression. The macros and explicit strings can be in the following format:

```
'a'         character constant (enclosed in single quotes)
123         Base-10 decimal integer
0123        Base-8 octal integer (indicated by the leading 0)
0x123       Base-16 hexadecimal (indicated by leading 0x)
```

Note that if MAKE cannot convert the macro or explicit string to a numerical value, it converts the string or macro to 0. If you need to test to see if a macro is defined, use the $d() macro.

Table 4-5 lists the operators supported by the MAKE utility for evaluating expressions in a conditional expression.

| UNARY | | | | BITWISE OR |
|---|---|---|---|---|
| - | Negation | ^ | | Bitwise XOR |
| ~ | Bitwise NOT | && | | Logical AND |
| ! | Logical NOT | \|\| | | Logical OR |
| | | > | | Greater than |
| Binary | | < | | Less than |
| + | Addition | >= | | Greater than or equal to |
| - | Subtraction | <= | | Less than or equal to |
| * | Multiplication | == | | Equal to |
| / | Division | != | | Not equal to |
| & | Remainder | | | |
| >> | Right bit-shift | Ternary | | |
| << | Left bit-shift | ?: | | Conditional |
| & | Bitwise AND | | | |

**Table 4-5 Operators that can be used in a conditional expression**

Note that conditional directives may not appear in the middle of a rule definition and that every !if directive must have a matching !endif directive in the same source file. This means that a conditional expression cannot start in one .MAK file and end in another. Condition directives can be nested to any depth.

Unlike the !if directive, the !ifdef and !ifndef directives only check to see if the macro is defined and do not expand the macro.

### See Also

| | |
|---|---|
| !error | Print Error and Abort Directive |
| D*symbol, symbol=string* | Macro Definition |

### Example
See the example used in the !error directive.


# !include                                    Include Makefile Directive

- MAKE    - MAKER

### Purpose
The !include directive is the MAKE utility equivalent of the #include directive in C and C++; that is, the !include directive tells the MAKE utility to incorporate the text of the included file as part of the .MAK file being processed.

### Syntax
```
!include "filename"
```
Include 'filename' as part of the .MAK file text.

```
!include <filename>
```
Same as above.

### Description
The MAKE utility gives you an easy method for sharing build algorithms and macros among many different .MAK files without having to explicitly copy the algorithms from one .MAK file to another. You can share these common items between .MAK files by placing them in distinct files and using the !include directive.

Note that the MAKE utility automatically includes any file in the current directory called BUILTINS.MAK just as if you had the following first line of every .MAK file:

```
!include "BUILTINS.MAK"
```

The MAKE utility will also include any BUILTINS.MAK file that is either in the same directory as the MAKE.EXE application or in the include path designated by the -i command line option.

### See Also

*!directory*    Designate a Default Directory for !include

### Example
Write a set of general implicit rules governing the build of .OBJ and .EXE files and use these rules as part of an !include directive.

**included\implicit.inc**

```
# Enable autodependency checking
.autodepend

# Implicit rule for .C, .CPP, and .ASM source files
.c.obj:
    bcc -c $(OPTIONS) { $< }

.cpp.obj:
    bcc -c $(OPTIONS) { $< }

.asm.obj:
    bcc -c $(OPTIONS) { $< }

# Implicit rule for .EXE target files
.obj.exe:
    bcc $(OPTIONS) $(OBJ_FILES)
```

**included\makefile.mak**

```
!include "implicit.inc"

OBJ_FILES = test.obj main.obj assembly.obj
OPTIONS   = -ms -v -vi

test.exe : $(OBJ_FILES)
```

The IMPLICIT.INC file provides a universal set of implicit rules for building .OBJ files from .C, .CPP, and .ASM source files. It also provides a general implicit rule for building .EXE files by simply listing the .OBJ targets in an OBJ_FILES macro.

## .path                                          File Search Path Directive and Macro

■ MAKE      ■ MAKER

### Purpose
When .path is used as a directive, it instructs the MAKE utility to designate a specific path as the default directory for a file ending with a given file extension. When used as a macro, .path expands to the directory for the given file extension.

### Syntax
```
.path.ext = directory
```
Use 'directory' as the default directory for '.ext' files.

`$(.path.ext)`

Expand the .path.*ext* macro to the default directory designated by '.ext'. The .path.*ext* term must be enclosed in parentheses.

## Description

The .path directive serves double duty as both a directive and a macro. This provides a convenient method for associating files ending with specific extensions with specific directories. It also provides a method for using these directories to create pathnames.

## See Also

I*directory*     Designate a Default Directory for !include

## Example

Write a .MAK file that uses .path as both a directive and a macro for the default directory.

**path\makefile.mak**

```
# Designate the default director for .C, .H, .OBJ, and .EXE files off
#   the current directory.

.path.c=SOURCE
.path.h=SOURCE
.path.obj = OBJECT
.path.exe = APP

.c.obj:
    bcc -c -o$(.path.obj)\$& -I$(.path.c) $<

test.exe : test.obj main.obj
    bcc -e$< $(.path.obj)\test.obj
```

# .precious                              Do Not Delete Certain Targets

- MAKE        - MAKER

## Purpose

You use the .precious directive to prevent MAKE from deleting a target file if a command returns an error, i.e., a nonzero exit status.

## Syntax

`.precious: target [target [. . .]]`

Do not delete *target* if a comand returns an error.

## Description

There are times when you do not want MAKE to delete the target file if an error occurs. For example, if you are adding an .OBJ file to a library and an error occurs, you do not want MAKE to delete the .LIB file! You should use the .precious directive to provide MAKE with a list of files that are important (precious) and should not be deleted.

**See Also**

.suffixes     Specify Implicit Rule Usage Precedence

**Example**

Write a .MAK file to add an .OBJ file to a library and instruct MAKE not to delete the library using the .precious directive. In the following .MAK file, TLIB attempts to add TEST.OBJ to TEST.LIB. TEST.OBJ is an invalid object code file, which causes TLIB to return an error. The TEST.LIB file is not deleted, however, because it is listed as a precious file using the .precious directive.

**precious\makefile.mak**

```
.precious: test.lib

test.lib : test.obj
   tlib test.lib —+test.obj
```

# .suffixes                    Specify Implicit Rule Usage Precedence

■ MAKE        ■ MAKER

**Purpose**

You should be able to use the .suffixes directive to provide MAKE with an order of precedence for evalutating implicit rules. However, this directive is not operational in MAKE Version 3.6. MAKE instead uses the precedence order of the first implicit rule listed to the last regardless of the .suffixes directive. Note that with the -N option enabled, MAKE will reverse that precedence order.

**See Also**

N             Set NMAKE Compatibility
.precious     Do Not Delete Certain Targets

# .swap, .noswap                Swap MAKE Out of Memory Directives

MAKE        ■ MAKER

**Purpose**

The .swap and .noswap directives, respectively, instruct the MAKER utility to remove itself from memory while executing a command or to remain resident. Note, however, that they are not operational in Version 3.6 of MAKER. You should use the -S or -S-command line options instaed.

**See Also**

d*directory*   Swap Directory
S             Swap MAKE Out of Memory

# !undef

- MAKE    - MAKER

## Purpose

The !undef directive undefines a previously defined macro definition.

## Syntax

!undef *macro*

    Undefine 'macro'

## Description

The !undef directive should be used whenever you want to undefine a macro. Note that you do not have to use the !undef directive to redefine a macro. Macro redefinitions can be performed by simply writing a new definition for the macro.

## See Also

U*macro*    Undefine Macro

## Example

Write a .MAK file that undefines a previously defined macro definition.

undef\makefile.mak

```
        WARNINGS = -wbbf -weas -wamb -wsig
        DEBUG    = -v -vi
        OPTIONS  = -ms $(DEBUG) $(WARNINGS)

        # Should we leave out debug information?
        !if($d(NO_DEBUG))
        # Undefine the DEBUG macro
        !undef DEBUG
        !endif

        OPTIONS  = -ms $(DEBUG) $(WARNINGS)

        test.exe : test.obj
           bcc $(OPTIONS) test.obj

        test.obj : test.c
           bcc -c $(OPTIONS) test.c
```

# BORLAND C++
# LINKER
# REFERENCE

The IDE has its own internal linker. The command line compiler, BCC, calls the Turbo Linker (TLINK) to perform the linking functions. There may be times, however, when you may want to perform the link process manually or modify the automatic linking options using the -lxxx command line option. This chapter covers how to perform manual linking with TLINK for both DOS and Windows applications, TLINK's command line options, and a reference section on the module definition file (.DEF) statements.

## COMMAND LINE SYNTAX

TLINK uses the following general command line syntax:

```
tlink [options] objects, exename, mapname, libaries, deffile
```

Just as BCC differentiates between library files and object files by the filename extension (.OBJ for object code files and .LIB for library files), TLINK differentiates between types of files by the position on the command line. For example, if you enter the following:

```
tlink cOs hello, hello, hello, cs
```

then TLINK appends the default extensions and assumes you actually mean the following:

```
tlink cOs.obj hello.obj, hello.exe, hello.map, cs.lib
```

The above command line tells TLINK to link the COS.OBJ startup code file with the HELLO.OBJ object code file, call the resulting application HELLO.EXE, generate a map file called HELLO.MAP, and also link the CS.LIB run-time library. Table 5-1 lists the file extensions TLINK appends to files listed on the command line without extensions based on their position in the command line syntax.

| objects | .OBJ |
| --- | --- |
| exename | .EXE |
| mapname | .MAP |
| libaries | .LIB |
| deffile | .DEF |

**Table 5-1 Default file extensions**

Note that the placement of commas is very important to the TLINK command line syntax. Commas separate the categories of files. If you were to separate your object code files with commas, TLINK would assume the second object code file in the list to be the name of the resulting executable file, the third to be the name of the map file, and so forth. By the same token, if you did not use any commas, then TLINK would assume that all the files listed were object code files even if you included .EXE and .LIB file extensions.

# LINKING DOS APPLICATIONS

TLINK needs a minimum of three items to create a DOS application: your application's object code, a startup code file, and the appropriate run-time library. For example, consider the following "Hello, World!" application:

**examp1\hello.c**
```
#include <stdio.h>

void main(void)
{
    printf("Hello, World!");
}
```

The source code is first compiled into an object code file using the command line compiler as follows:

```
bcc -c hello.c
```

The '-c' command line option instructs the compiler to compile HELLO.C into HELLO.OBJ. To create the HELLO.EXE application, the resulting object code file needs to be linked with a startup object code file and a run-time library file for the memory model used to compile HELLO.C. The compiler defaulted to using the small memory model because no memory model was explicitly stated in the BCC command line. This means HELLO.OBJ should be linked with the small memory model startup code file, C0S.OBJ, and the small memory model run-time library, CS.LIB as follows:

```
tlink c0s hello, hello, hello, cs
```

The C0S.OBJ startup code file contains the code necessary to start the application. It essentially sets up the computer to implement a C program by setting up the stack frame and data segment and then calling the main() function in your application. The CS.LIB run-time library contains the object code for the functions listed in the *Borland C++ Library Reference*. For our HELLO application, TLINK locates the object code module in the CS.LIB run-time library containing the printf() function and links it to the function call in main().

For each of the five memory models, tiny, small, medium, large, and huge, there is a corresponding startup code file and a run-time library file. Additionally, BC++ comes with a second set of startup code files that create a memory model where the stack segment is the same as the data segment. These startup code files are intended to provide compatibility with source code from third-party vendors. They are called automatically by BCC when you use either the -Fs or the -Fm command line compiler options. See Chapter 2 for a detailed description of their operation. Table 5-2 lists the startup code and run-time libraries that correspond to the different memory models for DOS applications.

| MODEL | STARTUP CODE | COMPATIBILITY STARTUP CODE | RUN-TIME LIBRARY | MATH LIBRARY |
|---|---|---|---|---|
| Tiny | C0T.OBJ | C0FT.OBJ | CS.LIB | MATHS.LIB |
| Small | C0S.OBJ | C0FS.OBJ | CS.LIB | MATHS.LIB |
| Compact | C0C.OBJ | C0FC.OBJ | CC.LIB | MATHC.LIB |
| Medium | C0M.OBJ | C0FM.OBJ | CM.LIB | MATHM.LIB |
| Large | C0L.OBJ | C0FL.OBJ | CL.LIB | MATHL.LIB |
| Huge | C0H.OBJ | C0FH.OBJ | CH.LIB | MATHH.LIB |

**Table 5-2 Startup code and run-time libraries for different DOS memory models**

Note that most C and C++ applications will require a case sensitive link using the -c command line option. Though not required for the HELLO application because of the symbols used, it is a good practice to normally include this option. The HELLO application is linked with case sensitivity as follows:

```
tlink -c cOs hello, hello, hello, cs
```

## THE TLINK CONFIGURATION FILE

In the linking of the preceding application there was no need for either the startup code file, C0S.OBJ, or the run-time library file, CS.LIB, to be in the current directory. This is because they are located in the library path listed in the default TLINK.CFG file. Upon installation, BC++ creates a file called TLINK.CFG in the same directory as TLINK that contains the following:

**tlink.cfg**
```
-LC:\BORLANDC\LIB
```

Whenever TLINK is invoked, it searches for a file called TLINK.CFG in the current directory and interprets the contents as command line options. If it does not find a TLINK.CFG file in the current directory, it searches for the file installed by BC++ in the \BORLANDC\BIN directory or whichever directory contains the TLINK.EXE file. The -LC:\BORLANDC\LIB command line option in the default TLINK.CFG file instructs TLINK to look for any object code files or library files that it cannot find in the current directory in the C:\BORLANDC\LIB directory.

The TLINK.CFG file provides a convenient mechanism for altering the default configuration for TLINK. Note, however, that because whitespaces are ignored in the TLINK.CFG file, the file can only contain command line options.

# FLOATING-POINT MATH LIBRARIES

Applications that use floating-point math need to also link one of two floating-point libraries, depending on whether you wish to use emulated floating-point or inline coprocessor instructions, and one of five math libraries. The choice of emulated floating-point or inline coprocessor instructions depends on whether the target machine is guaranteed to have an installed math coprocessor. The choice of math library depends on the memory model for the application. For example, consider the following application:

**examp2\test.c**
```
#include <stdio.h>

void main(void)
{
  double One, Two, Three;

  One = 1.0;
  Two = 2.0;
  Three = One + Two;
  printf("%g + %g = %g\n", One, Two, Three);
}
```

The application is compiled to an object code file using the default small memory model as follows:

```
bcc -c test.c
```

Because the above application uses floating-point, either the coprocessor emulation, EMU.LIB, or the inline coprocessor library, FP87.LIB, needs to be linked with the application along with the math library for the small memory model. Consider the following:

```
tlink c0s test, test, test, emu maths cs
```

Note that if you wish to use inline coprocessor instructions, it is not necessary to compile the application using the -f87 option. Instead, you would simply use the FP87.LIB library in place of the EMU.LIB library as follows:

```
tlink c0s test, test, test, fp87 maths cs
```

Table 5-2 lists the math libraries that correspond to the different memory models.

# LINKING WINDOWS APPLICATIONS

Linking Windows applications is in many respects similar to linking DOS applications. Like DOS applications, a Windows application needs a startup code file, the object code for the application, and a run-time library. Both the startup code and the run-time library need to be compatible with the memory model used for the application.

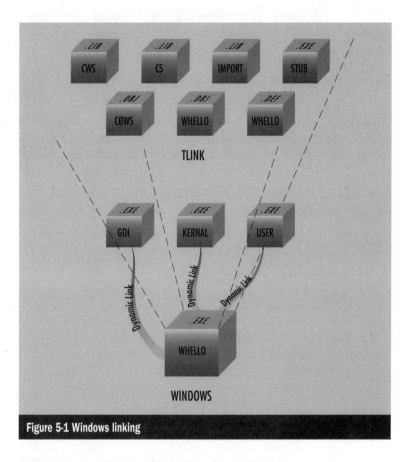

**Figure 5-1 Windows linking**

As shown in Figure 5-1, Windows applications also need to be linked with an additional Windows-specific run-time library, an Import library, a definition file, and a DOS stub.

## Windows-Specific Run-Time Libraries

The Windows-specific run-time library contains routines that are handled differently in the Windows environment than they are in DOS. This allows you to port your DOS applications to Windows with minimal modification. Table 5-3 lists the startup code and Windows-specific run-time libraries compatible with the different memory models. Note that you use a Windows math library instead of the DOS math library. Also note that there are no libraries for the tiny or huge memory models. This is because neither of these memory models is compatible with the Windows environment.

| MODEL | STARTUP CODE | WINDOWS LIBRARY | RUN-TIME LIBRARY | MATH LIBRARY |
|---|---|---|---|---|
| Small | COWS.OBJ | CWS.LIB | CS.LIB | MATHWS.LIB |
| Compact | COWC.OBJ | CWC.LIB | CC.LIB | MATHWC.LIB |
| Medium | COWM.OBJ | CWM.LIB | CM.LIB | MATHWM.LIB |
| Large | COWL.OBJ | CWL.LIB | CL.LIB | MATHWL.LIB |

Table 5-3 Startup code and run-time libraries for different Windows memory models

## Example Linking of a Windows Application

Consider the following "Hello, Windows!" application:

**examp3\hello.c**

```c
#include <windows.h>

char AppTitle[] = "Hello, Windows!";

/* Define the application window's message processing function */
long FAR PASCAL WndProc(HWND hWnd, unsigned msg, WORD wParam,
                        LONG lParam)
{
    RECT rect;
    PAINTSTRUCT ps;
    HDC hDC;

    switch(msg)
    {
       /* Paint the window */
       case WM_PAINT:
            hDC = BeginPaint(hWnd, &ps);

            /* Display the application title in the center of
               the window */
            GetClientRect(hWnd, &rect);
            DrawText(hDC, AppTitle, sizeof(AppTitle) - 1, &rect,
                         DT_SINGLELINE | DT_VCENTER | DT_CENTER);

            EndPaint(hWnd, &ps);
            break;

       /* Time to quit! */
       case WM_DESTROY:
            PostQuitMessage(0);
            break;

       /* All other messages go here. */
       default:
            return(DefWindowProc(hWnd, msg, wParam, lParam));
    }
    return(0);
}
```

```
/* Let the compiler know that we won't be using all the parameters
   in the WinMain() function
*/
#pragma argsused

int PASCAL WinMain(HANDLE hInstance, HANDLE hPrevInstance,
                   LPSTR lpCmdLine, int nCmdShow)
{
   int xDim, yDim;
   HWND hWnd;
   MSG msg;

   /* Register the application window class */
   if(!hPrevInstance)
   {
      WNDCLASS wc;

      wc.style           = CS_HREDRAW | CS_VREDRAW;
      wc.lpfnWndProc     = WndProc;
      wc.cbClsExtra      = 0;
      wc.cbWndExtra      = 0;
      wc.hInstance       = hInstance;
      wc.hIcon           = LoadIcon(NULL, IDI_HAND);
      wc.hCursor         = LoadCursor(NULL, IDC_ARROW);
      wc.hbrBackground   = GetStockObject(WHITE_BRUSH);
      wc.lpszMenuName    = NULL;
      wc.lpszClassName   = AppTitle;

      if(!RegisterClass(&wc))
          return(FALSE);
   }

   /* Get the screen dimensions */
   xDim = GetSystemMetrics(SM_CXSCREEN);
   yDim = GetSystemMetrics(SM_CYSCREEN);

   hWnd = CreateWindow(AppTitle, AppTitle, WS_OVERLAPPEDWINDOW,
          xDim / 4, yDim / 4, xDim / 2, yDim / 2,
          NULL, NULL, hInstance, NULL);

   if(hWnd == NULL)
     return(FALSE);

   /* Display the window */
   ShowWindow(hWnd, nCmdShow);

   /* Enter the message loop */
   while(GetMessage(&msg, 0, 0, 0))
   {
     TranslateMessage(&msg);
     DispatchMessage(&msg);
   }

   /* Exit the application */
   return(0);
}
```

The source code is first compiled into object code using the command line compiler, BCC, as follows:

```
bcc -c -WS hello.c
```

The -c option instructs the compiler to only compile the application and not call TLINK. The -WS option compiles the source code as a Windows application using smart callback prolog and epilog code (see Chapter 2). The following is used to link the application:

```
tlink -TW -c cOws hello, hello, hello, cws import
```

The -TW option instructs TLINK that the target is a Windows application. The -c tells TLINK to use case sensitive linking for nonimport functions, i.e., those functions not listed in an import library such as IMPORT.LIB. C0WS.OBJ is the Windows startup code for the small memory model. The first 'hello' specifies the object code file HELLO.OBJ, the second tells TLINK the application should be called HELLO.EXE, the third tells TLINK to call the map file HELLO.MAP. The CWS.LIB is the static Windows run-time library, CS.LIB is the static DOS run-time library, and IMPORT.LIB contains the list of import functions for the Windows system DLLs.

## The Module Definition File

When the above application is linked, TLINK will display the following warning message:

```
Warning: No module definition file specified: using defaults
```

This warning message is telling you that you did not include a module definition file (.DEF) in the call to TLINK. A module definition file contains information about a Windows application or DLL that the linker needs to create a file that is usable by Windows, such as the size of the stack, the initial size of the local data heap, the functions that should be exported, and the name of the DOS stub application. The default .DEF file used by TLINK if you do not supply your own is the following:

```
CODE        PRELOAD MOVEABLE DISCARDABLE
DATA        PRELOAD MOVEABLE MULTIPLE
HEAPSIZE    4096
STACKSIZE   5120
```

For Dynamic Link Libraries, TLINK uses the following default .DEF file:

```
CODE        PRELOAD MOVEABLE DISCARDABLE
DATA        PRELOAD FIXED SINGLE
HEAPSIZE    4096
```

The meanings for each of these items in the default .DEF file are located in the module definition file reference section.

These default settings are good for most simple applications. You should note, however, that Windows is a very stack-intensive environment. A stack size of 5120 is the minimum required stack size, not the recommend size. You should normally have a stacksize of at least twice the minimum (10240); otherwise, you will probably overflow the stack and encounter "Unrecoverable Application Errors" for no apparent reason.

# LINKING DYNAMIC LINK LIBRARIES

Not all the functions you use in a Windows application are linked by TLINK from the static libraries. Indeed, all the Windows-related functions, such as the CreateWindow() function, are located in Dynamic Link Libraries, called DLL. Functions in Dynamic Link Libraries are shared by all applications running in the Windows environment. When Windows loads your application, it links any required import functions to the function calls in your application—hence the term "dynamic" linking.

## The Windows System DLLs

Windows comes with many different Dynamic Link Libraries. Table 5-4 lists the different DLLs used with every Windows application and a general description of the types of functions stored in the DLL. As you can see, not all DLLs have a .DLL filename extension.

| DYNAMIC LINK LIBRARY | TYPES OF FUNCTIONS |
| --- | --- |
| GDI.EXE | Bitmaps, region, coordinate conversion, device context, pens, brushes, graphics drawing, fonts, metafiles, printing |
| KERNEL.EXE | Application loading and execution, resource loading, communication (COM and LPT), file I/O, memory management, sound, character conversion |
| USER.EXE | Window creation and management, clipboard, cursor, caret, dialog boxes, message management, keyboard, menus |
| WIN87EM.DLL | Coprocessor emulation functions |

Table 5-4 Windows Dynamic Link Libraries

The export functions in DLLs are made accessible by linking them with an Import Library. All export functions in a DLL need to be listed in an import library if they are to be imported into an application. TLINK uses the IMPORT.LIB library to link your applications with a function in one of the DLLs listed in Table 5-4.

## Linking the BC++ Run-Time DLL

Version 3.0 of the Borland C++ software package is shipped with an alternate run-time library for Windows applications, called CRTLDLL.LIB. This is a combination library that contains both normal object code modules and import function references to functions located in the Dynamic Link Library called BC30RTL.DLL. Many of the functions found in the static run-time library can be dynamically linked by Windows when your application is loaded. This greatly reduces the size of your application, because the code for the library functions is located in the DLL instead of linked as a part of your application.

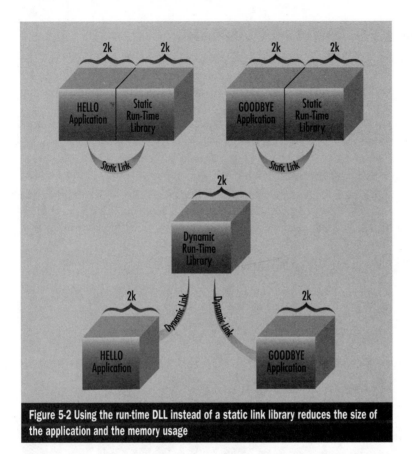

**Figure 5-2 Using the run-time DLL instead of a static link library reduces the size of the application and the memory usage**

Using the run-time DLL also allows more than one application to share the same library code, thus reducing the memory needed to run the application. Consider two similar applications: one that prints a "Hello" message to a window and the other that prints a "Goodbye" message. They would both use the same functions in the run-time library. With static linking, each application would be linked with a private copy of the run-time library object code, as shown in the top portion of Figure 5-2. Each application would be roughly 4K in size with 2K for the application object code and 2K for the run-time library code. Together, both applications would take up 8K of disk space and, if both were run concurrently in Windows, they would take up approximately 8K of memory space. If both applications were compiled using the run-time DLL instead of a static link library, then they would each be only 2K in size and share the same 2K run-time library.

One disadvantage to using the run-time DLL is that the end user must be given a copy of BC30RTL.DLL to use the application. Also, some function calls may operate more slowly if the user's memory is in short supply because the functions may not be resident in memory when called, requiring Windows to load the function off the hard disk.

This slowness when the user's memory is in short supply should be weighed against the possibility that the user may not be able to load an application at all if it also has to make room for all the static run-time routines. A second reason the application may run more slowly is that the run-time DLL uses far more function calls and far pointers.

If you intend to link an application using the run-time DLL and are compiling the application with BCC, the command line compiler, you must define the _RTLDLL macro either in the source code or, preferably, from the command line. The library include files are written to detect the _RTLDLL macro and declare prototypes using far function calls and far pointers where appropriate. For example, the "Hello, Windows!" application can be compiled to use the run-time DLL as follows:

```
bcc -c -D_RTLDLL hello.c
```

The -D command line option defines the _RTLDLL macro. To link an application so that it uses the run-time DLL instead of the static library, you simply replace the CWS.LIB with the CRTLDLL.LIB during the link step as follows:

```
tlink -Tw c0ws hello, hello, hello, crtldll import
```

Note that the IMPORT.LIB library still needs to be linked with the windows application. You do not need to link a math library if you are using the run-time DLL.

## Linking Custom-Written DLLs

When you write your own DLLs for your applications, you link them in a similar manner as you do for a regular Windows application, except you use one of the startup code files listed in Table 5-5 instead of the Windows application startup code. The library files for link DLLs are identical to the ones for Windows applications.

| MODEL | STARTUP CODE | WINDOWS LIBRARY | MATH LIBRARY |
|-------|--------------|-----------------|--------------|
| Small | CODS.OBJ | CWS.LIB | MATHWS.LIB |
| Compact | CODC.OBJ | CWC.LIB | MATHWC.LIB |
| Medium | CODM.OBJ | CWM.LIB | MATHWM.LIB |
| Large | CODL.OBJ | CWL.LIB | MATHWL.LIB |

Table 5-5 Startup code and run-time libraries for different DLL memory models

The following is an example DLL that uses the exported ExampDLLMsg() function to return a global atom to the string ""Hello from the Example DLL!":

**dll\examp.h**
```
#ifndef EXAMP_H
#define EXAMP_H

ATOM FAR PASCAL ExampDLLMsg(void);

#endif
```

**dll\examp.c**

```
#include <windows.h>
#include "examp.h"

ATOM MsgAtom;

/* Dynamic Link Library initialization routine. This function is
   called once when the DLL is first loaded by Windows.
*/
#pragma argsused
int FAR PASCAL LibMain(HANDLE hInstance, WORD wDataSegment,
                       WORD wHeapSize, LPSTR lpszCmdLine)
{
  /* Place our message on the global atom table */
  MsgAtom = GlobalAddAtom("Hello from the Example DLL!");

  /* Unlock the automatic data segment */
  if(wHeapSize != 0)
    UnlockData(0);

  /* Tell Windows the initialization was OK. */
  return(TRUE);
}


/* This function, called Windows Exit Procedure, is called by Windows
   just before the DLL is removed from memory.
*/
#pragma argsused
int FAR PASCAL WEP(int bSystemExit)
{
  /* Remove our message from the global atom table */
  GlobalDeleteAtom(MsgAtom);

  /* Return an 'All Clear' */
  return(1);
}


/* Designate this as an Export function so that it can be called from
   outside the DLL.
*/
ATOM FAR PASCAL _export ExampDLLMsg(void)
{
  return(MsgAtom);
}
```

The EXAMP.C source code is written to place the string "Hello from the Example DLL!" into the global atom table when it is initialized as shown in Figure 5-3. The EXAMP.C source code is compiled to an object code file as follows:

```
bcc -WDE -ms! -c examp.c
```

The -WDE option instructs the BC++ compiler to compile the source code as a Windows Dynamic Link Library with exports explicitly stated using the _export keyword. The -ms! option uses the small memory model, assuming that the Stack Segment register (SS) is not the same as the Data Segment (DS) register. This is true of all DLLs. See the -ms! option

**Figure 5-3 The EXAMP.DLL Dynamic Link Library places the message string onto the Global Atom Table. When HELLO.EXE calls the ExampDLLMsg() function in EXAMP.DLL, it receives the index to the message string which it then retrieves off the Atom Table and displays in the window**

in Chapter 2 for a detailed description of why this is necessary. The -c option compiles the source code to object code without calling TLINK. To link the EXAMP.OBJ object code, we call TLINK from the DOS command line as follows:

```
tlink -TWD -c c0ds examp, examp, examp, cws cs import
```

Except for the -TWD command line option and the C0DS startup code file, the linking of a DLL is the same as for a normal Windows application. The next step is to create an import library for EXAMP.DLL that contains the listing for the exported ExampDLLMsg() function. This is done using the IMPLIB.EXE utility as follows:

```
implib -v examp.lib examp.dll
```

The IMPLIB utility examines the exported functions in EXAMP.DLL and lists them in an import library called EXAMP.LIB. The HELLO.C source code below is compiled and linked using the command line compiler as follows:

```
bcc -WS hello.c examp.lib
```

The -WS option instructs BCC to compile the source code as a Windows application using smart callbacks. The command line compiler is also passed the EXAMP.LIB library created by the IMPLIB. This allows the linker to reference the ExampDLLMsg() function used in HELLO.EXE to its location in EXAMP.DLL.

**dll\hello.c**

```
#include <windows.h>
#include "examp.h"

char AppTitle[] = "Hello, DLL!";
char MsgStr[80];
ATOM MsgAtom;

/* Define the application window's message processing function */
```

```
long FAR PASCAL WndProc(HWND hWnd, unsigned msg, WORD wParam,
                        LONG lParam)
{
  RECT rect;
  PAINTSTRUCT ps;
  HDC hDC;

  switch(msg)
  {
      /* Paint the window */
      case WM_PAINT:
            hDC = BeginPaint(hWnd, &ps);

            /* Display the application title in the center of
               the window */
            GetClientRect(hWnd, &rect);
            DrawText(hDC, MsgStr, lstrlen(MsgStr), &rect,
                       DT_SINGLELINE | DT_VCENTER | DT_CENTER);

            EndPaint(hWnd, &ps);
            break;

      /* Time to quit! */
      case WM_DESTROY:
            PostQuitMessage(0);
            break;

      /* All other messages go here. */
      default:
            return(DefWindowProc(hWnd, msg, wParam, lParam));
  }
  return(0);
}

/* Let the compiler know that we won't be using all the parameters
   in the WinMain() function
*/
#pragma argsused

int PASCAL WinMain(HANDLE hInstance, HANDLE hPrevInstance,
                   LPSTR lpCmdLine, int nCmdShow)
{
  int xDim, yDim;
  HWND hWnd;
  MSG msg;

  /* Register the application window class */
  if(!hPrevInstance)
  {
    WNDCLASS wc;

    wc.style           = CS_HREDRAW | CS_VREDRAW;
    wc.lpfnWndProc     = WndProc;
    wc.cbClsExtra      = 0;
    wc.cbWndExtra      = 0;
    wc.hInstance       = hInstance;
    wc.hIcon           = LoadIcon(NULL, IDI_HAND);
    wc.hCursor         = LoadCursor(NULL, IDC_ARROW);
    wc.hbrBackground   = GetStockObject(WHITE_BRUSH);
    wc.lpszMenuName    = NULL;
    wc.lpszClassName   = AppTitle;
```

```c
  if(!RegisterClass(&wc))
    return(FALSE);
}

/* Grab the message ATOM from the DLL */
MsgAtom = ExampDLLMsg();

/* Get the string for the ATOM */
GlobalGetAtomName(MsgAtom, MsgStr, sizeof(MsgStr));

/* Get the screen dimensions */
xDim = GetSystemMetrics(SM_CXSCREEN);
yDim = GetSystemMetrics(SM_CYSCREEN);

hWnd = CreateWindow(AppTitle, AppTitle, WS_OVERLAPPEDWINDOW,
        xDim / 4, yDim / 4, xDim / 2, yDim / 2,
        NULL, NULL, hInstance, NULL);

if(hWnd == NULL)
  return(FALSE);

/* Display the window */
ShowWindow(hWnd, nCmdShow);

/* Enter the message loop */
while(GetMessage(&msg, 0, 0, 0))
{
  TranslateMessage(&msg);
  DispatchMessage(&msg);
}

/* Exit the application */
return(0);
}
```

# TLINK OPTIONS REFERENCE SECTION

Options for TLINK are specified on the command line preceded by either a '/' or a '-' character, however, they do not need to be separated by spaces. Some command line options for TLINK can be disabled by following the option with a '-'. If an option cannot be disabled using the '-' character, the Default section is listed as (disabled).

## @*filename*                                          Response File

### Purpose
The @*filename* option tells TLINK to use 'filename' for command line options and file parameters.

### Usage
```
TLINK @MY_APP.LNK
```
Use MY_APP.LNK as a response file.

## Description

The DOS command line is restricted to 128 characters, which is not enough room to list all the options, object code files, and libraries needed to link large applications. Using the *@filename* command line option, these items can be placed in a response file and the response file can then be used by TLINK. You can place text in the response file just as you would normally enter the items on the command line, or you can place each item on a new line instead of using a comma. For example, suppose the following were placed in a file called RESP.LNK:

```
c0s hello, hello
hello
cs
```

and TLINK were executed using 'tlink @resp.lnk'. TLINK would then interpret the above response file as if you had entered:

```
c0s hello, hello, hello, cs
```

You may also use the '+' character in the list of object code and library files to continue the listing over several lines. For example, the '+' character after the C0S entry in the following response file causes TLINK to interpret the HELLO entry as part of the object file list:

```
c0s +
hello
hello
hello
cs
```

The BCC command line compiler uses a response file called TURBOC.$LN when it executes TLINK. For example, to link the HELLO.EXE application for the DLL example earlier in the chapter, BCC created the following response file:

**dll\turboc.$ln**
```
C:\BORLANDC\LIB\c0ws.obj+
hello
hello
/c/x/Tw
examp.lib+
C:\BORLANDC\LIB\IMPORT.LIB+
C:\BORLANDC\LIB\mathws.lib+
C:\BORLANDC\LIB\cws.lib
```

and then executed TLINK as follows:

```
TLINK @TURBOC.$LN
```

BCC always erases the TURBOC.$LN file after TLINK completes its operations.

## See Also

Chapter 2: *@filename*      Use a Response File
TLIB: *@filename*      Response File

**Example**
See the examples in the description section.

## 3                                          Link Using 32-Bit Function Offsets

**Purpose**
Use the 3 option to link an application that uses 32-bit function calls. Currently, only TASM will generate code for 32-bit function calls for the 80386 and 80486 microprocessor.

**IDE Option**
None

**Default**
(disabled)
Link using 16-bit function offsets.

**Usage**
–3
Link SOURCE.OBJ using 32-bit function offsets.

**Description**
The 8086 and 80286 microprocessors operate in a memory space in which segments have a maximum offset of 16 bits. Near function calls are made within a segment using a 16-bit offset, and far function calls are made between segments using a combination of a 16-bit segment and a 16-bit offset.

The 80386 and 80486 microprocessor can operate when the memory space is configured such that segments have a maximum offset of 32 bits. In this memory model, near function calls use a 32-bit offset and far function calls between segments use a 48-bit combination of a 16-bit segment and a 32-bit offset. The Borland C and C++ compilers currently have no memory models for this configuration. However, TASM will generate code that uses 32-bit near space.

TLINK normally sets up its internal tables to link using 16-bit function offsets. If it encounters an object code record that uses 32-bit function offsets, it will generate an error message. You use the -3 command line option to instruct TLINK to set up its internal tables for 32-bit function offsets. If you use the -3 option and your application does not contain any 32-bit function offsets, TLINK will still link correctly, however, it will operate more slowly than if you used 16-bit linking.

Note that you cannot call functions with 32-bit offsets unless the processor is configured for protected mode operation. You can operate in a 32-bit near address space in the Windows environment when operating in the enhanced mode. This requires using the WINMEM32.DLL library to set up the code space and moving your application code into the created space. See Appendix E of Microsoft's *Software Developer's Kit Reference Manual* for more information.

### Example

Write an application that uses a 32-bit function offset and link it with the -3 option. The TEST.ASM file creates a segment using 32-bit offsets for the Fnct32Bit() function. The MAIN.C source code prints the 48-bit address for the function.

**3\test.asm**

```
.386

SEGMENT CODE

Fnct32Bit   PROC
    mov   ax, 1234h
    ret
Fnct32Bit   ENDP

ENDS

.8086

.model small, c

.data

public FnctOffset, FnctSeg
FnctOffset    DD    OFFSET   Fnct32Bit
FnctSeg             DW SEG   Fnct32Bit

END
```

**3\main.c**

```
#include <stdio.h>

extern unsigned long FnctOffset;
extern unsigned int  FnctSeg;

void main(void)
{
    printf("Fnct32Bit Address = %04X:%08lX", FnctSeg, FnctOffset);
}
```

The above application is linked using 32-bit function offsets as follows:

```
tlink /3 c--s test main, test, nul, cs
```

The application produces the following output when run:

```
Fnct32Bit Address = 0EBB:00000000
```

# A=*number* Align Code Segments

## Purpose
The -A command line option allows you to modify the code segment alignment. This option only applies to Windows applications and Dynamic Link Libraries.

## IDE Option
Options | Linker | Settings | Segment Alignment

## Default
−A=512

> Align each segment to start on a 512-byte boundary.

## Usage
−A=1024

> Align each segment to start on a 1024-byte boundary.

## Description
In DOS, each segment starts on a 16-byte boundary. This means that each segment has a minimum size of 16 bytes. In the Windows environment, you can specify the starting byte for each segment in your application or DLL to be any power of two using the -A=*number* option. If 'number' is not a power of two, TLINK will round the number up to the next nearest power of two. The value of 'number' must be 2 or more and must also be less than 65,535.

## See Also
Chapter 2: a Byte/Word Alignment

## Example
Link the "Hello, Windows!" application using a segment alignment of 1024 bytes. This is done as follows:

```
tlink −TW −c −A=1024 c0ws hello, hello, hello, cws cs import
```

# C Case Sensitive Imports

## Purpose
The -C option instructs TLINK to use case sensitivity when importing and exporting functions.

## IDE Option
Options | Linker | Settings | Case-sensitive exports

## Default

```
-C-
```

Import functions without sensitivity to case.

## Usage

```
-C
```

Import functions with sensitivity to the case.

## Description

The -C option instructs TLINK to use case sensitivity when linking imported functions. This option is rarely necessary, because most imported functions use the Pascal calling convention, which is case insensitive. The compiler converts all function names that use the Pascal calling convention to uppercase. If all the import functions use the Pascal calling convention, then they will all be uppercase anyway by the time their names are processed by TLINK.

This option has no effect on exported functions. Functions are always exported as they were compiled by the compiler, that is, in uppercase if they use the Pascal calling convention or with case sensitivity if they use standard C notation.

Note that if you do use case sensitive linking of import functions, you must also use the -c option for case sensitive publics and externals.

## See Also

| | |
|---|---|
| c | Case Sensitive Public and External Symbols |
| Chapter 2: p | Use the Pascal Calling Convention |

## Example

Rewrite the EXAMP.DLL library using the normal C (rather than Pascal) calling convention for the ExampDLLMsg() function and link using case sensitivity for the imports. The EXAMP.H and EXAMP.C files would be written as:

**c\examp.h**

```
#ifndef EXAMP_H
#define EXAMP_H

ATOM FAR ExampDLLMsg(void);

#endif
```

**c\examp.c**

```
#include <windows.h>
#include "examp.h"

ATOM MsgAtom;

/* Dynamic Link Library initialization routine. This function is
   called once when the DLL is first loaded by Windows.
*/
```

```
#pragma argsused
int FAR PASCAL LibMain(HANDLE hInstance, WORD wDataSegment,
                       WORD wHeapSize, LPSTR lpszCmdLine)
{
   /* Place our message on the global atom table */
   MsgAtom = GlobalAddAtom("Hello from the Example DLL!");

   /* Unlock the automatic data segment */
   if(wHeapSize != 0)
     UnlockData(0);

   /* Tell Windows the initialization was OK. */
   return(TRUE);
}

/* This function, called Windows Exit Procedure, is called by Windows
   just before the DLL is removed from memory.
*/
#pragma argsused
int FAR PASCAL WEP(int bSystemExit)
{
   /* Remove our message off the global atom table */
   GlobalDeleteAtom(MsgAtom);

   /* Return an 'All Clear' */
   return(1);
}

/* Designate this as an Export function so that it can be called from
   outside the DLL.
*/
ATOM FAR _export ExampDLLMsg(void)
{
    return(MsgAtom);
}
```

These files are compiled and linked as a normal DLL. Note that in the following case there is no need to link using the -C option, but it is necessary to link using the -c option for case sensitive publics and externals:

```
bcc -WDE -ms! -c examp.c
tlink -TWD -c cOds examp, examp, examp, cws cs import
```

The HELLO.C application is the same as that used in the DLL example in the tutorial section of the chapter. This file is recompiled normally using the new EXAMP.H header file as follows:

```
bcc -WS -c hello.c
```

The application is linked using case sensitive imports as follows:

```
tlink -Tw -C -c cOws hello, hello, nul, cws cs import examp
```

Note that both the -C and the -c options must be used to link using case sensitive imports. If the -c option were not used, TLINK would first convert all the public symbols to uppercase and then look for a case sensitive match.

# c Case Sensitive Public and External Symbols

## Purpose
The -c option instructs the compiler to use case sensitivity when linking public and external symbols. You normally use case sensitive linking for all C and C++ applications.

## IDE Option
Options | Linker | Settings | Case-sensitive link

## Default
-c-

Link public and external symbols without sensitivity to case.

## Usage
-c

Link public and external symbols using case sensitivity.

## Description
Without case sensitivity, TLINK will treat the function MyFnct() the same as MY-FNCT() and myfnct(). With case sensitivity, the two functions MyFnct() and MY-FNCT() are considered to be unique symbols.

## See Also
C                   Case-sensitive Imports
Chapter 2: p        Use the Pascal Calling Convention
Chapter 7: sc       Source Case Sensitivity

## Example
Link the "Hello, World!" application using case sensitivity:

```
tlink -c cOs hello, hello, hello, cs
```

# d Duplicate Symbols Warning

## Purpose
The -d option tells TLINK to warn you of duplicate symbol definitions between your object code and library files.

## IDE Option
Option | Linker | Settings | Warn duplicate symbols

## Default
(disabled)

Ignore duplicate symbols and use the first symbol definition encountered.

## Usage

-d

Warn of any duplicate symbols even if they are not used in the application.

## Description

This option is very useful for spotting duplicate symbol bugs, such as when there are two function definitions with the same name located in both an object code module and a library file. When the -d option is enabled, TLINK will issue a warning statement if it finds a symbol in your object code file that is duplicated in one of the library files or if it finds duplicate symbols between library files.

With the advent of EasyWindows, this option is very cumbersome to use in Windows applications as there are many symbols duplicated between the Windows and DOS run-time libraries. Both libraries are required for linking a Windows application.

This option is not related to the error generated when there are duplicated symbols in different object code files in your application.

## See Also

Chapter 2: Fc          Generate COMDEFs
Chapter 2: w           Display Warnings
Chapter 2: w*xxx*       Individual Warnings
Chapter 5: d           Duplicate Symbols Warning
Chapter 6: W           Warning Message Control

## Example

Write an application with duplicate symbols and link using the -d option. The following application defines a sin() function that uses the 80387 coprocessor instruction:

**d\test.c**

```
        /* Tell the compiler to compile via TASM */
        #pragma inline

        #include <stdio.h>
        #include <dos.h>

        double sin(double x)
        {
        double Ans;

           asm {
          .386
          .387
             fld   QWORD PTR x
             fsin
             fstp  QWORD PTR Ans
          .8086
           }
           return(Ans);
        }

        void main(void)
        {
```

```
if(_8087 < 3)
printf("This application requires an 80387 or compatible \
coprocessor.\n");
else
{
    double x = 2.0, Ans;

    /* Call the 80387 version of the sin() function. */
    Ans = sin(x);
    printf("sin(%g) = %g\n", x, Ans);
}
}
```

The above application is compiled and linked separately as follows:

```
bcc -c test.c
tlink -d -c cOs test, test, nul, fp87 maths cs
```

Because the application is linked with the -d option, TLINK generates the following warning statement:

```
Warning: _sin defined in module test.c is duplicated in library file
c:\borlandc\lib\maths.lib in module SIN
```

## e                    Do Not Use Extended Dictionary Information

### Purpose
This option is obsolete in Version 3.0 of BC++. For earlier versions, it disabled the use of extended dictionary information in libraries so as to allow debugging information to be linked into an application.

### IDE Option
None

### Default
(disabled)
Uses libraries extended dictionary information whenever it is available.

### Usage
-e
Ignore any extended dictionary information found in a library.

### Description
The Turbo Librarian (TLIB) has a feature that allows it to store extended information in a library file such that TLINK is able to load this information all at once. This enables TLINK to operate much more quickly, especially when using libraries on a floppy drive or a slow hard disk. TLINK will normally use this information if it is available in a li-

brary. Although this accelerates the linking time, in versions of TLINK before the release of BC++ Version 3.0, it also left out any debug information that might be in the library. The -e option would allow you to disable the use of extended dictionary information and thereby include any debug information in your application from the library if you are linking with the -v option. The version of TLINK shipped with BC++ 3.0 ignores this option, because it includes debugging information from a library even if it does use extended dictionary information.

### See Also
TLIB Reference Section

### Example
None

---

## i                                                    Initialize All Segments

### Purpose
The -i option instructs TLINK to initialize all segments. If a static variable in your application does not have an initializer, it is initialized to 0.

### IDE Option
Options | Linker | Settings | Initialize segments

### Default
(disabled)

    Do not initialize data without an initialized value specified in the source code.

### Usage
−i

    Initialize any data without an initializer to 0.

### Description
Some C and C++ language compilers initialize data to 0 even if there is no initializer specified. For example, consider the following:

```
int Initialized = 0;
int Unintialized;
```

In some C and C++ compilers, both the 'Initialized' and the 'Uninitialized' variables will be set to 0. However, in BC++, only the 'Initialized' integer will be set to 0 and the 'Uninitialized' variable will be left at the value found in that area of memory when the program was loaded. The -i option instructs the linker to initialize all uninitialized data to 0 for compatibility with source code written for other compilers.

Note that this option also increases the size of an application. Also, BC++ normally initializes variables to 0 for C++ applications.

## See Also

| | |
|---|---|
| Chapter 2: Fc | Generate COMDEFs |
| Chapter 2: Ff, Ff=size | Automatic Far Variables |
| Chapter 2: Fm | Use Fc, Ff, Fs Options |
| Chapter 2: Fs | Assume SS equals DS at Run Time |

## Example

Write an application with a large array and compare the sizes with and without the -i option:

**i\test.c**

```
#include <stdio.h>
char Array[32000];
void main(void)
{
    unsigned n;
    for(n = 0; n < sizeof(Array); n++)
    {
        if(Array[n] != 0)
        {
            printf("Array is uninitialized\n");
            break;
        }
        Array[n] = 1;
    }
}
```

The above application is compiled using the following:

```
bcc -c test.c
```

The following will link two applications called INIT.EXE and UNINIT.EXE with and without the -i option, respectively:

```
tlink -i cOs test, init,  nul, cs
tlink    cOs test, uninit, nul, cs
```

The resulting INIT.EXE is 38,656 bytes and the UNINIT.EXE application is 6456 bytes. Note that if the application is compiled as C++ source code, it would be 38,456 bytes in length if compiled without the -i option and 38,656 bytes with the option.

# Lpath                                              Set Library Search Path

## Purpose

The -L option is used to set the default library path for object code and library files.

## IDE Option
Options | Directories | Libraries Directories

## Default
-L

Search for libraries in the current directory only. Note that upon installation of the BC++ software package, a TLINK.CFG file is created that contains the -L option as follows:

-LC:\BORLANDC\LIB

## Usage
-Lc:\borlandc\lib;c:\mylib

## Description
TLINK will always look for .OBJ and .LIB files in the current directory. If it cannot find the required file in the current directory, it searches each of the directories listed in the -L option in turn from left to right until the .OBJ or .LIB file is found or it reaches the end of the list.

## See Also

| | |
|---|---|
| m, s, x | Map File Options |
| Chapter 2: I*path* | Set Include Files Directory |
| Chapter 2: L | Set the Location of Library Files |
| Chapter 6: I*path* | Set Include Path |
| Chapter 7: sd*Path* | Source Code Directory |
| Chapter 7: t*Path* | Startup Directory |

## Example
Modify the -L option in the TLINK.CFG file to set a default library path to include the Class library, Object Window, and Turbo Vision libraries:

**\borlandc\bin\tlink.cfg**
```
    -LC:\BORLANDC\LIB;c:\borlandc\classlib\lib;c:\borlandc\owl\lib;c:\borla
    ndc\tvision\lib
```

---

**l**                                   **Include Line Number Information**

---

## Purpose
The -l option includes line number information in the resulting .MAP file. This information is then available for use by debugging utilities that can use this information.

## IDE Option
None

## Default
(disabled)

Do not include line number information in the .MAP file.

## Usage
-l

Include line number information relating the source code text to the application code.

## Description
This option is a left-over from the days when debugging applications read .MAP files to relate the application code to the source code. This option is rarely used today. Note that the option is only effective if the source code is compiled using either the -y or -v option and linked so as to create a .MAP file.

## See Also
y              Compile Line Number Information
v, vi         Compile with Debug Information

## Example
Compile and link the "Hello, World!" application so as to include line number information in the HELLO.MAP file.

**l\hello.c**
```
1:   #include <stdio.h>
2:
3:   void main(void)
4:   {
5:   printf("Hello, World!");
6:   }
```

The compiling and linking of the above application is accomplished as follows:

```
bcc -y -c hello.c
tlink -l  cOs hello, hello, hello, cs
```

The -y option in the compile step includes line number information in the HELLO.OBJ file. The -l option in the link step extracts this line number information and places it in the HELLO.MAP file in the following format:

```
Line numbers for hello.obj(HELLO.C) segment _TEXT
     3 0000:0291     5 0000:0294    6 0000:029C
Program entry point at 0000:0000
```

The line numbers '3', '5', and '6' list address points in the application that correspond to the line numbers in the source code. This information can then be used by debuggers capable of extracting the line number information from a .MAP file.

## m, s, x                                           Map File Options

### Purpose

The -m, -s, and -x options tell TLINK how to handle .MAP file generation. The -m option causes TLINK to generate a .MAP file that contains an alphabetical listing of public symbols. The -s option is the same as the -m option, except that TLINK also creates a detailed segment map. The -x option tells TLINK not to generate any .MAP file.

### IDE Option

Options | Linker | Off          *for -x*
Options | Linker | Segments     *(TLINK default)*
Options | Linker | Publics      *for -m*
Options | Linker | Detailed     *for -s*

### Default

Generate a .MAP file containing only a list of segments.

### Usage

−x

  Do not generate a .MAP file.

−m

  Generate a .MAP file with a list of segments and public symbols.

−s

  Generate a .MAP file with a list of public symbols and a detailed list of segments.

### Description

Mapping the executable file is very useful for tracking down linking errors. For example, if you have an application that is unable to link a function call you have in one source module with a function definition in another module, you can create a .MAP file of both to see how the compiler is constructing your function names. This lets you check the name mangling performed in C++, the number of significant characters used, the case sensitivity, etc.

Normally, TLINK will generate a .MAP file with a list of segments, such as the following:

```
Start   Stop    Length  Name        Class

00000H  013CEH  013CFH  _TEXT       CODE
013D0H  013D0H  00000H  _FARDATA    FAR_DATA
013D0H  013D0H  00000H  _FARBSS     FAR_BSS
013D0H  013D0H  00000H  _OVERLAY_   OVRINFO
013D0H  013D0H  00000H  _1STUB_     STUBSEG
013D0H  016FFH  00330H  _DATA       DATA
01700H  01701H  00002H  _CVTSEG     DATA
01702H  01707H  00006H  _SCNSEG     DATA
```

```
01708H  01708H  00000H  _CONST     CONST
01708H  0170DH  00006H  _INIT_     INITDATA
0170EH  0170EH  00000H  _INITEND_  INITDATA
0170EH  0170EH  00000H  _EXIT_     EXITDATA
0170EH  0170EH  00000H  _EXITEND_  EXITDATA
0170EH  0174FH  00042H  _BSS       BSS
01750H  01750H  00000H  _BSSEND    BSSEND
01750H  017CFH  00080H  _STACK     STACK
```

Program entry point at 0000:0000

The Start and Stop columns designate the absolute address where each segment starts and stops. The Length column specifies the length of the segment in hexadecimal notation. The Name and Class columns correspond to the name and class of the segments specified using the -Zx compiler option. Many segments are created by the compiler and have no corresponding -Zx option. Other segments listed have a zero length, which means they are not used at all in the applications.

The -m option creates a more detailed .MAP file that includes a listing of public symbols in the application. For example, the following is a partial list of the public symbol portion of the "Hello, World!" .MAP file:

```
Address              Publics by Name

013D:0000            DATASEG@
0000:028D            DGROUP@
0000:0278            _ABORT
0000:029E            _ATEXIT
. . .
013D:009C            ___BRKLVL
013D:009A            ___HEAPBASE
0000:09FA            ___SBRK
0000:1283            ___WRITE

Address              Publics by Value

0000:0000  Abs       __CVTFAK
0000:000C  Abs       __AHINCR
0000:015C            __CLEANUP
. . .
013D:0328            __ROVER
013D:0330            __REALCVTVECTOR
013D:0332            __SCANTODVECTOR
013D:033E            __ATEXITTBL
```

Program entry point at 0000:0000

The first section of the public symbol list is alphabetical. Next, the public symbols are listed as they are ordered in the application. Both lists include the starting address of the symbol using segment:offset far pointer notation. The segment portion of the address can be used to identify which segment contains the symbol by multiplying the hexadecimal number by 16 to convert it to an absolute address and looking up the corresponding address in the list of segments.

The -s option is the same as the -m option except that TLINK generates a detailed listing of the segments instead of a summary, such as the following partial list generated for the "Hello, World!" application:

```
Detailed map of segments
0000:0000 0291 C=CODE     S=_TEXT    G=(none)  M=CO.ASM   ACBP=28
0000:0291 000D C=CODE     S=_TEXT    G=(none)  M=HELLO.C  ACBP=28
. . .
013D:037E 0000 C=BSS      S=_BSS     G=DGROUP  M=LSEEK    ACBP=48
013D:037E 0000 C=BSS      S=_BSS     G=DGROUP  M=SETUPIO  ACBP=48
013D:037E 0000 C=BSS      S=_BSS     G=DGROUP  M=VPRINTER ACBP=48
013D:037E 0000 C=BSS      S=_BSS     G=DGROUP  M=BRK      ACBP=48

013D:037E 0000 C=BSS      S=_BSS     G=DGROUP  M=MEMCPY   ACBP=48
013D:037E 0001 C=BSS      S=_BSS     G=DGROUP  M=PUTC     ACBP=48
013D:0380 0000 C=BSS      S=_BSS     G=DGROUP  M=WRITEA   ACBP=48
013D:0380 0000 C=BSSEND   S=_BSSEND  G=DGROUP  M=CO.ASM   ACBP=28
0175:0000 0080 C=STACK    S=_STACK   G=(none)  M=CO.ASM   ACBP=74
```

The source code modules used to link an application are listed with detailed information on each segment used in the module along with the segment's location and attributes. Table 5-6 lists the general format for the detailed segment listing.

*address* *length* C=*class* S=*segname* G=*group* M=*module* ACBP=*type*

| | |
|---|---|
| *address* | seg:offset address where TLINK placed the segment. |
| *length* | Length of the segment. The length is 0 if the segment was not used by the application. |
| C=*class* | The segment's class name. |
| S=*segname* | The name of the segment. |
| G=*group* | The segment's group name. Not all segments belong to a group. |
| M=*module* | Name of the source code module where the segment originated. |
| ACBP=*type* | Two-digit type code for the segment attributes. The first hexadecimal digit designates the following: |

| | |
|---|---|
| 0 | An absolute segment |
| 2 | BYTE: Aligned along any byte boundary |
| 4 | WORD: Aligned along word addresses |
| 6 | PARA: Paragraph alignment (16-byte boundary) |
| 8 | PAGE: Page aligned (256-byte boundary) |
| 7 | COMMON: undefined alignment |
| A | DWORD: Double-word aligned (4-byte boundary) |

The first two bits of the second digit represent the size of the segment:

| | |
|---|---|
| 0 | USE16: Segment is less than 64K (uses 16-bit offsets). |
| 1 | USE32: Segment is larger than 64K (uses 32-bit offsets). |
| 2 | USE16: Segment is exactly 64K (uses 16-bit offsets). |

*Table 5-6 (continued)*

| | |
|---|---|
| | The size bits are ORed with one of the following to designate how the segment is combined: |
| 0 | PRIVATE: Segment cannot be combined. |
| 4 | MEMORY: Same as public, designates a stack area. |
| 8 | PUBLIC: Segments with the same name are combined. |

**Table 5-6 General format for the detailed segment listing**

The -x option instructs TLINK not to generate a .MAP file. TLINK can perform faster linking if it does not have to generate a .MAP file. An alternative to using the -x option is to use the name NUL for the .MAP filename. DOS ignores application output to any file with the name NUL.

### See Also

| | |
|---|---|
| L*path* | Set Library Search Path |
| Chapter 2: *zXname* | Rename Segment |
| Chapter 7: TDUMP | File Structure |
| Chapter 7: TDMAP | Create Debug Information from .MAP File |

### Example
Link the "Hello, World!" application using the default, -m, and -s .MAP file options:

**m\link.bat**
```
tlink   cOs hello, hello, default, cs
tlink -m cOs hello,hello, m,      cs
tlink -s cOs hello,hello, s,      cs
```

The above .BAT file creates three .MAP files called DEFAULT.MAP, M.MAP, and S.MAP.

## n                                                    Do Not Use Default Libraries

### Purpose
The -n option instructs TLINK not to use the default libraries specified in the .OBJ file. This option only applies when linking object files generated by compilers other than BC++.

### IDE Option
Options | Linker | Settings | Default libraries

### Default
(disabled)
TLINK will search for all libraries specified in the .OBJ file.

## Usage

−n

TLINK will ignore any libraries specified in the .OBJ file.

## Description

Unlike BC++, many compilers, such as the Microsoft C compiler (MSC), generate .OBJ files that call for specific library files. For example, if you compile a small memory model application using MSC, the resulting .OBJ file contains information instructing the linker to use the SLIBCE.LIB library. You can use the -n option to instruct TLINK to ignore the default library information in the .OBJ files and use the libraries specified on the command line. This will enable you to link some .OBJ files compiled by foreign compilers into your BC++ applications. You should note that this cannot be done in all cases. For example, if an application is compiled by the MSC compiler with stack checking enabled, TLINK will not be able to link the .OBJ file because BC++ uses a different stack checking mechanism.

## See Also

| | |
|---|---|
| Chapter 2: Fc | Generate COMDEFs |
| Chapter 2: Ff, Ff=*size* | Automatic Far Variables |
| Chapter 2: Fm | Use Fc, Ff, Fs Options |
| Chapter 2: Fs | Assume SS equals DS at Run Time |

## Example

Write a "Hello, MSC!" application, compile using MSC, and link using TLINK and the BC++ libraries:

n\hello.c
```
    #include "stdio.h"
    void main(void)
    {
        printf("Hello, MSC!");
    }
```

The above file is compiled using MSC as follows:

```
cl -Gs -c hello.c
```

The -Gs option disables stack checking and the -c option instructs MSC not to call the linker. If the resulting HELLO.OBJ file were linked like a normal BC++ .OBJ file, TLINK would not be able to locate the library called for by the .OBJ file (that is, assuming the MSC libraries are not in your BC++ library path) and would generate the following error message:

```
Fatal: Unable to open file 'slibce.lib'
```

The HELLO.OBJ file is properly linked using TLINK and the BC++ libraries as follows:

```
tlink -n cOs hello, hello, hello, cs
```

## o, o*name*, o#*XX*                                 **Overlay Modules**

### Purpose
The -o option is used to tell TLINK to overlay all segments that have a class name end-ing with the letters 'CODE.' The -o*name* option tells TLINK to overlay all segment classes called 'name.' The -o#*XX* option tells TLINK which interrupt the Virtual Run-time Object-Oriented Memory Manager (VROOMM) should use when implementing overlay management. Overlays can only be used with DOS applications.

### IDE Option
Options | Linker | Settings | Overlaid DOS EXE

### Default
(disabled)
> Do not overlay the code segments in any module.

### Usage
-o
> Overlay all code segments with a class name ending in 'CODE' for the remaining .OBJ files.

-o-
> Do not overlay code segments for the remaining .OBJ files.

-oMY_OVL
> Overlay all code segments in the MY_OVL segment class.

-o#45
> Use interrupt 0x45 for implementing overlays.

### Description
You can write applications that are larger than a machine's available memory space by using overlays. An application that uses overlays consists of at least one or more base modules and one or more overlay modules. Those modules that are not one of the base modules, i.e. an overlay module, must be compiled using the -Yo option. When you explicitly use TLINK instead of relying on BCC to link the application, you do not need to compile using the -Y option, but you will need to compile overlay modules with the -Yo option and link them using the -o option. You will also have to link with the OVERLAY.LIB library, which contains the VROOMM code, as well as the normal run-time library. For information on general usage and restrictions associated with using overlays, see the -Y option in the command line compiler reference section of Chapter 2.

When you use the -o option without using a specific segment class, TLINK will gener-ate an overlay for all segments with a class name ending in 'CODE.' You can use a combina-tion of -o and -o- options to enable and disable overlaying specific modules as follows:

```
tlink c0m base -o source1 -o- source2 -o source3, test, nul, overlay cm
```

TLINK will overlay the code in the SOURCE1.OBJ and SOURCE3.OBJ files, but not the code in the C0S.OBJ, BASE.OBJ, or SOURCE2.OBJ files.

If you do specify a segment class name with the -o option, TLINK will only overlay those code segments that have that same class name. You can use as many -o options as you need to name all the code segment classes you'd like overlaid. For example, the following call to TLINK will link the MY_OVL and FOOBAR segment classes as overlays in the SOURCE1.OBJ module:

```
tlink cOm -oMY_OVL -oFOOBAR source1, test, nul, overlay cm
```

Functions in an overlay are executed via an interrupt. TLINK normally uses the 0x3F interrupt for this purpose, but you can instruct TLINK to use a different interrupt as follows:

```
tlink -o#F0 cOm base -o source, test, nul, cm
```

The -o#F0 option instructs TLINK to use the 0xF0 interrupt vector instead of the 0x3F interrupt vector.

### See Also

Chapter 2: Y, Yo     Overlay the Compiled Files
*zXname*            Rename Segment

### Example

Link the OVERLAY application from Chapter 2 using an explicit call to TLINK. The OVERLAY.C and BASE.C files are compiled as follows:

```
bcc -c -mm base.c -Yo overlay.c
```

The -Yo option compiles the OVERLAY.C file as an overlaid module, but not the BASE.C source file. Note that you do not have to compile using the -Y option. TLINK is executed as follows:

```
tlink cOm base -o overlay, test, nul, overlay cm
```

TLINK will create an application called TEST.EXE with the BASE.OBJ and C0M.OBJ code resident at all times and the OVERLAY.OBJ code overlaid.

## P, P=*size*               Pack Code Segments

### Purpose

The -P option tells TLINK to pack the code segments for a Windows application or DLL. The -P=*size* specifies the size limit for packing code segments. This option is ignored by TLINK for DOS applications.

### IDE Option

Options | Linker | Settings | Pack code segments

## Default

−P

Pack code segments using a limit of 8192 bytes per segment.

## Usage

−P=10240

Pack code segments using a limit of 10240 bytes per segment.

−P−

Do not pack code segments.

## Description

When TLINK creates a Windows application or DLL that uses multiple code segments, such as those compiled using the medium or large memory model, it will normally combine different code segments where possible until it reaches the default packing limit of 8192 bytes per segment. For example, consider a medium memory model Windows application that has the source files ONE.C, TWO.C, and THREE.C. BC++ will place the code associated with each of those source files into segments called ONE_TEXT, TWO_TEXT, and THREE_TEXT. If segment ONE_TEXT has 10,000 bytes, TWO_TEXT has 5000 bytes, and THREE_TEXT has 2000 bytes, then TLINK will combine the TWO_TEXT and THREE_TEXT segments into one physical segment of 7000 bytes. It will not combine segment ONE_TEXT, because it already has more than 8192.

The advantage to packing code segments is that Windows can manipulate code segments more efficiently if they are about 4K in size. BC++ uses the limit of 8192 so that the average size of the packed segments will be close to 4K. The only time you would not use code packing is when you are porting assembly language software to Windows that requires code to be placed in specific segments.

## See Also

| | |
|---|---|
| i | Initialize All Segments |
| Chapter 2: z*Xname* | Rename Segment |
| Chapter 6: A | Order Segments Alphabetically |
| Chapter 6: S | Order Segments Sequentially |

## Example

Write an EasyWindows application and link with the code packing enabled and disabled:

p\test.c

```
#include <stdio.h>
void PrintSomething(void)
{
    printf("Hello there!.\n");
}
```

p\main.c

```
#include <stdio.h>
void main(void)
{
    PrintSomething();
}
```

The preceding code is compiled as follows:

```
bcc -WS -c -mm test.c main.c
```

The following uses the -P option to link an application called PACK.EXE and the -P- option to link an application called NOPACK.EXE:

```
tlink -Tw  -P  cOwm test main, pack,   pack,   cwm import
tlink -Tw -P- cOwm test main, nopack, nopack, cwm import
```

The following excerpts from the .MAP files show how TLINK combined the separate MAIN_TEXT and TEST_TEXT segments in the NOPACK application into a single physical segment in the PACK application:

**p\nopack.map**

| Start | Length | Name | Class |
|-------|--------|------|-------|
| 0001:0000 | 2617H | _TEXT | CODE |
| 0002:0000 | 0018H | TEST_TEXT | CODE |
| 0003:0000 | 0013H | MAIN_TEXT | CODE |

**p\pack.map**

| Start | Length | Name | Class |
|-------|--------|------|-------|
| 0001:0000 | 2617H | _TEXT | CODE |
| 0002:0000 | 0018H | TEST_TEXT | CODE |
| 0002:0018 | 0013H | MAIN_TEXT | CODE |

In the NOPACK application, the TEST_TEXT segment is assigned selector 2 and the MAIN_TEXT segment is assigned selector 3. In the PACK application, both the TEST_TEXT and the MAIN_TEXT segments are assigned selector 2. Selector 1, which contains the C0M.OBJ code, is not packed because it has a length of 9751 bytes (0x2617), which is larger than the 8192 pack limit.

## Tw, Twd, Twe                    Link to a Windows Application or DLL

### Purpose
The -Tw and -Twe options both instruct TLINK to create a Windows application. The -Twd option instructs TLINK that the target application is a Windows Dynamic Link Library (DLL).

### IDE Option
Options | Linker | Settings | Windows EXE *for -Tw or -Twe*
Options | Linker | Settings | Windows DLL *for -Twd*

### Default
-Tde
    The target is a DOS .EXE application.

## Usage

`-Tw`

> The target is a Windows application.

`-Twe`

> Same as above.

`-Twd`

> The target is a Windows Dynamic Link Library.

## Description

Windows applications and DLLs require a special .EXE format. The header of a Windows .EXE is identical to a DOS .EXE file. This is the reason a Windows application can be executed from the DOS command line and not lock up the computer. The DOS header in a Windows application is referred to as the 'Old-Style' header. Windows applications and DLLs also have a second header called the 'New-Style' header, which contains the information needed for Windows to properly load the applications resources, code, and data. The -Tw and -Twe options instruct TLINK to create this second header and to use a module definition file to determine the characteristics of the code and data segments, the size of the stack and heap, and which DOS application (called the DOS 'stub') TLINK should use for the 'Old-Style' header.

The -Twd option instructs TLINK to create a Windows Dynamic Link Library. Windows DLLs are identical to Windows applications except for one bit in the 'New-Style' header. Everything else is the same. TLINK responds to the -Twd command line option in the same way it would for the -Tw or -Twe option, except that it sets this bit to indicate the file is a DLL and appends a .DLL extension if no extension is specified in the command line parameter for the name of the target file.

## See Also

t, Tdc, Tde   Compile to a DOS .COM or .EXE File.

## Example

See the examples used in the tutorial section at the beginning of this chapter.

# t, Tdc, Tde                                    Link to a DOS .COM or .EXE File

## Purpose

The -t option instructs TLINK to generate a .COM file. The -Tdc option is identical to the -t option. These option can only be used for DOS applications compiled using the small memory model. The -Tde option creates a DOS .EXE application.

## IDE Option

Options | Linker | Settings | Standard DOS EXE     *for -Tde*
Options | Linker | Settings | Overlaid DOS EXE     *for -Tde with -o*

> There is no IDE equivalent for the -t or -Tdc options.

## Default

−Tde

>   The target application is a DOS .EXE file.

## Usage

−t

>   The target application is a DOS .COM file.

−Tdc

>   Same as above.

## Description

There may be instances (such as for small utility programs) in which it is preferable to generate a .COM file instead of an .EXE file. To do this you must first compile the application code using the small memory model. The object code files are then linked as in a normal DOS application except that you use the -t or -Tdc option and the C0T.OBJ startup file.

Note that a .COM file cannot contain any debug information. If you need to debug a .COM file, first generate the application as an .EXE file and then use the TDSTRIP utility with the -s and -c options to create a .COM command file and a .TDS symbolic information file that can be used by the Turbo Debugger.

## See Also

Tw, Twe, Twd            Compile to a Windows Application or DLL

Chapter 7: TDSTRIP      Symbolic Information Stripper

## Example

Compile the "Hello, World!" application using the small memory model and link as a DOS .COM file. The HELLO.C source code is first compiled as follows:

```
bcc −c hello.c
```

The application is linked as a .COM file as follows:

```
tlink −t c0t hello, hello, hello, cs
```

## Vt                                        Compress Debug Information

## Purpose

The -Vt option compresses debug information placed in the target application. This option only applies to targets linked using the -v option.

## IDE Option

Options | Linker | Settings | Compress debug info

## Default

```
-Vt-
```
Do not compress debug information.

## Usage

```
-Vt
```
Compress debug information.

## Description

TLINK normally compiles the debug information in an uncompressed format. Use the -Vt option to compress the debug information. The advantage of compressing debug information is it reduces the size of the application and also loads more quickly into the debugger. The amount of the resulting compression varies between programs. You will see no compression at all in small programs, whereas you will see significant amounts of compression in large applications.

## See Also

| | |
|---|---|
| v | Include Full Symbolic Debug Information |
| Chapter 2: v, vi | Compile with Debug Information |
| Chapter 7: TDSTRIP | Utility |

## Example

Link the WFRACTAL application in Chapter 10 using the -Vt option to compress the debug information. The following is from the .MAK file for WFRACTAL:

```
wfractal.exe: wfractal.cfg $(Link_Include) $(Link_Exclude)
        $(TLINK) /v/x/c/P-/Vt/Twe/L$(LIBPATH) @&&|
cOws.obj+
atpoint.obj+
drawing.obj+
intro.obj+
palette.obj+
wfractal.obj+
zoom.obj
wfractal
fractdll.lib+
mathws.lib+
import.lib+
cws.lib
wfractal.def
|
RC wfractal.res wfractal.exe
```

The resulting application is 3K smaller with the -Vt option than when linked without compression.

| **V** | **Include Full Symbolic Debug Information** |

## Purpose
The -v option instructs TLINK to include symbolic information it finds in the .OBJ files in the target file.

## IDE Option
Options | Debugger | On

- or -

Options | Debugger | Standalone

## Default
(disabled)

Debug information is not included in the target.

## Usage
–v

Debug information is linked with the target.

## Description
The BC++ compiler will produce symbolic information that can be used by the debugger if you compile the source code using the -v option for the BCC command line compiler or mark the box in the [Options][Compiler][Advanced][Debug info in OBJs] IDE menu item. You also need to link using the -v option for this debugging information to be placed into the target application or DLL.

Note that you always have the option of removing this debugging information later using the TDSTRIP utility. You can also use TDSTRIP to move the debugging information into a separate symbolic information (.TDS) file that can be used by the Turbo Debugger.

## See Also
| Vt | Compress Debug Information |
| Chapter 2:  v, vi | Compile with Debug Information |
| Chapter 7:  TDSTRIP | Utility |

## Example
Compile and link the "Hello, World!" application with symbolic information for use by the Turbo Debugger. The HELLO.C source file is first compiled with the -v option for the command line compiler as follows:

```
bcc -c -v hello.c
```

Next the application is linked using the -v option for TLINK as follows:

```
tlink -v c0s hello, hello, hello, cs
```

# MODULE DEFINITION FILE REFERENCE

Module definition files (.DEF) define certain characteristics about a Windows application or Dynamic Link Library. The linker needs to know these characteristics to create an executable file or DLL that will operate as expected in the Windows environment. Module definition files can contain one or all of the following statements: CODE, DATA, Description, EXETYPE, EXPROTS, HEAPSIZE, IMPORTS, LIBRARY, NAME, SEGMENTS, STACKSIZE, STUB. If a particular statement is missing from the .DEF file, TLINK will use the defaults listed in the Default section for the statement. Note that the Default section is not the same as the default .DEF file used by TLINK if no .DEF file is specified. These defaults only apply if a .DEF file is specified and the statement is missing.

Comments may also be included in .DEF files using the semicolon (;). You use the semicolon as you would normally use it for comments in an assembly language file. TLINK will ignore any text following a semicolon to the end of the line. For example, consider the following:

```
; The CODE statement defining the attributes for the code segments
CODE MOVEABLE DISCARDABLE PRELOAD

; List of Export functions
EXPORTS
        MYDIALOGFNCT ; Export statement for MyDialogFnct() in the
                     ;  TEST.C file.
```

Adding comments to your .DEF file makes them much more readable.

One point to consider when using a module definition file is that the statement's syntax was developed by Microsoft for use by their linker to link both Windows and OS/2 applications. Borland uses the same syntax for compatibility even though not all statements or options apply to Windows 3.0 applications. Later revisions of Windows may use more attributes than are currently recognized by Windows 3.0. Any option or statement that is ignored by TLINK is noted in the description or purpose section for the statement.

# CODE

### Purpose

The CODE statement tells Windows how it should handle the code segments in your application. This includes information such as whether the code is moveable or whether the code should be loaded all at once or only when needed.

### Syntax

```
CODE    [FIXED/MOVEABLE]  [[NON]DISCARDABLE]   [PRELOAD/LOADONCALL]
        [[NO]IOPL]        [[NON]SHARED]        [[NON]CONFORMING]
        [EXECUTE[ONLY/READ]]
```

## Default

```
CODE FIXED NONDISCARDABLE LOADONCALL
```

If there is no CODE statement in a .DEF file, then TLINK uses the above defaults.

## Description

Windows has some very sophisticated memory management facilities. It can move your applications code to different locations in memory. It can also remove your code from memory entirely when memory gets tight and reload it from the disk when needed. You use the CODE statement in the .DEF file to tell Windows if these types of operations are permissible. For example, if you use the MOVEABLE attribute, then you are giving Windows permission to move your code in memory. The FIXED attribute tells Windows not to move the code in memory. When Windows moves your application's code in memory, it is a totally transparent operation even if your application uses far-function pointers. For this reason, the MOVEABLE attribute should normally be used so as to allow Windows the freedom to optimize memory usage.

The DISCARDABLE attribute tells Windows that if memory requirements get tight, it has your permission to remove your code from memory until it is needed. For example, the user could have loaded your application and then switched to another task. Some other action by the user may require more memory than is currently available on the machine. If your application gave permission for Windows to discard your code when required, the Windows would simply remove your application from memory to free up more space. When the user switched back to your application, it would be reloaded from the disk. Note that if your application were performing some background task, Windows would not remove it from memory. If you use the DISCARDABLE statement, TLINK defaults with the MOVEABLE attribute.

The NONDISCARDABLE attribute tells Windows that it does not have your permission to remove the code from memory. You would normally use this option if you store nonstatic data in a code segment which would be lost if Windows removed the code segment from memory.

The PRELOAD attribute tells Windows to load all the code into memory when the application is loaded. The LOADONCALL attribute operates in a similar manner to a DOS overlay in that the code is only loaded off the disk when a function in one of the unloaded segments is called.

The CODE statement operates globally on all code segments in your application. You can use the SEGMENTS statement to customize the attributes of individual segments.

The following attributes are only optional in OS/2 applications and are ignored by TLINK:

```
[NO]IOPL [NON]SHARED [NON]CONFORMING EXECUTE[ONLY/READ]
```

See the SEGMENTS statement description for details on which of these attributes are used by TLINK for Windows applications.

### Example

Write a CODE definition file statement for an application that permits discardable, moveable code segments that are all loaded with the application.

```
CODE MOVEABLE DISCARDABLE PRELOAD
```

# DATA

### Purpose

The DATA statement provides Windows with information on your application's standard data segment, such as whether it has one, whether it is fixed or moveable, and whether you are allowing more than one instance of the application to run at the same time.

### Syntax

```
DATA    [NONE/SINGLE/MULTIPLE] [FIXED/MOVEABLE] [PRELOAD]
        [READ[ONLY/WRITE]]
```

### Description

The application's standard data segments are the segments in the DGROUP segment group of the DATA segment class. This is the data segment group that is created automatically by Windows that contains the local heap and the stack.

The NONE attribute informs Windows that the module has no standard data segment and therefore no local heap or stack. This option can only be used for Dynamic Link Libraries, because a DLL will use the calling application's stack and does not use one for itself. Windows applications must have a stack and therefore cannot use the NONE option

You use the SINGLE attribute for Windows applications when you do not want the user to run more than one instance of your application concurrently. Windows will prevent the user from loading a second instance of an application if the standard data segment has the SINGLE attribute. You also use the single attribute for DLLs which require a local heap.

The MULTIPLE attribute gives Windows permission to create more than one instance of your application when requested by the user. When Windows creates a second instance, it does so by creating another copy of the application's initial data and stack. It does not create a second copy of the code segments, but instead uses the same function code loaded with the first instance.

The MULTIPLE attribute does not apply to Dynamic Link Libraries, because Windows will only load one instance of a DLL regardless of the number of applications using it.

The MOVEABLE and FIXED attributes either give or deny Windows permission to move the standard data segment once it is loaded. All Windows applications should use the MOVEABLE attribute whenever possible so as to give Windows the freedom to effectively manage the computer's memory resources. If, however, you are porting an application to Windows that uses long-term storage of far pointers to data in the standard data

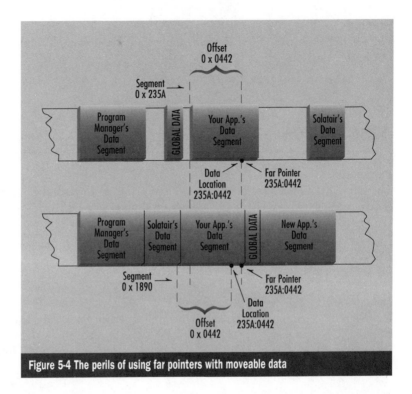

**Figure 5-4 The perils of using far pointers with moveable data**

segment, i.e., far pointers to local data, then you should use the FIXED attribute. The reason for this is shown in Figure 5-4. Suppose you've stored a far pointer to data located at offset 0x0442 in your application's local heap. The compiler generates the far pointer by using the segment location for the local heap and creating a far pointer with the value of 235A:0442. If at some later point in time the user loads another application and Windows needs to move your data segment to make room in memory, such as in segment 0x1890, then the far pointer no longer points to offset 0x0442 in your application's local heap. Using the FIXED attribute would prevent Windows from moving your local heap; however, in the above situation, it would also have prevented the user from loading another application.

Note that short-term storage of far pointers does not present a problem so long as you do not use the far pointer after control of the computer has been returned to Windows. Windows will only move the local heap while your application has control if your application calls a memory allocation function.

The standard data segment is always set with the PRELOAD attribute. You can, however, explicitly list this attribute as part of the DATA statement.

Windows applications can only use the READWRITE attribute. The READ ONLY attribute is used in OS/2 applications for restricting write access to specific data segments. The READONLY attribute is ignored by TLINK.

**Example**

Write a DATA statement for a Windows application that permits multiple instances and a moveable local heap:

```
DATA     MULTIPLE MOVEABLE
```

# DESCRIPTION

### Purpose

The DESCRIPTION statement allows you to place text towards the beginning of the binary executable file of either a Windows application or a DLL. This text is usually a copyright statement.

### Syntax

```
Description 'text string'
```

### Description

Copyright laws require a readable statement of copyright in executable files. The DESCRIPTION statement in a .DEF file allows you to place this statement into your executables. Only one DESCRIPTION statement is allowed in a .DEF file. Note that the statement cannot contain any (') or (") characters.

### Example

Write a copyright statement for the Fractal DLL and place it in the executable file:

```
Description 'Fractal DLL, Copyright (C) 1991 Mark Peterson'
```

# EXETYPE

### Purpose

The EXETYPE statement is not used by TLINK, but is allowed in a .DEF file to maintain compatibility with .DEF files written for the Microsoft linker.

### Syntax

```
EXETYPE WINDOWS
```

### Description

The Microsoft linker uses the .DEF file to link both Windows and OS/2 applications. In these .DEF files the EXETYPE can either be "WINDOWS" or "OS/2". TLINK will currently only accept an EXETYPE of "WINDOWS".

**Example**

Write an EXETYPE statement for a Windows application:

```
EXETYPE WINDOWS
```

# EXPORTS

**Purpose**

The EXPORTS statement allows you to list the functions you'd like exported that may or may not have been compiled using the _export keyword in the source code. The EXPORTS section also allows you to assign ordinal values to export functions as well as differentiate between the name used internally within the application and the name of the function actually exported. The EXPORT section can also be used to state the number of parameters that must be passed to the function.

**Syntax**

```
EXPORTS
    [FnctName[=InternalName][@ordinal][RESIDENTNAME] [NODATA]
    [NumParam]]
    [. . .]
```

**Description**

Any function you expect to be called by Windows must be exported. The reason for this is that the Windows system uses a different Data Segment (DS) register value than the one required by your application. If Windows calls an application's function that has not been exported, the DS register will not be set to the proper value and you will have problems accessing global data within the application. When a function is exported, TLINK places the function name in a special table that contains information on the proper value Windows should use for the DS register. Note that the exporting of functions is not required if your application uses the -WS (smart callbacks) when compiling the source code.

The 'NumParam' option is for use with OS/2 applications. This option is ignored by TLINK.

## Ordinal Values

The preferred method for exporting a function if you are not compiling with the -WS option is to use the _export keyword with the function definition in the source code. This will cause TLINK to place the function name in the export table just as if you had listed the function in the EXPORT section. However, you always have the option of listing the functions explicitly in the EXPORTS section of the .DEF file using an original value. There are several reasons why you may want to do this. One reason would be to save space. Exported functions are stored in the export table using character strings representing the function names. For example, the MyDialog() function name is stored in the export table as the string "MYDIALOG." Applications which have many exported functions with long function names, such as the long names assigned to functions in C++ applications, can take up a significant amount of space. Assigning the function an ordinal value in the EXPORTS section tells the linker not to place the character string in the export table, but to instead reference the function by using its ordinal number. For example, consider the following:

```
EXPORTS
  MYDIALOG        @1      ; The MyDialog() function
```

Instead of Windows referencing the MyDialog() function using the "MYDIALOG" string, it uses the ordinal value of the integer 1 to reference the function.

You can tell TLINK to export a function using both the ordinal value and the character string by using the RESIDENTNAME keyword. For example, the following causes TLINK to store both the ordinal value and the string for the functions name in the export table:

```
EXPORTS
  MYDIALOG        @1 RESIDENTNAME   ; The MyDialog() function
```

## Using the EXPORTS Statement with C++ Functions

Function naming conventions in C++ applications are not as straightforward as those for C because of the language's use of function overloading. To implement function overloading, the BC++ compiler performs 'name mangling' on the function names, that is, BC++ creates function names that represent the types of parameters passed to the function. For example, consider the following function prototypes:

```
void FAR PASCAL _export MyFunction(unsigned char);
void FAR PASCAL _export MyFunction(unsigned char, int, long);
void FAR PASCAL _export MyFunction(long);
```

C++ allows you to use functions that have the same name, but differ in the types and/or number of parameters passed to the function. Each of the names for the above functions is mangled by the BC++ compiler to reflect the number and types of parameters passed to the function. This name mangling allows TLINK to differentiate among the three of them. This can, however, create problems if you need to list a C++ function in the exports section, as you must use the mangled name recognized by TLINK. The easiest way to create a list of exports is to first compile and link the application or DLL, and then use the IMPDEF utility. This utility uses the following syntax:

```
impdef dest[.def] source[.dll]
```

The 'dest' parameter is the pathname for the .DEF file and the 'source' is the pathname for the source .DLL or .EXE file. If, for example, you have a TEST.EXE application which contained the above three functions, you could use the IMPDEF utility to create a .DEF file as follows:

```
impdef test.def test.exe
```

The IMPDEF utility would then create the following TEST.DEF file.

**exports\test.def**
```
LIBRARY    TEST
Description 'TEST.EXE                    '
EXPORTS
        @MYFUNCTION$QL      @1 ; myfunction(long)
        @MYFUNCTION$QUCIL   @2 ; myfunction(unsigned char,int,long)
        @MYFUNCTION$QUC     @3 ; myfunction(unsigned char)
```

## Internal Names for Export Functions

You can rename your export functions to something different when you export them via the EXPORTS statement. For example, the following exports the MyExport() function as FUNCTION:

```
EXPORTS
Function = MyExport
```

This allows you to use the function name MyExport() internally within your application, but any application calling the function from outside your application or DLL would use the name Function(). Keep in mind that since export functions normally use the Pascal calling convention, the function names are not case sensitive.

## Data Binding

Exported functions normally set the DS register to a value that corresponds to the function's data segment. There may be times, however, when you want the DS register to retain the value from the calling application. You do this by using the NODATA option. This would allow your application or DLL to access global near data in the calling application. For example, consider the following export:

```
EXPORTS
    MyFunction NODATA
```

In this example, MyFunction() is not bound to any particular data segment and will use data segment from the calling application. This is particularly useful if a DLL needs to allocate or modify local memory in the calling application.

Note that the NODATA export attribute will not operate correctly with applications compiled using the smart callbacks (-WS) option. When applications are compiled using smart callbacks, BC++ generates code for far functions that sets the DS register to the same value as the Stack Segment (SS) register, thus bypassing any export table created by TLINK.

### Example

See the individual examples in the preceding description section.

# HEAPSIZE

## Purpose
The HEAPSIZE statement informs Windows of the initial size to use for the local heap in bytes.

## Syntax
`HEAPSIZE bytes`

## Description
The initial value of an application's local heap is determined by the HEAPSIZE statement. Windows will expand the size of the local heap as needed, so this value has little importance. The initial heap size will be zero if there is no HEAPSIZE in the .DEF file. If a HEAPSIZE statement is used, then the minimum size is 256 bytes.

Note that the size specified by the HEAPSIZE statement and the STACKSIZE statement together plus any static data in your application's automatic data segment cannot exceed 64K.

## Example
Write a HEAPSIZE statement that sets the initial size of an application's local heap to 1024 bytes:

```
HEAPSIZE 102
```

# IMPORTS

## Purpose
The IMPORTS statement informs Windows of the names of the functions and Dynamic Link Libraries you wish to import for use in your application. This statement is not required if you are using an import library.

## Syntax
```
IMPORTS
[InternalName=]ModuleName.FnctName
```

## Description
TLINK will normally use the functions listed in an import library to create the import list needed by Windows. However, you have the option of listing the import functions in the IMPORTS section of the .DEF file. One reason for doing this is if you would like to call a function by a name other than the exported name or by its ordinal value. For example, suppose you would like to call the function MyDialog() in a DLL called OTHER.DLL, but you already have a function in your application called MyDialog(). The solution would be to use the following IMPORTS statement:

```
IMPORTS
    OtherDialog = Other.MyDialog
```

The above import tells TLINK to dynamically link the function calls referred to as OtherDialog() in your source code to the DLL function called MyDialog() in the OTHER.DLL Dynamic Link Library. This enables you to use a function in your application called MyDialog() and still call the MyDialog() function in the OTHER.DLL library file.

You may also import functions by the exported ordinal value. For example, if the MyDialog() function in the above example were exported as follows:

```
EXPORTS
    MyDialog @1
```

then you could import the MyDialog() function into your application using the ordinal value of '1' as follows:

```
IMPORTS
    OtherDialog = Other.1
```

Importing by ordinal values saves space, as only the integer, rather than the character string "MYDIALOG," is actually stored in the application's import table.

### Example

See the examples in the description section above.

# LIBRARY, NAME

### Purpose

The LIBRARY and NAME statements designate the name of the Dynamic Link Library and a Windows application, respectively. These statements are not used by TLINK.

### Syntax

LIBRARY *name*
NAME *name*

### Description

The Microsoft linker does not have command line switches that can be used to designate whether the target is a Windows application or a Dynamic Link Library. Instead, it uses the LIBRARY and NAME statements in the .DEF file. If the .DEF file contains the NAME statement, then the target is a Windows application. If the .DEF file contains a LIBRARY statement, then the target is a DLL. Because command line switches are used to designate the target, TLINK ignores these statements in a .DEF file. The two statements are permitted in .DEF files used by TLINK to provide compatibility with module definition files written for use with the Microsoft linker.

### Example

None

# PROTMODE, REALMODE

### Purpose

The PROTMODE statement directs TLINK to create an application or DLL that will not run in the real mode. The REALMODE statement allows the application to run in either the real mode or the protected mode.

### Syntax

PROTMODE

Application/DLL will only run with Windows operating in the standard or enhanced mode.

REALMODE

Application/DLL will run with Windows operating in any mode.

### Description

TLINK defaults to creating Windows applications and DLLs with the REALMODE attribute, which will operate with Windows operating in the read, standard, or enhanced modes. You may want some applications you write to only operate with Windows in the standard or enhanced mode. For those applications, you would use the PROTMODE attribute. The statement in the .DEF file causes TLINK to set a bit in the header file that tells Windows that it must be operating in the standard or enhanced mode to load the application. If Windows loads an application or DLL with this bit set and it is operating in the real mode, Windows will generate a message box informing the user that Windows should be run in the standard or enhanced mode to load your application.

### Example

Write a .DEF file for the "Hello, Windows!" application that will create an application that will not load with Windows in the real mode:

**examp3\hello.def**

```
CODE MOVEABLE DISCARDABLE
DATA MOVEABLE MULTIPLE

STACKSIZE 5120
HEAPSIZE  1024

PROTMODE
```

# SEGMENTS

### Purpose

The SEGMENTS statement is used to define the attributes of specific code and data segments by name.

## Syntax

```
SEGMENTS
    SegName [CLASS'name'][MinAlloc][FIXED/MOVEABLE][[NON]DISCARDABLE]
    [PRELOAD/LOADONCALL][READ[ONLY/WRITE]] [[NON]SHARED]
    [EXECUTE[ONLY/READ]] [[NO]IOPL] [[NON]CONFORMING] [[NON]SHARED]
    [ . . .]
```

## Description

The SEGMENTS statement allows you to modify the attributes of code segments individually by name rather than globally as with the CODE statement. The CLASS statement allows you to designate the segment class associated with SegName. If no CLASS is specified, then TLINK assumes that SegName belongs in the CODE class.

The MinAlloc parameter is used in the Microsoft linker to specify the minimum allocation size for the segment. This parameter is not used by TLINK.

See the CODE statement description for information on FIXED, MOVEABLE, DISCARDABLE, NONDISCARDABLE, PRELOAD, LOADONCALL.

The following options are only used for linking OS/2 applications and are ignored by TLINK:

| | |
|---|---|
| READ[ONLY/WRITE] | Used with data segments to set read/write access rights. Windows 3.0 only uses the READWRITE attribute. |
| [NON]SHARED | Used with code segments. Applications with NONSHARE attributes receive separate copies of the segment for each instance of the application. Windows 3.0 always uses the SHARED attribute for code segments. |
| EXECUTE[ONLY/READ] | Used with code segments to allow read access rights. Windows 3.0 always uses the EXECUTEREAD attribute. |
| [NO]IOPL | Used with code segments to determine I/O bus privileges. This attribute has no equivalent in Windows 3.0. Applications have full access to I/O ports in the real and standard mode and virtualized access to ports in the enhanced mode. |
| [NON]CONFORMING | This attribute only applies to code segments executed by an 80286 microprocessor. A CONFORMING code segment operates at the same privilege level as the caller when called from either Ring 2 or Ring 3. Windows 3.0 always uses NONCONFORMING; however, because all applications use the same privilege ring as the Windows system, this attribute has no effect. |

**Example**

Define the attributes of the MY_TEXT code segment to be moveable, discardable, and only loaded when needed:

```
SEGMENTS
    MY_TEXT CLASS 'CODE' MOVEABLE DISCARDABLE LOADONCALL
```

# STACKSIZE

**Purpose**

The STACKSIZE statement is used to specify the size of the stack in a Windows application. A Dynamic Link Library does not have a stack and should not use the STACKSIZE statement.

**Syntax**

```
STACKSIZE bytes
```

**Description**

The stack in a Windows application is used for the same purposes as the stack in a DOS application; that is, to provide space for function return addresses, parameter passing, and local (automatic) function variables. The size you set for your applications stack depends on how many function calls you make in the application, the number of parameters passed with each, and the size of your automatic variables within the functions. Windows is a very stack intensive environment and requires a minimum stack size of 5120 bytes. Windows will ignore any stacksize statement smaller than 5120 bytes and set the size of the stack to 5120 bytes. The recommended stack size for most applications is at least 10,240 bytes.

TLINK will ignore any STACKSIZE statement in the .DEF file of a DLL.

Note that the size specified by the STACKSIZE statement and the HEAPSIZE statement plus any static data in your application's automatic data segment cannot exceed 64K.

**Example**

Write a module definition statement that sets the size of the stack to 10,240 bytes:

```
STACKSIZE    10240
```

# STUB

**Purpose**

The STUB statement tells the linker which DOS application should be linked with the Windows application or Dynamic Link Library.

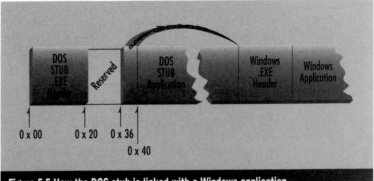

**Figure 5-5 How the DOS stub is linked with a Windows application**

### Syntax
STUB '*filename*'

### Description
Every Windows application and DLL contains a DOS application that can be executed from the DOS command line. The STUB statement tells TLINK which DOS application should be linked with the Windows application or DLL.

The DOS stub portion of a Windows application or DLL is actually linked as part of the executable code rather than just being called. As shown in Figure 5-5, the header portion of a Windows application is actually the header for the DOS stub executable file. This causes the Windows application to appear to DOS as a normal DOS application. This header information causes DOS to execute the DOS stub located at offset 0x40. When Windows loads the application, however, it ignores the DOS header information and looks at offset 0x3C for the starting address of the Windows header information. It uses this information to execute the Windows application code located immediately after the Windows header.

If the .DEF file does not contain a STUB statement, then TLINK will use the WINSTUB.EXE file. If it cannot find a file called WINSTUB.EXE in the current directory, then it will search the directories specified by the PATH environmental variable. This usually leads to the WINSTUB.EXE application located in the BORLANDC\BIN directory. This DOS application prints the following when executed and then exits:

```
This program must be run under Microsoft Windows.
```

### Example
When the user executes one of your programs from DOS, it would be convenient if it would automatically be executed again under Windows rather than printing a simple message. Write a DOS stub application that automatically executes your application in the Windows environment if it is called from DOS.

**stub\winstub.c**

```
#include <process.h>
/* WINSTUB.EXE, by Mark Peterson

   When used as a stub for a Windows application, this file will
   automatically call Windows and execute the intended application
   in the Windows environment.
*/

#pragma argsused
int main(int Num, char *Arg[])
{
   /* Arg[0] is the pathname of the application the user was trying
      to execute. */
   return(spawnlp(P_OVERLAY, "win", "win", Arg[0], OL));
}
```

Once the above application is compiled into an executable file, it can then be used as a DOS stub for a Windows application by explicitly listing the application as follows in your application's .DEF file:

```
STUB   'WINSTUB.EXE'
```

TLINK will then create a Windows application with the WINSTUB application configured to run if the user executes your application from the DOS command line. For example, if the WINSTUB.EXE file is used as the DOS stub for the "Hello, Windows!" application used earlier in the chapter, then when the user executes HELLO.EXE from the DOS command line, the WINSTUB portion will in turn execute the following:

```
win hello
```

This executes Windows and causes Windows to automatically run the HELLO application.

If you would like all your applications to execute automatically in Windows when executed from the DOS command line, then all you need to do is replace the WINSTUB.EXE application in the BORLANDC\BIN directory with the above WINSTUB application.

# TURBO LIBRARIAN REFERENCE

The Turbo Librarian Utility, TLIB.EXE, creates and maintains library (.LIB) files for use with the TLINK. A .LIB file is a collection of different .OBJ files and/or import function listings. If TLINK cannot locate a function in the .OBJ files you list on the command line, it will search the .LIB files you specify and use the first occurrence of the function it finds.

The TLIB utility uses the following command line syntax:

```
tlib library[.LIB] [options] [operation] [, listfile]
```

If you use a .LIB filename that does not exist, TLIB will automatically create a new library file. The TLIB utility will also create a *listfile* if one is specified. This is a text file that contains a list of all the functions and object code files in the library.

## Library List Files

You can generate a .LIB file listing of an existing library without performing any operations. For example, the following will generate a listing of all the functions in the CS.LIB run-time library file:

```
tlib \borlandc\lib\cs.lib, cs.lst
```

The above command line entry would generate a list that looks as follows:

```
Publics by module

ABS             size = 14
       _abs

ABSREAD         size = 276
       _absread                      _abswrite

ACCESS          size = 49
       _access

ALLOCA          size = 50
       _alloca
```

The names in capital letters on the far left are the names of the original .OBJ files, followed by the size of the entire .OBJ file, and immediately following this information is a list of the functions in the .OBJ file.

You may also generate a listing for import libraries. For example, to generate a listing of the functions in the IMPORT.LIB library, you would enter the following:

```
tlib \borlandc\lib\import, import.lst
```

This would create a file called IMPORT.LST that contains entries which look as follows:

```
Publics by module

A2OPROC          size = 0
ACCESSRESOURCE   size = 0
ADDATOM          size = 0
ADDFONTRESOURCE  size = 0
ADJUSTWINDOWRECT size = 0
```

Import library entries have no 'size.' They are in capital letters because the above functions use the Pascal calling convention. Import functions that use the normal C calling convention are listed with a leading underscore and are also case sensitive.

It is important to specify the directory location as part of the filename if the library is not in the current directory! TLIB does not use default directory paths. If you were to leave out the directory path and the IMPORT.LIB file were not in the current directory, the above command line for TLIB would create an empty library called IMPORT.LIB in the current directory and generate an empty list file.

## TLIB Operations

The following is a list of operators that can be used with TLIB. You can specify as many operations as you like. TLIB will first sort the operations so that it will perform all extractions first, followed by all removal operations, and then any additions.

**+**                                                                                    **Add .OBJ or .LIB File**

### Description

The '+' option is used to add an .OBJ file to a library. TLIB will add all the functions and data in the defined .OBJ file. If the file already exists, TLIB will issue a warning message and not add the file. Use the '-+' operator to replace existing .OBJ file entries.

The '+' operator can also be used to combine libraries. When the filename ends with a .LIB extension, TLIB will add all .OBJ file entries in the specifieD library. Note that you may combine import libraries with normal object code libraries. For example, you could combine the CWS.LIB library with the IMPORT library to create one small memory model import library called CWSI.LIB as follows:

```
tlib cwsi +\borlandc\lib\cws.lib +\borlandc\lib\import.lib
```

Note that if the '+' operator is used on a file without a filename extension, TLIB assumes it is an .OBJ file.

### Example
```
tlib mylib, +myfile.obj +other.lib
```
Add MYFILE.OBJ to MYLIB.LIB. Also add all the .OBJ file entries in OTHER-.LIB into MYLIB.LIB.

**-**                                                                                    **Remove an .OBJ File**

### Description

You use the '-' operator to instruct TLIB to remove an .OBJ file entry. TLIB issues a warning message if the file does not exist.

### Example
```
tlib mylib -myfile
```
Remove the MYFILE.OBJ entry from the library.

**\***                                                                                    **Extract an .OBJ File**

### Description

The '*' operator extracts an .OBJ file from a library. An extraction creates the .OBJ file in the current directory. If a directory path precedes the filename, TLIB will create the

.OBJ file in the specified directory. A warning message is issued if TLIB cannot find the .OBJ file entry. TLIB will overwrite the .OBJ file if it already exists in the specified directory. Note that an extraction does not remove the .OBJ file entry from the library.

### Example

```
tlib mylib *first *\myapp\lib\second
```

Extract the FIRST.OBJ file entry from MYLIB.LIB and place it in the current directory. Extract the SECOND.OBJ file entry and place it in the \MYAPP\LIB directory.

## -*, *-                                                              Extract and Remove

### Description

The '-*' and '*-' are both shorthand notation instructing TLIB to both extract and remove an .OBJ file entry. The file is first extracted and then removed from the library regardless of which operator is used. Like the * operator, you may specify a directory path in which TLIB will place the extracted .OBJ file. TLIB will overwrite the .OBJ file if it already exists in the specified directory.

### Example

```
tlib mylib *-first -*\myapp\lib\second
```

Extract the FIRST.OBJ file entry from MYLIB.LIB and place it in the current directory. Extract the SECOND.OBJ file entry and place it in the \MYAPP\LIB directory. Remove both the FIRST.OBJ and SECOND.OBJ file entries from MYLIB.LIB.

## -+, +-                                                                Replace .OBJ File

### Description

Both the '-+' and '+-' operators instruct TLINK to replace an .OBJ file entry with a new .OBJ file. A warning message is issued if the specified file entry does not already exist; however, the .OBJ file is still added. If either operator is used with an .LIB file, all .OBJ entries in the specified library file will replace those in the target library.

### Example

```
tlib mylib -+myfile -+other.lib
```

Replace the MYFILE.OBJ entry in MYLIB.LIB with the new MYFILE.OBJ. Add all the .OBJ file entries in OTHER.LIB to MYLIB.LIB and replace any that already exist.

## TLIB Command Line Options

The following is a listing of the command line options that can be used with TLIB.

## @Filemane Use Response File

### Purpose
The @*filename* instructs TLIB to use the text in 'filename' as if it were typed in on the command line.

### Default
None

### Description
The DOS command line is limited to 127 characters. This can be too small for lengthy operations. You can use a response file to get around this limitation. When TLIB encounters a response file specified on the command line, it will read the text in a file as it were typed on the command line. You can use the '&' character in the text of the file to continue entries over several lines.

### See Also
TLINK: *@filename*      Response File
Chapter 2: *@filename*      Use a Response File

### Example
Execute a list of library operations using a response file:

**tlib.rsp**
```
+one +two +three &
+four -+five &
*siz
```

The list of operations is executed for the MYLIB.LIB library as follows:

```
tlib mylib @tlib.rsp
```

## C Use Case Sensitivity

### Purpose
The /C option instructs TLIB to use case sensitivity when performing an operation.

### Default
(disabled)

### Description
The TLIB utility does not normally use case sensitivity when performing an operation. For example, it treats the Myfnct(), MyFnct(), and myfnct() functions as if they were

the same. You can use the /C option to tell TLIB to regard function names with different cases as different functions.

### See Also

| | |
|---|---|
| c | Case Sensitive Public and External Symbols |
| C | Case Sensitive Imports |
| Chapter 2: p | Use the Pascal Calling Convention |

### Example

Add an .OBJ file to a library using the case sensitivity option:

```
tlib /C mylib +myfile
```

---

## E                                     Create Extended Dictionary

---

### Purpose

The -E option instructs TLIB to add extended dictionary information to a .LIB file. This enables TLINK to perform linking operations more quickly.

### Default

(disabled)

### Description

Extended dictionary information in a .LIB file enables TLINK to perform linking operations more quickly. This speed increase is more noticeable on slow hard disks or when linking from a library file located on a floppy. On a slow floppy drive, the extended dictionary information can increase the linking speed by 30%. The effects of extended dictionary information are negligible on normal hard drives.

Note that the run-time libraries shipped with the BC++ compiler package do not contain extended dictionary information.

### See Also

TLINK: e    Do Not Use Extended Dictionary Information

### Example

Create a small memory model run-time library on a floppy drive called CSE.LIB that contains extended dictionary information:

```
tlib /E a:\cse.lib +\borlandc\lib\cs.lib
```

# P*size*                                             Set Page Size

## Purpose
The /P*size* option is used to specify the page size of library entries.

## Default
/P16

Set the page size of library entries to 16.

## Description
Library entries are aligned along page boundaries. This means with a default page boundary set at 16, library entries are entered in 16-byte increments, making the size of library file entries the next higher multiple of 16. For example, if the page size is set to 16 and you enter the library entries with sizes of 10 and 20 bytes, then the first entry will occupy 16 bytes of disk space and the second will occupy 32.

Setting a page size larger than 16 has the effect of creating larger library files. For example, changing the CS.LIB file from its default page size of 16 bytes to 32 increases the size of the file from 265K to 269K.

You may wish to increase the page size of a library if you are using very large library files. TLIB indexes library entries by page. This means that to locate an entry in the library with a page index of 1000, TLIB multiplies the page size 1000 times to determine the offset. These indexes are 16-bit integers, which means the maximum size a library can be is 65,535 times the page size. This limits the size of a library to 1 Meg for the default page size. You can increase the maximum size of a library by increasing the page size. For example, doubling the page size to 32 allows you use a 2 Meg library file.

## See Also
E                    Create Extended Dictionary

## Example
Create a small memory model run-time library called CSP32.LIB with a page size of 32:

```
tlib /P32 csp32 +\borlandc\lib\cs.lib
```

# BORLAND
# TURBO
# ASSEMBLER
# REFERENCE

Borland C++ allows you to embed assembly language instructions within your C and C++ source code. The BC++ compiler normally uses the built-in assembler (BASM) to process inline assembly language instructions. BASM, however, recognizes only the 8086 and 8087 microprocessor and floating-point coprocessor instruction set. To compile 32-bit inline assembly language instructions requires using the 80386 instruction set. You may also wish to use some of the 80387 specific coprocessor instructions in your inline assembly. This type of programming requires using the Turbo Assembler (TASM) instead of BASM to process your inline assembly language.

The first part of this chapter covers how to write inline assembly language instructions to manipulate data in C and C++ applications, how to enable the 80386 and 80387 instruction sets, and how to use TASM to compile the inline assembly instructions. The latter portion of this chapter is a reference section on the command line options for TASM. Unlike the *Turbo Assembler User's Guide*, which assumes you are writing your entire application (or at least an entire source code module) in assembly language, this reference section is written for programmers who are using BC++ with the -B command line option, the #pragma inline directive, or the IDE menu option equivalent, [Options][Compiler][Code][Compile via assembler], to compile their C or C++ source code via an external assembler, such as TASM, and using the -Txxx command line option for BC++ to control the operation of the assembler.

The inline assembly language portions of this chapter assume you have an intermediate knowledge level of assembly language programming.

## USING INLINE ASSEMBLY LANGUAGE IN C

You access C language data in an inline assembly language block just as you would if the data were in any normal .ASM file. BC++ translates the usage of automatic variables to offsets from the BP register. This means some data manipulations involving automatic variables will require you to use a data size specification such as BYTE, WORD, or DWORD if the size of the operation is not implied by the use of a register. For example, in the following function, the assembler assumes the size of 'MyData' is 16 bits with the MOV instruction because the instruction involves a 16-bit register:

```
int MyFnct(void)
{
```

```
    int MyData;

    asm {
        mov  ax, 0
        mov  MyData, ax
    }
    return(MyData);
}
```

However, the assembler does not "know" the operand size of the MOV in the following function because it does not use a register:

```
int MyFnct(void)
{
    int MyData;

    asm {
        mov MyData, 0
    }
    return(MyData);
}
```

This function should be rewritten as follows for proper compilation by the assembler:

```
int MyFnct(void)
{
    int MyData;

    asm {
        mov WORD PTR MyData, 0
    }
    return(MyData)
}
```

BC++ also translates C structure definitions into their assembly language STRUC counterparts. This enables accessing structure data members both directly and via pointers to the structures. For example, consider the following application, which accesses the data members in MyStruct directly and using a near and far pointer:

**examp1\test.c**

```
#include <stdio.h>

struct MY_STRUCT
{
    int One, Two, Three, Four;
};

void main(void)
{
    struct MY_STRUCT MyStruct, *NearPtr, far *FarPtr;

    /* Initialize the near and far pointers */
    FarPtr = NearPtr = &MyStruct;

    /* Initialize the 'One' and 'Two' data members directly */
    asm {
        mov     ax,    1
```

```
        mov  WORD PTR MyStruct.One, ax
        mov  ax, 2
        mov  WORD PTR MyStruct.Two, ax
    }

    /* Calculate the 'Three' data member using the near pointer */
    asm {
        mov     si,     NearPtr
        mov     ax,     [si].One
        add     ax,     [si].Two
        mov             [si].Three, ax
    }

    /* calculate the 'Four' data member using the far pointer */
    asm {
        les     si,     FarPtr
        mov     ax,     es:[si].Two
        add     ax,     es:[si].Two
        mov     es:     [si].Four, ax
    }

    /* Print the results */
    printf("One = %d\n", MyStruct.One);
    printf("Two = %d\n", MyStruct.Two);
    printf("One + Two = %d\n", MyStruct.Three);
    printf("Two + Two = %d\n", MyStruct.Four);
}
```

# ACCESSING C++ OBJECT CLASS MEMBERS

You access public data members in an object class outside of a member function using assembly language by employing the same methods as the preceding C language example. Accessing public member data from within a member function, as well as accessing protected and private data members, is accomplished using the *this* pointer. The 'this' pointer is a near pointer in the tiny, small, and medium memory models and a far pointer in the compact, large, and huge memory models. This means that you need to either write the code for a specific memory model, or write the code to detect the memory model being used by looking for one of the memory model macros as shown in the following example:

**examp2\test.cpp**
```
    #include <iostream.h>

    #ifndef __COMPACT__
    #  ifndef __LARGE__
    #    ifndef __HUGE__
    #      define NEARDATA      // Define the NEARDATA macro
    #    endif
    #  endif
    #endif

    class OBJECT
    {
        /* Private data members 'One' and 'Two' */
```

391

```
    int One, Two;
    void CalcThree(void);
public:
    int Three;

    OBJECT()
    {
        One = 1;
        Two = 2;
        CalcThree();
    }
};

void OBJECT::CalcThree(void)
{
    asm {
        /* Load the SI register with the 'this' pointer */
#ifndef NEARDATA
        push ds
        lds  si, this
#else
        mov  si, this
#endif

        /* Calculate the value of 'Three' */
        mov   ax,  [si].One
        add   ax,  [si].Two
        mov        [si].Three, ax

#ifndef NEARDATA
        pop   ds
#endif
    }
}

void main(void)
{
    OBJECT Object;

    cout << "Object.Three = " << Object.Three << "\n";
}
```

Note that BC++ Version 2.0 does not properly handle the 'this' pointer in inline assembly language. You should use BC++ 3.0 to compile inline assembly language in C++ source code, which uses the 'this' pointer.

Be aware that BC++ will not allow inline assembly language instructions in inline function definitions even if you are using the -vi option. Inline assembly language can only be used in explicit out-of-line function definitions.

# REGISTER VARIABLES AND INLINE ASSEMBLY LANGUAGE

You need to exercise caution if you write a function containing register variables. A register variable is one of the microprocessor's registers used by BC++ to store an integer value rather than storing it in computer memory. BC++ automatically uses register variables whenever possible unless you compile using the -r- command line option for BC++. Although BC++ will scan an inline assembly language block and not use any registers also being explicitly used, it does *not* look for any indirect register usage. For example, consider the following application:

**register\dx.c**

```
#pragma inline

int x, y, Ans;
unsigned NumTimes = 10;

void BadLoop(void)
{
    unsigned n;

    for(n = 0; n < NumTimes; n++)
    {
    asm {
    mov   ax, WORD PTR x
    imul  WORD PTR y
    mov   WORD PTR Ans, ax
      }
    }
}

void main(void)
{
    x = 2;
    y = 4;

    Fast();
}
```

BC++ will compile the BadLoop() function as follows:

**register\fast.asm**

```
_Fast    proc    near
         push    bp
         mov     bp,sp
    ;
    ;    {
    ;        unsigned n;
    ;
    ;        for(n = 0; n < NumTimes; n++)
    ;
         xor     dx,dx
         jmp     short @1@170
    @1@58:
    ;
    ;        {
    ;            asm {
    ;                mov   ax, WORD PTR x
    ;
         mov        ax, WORD PTR DGROUP:_x
    ;
    ;                imul  WORD PTR y
    ;
         imul       WORD PTR DGROUP:_y
```

393

```
;
;                       mov    WORD PTR Ans, ax
;
        mov             WORD PTR DGROUP:_Ans, ax
        inc             dx
@1@170:
        cmp             dx,word ptr DGROUP:_NumTimes
        jb              short @1@58
;                   }
;           }
;       }
;
        pop     bp
        ret
_Fast   endp
```

As shown, BC++ is using the DX register as a register variable for 'n.' However, the IMUL instruction modifies the value of the DX register with each execution, which overwrites the value of 'n.' The easiest way to prevent this situation from occurring is to explicitly use any registers modified by an assembly language instruction. In the case of the BadLoop() function, the problem is corrected by an instruction to store the value placed in the DX register by the IMUL instruction as follows:

```
long Ans;
. . .

    asm {
        mov   ax, WORD PTR x
        imul  WORD PTR y
        mov   WORD PTR Ans, ax
        mov   WORD PTR Ans+2, dx        /* Use the DX register */
    }
```

BC++ then sees the DX register being used and instead chooses the BX register as the register variable for 'n.'

# INLINE ASSEMBLY LANGUAGE IN WINDOWS APPLICATIONS

You write inline assembly language blocks for Windows applications in exactly the same way as you do for a DOS application with one exception: do not make any assumptions about the meaning of a value in a segment register or load a segment register with an arbitrary value. Segment values in Windows do not have the same meanings as they do in DOS. In DOS, a segment value corresponds to a specific physical location in memory. In Windows, a segment value is a *selector* and is used as a reference to an entry in the microprocessor's Global Descriptor Table (GDT). When Windows is operating in the protected mode, it relies on the microprocessor to translate a selector value in a segment register to a physical location in memory. This enables Windows to move some of the physical segments in memory without affecting the operation of running applications.

Many programmers sometimes use a segment register for temporary storage. If the user is running Windows in the protected mode, then the microprocessor is monitoring the values either placed or modified in the segment registers. This includes the ES register! Be aware that any segment register with a value that does not correspond to a selector owned by the application (i.e., does not correspond to a selector in the GDT) will cause a General Protection (GP) fault. The user sees a GP fault as an "Unrecoverable Application Error" followed by the automatic removal of the application from the Windows operating system. If you'd like your application to be able to run in the Windows standard or enhanced modes, only load segment registers with selectors provided by the Windows operating system, such as the high word of initialized far pointers or a value already in one of the other segment registers. Any modification of selector values should be avoided.

# 32-BIT INLINE ASSEMBLY LANGUAGE INSTRUCTIONS

Using 32-bit inline assembly language will significantly improve the performance of many applications. For example, consider the following application, which performs a left bit-shift on an array of long integers:

**examp3\test.c**

```
#define NUM_ELEM 15000
long Array[NUM_ELEM];

void Fast(void)
{
   asm {
         mov   cx, NUM_ELEM
         mov   bx, 4
         lea   si, Array
   }
   ShiftLoop: asm {
   .386
         shl   DWORD PTR [si], 1   /* Left bit-shift */
         add   si, bx
         loop  ShiftLoop
   .8086
   }
}

void Slow(void)
{
   unsigned n;

   for(n = 0; n < NUM_ELEM; n++)
      Array[n] <<= 1;                /* Left bit-shift */
}

void main(void)
{
```

```
  unsigned n;

  for(n = 0; n < NUM_ELEM; n++)
    Array[n] = 1;

  Fast();
  Slow();
}
```

The above application uses the Fast() and Slow() functions to left bit-shift each element in the array. The Slow() function uses the C bit-shift assignment operator to perform the bit-shift. The BC++ compiler translates the bit-shift assignment operator into a call to a function in the C library that performs the bit-shift using 16-bit 8086 compatible instructions. The Fast() function takes full advantage of operating on an 80386 machine 32-bit instruction set to perform the left bit-shift. This produces a 300% speed improvement over the code in the Slow() function.

There are many other 80386 processor instructions you can use in your C and C++ applications that will greatly improve their performance. These include instructions for 32-bit additions, subtraction, multiplication, division, bit testing, and bit scanning, and also 64-bit left and right shift instructions. See the *Turbo Assembler Quick Reference Guide* for information on 80386 specific functions.

## DETECTING A 32-BIT MICROPROCESSOR

Attempting to execute 80386 specific instructions on an 8086 or 80286 compatible machine will more than likely lock the computer. Your applications should include a routine to check for the presence of a 32-bit microprocessor. This can be done using the is32bit() function as shown in the following application:

**det_386\cpu.c**

```
#pragma inline

#include <stdio.h>

int is32bit(void)
{
  int NotAn8086 = 0;
  char GDT[6];

  asm {
    push  sp
    mov   ax, sp
    pop   bx
    cmp   ax, bx
    je    Exit

    mov   NotAn8086, 1

  .286P
    sgdt  FWORD PTR GDT
  .8086
  }
Exit:
  return(NotAn8086 && GDT[1] >= 0);
}
```

```
void main(void)
{
  if(is32bit())
    printf("This is a 32-bit machine.\n");
  else
    printf("This is an 8086, 80186, or an 80286.\n");
}
```

The first section of code in the is32bit() function performs a test to see if the machine is an 8086 or an 80186. In these microprocessors, the SP register is incremented before being placed on the stack. In all later microprocessors, such as the 80286 and 80386, the SP register is incremented after being pushed onto the stack. If the value of the BX register is equal to the value of the AX register, then the SP register was incremented before being pushed onto the stack and the machine is an 8086 or 80186.

The second part of the routine uses the protected mode instruction SGDT to load the global descriptor table into the GDT variable. A machine with an 80286 will place a -1 in the second byte of the table, whereas an 80386 or 80486 will place either a 0 or a +1. If the second byte of the table is greater than 0, then the machine is an 80386 or better.

In Windows applications it is much easier to determine the type of microprocessor available at run time by calling the GetWinFlags() function, as shown in the following EasyWindows application:

**det_386\wincpu.c**

```
#include <windows.h>
#include <stdio.h>

void main(void)
{
  BOOL is32bit;

  is32bit = !(GetWinFlags() & (WF_CPU086 | WF_CPU186 | WF_CPU286));
  if(is32bit)
    printf("This is a 32-bit machine.\n");
  else
    printf("This is an 8086, 80186, or 80286 machine.\n");
}
```

If the user's machine is an 80386 or better, then the value of is32bit will be TRUE (nonzero).

# COMPILING INLINE ASSEMBLY LANGUAGE VIA THE TURBO ASSEMBLER

The BC++ compiler will normally attempt to compile any inline assembly language in a source file using the built-in assembler (BASM). Because BASM is limited to the 8086 and 8087 instruction sets, it will generate errors when compiling inline assembly language that contains 80386 specific instructions and directives. You can instruct BC++ to compile the inline assembly language using an external assembler, such as TASM, by one of three methods and thereby allow full use of the assembly language instruction. One method you can use in the IDE is to set the [Options][Compiler][Code][Compile via assembler] menu option. The drawback to this method is that it will compile all source code modules in your project using TASM. This will slow down the build process by unnecessarily compiling some source code via TASM which either does not contain inline assembly language or contains inline assembly language that can be compiled by BASM. Another method is to use the -B command line option as a local option to a specific project file. The best method, however, is to use the #pragma inline directive at the beginning of any source code file that requires compilation via an external assembler. This will ensure that an external assembler, such as TASM, is used to compile the source code regardless of the IDE menu item settings or the command line options used. See the -B command line option in Chapter 2 for more information on compiling via an external assembler and the #pragma inline directive.

Note that neither Turbo C++ for Windows (TCW) nor Borland C++ for Windows (BCW) support compilation via an external assembler and will ignore the #pragma inline directive. Because of this, any source code compiled using TCW or BCW cannot contain 80386, 80387, or 80486 instructions in inline assembly language blocks.

## USING 80387 COPROCESSOR INSTRUCTIONS IN INLINE ASSEMBLY LANGUAGE

The 80387 and 80487 coprocessors, the 80486DX microprocessor, and many non-Intel math coprocessors can execute several instructions not supported by the 8087 and 80287 instruction set. These include the following:

| | |
|---|---|
| FCOS | Calculates the cosine of ST(0) |
| FSIN | Calculates the sine of ST(0) |
| FSINCOS | Calculates the sine and cosine of ST(0) |
| FUCOM | Unordered comparison |
| FUCOMP | Unordered comparison, pop ST(0) |
| FUCOMPP | Unordered comparison, pop ST(0) and ST(1) |

You need to enable the 80387 instruction set to use any of these instructions. This is done by including the .386 and .387 directives in your inline assembly block. For example, the following application uses the 80387 FSINCOS instruction to calculate the sine and cosine of the number 2.0:

387\test.c
```
/* Ensure the application is compiled using TASM */
#pragma inline

#include <stdio.h>
#include <dos.h>

void main(void)
{
    double Two = 2.0;
    double Sine, Cosine;
```

```c
if(_8087 < 3)
{
    printf("This application requires an 80387 or better \
coprocessor.\n");
    return;
}
asm {
.386
.387
    fld   QWORD PTR Two        /* Load the number 2.0 */
    fsincos                    /* Calculate the sine & cosine */
    fstp  QWORD PTR Cosine     /* Store the cos(2.0)  */
    fstp  QWORD PTR Sine       /* Store the sin(2.0)  */
.8087
.8086
}

printf("cos(%g) = %g\n", Two, Cosine);
printf("sin(%g) = %g\n", Two, Sine);
}
```

The built-in assemblers in the IDE and BCC compilers do not support 80387 in-structions, so the #pragma inline directive is included in the source code to ensure an external assembler is used for compilation.

Note that the BC++ floating-point emulation library does not support the emula-tion of 80387 specific instructions. Attempting to execute an 80387 specific instruction on a machine not equipped with an 80387 compatible coprocessor will cause a system lockup, or, if the machine has no coprocessor at all, a floating-point emulation error. If you are writing a DOS application, you must ensure the user's machine has an 80387 or better coprocessor by examining the _8087 global variable as shown in the preceding example. The _8087 declaration is in the DOS.H header file. You detect the presence of an 80387 compatible coprocessor in a Windows application using the GetWinFlags() function, as shown in the following EasyWindows application:

**387\wintest.c**

```c
#include <windows.h>
#include <stdio.h>

void main(void)
{
    DWORD Flags;
    BOOL is32bit;

    Flags = GetWinFlags();
    is32bit = !(Flags & (WF_CPU086 | WF_CPU186 | WF_CPU286));
    if(is32bit && (Flags & WF_80x87))
        printf("This machine can execute 80387 instructions.\n");
    else
        printf("This machine has an 8087, 80287 or no \
                coprocessor.\n");
}
```

The GetWinFlags() function is used to determine if the user has a 32-bit machine and, if so, if it also has a numerical coprocessor. If this is the case, then it is capable of executing 80387 specific instructions. Note that this test does not detect the presence of non-Intel coprocessors, such as the IIT 2C87, which are also capable of executing 80387 specific instructions.

## THE H2ASH UTILITY

BC++ comes with a utility called H2ASH which converts C and C++ header (.H) files to assembly language header (.ASH) files. This utility allows you to use your C and C++ header files in your .ASM source code files. However, you should note the utility does not support the following features available in BC++ Version 3.0:

- Multiple inheritance
- Virtual base classes
- Templates

A second problem with H2ASH is that it does not always translate your header files correctly. For example, consider the following C directive:

```
#define MY_MACRO   100
```

H2ASH should generate an EQU statement which equates MY_MACRO with 100. However, it instead generates the following incorrect EQU statement, which equates the macro to 10:

```
MY_MACRO          EQU    10
```

Considering the restrictions placed on C++ definitions and the current bugs in this utility, you are better off to use inline assembly language rather than relying on H2ASH to translate your C and C++ header files for use in pure assembly language source files.

## TASM COMMAND LINE OPTIONS

If you are using the -B option or the #pragma inline directive to instruct BCC or the IDE to compile via an external assembler, you pass the assembler options using the -Txxx option (see Chapter 2). The following section is a listing of the command line options that can be used with TASM to control the compilation of both inline assembly language and normal C and C++ code. The Default section lists the defaults passed to TASM when executed by either BCC or the IDE. For information on the defaults present when using TASM as a standalone compiler, see the *Turbo Assembler User's Guide*. The Directive section lists a directive that can be used in the inline assembly language source code to perform similar actions to that of the command line option if you are compiling using an external assembler. Directives in the inline assembly language block override command line option parameters.

The command line options passed to TASM are not case sensitive. Both upper- and lowercase command line options operate identically. Also, you may not use the '-' or '+'

characters to either disable or enable options. Many command line options for TASM have antonym options which have the opposite effect. For example, the /A option orders segments alphabetically, whereas the /S option orders segments sequentially. To override the /S option, you simply use the /A option or vice versa.

Only one option may be specified with each -T option, but you may use as many -Txxx options as you like on a command line. BC++ will pass each option listed in the separate -Txxx options to TASM. For example, consider the following BCC command line execution:

```
bcc -B -TL -TX SOURCE.C
```

The -B option instructs the compiler to create a temporary assembly language file and compile the object code file using TASM. The -TL and -TX options instruct BC++ to pass TASM the /L and /X options. These options will create a list file, called SOURCE.LST, which also includes any false conditional code blocks.

# /A, /S                Order Segments Alphabetically/Sequentially

| ■ MASM | ■ 2.0 | ■ 2.5 | ■ 3.0 |
| --- | --- | --- | --- |

## Purpose
The /A option instructs TASM to order segments alphabetically by segment name. The /S option orders the segments in the same order in which they occur in the source code. The /A and /S options have no useful purpose with respect to inline assembly language or compilation of C and C++ source code via an external assembler.

## Directive
.ALPHA
    Order segments alphabetically.

.SEQ
    Order segments sequentially.

## See Also
Chapter 2: zX*name*    Rename Segment
Chapter 5: P, P=*size*   Pack Code Segments

# /B*size*                                 Set Buffer Size

| ■ MASM | ■ 2.0 | ■ 2.5 | ■ 3.0 |
| --- | --- | --- | --- |

## Purpose
The -B*size* option is used in Microsoft's MASM to set the size of the buffer. This option is ignored by TASM.

## Description

The /Bsize option is accepted by TASM so as to maintain command line compatibility with Microsoft's MASM assembler.

## See Also

V              Display Extra Statistics

---

# /C                         Generate Cross-Reference Listing

- MASM         ■ 2.0         ■ 2.5         ■ 3.0

## Purpose

The /C option instructs TASM to add a cross-reference listing of functions in the source code to the generated list file.

## Directive

`.CREF (MASM), %CREF (Ideal)`
> Start accumulating cross-reference information for inclusion in the list file.

`.XCREF (MASM), &CREF (Ideal)`
> Stop accumulating cross-reference information.

## Default

(disabled)

## Usage

`BCC -B -TL -TC SOURCE.C`
> Generate a list file for SOURCE.C and include a function cross-reference listing.

## Description

The /C option instructs TASM to generate a cross-reference listing of function definitions as used in the compiled source code. This listing includes the line number for all function definitions and the lines numbers for function calls. The resulting cross-reference listing is placed in the list file generated by TASM. This option has no effect if no list file is called for using the /L option.

## See Also

| | |
|---|---|
| L, LA | Generate a List File |
| N | Suppress Generation of a List File |
| X | Include False Conditionals |

## Example

Write a "Hello, TASM!" application, compile using TASM, and generate a cross-reference listing.

**c\test.c**

```
#include <stdio.h>

void SayHello(void)
{
    printf("Hello, TASM!\n");
}

void main(void)
{
    SayHello();
}
```

The above application is compiled using TASM as follows:

```
bcc -B -TL -TC main.c
```

The -B option instructs BC++ to compile using an external assembler with TASM as the default assembler. The -TL and -TC options pass the /L and /C options to TASM, instructing it to generate the .LST file, called TEST.LST, which includes a cross-reference listing. The listing sections for the SayHello() and main() functions are as follows:

```
. . .
27 0000                        _SayHello       proc    near
28 0000 55                                     push    bp
29 0001 8B EC                                  mov     bp,sp
30 0003 B8 0000r                               mov     ax,offset DGROUP:s@
31 0006 50                                     push    ax
32 0007 E8 0000e                               call    near ptr _printf
33 000A 59                                     pop     cx
34 000B 5D                                     pop     bp
35 000C C3                                     ret
36 000D                        _SayHello       endp
37                                             assume  cs:_TEXT
38 000D                        _main   proc    near
39 000D 55                                     push    bp
40 000E 8B EC                                  mov     bp,sp
41 0010 E8 FFED                                call    near ptr _SayHello
42 0013 5D                                     pop     bp
43 0014 C3                                     ret
44 0015                        _main   endp
. . .
57                                             public  _main
58                                             public  _SayHello
59                                             extrn   _printf:near
```

The cross-reference listing for the main() and SayHello() functions is as follows:

```
_SayHello       Near    _TEXT:0000      #27     41  58
_main           Near    _TEXT:000D      #38     57
```

A normal .LST file without the /C option would produce a listing similar to the examples above except for the line number information to the righthand side of the SayHello() and main() function references. Any line number reference preceded by a '#' character refers to the line number where the function or data is declared or defined. A line number reference without the '#' character is the line number where the function or data is used. For example, the SayHello() function is defined on line 27 in the listing, used in a function call on line 41, and is the argument of a PUBLIC declaration on line 58.

## /Dsymbol, /Dsymbol = string      Macro String Definition

- MASM     ▪ 2.0     ▪ 2.5     ▪ 3.0

### Purpose
The /D*symbol* option instructs TASM to define a macro before compilation. The /D*symbol=string* option assigns a string to a macro that will be expanded whenever the macro is used.

### Directive
`symbol = string`
> Define a macro.

`PURGE symbol`
> Undefine a macro.

### Default
`/D__model__ /D__language__`
> Define a macro representing the memory model and the language. The model macro is either __TINY__, __SMALL__, __COMPACT__, __MEDIUM__, __LARGE__, or __HUGE__. The language macro is either __CDECL__ or __PASCAL__.

### Usage
`BCC -B -TDMY_MACRO=MyString SOURCE.C`
> Define MY_MACRO as MyString while TASM is compiling, but not while BC++ is compiling.

### Description
Because BC++ explicitly expands all macros in the temporary .ASM file used by TASM, it does not pass TASM any of the macros defined in the [Options][Compiler][Code][Defines] menu item or any macros defined using the -D command line option for BCC. You can use the /D*symbol* and /D*symbol=string* options to define macros that are only visible during the compilation by TASM.

### See Also
Chapter 2: D*tag*, D*tag=string* #define tag string

**Example**

Write an application using a macro that is defined differently when compiled by BCC and TASM.

**d\test.c**
```c
#include <stdio.h>

void main(void)
{
    int BCCNumber, TASMNumber;

    /* Use the MY_NUMBER macro definition seen by BCC */
    BCCNumber = MY_NUMBER;

    /* Remove the macro definition for MY_NUMBER */
    #undef MY_NUMBER

    asm {
        /* Use the MY_NUMBER macro definition seen by TASM */
        mov    ax, MY_NUMBER
        mov    WORD PTR TASMNumber, ax
    }
    printf(" BCC expanded MY_NUMBER as %d\n", BCCNumber);
    printf("TASM expanded MY_NUMBER as %d\n", TASMNumber);
}
```

The application is compiled with two different definitions for the MY_NUMBER macro as follows:

```
bcc -B -DMY_NUMBER=1 -TDMY_NUMBER=2
```

The -DMY_NUMBER=1 parameter defines the MY_NUMBER macro as one during the compilation by BC++. The MY_NUMBER macro is then undefined after its first usage by BC++ using the #undef directive in the source code. The next usage of MY_NUMBER is in an inline assembly language block processed by TASM. Because MY_NUMBER is undefined in the assembly language block, BC++ leaves the macro in the temporary .ASM file as is. The -TDMY_NUMBER=2 command line parameter passes TASM the /DMY_NUMBER=2 option defining the MY_NUMBER macro as the number 2. This creates an application that produces the following output:

```
BCC  expanded MY_NUMBER as 1
TASM expanded MY_NUMBER as 2
```

# /E, /R                          Emulated/Real Floating-Point Instructions

■ MASM            ■ 2.0              ■ 2.5              ■ 3.0

**Purpose**

The /E option instructs TASM to compile coprocessor instructions as floating-point emulation interrupts. The /R option instructs TASM to compile real coprocessor instructions.

## Directive

EMUL

Generate subsequent coprocessor instructions as emulated floating-point interrupts.

NOEMUL

Generate real coprocessor instructions.

## Default

/E

Compile coprocessor instructions as floating-point emulation interrupts.

/R

Compile actual coprocessor instructions if the -f87 or -f287 options are enabled or the -f option is disabled.

## Description

The BC++ compiler package can create applications using coprocessor instructions which emulate the operation of the 8087 and 80287 coprocessors. It does this by compiling interrupts which call the floating-point emulation library. If there is an actual coprocessor present on the user's machine, then the emulation library rewrites the application code at run time to use real floating-point instructions as the application is executed.

TASM can also compile coprocessor instructions as floating-point emulation interrupts using the /E option. The IDE and BCC will pass TASM either the /E option or the /R option, depending on the status of the -f, -f87, and -f287 options. This enables you to write coprocessor instructions that will execute on machines that are not equipped with a floating-point coprocessor.

The floating-point emulation library only supports coprocessor instructions for the 8087 and 80287 coprocessors.

Note that if you compile using an external assembler and use the -TE BC++ command line option to pass TASM the /E option, the entire source code module will be compiled using floating-point emulation regardless of the status of the -f, -f87, and -f287 options. This is because BC++ will only compile an assembly language text file, and TASM actually creates the .OBJ file. Use the EMUL and NOEMUL assembly language directives to control floating-point emulation within the source code file.

## See Also

Chapter 2:  f, f87, f287    Floating-Point Instruction Type

## Example

Write an application that uses inline floating-point instructions and compile using floating-point emulation. The following application uses a FastFactorial() and SlowFactorial() function to calculate the factorial of 64:

**e\test.c**

```
#include <stdio.h>

double FastFactorial(unsigned x)
{
```

```
    double Ans = x;

    asm {
        fld1                    /* Load 1.0 onto the FPU stack */
        fld         QWORD PTR Ans
        fld         st
    /* FPU Stack contents:  x, x, 1.0 */
    }
    while(--x)
    asm {
        fsub  st, st(2)    /* Decrement the index */
        fmul  st(1), st    /* Multiply the accumulator times the index */
    }
    asm {
        fstp  st(0)                 /* Remove the index */
        fstp  QWORD PTR Ans         /* Store the answer */
        fstp  st(0)                 /* Remove the 1.0 */
    }
    return(Ans);
}

double SlowFactorial(unsigned x)
{
    double Ans = x;

    while(--x)
        Ans *= x;
    return(Ans);
}

void main(void)
{
    printf("FastFactorial(64) = %g\n", FastFactorial(64));
    printf("SlowFactorial(64) = %g\n", SlowFactorial(64));
}
```

The language constraints of C force the compiler to update the value of 'Ans' with each iteration of the factorial loop in the SlowFactorial() function. The FastFactorial() function operates over 30% faster than the SlowFactorial() function because the inline emulated floating-point instructions enable it to leave the 'Ans' variable on the simulated FPU stack and only update the 'Ans' variable in the application after completing the factorial loop.

# /H, /?                                                    **Help Screen**

❶ MASM              ■ 2.0            ■ 2.5            ■ 3.0

❶ The /H option only.

## Purpose

The /H and /? options instruct TASM to display the help screen. These options should not be used as external assembler options.

## Directive

None

## Description

The /H and /? options should only be used when executing TASM directly. They produce the following output:

```
Turbo Assembler  Version 3.0  Copyright (c) 1988, 1991 Borland International

Syntax:  TASM      [options] source [,object] [,listing] [,xref]
/a,/s              Alphabetic or Source-code segment ordering
/c                 Generate cross-reference in listing
/dSYM[=VAL]        Define symbol SYM = O, or = value VAL
/e,/r              Emulated or Real floating-point instructions
/h,/?              Display this help screen
/iPATH             Search PATH for include files
/jCMD              Jam in an assembler directive CMD (eg. /jIDEAL)
/kh#               Hash table capacity # symbols
/l,/la             Generate listing: l=normal listing, la=expanded
                   listing
/ml,/mx,/mu        Case sensitivity on symbols: ml=all, mx=globals,
                   mu=none
/mv#               Set maximum valid length for symbols
/m#                Allow # multiple passes to resolve forward refer-
                   ences
/n                 Suppress symbol tables in listing
/o,/op             Generate overlay object code, Phar Lap-style 32-bit
                   fixups
/p                 Check for code segment overrides in protected mode
/q                 Suppress OBJ records not needed for linking
/t                 Suppress messages if successful assembly
/uxxxx             Set version emulation, version xxxx
/w0,/w1,/w2        Set warning level: w0=none, w1=w2=warnings on
/w-xxx,/w+xxx      Disable (-) or enable (+) warning xxx
/x                 Include false conditionals in listing
/z                 Display source line with error message
/zi,/zd,/zn        Debug info: zi=full, zd=line numbers only, zn=none
```

You can use the THELP utility to obtain detailed on-line help for TASM by entering the following:

```
THELP /f\borlandc\bin\tasm.tah
```

This will load the help file for TASM into the THELP utility. THELP is a memory-resident utility that is called up by pressing the ⑤ key on the keypad with (NumLock) off. (See Chapter 1.)

## See Also

Chapter 2:  H, ?    Display Help Screen
Chapter 8:  THELP utility

# /Ipath                                                      Set Include Path

▪ MASM            ▪ 2.0            ▪ 2.5            ▪ 3.0

## Purpose
The /I*path* option specifies a default path TASM should use when looking for include files.

## Directive
None

## Default
/I
> Look for include files in the current directory.

## Usage
```
BCC -B -TI\ASM_INC SOURCE.C
```
> Compile SOURCE.C using TASM as an external assembler and instruct TASM to look for include files in the \ASM_INC directory.

## Description
The /I*path* option is very useful if you have assembly language include files written for other applications that you'd like to use in your inline assembly language block. This enables you to use the INCLUDE directive in the assembly language block for include files located in another directory.

Note that the INCLUDE directive can only be used in an assembly language block if you are compiling using an external assembler.

## See Also
Chapter 2: Ip*ath* Set Include Files Directory

## Example
Write an application that uses the INCLUDE directive for a file located in a different directory. The following application uses the MY_MACROS.INC file located in a different directory than the source code file:

```
include\my_macros.inc
        MY_NUMBER = 2

i\test.c
        #include <stdio.h>

        void main(void)
        {
          int Number;
```

```
asm {
      INCLUDE MY_MACRO.INC

      mov  ax, MY_NUMBER
      mov  Number, ax
}
printf("MY_NUMBER = %d", Number);
}
```

The application is compiled by passing the /I..\INCLUDE option to TASM. This informs TASM as to where to look for the MY_MACRO.INC include file:

```
bcc -B -TI..\INCLUDE test.c
```

## /Jdirective                                                    Set Directive

| MASM | ■ 2.0 | ■ 2.5 | ■ 3.0 |
|------|-------|-------|-------|

### Purpose
The /J directive is used to pass TASM a directive it should execute before starting compilation.

### Default
None

### Usage
```
BCC -B -TJ.286 SOURCE.C
```
Compile the assembly language file generated by BC++ with the .286 directive executed.

### Description
The /J *directive* option allows you to globally set a directive that will apply to the entire source file, including normal C and C++ code, when you are compiling the source using an external assembler. You should exercise caution, as this could produce some undesirable results. For example, if you were to compile a source file via TASM and used the /J.386 option, TASM would compile the source using 32-bit segments. A better alternative is to use the appropriate directives as required in the assembly language block and then reset the defaults before exiting the block so as to prevent the directives from affecting the assembly language code generated by the BC++ compiler.

### See Also
I*path*          Set Include Path

### Example
Compile the example application for the /A option using the .ALPHA directive from the command line to organize the segments alphabetically. This is accomplished as follows:

```
bcc -B -TJ.ALPHA test.c
```

# /KH*number*                                    Set Maximum Symbol Level

| MASM | ▪ 2.0 | ▪ 2.5 | ▪ 3.0 |
|------|-------|-------|-------|

## Purpose
The /KH*number* specifies the maximum number of allowable symbols in a source file.

## Directive
None

## Default
/KH8192

The source file can contain no more than 8192 symbols.

## Usage
BCC –B –TKH15000 SOURCE.C

Compile the SOURCE.C file via TASM and allocate enough space in TASM to allow room for 15,000 symbols.

## Description
Very large source files which contain more than 8000 symbols may receive an "Out of hash space" error when compiling via TASM. The /KH*number* option can be used to increase the allowable number of symbols up to an absolute maximum of 32,768.

## See Also
MV*number*  Set Maximum Symbol Length

## Example
None

# /L, /LA, /N                                    List File Generation

| ▪ MASM | ▪ 2.0 | ▪ 2.5 | ▪ 3.0 |
|--------|-------|-------|-------|

## Purpose
The /L option instructs TASM to generate a list file. The /LA option instructs TASM to generate an expanded list file that includes an expansion of higher-level language directives. For example, the /LA option would expand the .MODEL directive to the appropriate SEGMENT and ASSUME statements. The BC++ compiler does not use higher language directives in its generated .ASM files, which means the /LA option is functionally equivalent to the /L option. The /N option instructs TASM to not generate a list file.

## Directive

`.LIST`

Enable listing of source lines.

`%NOLIST (Ideal), .XLIST (MASM)`

Disables output to a list file.

## Default

None

## Usage

`BCC -B -TL SOURCE.C`

Generate a list file called SOURCE.LST for the assembly language source file created by BC++.

`BCC -B -TLA SOURCE.C`

Generate an expanded list file for SOURCE.C that includes an expansion of the C language directives.

## Description

The BC++ compiler normally deletes any temporary .ASM file it creates for compilation by an external assembler. You can use the /L and /LA options to create a list file containing the source code created by BC++. You can use the /N option to override any previous /L or /LA option.

## See Also

| | |
|---|---|
| C | Generate Cross-Reference Listing |
| X | Include False Conditionals |
| Chapter 2: M | Create a .MAP File |
| Chapter 2: S | Compile to a .ASM File |

## Example

See the example used with the /C option.

# /ML, /MU, /MX                                    Symbol Case Sensitivity

| | | | |
|---|---|---|---|
| ▪ MASM | ▪ 2.0 | ▪ 2.5 | ▪ 3.0 |

## Purpose

The /ML option instructs TASM to use case sensitivity for all symbol names in the source file. The /MU option tells TASM to convert all symbol names to uppercase. The /MX option instructs TASM to use case sensitivity for all public and external symbols, but to convert all internally used symbols to uppercase.

**Directive**

None

**Default**

/ML

> Compile using case sensitivity for all symbols.

**Usage**

The /MU and /MX options should not be used when using an external assembler to compile code generated by BC++.

**Description**

C and C++ are case sensitive languages. A function defined as MyFnct() is different from a function called myfnct() or MYFNCT(). For this reason, only the default /ML option should be used when an external assembler is used to process inline assembly language.

**See Also**

Chapter 2: p      Use the Pascal Calling Convention

# /MV*number*                                            Set Maximum Symbol Length

| MASM | ■ 2.0 | ■ 2.5 | ■ 3.0 |
|------|-------|-------|-------|

**Purpose**

The /MV*number* option is used to specify the maximum length TASM should use for a symbol. Note, however, that TASM ignores this option and will not truncate the characters for symbols longer than *number*.

**Directive**

None

**See Also**

Chapter 2: i*n*      Use *n* Significant Characters for Tags

# /O, /OP                                            Generate TLINK/Phar Lap Overlay Code

| MASM | ■ 2.0 | ■ 2.5 | ■ 3.0 |
|------|-------|-------|-------|

**Purpose**

The /O option instructs TASM to compile overlay compatible object code. The /OP option causes TASM to compile overlay object code that is compatible with the Phar Lap linker, but not TLINK.

### Directive
None

### Default
/O

Compile source code as an overlay if the -Y option is used on the BC++ command line.

### Usage
`BCC -B -TOP -c SOURCE.C`

Compile the SOURCE .C file to an object code file via TASM with overlay code compatible with the Phar Lap linker.

### Description
The /O option is passed to TASM automatically by the BC++ compiler if you use the -Y option on the command line or select a DOS overlay application in the IDE. You can use the /OP option, however, to create an overlay object code file that is compatible with the Phar Lap linker. Note that an object code file compiled using the /OP option will not be compatible with Borland's TLINK.

### See Also
Chapter 2: Y, Yo Overlay the Compiled Files

### Example
Compile an overlaid application for linking with the Phar Lap linker. The overlaid application used in Chapter 2 for the -Y and -Yo command line options can be compiled for linking by the Phar Lap linker as follows:

```
bcc -B -TOP -c -Y -mm base.c -Yo overlay.c
```

The -B option instructs BC++ to compile the source code using an external assembler (the default is TASM) and the -TOP option passes TASM the /OP option, instructing it to generate Phar Lap compatible overlay code. This will compile the BASE.C and OVERLAY.C source code to overlaid code that can then be linked by the Phar Lap linker.

## /P                                                           Check for Impure Code

- MASM          ■ 2.0               ■ 2.5               ■ 3.0

### Purpose
The /P option tells TASM to check for "impure" code with a protected mode instruction set enabled, i.e., code which writes to memory with a CS register override.

### Directive
None

## Default
(disabled)

## Usage
```
BCC -B -TP SOURCE.C
```

## Description
Protected applications are only supposed to read or execute code in a code segment. Writing to a code segment is not permitted. The /P option tells TASM to issue a warning message if the code in a protected mode assembly language block has instructions that write to memory using the CS register override.

Note that TASM will not check for impure code unless a protected mode instruction set is enabled, such as by using the .286P directive.

## See Also
W           Warning Message Control

## Example
Write an application containing impure instructions and compile via TASM using the /P option. In the following application, a string is copied to a buffer located in the application's code segment. Note that the .286P directive is not required for the application to operate correctly, but it is required to get TASM to check for impure code.

**p\test.asm**
```
    .MODEL SMALL, C

    .CODE

    ; Code segment buffer
    CodeSegBuff    db      80 dup(0)

    ; Function to return the code segment pointer to the buffer
    PUBLIC GetCSPtr
    GetCSPtr PROC
            mov   ax, OFFSET CodeSegBuffret
    GetCSPtr ENDP

    END
```

**p\main.c**
```
    /* Compile via an external assembler */
    #pragma inline

    #include <stdio.h>

    /* Function to retrieve the code segment buffer pointer. */
    extern char _cs *GetCSPtr(void);

    void main(void)
    {
        char _cs *CSPtr;
        char Str[] = "This was placed in a code segment";
        unsigned n;
```

```
    CSPtr = GetCSPtr();

    /* Enable the protected mode instruction set */
    asm .286P

    /* Copy the string to the code segment buffer */
    for(n = 0; n < sizeof(Str); n++)
        CSPtr[n] = Str[n];

    /* Disable the protected mode instruction set */
    asm .8086

    /* Print the string in the code segment */
    printf("Str: '%Fs'\n", (char far *)CSPtr);
}
```

You enter the following to compile the previous source code files and check for impure code:

```
bcc -TP main.c test.asm
```

TASM will issue the following warning message when it compiles the MAIN.ASM file generated by BCC:

```
*Warning* main.ASM(96) CS override in protected mode
```

---

## /Q                    Suppress Autodependency and Copyright Information

| MASM | ▪ 2.0 | ▪ 2.5 | ▪ 3.0 |
|------|-------|-------|-------|

### Purpose
The /Q option tells TASM not to include dependency and copyright information in the object code file.

### Directive
None

### Default
(disabled)
Object code files are compiled with copyright and dependency information.

### Usage
```
BCC -B -TQ -X SOURCE.C
```
Compile SOURCE.C to an object code file and exclude copyright and all auto-dependency information.

### Description
The TASM will place autodependency information into an object code file that can be read by the IDE and MAKE utility to automatically rebuild the target file if one of the dependent include files has changed. TASM also places the string "Turbo Assembler

3.0" into the .OBJ file if the source code is compiled via an external assembler. You can tell the TASM to exclude this information using the /Q command line option so as to reduce the size of the resulting .OBJ file.

Note that when you compile via an external assembler, BC++ hard codes the include file information from the C and C++ source code autodependency in the form of ?debug statements that are not removed by TASM even if you do use the /Q option. For example, a source code file with the statement #include "stdio.h" will have the following debugging statements in the assembly language file generated by BC++:

```
?debug  C E9001044171B433A5C424F524C414E44435C494E434C5544455C73+
?debug  C 7464696F2E68
```

The first portion of the ?DEBUG directive is the time/date stamp for the STDIO.H include file. The remaining section is a hexadecimal dump of the pathname for STDIO.H:

```
43 3A 5C 42 4F 52 4C 41 4E 44 43 5C 49 4E 43 4C 55 44 45 5C 73 74 64 69
C  :  \  B  O  R  L  A  N  D  C  \  I  N  C  L  U  D  E  \  s  t  d  i

6F 2E 68
o  .  h
```

The only way this information can be excluded from the .OBJ file is to use the -X BC++ command line option with the /Q TASM option.

### See Also
Chapter 2:  X      Disable Autodependency Output

### Example
Compile the "Hello, TASM!" application in the C option example via TASM with and without autodependency and copyright information. The following will compile the application without autodependency and copyright information:

```
bcc -B -TQ -X test.c
```

This result in an .OBJ file that is 67% smaller than if the autodependency and copyright information were included. Note that the size of the executable file is unchanged.

---

## /T                                                    Suppress Messages

■ MASM          ■  2.0          ■  2.5          ■  3.0

### Purpose
The /T option is used to suppress the display of extraneous information during the compilation via TASM.

### Directive
None

## Default
(disabled)
> Display introductory and summary information regarding the compilation process.

## Usage
`BCC -B -TT SOURCE.C`
> Compile SOURCE.C via TASM and do not display extraneous information.

## Description
When BC++ compiles via an external assembler, TASM will display an introductory message and summary information, such as the following:

```
Turbo Assembler  Version 3.0  Copyright (c) 1988, 1991 Borland International
Assembling file:  test.ASM
Error messages:    None
Warning messages:  None
Passes:            1
Remaining memory:  368K
```

> You can use the /T option to suppress the display of this information. TASM will then only display any warning or error messages.

## See Also
W                   Warning Message Control
Chapter 4:  s Silent Mode

## Example
Compile the "Hello, TASM!" application in the C option example via TASM using the /T option to suppress the introductory and summary information:

```
bcc -B -TT test.c
```

---

## /V                                                   Display Extra Statistics

- MASM            ▪ 2.0              ▪ 2.5              ▪ 3.0

## Purpose
The /V option is used with Microsoft's assembler (MASM) to display extra statistics about the compilation process. This option is ignored by TASM.

## Description
The /V option is accepted by TASM so as to maintain command line compatibility with Microsoft's MASM assembler.

## See Also
B*size*            Set Buffer Size

# /W

## Warning Message Control

▪ MASM ▪ 2.0 ▪ 2.5 ▪ 3.0

## Purpose

The /W option is used to control the types of warning messages generated by TASM.

## Directive

```
WARN class
```
Enable a specific classification of warning messages.

```
NOWARN class
```
Disable a specific classification of warning messages.

## Default

```
/W /W-ICG
```
Enable all warning messages with the exception of messages in the "Inefficient code generation" classification.

## Usage

```
BCC -B -TW SOURCE.C
```
Compile SOURCE.C via TASM and enable all warning messages.

```
BCC -B -TW+ICG SOURCE.C
```
Same as above.

```
BCC -B -TW-RES SOURCE.C
```
Compile SOURCE.C via TASM and disable "Reserved word" warning messages.

```
BCC -B -TW- SOURCE.C
```
Compile SOURCE.C via TASM and disable all warning messages.

## Description

TASM will generate warning messages which fall into one of 14 different classifications represented by a three-character abbreviation:

| ABBREVIATION | CLASSIFICATION |
| --- | --- |
| ALN | Segment alignment |
| ASS | Assuming segment is 16 bit |
| BRK | Brackets needed |
| ICG | Inefficient code generation |
| LCO | Location counter overflow |
| OPI | Open IF conditional |
| OPP | Open procedure |

| OPS | Open segment |
|-----|--------------|
| OVF | Arithmetic overflow |
| PDC | Pass-dependent construction |
| PQK | Constant assumption |
| PRO | Writing to memory in protected mode |
| RES | Reserved word |
| TPI | Turbo Pascal illegal |

You can use the /W option by itself to enable all the warning message classifications or enable or disable individual classifications using the '+' and '-' options. Note that you must use a separate /W option for each warning group you need to enable/disable.

### See Also

| P | Check for Impure Code |
|---|----------------------|
| Chapter 2; w | Display Warnings |
| Chapter 2: w*xxx* | Individual Warnings |
| Chapter 5: d | Duplicate Symbols Warning |

### Example
Compile the "Hello, TASM!" application via TASM with all warning messages enabled:

```
bcc -B -TW test.c
```

## /X                                                    Include False Conditionals

■ MASM              ■ 2.0              ■ 2.5              ■ 3.0

### Purpose
The /X option instructs TASM to include false conditional blocks in the generated list file. This option is only effective if the /L option for generating a list file is also used.

### Directive
**.LFCOND**
　　List both true and false conditional blocks.

**.SFCOND**
　　List only statements which actually generate code.

**.TFCOND**
　　Toggle the mode for listing false conditionals.

## Default

(disabled)

Include only those lines that actually generate code in the source code portion of the list file.

## Usage

```
BCC -B -TL -TX SOURCE.C
```

Compile SOURCE.C via TASM and generate a list file that includes any false directive conditionals in the inline assembly language blocks.

## Description

You would normally use C or C++ preprocessor directives to control which blocks of code are compiled. Any false preprocessor directives are not included in the assembly language file generated by BC++ because they generate no code. If, however, you compile via an external assembler and use assembly language conditionals statements instead, such as IF instead of #if, these directives are evaluated by the assembler and are not filtered by BC++. You can then use the /X option to include any false conditional code blocks in a generated list file. Note that if no list file is generated, i.e., you did not also include the /L option, then the /X option is ignored.

## See Also

| | |
|---|---|
| C | Generate Cross-Reference Listing |
| L, LA, N | List File Generation |
| Chapter 2: M | Create a .MAP File |
| Chapter 2: S | Compile to a .ASM Fil |

## Example

Write an application that contains inline assembly language conditionals and create a .LST file that contains the false conditionals using the /X option.

**x\test.c**

```
#include <stdio.h>

/* This function counts the length of a string using inline
   assembly language */
unsigned MyStrLen(char *Str)
{
  asm {
  FAR_PTRS = 0
  IFNDEF(__TINY__)
     IFNDEF(__SMALL__)
        IFNDEF(__MEDIUM__)
           FAR_PTRS = 1
        ENDIF
     ENDIF
  ENDIF
```

```
    IF(FAR_PTRS)
       push ds
       lds  si, Str
    ELSE
       mov  si, Str
    ENDIF

       xor  bx, bx
       dec  bx
    }
    StrLoop: asm {
       inc  bx
       or   BYTE PTR [bx + si], 0
       jnz  StrLoop

    IF(FAR_PTRS)
       pop  ds
    ENDIF
    }
    return(_BX);
}

void main(void)
{
    char *Str = "This is a string";
    unsigned Length;

    Length = MyStrLen(Str);
    printf("The length of '%s' is %d bytes\n", Str, Length);
}
```

The above application contains the MyStrLen() function, which uses inline assembly language to determine the length of a string. The assembly language block uses a series of conditional directives to determine which memory model macro was passed to TASM and sets the FAR_PTRS macro to either 0 or 1. The application is compiled such that a listing file is created that includes false conditionals as follows:

```
bcc -B -TL -TX -ml test.c
```

The -ml option compiles the application via TASM. The -TL and -TX options are passed to TASM as the /L and /X options to create a list file containing false conditionals. The conditional statements in the above code are then generated in the TEST.LST file as follows:

```
41    0003 56             push    si
42          =0000          FAR_PTRS        = 0
3                          IFNDEF  (__TINY__)
44                         IFNDEF  (__SMALL__)
45                         IFNDEF  (__MEDIUM__)
46          =0001          FAR_PTRS     =  1
47                         ENDIF
48                         ENDIF
49                         ENDIF
50                         IF      (FAR_PTRS)
51    0004 1E              push    ds
52    0005 C5 76 06        lds     si,    [bp+6]
53                         ELSE
54                         mov     si,    [bp+6]
55                         ENDIF
```

Note that even though line 54 did not generate any code, it is still included in the TEST.LST file.

## /Z                                Include Source Lines with Error Messages

▪ MASM            ▪ 2.0            ▪ 2.5            ▪ 3.0

### Purpose
The /Z option instructs TASM to print the offending line of source code with each warning and error message.

### Directive
None

### Default
(disabled)
Print only line numbers when reporting warning and error messages.

### Usage
```
BCC -B -TZ SOURCE.C
```
Compile SOURCE.C via TASM and print the assembly language source code line with each warning and error message generated by TASM.

### Description
Normally, TASM will report only the line number associated with an assembly language warning or error message. Because BC++ generated the assembly language file, it is not always very easy to correlate the warning message with a particular line of code. For example, consider the following application:

**z\test.c**
```
void main(void)
{
   asm {
      mov   ax, BOGUS
   }
}
```

When the application is compiled via an external assembler, TASM will report the following:

```
**Error** test.ASM(35) Undefined symbol: BOGUS
```

The test.ASM(35) refers to line number 35 in the assembly language file generated by BC++. Because BC++ deletes the file after TASM exits, tracking down the error in a large source file can be difficult. When you pass TASM the /Z option, TASM will also print the offending source code as follows:

```
      mov       ax, BOGUS
**Error** test.ASM(35) Undefined symbol: BOGUS
```

While this will help you locate the line of source code, the best method is to first compile the file to assembly language using the -S BCC command line option. This will generate an .ASM file that contains the original C or C++ source code lines. Then invoke TASM manually and use the /L option to generate a .LST file. The warning and error messages will be shown in the .LST file as they occurred in the source, like the following:

```
21                              ;    void main(void)
22                              ;
23                                   assume cs:_TEXT
24 0000                         _main  proc    near
25 0000  55                            push    bp
26 0001  8B EC                         mov     bp,sp
27                              ;
28                              ;    {
29                              ;        asm {
30                              ;            mov    ax, BOGUS
31                              ;
32 0003  A1 0000                        mov        ax, BOGUS
**Error** test.ASM(43) Undefined symbol: BOGUS
33                              ;
34                              ;            }
35                              ;        }
36                              ;
37 0006  5D                            pop     bp
38 0007  C3                            ret
39 0008                         _main  endp
```

### See Also

| | |
|---|---|
| C | Generate Cross-Reference Listing |
| L, LA, N | List File Generation |
| Chapter 2:  M | Create a .MAP File |
| Chapter 2:  S | Compile to an .ASM File |

### Example

Compile the application in the description above so that the line of source code associated with the error message is also printed:

```
bcc -B -TZ test.c
```

# /ZD, /ZI, /ZN                    Debugging Information Options

| | | | |
|---|---|---|---|
| ▪ MASM | ▪ 2.0 | ▪ 2.5 | ▪ 3.0 |

### Purpose

The /ZD, /ZI, and /ZN options either include or exclude debugging information in the object code file compiled by TASM. The /ZD option only includes line number information. The /ZI option causes TASM to include all symbolic information. The /ZN option instructs TASM not to include any debugging information.

### Directive
None

### Default
None

### Usage
These options should not be used when TASM is called as an external assembler.

### Description
When you compile an application via an external assembler, BC++ creates a temporary assembly language file that is used by TASM to create the object code. BC++ then deletes the assembly language file. If you were to use the TASM debugging options, TASM would encode line number and symbolic information relating to the temporary assembly language file rather than the original source code. Because BC++ deletes the temporary .ASM file afterwards, however, any encoded line number information would be useless.

You can still have full symbolic debugging information in your .OBJ file even if you compile using an external assembler. When you use the -v command line option for BC++, the compiler hard codes debug information into an assembly language file using the ?debug assembly language directive. These directives are then used by TASM to encode the symbolic information as it relates to the original C or C++ source code. For example, compiling the SayHello() function from the "Hello, TASM!" application in the C option example using the -v option produces hard coded ?debug directives as follows:

```
;
;        void SayHello(void)
;
         ?debug  L 3
         assume  cs:_TEXT
_SayHello         proc    near
         ?debug  B
         push    bp
         mov     bp,sp
         ?debug  B
;
;        {
;                printf("Hello, TASM!\n");
;
         ?debug  L 5
         mov     ax,offset DGROUP:s@
         push    ax
         call    near ptr _printf
         pop     cx
;
;        }
;
         ?debug  L 6
         pop     bp
         ret
         ?debug  E
         ?debug  E
_SayHello         endp
```

Each of the ?debug directives followed by an 'L' refers to a line number in the original source code. At the end of the .ASM file is a series of ?debug directives that encode the symbolic text information used by the debuggers, such as the following:

```
?debug  C EC095F53617948656C6C6F191800
```

This statement is a hexadecimal series of numbers related to the SayHello() function. As shown below, much of the hexadecimal information refers to the character string for the function's name:

```
?debug  C EC 09 5F 53 61 79 48 65 6C 6C 6F 19 18 00
              _  S  a  y  H  e  l  l  o
```

BC++ will take care of including full symbolic information in your .OBJ files if you compile using the -v option. You should only use the TASM debug information options when you are directly compiling an .ASM assembly language file rather than compiling C or C++ source code files via an external assembler.

### See Also

| | |
|---|---|
| v, vi | Compile with Debug Information |
| y | Compile Line Number Information |
| Chapter 7: | Borland Turbo Debugger Reference |
| Chapter 7: | TDSTRIP Utility |

# BORLAND
# TURBO
# DEBUGGER/
# PROFILER
# REFERENCE

7

This chapter covers the requirements, features, and advantages of each of the debugger and profiler utilities and their associated command line parameters. The supporting utilities that aid in debugging and profiling an application are also discussed, including their command line parameters.

## THE TURBO DEBUGGER AND PROFILER UTILITIES

The BC++ compiler package comes with four standalone debuggers and three profilers:

**Debuggers**

| | |
|---|---|
| TD | Debugs DOS applications in the real mode |
| TD286 | Debugs DOS applications in the protected mode |
| TD386 | Debugs DOS applications in a virtual 8086 address space |
| TDW | Debugs Windows applications |

**Profilers**

| | |
|---|---|
| TPROF | Profiles DOS applications in the real mode |
| TF386 | Profiles DOS applications in a virtual 8086 address space |
| TPROFW | Profiles Windows applications |

### The Real-Mode Debugger and Profiler

The TD and TPROF utilities are the real-mode debugger and profiler for DOS applications. Each requires at lease 386K of memory and will work on any computer system. Although TD and TPROF utilities will load much faster than their protected mode and virtual counterparts, they operate much more slowly, as the breakpoints must be monitored using software rather than using the hardware interrupts available in the protected mode. As shown in Figure 7-1, the TD and TPROF utilities also utilize the same real memory space as the application. This results in a serious limitation on the size of the application you can debug or profile using the real-mode utilities.

Much of the 1 Meg of real memory space available on a machine is taken up by the system BIOS, video memory, EMS pages, DOS, any TSRs, and the TD or TPROF utilities themselves. This typically leaves only 270K available for the application code and data, thereby limiting the size of the application that can be loaded.

The TDINST utility is used to configure the TD.EXE utility. TFINST is used to configure TPROF.

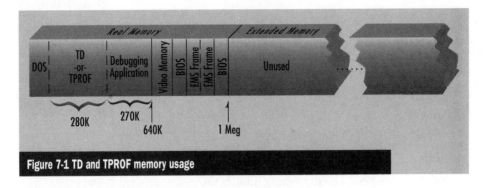

**Figure 7-1 TD and TPROF memory usage**

## The 80286 Protected Mode Debugger

The TD286 utility is a protected mode debugger that requires a machine with an 80286 or better microprocessor and at least 640K of extended memory. Under these conditions, TD286 will load a small driver into real memory and operate mainly from extended memory. This frees more real memory in the DOS 640K address space for use by the application as shown in Figure 7-2.

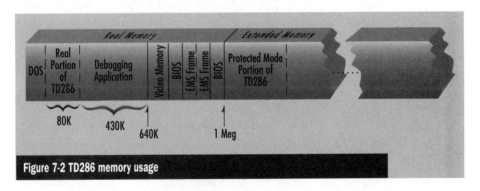

**Figure 7-2 TD286 memory usage**

If your system does not have an extended memory manager such as HIMEM.SYS, then you need to take a few precautions before running TD286. First you need to run the TD286INS utility to ensure that your system's characteristics are stored in the debugger's internal data base. TD286INS will run a series of tests to determine how to access extended memory on your machine if your system is not already in the data base. If TD286INS does run its series of tests, it will not only save the information to the TD286 debugger, but it will also place it in a file ending with a .DB extension. You should send this .DB file to Borland so the information on your machine can be placed in future versions of TD286.

Another precaution is necessary if you do not have an extended memory manager and you are using a RAMDISK or other piece of software utilizing extended memory. The TD286 utility needs to know how much extended memory is being used by other software. This is done by creating a text file called CONFIG.286 in the current drive's root directory. The text file should contain the statement "MEGS=" followed by the number of whole megabytes TD286 should skip over before utilizing the remainder of your system's extended memory. For example, if you have a 1.5-Meg RAMDISK, you need to have a CONFIG.286 file consisting of the following:

```
MEGS=2
```

The TD286 utility will then only utilize the extended memory beyond the first two megabytes so as not to interfere with the operation of the RAMDISK.

Note that you do not have to run the TD286INS utility or create a CONFIG.286 file if you have an extended memory manager that implements the XMS standard, such as the HIMEM.SYS DOS device driver supplied with Windows and DOS 5.0. However, if the application you are debugging uses extended memory, you may wish to use the CONFIG.286 file anyway so as to set aside extended memory for use by the application.

The TDINST utility is used to configure the operation of TD286. This is done by entering the following:

```
TDINST TD286.EXE
```

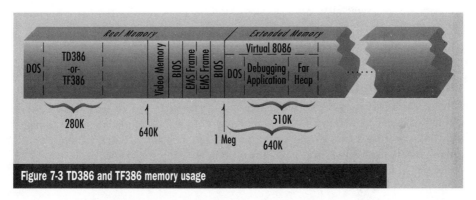

**Figure 7-3 TD386 and TF386 memory usage**

## The 80386 Virtual Debugger and Profiler

The TD386 debugger and the TF386 profiler utilities utilize the virtual 8086 capabilities of the 80386 microprocessor to create a virtual memory space in extended memory that appears to the DOS application as if it were real memory. As shown in Figure 7-3, this provides the DOS copy and the application with a full 640K of memory space. The application loads and executes exactly as if the debugger were not present. This means the application will load at the same address and have the same amount of far memory available as if it were running normally.

## The TDH386 DOS Device Driver

The TD386 debugger requires 640K of extended memory, whereas the TF386 profiler needs at least 700K of extended memory. Both utilities also require the TDH386.SYS DOS device driver to be loaded. This device driver makes the 80386's hardware debugging registers available for use by the two utilities and thereby enables them to configure the microprocessor to monitor break points on a hardware level rather than a software level. This greatly reduces the processing overhead required to monitor break points.

You load the TDH386.SYS device driver by adding the following statement to your CONFIG.SYS file and rebooting the computer:

```
device=\borlandc\bin\tdh386.sys
```

You may need to specify a different pathname for TDH386.SYS if you have your BC++ software in a different directory.

If your machine has an environmental table with more than the default 256 characters, then you will need to use the -e*Byte* command line option. The 'Bytes' parameter needs to be the same value as the -e:*Bytes* option used with the 'shell' statement in CONFIG.SYS. For example, if your CONFIG.SYS file contains the following statement:

```
shell=command /e:1024
```

then you should use the /e1024 parameter with the CONFIG.SYS device driver as follows:

```
device=\borlandc\bin\tdh386.sys /e1024
```

This allows the TDH386.SYS device driver to allocate the same size environmental table as the table used by DOS.

## Virtual Debugger and Profiler Extended Memory Management

As with the TD286 protected mode debugger, you will need to set aside a certain amount of extended memory if your system does not use an extended memory manager and you have other software using extended memory such as a RAMDISK or the application you are debugging/profiling. This is done by using the -e*kBytes* command line option when invoking TD386 or TF386. See the command line reference section for more information on this option.

## Virtual Debugger and Profiler Default Options

The TDINST utility is used to configure both TD and TD386. Likewise, the TFINST utility configures both TPROF and TF386. Unlike the method for configuring TD286, you do not specify either TD386.EXE or TF386.EXE on the command line when invoking the installation program. Any configuration changes you make to TD or TPROF will automatically be used by TD386 and TF386, respectively. This is because the virtual debugger and profiler use TD and TPROF, respectively, to do the actual debugging and profiling. After setting up the virtual 8086 environment, the TD386 and TF386 utilities hand over the application to their real-mode counterparts. They then restore the system to normal before the utilities exit.

## The Windows Debugger and Profiler

The TDW and TPROFW utilities are used for debugging and profiling Windows applications. You must have a computer with an 80286 or 80386 microprocessor, at least 1 Meg of

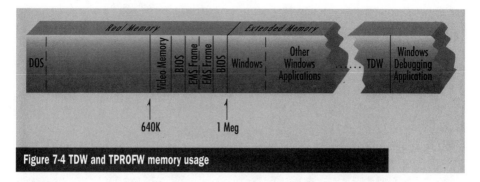

**Figure 7-4 TDW and TPROFW memory usage**

extended memory, and Windows 3.0 running in the standard or enhanced mode to use either TDW or TPROFW. These utilities operate best, however, when Windows is running in the Enhanced mode. As shown in Figure 7-4, the debugger, profiler, and the application all run entirely in extended memory.

## The TDDEBUG.386 Windows Device Driver

Although not required, the Windows debugger utility works best if the TDDEBUG.386 Windows driver is loaded when Windows is operating in the enhanced mode. This device driver enables you to interrupt a Windows application using the (Alt)-(Ctrl)-(SysRq) key while debugging just as you would use the (Ctrl)-(Break) key to interrupt a DOS application in one of the DOS debuggers. Note that when you interrupt a Windows application, it may be in the middle of a Windows function call. If you were to exit the debugger at that point, it is highly probable the system would crash. If you need to exit after interrupting a Windows application with the (Alt)-(Ctrl)-(SysRq) key, then set a break point somewhere in your source code, start the application again with the (F9) key, and then exit after reaching the break point.

## The WINDEBUG.DLL File

Both the TDW and TPROFW utilities use Microsoft's WINDEBUG.DLL Dynamic Link Library, which provides "hooks" into the Windows operating system needed by the debugger and profiler. This file needs to be located either in the same directory as the utilities or in the Windows directory. The WINDEBUG.DLL file is normally installed automatically in the same directory as the utilities.

The WINDEBUG.DLL file supplied with the BC++ compiler package is specific to Windows 3.0. If you upgrade your system to Windows 3.1, you will need to use a WINDEBUG.DLL file compatible with Windows 3.1. The WINDEBUG.DLL file in Microsoft's Software Developer's Kit (SDK) can be used by TDW and TPROFW. If you do not have Microsoft's SDK, contact Borland Technical Support for information on how to obtain an updated WINDEBUG.DLL file.

## Remote Debugging and Profiling

The BC++ compiler package comes with three utilities, TDREMOTE, TFREMOTE, and WREMOTE, which allow you to debug or profile DOS and Windows applications on a

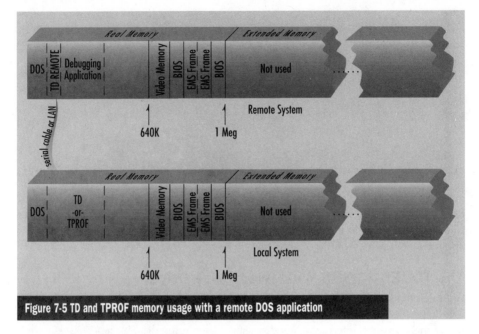

**Figure 7-5 TD and TPROF memory usage with a remote DOS application**

remote computer. The real-mode debugger and profiler, TD and TPROF, are used on the local computer and the connection is made to the remote computer either over a serial cable or via a Local Area Network (LAN). Remote debugging and profiling operations are the best method to use when you have two XT or AT computer systems, you are working with a memory-resident program or DOS device driver, or you are debugging on a network.

To debug a remote DOS application, you first start TDREMOTE on the remote computer. You would start TFREMOTE to profile a remote DOS application. These utilities then wait for either TD or TPROF to be started on the local computer using one of the -r command line options discussed in the reference section. As shown in Figure 7-5, the remote drivers are very small and leave quite a bit of room for running the application.

Debugging or profiling a remote Windows application is done in a similar manner. You first start Windows on the remote computer and then execute the WREMOTE utility. WREMOTE is used for both debugging and profiling. You then start either TD or TPROF as appropriate with one of the -r options and also the -w option to inform the utility that the remote application is running under Windows. Note that TDW and TPROFW are not used with remote operations. Figure 7-6 shows the memory usage when debugging or profiling a remote Windows application.

## Remote Serial Debugging and Profiling

A remote serial connection is physically made by connecting the serial ports of the remote and local computers with a NULL serial cable. A NULL serial cable is not the same as a straight-through serial cable such as one used to connect your computer to an external modem. A NULL serial cable has the transmit and receive pins reversed at one end. This sends

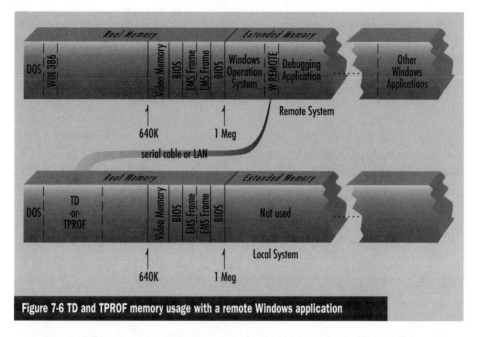

**Figure 7-6 TD and TPROF memory usage with a remote Windows application**

any data transmitted on the transmit pin on one computer to the receive pin on the other computer and vice versa. You can purchase a NULL serial cable from a computer store or you can modify an unused straight-through cable. A straight-through cable is converted to a NULL cable by disassembling one end and reversing the transmit and receive pins. As shown in Figure 7-7, these are pins 2 and 3 on both a 25- and 9-pin serial connector.

When you start the TDREMOTE, TFREMOTE, or WREMOTE application, you need to ensure it is running at the same baud rate you intend to use for the local computer. For example, if you want to use the slowest serial speed, 9600 baud, to debug an application called TEST.EXE, you would enter the following on each system:

```
tdremote -rs1          on the remote system
td -rs1 test           on the local system
```

## Remote Debugging or Profiling via a Local Area Network (LAN)

There are no special hardware requirements for remotely debugging or profiling an application over an existing LAN. You simply use the -rn command line option for the remote driver, TDREMOTE, TFREMOTE, or WREMOTE as appropriate, and also with the TD or TPROF utility on the local computer. However, if more than one person is also remotely debugging or profiling over the same network, then you each need to specify unique sets of identifiers with the -rn option when initiating the remote driver and local utility. For example, suppose a person named Fred is using TD on workstation #1 to debug an application called TEST.EXE on workstation #2 and you are using TD on workstation #3 to debug TEST.EXE on workstation #4. You would then execute the following at each workstation to ensure both you and Fred have unique identifiers:

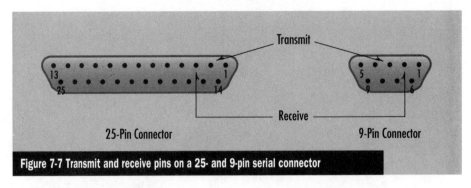

**Figure 7-7 Transmit and receive pins on a 25- and 9-pin serial connector**

```
tdremote -rnFredRemote          on workstation #2
td -rnFredLocal;FredRemote      on workstation #1

tdremote -rnMyRemote            on workstation #4
td -rnMyLocal;MyRemote          on workstation #3
```

This ensures the debugging messages sent to workstation #1 for Fred's debugging session are ignored by your debugging session on workstation #3.

## Debugger and Profiler Command Line Reference

All the debuggers and profilers use many of the same command line options. If a command line option can be used with a particular debugger or profiler utility, it will have an 'X' under the utility's name.

Some command line options only apply if you are debugging or profiling an application on a remote computer system. Others only apply if you are debugging or profiling an application locally on one computer system. Each option will have a ■ next to either the Remote or Local heading if the option can be used in either situation.

Note that the "Installation Menu Item" section refers to the TDINST or TFINST menu item, which corresponds to the command line option.

## b (Protected Mode Debuggers)                    Enable (Ctrl-Break)

| | | | | |
|---|---|---|---|---|
| ■ Local | Remote | TD | ■ TD286 | ■ TD386 |
| TDW | TPROF | TF386 | TPROFW | |

### Purpose
The -b option instructs the protected mode debuggers to enable the use of the (Ctrl)(Break) key even if interrupts are disabled.

### Installation Menu Item
None. Use the -w option to change the default setting in TD286.EXE and TD386.EXE.

## Default

–b–

Disable the (Ctrl)-(Break) key when interrupts are disabled.

## Usage

TD286 –b

Enable interruption of an application even if interrupts are disabled.

## Description

Some applications require using the CLI assembly language instruction to clear the microprocessor's interrupt flag and disable interrupts. This protects a section of code from any type of interrupt temporarily halting the execution until the STI assembly language instruction is executed to again enable interrupts. However, if there is a bug in the code somewhere between the CLI and STI instructions, such as an infinite loop, you cannot interrupt the debugger because the CLI instruction disabled all interrupts. For example, consider the following application:

```
b\test.c
void main(void)
{
   /* Disable interrupts */
   asm      cli

   /* Enter an infinite loop */
   while(1);

   /* Enable Interrupts */
   asm       sti
}
```

The CLI instruction disables interrupts including all keyboard interrupts. Once you trace beyond the CLI instruction and enter the infinite loop, you cannot interrupt the program. Even (Alt)-(Ctrl)-(Del) will not reboot the computer. You must perform a cold boot by either turning the computer off and then on again or by pressing a hardware reset button in order to regain control of the computer.

The -b option instructs the debugger to enable (Ctrl)-(Break) interrupts even if interrupts are disabled with the CLI instruction. This allows you to regain control of the computer again by pressing (Ctrl)-(Break), after which you can determine the location and nature of the infinite loop and then exit the debugger.

This option is only available with the TD286 and TD386 debuggers. The -b option cannot be used when debugging an application via a remote link.

## See Also

b (Profilers)   Batch Mode Profiling
TDNMI        Reset Periscope Breakout Switch

# b (Profilers)

**Batch Mode Profiling**

| | | | | |
|---|---|---|---|---|
| ■ Local | ■ Remote | TD | TD286 | TD386 |
| TDW | ■ TPROF | ■ TF386 | ■ TPROFW | |

## Purpose

The -b option is used with the profiler utilities to suppress the interactive operation of the profiler. This enables profiling using a batch file.

## Installation Menu Item

None

## Default

```
-b-
```

Enter the profiler in the interactive mode with the application inactive.

## Usage

```
TPROF -b MYAPP
```

Profile MYAPP.EXE, append the statistics to the MYAPP.TFS file, and exit the profiler.

## Description

If you are running a number of profiles for an application using different command line options, then it is sometimes easier to execute the profiler using the -b option rather than entering the profiler in the interactive mode. When you specify the -b option, the application is profiled using the profiling mode and selected areas defined in the application's .TFA file. As the profiler executes, the profiler's statistics for the application are appended to the end of the application's .TFS text file.

To define the profiling mode and selected areas stored in an application's .TFA file, first enter the profiler in the interactive mode without the -b option, set the desired mode, select the profiling areas, and then exit. The profiler will automatically create a .TFA file for the application if it does not already exist or update an existing .TFA file upon exiting.

The -b option enables you to use a DOS batch file to execute one of the DOS profiler utilities using a number of different parameters for your application. For example, if you have an application called MYAPP.EXE that accepts one to four numerical command line arguments, you could write a batch file called PROFILE.BAT, such as the following, to sequentially profile your application with different parameters:

```
tprof -b myapp 1 2 3 4
tprof -b myapp 3 2
tprof -b myapp 1
```

The PROFILE.BAT batch file will execute the profiler three times and each time provide your application with three different argument sets. The results of the three profiling sessions will be stored in the MYAPP.TFS text file.

Note that you may use the -b option with the Windows profiler, TPROFW, even though the Windows environment does not support batch file operations.

## See Also

| | |
|---|---|
| b (Protected Mode Debuggers) | Enable Ctrl-Break |
| Chapter 1: /b | Build Project |
| Chapter 1: /m | Make Project |

## *cfilename*                                                Load Configuration File

| | | | | |
|---|---|---|---|---|
| ▪ Local | ▪ Remote | ▪ TD | ▪ TD286 | ▪ TD386 |
| ▪ TDW | ▪ TPROF | ▪ TF386 | ▪ TPROFW | |

## Purpose
The -c*filename* option instructs the utility to load a configuration file.

## Installation Menu Item
None

## Default
```
-cTDCONFIG.TD
```
*for the debugger utilities*

Load the TDCONFIG.TD file in the current directory. If there is no TDCONFIG.TD file in the current directory, then load the TDCONFIG.TD file in the same directory as the utility.

```
-cTFCONFIG.TF
```
*for the profiler utilities*

Same as above for the TFCONFIG.TF file.

## Usage
```
TD -cMYCONFIG.TD          or          Tprof -cMYCONFIG.TF
```
Load the MYCONFIG.TD or MYCONFIG.TF configuration file.

## Description
The configuration file contains most of the default settings for the utility command line options, such as the display mode and source directory. The configuration file also contains the displayed screen colors and general window layout for the debugger/profiler screen.

One way to create a new configuration file is to use the TDINST or TFINST utility. These installation utilities can also be used to modify an existing configuration file. See "The Debugger and Profiler Installation Utilities" section in the tutorial for a detailed description of their operation.

You can also modify some of the command line option settings and save a configuration file from one of the debugger/profiler utilities. Simply modify the settings in the debugger or profiler utility and then select the [Options][Save Options] menu item.

## See Also
TDINST and TFINST Utility

## do, dp, ds

**Local Display Mode**

| ▪ Local | Remote | ▪ TD | ▪ TD286 | ▪ TD386 |
|---|---|---|---|---|
| ❶ TDW | ▪ TPROF | ▪ TF386 | ❶ TPROFW | |

❶ Only the -do and -ds options can be used with TDW and TPROFW. The -dp option is not supported for these utilities because Windows operates in a graphics video mode.

### Purpose
The -do, -dp, and -ds options instruct the debugger and profiler utility on how it is to handle the video display of the application's output and the debugger/profiler screen. The -do option displays the application's output on the primary monitor and the debugger/profiler output on a secondary monitory. The -dp option displays the application's output on one video text page and the utility's screen on a different page. The -ds option physically changes the video display mode and exchanges video memory when changing to or from the application screen to the debugger/profiler text screen.

### Installation Menu Item
Display | Other Display          *for -do*
Display | Flip pages            *for -dp*
Display | Swap                  *for -ds*

### Default
```
-ds
```
   Swap the display screen.

### Usage
```
TD -dp    or    TPROF -dp
```
   Place the debugging/profiler screen and the application screen on separate display pages.

```
TD -do    or    TPROF -do
```
   Display the debugger/profiler screen on the secondary monitor and the application screen on the primary monitor.

### Description
The -dp option sets the display paging mode. This mode uses the different display pages for the application and debugging screens. Color text display modes divide the video memory into several different areas with each area called a 'page.' The Debugger and Profiler utilities use the BIOS interrupt 10h function 5 to select one page while the application is active and another page for the debugger/profiler display while the application is inactive. This mode enables the fastest switching between the application and the debugger/profiler screen; however, it can only be used on a color system and only if the application leaves the video display in the text mode. The mode cannot be used with the Windows debugger or profiler because Windows operates in a graphics video mode.

The -ds option sets the display swapping screen mode. In this display mode the video display memory is saved to a memory buffer and the previous video mode set each time the application is made activate and inactive. This enables you to debug an application, which sets a graphics video mode.

The -ds option can also be used with the Windows debugger and profiler. If you are running Windows using a nonstandard video driver, i.e., Super VGA, Borland shipped several Dynamic Link Libraries that enable TDW and TPROFW to properly handle the screen swapping. These DLLs supplied with BC++ 3.0 support the following cards and video modes:

| FILE | VIDEO CARD AND MODE |
|------|---------------------|
| TSENG.DLL | TSENG based ET-3000 and ET-4000 cards |
| | 640 x 480 x 256 (except for Orchid ProDesigner II) |
| | 800 x 600 x 256 |
| | 1024 x 768 x 256 |
| ATI.DLL | ATI VGAWonder Card |
| | 640 x 480 x 256 |
| | 800 x 600 x 256 |

If you are using one of the above video cards and run Windows in one of the listed display modes, then copy or rename the appropriate DLL to TDVIDEO.DLL in the same directory as the TDW and TPROFW utilities. The Windows debugger and profiler will then use the DLL to swap the display screen when you load them with the -ds option.

BC++ 3.1 handles video swapping a little differently than Version 3.0. In 3.1 you set the "VideoDLL=*file*" line in the [Video Options] section of the TDW.INI. BC++ provides you with the following five video DLL files:

| FILE | VIDEO CARD AND MODE |
|------|---------------------|
| TSENG.DLL | TSENG based ET-3000 and ET-4000 |
| | 640 x 480 x 256 |
| ATI.DLL | ATI VGAWonder |
| | 640 x 480 x 256 |
| | 800 x 600 x 256 |
| TDVESA.DLL | All cards that support the VESA standard |
| STB.DLL | STB's MVP2 series of multi-screen video cards |
| ULTRA.DLL | ATI 8514/Ultra, 8514/Vantage, Graphics/Ultra, and Graphics/Vantage |

You must also set "IntF2Assist=yes" in TDW.INI for the TSENG and ATI libraries. Note that the following modes are supported directly by TDW and do not require any entries be made in the TDW.INI file:

| ATI | 1024 x 768 |
|-----|-----------|
| TSENG | 800 x 600 |
| TSENG | 1024 x 768 |

Screen swapping takes a noticeable amount of time in both the DOS and Windows debuggers and profilers. Also, there are many Super VGA cards and operating modes that are not supported by one of the video DLLs supplied by Borland. The best overall display mode to use to remedy these situations is the -do option. The -do option uses different monitors for the application and the debugger/profiler output. This is the ideal debugging/profiling environment, as it allows you to simultaneously view the application on one monitor and the application source in the debugger/profiler window on another monitor. The debugger and profiler recognize two dual monitor configurations: a system with both a color and a monochrome display and a system with a VGA and an 8514/a display.

Note that only BC++ 3.1 supports the VGA and 8514/a dual monitor configuration. If you do use this configuration, you must place the line "VideoDLL=DUAL8514.DLL" in TDW.INI. Also, if the 8514/a graphics card is not an ATI brand, then also set "ATI=no" in TDW.INI

Adding an 8514/a display to a machine is rather expensive. However, it is relatively inexpensive to add a secondary monochrome display screen to a color system. Simply purchase a monochrome monitor and display card and place the display card in a spare slot. Your existing color display card uses video memory located at address A000:0000 and the monochrome display will use memory at B000:000, so there will be no conflicts between the two. Most monochrome display cards come with a built-in printer port. This printer port will become LPT1 by default and any other printer ports on the system will be incremented by one LPT number.

The -do, -dp, and -ds options are ignored when debugging or profiling an application on a remote computer system or via a local area network.

### See Also

| r | Remote Operation |
|---|---|
| vg | Graphics Video Mode |
| vn | Disable 43/50-Line Display Mode |
| vp | Preserve Video Palette |
| Chapter 1: /d | Dual Monitor Display Mode |


## -e*kBytes*                                                    Extended Memory Usage

| ■ Local | Remote | TD | ■ TD286 | ■ TD386 |
|---|---|---|---|---|
| TDW | TPROF | ■ TF386 | TPROFW | |

### Purpose

The -e*kBytes* option instructs the debugger/profiler to only use the extended memory after the first *kBytes* on systems that do not have an extended memory manager. This prevents the debugger/profiler from using the same memory as a RAM disk. If there is an extended memory manager available, such as HIMEM.SYS, you use the -ek*Bytes* option to reserve extended memory for use by your application.

### kBytes Menu Item

None. Use the -w option to change the default setting in TD286.EXE, TD386.EXE, and TF386.EXE.

### Default

−e0

Use all available extended memory on the system.

### Usage

`TD386 −e2000 TEST.EXE`     *or*     `TF386 −e2000 TEST.EXE`

If there is no extended memory manager, the debugger/profiler will not use the first 2 Megs of extended memory. If there is an extended memory manager, the debugger/profiler leaves 2 Megs of extended memory free for use by TEST.EXE.

### Description

The protected mode debugger and profiler utilities will normally grab all the available extended memory. You should use the -e*kBytes* option if you are debugging an application that allocates extended memory according to the XMS standard.

The -e*kBytes* option has another use if you are debugging an application on the system that does not have an extended memory manager. In this case, the debugger/profiler will leave the first 'kBytes' of extended memory alone and instead use the remaining extended memory. This prevents the debugger/profiler from attempting to use the same extended memory for another application, such as a RAM disk.

### See Also

| | |
|---|---|
| -f*Segment* | EMS Emulation |
| y*kBytes*, ye*Pages* | Overlay Pool Size |

## -fSegment                                                    EMS Emulation

| | | | | |
|---|---|---|---|---|
| ▪ Local | Remote | TD | TD286 | ▪ TD386 |
| TDW | TPROF | ▪ TF386 | TPROFW | |

### Purpose

The -f*Segment* option instructs the virtual mode debugger/profiler to use *Segment* as the EMS frame or, if no expanded memory is available, to emulate EMS memory with that frame using extended memory.

### Installation Menu Item

None. Use the -w option to change the default setting in TD386.EXE and TF386.EXE.

### Default

−f−

Disable expanded memory emulation.

### Usage

`TD386 −fD000 TEST.EXE`     *or*     `TF386 −fD000 TEST.EXE`

Use the D000 segment as the EMS frame segment or, if no expanded memory is present, emulate EMS memory at the segment using extended memory.

## Description

Expanded memory is accessed by requesting the Expanded Memory Manager (EMM) to make a specific 16K page of the memory visible to the system in a segment of real memory called the 'frame segment.' The -f *Segment* option is used to tell the virtual mode debugger and profiler utilities to use a frame segment other than the frame segment used by the EMM. For example, if your EMM has the frame segment at 0xD000, you can use the -fE000 option to change the frame segment to 0xE000.

The protected mode debugger and profiler will also emulate expanded memory using your system's extended memory. For example, if your system does not have expanded memory, you can use the -fD000 to instruct the debugger/profiler to emulate expanded memory using the 0xD000 segment as the frame segment. The debugger/profiler will then respond to DOS expanded memory interrupts by emulating expanded memory using your system's extended memory.

You can use a combination of the -f *Segment* and the -e *kBytes* option to debug/profile an application with both extended and expanded memory available. For example, the following command line will provide TEST.EXE with 3 Megs of expanded memory at frame segment 0xD000 and 2 Megs of extended memory on a system that has 6 Megs of extended memory:

```
td386 -fD000 -e2000 test
```

The -e2000 option reserves 2 Megs of extended memory for use by the application and 3 Megs of extended memory will be used as emulated expanded memory. TD386 uses the remaining 1 Meg of extended memory.

## See Also

| | |
|---|---|
| -e *kBytes* | Extended Memory Usage |
| y *kBytes*, ye *Pages* | Overlay Pool Size |
| Chapter 1: /e[=*Pages*] | Swap with Expanded Memory |

# h, ?                                          Display Help Screen

- Local
- TDW
- Remote
- TPROF
- TD
- TF386
- TD286
- TPROFW
- TD386

## Purpose

The -h and -? options display the help screen for the respective utility. The help screen contains the command line syntax and command line options.

## Installation Menu Item

None

## Default

None

## Usage

TD -h          *or*          TPROF -h

Display the help screen for the debugger/profiler utility.

## Description

The help screens for the different debuggers and profilers display a list of the command line syntax and parameter options. For example, the TD.EXE utility displays the following help screen:

```
Syntax: TD [options] [program [arguments]]   -x- = turn option x off

    -c<file>     Use configuration file <file>
    -do,-dp,-ds  Screen updating: do=Other display, dp=Page flip,
                 ds=Screen swap
    -h,-?        Display this help screen
    -i           Allow process id switching
    -k           Allow keystroke recording
    -l           Assembler startup
    -m<#>        Set heap size to # kbytes
    -p           Use mouse
    -r           Use remote debugging
    -rn<L;R>     Debug on a network with local machine L and remote
                 machine R
    -rp<#>       Set COM # port for remote link
    -rs<#>       Remote link speed: 1=slowest, 2=slow, 3=medium,
                 4=fast
    -sc          No case checking on symbols
    -sd<dir>     Source file directory <dir>
    -sm<#>       Set spare symbol memory to # Kbytes (max 256K)
    -vg          Complete graphics screen save
    -vn          43/50 line display not allowed
    -vp          Enable EGA/VGA palette save
    -w           Debug remote Windows program (must use -r as well)
    -y<#>        Set overlay area size in K
    -ye<#>       Set EMS overlay area size to # 16K pages
```

## See Also

w (Virtual Debugger/Profiler)        Write Options
Chapter 1: /h, /?                    Display the BC Help Screen
Chapter 4:: W, ?, h                  Write/Display Default Options

---

# i                                          Process ID Switching

| ▪ Local | Remote | ▪ TD | ▪ TD286 | ▪ TD386 |
|---------|--------|------|---------|---------|
| TDW | TPROF | TF386 | TPROFW | |

## Purpose

The -i option instructs the debugger utilities to use a different Program Segment Prefix (PSP) for the application than the one used for the debugger. This allows the debugger to open files without restricting the number of file handles available to the application.

## Installation Menu Item
Options | Miscellaneous | Change process ID

## Default
–i

Use a separate PSP for the application and the debugger.

## Usage
TD –i– MYAPP

Use a single PSP shared by both MYAPP and the debugger.

## Description
DOS assigns each application a Program Segment Prefix (PSP) that has enough room for a fixed number of DOS file handles. If both the debugger utility and the application share the same PSP, then the file handles used by the debugger will limit the number of files that can be opened by the application. The -i option, which is enabled by default, tells the debugger to create a separate PSP for the application and to switch between the two whenever the application is either made active or inactive.

Switching between two different PSPs can cause problems if you set a break point somewhere within DOS or trace into a DOS interrupt using the (Alt-F7) key. The debugger switches between the application's PSP and the debugger's PSP using a DOS interrupt. Because DOS is not reentrant, executing a second DOS interrupt while still in the middle of the first DOS interrupt will cause the system to crash. You should disable PSP switching using the -i option whenever you need to debug inside of DOS.

## See Also
l             Startup in Assembly Language Mode

---

## k                                                    Keystroke Recording

---

| ▪ Local  | ▪ Remote | ▪ TD    | ▪ TD286 | ▪ TD386 |
|----------|----------|---------|---------|---------|
| TDW      | TPROF    | TF386   | TPROFW  |         |

## Purpose
The -k option enables keystroke recording of tracing steps and the setting of break points and watches for later playback.

## Installation Menu Item
Options | Input & prompting | Keystroke recording

## Default
–k–

Do not record keystrokes.

## Usage

`TD -k MYAPP`

Record the keystokes made during the debugging session.

## Description

With the -k option enabled, the debugger utility will record to a disk file all your keystrokes involving tracing and the setting of break points and watches. You can then replay these keystokes at any time during the debugging session and return to the selected point in the session even after you've exited the debugger and started the session over again. This is very useful if you need to leave the debugger to modify and recompile your application and then reenter the debugger. You can then replay the keystroke record to restore the previous session's break points and watches and also have the debugger trace to the exact point where you left off at some earlier point in the session.

To replay the keystrokes recorded using the -k option, select the [View][Execution History] window and press the (Tab) key once to move to the Keystroke Recording pane. Highlight the keystroke that will take you to the desired point in the debugging session, press (Alt)-(F10) to pull up the local menu, and select the [Keystroke restore] menu item. This will restart the application and replay the keystrokes up to the point you selected.

Keystroke recording is not available on the Windows version of the debugger, TDW.

## See Also

None

---

## l                                                    Debug Startup Code

| | | | | |
|---|---|---|---|---|
| ▪ Local | ▪ Remote | ▪ TD | ▪ TD286 | ▪ TD386 |
| ▪ TDW | TPROF | TF386 | TPROFW | |

## Purpose

The -l option instructs the debugger to start the session in the assembly language mode using the CPU window. This enables debugging an application's startup code and C++ static object constructors. If the application is a Windows application that uses a DLL, the -l option also enables debugging of the DLL's C++ static object constructors and the DLL's LibMain() function.

## Installation Menu Item

Display | Source                    *for -l-*
Display | Assembler                 *for -l*

## Default

`-l-`

Start the debugging session in the source code window.

## Usage

`TD -l TEST`

Start the session for TEST.EXE in the CPU window at the very beginning of the startup code.

## Description

When the debugger starts in the source code mode, it executes the application's startup code and starts at the first source code line listed in the debug information. This is normally the main() function in a DOS application or the WinMain() function in a Windows application. The -l option starts the debugging session in the CPU window and stops at the first instruction in the startup code. This enables you to either trace through the startup code or set break points in functions executed by the startup code. For example, the startup code for both DOS and Windows applications executes the constructors for any static C++ objects. Consider the following application:

**l\test.cpp**
```
#include <iostream.h>
#include <ltime.h>

/*  The APP_TIMES object class prints the current time when the
    application starts and immediately before exiting.
*/

struct APP_TIMES
{
    APP_TIMES();
    ~APP_TIMES();
}   AppTimes;

/*  Constructor */
APP_TIMES::APP_TIMES()
{
    cout << "Application started at: " << Time() << "\n";
}

/* Destructor */
APP_TIMES::~APP_TIMES()
{
    cout << " Application exited at: " << Time() << "\n";
}

void main(void)
{
    /* Count down from ten */
    for(int n = 10; n > 0; nñ)
    {
        /* Print the value of 'n' */
        cout << n << " ";

        /* Get the current seconds portion of the time */
        unsigned Seconds = Time().second();

        /* Wait until the current seconds is different than the
           saved seconds.
        */
        while(Seconds == Time().second());
    }
    cout << "O\n";
}
```

448

The above application, which counts down 10 seconds, prints the time when the application starts and exits. If a debugging session for the application were started in the source mode, then the debugger would execute the startup code to the point where the main() was entered which means the AppTimes constructor would have already executed and printed the start time. By using the -l option to start the session in the assembly language mode using the CPU window, you have an opportunity to switch back to the source code mode and set a break point in the APP_TIMES constructor before it is executed.

### See Also
tPa*th*        Startup Directory

## m*kBytes*                                                    Set Heap Size

| ■ Local | ■ Remote | ■ TD | ■ TD286 | ■ TD386 |
|---------|----------|------|---------|---------|
| TDW | ■ TPROF | ■ TF386 | TPROFW | |

### Purpose
The -m*kBytes* option sets the size of the working heap used by the debugger and profiler utilities.

### Installation Menu Item
None

### Default
−m18      *for TD and TD286*
    Set the working heap size to 18K.

−m40      *for TPROF*
    Set the working heap size to 40K.

### Usage
TD −m10 TEST      *or*      TPROF −m10 TEST
    Set the working heap size for debugging/profiling TEST.EXE to 10K.

### Description
The debugger and profiler utilities use a small memory heap for storing miscellaneous transient information such as the history list and callers. The heap for TD and TD286 can be as large as the default 18K or as small as 7K. If you set the debugger's heap size too small, you will receive an error message and the application will not load. The real-mode profiler, TPROF, will allow a heap size as large as 64K or one as small as 1K. The callers list will be truncated if the heap size is set too small when running TPROF. If you attempt to set the heap size to a value beyond the minimum or maximum range, the debugger and profiler will use the default value.

### See Also
sm*kByte*      Set Symbol Table Size

## p                                                            Enable/Disable Mouse

| ▪ Local | ▪ Remote | ▪ TD | ▪ TD286 | ▪ TD386 |
|---------|----------|------|---------|---------|
| ▪ TDW | ▪ TPROF | ▪ TF386 | ▪ TPROFW | |

### Purpose

The -p option enables or disables the use of the mouse in the debugging and profiling screen. This option has no effect on the application's use of the mouse.

### Installation Menu Item

Options | Input & prompting | Mouse enabled

### Default

`-p`

Enable use of the mouse when the application is inactive.

### Usage

`TD -p- TEST`   *or*   `TPROF -p- TEST`

Disable the mouse when the application is inactive. The mouse will still be usable when the application is active.

### Description

The -p option, which is enabled by default, uses the mouse to interact with the debugger/profiler display screen using the system's mouse driver. This would create problems if you are debugging a mouse driver or a section of code in your application that uses the mouse driver. In this case, you would use the -p- option to disable the debugger's/profiler's use of the mouse.

There are also some programmers who do not use the mouse at all when interacting with the debugger/profiler and find the mouse cursor in the middle of the screen a distraction. Disabling the mouse using the -p- option also removes the mouse cursor.

### See Also

`Installation Utilities -p option`

## r                                                            Remote Operation

| Local | ❶ Remote | ▪ TD | TD286 | TD386 |
|-------|----------|------|-------|-------|
| TDW | ▪ TPROF | TF386 | TPROFW | |

❶ Serial mode only.

### Purpose

The -r option instructs the real-mode debugger and profiler utilities to debug using default settings for the serial communication port.

## Installation Menu Item

Options | Miscellaneous | Serial

## Default

−r−

Debug/profile an application on the disk.

## Usage

TD −r  TEST    *or*    TPROF −r TEST

Debug/profile the TEST.EXE application on a remote system using the default settings for the speed and COM port.

## Description

The real-mode debugger and profiler, TD and TPROF, can debug a DOS or Windows application on a different computer system via a serial port. You must first start either the TDREMOTE or WREMOTE utility, depending on whether you are debugging a DOS or Windows application, on the system where the application is to be run. You then start either TD or TPROF using the -r. The -r option instructs the debugger/profiler to use the default serial port, usually COM1, at the default speed, 115,000 baud, to connect with the remote system. The default serial port and speed can be changed using the TDINST utility.

See the tutorial section for detailed information on remote debugging.

## See Also

| | |
|---|---|
| rn*LocalName;RemoteName* | Remote Network |
| rp*Port* | Remote COM Port |
| rs*Mode* | Remote Baud Rate |
| TDRF | Remote File/Directory Manipulation |
| WRSETUP | Set WREMOTE Defaults |

# rn*LocalName*;*RemoteName*                    Remote Network

| Local | ❶ Remote | ▪ TD | TD286 | TD386 |
|---|---|---|---|---|
| TDW | ▪ TPROF | TF386 | TPROFW | |

❶ Network mode only.

## Purpose

The -rn*LocalName;RemoteName* option instructs the real-mode debugger and profiler to debug an application located at a remote node on a Local Area Network (LAN).

## Installation Menu Item

| | |
|---|---|
| Options | Miscellaneous | Network | *must be enabled* |
| Options | Miscellaneous | Network local name | *for* LocalName |
| Options | Miscellaneous | Network remote name | *for* RemoteName |

451

## Default

`-rn-`

Do not debug/profile an application over a Local Area Network.

## Usage

`TD -rn TEST`          *or*          `TPROF -rn TEST`

Debug/profile TEST.EXE on a remote system connected via a Local Area Network. Call the remote system 'REMOTE' and the local system 'LOCAL.'

`TD -rnLNode TEST`     *or*          `TPROF -rnLNode`

Same as above except the local system is called 'LNode.'

`TD -rnLNode;RNode TEST`     *or*     `TPROF -rnLNode;RNode`

Same as above except the remote system is called 'RNode.'

## Description

The -rn option operates in the same way as the -r option except the connection is made using the Local Area Network rather than through a normal serial port.

If you use the -rn option without specifying a local or remote system name, then the debugger/profiler will default to using LOCAL and REMOTE. You can use these default names if you are the only person debugging on the LAN; otherwise, each person should use a unique set of local and remote identifiers. This will enable the debugger/profiler to distinguish between messages for your debugging/profiling session and those for another TD/TPROF user on the LAN.

## See Also

Remote Debugging in the Tutorial
r                   Remote Operation
rp*Port*            Remote COM Port
rsMode              Remote Baud Rate
TDRF Utility


# rp*Port*                                            Remote COM Port

| Local | ❶ Remote | ▪ TD | TD286 | TD386 |
|-------|----------|------|-------|-------|
| TDW   | ▪ TPROF  | TF386 | TPROFW | |

❶ Serial mode only.

## Purpose

The -rp option instructs the real-mode debugger and profiler utilities to debug using default settings for the serial communication speed and the port number designated by 'Port.'

## Installation Menu Item

Options | Miscellaneous | Serial          *must be enabled*
Options | Miscellaneous | COM1           *for rp1*
Options | Miscellaneous | COM2           *for rp2*

## Default

−r−

Debug/profile an application on the disk.

−rp1        *for -r*

Debug/profile an application over a remote link using the COM1 serial port.

## Usage

TD −rp2 TEST    *or*    TPROF −rp2 TEST

Debug/profile the TEST.EXE application on a remote system using COM2 and the default settings for the serial communication speed.

## Description

The -rp option operates identically to the -r option, except the debugger/profiler will use the serial port designated by the 'Port' parameter. You must first start either the TDREMOTE or WREMOTE utility, depending on whether you are debugging a DOS or Windows application, on the system where the application is to be run. You then start either TD or TPROF using the -rp*Port* option where 'Port' is the serial port on the local system connected to the remote system. The connection is made using the default speed if the -rs*Mode* option is not used. The default speed can be changed using the TDINST utility.

The local system does not have to use the same serial port as the remote system. For example, suppose you have a cable connected to COM1 on the remote system and COM2 on the local system. In this case, you would start TDREMOTE, TFREMOTE, or WREMOTE using the -rp1 option on the remote system and use the -rp2 option on the local system for TD/TPROF.

See the tutorial section for detailed information on remote debugging.

## See Also

Remote Debugging in the Tutorial

| | |
|---|---|
| r | Remote Operation |
| rn*LocalName,RemoteName* | Remote Network |
| rsMode | Remote Baud Rate |
| TDRF Utility | |

# *rsMode*                         **Remote Baud Rate**

| Local | ❶ Remote | ■ TD | TD286 | TD386 |
|---|---|---|---|---|
| TDW | ■ TPROF | TF386 | TPROFW | |

❶ Serial mode only.

## Purpose

The -rs option instructs the real-mode debugger and profiler utilities to debug using default settings for the serial communication port and the communication speed designated by 'Mode.'

### Installation Menu Item

| | |
|---|---|
| Options | Miscellaneous | Serial | *must be enabled* |
| Options | Miscellaneous | 9,600 baud | *for -rs1* |
| Options | Miscellaneous | 19,200 baud | *for -rs2* |
| Options | Miscellaneous | 38,400 baud | *for -rs3* |
| Options | Miscellaneous | 115,000 baud | *for -rs4* |

### Default

```
-r-
```
Debug/profile an application on the disk.

```
-rs4        for -r
```
Debug/profile an application over a remote link using a 115,000 baud rate.

### Usage

```
TD -rs1 TEST    or    TPROF -rs1 TEST
```
Debug/profile the TEST.EXE application on a remote system using the default communication port at 9,600 baud.

### Description

The -rs option operates identically to the -r option, except the debugger/profiler will use the serial port designated by the 'Port' parameter. You must first start either the TDREMOTE or WREMOTE utility, depending on whether you are debugging a DOS or Windows application, on the system where the application is to be run. Use the same -rs*Mode* option with the TDREMOTE or WREMOTE utility as you will be using with the debugger or profiler. You then start either TD or TPROF using the same -rs*Mode* option. The value for 'Mode' can be either 1, 2, 3, or 4, which correspond to 9,600, 19,200, 38,400, and 115,000, respectively. The connection is made using the default serial communication port if the -rs*Port* option is not used. Note that the default port can be changed using the TDINST utility.

The highest baud rate, mode 4 at 115,000 baud, is suitable for most systems except the PS/2. On a PS/2 system, you should use mode 1 for 9,600 baud. Your chosen baud rate may overdrive the capabilities of the serial card and the system could lock up. If this happens, or if it appears you are receiving faulty information from the remote computer, switch to a slower baud rate.

See the tutorial section for detailed information on remote debugging.

### See Also

Remote Debugging in the Tutorial

| | |
|---|---|
| r | Remote Operation |
| rn*LocalName,RemoteName* | Remote Network |
| rp*Port* | Remote COM Port |
| TDRF Utility | |

## SC
## Source Case Sensitivity

| | | | | |
|---|---|---|---|---|
| ▪ Local | ▪ Remote | ▪ TD | ▪ TD286 | ▪ TD386 |
| ▪ TDW | ▪ TPROF | ▪ TF386 | ▪ TPROFW | |

### Purpose

The -sc option is used to tell the debugger or profiler to ignore case sensitivity when setting break points and watches on symbols. This option has no effect if the application was linked without the /c (case sensitive link) option.

### Installation Menu Item

Options | Source debugging | Ignore symbol case

### Default

```
-sc-
```

Treat watches and break point symbols as case sensitive if the application was linked using the /c option.

### Usage

```
TD -sc TEST        or        TPROF -sc TEST
```

Treat watches and break point symbols as case insensitive even if the application was linked using the /c option.

### Description

If an application was linked using case sensitivity for public symbols, then the debugger and profiler will also use case sensitivity. You use the -sc option if you want to enter symbol names for break or watch points without regard to case sensitivity even if the application was created using a case sensitive link.

You should note that if you are debugging/profiling an application created with a case sensitive link and you are using the -sc option, then the debugger/profiler will only recognize the first occurrence of a symbol in a source file for two symbols that differ only by case. For example, consider the following application:

**sc\test.c**

```
#include <stdio.h>

int MyInt = 1;
int MYINT = 2;

void main(void)
{
    printf("MyInt = %d\n", MyInt);
    printf("MYINT = %d\n", MYINT);
}
```

The above application requires a case sensitive link because of the MYINT and MyInt variables. If the debugger is used with the -sc option and a watch is set on MYINT, the debugger will instead display the value for MyInt because it only differs from MYINT in case and it is defined earlier in the source code than MYINT is.

### See Also
Chapter 2: p    Use the Pascal Calling Convention
Chapter 5: C    Case Sensitive Imports
Chapter 5: c    Case Sensitive Public and External Symbols

## sd*Path*        Source Code Directory

- Local
- TDW
- Remote
- TPROF
- TD
- TF386
- TD286
- TPROFW
- TD386

### Purpose
The -sd option tells the debugger or profiler the directory location of the source code.

### Installation Menu Item
Options | Directories | Source directories

### Default
```
-sd
```
Look for source code files in the current directory. If the required source file is not in the current directory, then look in the application's directory.

### Usage
```
-sd\SUB_DIR;\MYAPP
```
Look for source code files in the SUB_DIR and MYAPP directories on the current disk. If the required source files are not in either of these directories, then look in the current directory and the application's directory.

### Description
When applications are linked for debugging, they contain debugging information regarding the name of the source code files, but not the directory location. The debugger and profiler utilities will search for the source code files in the directories listed using the -sd option. If they cannot be located in any of these directories, or you did not use the -sd option, then the utilities will look for the files in the current directory and also in the directory containing the application being debugged/profiled.

### See Also
t*Path*                    Startup Directory
Chapter 2: I*path*        Set Include Files Directory
Chapter 2: L               Set the Location of Library Files

## sm*kBytes*                                          **Set Symbol Table Size**

| | | | | |
|---|---|---|---|---|
| ■ Local | ■ Remote | ■ TD | ❶ TD286 | ■ TD386 |
| TDW | TPROF | TF386 | TPROFW | |

❶ The -sm*kBytes* option is ignored by the TD386.EXE utility.

### Purpose
The -sm*kBytes* option tells the DOS debugger utilities how much memory to allocate for loading the symbolic information in a .TDS file using the [Files][Symbol Load] menu item.

### Installation Menu Item
Options | Miscellaneous | Spare symbol memory (K)

### Default
−sm0
   Do not allocate any memory for loading a symbol table.

### Usage
TD −sm20
   Allocate 20K of memory for loading a .TDS symbolic information file using the [Files][Symbol Load] menu item.

### Description
The debuggers will automatically allocate the memory required to load the symbolic information if the information is available at startup, such as when the debugging information is in the .EXE file itself or in a .TDS file that is in the same directory as the application. If, however, you have to use the [Files][Symbol Load] menu item to load the file after TD.EXE is started, such as when you are debugging a DOS device driver or memory-resident portion of a TSR, then you need to use the -sm*kBytes* parameter to let the real and protected mode debugger know how much memory it must allocate for the symbolic information. This is normally about one and a half times the size of the .TDS file. For example, if the .TDS file is 10K, then you use a value of 15 for the 'kBytes' parameter. Loading the .TDS file for some applications may require more than one and a half times the .TDS file size. If this is the case, then the debugger will issue a "Not enough memory to load symbol table" error. You then need to exit the debugger and restart the session with a larger value for 'kBytes.'
   Note that the -sm*kBytes* command line option is not required if you are using the virtual mode debugger. TD386 will automatically allocate the required memory for loading a .TDS file when you use the [Files][Symbol Load] menu item.

### See Also
TDSTRIP          Symbolic Information Stripper

## t*Path*                                    Startup Directory

| | | | | |
|---|---|---|---|---|
| ▪ Local | Remote | TD | TD286 | TD386 |
| ▪ TDW | TPROF | TF386 | ▪ TPROFW | |

### Purpose
The -t*Path* option is used with TDW and TPROFW to specify a starting directory.

### Installation Menu Item
None

### Default
-t

Start the Windows debugging/profiling session in the current directory.

### Usage
TDW -t\my_app    *or*    TPROFW -t\my_app

Start the Windows debugging/profiling session in the \MY_APP directory on the current disk.

### Description
A Windows application needs to be started in a specific directory when it depends on a Dynamic Link Library or some other file located somewhere other than the current directory. Windows 3.0 only provides for starting an application in a specific directory if you write a .PIF file. You can use the -t*Path* option in the command line section of the Properties of the TDW or TPROFW Windows icon in lieu of creating a .PIF file.

Note that Windows 3.1 allows you to specify the starting directory as part of an icon's properties.

### See Also
| | |
|---|---|
| l | Debug Startup Code |
| sd*Path* | Source Code Directory |
| Chapter 2: I*path* | Set Include Files Directory |
| Chapter 2: L | Set the Location of Library Files |
| Chapter 5: L*path* | Set Library Search Path |
| Chapter 6: I*path* | Set Include Path |

## vg                                    Graphics Video Mode

| | | | | |
|---|---|---|---|---|
| ▪ Local | Remote | ▪ TD | ▪ TD286 | ▪ TD386 |
| TDW | ▪ TPROF | ▪ TF386 | TPROFW | |

### Purpose
The -vg option instructs the debugger and profiler to save the graphics area of video memory when swapping between a graphics application and the utility's text display.

This option only applies when using the -ds display mode and is ignored when using the -do or -dp display mode, or when debugging/profiling a remote application.

## Installation Menu Item
Display | Full graphics save

## Default
-vg-

Do not save complete graphics information.

## Usage
TD -vg    *or*    TPROF -vg

Save complete graphics information for the overwritten sections of video memory.

## Description
If you are debugging an application that uses a graphics video mode and you are using the -ds option to swap the video display between the application and debugging/profiling session screen, the top portion of the display screen will likely be corrupted. This is because the debugger or profiler overwrites that portion of video memory when it displays the text screen. You use the -vg option to instruct the debugger or profiler to save this section of video memory each time it swaps the display to the text mode for the debugging/profiling session and restore the top portion of the screen when the application is reactivated or the application's output is viewed. The -vg option requires an additional 8K of memory.

This option will not always work with some 256 color Super VGA modes.

## See Also
| | |
|---|---|
| do, dp, ds | Local Display Mode |
| vn | Disable 43/50-Line Display Mode |
| vp | Preserve Video Palette |

## vn             Disable 43/50-Line Display Mode

| | | | | |
|---|---|---|---|---|
| ▪ Local | Remote | ▪ TD | ▪ TD286 | ▪ TD386 |
| ▪ TDW | ▪ TPROF | ▪ TF386 | ▪ TPROFW | |

## Purpose
The -vn option instructs the debugger and profiler to allocate only enough memory for displaying the debugger and profiler in the 25-line mode. This option only applies when using the -ds or -dp display mode and is ignored when using the -do display mode or when debugging/profiling a remote application.

## Installation Menu Item
Display | Permit 43/50 lines

## Default

−vn−

Enable the 43/50-line display of the debugger/profiler text screen.

## Usage

TD−vn      *or*      TPROF −vn

Disable the option for the 43/50-line display of the debugger/profiler text screen.

## Description

The debugger and profiler by default allocate an additional 8K of memory to enable the display of their text screens in a 43- or 50-line mode. If you know you will not be using the 43- or 50-line display mode, you can save this 8K of memory by disabling the feature using the -vn option.

## See Also

do, dp, ds       Local Display Mode
vg                   Graphics Video Mode
vp                   Preserve Video Palette

---

## vp                                                Preserve Video Palette

| | | | | |
|---|---|---|---|---|
| ▪ Local | Remote | ▪ TD | ▪ TD286 | ▪ TD386 |
| TDW | ▪ TPROF | ▪ TF386 | TPROFW | |

## Purpose

The -vp option instructs the debugger and profiler utilities to save the VGA display palette on startup and restore the palette to its original state when exiting. This option only applies if you are debugging an application on a VGA or Super VGA system. The option is ignored on all other system display types.

## Installation Menu Item

None

## Default

−vp−

Do not preserve the display palette.

## Usage

TD −vp      *or*      TPROF −vp

Preserve the VGA display palette.

## Description

If you have a VGA system and the application you are debugging or profiling modifies the display palette, then you should use the -vp option to preserve the original palette. This option enables restoration of the original palette when you exit the debugger or profiler.

Note that the -vp option requires the debugger or profiler to use an additional 2K of memory.

## See Also

| | |
|---|---|
| vg | Graphics Video Mode |
| vn | Disable 43/50-Line Display Mode |
| Chapter 1: /p | Preserve Palette |

# w (Real-Mode Debugger/Profiler)   Remote Windows Operation

| Local | ▪ Remote | ▪ TD | TD286 | TD386 |
|---|---|---|---|---|
| TDW | ▪ TPROF | TF386 | TPROFW | |

## Purpose

The -w option is used with the real-mode debugger and profiler with one of the -r options to enable debugging of a remote Windows application.

## Installation Menu Item

None

## Default

-w-

Debug or profile a local or remote DOS application.

## Usage

TD -r -w test   *or*   TPROF -r -w test

Debug/profile the TEST.EXE Windows application on a remote computer.

## Description

TD and TPROF are also used to debug or profile remote Windows applications. Debugging a remote Windows application is identical to debugging a remote DOS application, except you also use the -w command line option. See the tutorial for more information on debugging a remote Windows application.

## See Also

| | |
|---|---|
| TDREMOTE, TFREMOTE, WREMOTE | Remote Debugging |
| TDRF | Remote File/Directory Manipulation |

# w (Virtual Debugger/Profiler)                    Write Options

| ▪ Local | Remote | TD | TD286 | ▪ TD386 |
|---------|--------|-----|-------|---------|
| TDW | TPROF | ▪ TF386 | TPROFW | |

## Purpose
The -w option is used with TD386 to write the -b, -e*kBytes*, and -f*Seg* option settings as the defaults. It is also used with TF386 to write the -e*kBytes* and -f*Seg* option settings as the defaults.

## Installation Menu Item
None

## Default
None

## Usage
`TD386 -b -e10 -fD000 -w`    *or*    `TF386 -e10 -fD000 -w`

Write the command line options listed to the virtual debugger/profiler as the defaults.

## Description
The TDINST, TFINST, and TDWINST installation utilities have no provisions for setting the defaults for the command line options specific to the virtual mode debugger and profiler. The -w option for TD386 and TF386 writes the options specified on the command line as the default options. The installation utilities are used to set the defaults for the command line options common to the debuggers and profilers. The -w option will not write a command line option that is installed using one of the TDINST, TFINST, or TDWINST installation utilities.

## See Also
TDINST, TFINST, TDWINST    Debugger/Profiler Installation
Chapter 4:: W, ?, h         Write/Display Default Options

# wd                                    Do Not Check for DLLs

| ▪ Local | ▪ Remote | TD | TD286 | TD386 |
|---------|----------|-----|-------|-------|
| ▪ TDW | TPROF | TF386 | ▪ TPROFW | |

## Purpose
The -wd option instructs the Windows debugger and profiler not to check for Dynamic Link Libraries (DLLs).

## Installation Menu Item
None

## Usage

```
TDW -wd test    or   TPROFW -wd test
```
Debug/profile TEST.EXE without checking for DLLs.

## Description

TDW and TPROFW will check for the presense of any DLL used by your Windows application. If your SYSTEM.INI file renames a DLL to something other than the name used when linking your application, then TDW and TPROFW will issue an error message. For example, if you linked your application with SOUND.DLL and your SYSTEM.INI contains the statement:

```
sound.dll=newsound.drv
```

to reference the file as NEWSOUND.DRV, then TDW and TPROFW will generate the error message, "Can't find sound.dll".

The -wd option instructs the debugger and profiler not to look for any DLLs linked with your application thereby eliminating this error.

## See Also

L             Debug Startup Code

# y*kBytes*, ye*Pages*          **Overlay Pool Size**

| ■ Local | ■ Remote | ■ TD | TD286 | TD386 |
|---------|----------|------|-------|-------|
| TDW | ■ TPROF | TF386 | TPROFW | |

## Purpose

The *-ykBytes* option instructs the real-mode debugger and profiler, TD and TPROF, to set aside 'kBytes' worth of real memory for use by the utility's overlay pool. The *-yePages* option instructs the utilities to limit the use of expanded memory to the number of pages specified by the 'Pages' option.

## Installation Menu Item

None

## Default

```
-y80
```
Use 80K of real memory for the TD and TPROF overlay pool.

```
-yeAll
```
Use all available expanded memory.

## Usage

```
TD -y200 -ye5    or   TPROF -y200 -ye5
```
Use 200K of memory for the TD/TPROF overlay pool and limit the usage of expanded memory for loading overlays to 5 EMS pages (80K).

## Description

The real-mode debugger and profiler use overlays for much of their code. This increases the amount of memory available to the application. The two utilities use an overlay pool to load and execute portions of the overlay in real memory. You set the size of this pool using the -y*kBytes* command line option. The maximum size you can set for the pool is 200K for TD or 250K for TPROF. The larger the size of the overlay pool, the faster the debugger/profiler will operate. However, the larger pool size limits the size of the application that can be loaded and the amount of far memory the application can allocate. By the same token, reducing the size of the overlay pool provides more memory for the application, but reduces the performance of the debugger and profiler. You can set the overlay pool to as small as 20K for either TD or TPROF.

The TD and TPROF utilities normally try to move all the overlays into expanded memory. This enables faster performance because they can then load the overlay from expanded memory into the overlay pool much more quickly than they can from the disk. TD uses approximately 240K of expanded memory when it is available and TPROF will use 192K. If you need this expanded memory for use by the application, you can limit the amount of expanded memory used to load the overlays with the -ye*Pages* option. Setting this option to zero will cause the debugger and profiler to load all overlays from the disk rather than the expanded memory. Note that even if you disable the overlay expanded memory usage to 0 with the -ye*Pages* option, the TD will still use 48k of expanded memory for other types of storage and TPROF will use 32K.

## See Also

| | |
|---|---|
| -e*kBytes* | Extended Memory Usage |
| -f*Segment* | EMS Emulation |
| Chapter 1: /e[=*Pages*] | Swap with Expanded Memory |
| Chapter 1: /x[=*kBytes*] | Extended Memory Allocation |

# SUPPORTING UTILITIES REFERENCE

The BC++ compiler package includes many supporting utilities that aid in debugging and profiling DOS and Windows applications. Each of the utilities listed in Table 7-1 has an entry in the reference section that follows.

| **DOS SPECIFIC** | |
|---|---|
| TD286INS | Adds a machine to the TD286 internal data base. |
| TDREMOTE | TSR used on one computer to link with the TD utility on another computer over a serial port or Local Area Network for debugging a DOS application. |
| TFREMOTE | TSR used on one computer to link with the TPROF utility on another computer over a serial port or Local Area Network for profiling a DOS application. |
| **WINDOWS SPECIFIC** | |
| TDWINST | Modifies the default settings of the Windows debugger, TDW. |
| WINSIGHT | Allows viewing the characteristics of all windows and window classes in the Windows operating system. Also allows monitoring of window messages. |

| WREMOTE | Windows application used on one computer to link with the TD or TPROF utility on another computer over a serial port or Local Area Network for debugging or profiling a Windows application. |
| WRSETUP | Modifies the default settings of the WREMOTE utility. |

**DOS AND WINDOWS**

| TDINST | Modifies the default settings of the debugger utilities: TD, TD286, TD386, and TDW. |
| TFINST | Modifies the default settings of the profiler utilities: TPROF, TF386, and TPROFW. |

**MISCELLANEOUS**

| EMSTEST | Tests the performance of the system's expanded memory manager. |
| TDDEV | Displays a list of loaded DOS device drivers. |
| TDUMP | Creates a text file detailing the structure of an .EXE, .OBJ, .LIB, or .TDS file. |
| TDMAP | Converts a .MAP file generated by a linker into symbolic debugging information and adds it to an .EXE file. |
| TDMEM | Displays the contents of real memory as well as available extended and expanded memory. |
| TDNMI | TSR program which enables the Periscope's breakout switch. |
| TDRF | Used to manipulate files and directories on the remote computer via a serial port or Local Area Network. |
| TDSTRIP | Removes symbolic debugging information from .EXE and .OBJ files and either discards the information or places it in a .TDS file. |

**Table 7-1 Utilities that aid in debugging and profiling**

# EMSTEST                                Expanded Memory Manager Testing

## Purpose
The EMSTEST utility tests the performance of the system's expanded memory manager.

## Syntax
EMSTEST

## Options
None

## Description
The EMSTEST utility will run all the functions for an expanded memory manager and verify that they are working properly. This is a three-part test. The first part determines if there is an expanded memory manager on the system, the frame segment it is using, and the total number of EMS pages. The second part of the test calls the basic EMS functions to allocate, page, and deallocate all the available expanded memory. The third

part of the test evaluates the EMS disk I/O functions by performing different types of I/O operations. The last test requires a few minutes to complete.

### See Also
| -ek*Bytes* | Extended Memory Usage |
| -f*Segment* | EMS Emulation |
| y*kBytes*, ye*Pages* | Overlay Pool Size |

## TD286INS                                          TD286 Machine Data Base Utility

### Purpose
The TD286INS utility adds a machine to the TD286 debugger's internal data base.

### Syntax
TD286INS

### Options
None

### Description
The TD286 debugger uses a variety of methods to access extended memory when run on a machine without an extended memory manager. If you do not run with an extended memory manager, then you need to run the TD286INS at least once to ensure your machine is in the debugger's internal data base. The TD286INS utility will first check to see if your machine is already in the data base and stop if it is. If not, then TD286INS will experiment with different methods for accessing extended memory and update the debugger's data base with the information resulting for its tests. It will also write the information to a separate file with a .DB extension. This file should be sent to Borland so your machine type can be included in future versions of TD286.

### See Also
TDINST, TFINST, TDWINST   Debugger/Profiler Installation

## TDDEV                                               Display DOS Device Drivers

### Purpose
The TDDEV utility displays a list of loaded DOS device drivers.

### Syntax
TDDEV [*options*]

### Options
-?

Display the help screen for TDDEV.
-R   Output a raw listing display.

## Description

The TDDEV utility is a useful tool when you are developing a DOS device driver. It will list all the device drivers loaded on the system sorted by their starting address. For example, the following is the normal output for TDDEV:

```
TDDEV  Version 1.0  Copyright (c) 1990 Borland International

   Address      Bytes  Name              Hooked vectors
   ---------    -----  ---------------   ---------------
   0070:0023      -    CON
   0070:0035      -    AUX
   0070:0047      -    PRN
   0070:0059      -    CLOCK$
   0070:006B      -    3 Block Units
   0070:007B      -    COM1
   0070:008D      -    LPT1
   0070:009       -    LPT2
   0070:00B8      -    LPT3
   0070:00CA      -    COM2
   0070:00DC      -    COM3
   0070:00EE      -    COM4
   0000:11A8    7760   NUL               1B 20 21 25 26 27 29
   0255:0000     416   SETVERXX
   026F:0000    1088   XMSXXXX0          15
   02B3:0000   22944   SMARTAAR          13
   084D:0000    7936   TDHDEBUG
   0A3D:0000   11136   MS$MOUSE          10 33
   0CF5:0000  -52944   DOS buffers
```

The 'Bytes' column indicates the size of the device driver listed as a decimal number. The utility lists the size as negative if the size is larger than 0x7ffff bytes. The 'Name' column lists the name listed in the device driver chain. The 'Hooked vectors' column indicates the interrupt vectors whose address points to somewhere in the device driver's memory space.

The starting address information is particularly important if you are debugging a DOS device driver and you need to load a .TDS file containing the device driver's symbolic debugging information using the [Files][Symbol Load] menu item. After the debugger has loaded the .TDS file, the symbolic information must then be segment aligned with DOS device drivers already loaded in memory using the [Files][Table Relocate] and the segment portion of the device driver's address. Once that is completed, you can then set break points in the source code. If you are debugging on a single system rather than debugging with the DOS device driver on a remote system, be sure to use the -i- command line option with the debugger so as to prevent reentering DOS.

The TDDEV utility will also display a raw output of the information such as the following when it is invoked with the -r command line option:

```
TDDEV  Version 1.0  Copyright (c) 1990 Borland International

   Starting     Next                 Strategy    Interrupt   Device
   Address      Hdr Addr    Attr     Entry Pnt   Entry Pnt   Name
   ---------    ---------   ----     ---------   ---------   -------
   0000:11A8    0A3D:0000   8004     0000:0DC6   0000:0DCC   NUL
```

```
0A3D:0000    084D:0000   8000   0000:0012   0000:0025   MS$MOUSE
084D:0000    02B3:0000   8000   0000:1776   0000:1781   TDHDEBUG
02B3:0000    026F:0000   C800   0000:00A2   0000:00AD   SMARTAAR
026F:0000    0255:0000   A000   0000:0043   0000:004E   XMSXXXX0
0255:0000    0070:0023   8000   0000:001E   0000:0029   SETVERXX
0070:0023    0070:0035   8013   0000:06F5   0000:0700   CON
0070:0035    0070:0047   8000   0000:06F5   0000:0721   AUX
0070:0047    0070:0059   A0C0   0000:06F5   0000:0705   PRN
0070:0059    0070:006B   8008   0000:06F5   0000:0739   CLOCK$
0070:006B    0070:007B   08C2   0000:06F5   0000:073E   3 Block Units
0070:007B    0070:008D   8000   0000:06F5   0000:0721   COM1
0070:008D    0070:009F   A0C0   0000:06F5   0000:070C   LPT1
0070:009F    0070:00B8   A0C0   0000:06F5   0000:0713   LPT2
0070:00B8    0070:00CA   A0C0   0000:06F5   0000:071A   LPT3
0070:00CA    0070:00DC   8000   0000:06F5   0000:0727   COM2
0070:00DC    0070:00EE   8000   0000:06F5   0000:072D   COM3
0070:00EE    0070:FFFF   8000   0000:06F5   0000:0733   COM4
```

In this format the device drivers are listed in the order in which they occur in the DOS device driver chain. For example, the first device driver in the chain is called "NUL." The starting address for NUL is listed as 0000:11A8. The "Next Hdr Addr" lists the starting address for the next device driver in the chain, which for NUL is the MS$MOUSE driver starting at address 0A3D:0000. The "Attr" is the IOCTL device driver attribute word for the device driver that specifies the device driver's characteristics. The "Strategy Entry Pnt" and "Interrupt Entry Pnt" sections list the offset to the strategy and interrupt functions called by DOS. You can convert these offsets to far pointer addresses by using the segment listed in the "Starting Address" column.

### See Also

i                  Process ID Switching
TDMEM              Memory Display

# TDUMP                                                File Structure

### Purpose
The TDUMP utility displays operating system and symbolic debugging information contained in an .OBJ, .EXE (both DOS and Windows), .COM, .LIB, .DLL, or .TDS file. TDUMP will display any file format it does not recognize in hexadecimal format.

### Syntax
TDUMP [options] filename [output]

### Options
-a         Display the file in an ASCII format.

-a7        Display a Wordstar file in ASCII format. This ASCII format ignores bit 7.

-bNum      Begin displaying information after offset 'Num.'

-e         Assume the filetype is an .EXE file.

-el       Assume the filetype is an .EXE file and ignore line number information.

-er       Assume the filetype is an .EXE file and ignore relocation table information.

-ex      Assume the filetype is a Windows .EXE file and ignore the Windows portion, i.e., the "New-Style" information. This option only displays information on the Windows application's DOS stub.

-h        Display the file in hexadecimal format (default for unrecognized filetypes).

-l         Assume the filetype is a .LIB file.

-m      Display the C++ filenames in their mangled form.

-o        Assume the filetype is an .OBJ file.

-oc      Assume the filetype is an .OBJ file and perform a CRC check to determine if the .OBJ file is corrupt.

-ox *Type*  Assume the filetype is an .OBJ file and exclude any records called 'Type.'

-oi *Type*  Assume the filetype is an .OBJ file and only list information on records called 'Type.'

-v        Display a verbose listing for .OBJ and .LIB files that includes an uncommented hexadecimal dump of the code and data in each record.

## Description

The TDUMP utility provides a wealth of information on the internal structure of many of the different filetypes such as the following:

| | |
|---|---|
| .BIN | Binary executable file |
| .COM | Command file |
| .DLL | Windows Dynamic Link Library |
| .EXE | DOS and Windows executable file |
| .LIB | Object code library and Import library file |
| .OBJ | Object code file |
| .TDS | Turbo Debugger symbolic information file |

When TDUMP does not recognize a file format, it displays the file as a hexadecimal dump. For example, consider the following "Hello, TDUMP!" application:

**tdump\hello.c**

```
#include <stdio.h>

void SayHello(void)
{
    printf("Hello, TDUMP!\n");
}

void main(void)
{
    SayHello();
}
```

The TDUMP utility displays the above file as follows:

```
Turbo Dump  Version 3.0 Copyright (c) 1988, 1991 Borland International
                   Display of File HELLO.C

000000: 23 69 6E 63 6C 75 64 65  20 3C 73 74 64 69 6F 2E #include <stdio.
000010: 68 3E 0D 0A 0D 0A 76 6F  69 64 20 53 61 79 48 65 h>....void SayHe
000020: 6C 6C 6F 28 76 6F 69 64  29 0D 0A 7B 0D 0A 20 20 llo(void)..{..
000030: 20 70 72 69 6E 74 66 28  22 48 65 6C 6C 6F 2C 20 printf("Hello,
000040: 54 44 55 4D 50 21 5C 6E  22 29 3B 0D 0A 7D 0D 0A TDUMP!\n");..}..
000050: 0D 0A 76 6F 69 64 20 6D  61 69 6E 28 76 6F 69 64 ..void main(void
000060: 29 0D 0A 7B 0D 0A 20 20  20 53 61 79 48 65 6C 6C )..{..   SayHell
000070: 6F 28 29 3B 0D 0A 7D 0D  0A 00 00 00 00 00 00 00 o();..}.........
```

You can force TDUMP to use the hexadecimal format even if it does recognize the file type by using the -h command line option.

The HELLO.C file can also be displayed in a pure ASCII format as follows using either the -a or -a7 command line option:

```
Turbo Dump  Version 3.0 Copyright (c) 1988, 1991 Borland International
                   Display of File HELLO.C

000000:     #include <stdio. h>....void SayHe llo(void)..{..
printf("Hello,
000040: TDUMP!\n");..}.. ..void main(void )..{..   SayHell o();..}..
```

The -b*Num* command line option instructs the TDUMP utility to start displaying information after the first 'Num' bytes into the file. The 'Num' parameter can either be a decimal number or, if it is preceded by a 0x prefix, it will be interpreted as a hexadecimal number. For example, the TDUMP utility will display the following for HELLO.C when you use the -b0x40 command line option:

```
Turbo Dump  Version 3.0 Copyright (c) 1988, 1991 Borland International
                   Display of File HELLO.C

000000: TDUMP!\n");..}.. ..void main(void )..{..   SayHell o();..}..
```

The TDUMP utility uses a different format when displaying an object code (.OBJ) file. For example, the following is a partial listing of the information displayed by TDUMP for the HELLO.OBJ file of the "Hello, TDUMP!" application:

```
Turbo Dump  Version 3.0 Copyright (c) 1988, 1991 Borland International
                   Display of File HELLO.OBJ

000000 THEADR  hello.c
00000C COMENT  Purge: Yes, List: Yes, Class: 0   (000h)
   Translator: TC86 Borland Turbo C++ 2.99
00002E COMENT  Purge: Yes, List: Yes, Class: 249 (0F9h)
   Debug information version 3.0
000036 COMENT  Purge: Yes, List: Yes, Class: 233 (0E9h)
   Dependency File: hello.c          11/19/91  06:16 pm
000048 COMENT  Purge: Yes, List: Yes, Class: 233 (0E9h)
   Dependency File: C:\BORLANDC\INCLUDE\stdio.h 10/04/91  02:00 am
 . . .
```

This lists the autodependency information included in the .OBJ file as a COMMENT record. Other types of records displayed by TDUMP are listed in Table 7-2.

| RECORD TYPE | DESCRIPTIONS |
|---|---|
| COMMENT | Miscellaneous information such as autodependency and debugging information |
| LNAMES | Segment names |
| SEGDEF | Segment definitions |
| GRPDEF | Group definitions |
| EXTDEF | External definitions |
| PUBDEF | Public definitions |
| LEDATA | Data |
| FIXUPP | Segment relocation information |
| LINNUM | Source code line number information |
| MODEND | Last record |

**Table 7-2 Types of records displayed by TDUMP for .OBJ and .LIB files**

You can instruct TDUMP to either include or exclude specific record types from the listing by using the -oi *Type* or -ox *Type* command line options, respectively.

The -v option when used with .OBJ and .LIB files produces a verbose listing that includes a hexadecimal dump of each record without informational comments. For example, the following is the display for the same records in the previous listing using the -v option:

```
000000 THEADR  hello.c
00000C COMENT  Purge: Yes, List: Yes, Class: 0   (000h)
    0000: 1B 54  43 38 36 20 42 6F  72 6C 61 6E 64 20 54 75   .TC86
Borland Tu
    0010: 72 62 6F 20 43 2B 2B 20  32 2E 39 39        rbo C++ 2.99
00002E COMENT  Purge: Yes, List: Yes, Class: 249 (OF9h)
    000: 03 00      ..
000036 COMENT Purge: Yes, List: Yes, Class: 233 (OE9h)
    0000: 15 92 73 17 07 68 65 6C 6C 6F 2E 63         ..s..hello.c
000048 COMENT Purge: Yes, List: Yes, Class: 233 (OE9h)
    0000: 00 10 44 17 1B 43 3A 5C 42 4F 52 4C 41 4E 44 43
..D..C:\BORLANDC
    0010: 5C 49 4E 43 4C 55 44 45 5C 73 74 64 69 6F 2E 68
\INCLUDE\stdio.h
```

The TDUMP utility displays as follows for executable files:

```
Turbo Dump Version 3.0 Copyright (c) 1988, 1991 Borland International
             Display of File HELLO.EXE

DOS File Size                                      2226h    (  8742. )
Load Image Size                                    17F0h    (  6128. )
Relocation Table entry count                       0001h    (     1. )
Relocation Table address                           003Eh    (    62. )
Size of header record        (in paragraphs)       0020h    (    32. )
Minimum Memory Requirement (in paragraphs)         0000h    (     0. )
Maximum Memory Requirement (in paragraphs)         FFFFh    ( 65535. )
File load checksum                                 0000h    (     0. )
```

Overlay Number                              0000h    (     0. )

Borland TLINK Version 5.00

Initial Stack Segment   (SS:SP)                    0177:0080
Program Entry Point     (CS:IP)                    0000:0000

Relocation Locations (1 Entry)

   0000:0001

Borland TLINK Symbol Table Present:

Symbolic Information Version:          3.10
Debugger Hook Address:                 0000:0000
Case Sensitive Link:                   Yes
Pascal Overlays Present:               No

Image Size                          0019F0h       (  6640. )
Name Pool Size (in bytes)           000364h       (   868. )
Number of Names                     005Dh         (    93. )
Number of Type Entries              001Ah         (    26. )
Number of Member Entries            0000h         (     0. )
Number of Symbols                   005Ah         (    90. )
Number of Global Symbols            0058h         (    88. )
Number of Source Modules            0001h         (     1. )
Number of Local Symbols             0000h         (     0. )
Number of Scopes                    0004h         (     4. )
Number of Line Number Entries       0006h         (     6. )
Number of Include Files             0001h         (     1. )
Number of Segments                  0001h         (     1. )
Number of Correlation Entries       0001h         (     1. )
Basic RTL String Segment Offset     0000h         (     0. )
Data Count                          0000h         (     0. )
Number of Class Entries             0000h         (     0. )
Mumber of Global Classes            0000h         (     0. )
Number of Parent Entries            0000h         (     0. )
Number of Overload Entries          0000h         (     0. )
Number of Scope Class Entries       0000h         (     0. )
Number of Module Class Entries      0000h         (     0. )
Number of Coverage Analysis Offsets 0006h         (     6. )
Number of Browser Entries           0000h         (     0. )
Number of Optimized Symbol Entries  0000h         (     0. )
Debug Flags                         0000h         (     0. )

Global Table           88. Entries (0058)  File Base: 01A40h

   0000:015C [001] __cleanup     Type: Unknown
   0000:016F [002] __checknull   Type: Unknown
   0000:0197 [003] __terminate   Type: Unknown
   0000:01EC [004] __restorezero Type: Unknown

   . . .

   Module: [05a] HELLO
      Language:  C         Underbars: Yes    Memory Model: Small

      Source Files:
      [05d] HELLO.C                        Time Stamp: 11/19/
91  06:16 pm

```
Module Type Definitions:
  [05b] fpos_t                                         typedef signed long
  [05c] size_t                                         typedef unsigned
int

  Correlation Records:
  File Name: HELLO.C
  Code Base:    0000:0291     Code Length:           0015 bytes

  Parent Scope:  0
    Scope Offset:  0291       Scope Length:          000D Bytes

  Parent Scope:  1
    Scope Offset:  0294       Scope Length:          000A Bytes

  Parent Scope:  0
    Scope Offset:  029E     Scope Length:   0008 Bytes

  Parent Scope:  3
    Scope Offset:  02A1     Scope Length:   0005 Bytes

  Line Numbers:
    3:0291h       5:0294h         6:029Ch         8:029Eh      10:02A1h
    11:02A4h
```

Much of the above information refers to symbolic debugging. The TDUMP utility will produce a similar output to the above display for a .TDS file.

The -el and -er options are used with executable files to instruct TDUMP to exclude information such as line number information and relocation table information, respectively. The -ex option is used with Windows executable code to tell TDUMP to display only information on the DOS stub and to exclude any "New-Style" executable information.

### See Also
Chapter 5: m, s, x     Map File Options

# TDINST, TFINST, TDWINST     Debugger/Profiler Installation

### Purpose
The TDINST, TFINST, and TDWINST utilities are DOS applications which customize the debugger's or profiler's default settings. These default settings can then be written to either a configuration file or to executable files for one of the utilities.

### Syntax
TDINST/TFINST [*options*] [*exefile*]

### Options
-cfilename
    Load a configuration file. The installation utility will load with the default settings stored in the configuration file.

473

**-h, -?**

Display the help screen for TDINST, TFINST, or TDWINST.

**-p**

Enable/disable the mouse. This option is not operational in the utilities shipped with the BC++ Version 3.0 compiler package.

**-w**

The target is a Windows utility (TDW or TPROFW). This option is only available with the TDINST and TFINST utilities. It is identical to calling TDWINST when used with the TDINST utility.

## Description

The 'exefile' parameter is the pathname for a debugger or profiler executable file. If there is no debugger or profiler utility corresponding to the 'exefile' pathname, then the installation utility will create one. You can also specify a configuration file pathname instead of an executable file using the *-cfilename* option. Again, if the configuration file does not exist, the installation utility will create one. Otherwise it will load with the default settings specified in the configuration file. If you do not specify a debugger/profiler executable file or a configuration file, then the installation utility will load the TDCONFIG.TD or TFCONFIG.TF configuration file located in the current directory; otherwise, it will load with the options currently saved in the debugger and profiler utilities.

You have the option of saving your changes to either a configuration file or directly to the utility's .EXE file as the debugger/profiler utility's defaults. Saving the changes to a configuration file in a specific directory means your option settings will only be used when debugging or profiling in that directory. If you save the options settings to the executable file, the changes are written directly to the debugger or profiler utility. If you loaded the utility without an 'exefile' parameter, then this will also write the options to the 386 version of the debugger or profiler. To modify the TD286 utility, you need to explicitly use 'TD286.EXE' as the 'exefile' parameter. If you used the -w command line option with TDINST or TFINST, then the changes are saved directly in either TDW or TPROFW as the default settings. Likewise, saving to an .EXE file from the TDWINST utility will save the changes directly in TDW as the default options.

See the *Turbo Debugger User's Guide* and the *Turbo Profiler User's Guide* for information on the internal operation of the utilities.

## See Also

w (Virtual Debugger/Profiler)  Write Options
TD286INS                        TD286 Machine Data Base Utility

## TDMAP                                    Create Debug Information from .MAP File

## Purpose

Converts a .MAP file generated by a linker into symbolic debugging information and creates a .TDS file that can be loaded by the Turbo debugger utilities.

## Syntax

```
TDMAP [options] filename[.MAP] [filename[.TDS]]
```

## Options

−b

Align all symbols along a byte boundary.

−c

Generate case sensitive symbols.

−w

The .MAP file is for a Windows executable or Dynamic Link Library.

−q

Suppress status reporting.

## Description

The TDMAP utility will read the information contained in a detailed .MAP file, i.e., a .MAP file generated using the linker's /s command line option, and convert it into a .TDS file, which can be loaded by the debugger utilities. This utility is used when you have an executable file linked without symbolic information. For example, consider the following "Hello, TDMAP!" application:

**tdmap\hello.c**

```
#include <stdio.h>

void main(void)
{
    printf("Hello, TDMAP!\n");
}
```

A .MAP file which can be read by the TDMAP utility is generated as follows:

```
bcc −v −y −c hello.c
tlink −s cOs hello, hello, hello, cs
```

The -v and -y options for BCC create an object code file that contains both symbolic information and line number information. The -s option for TLINK instructs the linker to generate the detailed .MAP file required by TDMAP. Note that since the -v option the resulting HELLO.EXE file contains no symbolic information. A .TDS file containing this information can be generated from the HELLO.MAP file as follows:

```
TDMAP HELLO
```

The above will generate a file called HELLO.TDS that will be automatically loaded by the debugger along with the HELLO.EXE file. Note that if you create a .TDS file with a different name than that of the .EXE file, you will have to load the file into the debugger manually using the [Files][Symbol Load] menu option. If you are using the real-mode debugger, TD, you will also have to start it with the -sm*kBytes* option. After the file is loaded into the debugger, you must then align the symbolic information with the executable file in memory using the [Files][Table Relocate] menu option with the value displayed for the CS register.

### See Also

| | |
|---|---|
| sm *kBytes* | Set Symbol Table Size |
| TDUMP | File Structure |
| TDSTRIP | Symbolic Information Stripper |
| Chapter 5: m, s, x | Map File Options |

# TDMEM Memory Display

### Purpose

The TDMEM utility displays the contents of real memory as well as available expanded memory.

### Syntax

TDMEM [*options*]

### Options

−?

> Displays the help screen for TDMEM.

−v

> Displays a verbose listing.

### Description

The TDMEM utility displays information on the contents of your system's memory, as follows:

```
TDMEM  Version 1.0  Copyright (c) 1991 Borland International

PSP    blks   bytes   owner   command line      hooked vectors
____   ____   _____   _____ _____      _____
0008    2     48224   command
0E1C    2     2624    N/A                         22 2E
0ED3    1     4128    N/A                         2F FF
0FE3    2     590288  free
```

This display lists all the memory-resident applications along the Program Segment Prefix (PSP) chain. It includes information on the size of each application in the chain, its name, and any interrupt vectors pointing to the application's address space.

The -v command line option when used with TDMEM displays a verbose listing such as the following, which lists all the applications along the Memory Control Block (MCB) chain:

```
TDMEM  Version 1.0  Copyright (c) 1991 Borland International (verbose)

PSP    MCB    files  bytes   owner       command line   hooked vectors
____   ____   _____  _____   _____     _____  _____
_____
0008   0253   0      48160   command
0008   0E16   0      64      command
```

| | | | | | | | |
|------|------|---|--------|------|-----|----------------------|
| OE1C | OE1B | 1 | 2368   | N/A  | −v  | 22 2E                |
| 0000 | OEBO | 0 | 64     | N/A  | N/A |                      |
| OE1C | OEB5 | 1 | 256    | N/A  | −v  |                      |
| 0000 | OEC6 | 0 | 176    | N/A  | N/A |                      |
| OED3 | OED2 | 0 | 4128   | N/A  |     | 2F FF                |
| OFE3 | OFD5 | 1 | 192    | free | −v  |                      |
| OFE3 | OFE2 | 1 | 590288 | free | 00  | 23 24 30 3F EC EF F7 F9 |

This list includes any PSP associated with the Memory Control Block.

### See Also
TDDEV      Display DOS Device Drivers


# TDNMI      Reset Periscope Breakout Switch

### Purpose
The TDNMI utility is a TSR program that enables the Periscope board's breakout switch twice a second.

### Syntax
TDNMI

### Options
−p*Addr*
     Set Periscope board base address.

### Description
The TDNMI utility is used to reset the breakout switch twice a second when your system contains a Periscope board for hardware debugging. You should use the *-pAddr* command line option to set the board's base address.

     The TDNMI is also used on PC clones, such as the PC's limited systems, to enable the breakout switch.

### See Also
b (Protected Mode Debuggers)      Enable (Ctrl-Break)


# TDREMOTE, TFREMOTE, WREMOTE      Remote Debugging

### Purpose
TSR is used on one computer to link with the TD or TPROF utility on another computer over a serial port or Local Area Network.

### Syntax
TDREMOTE [*options*]
TFREMOTE [*options*]
WREMOTE [*options*]

## Options

**-rn**

Tells the utilities the remote computer is connected via a Local Area Network (LAN).

**-rn*rID***

Same as above. The 'rID' is the identifier for the driver. The 'rID' parameter must be the same identifier used with the local debugger's -rn*rID* option. If the 'rID' is omitted, the driver defaults to REMOTE.

**-rp*Port***

The 'Port' parameter is either a numerical '1' or '2' that instructs the utilities to use either COM1 or COM2 as the serial port for the remote link.

**-rs*Mode***

The 'Mode' parameter tells the utilities which baud rate to use. The 'Mode' parameter should be the same numerical value used with the debugger or profiler -rs*Mode* command line option.

**-w**

Write the options listed to the executable file to use as the defaults. This option only applies to TDREMOTE and TFREMOTE. The WREMOTE utility uses a configuration file written by the WRSETUP utility as the defaults.

*Options specific to WREMOTE:*

**-c*filename***

Use a initialization (.INI) file other than WREMOTE.INI.

**-d*Path***

Use 'Path' as the startup directory.

**-rq0**

Remain on-line after TD or TPROF exits.

**-rq1**

Terminate when TD or TPROF exits.

## Description

The TDREMOTE application is the driver you run on the remote computer when you are debugging a DOS application. You use the TFREMOTE utility on the remote computer when you are profiling a DOS application. The WREMOTE utility is run on the remote computer when you are either debugging or profiling a Windows application. See the tutorial for detailed information on remote debugging and profiling.

## See Also

| | |
|---|---|
| r | Remote Operation |
| rn*LocalName, RemoteName* | Remote Network |
| rp*Port* | Remote COM Port |

| rsMode | Remote Baud Rate |
|--------|------------------|
| TDRF | Remote File/Directory Manipulation |
| WRSETUP | Set WREMOTE Defaults |

## TDRF                                    Remote File/Directory Manipulation

### Purpose
The TDRF utility is used to manipulate files and directories on the remote computer via a serial connection or over a Local Area Network.

### Syntax
`TDRF [options] command [arg1 [arg2]]`

### Options
`-rn`

Tells the TDRF utility the remote computer is connected via a Local Area Network (LAN).

`-rn[lID;rID'`

Same as above. The 'lID' parameter is the identifier for the local computer and the 'rID' is the identifier for the remote computer. The 'rID' parameter must be the same identifier used with the remote driver's -rn*rID* option. If either the 'lID' or the 'rID' is omitted, TDRF defaults to an identifier of either LOCAL or REMOTE, respectively.

`-rpPort`

The 'Port' parameter is either a numerical '1' or '2' that instructs the TDRF utility to use either COM1 or COM2 as the serial port for the remote link.

`-rsMode`

The 'Mode' parameter tells TDRF which baud rate the TDREMOTE, TFREMOTE, or WREMOTE driver is using. The 'Mode' parameter should be the same numerical value used with the remote driver -rs*Mode* command line option.

`-w`

Write the options listed to the TDRF file for use as the defaults. This allows you to set the speed, port, or network options once and not have to enter them again each time you use TDRF.

### Description
The TDRF utility is used on a local system to transfer files to or from the remote system, to rename, move, or delete files on the remote system, or to create, delete, display, or change directories on the remote system. TDRF uses a command set similar, but not identical, to the DOS commands for file and directory manipulation. Each command has both a full name and a one-letter abbreviation. The CopyTo command is also the

same as the Copy command. TDRF commands are not case sensitive. As with DOS file commands, the '?' and '*' wildcards can be used with the CopyTo, CopyFrom, DEL, and DIR commands.

The TDREMOTE, TFREMOTE, or the WREMOTE driver must be operating on the remote system for the TDRF utility to function and the two systems must be connected either through a NULL serial cable or via a Local Area Network (LAN) as described in the tutorial in the beginning of this chapter. You can then execute TDRF directly from the DOS command line. If you are in either TD or TPROF on the local system, you must first shell to DOS by selecting the [Files][DOS Shell] menu item before executing TDRF.

The following is a list of commands supported by TDRF and an example of their usage:

CD, C

Changes the current drive and/or directory on the remote system. The following changes the current drive and directory on the remote system to the B drive's root directory:

```
tdrf cd b:\
```

CopyFrom, F

Copies files from the remote system to the local system. The following copies the TEST.EXE file from the root directory on the C drive of the remote system to the MY_APP directory on the local system:

```
tdrf copyfrom c:\test.exe \my_app
```

Copy, CopyTo, T

Copy files from the local system to the remote system. For example, the following copies the TEST.EXE file in the MY_APP directory on the local computer to the root directory on the C drive on the remote computer:

```
tdrf copyto \my_app\test.exe c:\
```

DEL, E

Deletes a file on the remote system. The following deletes the TEST.EXE file located in the root directory on the C drive of the remote system:

```
tdrf del c:\test.exe
```

DIR, D

Displays a directory listing of files on the remote system. The following displays the executable (.EXE) files on the remote system located in the root directory on the C drive of the remote computer:

```
tdrf dir c:\*.exe
```

MD, M

Makes a new directory on the remote system. The following creates the NEW_DIR directory from the root directory on the remote system:

```
tdrf md \new_dir
```

## RD, D

Removes a directory on the remote system. The following removes the NEW_DIR directory located off the root directory on the remote system:

```
tdrf rd \new_dir
```

## REN, R

Renames and/or moves a file on the remote system. The following moves the TEST.EXE file from the root directory on the remote system to the TEMP directory also on the remote system:

```
tdrf ren c:\test.exe c:\temp\test.exe
```

### See Also

| | |
|---|---|
| r | Remote Operation |
| rnLocal*Name*, *RemoteName* | Remote Network |
| rp*Port* | Remote COM Port |
| rsMode | Remote Baud Rate |
| TDREMOTE, TFREMOTE, WREMOTE | Remote Debugging |
| WRSETUP | Set WREMOTE Defaults |

## TDSTRIP                                        Symbolic Information Stripper

### Purpose

The TDSTRIP utility will remove symbolic debugging information from an .OBJ or .EXE file. It will also generate a .TDS file from the symbolic information in an .EXE file for use by the debugger utilities. It will also convert a tiny memory model .EXE file with debug information into a .COM and .TDS file.

### Syntax

```
TDSTRIPT [options] filename[.EXE/.OBJ] [output[.TDS]]
```

### Options

−s

Place the debugging information in an .EXE file into a separate .TDS file. The debugging information in the .EXE file is not removed. This option is ignored with .OBJ files.

−c

Remove the debugging information from an .EXE file and convert it to a .COM file. A .TDS file is also generated if this option is used with the -s option.

### Description

When you use the TDSTRIP utility without any options, it will remove any debugging information contained in the specified file. You can optionally place the debugging information contained in an .EXE file into a .TDS file that can then be used by the debuggers and profilers. If the application uses the tiny memory model, TDSTRIP will also convert it to a .COM file when you use the -c option. This enables debugging .COM files and DOS device drivers that cannot contain debugging information. For example, consider the following "Hello, TDSTRIP!" application:

**tdstrip\hello.c**
```
#include <stdio.h>

void main(void)
{
    printf("Hello, TDSTRIP!\n");
}
```

If this application were compiled and then linked directly to a .COM file, the linker would discard all the debugging information in the .OBJ file. Instead, you can create a .TDS file for the debugger and profiler by first creating a tiny memory model .EXE application with debugging information and then using TDSTRIP to create the .COM and .TDS file. This is done as follows:

```
bcc -v -mt hello.c
tdstrip -s -c hello
```

The above entries will create HELLO.COM and HELLO.TDS. You can then load the HELLO.COM application into any debugger or profiler utility and they will automatically load the associated HELLO.TDS file provided it is located in the current directory.

**See Also**

Chapter 5: t, Tdc, Tde     Compile to a DOS .COM or .EXE File

# WINSIGHT                                         Window Inspection

**Purpose**

Allows viewing the characteristics of the created windows on the system and the associated window classes. It also provides monitoring of window messages.

**Syntax**

WINSIGHT

**Options**

None

**Description**

The WINSIGHT utility contains three main window panes: a Window Tree pane that displays the hierarchy of parent and child windows, a Class List pane that lists all the registered window classes, and a Message Trace pane that logs selected messages sent to the different windows on the system. You view one or all three of the different windows by selecting the [View] menu and then checking either the [Class List], [Window Tree], or [Message Trace] menu items. The utility is activated by selecting the [Start] menu item and deactivated by selecting the [Stop] menu item.

## The Window Tree Pane

As shown in Figure 7-8, the Window Tree pane diagrams the hierarchy of the windows on the system.

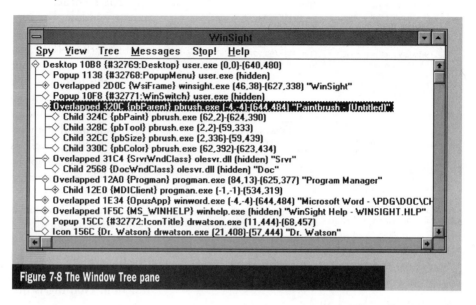

**Figure 7-8 The Window Tree pane**

Each window, either hidden or displayed, is listed in relation to its parent, siblings, and children in the following format:

*Tree     Style     Handle     (Class)     Module     Position     "Title"*

The 'Tree' parameter is a diamond symbol that displays in an inverted color whenever a message is sent to a window. For example, if you move the cursor over the desktop window, you will see the diamond displayed in an inverted color as the desktop window is sent WM_MOUSEMOVE messages. The diamond symbol is empty if the window has no children, otherwise it contains either a '+' or '-' indicating the tree can either be expanded or collapsed. You expand or collapse the tree by either clicking the diamond symbol or selecting the [Tree] menu items.

The 'Style' parameter is the window type. This corresponds to the window type used with the 'dwStyle' for the CreateWindow() function when the window was created. For example, if the window was created with the WS_CHILD style, then the 'Style' parameter will display as 'Child'. Likewise, if the WS_OVERLAPPED style was used, then the 'Style' parameter will display as 'Overlapped'.

The 'Handle' parameter is the handle returned by the CreateWindow() function.

The 'Class' parameter is the name of the window class. Note that many predefined windows, such as push-buttons and the desktop, start with a numerical value.

The 'Module' parameter is the name of the module that created the window.

The 'Position' parameter shows the window's position and extent in rectangular coordinates. The first coordinate pair is the position of the upper-left corner and the second pair is

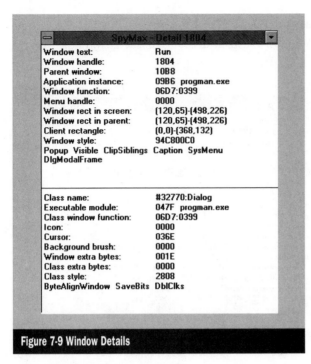

**Figure 7-9 Window Details**

the position of the lower-right corner. These coordinates are relative to the upper-left corner of the parent window. For top-level windows, i.e., those created with a NULL parameter for a parent handle, this is the absolute position on the screen because their parent window is the desktop. If the window is hidden, such as when a call is made to the SetWindowPos() function with the SWP_HIDEWINDOW flag, the position is displayed as '(hidden)'.

The 'Title' parameter is the 'lpWindowName' used with the CreateWindow() function. Nothing is displayed if the window is a NULL.

Figure 7-9 shows the Window Details window displayed when either the mouse is double clicked on a window listing or the [Spy][Open Detail] menu item is selected. This window provides the same information as the Window Tree pane and also many of the details regarding the window's style and the details on the window's class.

## The Class List Pane

Figure 7-10 shows the class list pane, which lists all the window classes registered on the system using the RegisterClass() function.

Each window class registered on the system is listed in the following format:

*Message*        *Name*        (*Module*)        *Function*        *Style*

The 'Message' parameter is a diamond symbol that is displayed in an inverted color when a window created from the class receives a message.

The 'Name' parameter is the name of the class.

The 'Module' parameter is the name of the module that registered the class.

The 'Function' parameter is the same as the 'lpfnWndProc' parameter used to register the class.

The 'Style' parameter is a list of style attributes associated with the class. For example, a class registered with the CS_DBCLKS and the CS_HREDRAW style bits would be listed with the 'DblClks' and 'HorzRedraw' style attributes.

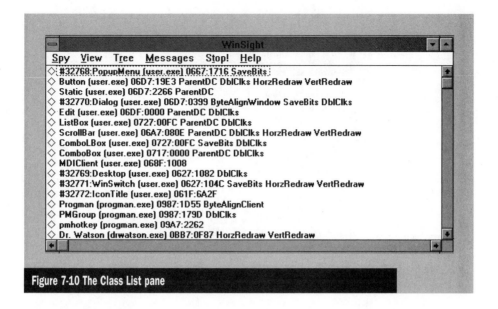

**Figure 7-10 The Class List pane**

The details of each class can be viewed by either double clicking a particular class or selecting the [Spy][Open Details] menu item. This will display a window identical to the bottom half of the Window Details window.

## The Message Trace Pane

Figure 7-11 shows the Message Trace pane. The message tracing feature is initially disabled. You will need to select either the [Selected Classes], [Selected Windows], or the [All Windows] menu item in the [Messages] window to start tracing, and select the [Start] menu item.

The messages are indented depending on how deeply the messages are nested. For example, Figure 7-11 shows a window of the {MIDClient} class sending a WM_MOUSE-MOVE message. Before the receiving window completes its processing of the message, it sends its own WM_USER+0x00C9 message to another window. This nested message is indented by two spaces.

## Message Trace Format

Each message is displayed in the following format:

*Destination* [" *Title*" or {*Class*}]        *Message*        *Status*        *Values*

The 'Destination' parameter is the handle for the window receiving the message.

The second parameter is either the sending window's 'Title' displayed in quotations or, if it does not have a title, then the window's class name displayed in curly braces.

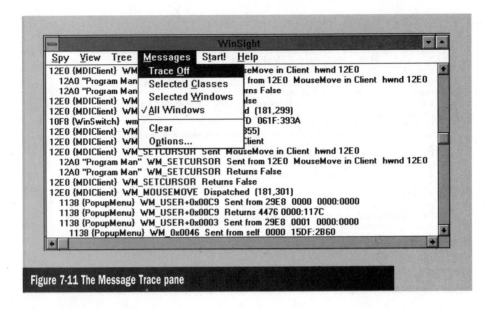

**Figure 7-11 The Message Trace pane**

The 'Message' parameter corresponds to the 'wCmd' parameter sent to the window's message processing function. This is usually one of the message names defined in WINDOWS.H, in which case it is displayed in all capitals. If it is a known Windows message not listed in WINDOW.H, then the message is displayed in lowercase. Messages that were registered using the RegsiterWindowMessage() function are displayed in single quotes. Any unknown messages are displayed as an offset from the WM_USER message. For example, if the numerical value of the message is 5 greater than the value of WM_USER, then it is displayed as WM_USER+0x0005. A message with a value of 5 lower than WM_USER is displayed as WM_USER_0x0005.

The 'Status' parameter is displayed as either 'Dispatched', 'Sent', or 'Return':

**Dispatched**  This means the message was dispatched to the window's message processing function via the DispatchMessage() function in the application's message loop. These messages originate from the PostMessage() function.

**Sent**  The message was sent directly to the window's message processing function using the SendMessage() function. All messages with this status have a corresponding 'Return' message status, which is indented to the same level.

**Return**  This is the value from a window's message processing function that received a 'Sent' message. This is either the value returned when the message processing function returns (usually TRUE or FALSE) or the value returned via the ReplyMessage() function.

If the message was either 'Dispatched' or 'Sent' and it is a known message, such as WM_SETFOCUS or WM_MOUSEMOVE, then the 'Value' parameter will be the name and values for the 'wParam' and 'lParam' associated with the message. Only the value is displayed for unknown messages and messages registered using the RegisterWindowMessage() function.

The 'Value' parameter for messages with a 'Return' status can be the raw numerical value for the returned DWORD. Or, if the return corresponds to a known 'Sent' message, then more specific information is displayed. For example, if the WM_GETTEXT message is sent to a list box and there are no items selected, then the 'Value' parameter will display as LB_ERR.

## Message Trace Options

The [Messages][Options] menu item displays the dialog box shown in Figure 7-12. Changes made in this dialog box are written to the WINSIGHT.INI file.

The [Hex Only] check box instructs WINSIGHT not to interpret the numerical values associated with the 'Value' parameter of a message.

The [Log File] check box

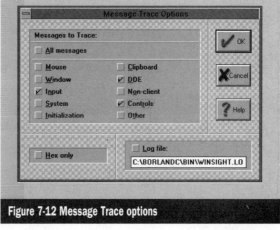

**Figure 7-12 Message Trace options**

tells WINSIGHT to write all the messages to both the window and to the file listed in the edit box.

The check boxes in the "Messages to Trace:" area instruct WINSIGHT to only display messages that fall into the categories listed in Table 7-3. Note that the messages listed in lowercase are not defined in WINDOWS.H.

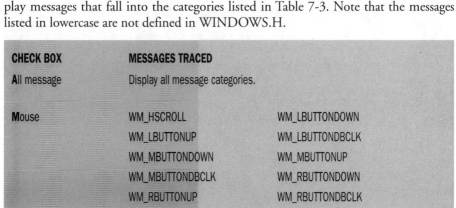

| CHECK BOX | MESSAGES TRACED | |
| --- | --- | --- |
| All message | Display all message categories. | |
| Mouse | WM_HSCROLL | WM_LBUTTONDOWN |
| | WM_LBUTTONUP | WM_LBUTTONDBCLK |
| | WM_MBUTTONDOWN | WM_MBUTTONUP |
| | WM_MBUTTONDBCLK | WM_RBUTTONDOWN |
| | WM_RBUTTONUP | WM_RBUTTONDBCLK |
| | WM_SETCURSOR | WM_VSCROLL |

*Table 7-3 (continued)*

| CHECK BOX | MESSAGES TRACED | |
|---|---|---|
| Window | WM_ACTIVATE | WM_ACTIVATEAPP |
| | WM_CANCELMODE | WM_CHILDACTIVATE |
| | WM_CLOSE | WM_CREATE |
| | WM_CTRLCOLOR | WM_DESTROY |
| | WM_ENABLE | WM_ENDSESSION |
| | WM_ERASEBKGND | WM_GETDLGCODE |
| | WM_GETMINMAXINFO | WM_GETTEXT |
| | WM_GETTEXTLENGTH | WM_ICONERASEBKGND |
| | WM_KILLFOCUS | WM_MOVE |
| | WM_PAINT | WM_PAINTICON |
| | WM_QUERYDRAGICON | WM_QUERYENDSESSION |
| | WM_QUERYNEWPALETTE | WM_QUERYOPEN |
| | WM_QUIT | WM_SETFOCUS |
| | WM_SETFONT | WM_SETREDRAW |
| | WM_SETTEXT | WM_SHOWWINDOW |
| | WM_SIZE | |
| Input | WM_CHAR | WM_CHARTOITEM |
| | WM_COMMAND | WM_DEADCHAR |
| | WM_KEYDOWN | WM_KEYLAST |
| | WM_KEYUP | WM_MENUCHAR |
| | WM_MENUSELECT | WM_PARENTNOTIFY |
| | WM_SYSCHAR | WM_SYSDEADCHAR |
| | WM_SYSKEYDOWN | WM_SYSKEYUP |
| | WM_TIMER | WM_VKEYTOITEM |
| System | WM_COMPACTING | WM_DEVMODECHANGE |
| | WM_FONTCHANGE | WM_ENTERIDLE |
| | WM_NULL | WM_PALETTEISCHANGING |
| | WM_PALETTECHANGED | WM_QUEUESYNCH |
| | WM_SPOOLERSTATUS | WM_SYSCOLORCHANGE |
| | WM_SYSCOMMAND | WM_TIMECHANGE |
| | WM_WININICHANGE | |

| CHECK BOX | MESSAGES TRACED | |
|---|---|---|
| Initialization | WM_INITDIALOG | WM_INIMENU |
| | WM_INITMENUPOPUP | |
| Clipboard | WM_ASKCBFORMATNAME | WM_CHANGECBCHAIN |
| | WM_CLEAR | WM_COPY |
| | WM_CUT | WM_DESTROYCLIPBOARD |
| | WM_DRAWCLIPBOARD | WM_HSCROLLCLIPBOARD |
| | WM_PAINTCLIPBOARD | WM_PASTE |
| | WM_RENDERALLFORMATS | WM_RENDERFORMAT |
| | WM_SIZECLIPBOARD | WM_UNDO |
| | WM_VSCROLLCLIPBOARD | |
| DDE | WM_DDE_ACK | WM_DDE_ADVISE |
| | WM_DDE_DATA | WM_DDE_EXECUTE |
| | WM_DDE_INITIATE | WM_DDE_POKE |
| | WM_DDE_REQUEST | WM_DDE_TERMINATE |
| | WM_DDE_UNADVISE | |
| Nonclient | WM_NCACTIVATE | WM_NCCALCSIZE |
| | WM_NCCREATE | WM_NCDESTROY |
| | WM_NCHITTEST | WM_NCLBUTTONDBLCLK |
| | WM_NCLBUTTONDOWN | WM_NCLBUTTONUP |
| | WM_NCMBUTTONDBLCLK | WM_NCMBUTTONDOWN |
| | WM_NCMBUTTONUP | WM_NCMOUSEMOVE |
| | WM_NCPAINT | WM_NCRBUTTONDBLCLK |
| | WM_NCRBUTTONDOWN | WM_NCRBUTTONUP |
| Controls | All messages begining with BM_, CB_, DM_, EM_, or LB_. | |
| Other | Messages in lowercase are not defined in WINDOWS.H. | |
| | wm_alttabactive | wm_begindrag |
| | WM_COMPAREITEM | wm_convertrequest |
| | wm_convertresult | WM_DELETEITEM |
| | wm_dragloop | wm_dragmove |
| | wm_dragselect | WM_DRAWITEM |

*Table 7-3 (continued)*

| CHECK BOX | MESSAGES TRACED | |
|-----------|-----------------|--|
| | wm_dropobject | wm_entermenuloop |
| | wm_entersizemove | wm_exitmenuloop |
| | wm_exitsizemove | wm_filesyschange |
| | WM_GETFONT | wm_isactiveicon |
| | wm_lbtrackpoint | WM_MDIACTIVATE |
| | WM_MDICASCADE | WM_MDICREATE |
| | WM_MDIDESTROY | WM_MDIGETACTIVE |
| | WM_MDIICONARRANGE | WM_MDIMAXIMIZE |
| | WM_MDINEXT | WM_MDIRESTORE |
| | WM_MDISETMENU | WM_MDITILE |
| | WM_MEASUREITEM | WM_NEXTDLGCTL |
| | wm_nextmenu | wm_null |
| | wm_querydropobject | wm_queryparkicon |
| | wm_setvisible | wm_systemerror |
| | wm_syncpaint | wm_synctask |
| | wm_systimer | wm_testing |

**Table 7-3 Message Trace categories**

## See Also
The Windows Debugger and Profiler

# WRSETUP                                          Set WREMOTE Defaults

## Purpose
The WRSETUP utility creates a configuration file that modifies the default settings of the WREMOTE utility.

## Syntax
WRSETUP

## Options
None

## Description
The WRSETUP utility is a simple Windows application that creates a WREMOTE.INI text file containing the default settings for the WREMOTE utility.

The WREMOTE utility will then use these settings if the file is located in the same directory as the WREMOTE startup directory or if you execute WREMOTE with the *-cfilename* command line option specifying the name and directory for the configuration file.

### See Also

| | |
|---|---|
| r | Remote Operation |
| rn *LocalName*, *RemoteName* | Remote Network |
| rp *Port* | Remote COM Port |
| rsMode | Remote Baud Rate |
| TDREMOTE, TFREMOTE, WREMOTE | Remote Debugging |
| TDRF | Remote File/Directory Manipulation |

## Windows Debugging Support Libraries

Borland C++ 3.1 comes with two Dynamic Link Libraries (DLLs) that aid in debugging and testing applications: TOOLHELP.DLL and STRESS.DLL. The TOOLHELP library contains routines that provide you with information not normally available with the regular Windows API functions. The STRESS library contains routines that will artificially consume various Windows resources to simulate scarce resource situations in order to test your application's response to these conditions.

The following is a reference to the structures and functions in the TOOLHELP and STRESS libraries. Note that there are additional functions in the TOOLHELP library that are not covered in this reference. These functions are only useful if you are writing a debugging application similar to TDW which debugs other Windows applications or DLLs. Table 7-4 lists these debugging functions.

| FUNCTION | DESCRIPTION |
|---|---|
| InterruptRegister | Installs a function which will intercept all system interrupts. |
| InterruptUnRegister | Removes a function installed by the InterruptRegister() function. |
| MemoryWrite | Write to any area of Windows memory. |
| NotifyRegister | Installs a function which will receive notification of changes in system conditions. |
| NotifyUnRegister | Removes a function installed by the NotifyRegister() function. |
| StackTraceCSIPFirst | Begin a stack trace on an active task. |
| StackTraceFirst | Begin a stack trace on an inactive task. |
| StackTraceNext | Walk through a stack trace. |
| TaskGetCSIP | Retrieves an inactive task's CS:IP value. |
| TaskSetCISP | Sets an inactive task's CS:IP value. |
| TaskSwitch | Activates a task starting at a specific CS:IP location. |
| TerminateApp | Terminates an application via a GP fault. |

**Table 7-4 List of functions in the TOOLHELP library that are only useful when writing a debugging application similar to TDW**

# AllocDiskSpace

**STRESS.DLL Function**

### Purpose
You use the AllocDiskSpace() function to stress the disk space available to an application.

### Syntax
```
int WINAPI AllocDiskSpace(LONG lLeft, UINT uDrive);
```

LONG *lLeft*
> Specifies how much free disk space the TOOLHELP library should leave on the designated drive.

UINT *uDrive*
> Designates a disk drive. The *uDrive* parameter should be one of the following values:

| | |
|---|---|
| EDS_CUR | *Allocates space on the current drive.* |
| EDS_TEMP | *Allocates space on the drive specified by the TEMP variable or the Windows system drive if no TEMP variable is defined.* |
| EDS_WIN | *Allocates space on the Windows system drive.* |

### Returns
Returns a -1 if a parameter is invalid, zero if it could not create the STRESS.EAT file to allocate the disk space, or a nonzero number other than -1 if the function was successful.

### Description
The end user of your application may not have as much disk space available as you do on your development system. The AllocDiskSpace() function allows you to temporarily eat away the available space on your development system so as to test your application in a worst case scenario. The AllocDiskSpace() function does this by creating a file called STRESS.EAT that is sized to leave free the amount of disk space specified by the lLeft parameter. The AllocDiskSpace() function will first delete any STRESS.EAT file on the specified drive if it already exists and then create a new one based on the *lLeft* parameter. Note that this feature allows you to call AllocDiskSpace() for each drive path even if one or more of them are the same.

### See Also
| | |
|---|---|
| AllocFileHandles | STRESS.DLL Function |
| AllocGDIMem | STRESS.DLL Function |
| AllocMem | STRESS.DLL Function |
| AllocUserMem | STRESS.DLL Function |
| UnAllocDiskSpace | STRESS.DLL Function |

### Example
Write an application that leaves only 100k available on the current drive, 50k on the temporary drive, and 25k on the Windows system drive.

**stress\disk\test.c**

```c
#include <windows.h>
#include <stress.h>
#include <dos.h>
#include <stdio.h>
#include <ctype.h>
#include <string.h>

WORD DriveSpace(BYTE Drive)
{
   struct dfree Info;
   DWORD Space;

   getdfree(Drive, &Info);
   Space = ((DWORD)Info.df_avail * Info.df_bsec) * Info.df_sclus;
   return(Space / 1000);
}

BYTE GetTempVariable(void)
{
   LPSTR EnvStr;

   /* Get the DOS environment string */
   EnvStr = GetDOSEnvironment();
   while(EnvStr[0] != 0)
   {
     /* Is this the TEMP variable? */
     if(_fstrnicmp(EnvStr, "TEMP", 4) == 0)
       return(toupper(EnvStr[5]));

     /* Point to the next environment string */
     EnvStr += lstrlen(EnvStr) + 1;
   }
   /* No TEMP variable defined.  Return the system drive */
   return(GetTempDrive(0));
}

void PrintDriveSpace(void)
{
   struct dfree CurrDriveInfo, TempDriveInfo, WindowsDriveInfo;
   UINT TempDrive, WindowsDrive;

   /* Print the free space on the current drive */
   printf("Current drive:       %uk\n", DriveSpace(0));

   /* Print the free space on the temporary drive */
   TempDrive = GetTempVariable() - 'A' + 1;
   printf("Temporary drive:      %uk\n", DriveSpace(TempDrive));

   /* Print the free space on the Windows system drive */
   WindowsDrive = GetTempDrive(0) - 'A' + 1;
   printf("Windows system drive: %uk\n", DriveSpace(WindowsDrive));
}
```

```
void main(void)
{
  printf("Initial drive space\n");
  PrintDriveSpace();

  /* Leave only 100k on the current drive */
  AllocDiskSpace(100000L, EDS_CUR);
  /* Leave only 50k on the temporary drive */
  AllocDiskSpace(50000L, EDS_TEMP);
  /* Leave only 25k on the Windows system drive */
  AllocDiskSpace(25000L, EDS_WIN);

  printf("\nAfter calling the AllocDiskSpace() function\n");
  PrintDriveSpace();

  /* Remove the STRESS.EAT files */
  UnAllocDiskSpace(EDS_CUR);
  UnAllocDiskSpace(EDS_TEMP);
  UnAllocDiskSpace(EDS_WIN);

  printf("\nAfter calling the UnAllocDiskSpace() function\n");
  PrintDriveSpace();
}
```

Figure 7-13 shows the output from the TEST.EXE.

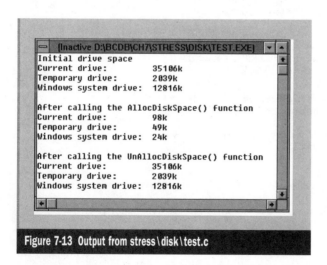

Figure 7-13 Output from stress\disk\test.c

# AllocFileHandles

## Purpose

You use the AllocFileHandles() function to stress the number of file handles available to an application.

### Syntax

```
int WINAPI AllocFileHandles(int iLeft);
```

INT *iLeft*

The *iLeft* parameter designates how many file handles to leave available to the application when the function returns.

### Returns

Returns -1 if the *iLeft* parameter is invalid, greater than zero if the function is able to allocate at least one file handle. Returns zero if the function fails such as when the *iLeft* parameter equals or is less than the number of free file handles.

### Description

Opening a file for either reading or writing always uses an available file handle. The more files you have open at one time, the more file handles your application uses. If the end user runs several applications concurrently that open many files, then there may not be any file handles available for your application. In this situation an attempt to open a new file will fail. You can use the AllocFileHandles() function to ensure your application properly handles this situation and responds accordingly. The AllocFile-Handles() function allocates file handles until only the number specified by the *iLeft* parameter remain free.

Use the UnAllocFileHandles() to free the handles allocated by AllocFileHandles(). You do not need to call UnAllocFileHandles() between subsequent calls to AllocFileHandles() as the AllocFileHandles() function automatically deallocates any file handles previously allocated by an earlier call to AllocFileHandles().

Note that the AllocFileHandles() function will not allocate more than 256 handles.

### See Also

| | |
|---|---|
| AllocDiskSpace | STRESS.DLL Function |
| AllocGDIMem | STRESS.DLL Function |
| AllocMem | STRESS.DLL Function |
| AllocUserMem | STRESS.DLL Function |
| GetFreeFileHandles | STRESS.DLL Function |

### Example

Write an application that leaves only 3 and then 10 file handles free.

**stress\files\test.c**

```
#include <windows.h>
#include <stress.h>
#include <stdio.h>

void main(void)
{
  printf("Initial free file handles = %d\n", GetFreeFileHandles());
```

```
/* Leave only 3 file handles free */
AllocFileHandles(3);
printf("Free handles after calling AllocFileHandles(3) = %d\n",
  GetFreeFileHandles());

/* Leave only 3 file handles free */
AllocFileHandles(10);
printf("Free handles after calling AllocFileHandles(10) = %d\n",
  GetFreeFileHandles());

/* Restore original number of free file handles */
UnAllocFileHandles();
printf("Free handles after calling UnAllocFileHandles() = %d\n",
  GetFreeFileHandles());
}
```

Figure 7-14 shows the output from the TEST.EXE.

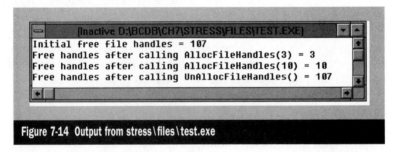

Figure 7-14 Output from stress\files\test.exe

# AllocGDIMem                                         STRESS.DLL Function

### Purpose
You use the AllocGDIMem() function to stress the GDI memory heap.

### Syntax
```
BOOL WINAPI AllocGDIMem(UINT uLeft);
```

UNIT *uLeft*

The *uLeft* parameter designates how many bytes of memory to leave available in the GDI heap when the function returns.

### Returns
Returns zero if the function fails, such as when the *uLeft* parameter is greater than the memory available in the GDI heap. Returns a nonzero value if successful.

### Description
When your application creates graphics objects, such as brushes and pens, you use a small amount of memory in the GDI heap. For example, Table 7-5 lists the amount of memory used for the creation of different graphic objects.

| OBJECT | MEMORY USAGE |
|--------|--------------|
| Bitmap | 28–32 bytes |
| Brush | 32 bytes |
| Font | 40–44 bytes |
| Palette | 28 bytes |
| Pen | 28 bytes |
| Region | 28 to several kBytes |

**Table 7-5 Memory used in the GDI heap by different graphic objects**

If the end user is running several graphics-intensive applications concurrent with your application, it is possible that the call to a graphics function, such as CreatePattern-Brush() or CreatePalette(), will fail due to a lack of free GDI memory and return a NULL handle. You can use the AllocGDIMem() function to simulate this situation and test your application's response to low GDI memory situations. The AllocGDIMem() function allocates GDI memory until only the number of bytes specified by the *uLeft* are available. Subsequent calls to AllocGDIMem() automatically free any memory previously allocated by an earlier call to the AllocGDIMem() by your application.

Be sure to call the FreeAllGDIMem() function before your application exits or you will be unable to unallocate the memory. For example, if you call AllocGDIMem() in a debugging session and terminate the session before calling the FreeAllGDIMem() function, you will need to exit and restart Windows in order to recover the lost GDI memory.

### See Also
| | |
|--|--|
| AllocDiskSpace | STRESS.DLL Function |
| AllocFileHandles | STRESS.DLL Function |
| AllocMem | STRESS.DLL Function |
| AllocUserMem | STRESS.DLL Function |
| FreeAllGDIMem | STRESS.DLL Function |

### Example
Write an application which leaves only 5000 bytes of GDI memory available using the AllocGDIMem() function:

**stress\gdi\test.c**
```
#include <windows.h>
#include <stress.h>
#include <toolhelp.h>
#include <stdio.h>

void PrintSysMemSpace(void)
{
  SYSHEAPINFO Info;

  Info.dwSize = sizeof(SYSHEAPINFO);
```

```
SystemHeapInfo(&Info);

printf("GDI Free Memory Space:  %u%%\n", Info.wGDIFreePercent);
printf("User Free Memory Space: %u%%\n", Info.wUserFreePercent);
}

void main(void)
{
  printf("Initial System memory space\n");
  PrintSysMemSpace();

  /* Leave only 5000 bytes free in the GDI system module */
  AllocGDIMem(5000);
  printf("\nAfter calling AllocGDIMem(5000)\n");
  PrintSysMemSpace();

  /* Restore system to normal */
  FreeAllGDIMem();
  printf("\nAfter calling FreeAllGDIMem()\n");
  PrintSysMemSpace();
}
```

Figure 7-15 shows the output from the TEST.EXE.

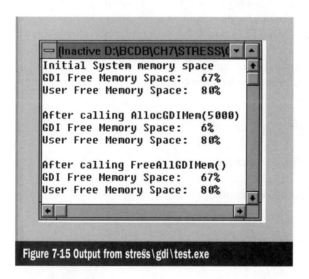

Figure 7-15 Output from stress\gdi\test.exe

# AllocMem                                       STRESS.DLL Function

## Purpose

You use the AllocMem() function to stress the global memory heap.

## Syntax

```
BOOL WINAPI AllocMem(DWORD dwLeft);
```

DWORD *dwLeft*

The *dwLeft* parameter designates how many bytes of memory to leave available in global memory when the function returns.

### Returns

Returns zero if the function fails such as using a *dwLeft* parameter that is greater than the available global memory. Returns a nonzero value if successful.

### Description

Almost all Windows applications dynamically allocate global memory at run time by either calling the GlobalAlloc() function, using the *new* keyword with a far object class, or by calling the farmalloc() function. It is highly likely that some of your end users will run low on global memory. This will cause one of these function calls to fail and return either a NULL handle or pointer. You can test how your application responds to this condition by using the AllocMem() function. This function allocates all available global memory and leaves only the amount of memory specified by the *dwLeft* parameter. Subsequent calls to AllocMem() automatically free any memory previously allocated by a call to the AllocMem() by your application.

Note that the *dwLeft* parameter specifies total global memory free. This will most likely not correspond to the largest contiguous block of memory available.

Windows automatically frees the global memory allocated by the AllocMem() function when your application terminates. Calling the FreeAllMem() function will also release the memory allocated by the AllocMem() function.

### See Also

| | |
|---|---|
| AllocDiskSpace | STRESS.DLL Function |
| AllocFileHandles | STRESS.DLL Function |
| AllocGDIMem | STRESS.DLL Function |
| AllocUserMem | STRESS.DLL Function |
| FreeAllMem | STRESS.DLL Function |

### Example

Write an application that allocates all but 500K bytes of global memory using the AllocMem() function:

**stress\global\test.c**

```
#include <windows.h>
#include <stress.h>
#include <toolhelp.h>
#include <stdio.h>

void PrintGlobalMemSpace(void)
{
    printf("Free Global memory:  %luk\n", GetFreeSpace(0) / 1000);
}
```

```
void main(void)
{
   DWORD Size = 500000L;
   printf("Initial global memory space\n");
   PrintGlobalMemSpace();

   /* Leave only 500k byte block of global memory free */
   AllocMem(Size);
   printf("\nAfter calling AllocMem(%lu)\n", Size);
   PrintGlobalMemSpace();

   /* Restore system to normal */
   FreeAllMem();
   printf("\nAfter calling FreeAllMem()\n");
   PrintGlobalMemSpace();
}
```

Figure 7-16 shows the output from the TEST.EXE.

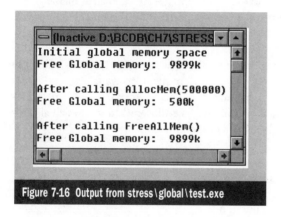

Figure 7-16  Output from stress\global\test.exe

# AllocUserMem
STRESS.DLL Function

## Purpose
You use the AllocUserMem() function to stress the USER module memory heap.

## Syntax
```
BOOL WINAPI AllocUserMem(UINT uContig);
```

## Returns
Returns zero if the function fails, such as when the *uContig* parameter is greater than the largest contiguous free memory block available in the USER module memory heap. Returns a nonzero value if successful.

## Description

When your application creates objects from the USER module, such as menus and windows, you use a small amount of memory in the USER module's local memory heap. For example, Table 7-6 lists the memory required by different objects in the USER module.

| OBJECT | MEMORY USAGE |
|---|---|
| Popup Menu | 20 bytes |
| Menu Item | 20 bytes |
| Window | 60–70 bytes |
| Window class | 40–50 bytes |

**Table 7-6 Memory used by objects in the USER module**

If the end user is running several applications concurrent with your application, it is possible that a call to one of the USER module functions will fail and return a NULL handle. You should use the AllocUserMem() function to simulate this situation and test your application's response to low USER module memory situations. The AllocUserMem() function allocates USER module memory until the largest contiguous block of free memory in the module is less than or equal to the value of *uContig*. Subsequent calls to AllocUserMem() automatically free any memory previously allocated by a call to AllocUserMem() by your application.

Be sure to call the FreeAllUserMem() function before your application exits or you will be unable to unallocate the memory. For example, if you call AllocUserMem() in a debugging session and terminate the session before calling the FreeAllUserMem() function, you will need to exit and restart Windows in order to recover the lost memory from the USER module.

## See Also

| | |
|---|---|
| AllocDiskSpace | STRESS.DLL Function |
| AllocFileHandles | STRESS.DLL Function |
| AllocGDIMem | STRESS.DLL Function |
| AllocMem | STRESS.DLL Function |
| FreeAllUserMem | STRESS.DLL Function |

## Example

Write an application that leaves 5000 bytes as the largest contiguous block of memory in the USER module:

**stress\user\test.c**
```
#include <windows.h>
#include <stress.h>
#include <toolhelp.h>
```

```c
#include <stdio.h>

void PrintSysMemSpace(void)
{
   SYSHEAPINFO Info;

   Info.dwSize = sizeof(SYSHEAPINFO);
   SystemHeapInfo(&Info);

   printf("GDI Free Memory Space:   %u%%\n", Info.wGDIFreePercent);
   printf("User Free Memory Space:  %u%%\n", Info.wUserFreePercent);
}

void main(void)
{
   printf("Initial System memory space\n");
   PrintSysMemSpace();

   /* Leave only 5000 byte block of memory free in the User module */
   AllocUserMem(5000);
   printf("\nAfter calling AllocUserMem(5000)\n");
   PrintSysMemSpace();

   /* Restore system to normal */
   FreeAllUserMem();
   printf("\nAfter calling FreeAllUserMem()\n");
   PrintSysMemSpace();
}
```

Figure 7-17 shows the output from the TEST.EXE.

**Figure 7-17 Output from stress\user\test.exe**

# CLASSENTRY                                        TOOLHELP.H Structure

### Purpose
The CLASSENTRY structure is used by the ClassFirst() and ClassNext() functions to enumerate the registered window class names.

**Definition**

```
typedef struct tagCLASSENTRY
{
   DWORD dwSize;
   HMODULE hInst;
   char szClassName[MAX_CLASSNAME + 1];
   WORD wNext;
} CLASSENTRY;
```

DWORD *dwSize*

Size of the CLASSENTRY structure in bytes. Set this member using sizeof(CLASSENTRY) before calling the ClassFirst() function.

HMODULE *hInst*

The ClassFirst() and ClassNext() functions set this value with the instance handle of the module that registered the window class. You can use this value to obtain more detailed information on the window class by calling the GetClassInfo() function.

char *szClassName*

A character array containing the name of the window class.

WORD *wNext*

Used internally by the ClassNext() function to fill the CLASSENTRY structure with the next window class.

**See Also**

ClassFirst     TOOLHELP.DLL Function
ClassNext      TOOLHELP.DLL Function

# ClassFirst                                    TOOLHELP.DLL Function

**Purpose**

You call the ClassFirst() function to fill a CLASSENTRY structure with the first entry in the list of registered window classes. You'd normally use this function in conjunction with the ClassNext() function to walk through the list of registered window class names.

**Syntax**

```
BOOL WINAPI ClassFirst(CLASSENTRY FAR* lpClass);
```

CLASSENTRY FAR *\*lpClass*

Far pointer to a CLASSENTRY structure. The ClassFirst() function fills the *hInst*, *szClassName*, and *wNext* members of the structure.

**Returns**

Returns zero if the function fails, such as when the *dwSize* structure member for *lpClass* is not initialized. Returns a nonzero value if successful.

## Description

You use the ClassFirst() function to fill a CLASSENTRY structure with information on the name and module instance handle of the first registered window class. You would then call the ClassNext() function to fill the structure with the next name and module instance handle of the next window class. Note that you must initialize the *dwSize* member with the size of the CLASSENTRY structure before calling ClassFirst().

Call the GetClassInfo() Windows API function using the *szClassName* and *hInst* members of the CLASSENTRY structure to retrieve more detailed information on each window class.

## See Also

CLASSENTRY    TOOLHELP.H Structure
ClassNext        TOOLHELP.DLL Function

## Example

Write an application that prints the names of all registered window classes:

**toolhelp\class\test.c**
```c
#include <windows.h>
#include <toolhelp.h>
#include <stdio.h>

void main(void)
{
  CLASSENTRY Entry;
  BOOL Status;

  /* Initialize the CLASSENTRY structure */
  Entry.dwSize = sizeof(CLASSENTRY);

  /* Get the first class entry */
  Status = ClassFirst(&Entry);

  /* Walk through the class list */
  while(Status != FALSE)
  {
    printf("%20s - %04X\n", Entry.szClassName, Entry.hInst);
    Status = ClassNext(&Entry);
  }
  printf("End of class list\n");
}
```

Figure 7-18 shows the output from the TEST.EXE.

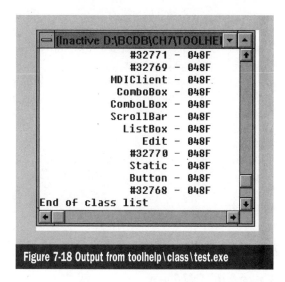

Figure 7-18 Output from toolhelp\class\test.exe

# ClassNext

TOOLHELP.DLL Function

## Purpose

Applications, such as Borland's WINSIGHT, call this function to enumerate the names and module handles of the registered window classes.

## Syntax

```
BOOL WINAPI ClassNext(CLASSENTRY FAR* lpClass);
```

CLASSENTRY FAR* *lpClass*

Far pointer to a CLASSENTRY structure. The ClassNext() function uses the *wNext* member to determine the next window class and then fills the *hInst*, *szClassName*, and *wNext* members of the structure.

## Returns

Returns zero if the function fails, such as when the *dwSize* structure member for *lpClass* is not initialized. Returns a nonzero value if successful.

## Description

You use the ClassFirst() function to first fill a CLASSENTRY structure with information on the name and module instance handle of the first registered window class. You would then call the ClassNext() function to fill the structure with the next name and module instance handle of the next window class. Note that you must initialize the CLASSENTRY structure with a prior call to either the ClassNext() or ClassFirst() function before calling ClassNext().

Call the GetClassInfo() Windows API function using the *szClassName* and *hInst* members of the CLASSENTRY structure to retrieve more detailed information on each window class.

### See Also
CLASSENTRY    TOOLHELP.H Structure
ClassFirst         TOOLHELP.DLL Function

### Example
See the example for the ClassFirst() function.

## FreeAllGDIMem                                      STRESS.DLL Function

### Purpose
Use the FreeAllGDIMem() function to free any GDI memory allocated by a previous call to the AllocGDIMem() function.

### Syntax
```
void WINAPI FreeAllGDIMem(void);
```

### Returns
```
void
```

### Description
Calling this function will release all the GDI memory allocated when your application instance called the AllocGDIMem() function. Note that it will not release any GDI memory allocated when other application instances called AllocGDIMem().

### See Also
AllocGDIMem           STRESS.DLL Function
FreeAllUserMem        STRESS.DLL Function
UnAllocDiskSpace      STRESS.DLL Function
UnAllocFileHandles    STRESS.DLL Function

### Example
See the example for the AllocGDIMem() function.

# FreeAllMem

**STRESS.DLL Function**

## Purpose

Use the FreeAllMem() function to free any global memory allocated by your application from a call to the AllocMem() function.

## Syntax

```
void WINAPI FreeAllMem(void);
```

## Returns

void

## Description

Calling this function will release all global memory allocated when your application instance called the AllocMem() function. Note that Windows will automatically release the memory allocated by AllocMem() when your application terminates.

## See Also

| | |
|---|---|
| AllocMem | STRESS.DLL Function |
| FreeAllUserMem | STRESS.DLL Function |
| UnAllocDiskSpace | STRESS.DLL Function |
| UnAllocFileHandles | STRESS.DLL Function |

## Example

See the example for the AllocMem() function.


# FreeAllUserMem

**STRESS.DLL Function**

## Purpose

Use the FreeAllGDIMem() function to free any GDI memory allocated when your application called the AllocGDIMem() function.

## Syntax

```
void WINAPI FreeAllUserMem(void);
```

## Returns

void

## Description

Calling this function will release all the User memory allocated when your application instance called the AllocUserMem() function. Note that this function will not release any User memory allocated when a different application instances called AllocUser-Mem().

## See Also

| | |
|---|---|
| AllocUserMem | STRESS.DLL Function |
| FreeAllGDIMem | STRESS.DLL Function |
| UnAllocDiskSpace | STRESS.DLL Function |
| UnAllocFileHandles | STRESS.DLL Function |

## Example

See the example for the AllocUserMem() function.

# GetFreeFileHandles                                        STRESS.DLL Function

## Purpose

You call the GetFreeFileHandles() function to determine the number of file handles available for your application.

## Syntax

```
int WINAPI GetFreeFileHandles(void);
```

## Returns

Returns the number of file handles available in this instance of your application.

## Description

You'd normally use the GetFreeFileHandles() while debugging your application to ensure that you've closed all the files opened by your application.

## See Also

| | |
|---|---|
| AllocFileHandles | STRESS.DLL Function |
| UnAllocFileHandles | STRESS.DLL Function |

## Example

Write an application that displays an error message if any files are left open:

**stress\handles\test.c**
```
    #include <windows.h>
    #include <stress.h>
    #include <stdio.h>

    #define DEBUG

    void main(void)
    {
```

```
    int FreeHandles;

#ifdef DEBUG
    FreeHandles = GetFreeFileHandles();
#endif

    fopen("test.c", "rt");

#ifdef DEBUG
    if(FreeHandles != GetFreeFileHandles())
        MessageBox(NULL, "You've left some files open!", NULL, MB_OK);
#endif
}
```

The above application opens the TEST.C file, but never closes it.

# GLOBALENTRY                                      TOOLHELP.H Structure

## Purpose

You use the GLOBALENTRY structure with the GlobalFirst(), GlobalNext(), GlobalEntryHandle, and GlobalEntryModule() functions to retrieve information on a global memory object such as the size of the object, the object's location in linear memory, the owning module, the type of object and its lock counts.

## Definition

```
typedef struct tagGLOBALENTRY
{
    DWORD dwSize;
    DWORD dwAddress;
    DWORD dwBlockSize;
    HGLOBAL hBlock;
    WORD wcLock;
    WORD wcPageLock;
    WORD wFlags;
    BOOL wHeapPresent;
    HGLOBAL hOwner;
    WORD wType;
    WORD wData;
    DWORD dwNext;
    DWORD dwNextAlt;
} GLOBALENTRY;
```

DWORD *dwSize*

Size of the GLOBALENTRY structure in bytes. This member must be initialized before calling any function that uses the GLOBALENTRY structure.

DWORD *dwAddress*
Linear address of the global memory object in memory.

DWORD *dwBlockSize*
Size of the global memory object in bytes.

HGLOBAL *hBlock*
Handle to the global memory object.

WORD *wcLock*
Lock count for the object.

WORD *wcPageLock*
Page lock count for the memory object.

WORD *wFlags*
If the global object is a task, then the most significant byte equals GF_PDB_OWNER indicating the memory object is the owner of a Process Data Block (PDB). Otherwise, the byte is set to zero. The least significant byte contains flags used by the KERNEL module.

BOOL *wHeapPresent*
Set to FALSE if the object does not contain a local heap. Otherwise, the global object contains a local heap. You can then use the value of the *hBlock* member with the LocalFirst() and LocalInfo() functions to walk through the local heap.

HGLOBAL *hOwner*
Handle to the module or task that owns the object. You can use the value of *hOwner* to obtain more detailed information on the module or task which owns the object such as the name and execution path. If the value of *wType* is set to GT_TASK, use the value of *hOwner* as a task handle and call the TaskFindHandle() function. Otherwise, treat it as a module handle and call the ModuleFindHandle() function.

WORD *wType*
Contains information on the type of global memory object. The value is one of the following:

| VALUE | DESCRIPTION |
| --- | --- |
| GT_BURGERMASTER | The memory object is a map of selectors to arena handles. |
| GT_CODE | The memory object is a code segment. The *wData* member contains the segment number. |
| GT_DATA | Program data segment. This may contain either the stack and/or the local heap for the application. The *wData* member contains the segment number. |
| GT_DGROUP | The object is the default data segment. This object contains the stack segment. The *wData* member contains the segment number. |

| | |
|---|---|
| GT_FREE | The memory object is a part of the free memory pool. |
| GT_INTERNAL | This memory object type is reserved for internal use by Windows. |
| GT_MODULE | The memory object is the Windows database on modules. |
| GT_RESOURCE | The memory object is a resource. The *wData* member contains a value representing the type of resource. |
| GT_SENTINEL | The memory object is either the first and/or last object in the global heap. |
| GT_TASK | The memory object the Windows database on the tasks. |
| GT_UNKNOWN | Unknown memory type. |

WORD *wData*

Set to zero if the *wType* member is not GT_CODE, GT_DATA, GT_DGROUP, or GT_RESOURCE. If *wType* is GT_CODE, GT_DATA, or GT_DGROUP, then *wData* contains the segment number for the memory object. Type GT_RESOURCE memory objects contain one of the following values describing the type of memory object:

| VALUE | DESCRIPTION |
|---|---|
| GD_ACCELERATORS | An Accelerator table. |
| GD_BITMAP | A bitmap (including palette and bitmap bits). |
| GD_CURSOR | A group of cursors. |
| GD_CURSORCOMPONENT | A single cursor. |
| GD_DIALOG | A dialog box description. |
| GD_ERRTABLE | An error table. |
| GD_FONT | A single font. |
| GD_FONTDIR | A group of fonts. |
| GD_ICON | A group of icons. |
| GD_ICONCOMPONENT | A single icon. |
| GD_MENU | A menu. |
| GD_NAMETABLE | A name table. |
| GD_RCDATA | A user-define resource. |
| GD_STRING | A string table. |
| GD_USERDEFINED | A user-defined resource. |

DWORD *dwNext*

Reserved for use by Windows.

DWORD *dwNextAlt*

Reserved for use by Windows.

## See Also

# GlobalEntryHandle                      TOOLHELP.DLL Function

## Purpose

You use the GlobalEntryHandle() function to obtain information on a memory object (such as the size of the object, the object's location in linear memory, the owning module, the type of object, and its lock counts) associated with given global handle.

## Syntax

```
BOOL WINAPI GlobalEntryHandle(GLOBALENTRY FAR* lpGlobal, HGLOBAL hItem);
```

GLOBALENTRY FAR* *lpGLobal*

Far pointer to GLOBALENTRY structure. You must initialize the *dwSize* member of the structure with the size of the GLOBALENTRY structure before calling the GlobalEntryHandle() function.

HGLOBAL *hItem*

Handle or selector for a global memory object.

## Returns

Zero if the function fails. Otherwise, GlobalEntryHandle() returns a nonzero value.

## Description

The GlobalEntryHandle() function allows you to extract information on a global memory object using the handle for the object. This information includes the size of the object, the object's location in linear memory, the owning module, the type of object, and its lock counts.

Note that most handles that are global in nature, such as task and module handles, are also global memory handles. You can also use selectors with this function in lieu of a global handle so long it is not tiled or part of a selector array, i.e., you did not extract the selector value from a far pointer.

## See Also

## Example

Write an application that displays the information retrieve on its own data segment and task module global memory objects using the GlobalHandleEntry() function:

**toolhelp\handle\test.c**

```c
#include <windows.h>
#include <toolhelp.h>
#include <stdio.h>

#define pFlag(value, flag) \
  if((value) == (flag)) \
    printf("%s", #flag)

void PrintGlobalEntryInfo(GLOBALENTRY *GlobalEntry)
{
  printf("   dwAddress: 0x%08lx\n",  GlobalEntry->dwAddress);
  printf(" dwBlockSize: %ld bytes\n", GlobalEntry->dwBlockSize);
  printf("      hBlock: 0x%04x\n",  GlobalEntry->hBlock);
  printf("      wcLock: 0x%04x\n",  GlobalEntry->wcLock);
  printf("  wcPageLock: 0x%04x\n",  GlobalEntry->wcPageLock);

  printf("wHeapPresent: %s\n",
    GlobalEntry->wHeapPresent ? "TRUE" : "FALSE");

  /* Display information on the owner of the object */
  printf("      hOwner: ");
  if(GlobalEntry->wType != GT_TASK)
  {
    MODULEENTRY ModuleEntry;

    ModuleEntry.dwSize = sizeof(MODULEENTRY);
    ModuleFindHandle(&ModuleEntry, GlobalEntry->hOwner);
    printf("%s module\n", ModuleEntry.szModule);
  }
  else
  {
    TASKENTRY TaskEntry;

    TaskEntry.dwSize = sizeof(TASKENTRY);
    TaskFindHandle(&TaskEntry, GlobalEntry->hOwner);
    printf("%s module\n", TaskEntry.szModule);
  }

  printf("      wFlags: ");
  pFlag(HIBYTE(GlobalEntry->wFlags) << 8, GF_PDB_OWNER);
  if(!HIBYTE(GlobalEntry->wFlags))
    printf("<none>");

  printf("\n       wType: ");
  pFlag(GlobalEntry->wType, GT_UNKNOWN);
  pFlag(GlobalEntry->wType, GT_DGROUP);
  pFlag(GlobalEntry->wType, GT_DATA);
  pFlag(GlobalEntry->wType, GT_CODE);
  pFlag(GlobalEntry->wType, GT_TASK);
  pFlag(GlobalEntry->wType, GT_RESOURCE);
  pFlag(GlobalEntry->wType, GT_MODULE);
  pFlag(GlobalEntry->wType, GT_FREE);
```

```
    pFlag(GlobalEntry->wType, GT_INTERNAL);
    pFlag(GlobalEntry->wType, GT_SENTINEL);
    pFlag(GlobalEntry->wType, GT_BURGERMASTER);

    if(GlobalEntry->wType == GT_RESOURCE)
    {
      printf("\n      wData: ");
      pFlag(GlobalEntry->wType, GD_ACCELERATORS);
      pFlag(GlobalEntry->wType, GD_BITMAP);
      pFlag(GlobalEntry->wType, GD_CURSOR);
      pFlag(GlobalEntry->wType, GD_CURSORCOMPONENT);
      pFlag(GlobalEntry->wType, GD_DIALOG);
      pFlag(GlobalEntry->wType, GD_ERRTABLE);
      pFlag(GlobalEntry->wType, GD_FONT);
      pFlag(GlobalEntry->wType, GD_FONTDIR);
      pFlag(GlobalEntry->wType, GD_ICON);
      pFlag(GlobalEntry->wType, GD_ICONCOMPONENT);
      pFlag(GlobalEntry->wType, GD_MENU);
      pFlag(GlobalEntry->wType, GD_NAMETABLE);
      pFlag(GlobalEntry->wType, GD_RCDATA);
      pFlag(GlobalEntry->wType, GD_STRING);
      pFlag(GlobalEntry->wType, GD_USERDEFINED);
    }
    else if( GlobalEntry->wType == GT_CODE ||
             GlobalEntry->wType == GT_DATA ||
             GlobalEntry->wType == GT_DGROUP)
      printf("(%d)", GlobalEntry->wData);
}

void main(void)
{
  GLOBALENTRY GlobalEntry;
  TASKENTRY TaskEntry;
  HMODULE hThisModule;

  /* Initialize the GLOBALENTRY and TASKENTRY structures */
  GlobalEntry.dwSize = sizeof(GLOBALENTRY);
  TaskEntry.dwSize  = sizeof(TASKENTRY);

  /* Get the task handle for this data segment */
  GlobalEntryHandle(&GlobalEntry, _DS);
  printf("Information on this data segment\n");
  PrintGlobalEntryInfo(&GlobalEntry);

  /* Print information on the task memory object */
  TaskFindHandle(&TaskEntry, GetCurrentTask());
  GlobalEntryHandle(&GlobalEntry, TaskEntry.hTask);
  printf("\n\nTask object information\n");
  PrintGlobalEntryInfo(&GlobalEntry);
}
```

Figure 7-19 shows the output from the TEST.EXE.

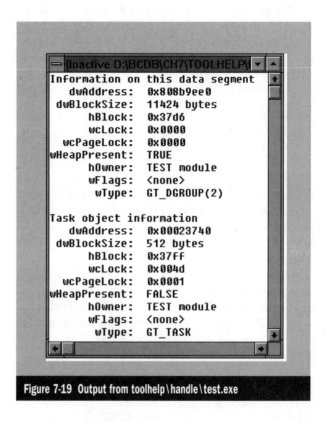

**Figure 7-19  Output from toolhelp\handle\test.exe**

# GlobalEntryModule

**TOOLHELP.DLL Function**

### Purpose

You use the GlobalEntryModule() function to obtain information on the memory object (such as the size of the object, the object's location in linear memory, the owning module, the type of object, and its lock counts) associated with a given module segment.

### Syntax

```
BOOL WINAPI GlobalEntryModule(GLOBALENTRY FAR* lpGlobal, HMODULE hModule,
WORD wSeg);
```

GLOBALENTRY FAR* *lpGlobal*

Far pointer to a GLOBALENTRY structure. Note that the *dwSize* member of this structure must be set to the size of the GLOBALENTRY structure before calling GlobalEntryModule().

HMODULE *hModule*
  Handle to a module.

WORD *wSeg*
  The segment number you would like information on. This should be a number between 1 and the number of segments in the module, both code and data.

## Returns
Returns a nonzero value if successful. Returns zero if the function fails such as when the *wSeg* parameter exceeds the number of segments in the module or the *hModule* parameter is invalid.

## Description
The GlobalEntryModule() function retrieves information on the global memory objects Windows loaded each of an application's segments into. The numbering sequence is contiguous and always starts with the number '1'. For example, if an application has a total of 10 code and data segments, then the segments will be numbered '1' through '10'.

## See Also
GlobalEntryHandle    TOOLHELP.DLL Function
GlobalFirst          TOOLHELP.DLL Function
GlobalHandleToSel    TOOLHELP.DLL Function
GlobalInfo           TOOLHELP.DLL Function
GlobalNext           TOOLHELP.DLL Function

## Example
Write an application that prints information on each of its segments using the GlobalEntryModule() function:

**toolhelp\gmodule\test.c**

```
#include <windows.h>
#include <toolhelp.h>
#include <stdio.h>

#define pFlag(value, flag) \
  if((value) == (flag)) \
    printf("%s", #flag)

void PrintGlobalEntryInfo(GLOBALENTRY *GlobalEntry)
{
  printf("  dwAddress: 0x%08lx\n",  GlobalEntry->dwAddress);
  printf(" dwBlockSize: %ld bytes\n", GlobalEntry->dwBlockSize);
  printf("     hBlock: 0x%04x\n",  GlobalEntry->hBlock);
  printf("     wcLock: 0x%04x\n",  GlobalEntry->wcLock);
  printf(" wcPageLock: 0x%04x\n",  GlobalEntry->wcPageLock);
```

```c
printf("wHeapPresent: %s\n",
  GlobalEntry->wHeapPresent ? "TRUE" : "FALSE");

/* Display information on the owner of the object */
printf("    hOwner: ");
if(GlobalEntry->wType != GT_TASK)
{
  MODULEENTRY ModuleEntry;

  ModuleEntry.dwSize = sizeof(MODULEENTRY);
  ModuleFindHandle(&ModuleEntry, GlobalEntry->hOwner);
  printf("%s module\n", ModuleEntry.szModule);
}
else
{
  TASKENTRY TaskEntry;

  TaskEntry.dwSize = sizeof(TASKENTRY);
  TaskFindHandle(&TaskEntry, GlobalEntry->hOwner);
  printf("%s module\n", TaskEntry.szModule);
}

printf("    wFlags: ");
pFlag(HIBYTE(GlobalEntry->wFlags) << 8, GF_PDB_OWNER);
if(!HIBYTE(GlobalEntry->wFlags))
  printf("<none>");

printf("\n    wType: ");
pFlag(GlobalEntry->wType, GT_UNKNOWN);
pFlag(GlobalEntry->wType, GT_DGROUP);
pFlag(GlobalEntry->wType, GT_DATA);
pFlag(GlobalEntry->wType, GT_CODE);
pFlag(GlobalEntry->wType, GT_TASK);
pFlag(GlobalEntry->wType, GT_RESOURCE);
pFlag(GlobalEntry->wType, GT_MODULE);
pFlag(GlobalEntry->wType, GT_FREE);
pFlag(GlobalEntry->wType, GT_INTERNAL);
pFlag(GlobalEntry->wType, GT_SENTINEL);
pFlag(GlobalEntry->wType, GT_BURGERMASTER);

if(GlobalEntry->wType == GT_RESOURCE)
{
  printf("\n    wData: ");
  pFlag(GlobalEntry->wType, GD_ACCELERATORS);
  pFlag(GlobalEntry->wType, GD_BITMAP);
  pFlag(GlobalEntry->wType, GD_CURSOR);
  pFlag(GlobalEntry->wType, GD_CURSORCOMPONENT);
  pFlag(GlobalEntry->wType, GD_DIALOG);
  pFlag(GlobalEntry->wType, GD_ERRTABLE);
  pFlag(GlobalEntry->wType, GD_FONT);
  pFlag(GlobalEntry->wType, GD_FONTDIR);
  pFlag(GlobalEntry->wType, GD_ICON);
  pFlag(GlobalEntry->wType, GD_ICONCOMPONENT);
  pFlag(GlobalEntry->wType, GD_MENU);
  pFlag(GlobalEntry->wType, GD_NAMETABLE);
  pFlag(GlobalEntry->wType, GD_RCDATA);
  pFlag(GlobalEntry->wType, GD_STRING);
  pFlag(GlobalEntry->wType, GD_USERDEFINED);
}
```

```
    else if( GlobalEntry->wType == GT_CODE ||
             GlobalEntry->wType == GT_DATA ||
             GlobalEntry->wType == GT_DGROUP)
      printf("(%d)", GlobalEntry->wData);
}

void main(void)
{
   TASKENTRY TaskEntry;
   GLOBALENTRY GlobalEntry;
   BOOL Status;
   WORD Segment;
   HMODULE hModule;

   /* Initialize the TASKENTRY and GLOBALENTRY structures */
   TaskEntry.dwSize = sizeof(TASKENTRY);
   GlobalEntry.dwSize = sizeof(GLOBALENTRY);

   /* Get the module handle */
   TaskFindHandle(&TaskEntry, GetCurrentTask());
   hModule = TaskEntry.hModule;

   /* Print information on each module segment */
   for(Segment = 1, Status = TRUE; Status != FALSE; Segment++)
   {
      /* Status will be set to FALSE when we run out of segments */
      Status = GlobalEntryModule(&GlobalEntry, hModule, Segment);
      if(Status != FALSE)
      {
         printf("\n\n%s Segment #%d\n", TaskEntry.szModule, Segment);
         PrintGlobalEntryInfo(&GlobalEntry);
      }
   }
}
```

Figure 7-20 shows the output from the TEST.EXE.

# GlobalFirst                               TOOLHELP.DLL Function

## Purpose
You call the GlobalFirst() function when you wish to walk through the global heap. This function fills a GLOBALENTRY structure with information on the first global memory object from either the complete list, the free list, or the least-recently-used list.

## Syntax
```
BOOL WINAPI GlobalFirst(GLOBALENTRY FAR* lpGlobal, WORD wFlags);
```

GLOBALENTRY FAR* *lpGlobal*

   Far pointer to a GLOBALENTRY structure. Note that the *dwSize* member of this structure must be set to the size of the GLOBALENTRY structure before calling GlobalFirst().

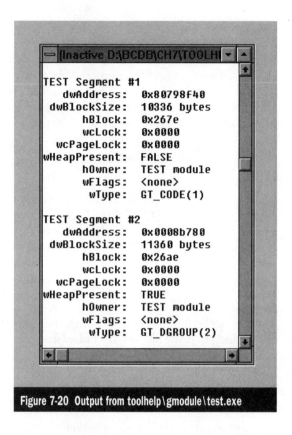

Figure 7-20  Output from toolhelp\gmodule\test.exe

WORD *wFlags*

Flag indicating which list will be used to fill the GLOBALENTRY structure. This value must be one of the following:

| VALUE | DESCRIPTION |
|---|---|
| GLOBAL_ALL | Retrieve information on the first object in the complete global heap list. |
| GLOBAL_FREE | Retrieve information on the first object in the list of free global objects list. |
| GLOBAL_LRU | Retrieve information on the first object in the list of least-recently-used global objects list. |

**Returns**

Returns a nonzero value if successful. Returns zero if the function fails, such as when the *wFlags* parameter or the *dwSize* member of the GLOBALENTRY structure is invalid.

## Description

The GlobalFirst() function provides you access to three lists in the Windows operating system concerning global memory objects: the complete list of global memory objects, another list containing all the memory objects that are currently free, and a third list of the least-recently-used objects. The GlobalFirst() function fills the GLOBALENTRY structure with information on the first item from one of these lists. You would then use the GlobalNext() function to retrieve information on subsequent items in the list. Note that you must call the GlobalNext() function using the same *wFlags* parameter as you did with the call to GlobalFirst().

## See Also

| | |
|---|---|
| GlobalEntryHandle | TOOLHELP.DLL Function |
| GlobalEntryModule | TOOLHELP.DLL Function |
| GlobalHandleToSel | TOOLHELP.DLL Function |
| GlobalInfo | TOOLHELP.DLL Function |
| GlobalNext | TOOLHELP.DLL Function |
| LocalFirst | TOOLHELP.DLL Function |

## Example

Write an application that walks through the least-recently-used list of global memory objects and prints the object's size and owner:

**toolhelp\global\test.c**

```c
#include <windows.h>
#include <toolhelp.h>
#include <stdio.h>

void PrintOwnerAndSize(GLOBALENTRY *GlobalEntry)
{
  if(GlobalEntry->wType != GT_TASK)
  {
    MODULEENTRY ModuleEntry;

    ModuleEntry.dwSize = sizeof(MODULEENTRY);
    ModuleFindHandle(&ModuleEntry, GlobalEntry->hOwner);
    printf("%s module: ", ModuleEntry.szModule);
  }
  else
  {
    TASKENTRY TaskEntry;

    TaskEntry.dwSize = sizeof(TASKENTRY);
    TaskFindHandle(&TaskEntry, GlobalEntry->hOwner);
    printf("%s task: ", TaskEntry.szModule);
  }
  printf("%ld bytes\n", GlobalEntry->dwBlockSize);
}

void main(void)
{
  GLOBALENTRY GlobalEntry;
```

```
BOOL Status;
WORD List = GLOBAL_LRU;

/* Initialize the GLOBALENTRY structure */
GlobalEntry.dwSize = sizeof(GLOBALENTRY);

/* Get information on the first object in the LRU list */
Status = GlobalFirst(&GlobalEntry, List);

/* Walk through the LRU list */
while(Status != FALSE)
{
   PrintOwnerAndSize(&GlobalEntry);
   Status = GlobalNext(&GlobalEntry, List);
}
}
```

Figure 7-21 shows the output from the TEST.EXE.

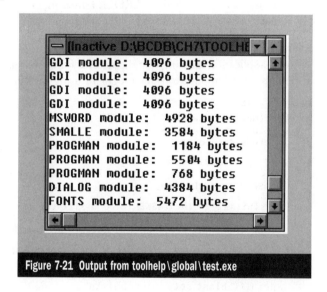

**Figure 7-21  Output from toolhelp\global\test.exe**

# GlobalHandleToSel                                    TOOLHELP.DLL Function

### Purpose

You use the GlobalHandleToSel() to convert a handle to a global memory object to a selector.

### Syntax

```
WORD WINAPI GlobalHandleToSel(HGLOBAL hMem);
```

HGLOBAL *hMem*
   Handle to a global memory object.

### Returns

Returns the selector for the global memory object. Returns zero if the value of *hMem* is invalid.

### Description

There may be times when you simply want to know the value of a selector for a global memory object. The GlobalHandleToSel() returns the value of that selector which is appropriate for both Windows Versions 3.0 and 3.1. Note that calling this function does not lock the memory object.

### See Also

| | |
|---|---|
| GlobalEntryHandle | TOOLHELP.DLL Function |
| GlobalEntryModule | TOOLHELP.DLL Function |
| GlobalFirst | TOOLHELP.DLL Function |
| GlobalInfo | TOOLHELP.DLL Function |
| GlobalNext | TOOLHELP.DLL Function |

### Example

Write an application showing that the selector for the handle for an application instance is the same as the applications data segment using the GlobalHandleToSel() function:

**toolhelp\sel\test.c**

```c
#include <windows.h>
#include <toolhelp.h>
#include <stdio.h>

void main(void)
{
  TASKENTRY TaskEntry;

  /* Initialize the TASKENTRY and fill the structure */
  TaskEntry.dwSize = sizeof(TASKENTRY);
  TaskFindHandle(&TaskEntry, GetCurrentTask());

  /* Compare the selector for the hInstance handle to the
     current data segment */
  printf(" Data Segment: %04x\n", _DS);
  printf("hInst selector: %04x\n",
GlobalHandleToSel(TaskEntry.hInst));
}
```

Figure 7-22 shows the output from the TEST.EXE.

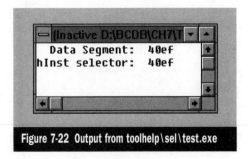

**Figure 7-22 Output from toolhelp\sel\test.exe**

# GLOBALINFO                                  **TOOLHELP.H Structure**

## Purpose

The GLOBALINFO structure is used by the GlobalInfo() function to return information on the number of items in the complete, free, and least-recently-used global memory object lists. You can then use this information to allocate any necessary memory prior to walking through the global heap.

## Definition

```
typedef struct tagGLOBALINFO
{
    DWORD dwSize;
    WORD wcItems;
    WORD wcItemsFree;
    WORD wcItemsLRU;
} GLOBALINFO;
```

DWORD *dwSize*

Size of the GLOBALINFO structure in bytes. Set this member using sizeof(GLOBALINFO) before calling the GlobalInfo() function.

WORD *wcItems*

Number of items in the complete global heap list. You access this list using the GlobalFirst() and GlobalNext() functions with GLOBAL_ALL for the *wFlags* parameter.

WORD *wcItemsFree*

Number of items in the free global heap list. You access this list using the GlobalFirst() and GlobalNext() functions with GLOBAL_FREE for the *wFlags* parameter.

WORD *wcItemsLRU*

Number of items in the least-recently-used (LRU) global heap list. You access this list using the GlobalFirst() and GlobalNext() functions with GLOBAL_LRU for the *wFlags* parameter.

## See Also

| | |
|---|---|
| GlobalFirst | TOOLHELP.DLL Function |
| GlobalInfo | TOOLHELP.DLL Function |
| GlobalNext | TOOLHELP.DLL Function |

# GlobalInfo                                  **TOOLHELP.DLL Function**

## Purpose

You use the GlobalInfo() function to retrieve information on the number of items in the three global heap lists. You can then use this information to allocate any necessary memory prior to walking through the global heap.

## Syntax

```
BOOL WINAPI GlobalInfo(GLOBALINFO FAR* lpGlobalInfo);
```

*GLOBALINFO FAR \* lpGlobalInfo*
    Far pointer to a GLOBALINFO structure. Note that the *dwSize* member of this structure must be set to the size of the GLOBALINFO structure before calling the GlobalInfo() function.

## Returns

Returns a nonzero value if successful. Returns zero if the function fails, such as when the *dwSize* member of the structure is not initialized.

## Description

Windows maintains three lists on the items in the global heap: the complete list, a list of free objects, and a list of the least-recently-used (LRU) items. You use the GlobalInfo() function to determine the number of items on each of these lists. You'd normally use this information for allocating memory before walking the global heap using the GlobalFirst() and GlobalNext() functions.

## See Also

| | |
|---|---|
| GlobalFirst | TOOLHELP.DLL Function |
| GLOBALINFO | TOOLHELP.H Structure |
| GlobalNext | TOOLHELP.DLL Function |

## Example

Write an application that prints the number of items in the complete, free, and LRU lists:

**toolhelp\lists\test.c**

```c
#include <windows.h>
#include <toolhelp.h>
#include <stdio.h>

void main(void)
{
  GLOBALINFO Info;

  /* Initialize the GLOBALINFO structure */
  Info.dwSize = sizeof(GLOBALINFO);

  /* Print the number of items in each of the three
     global heap lists */
  GlobalInfo(&Info);
  printf("Complete list: %d items\n", Info.wcItems);
  printf("    Free list: %d items\n", Info.wcItemsFree);
  printf("     LRU list: %d items\n", Info.wcItemsLRU);
}
```

Figure 7-23 shows the output from the TEST.EXE.

**Figure 7-23  Output from toolhelp\lists\test.exe**

# GlobalNext

**TOOLHELP.DLL Function**

## Purpose

You use the GlobalNext() function after first calling the GlobalFirst() function when you want to walk the global heap.

## Syntax

```
BOOL WINAPI GlobalNext(GLOBALENTRY FAR* lpGlobal, WORD wFlags);
```

GLOBALENTRY FAR* *lpGlobal*

Far pointer to a GLOBALENTRY structure. Note that this must be a pointer to a structure initialized by a call to either GlobalFirst() or a previous call to GlobalNext().

WORD *wFlags*

Flag indicating which list will be used to fill the GLOBALENTRY structure. This value must be one of the following:

| VALUE | DESCRIPTION |
| --- | --- |
| GLOBAL_ALL | Retrieve information on the first object in the complete global heap list. |
| GLOBAL_FREE | Retrieve information on the first object in the list of free global objects list. |
| GLOBAL_LRU | Retrieve information on the first object in the list of least-recently-used global objects list. |

## Returns

Returns a nonzero value if successful. Returns a zero if the function fails, such as when there are no more objects on the global heap list, when the *dwSize* member of the GLOBALENTRY structure is invalid, or when the *wFlags* parameter is invalid or does not match the *wFlags* parameter used with the call to the GlobalFirst() function.

## Description

The GlobalNext() function allows you to walk through one of the three lists in the Windows operating system for global memory objects:  the complete list of global memory objects, another list containing all the memory objects which are currently free, and a third list of the least-recently-used objects. You first call the GlobalFirst() function to initially fill the GLOBALENTRY structure with information on the first item from one of these lists. You would then use the GlobalNext() function to fill the same structure information on subsequent items in the list. Note that you must call the GlobalNext() function using the same *wFlags* parameter as you did with the call to GlobalFirst().

## See Also

| | |
|---|---|
| GlobalEntryHandle | TOOLHELP.DLL Function |
| GlobalEntryModule | TOOLHELP.DLL Function |
| GlobalFirst | TOOLHELP.DLL Function |
| GlobalInfo | TOOLHELP.DLL Function |
| LocalNext | TOOLHELP.DLL Function |

## Example

See the example for the GlobalFirst() function.

# LOCALENTRY                                    TOOLHELP.H Structure

## Purpose

You use the LOCALENTRY structure with the LocalFirst() and LocalNext() functions to walk the local heap. The two functions fill the structure with information on each object in the local heap such as the object's size, address, lock count, and type.

## Definition

```
typedef struct tagLOCALENTRY
{
    DWORD dwSize;
    HLOCAL hHandle;
    WORD wAddress;
    WORD wSize;
    WORD wFlags;
    WORD wcLock;
    WORD wType;
    WORD hHeap;
    WORD wHeapType;
    WORD wNext;
} LOCALENTRY;
```

DWORD *dwSize*

Size of the LOCALENTRY structure in bytes. You must initialize this member before calling the LocalFirst() function.

HLOCAL *hHandle*
Handle to the object on the local heap.

WORD *wAddress*
Near address of the object within the owning global memory object.

WORD *wSize*
Size of the object in bytes.

WORD *wFlags*
Attributes for the object. This value is one of the following:

| VALUE | DESCRIPTION |
| --- | --- |
| LF_FIXED | Object is fixed. |
| LF_FREE | Object has been freed. |
| LF_MOVEABLE | Object is moveable. |

WORD *wcLock*
Number of lock counts on the object. This value is zero if the object is not locked.

WORD *wType*
Type of object. For local heaps other than the GDI and User modules, this value is one of the following:

| VALUE | DESCRIPTION |
| --- | --- |
| LT_FREE | Object has been freed. |
| LT_NORMAL | Normal local object. |

The debugging version of Windows uses different *wType* values for local objects on the GDI and User local heaps. These values are only for informational purposes and may change in future versions of Windows:

| VALUE | DESCRIPTION |
| --- | --- |
| LT_GDI_BITMAP | Bitmap structure |
| LT_GDI_BRUSH | Brush structure |
| LT_GDI_DC | Device context structure |
| LT_GDI_DISABLED_DC | Reserved for internal use by Windows |
| LT_GDI_FONT | Font structure |
| LT_GDI_MAX | Reserved for internal use by Windows |
| LT_GDI_METADC | Metafile device context structure |
| LT_GDI_METAFILE | Metafile structure |

| | |
|---|---|
| LT_GDI_PALETTE | Palette structure |
| LT_GDI_PEN | Pen structure |
| LT_GDI_RGN | Region structure |
| LT_USER_ATOMS | Atom structure |
| LT_USER_BWL | Reserved for internal use by Windows |
| LT_USER_CBOX | Combo-box structure |
| LT_USER_CHECKPOINT | Reserved for internal use by Windows |
| LT_USER_CLASS | Class structure |
| LT_USER_CLIP | Clip structure |
| LT_USER_DCE | Reserved for internal use by Windows |
| LT_USER_ED | Edit control structure |
| LT_USER_HANDLETABLE | Reserved for internal use by Windows |
| LT_USER_HOOKLIST | Reserved for internal use by Windows |
| LT_USER_HOTKEYLIST | Reserved for internal use by Windows |
| LT_USER_LBIV | Reserved for internal use by Windows |
| LT_USER_LOCKINPUTSTATE | Reserved for internal use by Windows |
| LT_USER_MENU | Menu structure |
| LT_USER_MISC | Reserved for internal use by Windows |
| LT_USER_MWP | Reserved for internal use by Windows |
| LT_USER_OWNERDRAW | Reserved for internal use by Windows |
| LT_USER_PALETTE | Reserved for internal use by Windows |
| LT_USER_POPUPMENU | Reserved for internal use by Windows |
| LT_USER_PROP | Property structure |
| LT_USER_SPB | Reserved for internal use by Windows |
| LT_USER_STRING | Reserved for internal use by Windows |
| LT_USER_USERSEEUSERDOALLOC | Reserved for internal use by Windows |
| LT_USER_WND | Window structure |

WORD *hHeap*

Handle to the global memory object owning the local heap.

WORD *wHeapType*

Type of local heap. This value is one of the following:

| VALUE | DESCRIPTION |
| --- | --- |
| GDI_HEAP | Local heap belongs to the GDI module |
| NORMAL_HEAP | Default local heap for an application |
| USER_HEAP | Local heap belongs to the User module |

WORD *wNext*
  Used by the LocalNext() function to determine the next item on the local heap.

**See Also**
LocalFirst    TOOLHELP.DLL Function
LocalNext    TOOLHELP.DLL Function


# LocalFirst                                         **TOOLHELP.DLL Function**

**Purpose**
You use the LocalFirst() to retrieve information on the first item in a local heap such as the object's size, address, lock count, and type.

**Syntax**
```
BOOL WINAPI LocalFirst(LOCALENTRY FAR* lpLocal, HGLOBAL hHeap);
```

LOCALENTRY FAR* *lpLocal*
  Far pointer to a LOCALENTRY structure. Note that the *dwSize* member of this structure must be set to the size of the LOCALENTRY structure before calling LocalFirst().

HGLOBAL *hHeap*
  Handle or selector to a global memory object containing a local heap. Use the GlobalEntryHandle() function to determine if a global memory object contains a local heap. The GlobalEntryHandle() function will fill a GLOBALENTRY structure. The *wHeapPresent* member of this structure will be a nonzero value if the global memory object contains a local heap.

**Returns**
Returns a nonzero value if the function is successful. Returns a zero if the function fails, such as when the *dwSize* member of the LOCALENTRY structure is not initialized, the *hHeap* value is invalid or does not contain a local heap.

## Description

Some global memory objects, such as the DGROUP segment for an application, contain a local heap. The LocalFirst() and LocalNext() functions allow you to step through each object in the local heap and extract information such as its size, handle, lock count, address, and type.

You walk through the local heap by initially calling the LocalFirst() function and passing it a pointer to a LOCALENTRY structure. The LocalFirst() function will fill the structure with information on the first item in the local heap. You then call the LocalNext() function and pass it the same structure. The LocalNext() function will use the value of the *wNext* structure member to locate the next object on the local heap.

## See Also

| | |
|---|---|
| GlobalFirst | TOOLHELP.DLL Function |
| LOCALENTRY | TOOLHELP.H Structure |
| LocalInfo | TOOLHELP.DLL Function |
| LocalNext | TOOLHELP.DLL Function |

## Example

Write an application that walks through its own local heap using the LocalFirst() and LocalNext() functions. Print the information extracted on each object on the local heap. Note that the application below passes the selector in the DS register to the LocalFirst() in lieu of the application's instance handle.

**toolhelp\local\test.c**

```c
#include <windows.h>
#include <toolhelp.h>
#include <stdio.h>

#define pFlag(value, flag) \
  if((value) == (flag)) \
    printf("%s", #flag)

void PrintOwner(WORD hHeap)
{
  GLOBALENTRY GlobalEntry;

  GlobalEntry.dwSize = sizeof(GLOBALENTRY);
  GlobalEntryHandle(&GlobalEntry, hHeap);

  printf("\n   Owner: ");
  if(GlobalEntry.wType != GT_TASK)
  {
    MODULEENTRY ModuleEntry;

    ModuleEntry.dwSize = sizeof(MODULEENTRY);
    ModuleFindHandle(&ModuleEntry, GlobalEntry.hOwner);
    printf("%s module", ModuleEntry.szModule);
  }
  else
  {
    TASKENTRY TaskEntry;
```

```
      TaskEntry.dwSize = sizeof(TASKENTRY);
      TaskFindHandle(&TaskEntry, GlobalEntry.hOwner);
      printf("%s module", TaskEntry.szModule);
   }
}

void PrintLocalEntryInfo(LOCALENTRY *LocalEntry)
{
   PrintOwner(LocalEntry->hHeap);

   printf("\n  hHandle: %04x", LocalEntry->hHandle);
   printf("\n  wAddress: %04x", LocalEntry->wAddress);
   printf("\n    wSize: %d bytes", LocalEntry->wSize);
   printf("\n    wcLock: %d", LocalEntry->wcLock);

   printf("\n wHeapType: ");
   pFlag(LocalEntry->wHeapType, NORMAL_HEAP);
   pFlag(LocalEntry->wHeapType, USER_HEAP);
   pFlag(LocalEntry->wHeapType, GDI_HEAP);


   printf("\n   wFlags: ");
   pFlag(LocalEntry->wFlags, LF_FIXED);
   pFlag(LocalEntry->wFlags, LF_FREE);
   pFlag(LocalEntry->wFlags, LF_MOVEABLE);

   printf("\n    wType: ");
   if(LocalEntry->wHeapType == NORMAL_HEAP)
   {
      pFlag(LocalEntry->wType, LT_FREE);
      pFlag(LocalEntry->wType, LT_NORMAL);
   }
   else if(LocalEntry->wHeapType == GDI_HEAP)
   {
      pFlag(LocalEntry->wType, LT_FREE);
      pFlag(LocalEntry->wType, LT_NORMAL);
      pFlag(LocalEntry->wType, LT_GDI_BITMAP);
      pFlag(LocalEntry->wType, LT_GDI_BRUSH);
      pFlag(LocalEntry->wType, LT_GDI_DC);
      pFlag(LocalEntry->wType, LT_GDI_DISABLED_DC);
      pFlag(LocalEntry->wType, LT_GDI_FONT);
      pFlag(LocalEntry->wType, LT_GDI_MAX);
      pFlag(LocalEntry->wType, LT_GDI_METADC);
      pFlag(LocalEntry->wType, LT_GDI_METAFILE);
      pFlag(LocalEntry->wType, LT_GDI_PALETTE);
      pFlag(LocalEntry->wType, LT_GDI_PEN);
      pFlag(LocalEntry->wType, LT_GDI_RGN);
   }
   else if(LocalEntry->wHeapType == USER_HEAP)
   {
      pFlag(LocalEntry->wType, LT_FREE);
      pFlag(LocalEntry->wType, LT_NORMAL);
      pFlag(LocalEntry->wType, LT_USER_ATOMS);
      pFlag(LocalEntry->wType, LT_USER_BWL);
      pFlag(LocalEntry->wType, LT_USER_CBOX);
      pFlag(LocalEntry->wType, LT_USER_CHECKPOINT);
      pFlag(LocalEntry->wType, LT_USER_CLASS);
      pFlag(LocalEntry->wType, LT_USER_CLIP);
      pFlag(LocalEntry->wType, LT_USER_DCE);
```

```
      pFlag(LocalEntry->wType, LT_USER_ED);
      pFlag(LocalEntry->wType, LT_USER_HANDLETABLE);
      pFlag(LocalEntry->wType, LT_USER_HOOKLIST);
      pFlag(LocalEntry->wType, LT_USER_HOTKEYLIST);
      pFlag(LocalEntry->wType, LT_USER_LBIV);
      pFlag(LocalEntry->wType, LT_USER_LOCKINPUTSTATE);
      pFlag(LocalEntry->wType, LT_USER_MENU);
      pFlag(LocalEntry->wType, LT_USER_MISC);
      pFlag(LocalEntry->wType, LT_USER_MWP);
      pFlag(LocalEntry->wType, LT_USER_OWNERDRAW);
      pFlag(LocalEntry->wType, LT_USER_PALETTE);
      pFlag(LocalEntry->wType, LT_USER_POPUPMENU);
      pFlag(LocalEntry->wType, LT_USER_PROP);
      pFlag(LocalEntry->wType, LT_USER_SPB);
      pFlag(LocalEntry->wType, LT_USER_STRING);
      pFlag(LocalEntry->wType, LT_USER_USERSEEUSERDOALLOC);
      pFlag(LocalEntry->wType, LT_USER_WND);
   }
}

void main(void)
{
   LOCALENTRY LocalEntry;
   BOOL Status;
   WORD Item;

   /* Initialize the LOCALENTRY structure */
   LocalEntry.dwSize = sizeof(LOCALENTRY);

   /* Get the first item on the local heap */
   Status = LocalFirst(&LocalEntry, _DS);

   Item = 1;
   while(Status != FALSE)
   {
      printf("\n\nItem #%d", Item++);
      /* Print the item information */
      PrintLocalEntryInfo(&LocalEntry);

      /* Walk to the next item in the local heap */
      Status = LocalNext(&LocalEntry);
   }
   printf("\nEnd of local heap walk\n");
}
```

Figure 7-24 shows the output for the last two items in the local heap.

# LOCALINFO                                    TOOLHELP.H Structure

## Purpose

You use the LOCALINFO structure with the LocalInfo() function to determine the number of items on the local heap. You'd normally use this information to allocate any memory you require before walking the local heap.

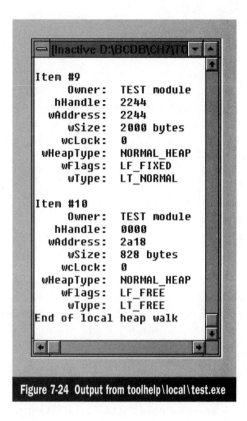

**Figure 7-24 Output from toolhelp\local\test.exe**

### Definition

```
typedef struct tagLOCALINFO
{
    DWORD dwSize;
    WORD wcItems;
} LOCALINFO;
```

DWORD *dwSize*

The size of the LOCALINFO structure in bytes. You must initialize this structure member before calling the LocalInfo() function.

WORD *wcItems*

Number of objects on the local heap.

### See Also

| | |
|---|---|
| GlobalInfo | TOOLHELP.DLL Function |
| LocalFirst | TOOLHELP.DLL Function |
| LocalInfo | TOOLHELP.DLL Function |
| LocalNext | TOOLHELP.DLL Function |

# LocalInfo

## Purpose

You use the LocalInfo() function to determine the number of objects on the local heap. You'd normally use this information to allocate any required memory before walking the local heap using the LocalFirst() and LocalNext() functions.

## Syntax

```
BOOL WINAPI LocalInfo(LOCALINFO FAR* lpLocal, HGLOBAL hHeap);
```

LOCALINFO FAR* *lpLocal*

Far pointer to a LocalInfo structure. You must initialize the *dwSize* parameter with the size of the LOCALINFO structure before calling the LocalInfo() function.

HGLOBAL *hHeap*

Handle or selector to a global memory object containing a local heap. Use the GlobalEntryHandle() function to determine if a global memory object contains a local heap. The GlobalEntryHandle() function will fill a GLOBALENTRY structure. The *wHeapPresent* member of this structure will be a nonzero value if the global memory object contains a local heap.

## Returns

Returns a nonzero value if successful. Returns zero if the function fails such as when the *dwSize* member of the LOCALINFO structure is not initialized or the *hHeap* parameter is invalid.

## Description

If you're writing an application that walks through a local heap, you will probably want to save some of the information in an array. You can use the LocalInfo() function to determine the number of items in the local heap. You would then use this information to calculate the amount of memory space you'd need for the array.

## See Also

| | |
|---|---|
| GlobalInfo | TOOLHELP.DLL Function |
| LocalFirst | TOOLHELP.DLL Function |
| LOCALINFO | TOOLHELP.H Structure |
| LocalNext | TOOLHELP.DLL Function |

## Example

Write an application that walks through the local memory heap and saves the information into an array of LOCALENTRY structures. Use the LocalInfo() function to calculate the size of the array:

**toolhelp\linfo\test.c**

```c
#include <windows.h>
#include <toolhelp.h>
#include <stdio.h>

HGLOBAL hLocalEntries = NULL;
LOCALENTRY FAR *LocalEntry;

WORD LoadLocalEntries(HGLOBAL hGlobal)
{
  LOCALINFO Info;
  GLOBALENTRY GlobalEntry;
  LOCALENTRY Entry;
  WORD n;
  BOOL Status;

  /* Does the global object contain a local heap? */
  GlobalEntry.dwSize = sizeof(GLOBALENTRY);
  GlobalEntryHandle(&GlobalEntry, hGlobal);
  if(GlobalEntry.wHeapPresent == FALSE)
    return(FALSE);

  /* How many items are in the local heap? */
  Info.dwSize = sizeof(LOCALINFO);
  LocalInfo(&Info, hGlobal);

  /* Allocate global memory to hold a LOCALENTRY array */
  hLocalEntries = GlobalAlloc(GMEM_MOVEABLE,
              ((long)Info.wcItems) * sizeof(LOCALENTRY));
  if(hLocalEntries == NULL)
    return(FALSE);
  LocalEntry = (LOCALENTRY FAR *)GlobalLock(hLocalEntries);
  if(LocalEntry == NULL)
    return(FALSE);

  /* Load the LOCALENTRY structure for each item into the array */
  Entry.dwSize = sizeof(LOCALENTRY);
  Status = LocalFirst(&Entry, hGlobal);
  for(n = 0; n < Info.wcItems; n++)
  {
    if(Status == FALSE)
    {
      GlobalFree(hLocalEntries);
      return(FALSE);
    }
    LocalEntry[n] = Entry;
    LocalNext(&Entry);
  }

  /* Return the number of items in the local heap */
  return(n);
}

void main(void)
{
  WORD NumItems, n, FreeItems;
  WORD NumFreeItems, NumAllocItems, FreeSize, AllocSize;
  WORD NumLockItems;
```

```
/* Create and load the LOCALENTRY array for this data segment */
NumItems = LoadLocalEntries(_DS);
if(NumItems != 0)
{
  /* Initialize the totals */
  NumFreeItems = NumAllocItems = FreeSize = 0;
  AllocSize = NumLockItems = 0;

  /* Calculate totals */
  for(n = 0; n < NumItems; n++)
  {
    if(LocalEntry[n].wType == LT_FREE)
    {
      NumFreeItems++;
      FreeSize += LocalEntry[n].wSize;
    }
    else
    {
      NumAllocItems++;
      AllocSize += LocalEntry[n].wSize;
    }
    if(LocalEntry[n].wcLock != 0)
      NumLockItems++;
  }

  /* Print the totals */
  printf("Local heap statistics\n");
  printf(" Total number of objects: %d\n", NumItems);
  printf("          Free objects: %u objects, %u bytes\n",
      NumFreeItems, FreeSize);
  printf("     Allocated objects: %u objects, %u bytes\n",
      NumAllocItems, AllocSize);
  printf("Number of locked objects: %u\n", NumLockItems);
}

/* Free the LOCALENTRY array */
if(hLocalEntries != NULL)
  GlobalFree(hLocalEntries);
}
```

Figure 7-25 shows the output for the above application.

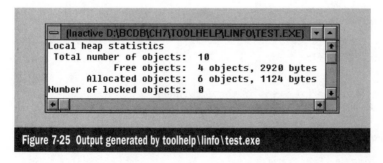

**Figure 7-25** Output generated by toolhelp\linfo\test.exe

# LocalNext

## Purpose

You use the LocalNext() to walk through the local heap. This function fills a LOCALENTRY structure with information on the next object in the local heap, such as the object's size, address, lock count, and type.

## Syntax

```
BOOL WINAPI LocalNext(LOCALENTRY FAR* lpLocal);
```

LOCALENTRY FAR* *lpLocal*

Far pointer to a LOCALENTRY structure. Note that this must be a pointer to a structure initialized by a call to either LocalFirst() or a previous call to LocalNext().

## Returns

Returns a nonzero value if successful. Returns a zero if the function fails such as when there are no more objects on the local heap or the LOCALENTRY structure is invalid.

## Description

Some global memory objects, such as the DGROUP segment for an application, contain a local heap. The LocalFirst() and LocalNext() functions allow you to step through each object in the local heap and extract information such as its size, handle, lock count, address, and type.

You walk through the local heap by initially calling the LocalFirst() function and passing it a pointer to a LOCALENTRY structure. The LocalFirst() function will fill the structure with information on the first item in the local heap. You then call the LocalNext() function and pass it the same structure. The LocalNext() function will use the value of the *wNext* structure member to locate the next object on the local heap.

## See Also

GlobalNext        TOOLHELP.DLL Function
LOCALENTRY  TOOLHELP.H Structure
LocalFirst        TOOLHELP.DLL Function
LocalInfo         TOOLHELP.DLL Function

## Example

Write an application that walks through the first 20 objects of the User module's local heap:

**toolhelp\user\test.c**
```
#include <windows.h>
#include <toolhelp.h>
#include <stdio.h>
```

```
#define pFlag(value, flag) \
  if((value) == (flag)) \
    printf("%s", #flag)

void PrintOwner(WORD hHeap)
{
   GLOBALENTRY GlobalEntry;

   GlobalEntry.dwSize = sizeof(GLOBALENTRY);
   GlobalEntryHandle(&GlobalEntry, hHeap);

   printf("\n   Owner: ");
   if(GlobalEntry.wType != GT_TASK)
   {
     MODULEENTRY ModuleEntry;

     ModuleEntry.dwSize = sizeof(MODULEENTRY);
     ModuleFindHandle(&ModuleEntry, GlobalEntry.hOwner);
     printf("%s module", ModuleEntry.szModule);
   }
   else
   {
     TASKENTRY TaskEntry;

     TaskEntry.dwSize = sizeof(TASKENTRY);
     TaskFindHandle(&TaskEntry, GlobalEntry.hOwner);
     printf("%s module", TaskEntry.szModule);
   }
}


void PrintLocalEntryInfo(LOCALENTRY *LocalEntry)
{
   PrintOwner(LocalEntry->hHeap);

   printf("\n  hHandle: %04x", LocalEntry->hHandle);
   printf("\n wAddress: %04x", LocalEntry->wAddress);
   printf("\n    wSize: %d bytes", LocalEntry->wSize);
   printf("\n   wcLock: %d", LocalEntry->wcLock);


   printf("\n wHeapType: ");
   pFlag(LocalEntry->wHeapType, NORMAL_HEAP);
   pFlag(LocalEntry->wHeapType, USER_HEAP);
   pFlag(LocalEntry->wHeapType, GDI_HEAP);

   printf("\n   wFlags: ");
   pFlag(LocalEntry->wFlags, LF_FIXED);
   pFlag(LocalEntry->wFlags, LF_FREE);
   pFlag(LocalEntry->wFlags, LF_MOVEABLE);

   printf("\n    wType: ");
   if(LocalEntry->wHeapType == NORMAL_HEAP)
   {
     pFlag(LocalEntry->wType, LT_FREE);
     pFlag(LocalEntry->wType, LT_NORMAL);
   }
   else if(LocalEntry->wHeapType == GDI_HEAP)
   {
```

```
      pFlag(LocalEntry->wType, LT_FREE);
      pFlag(LocalEntry->wType, LT_NORMAL);
      pFlag(LocalEntry->wType, LT_GDI_BITMAP);
      pFlag(LocalEntry->wType, LT_GDI_BRUSH);
      pFlag(LocalEntry->wType, LT_GDI_DC);
      pFlag(LocalEntry->wType, LT_GDI_DISABLED_DC);
      pFlag(LocalEntry->wType, LT_GDI_FONT);
      pFlag(LocalEntry->wType, LT_GDI_MAX);
      pFlag(LocalEntry->wType, LT_GDI_METADC);
      pFlag(LocalEntry->wType, LT_GDI_METAFILE);
      pFlag(LocalEntry->wType, LT_GDI_PALETTE);
      pFlag(LocalEntry->wType, LT_GDI_PEN);
      pFlag(LocalEntry->wType, LT_GDI_RGN);
    }
    else if(LocalEntry->wHeapType == USER_HEAP)
    {
      pFlag(LocalEntry->wType, LT_FREE);
      pFlag(LocalEntry->wType, LT_NORMAL);
      pFlag(LocalEntry->wType, LT_USER_ATOMS);
      pFlag(LocalEntry->wType, LT_USER_BWL);
      pFlag(LocalEntry->wType, LT_USER_CBOX);
      pFlag(LocalEntry->wType, LT_USER_CHECKPOINT);
      pFlag(LocalEntry->wType, LT_USER_CLASS);
      pFlag(LocalEntry->wType, LT_USER_CLIP);
      pFlag(LocalEntry->wType, LT_USER_DCE);
      pFlag(LocalEntry->wType, LT_USER_ED);
      pFlag(LocalEntry->wType, LT_USER_HANDLETABLE);
      pFlag(LocalEntry->wType, LT_USER_HOOKLIST);
      pFlag(LocalEntry->wType, LT_USER_HOTKEYLIST);
      pFlag(LocalEntry->wType, LT_USER_LBIV);
      pFlag(LocalEntry->wType, LT_USER_LOCKINPUTSTATE);
      pFlag(LocalEntry->wType, LT_USER_MENU);
      pFlag(LocalEntry->wType, LT_USER_MISC);
      pFlag(LocalEntry->wType, LT_USER_MWP);
      pFlag(LocalEntry->wType, LT_USER_OWNERDRAW);
      pFlag(LocalEntry->wType, LT_USER_PALETTE);
      pFlag(LocalEntry->wType, LT_USER_POPUPMENU);
      pFlag(LocalEntry->wType, LT_USER_PROP);
      pFlag(LocalEntry->wType, LT_USER_SPB);
      pFlag(LocalEntry->wType, LT_USER_STRING);
      pFlag(LocalEntry->wType, LT_USER_USERSEEUSERDOALLOC);
      pFlag(LocalEntry->wType, LT_USER_WND);
    }
  }

  void WalkLocalHeap(HGLOBAL hGlobal)
  {
    LOCALENTRY LocalEntry;
    BOOL Status;
    WORD n;

    /* Initialize the LOCALENTRY structure */
    LocalEntry.dwSize = sizeof(LOCALENTRY);

    /* Get the first item on the local heap */
    Status = LocalFirst(&LocalEntry, hGlobal);

    for(n = 0; n < 20 && Status != FALSE; n++)
    {
```

```
        printf("\n\nItem #%d", n+1);
        /* Print the item information */
        PrintLocalEntryInfo(&LocalEntry);

        /* Walk to the next item in the local heap */
        Status = LocalNext(&LocalEntry);
    }
}

void main(void)
{
    SYSHEAPINFO SysHeapInfo;

    /* Initialize the SYSHEAPINFO structure */
    SysHeapInfo.dwSize = sizeof(SYSHEAPINFO);

    /* Get the selector for the USER segment */
    SystemHeapInfo(&SysHeapInfo);

    /* Print the first 20 objects on the local heap */
    WalkLocalHeap(SysHeapInfo.hUserSegment);
}
```

Figure 7-26 shows the output for the last two objects printed.

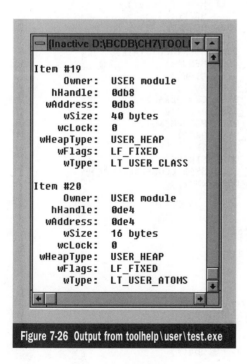

Figure 7-26 Output from toolhelp\user\test.exe

# MEMMANINFO

## Purpose

You use the MEMMANINFO structure with the MemManInfo() function to retrieve information on the Windows memory manager.

## Definition

```
typedef struct tagMEMMANINFO
{
    DWORD dwSize;
    DWORD dwLargestFreeBlock;
    DWORD dwMaxPagesAvailable;
    DWORD dwMaxPagesLockable;
    DWORD dwTotalLinearSpace;
    DWORD dwTotalUnlockedPages;
    DWORD dwFreePages;
    DWORD dwTotalPages;
    DWORD dwFreeLinearSpace;
    DWORD dwSwapFilePages;
    WORD wPageSize;
} MEMMANINFO;
```

DWORD *dwSize*

  Size of the MEMMANINFO structure in bytes. You must initialize this value before calling the MemManInfo() function.

DWORD *dwLargestFreeBlock*

  Size of the largest contiguous memory block. This is not the same value returned by a call to GlobalCompact(0) as this value also includes the swap file space.

DWORD *dwMaxPagesAvailable*

  Number of pages available. Windows calculates this value by dividing the *dwLargestFreeBlock* member by *wPageSize*.

DWORD *dwMaxPagesLockable*

  Number of pages which can be locked. This value represents the number of free pages in actual memory (RAM) rather than virtual memory (RAM and swap file).

DWORD *dwTotalLinearSpace*

  Total number of RAM and swap file pages available to Windows.

DWORD *dwTotalUnlockedPages*
Number of unlocked RAM pages. This value includes allocated pages that are not locked and free pages.

DWORD *dwFreePages*
Number of free RAM pages.

DWORD *dwTotalPages*
Total number of RAM pages available to Windows including all free, locked, and unlocked pages. This value represents the total amount of RAM available to Windows.

DWORD *dwFreeLinearSpace*
Number of free RAM and swap file pages.

DWORD *dwSwapFilePages*
Total number of pages in a permanent swap file.

WORD *wPageSize*
Number of bytes per page. Multiply by a value in pages to convert to bytes. For example, multiply *dwTotalPages* by *wPageSize* to determine how many bytes of RAM are reserved by Windows.

### See Also
MemManInfo     TOOLHELP.DLL Function

# MemManInfo                                    **TOOLHELP.DLL Function**

### Purpose
You use the MemManInfo() function to retrieve information on the Windows memory manager.

### Syntax
```
BOOL WINAPI MemManInfo(MEMMANINFO FAR* lpEnhMode);
```

MEMMANINFO FAR* *lpEnhMode*
Far pointer to a MEMMANINFO structure. The *dwSize* parameter of the structure must be initialized before calling the MemManInfo() function.

### Returns
Returns a nonzero value if successful. Returns zero if the function fails, such as when the *dwSize* parameter of the MEMMANINFO structure is not initialized.

### Description
When you run Windows 3.0 or 3.1 in the enhanced mode, it uses both physical memory and virtual memory. Physical memory is your system RAM. Virtual memory is

a combination of physical memory and memory space on your hard drive. The Windows Memory Manager is a portion of Windows that keeps track of how your *linear* memory (memory space as seen by your application) is mapped between physical memory and the hard disk. When your application accesses a portion of virtual memory that is located on the hard drive, the Windows Memory Manager automatically intervenes to move the block of memory (called a *page*) from the disk to your system RAM where it is then accessible. This movement is totally transparent to your application other than the delay time needed to reload the memory into RAM.

You can use the MemManInfo() function to retrieve information on the virtual memory in the system, including how the memory is divided between RAM and disk space. For example, the *dwTotalPages* member of the MEMMANINFO structure represents the total amount of physical RAM available to Windows. The *dwTotalLinearSpace* member represents the total amount of virtual memory available on the system, both physical RAM and hard disk space, used by the Windows Memory Manager.

**See Also**

| | |
|---|---|
| MEMMANINFO | TOOLHELP.H Structure |
| SystemHeapInfo | TOOLHELP.DLL Function |

**Example**
Write an application that prints the information contained in a MEMMANINFO structure:

toolhelp\memman\test.c
```c
#include <windows.h>
#include <toolhelp.h>
#include <stdio.h>

void main(void)
{
  MEMMANINFO Info;

  /* Initialize MEMMANINFO structure */
  Info.dwSize = sizeof(MEMMANINFO);

  /* Fill the MEMMANINFO stucture */
  MemManInfo(&Info);

  printf("Memory Manager Information\n");
  printf(" dwLargestFreeBlock: %lu bytes\n",
    Info.dwLargestFreeBlock);
  printf(" dwMaxPagesAvailable: %lu pages\n",
    Info.dwMaxPagesAvailable);
  printf(" dwMaxPagesLockable: %lu pages\n",
    Info.dwMaxPagesLockable);
  printf(" dwTotalLinearSpace: %lu pages\n",
    Info.dwTotalLinearSpace);
  printf("dwTotalUnlockedPages: %lu pages\n",
    Info.dwTotalUnlockedPages);
  printf("        dwFreePages: %lu pages\n",
    Info.dwFreePages);
```

```
    printf("        dwTotalPages: %lu pages\n",
      Info.dwTotalPages);
    printf(" dwFreeLinearPages: %lu pages\n",
      Info.dwFreeLinearSpace);
    printf("     dwSwapFilePages: %lu pages\n",
      Info.dwSwapFilePages);
    printf("            wPageSize: %u bytes\n",
      Info.wPageSize);
}
```

Figure 7-27 shows the output from the above application.

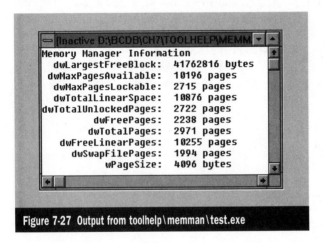

**Figure 7-27  Output from toolhelp\memman\test.exe**

# MemoryRead                                   TOOLHELP.DLL Function

### Purpose
You use the MemoryRead() function to copy the contents of a global memory object into a buffer.

### Syntax
`DWORD WINAPI MemoryRead(WORD wSel, DWORD dwOffset, void FAR* lpBuffer,`
`DWORD dwcb);`

WORD *wSel*
    Selector for the memory area you want to read. You should not use the FP_SEG() macro to extract the selector from a far pointer as the MemoryRead() function call will fail if the selector is an alias or part of a tiled selector array. You should only use selectors to objects on the global memory heap.

DWORD *dwOffset*
    Starting offset within the global memory object.

void FAR* *lpBuffer*

Far pointer to the buffer the memory will be read into. This should be a fixed memory object if the system is running low on memory.

DWORD *dwcb*

Size of the buffer pointed to by *kpBuffer* in bytes.

## Returns

Returns the number of bytes read into *lpBuffer*. The value is zero if the *wSel* parameter is invalid or the *swOffset* parameter is beyond the range of the selector.

## Description

Windows prevents your application from directly reading any portion of Windows that is not associated with your application. For example, if you were to attempt to read a portion of the GDI memory heap using the normal methods available in C, your application would generate a general protection fault and be terminated by Windows. The MemoryRead() function, on the other hand, provides a way around this restriction. With it you can read the memory area of virtually any part of Windows.

## See Also

| | |
|---|---|
| GlobalFirst | TOOLHELP.DLL Function |
| GlobalHandleToSel | TOOLHELP.DLL Function |
| GlobalNext | TOOLHELP.DLL Function |

## Example

Write an application that reads the first 256 bytes of the GDI data segment:

**toolhelp\memread\test.c**

```c
#include <windows.h>
#include <toolhelp.h>
#include <stdio.h>

void main(void)
{
  SYSHEAPINFO SysHeapInfo;
  BYTE Buffer[256];
  WORD Line, Row, n;

  /* Determine the selector for the GDI data segment */
  SysHeapInfo.dwSize = sizeof(SYSHEAPINFO);
  SystemHeapInfo(&SysHeapInfo);

  MemoryRead(SysHeapInfo.hGDISegment, 0, Buffer, sizeof(Buffer));
  printf("First 256 bytes of the GDI data segment\n");
  for(n = Line = 0; Line < 16; Line++)
  {
    for(Row = 0; Row < 16; Row++)
    {
      printf("%02x ", (WORD)(Buffer[n++]));
```

```
    }
    printf("\n");
  }
}
```

Figure 7-28 shows the output for the above application.

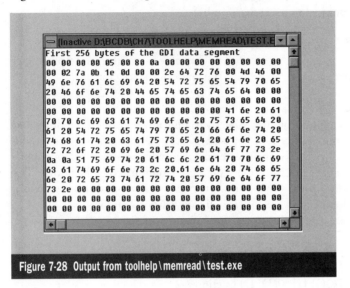

Figure 7-28 Output from toolhelp\memread\test.exe

# MODULEENTRY
**TOOLHELP.H Structure**

### Purpose
You use the MODULEENTRY structure with the ModuleFindHandle() and ModuleFindName() functions to retrieve information on a specific module. You use the structure with the ModuleFirst() and ModuleNext() functions to walk through the list of modules loaded in Windows.

### Definition
```
typedef struct tagMODULEENTRY
{
    DWORD dwSize;
    char szModule[MAX_MODULE_NAME + 1];
    HMODULE hModule;
    WORD wcUsage;
    char szExePath[MAX_PATH + 1];
    WORD wNext;
} MODULEENTRY;
```

DWORD *dwSize*

Size of the MODULEENTRY structure in bytes. You must initialize this value before calling the ModuleFindHandle(), ModuleFindName(), or ModuleFirst() function.

char *szModule*

A NULL terminated character array containing the name of the module.

HMODULE *hModule*

Handle for the module. Use this value with the GlobalEntryModule() function to retrieve information on each of the segments in the module.

WORD *wcUsage*

Number of locks on the module. This value increments each time an application or Windows calls LoadModule() to load the module and decrements each time an application or Windows calls FreeModule(). The value of *wcUsage* is also returned by the GetModuleUsage() function.

char *szExePath*

A NULL terminated character array containing the complete pathname for the module. You can use the pathname to determine the directory and drive where Windows loaded the module.

WORD *wNext*

Used by the ModuleNext() function to determine the next module in the module list.

### See Also
| | |
|---|---|
| ModuleFindHandle | TOOLHELP.DLL Function |
| ModuleFindName | TOOLHELP.DLL Function |
| ModuleFirst | TOOLHELP.DLL Function |
| ModuleNext | TOOLHELP.DLL Function |


## ModuleFindHandle                                    TOOLHELP.DLL Function

### Purpose
You use the ModuleFindHandle() function to retrieve information on a module for a given module handle. The function fills a MODULEENTRY structure which contains the modules filename, pathname, and lock count.

### Syntax
```
HMODULE WINAPI ModuleFindHandle(MODULEENTRY FAR* lpModule, HMODULE
hModule);
```

MODULEENTRY FAR* *lpModule*

Far pointer to a MODULEENTRY structure. You must initialize the *dwSize* pointer of this structure before calling the ModuleFindHandle() function. The ModuleFindHandle() function will fill the MODULEENTRY structure with information on the module.

HMODULE *hModule*

Handle to a module.

### Returns

Returns the *hModule* parameter if the function is successful. Returns zero if the function fails, such as when the *hModule* parameter is invalid or the *dwSize* member of the MODULEENTRY structure is not initialized.

### Description

Modules are the executable files loaded by Windows using the LoadModule() function. These files include applications, drivers, and dynamic link libraries. Note a module is not the same as a *task*. A module is typically shared by many different tasks whereas a task is unique to each instance of an application. For example, if a user runs five instances of CLOCK.EXE, Windows will load one CLOCK module and assign it five lock counts (the *wcUsage* member of the MODULEENTRY structure represents the lock count). Windows will also create a unique task for each execution of the module. This means there would be five tasks sharing one CLOCK module. Another way of looking at the task/module relationship is that a module contains the code for an application, whereas each task contains a unique data set for each application instance. Keep in mind that a given task may have more than one module. For example, if an application uses one or more dynamic link libraries, the application itself is one module and each dynamic link library is another module.

The ModuleFindHandle() function retrieves the filename and pathname for a given module handle by filling a MODULEENTRY structure.

Note that Windows loads each segment of an application into a separate global memory object. The owner of these global memory objects is the application module. For example, if you fill a GLOBALENTRY structure for a memory object and the *wType* member of the structure is not equal to GT_TASK, then the *hOwner* member is a handle to the owning module. You can then use the value of the *hOwner* member with the ModuleFindHandle() to determine the name and path of the module which owns.

### See Also

| | |
|---|---|
| ModuleFindName | TOOLHELP.DLL Function |
| ModuleFirst | TOOLHELP.DLL Function |
| ModuleNext | TOOLHELP.DLL Function |
| TaskFindHandle | TOOLHELP.DLL Function |

### Example

See the usage in the GlobalFirst() example.

# ModuleFindName

TOOLHELP.DLL Function

## Purpose
You use the ModuleFindName() function to determine if a specific module has been loaded into windows.

## Syntax
```
HMODULE WINAPI ModuleFindName(MODULEENTRY FAR* lpModule, LPCSTR
lpstrName);
```

MODULEENTRY FAR* *lpModule*
    Far pointer to a MODULEENTRY structure. You must initialize the *dwSize* member of the structure with the size of the MODULEENTRY structure before calling the ModuleFindName() function.

LPCSTR *lpstrName*
    Null terminated string for the module you wish to find.

## Returns
Returns the handle to the module specified by the *lpstrName* parameter. Returns a NULL handle if the module was has not been loaded or the *dwSize* member of the MODULEENTRY structure is not initialized.

## Description
The ModuleFindName() function is similar to the GetModuleHandle() function in that it will return a module handle for a given module name. However, the ModuleFindName() function also fills the MODULEENTRY structure which also contains the full pathname for the module and the lock (usage) count.

See the ModuleFindHandle() function for a description of the differences between a task and a module.

## See Also
MODULEENTRY        TOOLHELP.H Structure
ModuleFindHandle   TOOLHELP.DLL Function
ModuleFirst        TOOLHELP.DLL Function
ModuleNext         TOOLHELP.DLL Function

## Example
Write an application that prints the information contained in a MODULEENTRY structure using the ModuleFindName() function:

**toolhelp\modname\test.c**
```
#include <windows.h>
#include <toolhelp.h>
#include <stdio.h>
```

```
void PrintModuleInfo(MODULEENTRY *ModuleEntry)
{
  printf(" szModule: %s\n", ModuleEntry->szModule);
  printf(" hModule: %04x\n", ModuleEntry->hModule);
  printf(" wcUsage: %d\n", ModuleEntry->wcUsage);
  printf(" szExePath: %s\n\n", ModuleEntry->szExePath);
}

void main(void)
{
  MODULEENTRY ModuleEntry;
  HMODULE hModule;

  /* Initialize the MODULEENTRY structure */
  ModuleEntry.dwSize = sizeof(MODULEENTRY);

  hModule = ModuleFindName(&ModuleEntry, "TEST");
  if(hModule != NULL)
  {
    printf("TEST module info\n");
    PrintModuleInfo(&ModuleEntry);
  }
}
```

Figure 7-29 shows the output for the above application.

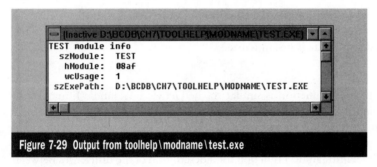

**Figure 7-29  Output from toolhelp\modname\test.exe**

# ModuleFirst                                TOOLHELP.DLL Function

### Purpose

You use the ModuleFirst() function to fill a MODULEENTRY structure with the first entry in the list of currently loaded modules maintained by Windows. You'd typically use this function with the ModuleNext() function to walk through the module list.

### Syntax

`BOOL WINAPI ModuleFirst(MODULEENTRY FAR* lpModule);`

MODULEENTRY FAR* *lpModule*

Far pointer to a MODULEENTRY structure. Note that you must initialize this *dwSize* member of this structure with the size of the MODULEENTRY structure before calling the ModuleFirst() function.

## Returns

Returns a nonzero value if the function is successful. Returns zero if the function fails such as when the *dwSize* parameter of the MODULEENTRY structure is not initialized.

## Description

Windows maintains a list of all currently loaded modules. You use the ModuleFirst() function to fill a MODULEENTRY structure with information on the first module in this list. You can then use the ModuleNext() function to fill the same structure with information on subsequent modules in the list.

See the ModuleFindHandle() function for a description on the differences between a task and a module.

## See Also

| | |
|---|---|
| MODULEENTRY | TOOLHELP.H Structure |
| ModuleFindHandle | TOOLHELP.DLL Function |
| ModuleFindName | TOOLHELP.DLL Function |
| ModuleNext | TOOLHELP.DLL Function |

## Example

Write an application that walks through the list of currently loaded modules and print the associated information on each entry in the list:

**toolhelp\modlist\test.c**

```c
#include <windows.h>
#include <toolhelp.h>
#include <stdio.h>

void PrintModuleInfo(MODULEENTRY *ModuleEntry)
{
  printf(" szModule: %s\n", ModuleEntry->szModule);
  printf("  hModule: %04x\n", ModuleEntry->hModule);
  printf("  wcUsage: %d\n", ModuleEntry->wcUsage);
  printf(" szExePath: %s\n\n", ModuleEntry->szExePath);
}

void main(void)
{
  MODULEENTRY ModuleEntry;
  BOOL Status;

  /* Initialize the MODULEENTRY structure */
  ModuleEntry.dwSize = sizeof(MODULEENTRY);

  /* Fill the MODULEENTRY structure with information on the
     first module in the list */
  Status = ModuleFirst(&ModuleEntry);
  while(Status != FALSE)
  {
    PrintModuleInfo(&ModuleEntry);
    Status = ModuleNext(&ModuleEntry);
  }
  printf("End of module list\n");
}
```

Figure 7-30 shows the output for the above application.

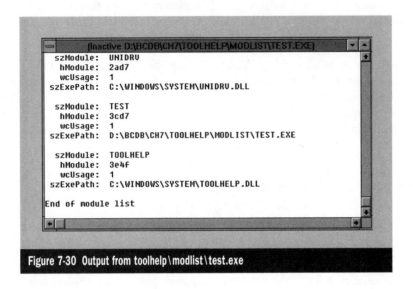

Figure 7-30 Output from toolhelp\modlist\test.exe

# ModuleNext                                         TOOLHELP.DLL Function

## Purpose
You use the ModuleNext() function to fill a MODULEENTRY structure with information on the next module in the list of currently loaded modules maintained by Windows.

## Syntax
```
BOOL WINAPI ModuleNext(MODULEENTRY FAR* lpModule);
```

MODULEENTRY FAR* *lpModule*
    Far pointer to a MODULEENTRY structure. Note that the structure must have been initialized by a prior call to ModuleNext(), ModuleFirst(), ModuleFindHandle(), or ModuleFindName() function.

## Returns
Returns a nonzero value if the function is successful. Returns a zero if the function fails, such as when the MODULEENTRY structure has not been initialized or there are no more entries in the list of currently loaded modules.

## Description
Windows maintains a list of all currently loaded modules. To walk through this list you'd normally use the ModuleFirst() function to fill a MODULEENTRY structure with information on the first module in this list. You'd then use the ModuleNext() function to fill the same structure with information on subsequent modules in the list.

Note that you can also use the ModuleNext() function when the MODULEENTRY structure has been initialized by the ModuleFindHandle() or ModuleFindName() function.

This is useful when you want to determine the modules loaded by Windows after a given module.

See the ModuleFindHandle() function for a description on the differences between a task and a module.

### See Also
| | |
|---|---|
| MODULEENTRY | TOOLHELP.H Structure |
| ModuleFindHandle | TOOLHELP.DLL Function |
| ModuleFindName | TOOLHELP.DLL Function |
| ModuleFirst | TOOLHELP.DLL Function |

### Example
See the example for the ModuleFirst() function.

# SYSHEAPINFO                                      TOOLHELP.H Structure

### Purpose
You use the SYSHEAPINFO structure with the SystemHeapInfo() function to retrieve information on the GDI and User memory heaps.

### Definition
```
typedef struct tagSYSHEAPINFO
{
    DWORD dwSize;
    WORD wUserFreePercent;
    WORD wGDIFreePercent;
    HGLOBAL hUserSegment;
    HGLOBAL hGDISegment;
} SYSHEAPINFO;
```

DWORD *dwSize*
    Size of the SYSHEAPINFO structure in bytes. You must initialize this value prior to calling the SystemHeapInfo() function.

WORD *wUserFreePercent*
    Percentage of free memory space in the User memory heap.

WORD *wGDIFreePercent*
    Percentage of free memory space in the GDI memory heap.

HGLOBAL *hUserSegment*
    Global memory handle for the User data segment. Note that you can use this value with the LocalFirst() and LocalNext() functions to walk through the User heap.

HGLOBAL *hGDISegment*
    Global memory handle for the GDI data segment. Note that you can use this value with the LocalFirst() and LocalNext() functions to walk through the GDI heap.

## See Also

| | |
|---|---|
| AllocGDIMem | STRESS.DLL Function |
| AllocUserMem | STRESS.DLL Function |
| SystemHeapInfo | TOOLHELP.DLL Function |

# SystemHeapInfo                                                 TOOLHELP.DLL Function

## Purpose
You use the SystemHeapInfo() function to fill a SYSHEAPINFO structure with information on the GDI and User memory heaps.

## Syntax
`BOOL WINAPI SystemHeapInfo(SYSHEAPINFO FAR* lpSysHeap);`

SYSHEAPINFO FAR* *lpSysHeap*
    Far pointer to a SYSHEAPINFO structure. Note that you must initialize the *dwSize* member of the structure with the size of the SYSHEAPINFO structure prior to calling the SystemHeapInfo() function.

## Returns
Returns a nonzero value if successful. Returns zero if the function fails, such as when the *dwSize* member of the SYSHEAPINFO structure is not initialized.

## Description
Many Windows API functions use memory in the GDI and User memory heaps. For example, when you create a palette or bitmap, you use memory in the GDI heap. When you create a window or register a window class, you use memory in the User heap. The GDI and User heaps are a limited Windows resource. It is possible that the memory in these heaps will run out which will cause a call to a function to fail.

The SystemHeapInfo() function fills a SYSHEAPINFO structure with the amount of free space in the User and GDI heaps. You can use this information when debugging an application to determine the cause of a function failure. For example, if one of the Windows API functions is failing in your application, you could call the SystemHeapInfo() function to see how much free memory is actually available at the time of the function failure.

The SystemHeapInfo() function also provides you with the data segment handles for the GDI and User modules. You can use these handles to walk through the respective local memory heaps.

Use the MemManInfo() function to retrieve information on the global memory heap.

## See Also

| | |
|---|---|
| AllocGDIMem | STRESS.DLL Function |
| AllocUserMem | STRESS.DLL Function |
| MemManInfo | TOOLHELP.DLL Function |
| SYSHEAPINFO | TOOLHELP.H Structure |

## Example

Write an application that prints the information returned by the SystemHeapInfo() function:

**toolhelp\sysinfo\test.c**

```
#include <windows.h>
#include <toolhelp.h>
#include <stdio.h>

void main(void)
{
  SYSHEAPINFO SysInfo;

  /* Initialize the SYSHEAPINFO structure */
  SysInfo.dwSize = sizeof(SYSHEAPINFO);

  /* Fill the SYSHEAPINFO structure */
  SystemHeapInfo(&SysInfo);

  /* Print the information in the SYSHEAPINFO structure */
  printf("System heap information\n");
  printf(" wUserFreePercent: %u%%\n", SysInfo.wUserFreePercent);
  printf(" wGDIFreePercent: %u%%\n", SysInfo.wGDIFreePercent);
  printf("    hUserSegment: %04x\n", SysInfo.hUserSegment);
  printf("    hGIDSegment: %04x\n", SysInfo.hGDISegment);
}
```

Figure 7-31 shows the output for the above application.

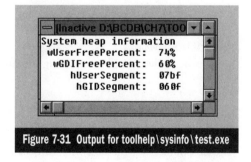

**Figure 7-31** Output for toolhelp\sysinfo\test.exe

# TASKENTRY
**TOOLHELP.H Structure**

## Purpose

You use the TASKENTRY structure with the TaskFindHandle(), TaskFirst(), and TaskNext() functions to retrieve information on a task. This information includes the task's parent, instance handle, top and bottom of the stack, stack segment and stack pointer, module handle of the currently executing function, and the number of pending events.

## Definition

```
typedef struct tagTASKENTRY
```

```
{
    DWORD dwSize;
    HTASK hTask;
    HTASK hTaskParent;
    HINSTANCE hInst;
    HMODULE hModule;
    WORD wSS;
    WORD wSP;
    WORD wStackTop;
    WORD wStackMinimum;
    WORD wStackBottom;
    WORD wcEvents;
    HGLOBAL hQueue;
    char szModule[MAX_MODULE_NAME + 1];
    WORD wPSPOffset;
    HANDLE hNext;
} TASKENTRY;
```

DWORD *dwSize*

Size of the TASKENTRY handle in bytes. You must initialize this value before calling the TaskFindHandle() or TaskFirst() function.

HTASK *hTask*

Handle to the task.

HTASK *hTaskParent*

Handle to the parent task.

HINSTANCE *hInst*

Handle the data segment for the task.

HMODULE *hModule*

Handle to the module containing the function currently being executed.

WORD *wSS*

Stack segment for the task when it became inactive.

WORD *wSP*

Stack pointer for the task when it became inactive.

WORD *wStackTop*

Offset to the top of the stack area (lowest possible stack pointer value).

WORD *wStackMinimum*

The lowest stack segment number during task execution.

WORD *wStackBottom*

Offset to the bottom of the stack (highest possible stack pointer value).

WORD *wcEvents*

Number of pending events.

HGLOBAL *hQueue*

Handle to the global memory object containing the task queue.

char *szModule*

A NULL terminated character array containing the name of the module containing the currently executing function.

WORD *wPSPOffset*

Offset from the program segment prefix (PSP) to the beginning of the executable portion of the code segment.

HANDLE *hNext*

Handle to the next task in the task list. The TaskNext() function uses this value to file the TASKENTRY structure with information on the next task in the task list maintained by Windows.

### See Also

| | |
|---|---|
| TaskFindHandle | TOOLHELP.DLL Function |
| TaskFirst | TOOLHELP.DLL Function |
| TaskNext | TOOLHELP.DLL Function |

# TaskFindHandle                                      TOOLHELP.DLL Function

### Purpose

You use the TaskFindHandle() function to retrieve information on a given task, such as task's parent, instance handle, top and bottom of the stack, stack segment and stack pointer, module handle of the currently executing function, and the number of pending events.

### Syntax

```
BOOL WINAPI TaskFindHandle(TASKENTRY FAR* lpTask, HTASK hTask);
```

TASKENTRY FAR* *lpTask*

Far pointer to a TASKENTRY structure. The TaskFindHandle() function will fill this structure with information on the task associated with the *hTask* parameters. You must initialize the *dwSize* member of this structure with the size of the TASKENTRY structure before calling the TaskFindHandle() function.

HTASK *hTask*

The handle to a task.

### Returns

Returns a nonzero value if successful. Returns zero if the function fails, such as when the *hTask* parameter is invalid or the *dwSize* parameter of the TASKENTRY structure is not initialized.

## Description

A task in Windows 3.1 on down is an application instance. Note that a task is not the same as a module. Modules are the executable files loaded by Windows such as applications, drivers, and dynamic link libraries. A module is typically shared by different tasks whereas a task is unique to each instance of an application. For example, if a user runs five instances of CLOCK.EXE, Windows creates five tasks—one for each application instance. However, Windows will only load one CLOCK module. This module will be assigned five lock counts. Windows will also create a unique task for each execution of the module. This means there would be five tasks sharing one CLOCK module. Another way of looking at the task/module relationship is that a module contains the code for an application, whereas each task contains a unique data set for each application instance. Keep in mind that a given task may have more than one module. For example, if an application uses one or more dynamic link libraries, the application itself is one module and each dynamic link library is another module.

You use the TaskFindHandle() function to fill a TASKENTRY structure with information on a given task. See the preceding TASKENTRY structure reference for a detailed explanation of this information.

## See Also

| | |
|---|---|
| TASKENTRY | TOOLHELP.H Structure |
| TaskFirst | TOOLHELP.DLL Function |
| TaskNext | TOOLHELP.DLL Function |

## Example

Write an application that prints information on its own task:

**toolhelp\taskent\test.c**

```c
#include <windows.h>
#include <toolhelp.h>
#include <stdio.h>

void PrintTaskEntryInfo(TASKENTRY *TaskEntry)
{
  TASKENTRY ParentTask;

  printf("     szModule: %s\n", TaskEntry->szModule);
  printf("  Parent Task: ");
  if(TaskEntry->hTaskParent != NULL)
  {
    /* Load the Parent Task information */
    ParentTask.dwSize = sizeof(TASKENTRY);
    TaskFindHandle(&ParentTask, TaskEntry->hTaskParent);
    printf("%s\n", ParentTask.szModule);
  }
  else
    printf("<none>\n");
```

```
    printf("      hTask: %04x\n", TaskEntry->hTask);
    printf("      hInst: %04x\n", TaskEntry->hInst);
    printf("    hModule: %04x\n", TaskEntry->hModule);
    printf("        wSS: %04x\n", TaskEntry->wSS);
    printf("        wSP: %04x\n", TaskEntry->wSP);
    printf("   wStackTop: %04x\n", TaskEntry->wStackTop);
    printf(" wStackMinimum: %04x\n", TaskEntry->wStackMinimum);
    printf(" wStackBottom: %04x\n", TaskEntry->wStackBottom);
    printf("    wcEvents: %d\n",  TaskEntry->wcEvents);
    printf("     hQueue: %04x\n", TaskEntry->hQueue);
    printf("  wPSPOffset: %04x\n", TaskEntry->wPSPOffset);
}

void main(void)
{
  TASKENTRY TaskEntry;

  /* Initialize TASKENTRY structure */
  TaskEntry.dwSize = sizeof(TASKENTRY);

  /* Fill the TASKENTRY structure with information on the
     current task */
  TaskFindHandle(&TaskEntry, GetCurrentTask());

  /* Print the information in the TASKENTRY structure */
  PrintTaskEntryInfo(&TaskEntry);
}
```

Figure 7-32 shows the output for the above application.

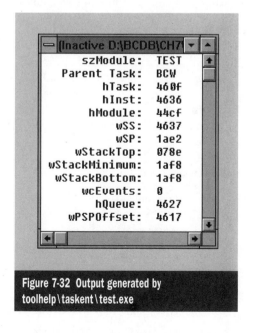

**Figure 7-32 Output generated by toolhelp\taskent\test.exe**

# TaskFirst

**TOOLHELP.DLL Function**

## Purpose
You use the TaskFirst() function to fill a TASKENTRY structure with the first task on the task list. You'd normally use this function with the TaskNext() function to walk through the Windows task list.

## Syntax
```
BOOL WINAPI TaskFirst(TASKENTRY FAR* lpTask);
```

TASKENTRY FAR* *lpTask*

Far pointer to a TASKENTRY structure. The TaskFirst() function will fill this structure with information on the first task in the task list. You must initialize the *dwSize* member of this structure with the size of the TASKENTRY structure before calling the TaskFirst() function.

## Returns
Returns a nonzero value if successful. Returns a zero if the function fails, such as when the *dwSize* member of the TASKENTRY structure is not initialized.

## Description
Windows maintains a list of all currently executing tasks. You use the TaskFirst() function to fill a TASKENTRY structure with information on this task. You can then call the TaskNext() function to fill the same structure with information on the next task in the list.

## See Also
| | |
|---|---|
| TASKENTRY | TOOLHELP.H Structure |
| TaskFindHandle | TOOLHELP.DLL Function |
| TaskNext | TOOLHELP.DLL Function |

## Example
Write an application that walks through the Windows task list. Print the module name and parent task for each entry:

**toolhelp\tasklist\test.c**
```c
#include <windows.h>
#include <toolhelp.h>
#include <stdio.h>

void main(void)
{
  TASKENTRY TaskEntry;
  BOOL Status;
  WORD n;

  /* Initialize the TASKENTRY structure */
  TaskEntry.dwSize = sizeof(TASKENTRY);

  /* Load TaskEntry with information on the first task in the
```

```
      task list */
   Status = TaskFirst(&TaskEntry);

   /* Walk through the task list */
   for(n = 1; Status != FALSE; n++)
   {
     printf("#%d:  Module - %-10s Parent - ", n, TaskEntry.szModule);
     if(TaskEntry.hTaskParent != NULL)
     {
       TASKENTRY ParentTask;

       ParentTask.dwSize = sizeof(TASKENTRY);
       TaskFindHandle(&ParentTask, TaskEntry.hTaskParent);
       printf("%s\n", ParentTask.szModule);
     }
     else
       printf("<none>\n");
     Status = TaskNext(&TaskEntry);
   }
   printf("End of task list\n");
}
```

Figure 7-33 shows the output for the above application.

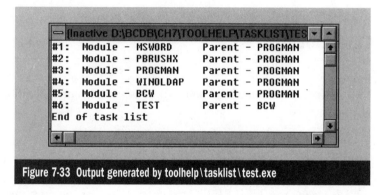

**Figure 7-33 Output generated by toolhelp\tasklist\test.exe**

# TaskNext                                      TOOLHELP.DLL Function

### Purpose
You use the TaskNext() function to fill a TASKENTRY structure with the next task in the task list. You can only use this function following a previous call to TaskFirst(), TaskNext(), or TaskFindHandle() function.

### Syntax
`BOOL WINAPI TaskNext(TASKENTRY FAR* lpTask);`

TASKENTRY FAR* *lpTask*

Far pointer to a TASKENTRY structure. The TaskNext() function will fill this structure with information on the next task in the task list. You must initialize the TASKENTRY structure with a call to either TaskFirst(), TaskFindHandle(), or a previous call to TaskNext() before calling the TaskNext() function.

### Returns

Returns a nonzero value if successful. Returns zero if the function fails, such as when the TASKENTRY structure has not been initialized by a previous call to a TaskFirst(), TaskNext(), or TaskFindHandle() function.

### Description

Windows maintains a list of all currently executing tasks. You use the TaskNext() function to fill a TASKENTRY structure with information on the next task in the list. The TaskNext() function uses the information in the *wNext* member of the TASKENTRY structure to determine the next task in the list.

### See Also

| | |
|---|---|
| TASKENTRY | TOOLHELP.H Structure |
| TaskFindHandle | TOOLHELP.DLL Function |
| TaskFirst | TOOLHELP.DLL Function |

### Example

See the example for the TaskFirst() function.

## TimerCount                                          TOOLHELP.DLL Function

### Purpose

You use the TimerCount() function to time aspects of your application to an accuracy of 1 millisecond.

### Syntax

```
BOOL WINAPI TimerCount(TIMERINFO FAR* lpTimer);
```

TIMERINFO FAR* *lpTimer*

Far pointer to a TIMERINFO structure. Note that you must initialize the *dwSize* member of this structure with the size of the TIMERINFO structure before calling the TimerCount() function.

### Returns

Returns a nonzero value if successful. Returns zero if the function fails, such as when the *dwSize* member of TIMERINFO is not initialized to the size of the TIMERINFO structure.

### Description

The regular timer function in Windows, GetTickCount(), will return the time since Windows started in milliseconds. However, the function uses the DOS timer which is updated 18.2 times a second. This means the timer value returned by GetTickCount only has an effective accuracy of 55 milliseconds.

The TimerCount() function, on the other hand, uses an algorithm which examines the hardware timer to estimate the time between clock ticks. This allows the function to fill the TIMERINFO structure with values to within 1 millisecond.

**See Also**

TIMERINFO     TOOLHELP.H Structure

**Example**

Write an application that prints the seconds since Windows started using the TimerCount() function:

**toolhelp\timer\test.c**

```c
#include <windows.h>
#include <toolhelp.h>
#include <stdio.h>

void PrintTimerInfo(TIMERINFO *TimerInfo)
{
  printf("dwmsSinceStart: %.03f Seconds\n",
    (double)TimerInfo->dwmsSinceStart / 1000);
  printf("   dwmsThisVM: %.03f Seconds\n",
    (double)TimerInfo->dwmsThisVM / 1000);
}

void main(void)
{
  TIMERINFO TimerInfo;

  /* Initialize the TIMERINFO structure */
  TimerInfo.dwSize = sizeof(TIMERINFO);

  /* Fill the TIMERINFO structure */
  TimerCount(&TimerInfo);

  /* Print the information in the TIMERINFO structure */
  PrintTimerInfo(&TimerInfo);
}
```

Figure 7-34 shows the output for the above application.

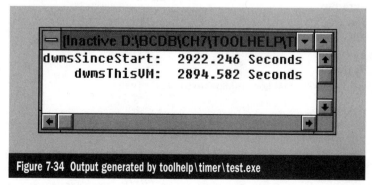

**Figure 7-34 Output generated by toolhelp\timer\test.exe**

# TIMERINFO

## Purpose

You use the TIMERINFO structure with the TimerCount() function to retrieve a timer count accurate to within 1 millisecond.

## Definition

```
typedef struct tagTIMERINFO
{
    DWORD dwSize;
    DWORD dwmsSinceStart;
    DWORD dwmsThisVM;
} TIMERINFO;
```

DWORD *dwSize*

Size of the TIMERINFO structure in bytes. You must initialize this value before calling the TimerCount() function.

DWORD *dwmsSinceStart*

Number of milliseconds since the start of Windows.

DWORD *dwmsThisVM*

Number of milliseconds since the start of Windows on the Virtual Machine. Note that this value is the same as *dwmsSinceStart* when Windows is operating in the standard mode.

## See Also

TimerCount      TOOLHELP.DLL Function

# UnAllocDiskSpace

## Purpose

You call the UnAllocDiskSpace() to delete the STRESS.EAT file created by the AllocDiskSpace() function.

## Syntax

```
void WINAPI UnAllocDiskSpace(UINT uDrive);
```

UINT *uDrive*

Designates a disk drive. The *uDrive* parameter should be one of the following values:

| | |
|---|---|
| EDS_CUR | *Allocates space on the current drive.* |
| EDS_TEMP | *Allocates space on the drive specified by the TEMP variable or the Windows system drive if no TEMP variable is defined.* |
| EDS_WIN | *Allocates space on the Windows system drive.* |

### Returns
void

### Description
The UnAllocDiskSpace() provides a convenient method for removing the STRESS.EAT file created by the AllocDiskSpace() function. Note that you do not have to call this function if you only wish to make another call to AllocDiskSpace(). The AllocDiskSpace() function will automatically delete the STRESS.EAT file before creating a new one.

### See Also
FreeAllGDIMem        STRESS.DLL Function
FreeAllUserMem       STRESS.DLL Function
UnAllocFileHandles   STRESS.DLL Function

### Example
See the example for the AllocDiskSpace() function.

# UnAllocFileHandles                          STRESS.DLL Function

### Purpose
You call the UnAllocFileHandles() function to release the file handles reserved by the AllocFileHandles() function.

### Syntax
```
void WINAPI UnAllocFileHandles(void);
```

### Returns
void

### Description
The UnAllocFileHandles() provides a convenient method for freeing the file handles reserved by the AllocFileHandles() function. Note that you do not have to call this function if you only wish to make another call to AllocFileHandles(). The AllocFileHandles() function will automatically release all the file handles reserved in a previous call to AllocFileHandles() before reserving new ones.

### See Also
AllocFileHandles     STRESS.DLL Function
FreeAllGDIMem        STRESS.DLL Function
FreeAllUserMem       STRESS.DLL Function
GetFreeFileHandles   STRESS.DLL Function
UnAllocDiskSpace     STRESS.DLL Function

### Example
See the example for the AllocFileHandles() function.

# HELP
# COMPILER
# REFERENCE

# 8

The BC++ 3.0 compiler package is distributed with Microsoft's Help Compiler version 3.0. BC++ Version 3.1 ships with a later version of the help compiler for Windows 3.1. The first portion of this chapter covers the features common in both versions of the Help Compiler. The second portion covers the features unique to Version 3.1. The last part of the chapter is a reference section covering both versions and the Rich Text Format (RTF).

You use the Help Compiler utilities to create Windows help (.HLP) files that are used by the WINHELP.EXE application supplied to all Windows users. WINHELP loads the .HLP file and displays the various topics within the .HLP file as requested by either the user or by your application. For example, when you call up the [Help][Index] option in Turbo C++ for Windows (TCW), TCW executes your WINHELP, which in turn loads the TCWHELP.HLP file. Once the WINHELP application executes, it will load the TCWHELP.HLP and display the index as shown in Figure 8-1.

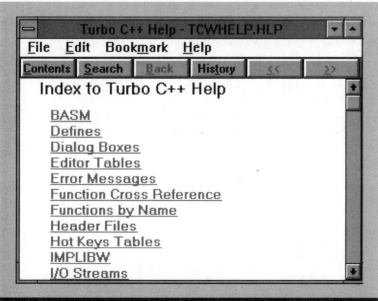

**Figure 8-1 The WINHELP.EXE displaying the TCWHELP.HLP Index**

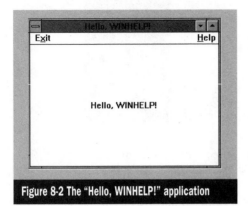

**Figure 8-2 The "Hello, WINHELP!" application**

You can also manually execute WINHELP and have it display the index for the TCW help system from the Program Manager. This is done by entering the following from the Program Manager's [Files][Run] menu item:

```
winhelp tcwhelp
```

# EXECUTING WINHELP FROM AN APPLICATION

You can also execute the WINHELP application from your application and load it with a specific help file by calling the WinHelp() function. As shown in the following "Hello, WINHELP!" application, you do not necessarily need to know anything about the .HLP file to call up its main index. Figure 8-2 shows the main window displayed by the application.

**examp1\hello.h**

```
#include <windows.h>

/* Define the menu item macros */
#define IDM_ABOUT      1000
#define IDM_EXIT       2000
#define ID_OK          3000
#define IDM_HTCW       4000
```

**examp1\hello.c**

```
#include "hello.h"

char AppTitle[] = "Hello, WINHELP!";
HANDLE hThisInstance;

/* We know not all the variables are used, so we may as well disable
   the warning message. */
#pragma warn -par

/* Define the application window's message processing function */
long FAR PASCAL WndProc(HWND hWnd, unsigned msg, WORD wParam,
                        LONG lParam)
{
  RECT rect;
  PAINTSTRUCT ps;
  HDC hDC;

  switch(msg)
  {
    /* Is it a menu command? */
    case WM_COMMAND:
        switch(wParam)
        {
        case IDM_EXIT:
```

```
                    /* Leave the application by destroying the main
                       window */
                    DestroyWindow(hWnd);
                    break;

              case IDM_HTCW:
                    WinHelp(hWnd, "tcwhelp.hlp", HELP_INDEX, wParam);
                    break;
              }
              break;

        /* Paint the window */
        case WM_PAINT:
              hDC = BeginPaint(hWnd, &ps);

              /* Display the application title in the center of
                 the window */
              GetClientRect(hWnd, &rect);
              DrawText(hDC, AppTitle, sizeof(AppTitle) - 1, &rect,
                  DT_SINGLELINE | DT_VCENTER | DT_CENTER);

              EndPaint(hWnd, &ps);
              break;

        /* Time to quit! */
        case WM_DESTROY:
              /* Let the WINHELP application know we're exiting */
              WinHelp(hWnd, NULL, HELP_QUIT, NULL);

              PostQuitMessage(0);
              break;

        /* All other messages go here. */
        default:
              return(DefWindowProc(hWnd, msg, wParam, lParam));
        }
        return(0);
}

int PASCAL WinMain(HANDLE hInstance, HANDLE hPrevInstance,
                   LPSTR lpCmdLine, int nCmdShow)
{
   int xDim, yDim;
   HWND hWnd;
   MSG msg;

   /* Make the instance handle globally available */
   hThisInstance = hInstance;

   /* Register the application window class */
   if(!hPrevInstance)
   {
       WNDCLASS wc;

       wc.style            = CS_HREDRAW | CS_VREDRAW;
       wc.lpfnWndProc      = WndProc;
       wc.cbClsExtra       = 0;
       wc.cbWndExtra       = 0;
       wc.hInstance        = hInstance;
       wc.hIcon            = LoadIcon(NULL, IDI_HAND);
```

```
        wc.hCursor         = LoadCursor(NULL, IDC_ARROW);
        wc.hbrBackground   = GetStockObject(WHITE_BRUSH);
        wc.lpszMenuName    = "MainMenu";
        wc.lpszClassName   = AppTitle;

        if(!RegisterClass(&wc))
            return(FALSE);
    }

    /* Get the screen dimensions */
    xDim = GetSystemMetrics(SM_CXSCREEN);
    yDim = GetSystemMetrics(SM_CYSCREEN);

    hWnd = CreateWindow(AppTitle, AppTitle, WS_OVERLAPPEDWINDOW,
        xDim / 4, yDim / 4, xDim / 2, yDim / 2,
        NULL, NULL, hInstance, NULL);

    if(hWnd == NULL)
        return(FALSE);

    /* Display the window */
    ShowWindow(hWnd, nCmdShow);

    /* Enter the message loop */
    while(GetMessage(&msg, 0, 0, 0))
    {
        TranslateMessage(&msg);
        DispatchMessage(&msg);
    }

    /* Exit the application */
    return(0);
}
```

**examp1\hello.rc**

```
    #include "hello.h"

    MainMenu MENU
    {
      MENUITEM "E&xit",   IDM_EXIT
      POPUP "\a&Help"
      {
        MENUITEM "&Help on TCW",   IDM_HTCW
      }
    }
```

The application executes the WinHelp() function whenever the [Help][Help on TCW] menu item is selected. The WinHelp() function actually executes the WINHELP application in the same way we did earlier from the Program Manager. WINHELP then displays the same index shown in Figure 8-1. The application calls WinHelp() elsewhere in the application when the window is destroyed, this time informing WINHELP that we no longer need the TCWHELP.HLP file.

The WinHelp() function can also be used to display specific topics in a .HLP file, a list of topic titles that match a keyword or list of multiple keywords. Unlike using WinHelp() to display the main index for a .HLP file, these usages of the WinHelp() function require a

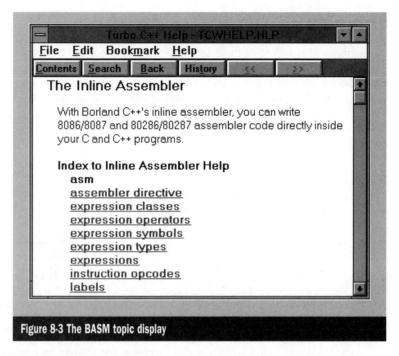

**Figure 8-3 The BASM topic display**

knowledge of the internal structure of the .HLP file, which, of course, you'll have when you are the one who wrote and compiled the .HLP file using the HC utility!

## HELP TOPICS

Help (.HLP) files are organized into individual 'topics', and within these topics you place *hyperlinks* to other topics. The main index shown in Figure 8-1 is a topic that contains links to other topics in the .HLP file. For example, Figure 8-3 shows the topic for the BASM topic, which contains another index of hyperlinked topics.

## THE HELP PROJECT FILE

The Help Compiler uses Help Project (.HPJ) files to create a .HLP file. The .HPJ file is a text file that defines how to build the help file. The .HPJ file can contain any of six different sections: Files, Options, BuildTags, Alias, Map, and Bitmaps. The only one of these sections that is required in all .HPJ files is the [Files] section. This section lists the files containing the topics. For example, the following .HPJ file tells HC to compile the TOPICS.RTF topic file:

**examp2\example.hpj**
```
    [Files]
       topics.rtf
```

See the "Help Project Reference" for details on the six .HPJ sections.

573

# TOPIC FILES AND THE RTF FORMAT

Topic files are the files in your project that contain the topics for your compiled .HLP
file with page breaks between the different topics. The Help Compiler expects each topic
file to be a Rich Text Format (.RTF) file. This is a word processing format composed
entirely of text. Instead of the normal control characters, an .RTF file contains control
words that are preceded by a '\' character. The formatting and font controls are enclosed
within text groupings consisting of the '{' and '}' characters. The following is an example
.RTF file:

**examp2\topics.rtf**

```
{\rtf1\ansi {\fonttbl{\f0\fswiss Helv;}}\f0 \fs20 {
This is an example topic file. All topic files must be saved as RTF
(Rich Text Format) files. \par
\par
Each paragraph in a .RTF file ends with a '\\par' control word.
Designating paragraphs enables the WINHELP.EXE application to
reformat the text in the topic whenever the user changes the size
of the help window. Other control words, such as \\f0 which calls
for font number zero and \\fs20, which calls for a font size of 10
points (20 half points), are always preceded by the '\\' symbol. The
'\{' and '\}' symbols designate text groupings. Some formatting
control words are visible only within the scope of a group. For
example, to temporarily change the font size to a 12 point font, you
start a new group with the '\{' symbol and change the font: \par
\par { \fs28\qc
Fourteen Point Helv \par
}
\par\ql
The \\fs28 control word calls for a font size of 28 half points, i.e.,
a 14 point font size. The \\qc control word calls for centering the
"Fourteen Point Helv" paragraph. The formatting returns to its
previous 10-point font size after the terminating '\}' symbol.\par}
}
```

The entire RTF file is enclosed within an RTF signature grouping, {\rtf1...}, where
the \rtf1 designates an RTF file that adheres to the Version 1 standard. The '}' on the last
line designates the end of the RTF file. The rest of the first line in the text defines the
characteristics of the file as a series of control words. The \ansi control word designates
the ANSI character set. The {\fonttbl ...} text grouping encloses a font table definition.
The {\f0\fswiss Helv;} designates font number zero as the Helv font in the Swiss family
of fonts. The last part of the first line opens the text grouping for the topic with \f0 calling for font number zero as the displayed font and \fs20 calling for a font size of 20 half
points, i.e., a font size of 10 points. The "Rich Text Format Reference" section at the
end of this chapter lists the different control words that can be used in your RTF file.
The line breaks in an RTF file are not significant.

Note that some of the .RTF examples used later in this chapter display some of the
text in bold. This is so that you, as the reader, can pick out aspects of the .RTF file under

discussion. All .RTF files are stored as DOS text files, which, of course, do not support boldfaced text.

A few word processors, such as Word for Windows and Microsoft Word 5.0, allow you to save your documents in the Rich Text Format. This is very convenient, as it allows you to write your topic files as normal documents and view them as they will appear in WINHELP. For example, the above .RTF file would display in Word for Windows as follows:

> This is an example topic file. All topic files must be saved as RTF (Rich Text Format) files.

> Each paragraph in a .RTF file ends with a '\par' control word. Designating paragraphs enables the WINHELP.EXE application to reformat the text in the topic whenever the user changes the size of the help window. Other control words, such as \f0, which calls for font number zero and \fs20, which calls for a font size of 10 point (20 half points), are always preceded by the '\' symbol. The '{' and '}' symbols designate text groupings. Some formatting control words are visible only within the scope of a group. For example, to temporarily change the font size to a 12-point font, you start a new group with the '{' symbol and change the font:

> ### Fourteen Point Helv

> The \fs28 control word calls for a font size of 28 half points, i.e., a 14 -point font size. The \qc control word calls for centering the "Fourteen Point Helv" paragraph. The formatting returns to its previous 10-point font size after the terminating '}' symbol.

## COMPILING THE HELP PROJECT

The following is the syntax for the Help Compiler:

```
hc filename[.HPJ]
```

The Help Compiler will read the project file listed on the command line and create a .HLP file with the same base name. For example, to compile the EXAMPLE.HPJ project file, you enter the following:

```
hc example
```

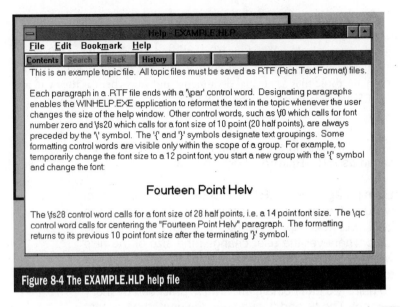

**Figure 8-4 The EXAMPLE.HLP help file**

This will create a file called EXAMPLE.HLP, which displays in the WINHELP application as shown in Figure 8-4.

## CONTEXT STRINGS

Individual topics are internally referenced by the Help Compiler through a unique context string assigned by you at the beginning of each topic. A context string enables you to reference the topic so as to create links that allow the user to jump between topics, such as with the main index for TCW help, or display a lookup box containing a phrase definition or other short topic. A context string also enables you to call for the display of a specific topic from your application using the WinHelp() function. This can be used to provide "context sensitive" help to your applications.

Context strings are assigned by placing a footnote at the very beginning of the topic using the '#' character as the footnote reference. The context string itself is placed in the text for the footnote. Footnotes are inserted in Word for Windows using the [Insert][Footnote] menu item. For example, in Word for Windows, a topic file with a context string of "ExampleTopic" would look as follows:

#This is an example topic with a context string. The context string enables you to place jumps in your help file to related topics. These jumps are known as a hyperlink.

---

#ExampleTopic

The above appears as follows in an RTF format:

**examp3\topics.rtf**

```
{\rtf1\ansi {\fonttbl{\f0\fswiss Helv;}}\f0 \fs20 {
#{\footnote ExampleTopic}
This is an example topic with a context string. The context string
enables you to place jumps in your help file to related topics.
These jumps are known as a hyperlink.\par}
}
```

The footnote is on the second line of the above RTF text. Immediately following the '#' character is the footnote text grouping using the \footnote control word. The footnote text is enclosed within a text grouping so as to distinguish it from the normal text.

Note that the case of context strings is not significant. The Help Compiler will treat "ExampleTopic" the same as it would "EXAMPLETOPIC." Also, a context string may not contain any spaces and is limited to 255 characters.

# HYPERLINKS

You place a hyperlink in your help files to allow the user to jump to related topics. The hyperlink text will appear in green with a color system and display the hand-pointer cursor when the mouse is placed over the text. When the user clicks on the hyperlink, the WINHELP application automatically displays the associated topic.

You designate hyperlink text by double-underlining the text. The hyperlink text is then immediately followed by the context string as hidden text. In Word for Windows, the double underline is toggled on and off using the (Ctrl)-(D) key. Hidden text is toggled using the (Ctrl)-(H) key. The hidden text is viewed by selecting the [View][Preferences][Hidden Text] menu item. For example, the following two topics

#This is an example topic with a context string. The context string enables you to place jumps in your help file to related topics. These jumps are known as a hyperlinkHyperLink.

#There is a hyperlink to this topic from the topic with the ExampleTopicExampleTopic context string.

#ExampleTopic
#HyperLink

One of the disadvantages to using a word processor such as Word for Windows is that the footnotes for the context strings, and, as you'll see later, the keywords, titles, and browse sequence, become separated from the actual topic. It can get very confusing associating these items with the topic text when the topic file contains more than three or four topics. If you write your topic files directly as RTF text files, the placement of the footnotes immediately before the topic tends to make the text more readable. Another advantage is you can edit your RTF file from your text editor as you make changes to your application. The above Word for Windows text can be written as the following RTF text:

**examp4\topics.rtf**

```
{\rtf1\ansi {\fonttbl{\f0\fswiss Helv;}}\f0 \fs20 {

#{\footnote ExampleTopic}
This is an example topic with a context string. The context string
enables you to place jumps in your help file to related topics.
A jump to another topic is known as a {\uldb hyperlink}
{\v HyperLink}.\par

\page
#{\footnote HyperLink}
There is a hyperlink to this topic from the topic with the
{\uldb ExampleTopic}{\v ExampleTopic} context string.\par}
}
```

The \uldb control word designates a double-underline. The \v control word is used to designate hidden text. Again, both the double-underlined text and the hidden text are enclosed with text groupings so as to prevent character attributes from affecting the remaining topic text. Note that the \page control word designates the page break that separates the two topics.

The previous EXAMPLE.HPJ help project file can be used to compile the above TOPICS.RTF file. Figure 8-5 shows how the resulting help file displays the two topics in the WINHELP application.

A hyperlink can also be defined as a popup box. This is very useful when you only need to explain a term rather than open a window for an entirely new topic. A hyperlink to a

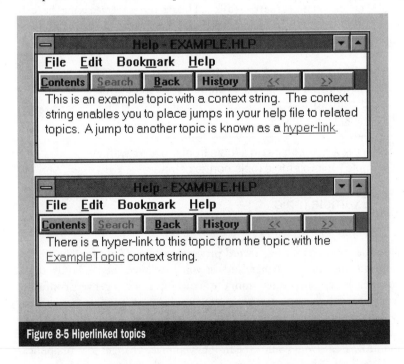

**Figure 8-5 Hiperlinked topics**

popup box is declared in the same way as with a normal topic hyperlink except that a single underline is used rather than a double underline. For example, the following RTF file adds a term definition for "context string":

**examp4\topics2.rtf**

```
{\rtf1\ansi {\fonttbl{\f0\fswiss Helv;}}\f0 \fs20 {

#{\footnote ExampleTopic}
This is an example topic with a context string. The
{\ul context string}{\v ContextString} enables you to place jumps in
your help file to related topics. A jump to another topic is known
as a {\uldb hyperlink}
{\v HyperLink}.\par

\page
#{\footnote HyperLink}
There is a hyperlink to this topic from the topic with the
{\uldb ExampleTopic}{\v ExampleTopic} context string.\par

\page
#{\footnote ContextString}
A context string is used by the Help Compiler as an internal
reference to a topic.}
}
```

In the above RTF file, the underlining of the term "context string" is done using the \ul control word instead of the \uldb control word. This is equivalent to the single underline in Word for Windows.

## THE MAIN INDEX

An index is a topic file that generally contains a list of hyperlinks. For example, the main index for the TCW help system shown in Figure 8-1 is nothing more than a topic file with a list of hyperlinks. You can instruct the Help Compiler to designate a specific topic file as the *main index*. The main index is the topic displayed by WINHELP when a help file is called up by the user, you execute the WinHelp() function with the HELP_INDEX keyword, or the user pushes the [Contents] or [Index] push-button in the help window. The Help Compiler assumes that the first topic in the first topic file is the main index. However, the main index can be placed anywhere in any of your topic files if you use the INDEX option in your project file. For example, consider the following RTF topic file:

**example5\topics.rtf**

```
{\rtf1\ansi {\fonttbl{\f0\fswiss Helv;}}\f0 \fs20 {

#{\footnote ExampleTopic}
This is an example topic with a context string. The context string
enables you to place jumps in your help file to related topics.
A jump to another topic is known as a {\uldb hyperlink}
{\v HyperLink}.\par
```

```
\page
#{\footnote HyperLink}
There is a hyperlink to this topic from the topic with the
{\uldb ExampleTopic}{\v ExampleTopic} context string.\par}

\page
#{\footnote MainIndex}
{\b\fs24 The Main Index}\par
\par
The following topics are available in this help file:\par
\par
    {\uldb Example Topic}{\v ExampleTopic}\par
    {\uldb HyperLink Topic}{\v HyperLink}\par
}
```

Note that the control word in the first line of text for the MainIndex topic, \b\fs24, displays the text "The Main Index" in bold 12 point.

Because the main index for this help file is not the first topic, then the .HPJ file needs to contain the INDEX option as follows:

**examp5\example.hpj**
```
[Files]
    topics.rtf

[Options]
    INDEX=MainIndex
```

Setting the INDEX option to "MainIndex" tells the Help Compiler that the MainIndex topic should be used as the help file's main index. Figure 8-6 shows the initial screen for the resulting help file.

Note that Version 3.1 of the Help Compiler uses the CONTENTS option rather than INDEX.

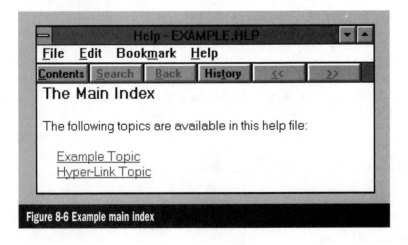

Figure 8-6 Example main index

## TOPIC TITLES

Where context strings are used as the Help Compiler's internal reference, a topic's title is displayed by WINHELP for the user as the topic's reference. For example, if you were to select a few topics in WINHELP using the previous help file and then select the WINHELP [History] push-button, WINHELP would display each topic previously viewed as an >> Untitled Topic << as shown in Figure 8-7. This is because we haven't assigned titles yet to our two example topics.

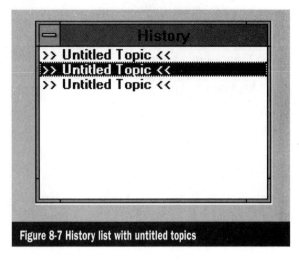

**Figure 8-7 History list with untitled topics**

You add a title to a topic in the same way you add a context string, except that the you use the '$' character instead of the '#' character. The following RTF file creates a help file, which will contain titles:

**example5\topics.rtf**

```
{\rtf1\ansi {\fonttbl{\f0\fswiss Helv;}}\f0 \fs20 {

#{\footnote ExampleTopic}
${\footnote An Example Topic}
This is an example topic with a context string. The context string
enables you to place jumps in your help file to related topics.
A jump to another topic is known as a {\uldb hyperlink}
{\v HyperLink}.\par

\page
#{\footnote HyperLink}
${\footnote A HyperLink Topic}
There is a hyperlink to this topic from the topic with the
{\uldb ExampleTopic}{\v ExampleTopic} context string.\par}

\page
#{\footnote MainIndex}
${\footnote The Main Index}
{\b\fs24 The Main Index}\par
\par
The following topics are available in this help file:\par
\par
    {\uldb Example Topic}{\v ExampleTopic}\par
    {\uldb HyperLink Topic}{\v HyperLink}\par
}
```

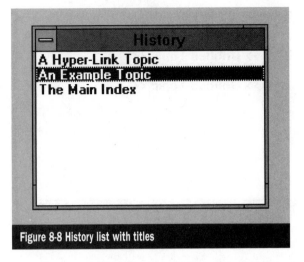

**Figure 8-8 History list with titles**

Figure 8-8 shows the history list generated when topics are assigned titles.

Note that the length of a title string cannot exceed 128 characters.

## CALLING INDIVIDUAL TOPICS FROM AN APPLICATION

Context strings are used by the Help Compiler to internally reference topics within a help project. Titles are assigned to topics to provide the user with a means of referencing a topic. To allow topics to be referenced by your application, each context string for the topics you want made accessible from your application must be mapped to a numerical value in the [Map] section of the project file. The *Borland languages Help Compiler* reference manual lists several methods for accomplishing this; however, the best method to use is to map the context strings as macro definitions that are readable by the BC++ compiler. For example, the following .HMP file maps the context strings for the topics in the previous example to three unique numerical values:

**examp6\example.hmp**

```
#define MainIndex     0x4000
#define ExampleTopic  0x4100
#define HyperLink     0x4200
```

Note that the numerical values assigned to the #define statements must be in a hexadecimal format.

The .HPJ file is also modified to add the [Map] section as follows:

**examp6\example.hpj**

```
[Files]
    topics.rtf

[Options]
    INDEX=MainIndex

[Map]
    #include <example.hmp>
```

Now when the help file is compiled, the Help Compiler will create an internal table that maps the numerical values in the EXAMPLE.HMP file to the topics associated with the context strings in the #define statement. The advantage of this mapping method is it allows the same .HMP file to be used with not only the help project file, but also the application source code and the resource file, as shown in the following application:

**examp6\hello.h**

```
#include <windows.h>

/* Define the menu item macros */
#define IDM_ABOUT    1000
#define IDM_EXIT     2000
#define ID_OK        3000

#include "example.hmp"
```

**examp6\hello.rc**

```
#include "hello.h"

MainMenu  MENU
{
  MENUITEM "E&xit",   IDM_EXIT
  POPUP "\a&Help"
  {
    MENUITEM "&Index",      MainIndex
    MENUITEM "&Example",    ExampleTopic
    MENUITEM "&HyperLink",  HyperLink
  }
}
```

The HELLO.C file for this application is identical to the application shown earlier in this chapter, except for the following change to the WM_COMMAND case:

**examp6\hello.c**

```
  . . .
        case WM_COMMAND:
            switch(wParam)
            {
                case IDM_EXIT:
                    /* Leave the application by destroying the main
                       window */
                    DestroyWindow(hWnd);
                    break;

                /* Was one of the help menu items selected? */
                case MainIndex:
                case ExampleTopic:
                case HyperLink:
                    WinHelp(hWnd, "example.hlp", HELP_CONTEXT, wParam);
                    break;
            }
            break;
  . . .
```

Whereas the Help Compiler interpreted the #define statements in EXAMPLE.HMP as relating context strings to numerical values, the BC++ and resource compilers interpret the statements as macro definitions for the numerical values. This creates a hard tie between the context string as seen by the Help Compiler and the numerical values for the menu items and the values passed to the WinHelp() function.

# DETECTING WHEN THE Ⓕ⒈ KEY IS PRESSED

All quality Windows applications adhere to the Common User Access (CUA) standard. According to this standard, when the user presses the Ⓕ⒈ key, your application should respond by displaying some form of help—either context sensitive help or, at a minimum, your application's help index. Detecting when the user presses the Ⓕ⒈ key is trivial while the application window has the focus. However, detecting when the Ⓕ⒈ key is being pressed while the user has a menu pulled down or while a dialog box is active is another matter. Detecting the depression of the Ⓕ⒈ key under these situations is accomplished by setting a "hook" in the message dispatching function for your application. Consider the following functions:

```
FARPROC lpMsgHookFnct = NULL;
FARPROC lpNextHookFnct = NULL;
#define WM_HELPKEY WM_USER

/* Hook Procedure */
int FAR PASCAL _export MessageHook(int iCode, WORD wParam,
                    LONG lParam)
{
    LPMSG pMsg = (LPMSG)lParam;

    /* Was the F1 key pressed down? */
    if((pMsg->message == WM_KEYDOWN) && (pMsg->wParam == VK_F1))
    {
        if(iCode == MSGF_DIALOGBOX)
        {
            HWND hParent = GetParent(pMsg->hwnd);

            /* Send a message to the parent window */
            PostMessage(hParent, WM_HELPKEY, iCode, pMsg->hwnd);
        }
        else if(iCode == MSGF_MENU)
        {
            /* The should have monitoring of which menu items were
               selected. Send a message to the window that owns the
               menu that the help key was pressed. */
            PostMessage(pMsg->hwnd, WM_HELPKEY, iCode, NULL);
        }
    }

    /* Call the next hook in the chain */
    DefHookProc(iCode, wParam, lParam, &lpNextHookFnct);
    return(0);
}

BOOL SetMessageHook(HANDLE hInstance)
{
    lpMsgHookFnct = MakeProcInstance(MessageHook, hInstance);
    if(lpMsgHookFnct != NULL)
    {
        lpNextHookFnct = SetWindowsHook(WH_MSGFILTER, lpMsgHookFnct);
        return(TRUE);
    }
    return(FALSE);
```

```
}
void UnhookMessageHook(void)
{
    if(lpMsgHookFnct != NULL)
    {
        UnhookWindowsHook(WH_MSGFILTER, lpMsgHookFnct);
        FreeProcInstance(lpMsgHookFnct);
    }
}
```

The SetMessageHook() function should be called whenever your application is ready to start monitoring the F1 key. This function places the MessageHook() function in the WH_MSGFILTER hook chain. Once the hook is in place, all keyboard interaction messages dealing with the menu or a dialog box will be sent through this function. Any time the F1 key is pressed while a menu is pulled down or the application has a dialog box displayed, the MessageHook() function will send the owner of the menu or the parent of the dialog box a WM_HELPKEY message.

With the MessageHook() function in place, it is fairly straightforward to respond to a WM_HELPKEY message when the user presses the F1 key from a dialog box. When this happens, the wParam of the message will equal MSGF_DIALOGBOX and the low word of the lParam will contain the handle to the control window that had the focus at the time of the F1 keypress. You can then use the control window handle to determine the ID of the control using the GetDlgCtrlID() function. You then determine the appropriate topic associated with that control and call the WinHelp() function.

Detecting which menu item was selected when the F1 key was pressed is accomplished in a more roundabout manner. The message processing function for the window owning the menu should detect the WM_MENUSELECT message and keep track of which menu item the user has selected. For example, the following code keeps the MenuSelectID current with the menu item selected by the user:

```
static MenuSelectID;
. . .
            case WM_MENUSELECT:
                MenuSelectID = wParam;
                break;
        . . .
```

When the window with the menu receives the WM_HELPKEY message from the MessageHook() function, the wParam of the message will be equal to MSGF_MENU. At this point the MenuSelectID variable can be checked to determine which menu item was last selected.

# BROWSE SEQUENCES

The browse sequence allows the user to select the [<<] or [>>] push-buttons and page through the topics in the order you define. Adding keywords and a browse sequence to a help file is accomplished by adding footnotes at the beginning of a topic in the same manner as the context string and title.

A browse sequence uses the '+' character as the footnote reference. For the text portion of the footnote, you assign the browse sequence a subject and a number as follows:

`Subject:Num`

The Help Compiler will group topics with the same subject into a browse sequence ordered numerically by the values of the different 'Num' parameters. This allows the user to browse through related topics in an order specified by you. For example, suppose you had a series of topics that could be grouped into three related subjects, Files, Editing, and Windows. You could organize a browse sequence for the topics that fall under these subjects as follows:

| Context String | Browse footnote text |
|---|---|
| NewFiles | files:010 |
| OpenFiles | files:020 |
| CloseFiles | files:030 |
| SaveFiles | files:040 |
| Cut | edit:010 |
| Paste | edit:020 |
| FontSize | edit:030 |
| Tiling | windows:010 |
| Icons | windows:020 |
| Cascading | windows:030 |
| NewWindow | windows:040 |

With the above browse sequences for the three subjects, if the user were to pull up the topic for "OpenFiles," the "NewFiles" topic would be selected with the [<<] push-button and the [>>] push-button would select the "CloseFiles" topic. When the user reached the end of a browse sequence for a particular subject, the appropriate push-button would be disabled.

Note that the number parameter assigned to a browse sequence cannot exceed 999. Also, the Help Compiler sorts the numerical values as ASCII strings rather than actual numbers. This causes the Help Compiler to place a topic with a sequence number of 100 before a topic with a number of 99 because it compares the first character of each and determines that the character '1' comes before '9'. For this reason, you should use browse sequence numbers with leading zeros. This will ensure the Help Compiler places the topic with sequence number 099 before topic 100.

# HELP KEYWORDS

Associating keywords with topics allows the user to select the [Search] push-button and retrieve a list of topic titles. A list of topics relating to a specific keyword can also be

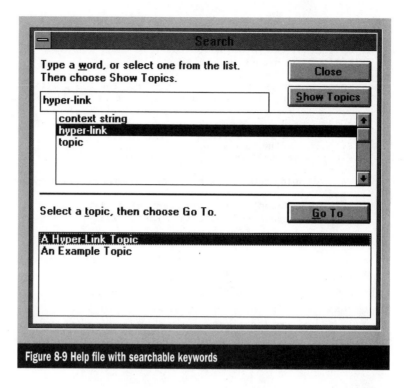

**Figure 8-9 Help file with searchable keywords**

generated from the application using the HELP_KEYWORD parameter with the WinHelp() function.

You use the 'K' character as the footnote reference for keywords. The footnote text then contains the list of keywords separated by semicolons. You can use any character in the individual keywords except for the semicolon. This allows you to use the space character to create a phrase keyword, such as "paint brush." Note that keywords are not case sensitive. Also, the list of keywords for one topic, including any imbedded spaces, cannot exceed 255 characters.

The following RTF file is an example of a topic file with both a browse sequence and keywords:

**examp7\topics.rtf**

```
{\rtf1\ansi {\fonttbl{\f0\fswiss Helv;}}\f0 \fs20 {

#{\footnote ExampleTopic}
${\footnote An Example Topic}
K{\footnote topic;context string;hyperlink}
+{\footnote topic:010}
This is an example topic with a context string. The context string
enables you to place jumps in your help file to related topics.
A jump to another topic is known as a {\uldb hyperlink}
{\v HyperLink}.\par
```

```
\page
#{\footnote HyperLink}
${\footnote A HyperLink Topic}
K{\footnote hyperlink;topic}
+{\footnote topic:020}
There is a hyperlink to this topic from the topic with the
{\uldb ExampleTopic}{\v ExampleTopic} context string.\par}

\page
#{\footnote MainIndex}
${\footnote The Main Index}
{\b\fs24 The Main Index}\par
\par
The following topics are available in this help file:\par
\par
    {\uldb Example Topic}{\v ExampleTopic}\par
    {\uldb HyperLink Topic}{\v HyperLink}\par
}
```

With keywords assigned to the topics in the above RTF file, the user can utilize the search dialog box. The keywords are sorted alphabetically and displayed. As shown in Figure 8-9, selecting the "hyper-link" keyword displays the topic titles for both "A HyperLink Topic" and "An Example Topic".

You can also access topics from your application using keywords. For example, the following Easy Windows application calls the WinHelp() function and looks for topics relating to the "Constants" keyword:

**examp7\test.c**
```c
#include <windows.h>

void main(void)
{
    WinHelp(NULL, "tcwhelp.hlp", HELP_KEY,
    (DWORD)((LPSTR)"Constants"));
}
```

The above application displays the "Inline Assembler String Constants" topic in the TCWHELP.HLP file. Note that there are actually two topics relating to "Constants" in the .HLP file; however, WINHELP will only display the first topic it encounters that matches the requested keyword.

# MULTIPLE KEYWORD LISTS

The Help Compiler supports help files that contain up to four additional keyword lists besides the main keyword list. These additional keyword lists are not accessible by the user from the WINHELP application. They can only be accessed from a call to the WinHelp() function using the HELP_MULTIKEY command. This is useful when you would like to call for specific topics from your application via a keyword, but you do not want the keywords accessible to the user.

Topics related to one of these additional lists are given a footnote similar to the normal keyword footnote except a letter other than 'K' is used for the footnote reference. For example, the following RTF file uses the letter 'L' as the footnote reference for the "ExampleTopic":

**examp7\topics2.rtf**

```
{\rtf1\ansi {\fonttbl{\f0\fswiss Helv;}}\f0 \fs20 {

#{\footnote ExampleTopic}
${\footnote An Example Topic}
L{\footnote topic;context string;hyperlink}
+{\footnote topic:010}
This is an example topic with a context string.  The context string
enables you to place jumps in your help file to related topics.
A jump to another topic is known as a {\uldb hyperlink}
{\v HyperLink}.\par

\page
#{\footnote HyperLink}
${\footnote A HyperLink Topic}
K{\footnote hyperlink;topic}
+{\footnote topic:020}
There is a hyperlink to this topic from the topic with the
{\uldb ExampleTopic}{\v ExampleTopic} context string.\par}

\page
#{\footnote MainIndex}
${\footnote The Main Index}
{\b\fs24 The Main Index}\par
\par
The following topics are available in this help file:\par
\par
    {\uldb Example Topic}{\v ExampleTopic}\par
    {\uldb HyperLink Topic}{\v HyperLink}\par
}
```

The 'L' footnote reference for the ExampleTopic places the list of keywords in a separate keyword list. Note that the code in the *Borland Languages Help Compiler* reference manual for accessing additional keyword lists is incorrect. Multiple keyword lists are accessed using the following code example:

**examp7\hello.c**

```
char Keyword[] = "topic";
. . .
        case WM_COMMAND:
            switch(wParam)
            {
                HANDLE hMem;
                MULTIKEYHELP FAR *pKey;
                unsigned Size;

                case IDM_TOPIC:
                    /* Determine the size of the structure */
                    Size = sizeof(MULTIKEYHELP) + lstrlen(Keyword);
```

```
                /* Allocate the MULTIKEYHELP structure */
                hMem = GlobalAlloc(GMEM_MOVEABLE | GMEM_ZEROINIT,
                    Size);
                pKey = (MULTIKEYHELP FAR *)GlobalLock(hMem);

                /* Fill in the details */
                pKey->mkSize= Size;
                pKey->mkKeylist = 'L';
                lstrcpy(pKey->szKeyphrase, Keyword);

                /* Call the WinHelp() function */
                WinHelp(hWnd, "multi.hlp", HELP_MULTIKEY,
                    (DWORD)((LPSTR)pKey));

                /* Free the global memory */
                GlobalUnlock(hMem);
                GlobalFree(hMem);
                break;

            case IDM_EXIT:
            . . .
```

Note that the HELP_MULTIKEY command for the WinHelp() function operates in a similar fashion to the HELP_KEY command in that if more than one topic has the same keyword, the WINHELP application will only display the first topic in the help file for that keyword.

## PLACING BITMAPS IN A HELP FILE

Bitmap figures add color and easy-to-follow visual references to your help files. There are two ways of placing a bitmap in a help file. One method is to use a word processor to import a picture into the topic text. This is generally not the best method, as you will generally be limited to monochrome bitmap files. It is also difficult to change a drawing once it has been placed into the text. The better method is to reference the bitmap using one of the following statements in the topic text:

| Bitmap Reference | Description |
| --- | --- |
| {bmc *filename*.BMP} | Places the bitmap in the text as a normal word. Text can both precede and follow the bitmap. The bitmap is moved with the text on reformatting to keep it between the text immediately before and after the bitmap. |
| {bml *filename*.BMP} | Places the bitmap flush with the left side of the help window. Words are wrapped around the bitmap. |
| {bmr *filename*.BMP} | Places the bitmap flush with the right side of the help window. Words are wrapped around the bitmap. |

If you are writing in Word for Windows, you can place the bitmap references in your topic text exactly as listed above. However, if you are writing your topics directly in as RTF files, you will need to use the '\' escape character so that the Help Compiler does not interpret the '{' and '}' characters of the bitmap reference as text groupings. For example, consider the following RTF file:

**examp8\topics.rtf**

```
{\rtf1\ansi {\fonttbl{\f0\fswiss Helv;}}\f0 \fs20 {
Bitmap references are placed in a topic text using either the bmc,
bml, or bmr, reference statements. For example, the TPROFW icon
bitmap, \{bmc tprofw.bmp\}, was placed into this topic text using
the bmc bitmap reference. \par
\par
\{bml tdw.bmp\}The TDW icon bitmap was placed flush left with this
block of text using the bml bitmap reference. As shown, the words
wrap around the bitmap reference as required.\par
\par
\{bmr workshop.bmp\}The WORKSHOP icon bitmap was placed flush with
the right side of this text using the bmr bitmap reference. As with
the bml reference, the words are wrapped around the bitmap as
required.\par}
}
```

The above RTF text would appear as follows when using Word for Windows or some other word processor:

Bitmap references are placed in a topic text using either the bmc, bml, or bmr reference statements. For example, the TPROFW icon bitmap, {bmc tprofw.bmp}, was placed into this topic text using the bmc bitmap reference.

{bml tdw.bmp}The TDW icon bitmap was placed flush left with this block of text using the bml bitmap reference. As shown, the words wrap around the bitmap reference as required.

{bmr workshop.bmp}The WORKSHOP icon bitmap was placed flush with the right side of this text using the bmr bitmap reference. As with the bml reference, the words are wrapped around the bitmap as required.

You must also list all the bitmaps referenced in the topic text in the [Bitmaps] section of the help project file. Also, you do not use directory path locations with the bitmap references in the topic text, but instead place the required path in the [Bitmaps] section of the help project file. For example, if the bitmaps referenced in the above text were located in the parent directory, then the path for the filename would be included as part of the listing in the [Bitmap] section of the project file as follows:

**examp8\example.hpj**
```
[Files]
    topics.rtf

[Bitmaps]
    ..\tdw.bmp
    ..\tprofw.bmp
    ..\workshop.bmp
```

Figure 8-10 shows the resulting help file.

If you use multiple references to a single bitmap, it should only be listed once in the [Bitmaps] section. Also note that the WINHELP application will display any type of Device Independent Bitmap, including 24-bit RGB color. The WINHELP utility and the user's Windows display driver will remap the bitmap colors as required.

# CONDITIONAL COMPILATION USING BUILD TAGS

If you are writing similar applications that use many of the same topics in a help file, such as an application with an introductory and a professional version, you should consider writing one set of topic files and using build tags to control which topics are actually placed in the resulting help file. This allows you to share many of the same topics between the two help files without having to create and maintain separate topic file sets. For example, suppose your professional level application had the same menu items as the introductory version except that it also included an "Advanced Options" menu item. You could then create a single topic file covering all the menu items, place a build tag on the topic for the "Advanced Options," and exclude the topic from the build for the introductory version.

Build tags are added to topics by placing a footnote at the beginning of the topic using the '*' character as the footnote reference. The footnote text contains the list of tags. Build tags have several restrictions:

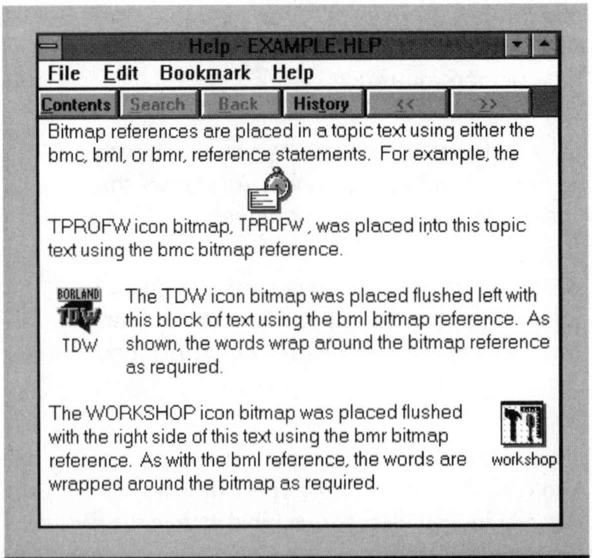

**Figure 8-10 Help file with color bitmaps**

1. The build tag footnote must be the first footnote for the topic.

2. The tags listed in the footnote text cannot contain any spaces and must be separated by semicolons.

3. The list of footnote tags is restricted to 255 characters.

4. Build tags are not case sensitive.

The following RTF file places the "Professional" build tag on the "Advanced Options" topic:

**examp9\topics.rtf**

```
{\rtf1\ansi {\fonttbl{\f0\fswiss Helv;}}\f0 \fs20 {

#{\footnote Options}
${\footnote Options Menu Item}
K{\footnote menu items;options}
+{\footnote menu:010}
The "Options" menu contains a list of optional settings for the
application.\par

\page
*{\footnote Professional}
#{\footnote AdvOpt}
${\footnote Advanced Options Menu Item}
K{\footnote menu items;advanced;options}
+{\footnote menu:020}
The "Advanced Options" menu contains a list of optional settings
specific to the professional version of the application.\par}
 }
```

To compile the topic file so as to include the topics with the "Professional" build tag, the tag is listed as part of the BUILD statement in the [Options] section of the project file. The tag is also listed in the [BuildTags] section. For example, the following is the help project file for the professional version of the application, which includes the professional level topic:

**examp9\prof.hpj**

```
[Files]
    topics.rtf

[BuildTags]
    Professional          ; Topics that are specific to the
                          ;    professional version.

[Options]
    BUILD=Professional    ; Include professional level topics in the
                          ;    help file
```

The help project file for the introductory version is slightly different. This time you need the professional level topics excluded from the help file so the BUILD statement uses the '~' operator instructing the Help Compiler to exclude those topics. The following help project builds a help file that excludes the professional level topics:

**examp9\intro.hpj**

```
[Files]
    topics.rtf

[BuildTags]
    Professional        ; Topics that are specific to the
                        ;    professional version.

[Options]
    BUILD=~Professional  ; Exclude professional version topics
```

Note that all the topics containing build tags must be listed in the [BuildTags] section even if they are not to be included in the help file.

# NEW FEATURE IN HELP COMPILER VERSION 3.1

BC++ 3.1 includes Version 3.1 of the Help Compiler. This version is almost fully compatible with Version 3.0 and also includes the following new features:

- Hot-Spot Bitmaps
- Multiple Resolution Bitmaps
- Macro Execution
- Secondary Help Window
- CD-ROM Optimizations

The one incompatibility with the older 3.0 version is that the INDEX option is no longer recognized. You should use the new CONTENTS option instead.

## Hot-Spot Bitmaps

Version 3.1 of the Help Compiler lets you use a bitmap as a hyper-link. For example, consider the following topic text:

```
#{\footnote ExampleTopic}
Borland C++ for Windows {\strike \{bmc BCW.BMP\}}{\v BCWTopic}
contains almost all of the functionality of the DOS version.
```

The "\strike" designates the BCW.BMP bitmap as a hot-spot bitmap. The "\v BCWTopic" links the hot spot to the topic associated with the "BCWTopic" context string. WINHELP will then treat the bitmap as it would a normal hyper-link hot-spot, i.e. pressing the (tab) key will highlight the bitmap, the cursor is displayed as a hand when it moves over the bitmap, and selecting the bitmap will display the topic associated with the "BCWTopic" context string.

## The Hot Spot Editor

You can also create bitmaps with multiple hot-spots using the SHED.EXE utility, also known as the "Hot Spot Editor". This Windows editor allows you to designate different areas of a bitmap as hot-spot areas. You do this by clicking the mouse on an area and then dragging the mouse to set the size of the hot-spot. Once you've designated the area, you can move the hot-spot by clicking the mouse somewhere in the center and moving it to a new location. You can also change

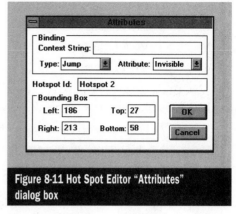

Figure 8-11 Hot Spot Editor "Attributes" dialog box

the size by clicking on one of the corner or side blocks and then resizing. You can display the "Attribute" dialog box shown in Figure 8-11 by either double clicking the hot-spot or by selecting the [Edit][Attributes] menu item. This dialog box allows you to set the context string associated with the hot-spot, the type of hot-spot, and its visibility. The type parameter allows you to select either "Jump", "Pop-up", or "Macro". A "Jump" hot-spot creates a hyperlink which jumps to the topic associated with a context string whereas a "Pop-up" displays a popup window for the topic. Selecting a "Macro" type interprets the text in the "Context String" box as a macro (see "Help Macros" section later in this chapter).

## Multiple Resolution Bitmaps

BC++ 3.1 includes a utility called the Multiple Resolution Bitmap Compiler (MRBC.EXE). This is a DOS utility that combines two or more bitmaps intended for display on different adapters typed into a single file. For example, you can create separate bitmaps for CGA, EGA, VGA, and 8514 screens and combine them into a single bitmap. You can then use this bitmap in a help file and WINHELP will select the appropriate bitmap for the user's display.

The MRBC utility uses the following syntax:

```
mrbc [/s] [file.CGA] [file.EGA] [file.VGA] [file.854]
```

The MRBC utility will normally attempt to determine the type of display to associate with a bitmap by examining the bitmaps *biXPelsPerMeter* and *biYPelsPerMeter* members of the BITMAPINFOHEADER structure within the bitmap. It will prompt you for the proper display type if it cannot determine the intended display from this information.

The /s option instructs the utility to ignore the information in the bitmap and to base the bitmap's intended display type on the first letter of the filename extension as follows:

| Letter | Display Type |
|--------|--------------|
| C | CGA Display |
| E | EGA Display |
| V | VGA Display |
| 8 | 8514 Display |

For example, the following will compile the BCW.CGA, BCW.EGA, BCW.VGA and BCW.854 bitmaps into a single BCW.MRB file:

```
mrbc /s bcw.cga bcw.ega bcw.vga bcw.854
```

You can find the resulting BCW.MRB file in a help file as you would a normal bitmap.

## Help Macros

The Help Compiler now implements a complete macro language. There are 55 predefined macros and also provisions for calling functions in a Dynamic Link Library (DLL). The predefined macros are listed in a reference section towards the end of this chapter.

When WINHELP actually executes a macro depends on usage:

| MACRO USAGE | WHEN THE MACRO IS EXECUTED |
|-------------|----------------------------|
| In the [CONFIG] section of a project file | When WINHELP loads the help file |
| As a footnote to a topic | When WINHELP displays the topic |
| As a topic hot-spot | When the user selects the hot-spot |
| As a menu item | When the user selects the menu item |
| As a push-button | When the user presses the button |
| As an accelerator key | When the user presses the key combination |
| As a bitmap | When the user selects the bitmap |
| As a hot-spot on a bitmap | When the user selects the hot-spot |

*Executing macros when WINHELP loads a help file*

You list all the macros you'd like executed when WINHELP initially loads a help file in the [CONFIG] section of a project file. For example, since the following macro is in the [CONFIG] section of a project file, WINHELP will execute the macro when it loads the help file and jump to the topic the a context string of "FirstTopic":

```
[CONFIG]
    JumpId("", "FirstTopic")
```

You can list as many macros as you like in the [CONFIG] section. The entire macro must appear on the same line. You can only list one macro per line.

*Executing macros when WINHELP displays a topic*

You assign a macro to a topic using a footnote in the same way that you assign a browse sequence or keyword to a topic. WINHELP will then execute the macros you've assigned each time it displays the topic.

Instead of the '#', you use '!' as the footnote character for a macro. For example, the following topic footnotes instruct WINHELP to execute the PopupId() macro each time it displays the topic for the "ExampleTopic" context string::

```
#{\footnote ExampleTopic}
!{\footnote PopupId("", "HyperLink")}
```

You can list more than one macro in a footnote provided you separate the macros with a semicolon or you can list each macro as a separate footnote. For example, the following topic heading executes the CLOCK application and also displays the "HyperLink" topic in a popup window:

```
#{\footnote ExampleTopic}
!{\footnote ExecProgram("CLOCK.EXE", 0)}
!{\footnote PopupId("", "HyperLink")}
```

*Assigning a macro to a topic hot-spot*

Just as a you can create a hot-spot in a topic that jumps to another topic, you can also create a hot-spot in a topic that will execute a macro. For example, consider the following topic text:

```
Selecting {\uldb BCW}{\v !ExecProgram("BCW", 0)} will execute the
BCW application.
```

The above topic text creates a hot-spot for "BCW" and displays the text as if it were a hyper-link to another topic. However, when the user selects the hot-spot, WINHELP will execute the ExecProgram() macro rather than jump to another topic. Note that you must precede the macro with a '!' character so as to distinguish the macro from a hyper-link jump reference. You can list more than one macro provided you separate each macro with a semicolon.

*Assigning a macro to a menu item*

You execute one of three macros to assign a macro to a menu item: AppendItem(), InsertItem(), and ChangeItemBinding(). Both the AppendItem() and InsertItem() macros create a new menu item in a popup menu and assign the item a macro. WINHELP will then execute the macro whenever the user selects the item. For example, consider the following:

```
[CONFIG]
    InsertMenu("MY_MENU", "M&y Menu", 3)
    AppendItem("MY_MENU", "IDM_EXIT", "E&xit", "Exit()")
```

The InsertMenu() macro creates a popup menu called [My Menu] as the third menu on WINHELP's menu bar. The AppendItem() macro adds the [Exit] menu item. Whenever the user selects the [My Menu][Exit] menu item, WINHELP will execute the Exit() macro.

You change the macro assignment for a menu item using the ChangeItemBinding() macro. For example, the following macro will assign the CloseWindow() macro to the [My Menu][Exit] menu item:

```
ChangeItemBinding("IDM_EXIT", "CloseWindow(`main')")
```

Note that when you list a macro that uses a string parameter as the parameter of another macro, you use open and close single quotes for the string rather than double quotes. The open single quote character, ('), is located on the same key as the tilde (~) character. The close single quote, ('), is located on the same key as the double quote (") character. The help compiler will generate an error message if you do not use the proper set of quotes.

Other related macros include the CheckItem(), DeleteItem(), DisableItem(), EnableItem(), and UncheckItem() macros.

### Assigning a macro to a pushbutton

You execute one of two macros to assign a macro to a pushbutton. The CreateButton() macro creates a new pushbutton and assigns it a macro. The Change-ButtonBinding() macro changes the macro assigned to a pushbutton. For example, consider the following:

```
CreateButton("BTN_EXIT", "E&xit", "Exit()")
```

The above macro creates an [Exit] pushbutton on WINHELP's button bar. WINHELP will execute the Exit() macro whenever the user pushes the button.

Note that you can also use the ChangeButtonBinding() macro to change the macro executed by WINHELP's standard [Back], [Contents], [History], [>>], [<<], and [Search] buttons. Other related macros include the DestroyButton(), DisableButton(), and EnableButton() macros.

### Assigning a macro to an accelerator

You can create an accelerator key that executes a macro using the AddAccelerator() macro. This macro allows you to create accelerators using the (Ctrl), (Alt), and (Shift) keys in combination with a virtual key. For example, the following creates an accelerator that executes the Exit() macro when the user presses the (Alt)-(X) key:

```
[config]
    AddAccelerator(0x58, 4, "Exit()")
```

### Assigning a macro to a bitmap

You can assign a macro to a bitmap in the same way you assign a hyperlink to a bitmap. The only difference is that you precede the macro with a '!' character. For example, the following topic text creates a hot-spot for the BCW.BMP bitmap and jumps to the TCWHELP.HLP help file contents topic when selected by the user:

```
#{\footnote ExampleTopic}
Borland C++ for Windows
 {\strike \{bmc BCW.BMP\}}{\v !JumpContents("TCWHELP.HLP")} contains
 almost all of the functionality of the DOS version.
```

You can assign more than one macro to a bitmap by separating the macros with a semicolon.

The Hot Spot Editor allows you to assign macros to multiple hot-spots in a bitmap. See the "Hot Spot Editor" section earlier in this chapter for details.

*Creating custom macros*

The RegisterRoutine() macro allows you to create your own custom macros that you can call as you would one of the Help Compiler's predefined macros. With this macro you register a routine in a Dynamic Link Library (DLL). Then, when you execute the macro, WINHELP will call the DLL routine using the parameters you pass to the macro.

You can also use this routine to create a macro that calls one of the Windows API functions. For example, the following allows you to call the MessageBeep() API function from within the help file:

```
[CONFIG]
    RegisterRoutine("USER", "MessageBeep", "I")
```

With the MessageBeep() routine registered, you can then use the routine as you would a predefined macro as shown in the following:

```
#{\footnote ExampleTopic}
!{\footnote MessageBeep(0)}
```

With the above macro in the topic heading, WINHELP will execute the MessageBeep() macro whenever it displays the topic.

## Secondary Windows

Another feature new to Version 3.1 of the Help Compiler allows you to display a secondary help window. This secondary window operates similar to WINHELP's main window except that it does not contain any menu or button bar. You create a secondary window by first defining the window attributes in the [WINDOWS] section of the project file as follows:

```
[WINDOWS]
    sec="Secondary Window", (256, 256, 512, 128), 0
```

The above defines a secondary window, called "sec". The remaining parameters set the window's size and position (see [WINDOWS] in the reference section for details). You can request WINHELP to display this secondary window instead of the normal main window by calling WinHelp from an application as follows:

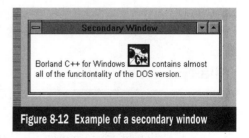

**Figure 8-12  Example of a secondary window**

```
WinHelp(hWnd, "example.hlp>sec", HELP_CONTENTS, OL);
```

The "example.hlp>sec" requests WINHELP to load the EXAMPLE.HLP help file and use the "sec" window defined in the help file's [WINDOWS] section. Figure 8-12 shows the resulting display.

You can also request WINHELP to display a secondary window by executing one of the jump macros and including the name of the secondary window as part of the file-name specification. For example, the following macro displays the topic associated with the "HyperLink" context string in a secondary window:

```
JumpId("example.hlp>sec", "HyperLink")
```

Unlike the call from an application, when you request a secondary window using a macro, WINHELP's main window remains open. WINHELP executes the secondary window as a separate task. Execute the CloseWindow("main") macro to close the main window.

Note that you can only have one secondary window open at a time. If you attempt to open a secondary window when one is already open, WINHELP will close the first secondary window before opening the new one.

## Optimizations for CD-ROM

Version 3.1 of the Help Compiler contains two features that help optimize the generation of help files that will be stored on CD-ROM. One feature is the OPTCDROM option. When this option is set, the Help Compiler will align topics on predefined block boundaries. The second feature is the storage of bitmaps in the [BAGGAGE] section of the project file. WINHELP has to read the file allocation table when it uses a bitmap. This operation takes time and is exaggerated by the slower access times of CD-ROM. When you list the files in the [BAGGAGE] section, however, the Help Compiler uses its own internal file storage system which bypasses the use of the file allocation table. The following instructs the Help Compiler to store the BCW.BMP file using its own internal filing system:

```
[BAGGAGE]
    BCW.BMP
```

# HELP COMPILER PROJECT REFERENCE

The project file for a help system contains all the information that is needed to correctly build the help file. The following reference section provides details on the six different sections in a help project file listed within square brackets. Reference listings in all capitals refer to statements that are used in the [Options] section of the project file.

## [Alias]                                          Context String Aliases

- 3.0    - 3.1

### Purpose
The [Alias] section of a help project file lists alternative names for different context strings. This section is optional, but if it is included, it should be listed before any section that uses one of the alternative names.

### Description
When you move topics between help projects, some of the embedded hyperlinks may reference topics which either do not exist or use a different context string. Rather than

going through each individual topic to change the hyperlinks, it may be easier to instead instruct the Help Compiler to interpret hyperlink references to one context string as a different context string entirely. For example, suppose you move a series of topics that contains references to "Cut," "Paste," and "Copy" context strings, and your new help project only contains a topic on "CutAndPaste." Rather than changing all the references in the topics, you can instead list the following [Alias] section:

```
[Alias]
    Cut=CutAndPaste
    Paste=CutAndPaste
    Copy=CutAndPaste
```

The Help Compiler will then link any references to "Cut," "Paste," or "Copy" to the "CutAndPaste" topic.

### See Also
Tutorial:       Context Strings
[Map]           Map Context Strings to Numerical Values

## [BAGGAGE]                                         Internal Files

3.0        ■ 3.1

### Purpose
You list files in the [BAGGAGE] section when the help file you're creating will be stored on a CD-ROM disk.

### Description
WINHELP must access the DOS file allocation table when it displays a bitmap in a topic window that slows down the performance, especially when the help file is on a CD-ROM drive. Listing a file in the [BAGGAGE] section instructs the Help Compiler to create an internal file storage system that bypasses the use of the DOS file allocation table and thereby enhances performance.

### See Also
OPTCDROM     CD-ROM Option

## [Bitmaps]                                         Bitmap References

■  3.0        ■ 3.1

### Purpose
The [Bitmaps] project file section lists all the bitmap references used in the topic files and specifies their directory locations.

## Description

All bitmap references used in the topic files must also be listed in the [Bitmaps] section of a Version 3.0 help project file. You can either list the filenames as they were used in the topic files if they are located in the help directory (i.e., either the current directory or the directory and drive listed in the ROOT statement), or you can use explicit pathnames. Note that if the topic files contain several references to the same bitmap, the bitmap should only be listed once in the [Bitmaps] section. Listing bitmap files in this section is optional in Version 3.1 of the Help Compiler.

## See Also

Tutorial: Placing Bitmaps in a Help File
BM ROOT       Default Bitmap Path Option

# BMROOT                                        Default Bitmap Path Option

3.0        ■  3.1

## Purpose

You use the BMROOT option in the [OPTIONS] section of a project file to specify the root directory for bitmap files.

## Default

```
BMROOT=root_dir
```
   *root_dir* is the directory specified by the ROOT option

## Usage

```
[OPTIONS]
  BMROOT=C:\MYPROJ, D:\BITMAPS
```
   Instructs the Help Compiler to first look in the C:\MYPROJ directory and then the D:\BITMAPS directory.

## Description

The BMROOT option allows you to place your bitmap files in a directory other than the current directory. The Help Compiler will then use that directory unless an absolute pathname is used with the file listing in either the [Files] or [Bitmap] section of the project file.

## See Also

[Bitmaps]    Bitmap References
[Files]      Topic Files
ROOT         Drive and Directory Path for Help Project Files

# BUILD

**Conditional Build Option**

■ 3.0 ■ 3.1

## Purpose

The BUILD statement is used in the [Options] section to either include or exclude topics with specific build tags.

## Default

None. Include all topics in the help file.

## Usage

```
[Options]
  BUILD= (Professional | Introductory) & ~Testing
```

Build all topics that have either the "Professional" or "Introductory" build tags, but not the "Testing" build tag.

## Description

As the Help Compiler reads through the topic files, it checks for any build tags, and if one is listed for the topic, it then compares it against the BUILD statement listed in the [Options] section of the help project file. The BUILD statement is evaluated as follows:

| | |
|---|---|
| *tag* | If a tag listed in the BUILD statement is listed as a build tag for the topic, then the 'tag' evaluates as a Boolean TRUE. If the tag is not listed as one of the topic's build tags, then the 'tag' evaluates as FALSE. |
| & | Boolean AND |
| \| | Boolean OR |
| ~ | Boolean NOT |

If the BUILD statement for the topic with a build tag evaluates as true, then the topic is included as part of the help file. For example, consider the following BUILD statement for a topic that has the "Professional" and "Testing" build tags:

```
BUILD=(Professional | Introductory) & ~Testing
```

Because the topic has both the "Professional" and "Testing" build tags, the BUILD statement evaluates as follows:

```
BUILD = (TRUE | FALSE) & ~(TRUE)
      = TRUE & FALSE
      = FALSE
```

The topic is then not included in the help file size and the statement is evaluated as FALSE. Note that any topics that do not have any build tags are always included in the help file. Also, topics with build tags are included in the help file if there is no BUILD statement listed in the project file.

BUILD statements are limited to 255 characters.

### See Also
Tutorial: Conditional Compilation Using Build Tags
[BuildTags]   Topic Build Tags


# [BuildTags]                                    Topic Build Tags

■  3.0      ■  3.1

### Purpose
The [BuildTags] section in a project file lists the build tags used in the topic files.

### Description
Any build tags assigned to topics must also be listed in the [BuildTags] section of the project file. This section is limited to 30 tags. Note that build tags are not case sensitive.

### See Also
Tutorial: Conditional Compilation Using Build Tags
BUILD   Conditional Build Option


# COMPRESS                                   Help File Compression Flag

■  3.0      ■  3.1

### Purpose
The COMPRESS statement is used in the [Options] section to specify compression of the help file. This not only reduces the size of the help file, but also enables it to run more quickly.

### Default
```
COMPRESS=FALSE
```

### Usage
```
[Options]
   COMPRESS=TRUE
```

### Description
The Help Compiler will use a compression algorithm to reduce the size of a help file. The help file is automatically expanded by WINHELP as required. The amount of the

compression depends on the size of the help file. Small help files will see little compression, whereas larger help files will have more significant compression ratios. Another advantage is that compressed help files are loaded more quickly than uncompressed files. The only disadvantage to using compression is that it takes longer than an uncompressed build.

The first time the Help Compiler builds a help file using the COMPRESS option, it creates a .PH file containing repetitive phrases used in the topic files. The Help Compiler then uses the .PH file on subsequent builds to speed the compilation process. To receive full compression on subsequent builds with the COMPRESS statement set to TRUE, you should erase the associated .PH file.

**See Also**
[Options]   Build Options
OLD KEY PHRASE        Old Key=Phrase File Usage

## [CONFIG]                                    Initial Macro Executions

3.0        ▪ 3.1

**Purpose**
You use the [CONFIG] section to list any macros you'd like executed when WINHELP loads the help file.

**Description**
WINHELP will execute all the macros listed under the [CONFIG] section of the help project when it loads the help file. You'd typically register DLL functions and create menus and pushbuttons in this section.

Note that each macro entry must be on a separate line and must be no more than 254 characters in length.

**See Also**
[WINDOWS]    Secondary Help Windows

## CONTENTS                                    Ver 3.1 Main Index Topic

3.0        ▪ 3.1

**Purpose**
The CONTENTS statement in the [OPTIONS] section specifies which topic WINHELP should use as the display when it first opens the help file and when the user presses the [Contents] button.

## Default

None. Uses the first topic as the contents topic.

## Usage

```
[Options]
  CONTENTS=MainIndex
```
Use the topic with the MainIndex context string as the help file's contents topic.

## Description

The Help Compiler will normally use the first topic in the help file as the contents topic. The CONTENTS statement allows you to specify some other topic file referenced by its context string.

Note that this option is the equivalent of the INDEX option in HC Version 3.0.

## See Also

INDEX     Ver 3.0 Main Index Topic

# COPYRIGHT                                          Copyright String

3.0        ▪ 3.1

## Purpose

You use the COPYRIGHT statement in the [OPTIONS] section of a project file to have WINHELP display a copyright string when it displays the "About" dialog box.

## Default

None

## Usage

```
[OPTIONS]
  COPYTRIGHT=Copyright (C) 1992, The Yankee Programmer
```

## Description

WINHELP will display the string you specify with the COPYRIGHT option in the "About" dialog box as shown in Figure 8-13. Note that the string should be less then 35 characters in length.

## See Also

ICON      Help Icon Option

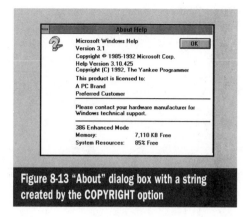

**Figure 8-13 "About" dialog box with a string created by the COPYRIGHT option**

# ERRORLOG
**Error Log File Option**

3.0 ▪ 3.1

## Purpose
The ERRORLOG option directs the Help Compiler to send any error message to the designated file.

## Usage
```
[OPTIONS]
  ERRORLOG=ERRLIST.TXT
```

## Description
The Help Compiler normally sends error messages to the screen. This can be unwieldy when compiling with large help files that contain numerous errors. The ERRORLOG option instructs the Help Compiler to send these error messages to a file.

## See Also
REPORT     Display Compilation Messages

# [Files]
**TOPIC FILES**

▪ 3.0 ▪ 3.1

## Purpose
The [Files] section of a project file lists the topic files the Help Compiler should use to build the help file. This section must be included in all help project files.

## Description

The Help Compiler reads the list of topic files in the [Files] section and compiles them into the help file. Only files in the RTF format should be listed. The compiler looks for the files in either the current directory or the directory specified by the ROOT statement in the [Options] section. For example, the following instructs the Help Compiler to use the topics listed in the MAIN.RTF and TOPICS.RTF files:

```
[Files]
main.rtf
topics.rtf
```

The list of filenames can be located in a file other than the project file and included using a C style #include directive. For example, the following includes the TOPICS.LST file as the list of topic files:

```
[Files]
#include <topics.lst>
```

## See Also

[Alias]         Context String Aliases
[Options]       Build Options

# FORCEFONT                    Compile the Topics Using a Specific Font

- 3.0    - 3.1

## Purpose

The FORCEFONT statement is used in the [Options] section of a project file to force the Help Compiler to ignore the fonts used in the topic files and to use a different font instead.

## Default

None. Use the fonts written into the topic files.

## Usage

```
[Options]
    FORCEFONT=Helv
```
Ignore the fonts used in the topic files and compile the help file using the Helv font.

## Description

Windows is shipped with a limited number of fonts. These include the following fonts and sizes:

| Font | Sizes |
|------|-------|
| Courier | 10, 12, 15 |

| Helv | 8, 10, 12, 14, 18, 24 |
| Modern | |
| Roman | |
| Script | |
| Symbol | 8, 10, 12, 14, 18, 24 |
| Tms Rmn | 8, 10, 12, 14, 18, 24 |

Windows will attempt to display help files that use fonts not available on the user's system by matching the font to the closest font available, but this often results in ragged text quality.

If you have topic files written using nonstandard fonts, you can instruct the Help Compiler to ignore the fonts used in the topic files and to instead use one of the native fonts available to the user. An error will result if you list a font that is not one of the fonts listed above. Note that the FORCEFONT statement may not contain any spaces and that the "Tms Rmn" font may not be used.

**See Also**

| MAPFONTSIZE | Use a Specific Set of Font Sizes |
| [Options] | Build Options |

# ICON
**Help Icon Option**

3.0      ■  3.1

**Purpose**
You use the ICON option to change the icon WINHELP displays when minimized.

**Usage**
```
[OPTIONS]
  ICON=MYAPP.ICO
```

**Description**
The Help Compiler normally displays the icon shown in Figure 8-14 when minimized. The ICON statement instructs WINHELP to display a different icon. Note that this option does not change the icon displayed in WINHELP's "About" dialog box.

Figure 8-14
Normal
WINHELP icon

**See Also**
COPYRIGHT    Copyright String

# INDEX                                    Ver 3.0 Main Index Topic

- 3.0      - 3.1

## Purpose
The INDEX statement in the [Options] section specifies a topic the Help Compiler should list as the main index for the help file.

## Default
None. Use the first topic as the main index.

## Usage
```
[Options]
    INDEX=MainIndex
```
Use the topic with the MainIndex context string as the help file's main index.

## Description
The Help Compiler will normally use the first topic in the help file as the main index. The INDEX statement allows you to specify some other topic file referenced by its context string.

## See Also
Tutorial: The Main Index
[Alias]            Context String Aliases
CONTENTS        Ver 3.1 Main Index Topic


# LANGUAGE                                  Language Sort Order

3.0      - 3.1

## Purpose
You use the LANGUAGE option to specify which language WINHELP should assume when sorting keywords in the Search dialog box.

## Default
```
LANGUAGE=english
```

## Usage
```
[OPTIONS]
  LANGUAGE=scandanavian
```

## Description
Different languages use differing sort criteria. You use the LANGUAGE option to ensure WINHELP sorts the keyword strings according to the criteria for a given language. Note that "scandanavian" is the only other language currently supported by WINHELP.

**See Also**

MULTIKEY     Additional Keyword Footnote References


# [Map]                    Map Context Strings to Numerical Values

■ 3.0    ■ 3.1

## Purpose

The [Map] section of a project file relates the topic context strings to numerical values that can be used by an application to call up specific topics.

## Description

Context strings can be mapped to numerical values by one or more of the following methods:

```
[Map]
    ExampleTopic       0x1000; Context string and a hexadecimal number
    HyperLink            2000; Context string and a decimal number
    #define MainIndex 0x3000; #define directive and a hexadecimal
                        ;        number
    #include <file.hmp>   ; #include directive
```

    The best method to use is the #include directive with the context strings mapped using the #define directive in the included file. This allows the include file to also be used with the application source code.

## See Also

Tutorial: Calling Individual Topics from an Application
[Alias]                Context String Aliases
MAPFONTSIZE        Use a Specific Set of Font Sizes


# MAPFONTSIZE                    Use a Specific Set of Font Sizes

■ 3.0    ■ 3.1

## Purpose

The MAPFONTSIZE statement in the [Options] section instructs the Help Compiler to translate certain font size references in the topic files to other font sizes.

## Default

None. Use the font sizes specified in the topic files.

## Usage

```
[Options]
  MAPFONTSIZE=12-18:10
```

Convert all font sizes in the topic files from 12 point through 18 point to a 10 point font size.

## Description

Some of the font sizes used in a topic file may not be appropriate for all help files. For example, you could build a help file designed to display well on a VGA system and another for a CGA system. Large fonts which display well on a VGA system will not display as well as the smaller fonts on the CGA system. The MAPFONTSIZE statement allows you to create a help file for the CGA system using the same topic files as the VGA help file using smaller fonts.

You may use as many MAPFONTSIZE statements as you need. Note, however, that a specific font size can only be mapped once and any subsequent attempt at remapping will be ignored. For example, consider the following:

```
[Options]
    MAPFONTSIZE=12-18:10
    MAPFONTSIZE=16:12
```

The first MAPFONTSIZE statement maps fonts 12 through 18. The second statement attempts to map font 16, however, font size 16 was already mapped by the first statement so this second statement is ignored.

### See Also

FORCEFONT    Compile the Topics Using a Specific Font
[Map]        Map Context Strings to Numerical Values

# MULTIKEY                          Additional Keyword Footnote References

- 3.0     - 3.1

## Purpose

The MULTIKEY option in a project file specifies a footnote reference for an alternative keyword list.

## Default

None. Use the normal keyword list only.

## Usage

```
[Options]
    MULTIKEY=L
```

Create an additional keyword list consisting of the topics listed with the 'L' footnote reference.

## Description

Alternative keyword lists are used when you would like to create a list of keywords for use by the application via the WinHelp() function, but do not want the keywords directly accessible by the user. See the tutorial for a detailed description of alternative keyword lists.

**See Also**
Tutorial: Multiple Keyword Lists

# OLDKEYPHRASE                                    Old Key-Phrase File Usage

3.0        ■ 3.1

**Purpose**
The OLDKEYPHRASE option tells the Help Compiler whether or not it should use any old key-phrase files.

**Default**
OLDKEYPHRASE=NO

**Usage**
[OPTIONS]
  OLDKEYPHRASE=YES

**Description**
The Help Compiler normally uses an old key-phrase file if one exists. You use the OLDKEYPHRASE option to instruct the Help Compiler to build a new key-phrase file.

**See Also**
COMPRESS        Help File Compression Flag

# OPTCDROM                                        CD-ROM Option

3.0        ■ 3.1

**Purpose**
The OPTCDROM instructs the Help Compiler to align topic files on block boundaries.

**Default**
OPTCDROM=NO

**Usage**
[OPTIONS}
  OPTCDROM=YES

**Description**
CD-ROM access is more efficient if WINHELP can locate topic files on predefined block boundaries. Setting the OPTCDROM option to YES ensures the topic file alignment is optimized for storage in a CD-ROM disk.

## See Also
[BAGGAGE]  Internal Files


# [Options]         Build Options

- 3.0   - 3.1

## Purpose
The [Options] section of the help project lists one or more of the following statements that are used to control the build process of the help file: BUILD, COMPRESS, FORCEFONT, INDEX, MAPFONTSIZE, MULTIKEY, ROOT, TITLE, and WARNING.

## Description
See the individual descriptions for the [Options] section statements.

## See Also
| | |
|---|---|
| BUILD | Conditional Build Option |
| COMPRESS | Help File Compression Flag |
| FORCEFONT | Compile the Topics Using a Specific Font |
| INDEX | Main Index Topic |
| MAPFONTSIZE | Use a Specific Set of Font Sizes |
| MULTIKEY | Additional Keyword Footnote References |
| ROOT | Drive and Directory Path for Help Project Files |
| TITLE | Assign a Title to the Help Window |
| WARNING | Set a Warning Level |


# REPORT      Display Compilation Messages

3.0   - 3.1

## Purpose
You enable the REPORT option when you want to monitor the progress of the help file compilation.

## Default
REPORT=NO

## Usage
```
[OPTIONS]
  REPORT=YES
```

## Description

Compiling large help files can sometimes take a considerable amount of time. You can use the REPORT option to monitor the progress of the compilation. With this option enabled, the Help Compiler will send periodic progress reports to the screen.

## See Also

ERRORLOG    Error Log File Option

# ROOT          Drive and Directory Path for Help Project Files

■ 3.0    ■ 3.1

## Purpose

The ROOT statement in the [Options] section of a project file specifics the drive and directory location of topic and bitmap files.

## Default

```
ROOT=
```
    Look for help project files in the current directory.

## Usage

```
[Options]
    ROOT=c:\helpdir
```
    Look for any files needed by the help project in the C:\HELPDIR directory.

## Description

The ROOT option allows you to place your topic files and bitmap files in a directory other than the current directory. The Help Compiler will then use that directory unless an absolute pathname is used with the file listing in either the [Files] or [Bitmap] section of the project file.

## See Also

[Bitmaps]    Bitmap References
[Files]    Topic Files

# TITLE          Assign a Title to the Help Window

■ 3.0    ■ 3.1

## Purpose

The TITLE statement in the [Options] section assigns a title to the help file that is displayed in the title bar of the WINHELP window.

### Default

None. Only display the name of the help file.

### Usage

```
[Options]
   TITLE=My Application
```

Display the help window title as "My Application Help - *filename*" where 'filename' is the name of the help file.

### Description

Any title you list using the TITLE statement will be displayed in the caption bar of the help window. Note that the WINHELP application will append a 'Help - *filename*' string to the end of the title. If the project file does not contain a TITLE statement, then only the help file's filename is listed. Titles are restricted to 32 characters.

### See Also

[Options]    Build Options
BM ROOT  Default Bitmap Path Option

# WARNING                         Set a Warning Level

- 3.0     ■ 3.1

### Purpose

The WARNING statement in the [Options] section sets the warning level the Help Compiler should use when reporting warning messages.

### Default

```
WARNING=3
```

Display all warning messages.

### Usage

```
[Options]
WARNING=1
```

Only generate warning messages for the most severe warnings.

### Description

The Help Compiler uses three levels of warning messages:

| Level | Description |
|-------|-------------|
| 1 | Generate warning messages for the most severe warnings. |
| 2 | Generate warning messages that have an intermediate impact on help file compilation. |
| 3 | Generate all warning messages. |

For example, if your project file contains build tags and your project file does not contain a BUILD statement, then the "Build expression missing from project file." warning message will be generated telling you that all topics in the file will be included in the help file. If you want all the topics to be included, but do not want this warning message, you can either include a BUILD statement or set the WARNING message to level 1 to suppress the message.

**See Also**
[Options]    Build Options

# [WINDOWS]                                    **Secondary Help Windows**

3.0      ■  3.1

**Purpose**
You use the [WINDOWS] section of the project file to define the window attributes for the main and secondary windows.

**Description**
The [WINDOWS] section allows you to specify the initial size, position, and color of the main and secondary windows. This section expects the following syntax:

```
name="title", (x, y, width, height), ShowMax, NormalColor,
    NonScrollColor
```

*name*
    Name used to internally reference the window. Use "main" when defining the attributes for WINHELP's main window.

*"title"*
    The title WINHELP should display in the window's caption bar.

*x, y*
    Position of the upper-lefthand corner of the window in help units. One help unit is 1/1024th of the screen resolution.

*width, height*
    Size of the window in help units. One help unit is 1/1024th of the screen resolution.

*ShowMax*
    Boolean flag indicating the window should be shown maximized. WINHELP ignores the *x, y, width,* and *height* parameters if this value is set to 1.

*NormalColor*
    This parameter is an RGB triplet defining the background color for the scrolling portions of the window. For example, a parameter of (0, 255, 255) displays cyan. This

parameter is optional. If no color is specified, WINHELP displays the user's default window colors.

*NonScrollColor*

This parameter is an RGB triplet defining the background color for the non-scrolling portions of the window. For example, a parameter of (0, 255, 255) displays cyan. This parameter is optional. If no color is specified, WINHELP displays the user's default window colors.

**See Also**

TITLE      Assign a Title to the Help Window

# HELP FILE MACRO REFERENCE

The following reference section covers the help file macros available in Version 3.1 of the Help Compiler. Note that macros are not supported in Version 3.0. The following is a list of general rules concerning macros:

- The total length of any macro including all parameters may not be more than 254 characters.

- Macro names are not case sensitive. Differences between upper and lower case are ignored.

- All macro parameters must be enclosed within double quotes unless the parameter is a numerical value.

- When you use a macro as the parameter of another macro, you must use open and close single quotes for the string parameters of the enclosed macro.

- You always have the option of listing more than one macro by separating them with a semicolon (;). The only exception to this rule is that you use a full colon (:) when you are listing more than one macro as the parameter of another macro.

- You should not execute macros which create menus, pushbuttons, or display dialog boxes when a secondary window has the focus.

# About

**Purpose**

The About() macro displays the WINHELP "About" dialog box shown in Figure 8-13. Executing this macro is equivalent to the user selecting WINHELP's [Help][About Help...] menu item. You should not execute this macro when a secondary window has the focus.

## Syntax

About()

## See Also

Annotate, CopyDialog, FileOpen, HelpOn, History, PrinterSetup, Search

# AddAccelerator (AA)

## Purpose

With the AddAccelerator() macro you can set up your help file to execute a macro when the end user presses a particular key sequence.

## Syntax

AddAccelerator(*key, ShiftState, "macro[:macro:...]"*)
AA(*key, ShiftState, "macro[:macro:...]"*)

*key*

 The virtual keycode for the accelerator. This *key* parameter should be one of the following hexadecimal values:

| Value | Virtual Key | Value | Virtual Key |
|-------|-------------|-------|-------------|
| 6A | VK_ADD | 08 | VK_BACK |
| 03 | VK_CANCEL | 14 | VK_CAPITAL |
| 0C | VK_CLEAR | 11 | VK_CONTROL |
| 6E | VK_DECIMAL | 2E | VK_DELETE |
| 6F | VK_DIVIDE | 28 | VK_DOWN |
| 23 | VK_END | 2B | VK_EXECUTE |
| 1B | VK_ESCAPE | 70 | VK_F1 |
| 71 | VK_F2 | 72 | VK_F3 |
| 73 | VK_F4 | 74 | VK_F5 |
| 75 | VK_F6 | 76 | VK_F7 |
| 77 | VK_F8 | 78 | VK_F9 |
| 79 | VK_F10 | 7A | VK_F11 |
| 7B | VK_F12 | 7C | VK_F13 |
| 7D | VK_F14 | 7E | VK_F15 |
| 7F | VK_F16 | 2F | VK_HELP |
| 24 | VK_HOME | 2D | VK_INSERT |
| 25 | VK_LEFT | 01 | VK_LBUTTON |
| 04 | VK_MBUTTON | 12 | VK_MENU |
| 6A | VK_MULTIPLY | 22 | VK_NEXT |
| 60 | VK_NUMPAD0 | 61 | VK_NUMPAD1 |
| 62 | VK_NUMPAD2 | 63 | VK_NUMPAD3 |
| 64 | VK_NUMPAD4 | 65 | VK_NUMPAD5 |

*(continued)*

| Value | Virtual Key | Value | Virtual Key |
|-------|-------------|-------|-------------|
| 66 | VK_NUMPAD6 | 67 | VK_NUMPAD7 |
| 68 | VK_NUMPAD8 | 69 | VK_NUMPAD9 |
| 90 | VK_NUMLOCK | 13 | VK_PAUSE |
| 2A | VK_PRINT | 21 | VK_PRIOR |
| 02 | VK_RBUTTON | 0D | VK_RETURN |
| 27 | VK_RIGHT | 29 | VK_SELECT |
| 6C | VK_SEPARATOR | 10 | VK_SHIFT |
| 2C | VK_SNAPSHOT | 20 | VK_SPACE |
| 6D | VK_SUBTRACT | 09 | VK_TAB |
| 26 | VK_UP | 30 | VK_0 |
| 31 | VK_1 | 32 | VK_2 |
| 33 | VK_3 | 34 | VK_4 |
| 35 | VK_5 | 36 | VK_6 |
| 37 | VK_7 | 38 | VK_8 |
| 39 | VK_9 | 41 | VK_A |
| 42 | VK_B | 43 | VK_C |
| 44 | VK_D | 45 | VK_E |
| 46 | VK_F | 47 | VK_G |
| 48 | VK_H | 49 | VK_I |
| 4A | VK_J | 4B | VK_K |
| 4C | VK_L | 4D | VK_M |
| 4E | VK_N | 4F | VK_O |
| 50 | VK_P | 51 | VK_Q |
| 52 | VK_R | 53 | VK_S |
| 54 | VK_T | 55 | VK_U |
| 56 | VK_V | 57 | VK_W |
| 58 | VK_X | 59 | VK_Y |
| 5A | VK_Z | | |

*ShiftState*

This value adds a combination of the (Shift), (Ctrl), and (Alt) keys to the base virtual character represented by the *key* parameter. This parameter should be one of the following values:

| Value | Key Combination |
|-------|-----------------|
| 0 | None |
| 1 | (Shift) |
| 2 | (Ctrl) |
| 3 | (Shift+Ctrl) |
| 4 | (Alt) |
| 5 | (Alt+Shift) |
| 6 | (Alt+Ctrl) |
| 7 | (Alt+Shift+Ctrl) |

*"macro[:macro:...]"*

Macro WINHELP should execute when the user presses the given key combination. You must enclose the macro within quotation marks. If the macro you are executing also requires the use of quotation marks, use single (both open and close) quotes for the embedded macro. You can execute more than one macro provided you separate each macro with a full colon.

### See Also
CreateButton

### Example
Write a macro that will create an accelerator for the (Alt)-(X) key combination that will exit WINHELP when pressed:

```
[config]
    AddAcclerator(0x58, 4, "Exit()")
```

# Annotate

### Purpose
The Annotate() macro displays the WINHELP "Annotate" dialog box shown in Figure 8-15. Executing this macro is equivalent to the user selecting WINHELP's [Edit][Annotate...] menu item. Note that you should not use this macro when a secondary window has the focus.

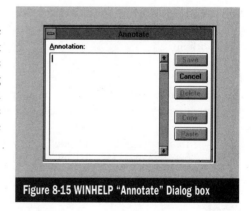

**Figure 8-15 WINHELP "Annotate" Dialog box**

### Syntax
Annotate()

### See Also
About, BookmarkDefine, BookmarkMore, CopyDialog, FileOpen, History, PrinterSetup, Search

# AppendItem

### Purpose
You use the AppendItem() macro to add a menu item to a menu created by the InsertMenu() macro. The AppendItem() macro will place the new menu item as the last item in the popup menu.

**Syntax**
```
AppendItem("MenuId", "ItemId", "ItemName", "macro[:macro:...]")
```

*"MenuId"*
    ID string for the popup menu created by the InsertMenu() macro.

*"ItemId"*
    ID string for the menu item. You use this ID string with the DisableItem(), EnableItem(), and DeleteItem() macros to reference the new menu item.

*"ItemName"*
    Character string for the menu item as it should appear in the popup menu. Place an '&' character before the character WINHELP should use as the menu item's hot-key.

*"macro[:macro:...]"*
    Macro WINHELP should execute when the user selects the menu item. You must enclose the macro within quotation marks. If the macro you are executing also requires the use of quotation marks, use single (both open and close) quotes for the embedded macro. You can execute more than one macro provided you separate each macro with a full colon.

**See Also**
ChangeItemBinding, CheckItem, DeleteItem, EnableItem, DisableItem, InsertItem UncheckItem

**Example**
Write a macro set that creates a custom popup menu called "My Menu" with a "My Exit" menu item which, when selected, will exit WINHELP:

```
[config]
   InsertMenu("IDM_MYMENU", "M&y Menu", 0)
   AppendItem("IDM_MYMENU", "IDM_MYEXIT", "&My Exit", "Exit()")
```

# Back

**Purpose**
Executing the Back() macro is equivalent to pressing the WINHELP [Back] button. This macro displays the previous topic selected by the user.

**Syntax**
```
Back()
```

**See Also**
Contents, Next, Prev

# BookmarkDefine

### Purpose

The BookmarkDefine () macro displays the WINHELP "Bookmark Define" dialog box shown in Figure 8-16. Executing this macro is equivalent to the user selecting WINHELP's [Bookmark][Define...] menu item. You should not execute this macro from a secondary window.

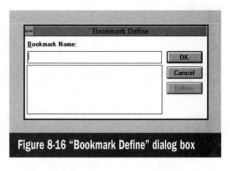

Figure 8-16 "Bookmark Define" dialog box

### Syntax

```
BookmarkDefine()
```

### See Also

About, Annotate, BookmarkMore, CopyDialog, FileOpen, History, PrinterSetup, Search

# BookmarkMore

### Purpose

The BookmarkMore() macro displays the WINHELP "Bookmark" dialog box shown in Figure 8-17. You should not execute this macro from a secondary window.

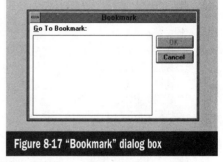

### Syntax

```
BookmarkMore()
```

Figure 8-17 "Bookmark" dialog box

### See Also

About, Annotate, BookmarkDefine, CopyDialog, FileOpen, History, PrinterSetup, Search

# BrowseButtons

### Purpose

The BrowseButtons() macro places the [<<] and [>>] buttons to the button bar. WINHELP will place these buttons at the end of the button bar.

**Syntax**
BrowseButtons()

**See Also**
CreateButton, DestroyButton, DisableButton, EnableButton

# ChangeButtonBinding (CBB)

**Purpose**
You use the ChangeButtonBinding() macro to change the macro WINHELP to execute when the user presses a button. You can use this macro to change the macro assignment for either the buttons you create using the CreateButton() macro or the standard WINHELP buttons.

**Syntax**
ChangeButtonBinding("ButtonId", "macro[:macro:...]")
CBB("ButtonId", "macro[:macro:...]")

*"ButtonId"*
     The ID for the button to change. This is either the *"ButtonId"* parameter you used with an earlier call to the CreateButton() macro or, if you would like to change the macro assignment for a standard WINHELP button, it should be one of the following button IDs:

| ID | Button |
|----|--------|
| BTN_BACK | [Back] |
| BTN_CONTENTS | [Contents] |
| BTN_HISTORY | [History] |
| BTN_NEXT | [>>] |
| BTN_PREVIOUS | [<<] |
| BTN_SEARCH | [Search] |

*"macro[:macro:...]"*
     Macro WINHELP should execute when the user presses the button. You must enclose the macro within quotation marks. If the macro you are executing also requires the use of quotation marks, use single (both open and close) quotes for the embedded macro. You can execute more than one macro provided you separate each macro with a full colon.

**See Also**
ChangeItemBinding, CreateButton

**Example**
Write a macro that will assign the [Search] button to a macro which will display a "My-Index" topic in the MYHELP.HLP help file:

```
ChangeButtonBinding("BTN_SEARCH", "JumpId(`MYHELP.HLP', `MyIndex')")
```

# ChangeItemBinding (CIB)

### Purpose
You use the ChangeItemBinding() macro to change the macro WINHELP to execute when the user selects a menu item created by either the AppendItem() or InsertItem() macro.

### Syntax
```
ChangeItemBinding("ItemId", "macro[:macro:...]")
CIB("ItemId", "macro[:macro:...]")
```

*"ItemId"*
    The ID for the menu item to change. This should be the *"ItemId"* parameter you used with an earlier call to the InsertItem() or AppendItem() macro.

*"macro[:macro:...]"*
    Macro WINHELP should execute when the user selects the menu item. You must enclose the macro within quotation marks. If the macro you are executing also requires the use of quotation marks, use single (both open and close) quotes for the embedded macro. You can execute more than one macro provided you separate each macro with a full colon.

### See Also
AppendItem, ChangeButtonBinding, InsertItem

# CheckItem (CI)

### Purpose
The CheckItem() macro places a check mark next to a menu item created by either the AppendItem() or InsertItem() macro.

### Syntax
```
CheckItem("ItemId")
CI("ItemId")
```

*"ItemId"*
    The ID for the menu item to check. This should be the *"ItemId"* parameter you used with an earlier call to the InsertItem() or AppendItem() macro.

### See Also
AppendItem, ChangeItemBinding, DeleteItem, DisableItem, EnableItem, InsertItem, UncheckItem

# CloseWindow

### Purpose
The CloseWindow() macro closes either a secondary window or the WINHELP main window.

### Syntax
`CloseWindow("WindowName")`

*"WindowName"*
    Name of the window to close. This should be the name declared in the [WINDOWS] section of the project file. Using "main" to close WINHELP's main window is equivalent to executing the Exit() macro.

### See Also
FocusWindow, PositionWindow

# Contents

### Purpose
The Contents() macro displays the topic specified by the CONTENTS option in the [OPTIONS] section of the project file.

### Syntax
`Contents()`

### See Also
Back, JumpContents, Next, Prev

# CopyDialog

### Purpose
The CopyDialog() macro displays the WINHELP "Copy" dialog box shown in Figure 8-18. Executing this macro is equivalent to the user selecting WINHELP's [Edit][Copy...] menu item. You should not use this macro when a secondary window has the focus.

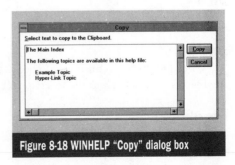

**Figure 8-18 WINHELP "Copy" dialog box**

### Syntax
`CopyDialog()`

### See Also
About, Annotate, BookmarkDefine, BookmarkMore, CopyTopic, FileOpen, History, PrinterSetup, Search

# CopyTopic

### Purpose
The CopyTopic() macro copies the displayed topic to the Windows clipboard. You should not use this macro when a secondary window has the focus.

### Syntax
```
CopyTopic()
```

### See Also
CopyDialog, Print

# CreateButton (CB)

### Purpose
You use the CreateButton() macro to add a new button to the end of WINHELP's button bar.

### Syntax
```
CreateButton("ButtonId", "ButtonName", "macro[:macro:...]")
CB("ButtonId", "ButtonName", "macro[:macro:...]")
```

*"ButtonId"*

Text ID for the new button. You would use this ID when referencing any of the other macros for a button such as DestroyButton and DisableButton.

*"ButtonName"*

Name of the button as it should appear to the user. Place a '&' character before the letter you want to use as a hot-key for the new button.

*"macro[:macro:...]"*

Macro WINHELP should execute when the user presses the button. You must enclose the macro within quotation marks. If the macro you are executing also requires the use of quotation marks, use single (both open and close) quotes for the embedded macro. You can execute more than one macro provided you separate each macro with a full colon.

**See Also**
BrowseButtons, ChangeButtonBinding, DestroyButton, DisableButton, EnableButton

**Example**
Write a macro to add an [Exit] button to WINHELP's button bar:

```
CreateButton("BTN_EXIT", "E&xit", "Exit()")
```

# DeleteItem

**Purpose**
The DeleteItem() macro removes a menu item created by either the AppendItem() or InsertItem() macro.

**Syntax**
```
DeleteItem("ItemId")
```

*"ItemId"*
    The ID for the menu item to delete. This should be the *"ItemId"* parameter you used with an earlier call to the InsertItem() or AppendItem() macro.

**See Also**
AppendItem, ChangeItemBinding, CheckItem, DisableItem, EnableItem, InsertItem, UncheckItem

# DeleteMark

**Purpose**
The DeleteMark() macro removes a marker created by the SaveMark() macro.

**Syntax**
```
DeleteMark("MarkerText")
```

*"MarkerText"*
    A text marker defined earlier by the SaveMark() macro.

**See Also**
GotoMark, IsMark, SaveMark

# DestroyButton

### Purpose

The DestroyButton() macro removes a button placed on the button bar by the Create-Button() macro. You should not use this macro to delete one of the standard WINHELP buttons. You should also not use this macro when a secondary window has the focus.

### Syntax

```
DestroyButton("ButtonId")
```

*"ButtonId"*

Text ID for the button. This should be the same as the *"ButtonId"* parameter used with the CreateButton() macro.

### See Also

BrowseButtons, ChangeButtonBinding, CreateButton, DisableButton, EnableButton

# DisableButton (DB)

### Purpose

The DisableButton() macro disables a button placed on the menu bar by the CreateButton() macro or one of the standard WINHELP buttons. WINHELP will display the text for the disabled button using a light gray color indicating the disabled state.

### Syntax

```
DisableButton("ButtonId")
DB("ButtonId")
```

*"ButtonId"*

Text ID for the button. This should be the same as the *"ButtonId"* parameter used with the CreateButton() macro or, if you would like to disable a standard WINHELP button, it should be one of the following button IDs:

| ID | Button |
|---|---|
| BTN_BACK | [Back] |
| BTN_CONTENTS | [Contents] |
| BTN_HISTORY | [History] |
| BTN_NEXT | [>>] |
| BTN_PREVIOUS | [<<] |
| BTN_SEARCH | [Search] |

**See Also**

BrowseButtons, ChangeButtonBinding, CreateButton, DestroyButton, EnableButton

# DisableItem (DI)

**Purpose**

The DisableItem() macro disables a menu item created by either the AppendItem() or InsertItem() macro.

**Syntax**
```
DisableItem("ItemId")
DI("ItemId")
```

*"ItemId"*

The ID for the menu item to disable. This should be the *"ItemId"* parameter you used with an earlier call to the InsertItem() or AppendItem() macro.

**See Also**

AppendItem, ChangeItemBinding, CheckItem, DeleteItem, EnableItem, InsertItem, UncheckItem

# EnableButton (EB)

**Purpose**

The EnableButton() macro enables a button placed on the menu bar by the Create-Button() macro or one of the standard WINHELP buttons. WINHELP will display the text for the enabled button in black indicating the enabled state.

**Syntax**
```
EnableButton("ButtonId")
EB("ButtonId")
```

*"ButtonId"*

Text ID for the button. This should be the same as the *"ButtonId"* parameter used with the CreateButton() macro or, if you would like to enable a standard WINHELP button, it should be one of the following button IDs:

| ID | Button |
|---|---|
| BTN_BACK | [Back] |
| BTN_CONTENTS | [Contents] |

| BTN_HISTORY | [History] |
| BTN_NEXT | [>>] |
| BTN_PREVIOUS | [<<] |
| BTN_SEARCH | [Search] |

**See Also**
BrowseButtons, ChangeButtonBinding, CreateButton, DestroyButton, DisableButton


# Enableltem (EI)

**Purpose**
The EnableItem() macro enables a menu item created by either the AppendItem() or InsertItem() macro.

**Syntax**
```
EnableItem("ItemId")
EI("ItemId")
```

*"ItemId"*
    The ID for the menu item to enable. This should be the *"ItemId"* parameter you used with an earlier call to the InsertItem() or AppendItem() macro.

**See Also**
AppendItem, ChangeItemBinding, CheckItem, DeleteItem, DisableItem, InsertItem, UncheckItem


# ExecProgram (EP)

**Purpose**
The ExecProgram() macro executes a Windows application or .PIF file.

**Syntax**
```
ExecProgram("CommandLine", DisplayState)
EP("CommandLine", DisplayState)
```

*"CommandLine"*
    Command line for the program to execute. Do not use the '\' escape character for quotes in the command line. Enclose the command in single (both open and close) quotes instead and then use any required full quotes in the command line.

*DisplayState*

Specifies how the application should be displayed by Windows. This parameter should be one of the following:

| Value | Description |
|-------|-------------|
| 0 | Normal |
| 1 | Minimized |
| 2 | Maximized |

### See Also
RegisterRoutine

### Example
Create a button which will execute BCW when pressed:

```
[CONFIG]
   CreateButton("BTN_BCW", "&BCW", "ExecProgram(`BCW', 2)")
```

# Exit

### Purpose
The Exit() macro instructs WINHELP to exit. Executing this macro is equivalent to the user selecting WINHELP's [File][Exit] menu item.

### Syntax
```
Exit()
```

### See Also
Print

# FileOpen

### Purpose
The FileOpen() macro displays the WIN-HELP "Open" dialog box shown in Figure 8-19. Executing this macro is equivalent to the user selecting WINHELP's [File][Open...] menu item. You should not use this macro when a secondary window has the focus.

### Syntax
```
FileOpen()
```

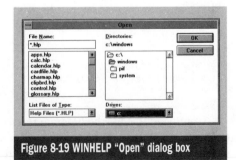

**Figure 8-19 WINHELP "Open" dialog box**

**See Also**

About, Annotate, BookmarkDefine, BookmarkMore, CopyDialog, History, PrinterSetup, Search

# FocusWindow

## Purpose

You use the FocusWindow() macro to set the focus to either the main or secondary window. The window specified by the *"WindowName"* parameter must already be open.

## Syntax

```
FocusWindow("WindowName")
```

*"WindowName"*

Name of the secondary window. This should be the same name as the *type* parameter listed in the [WINDOWS] section of the project file. Use "main" to set the focus on WINHELP's main window.

## See Also

CloseWindow, PositionWindow

## Example

Write a set of macros that will create a secondary window and then shift the focus back to the main window:

```
[WINDOWS]
  ; set the size and position of the main window
  main=, (0, 0, 1000, 600), 0

  ; set the size, position, and color of the secondary window
  sec= "Secondary Help Window", (250, 300, 500, 350), 0, (0, 255,
  255)

[CONFIG]
  ; Open the secondary window
  JI("example.hlp>sec", "ExampleTopic");

  ; Return focus to the main window
  FocusWindow("main")
```

# GotoMark

## Purpose

You use the GotoMark() macro to jump to a topic previously marked using the SaveMark() macro.

**Syntax**
```
GotoMark("MarkerText")
```

*"Marker Text"*
> A text marker defined earlier by the SaveMark() macro.

**See Also**
DeleteMark IsMark, SaveMark

# HelpOn

**Purpose**
You use the HelpOn() macro to open the WINHELP.HLP file. Executing this macro is equivalent to the user selecting WINHELP's [Help][How to Use Help] menu item.

**Syntax**
```
HelpOn()
```

**See Also**
JumpHelpOn, SetHelpOn

# HelpOnTop

**Purpose**
You execute the HelpOnTop() macro when you want WINHELP as the top-most window regardless of which application window has the focus. Executing this macro is equivalent to the user selecting WINHELP's [Help][Always on Top] menu item.

**Syntax**
```
HelpOnTop()
```

**See Also**
HelpOn

# History

**Purpose**
The History() macro displays the WINHELP "History" dialog box shown in Figure 8-8. Executing this macro is equivalent to the user pressing WINHELP's [History] button. You should not use this macro when a secondary window has the focus.

**Syntax**
```
History()
```

**See Also**
About, Annotate, BookmarkDefine, BookmarkMore, CopyDialog, FileOpen,
PrinterSetup, Search

# IfThen

**Purpose**
You use the IfThen() macro when you want a macro executed if a text marker has or has
not been set by the SaveMark() macro.

**Syntax**
```
IfThen(boolean, "macro[:macro:...]")
```

*boolean*
 Boolean flag returned by either the IsMark() or Not(IsMark()) macro.

*"macro[:macro:...]"*
 The macro WINHELP should execute if the boolean flag is true. You must enclose
the macro within quotation marks. If the macro you are executing also requires the use of
quotation marks, use single (both open and close) quotes for the embedded macro. You can
execute more than one macro provided you separate each macro with a full colon.

**See Also**
IfThenElse, IsMark, Not, SaveMark

# IfThenElse

**Purpose**
You use the IfThenElse() macro when you want to execute one of two macros depending on whether a text marker has or has not been set by the SaveMark() macro.

**Syntax**
```
IfThenElse(boolean, "IfMacro", "ElseMacro")
```

*boolean*
 Boolean flag returned by either the IsMark() or Not(IsMark()) macro.

*"IfMacro"*
 The macro WINHELP should execute if the boolean flag is true. You must enclose
the macro within quotation marks. If the macro you are executing also requires the use of

quotation marks, use single (both open and close) quotes for the embedded macro. You can execute more than one macro provided you separate each macro with a full colon.

*"ElseMacro"*

The macro WINHELP should execute if the boolean flag is false.

### See Also

IfThen, IsMark, Not, SaveMark

# InsertItem

### Purpose

The InsertItem() macro inserts a menu item into a menu created by the InsertMenu() macro. You should not execute this macro when a secondary window has the focus.

### Syntax

```
InsertItem("MenuId", "ItemId", "ItemName", "macro[:macro:...]", position)
```

*"MenuId"*

Identification string for the menu. This should be the same *"MenuId"* parameter used with an earlier call to the InsertMenu() macro.

*"ItemId"*

The ID for the menu item to insert. This should be the *"ItemId"* parameter you used with an earlier call to the InsertItem() or AppendItem() macro.

*"macro[:macro:...]"*

The macro WINHELP should execute when the user selects the menu item. You must enclose the macro within quotation marks. If the macro you are executing also requires the use of quotation marks, use single (both open and close) quotes for the embedded macro. You can execute more than one macro provided you separate each macro with a full colon.

*position*

Integer value representing the position of the item in the menu. For example, using a value of 0 will place the new item as the first item in the menu. Use the AppendItem() macro to place an item as the last item in the menu.

### See Also

AppendItem, ChangeItemBinding, CheckItem, DeleteItem, DisableItem, EnableItem, UncheckItem

# InsertMenu

### Purpose
You use the InsertMenu() macro to add a new popup menu to WINHELP's menu bar. You should not execute this macro when a secondary window has the focus.

### Syntax
`InsertMenu("MenuId", "MenuName", position)`

*"MenuId"*
 Text identification string for the menu. You'd use this string to reference the menu later with a call to the AppendItem() or InsertItem() macros.

*"MenuName"*
 Character string for the menu as it should appear on the menu bar. Place an '&' character before the character WINHELP should use as the menu's hot-key.

*position*
 Position on the menu bar. Use a value of 0 to place the menu as the first menu on the menu bar.

### See Also
AppendItem, InsertItem

# IsMark

### Purpose
You use the IsMark() macro within the IfThen() and IfThenElse() macros to conditionally execute a macro. The IsMark() macro will return a TRUE if the SaveMark() macro created the marker identified by *"MarkerText"*. Use the Not() macro to negate the boolean flag returned by IsMark().

### Syntax
`IsMark("MarkerText")`

*"MarkerText"*
 A text marker defined earlier by the SaveMark() macro.

### See Also
DeleteMark GotoMark, IfThen, IfThenElse, Not(), SaveMark

# JumpContents

## Purpose

You use the JumpContents() macro to jump to the Contents topic of a new help file. Use the Contents() macro to jump to the Contents topic of the current help file.

## Syntax

```
JumpContents("HelpFile")
```

*"HelpFile"*
    Name of the new help file.

## See Also

Contents, JumpContext, JumpHelpOn, JumpId, JumpKeyword

# JumpContext (JC)

## Purpose

You use the JumpContext() macro to display the topic in a help file associated with a context number. You can also use this macro to create a secondary window.

## Syntax

```
JumpContext("HelpFile", ContextNumber)
JC("HelpFile", ContextNumber)

JumpContext("HelpFile>window", ContextNumber)
JC("HelpFile>window", ContextNumber)
```

*"HelpFile"*
    Name of the new help file.

*"HelpFile>window"*
    Name of the new help file and secondary window where *window* is the name used in the [WINDOWS] section of the project file. WINHELP will close any secondary window if it exists before creating a new secondary window.

*ContextNumber*
    Context number for the topic.

## See Also

JumpContents, JumpHelpOn, JumpId, JumpKeyword

# JumpHelpOn

## Purpose

You call the JumpHelpOn() macro to load the WINHELP help file. This macro is equivalent to the HelpOn() macro unless you've designated a different file with the Set-HelpOnFile() macro.

## Syntax
```
JumpHelpOn()
```

## See Also

HelpOn, JumpContents, JumpContext, JumpId, JumpKeyword, SetHelpOnFile

# JumpId (JI)

## Purpose

You use the JumpId() macro to display the topic in a help file associated with a context string. You can also use this macro to create a secondary window.

## Syntax
```
JumpId("HelpFile", "ContextString")
JI("HelpFile", "ContextString")

JumpId("HelpFile>window", "ContextString")
JI("HelpFile>window", "ContextString")
```

*"HelpFile"*
 Name of the new help file.

*"HelpFile>window"*
 Name of the new help file and secondary window where *window* is the name used in the [WINDOWS] section of the project file. WINHELP will close any secondary window if it exists before creating a new secondary window.

*ContextString*
 Context string for the topic.

## See Also

JumpContents, JumpContext, JumpId, JumpHelpOn, JumpKeyword

# JumpKeyword (JK)

### Purpose
You use the JumpKeyword() macro to display the topic in a help file associated with a keyword. You can also use this macro to create a secondary window.

### Syntax
```
JumpKeyword("HelpFile", "Keyword")
JK("HelpFile", "Keyword")

JumpKeyword("HelpFile>window", "Keyword")
JK("HelpFile>window", "Keyword")
```

*"HelpFile"*
     Name of the new help file.

*"HelpFile>window"*
     Name of the new help file and secondary window where *window* is the name used in the [WINDOWS] section of the project file. WINHELP will close any secondary window if it exists before creating a new secondary window.

*"Keyword"*
     The keyword associated with a topic.

### See Also
JumpContents, JumpContext, JumpId, JumpHelpOn

# Next

### Purpose
The Next() macro will display the next topic in a browse sequence. WINHELP ignores this macro if there is no browse sequence or the user is on the last topic in the sequence. Executing this macro is equivalent to the user pressing the [>>] button.

### Syntax
```
Next()
```

### See Also
Back, Contents, Prev

# Not

### Purpose

You use the Not() macro with the IfThen() and IfThenElse() macros to negate the boolean flag returned by the IsMark() macro.

### Syntax

```
Not(IsMark("MarkerText"))
```

### See Also

IfThen, IfThenElse, IsMark, SaveMark

# PopupContext (PC)

### Purpose

You use the PopupContext() macro to display a popup window for a topic associated with a context number.

### Syntax

```
PopupContext("HelpFile", ContextNumber)
PC("HelpFile", ContextNumber)
```

*"HelpFile"*
  Help file containing the topic.

*ContextNumber*
  Context number for the topic

### See Also

PopupId

# PopupId (PI)

### Purpose

You use the PopupId() macro to display a popup window for a topic associated with a context string.

**Syntax**

```
PopupId("HelpFile", "ContextString")
PI("HelpFile", "ContextString")
```

*"HelpFile"*
> Help file containing the topic.

*"ContextString"*
> Context string for the topic

**See Also**

PopupContext

# PositionWindow (PW)

**Purpose**

You use the PositionWindow() macro to change the size and/or position of either the main or secondary window. Note that WINHELP uses a base resolution of 1024 x 1024 for the position and width. This allows you to place and size the window independent of the end user's screen resolution.

**Syntax**

```
PositionWindow(x, y, width, height, state, "Name")
PW(x, y, width, height, state, "Name")
```

*x*
> Horizontal position for the window's upper-lefthand corner in units of 1/1024 of the screen's horizontal resolution.

*y*
> Vertical position of the window's upper-lefthand corner in units of 1/1024 of the screen's vertical resolution.

*width*
> Width of the window in units of 1/1024 of the screen's horizontal resolution.

*height*
> Height of the window in units of 1/1024 of the screen's vertical resolution.

*state*
> How WINHELP should display the window. This parameter should be one of the following values:

| Value | Description |
| --- | --- |
| 1 | Normal |
| 2 | Minimized |
| 3 | Maximized |

Note that WINHELP will ignore the position and size parameters if you use a value of '2' or '3' for the *state* parameter.

*"Name"*

Name of the window. This should be the same name as the *type* parameter listed in the [WINDOWS] section of the project file. Use "main" to set the size/position of WINHELP's main window.

**See Also**

CloseWindow, FocusWindow

**Example**

Write a macro which will size and position a secondary window in the center of the screen at 1/4 the size of the screen resolution:

```
PositionWindow(256, 256, 512, 512, 1, "sec")
```

# Prev

**Purpose**

The Prev() macro will display the previous topic in a browse sequence. WINHELP ignores this macro if there is no browse sequence or the user is on the first topic in the sequence. Executing this macro is equivalent to the user pressing WINHELP's [<<] button.

**Syntax**

```
Prev()
```

**See Also**

Back, Contents, Next

# Print

**Purpose**

The Print() macro will print the current topic. Executing this macro is equivalent to the user selecting WINHELP's [File][Print Topic] menu item.

**Syntax**

```
Print()
```

**See Also**

PrinterSetup

# PrinterSetup

### Purpose

The PrinterSetup() macro displays the WINHELP "Print Setup" dialog box shown in Figure 8-20. Executing this macro is equivalent to the user selecting WINHELP's [File][Print Setup...] menu item. You should not use this macro when a secondary window has the focus.

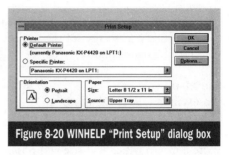

**Figure 8-20 WINHELP "Print Setup" dialog box**

### Syntax

```
PrintSetup()
```

### See Also

About, Annotate, BookmarkDefine, BookmarkMore, CopyDialog, FileOpen, History, Search

# RegisterRoutine (RR)

### Purpose

You use the RegisterRoutine() macro in the [CONFIG] section of a project file to create your own custom macros. This allows you to call a function in a DLL from anywhere in the help file as you would with any other WINHELP macro.

### Syntax

```
RegisterRoutine("DLLFile", "FunctionName", "FunctionFormat")
RR("DLLFile", "FunctionName", "FunctionFormat")
```

*"DLLFile"*

The name of the Dynamic Link Library (DLL) containing the function.

*"FunctionName"*

The name of the function in the DLL.

*"FunctionFormat"*

A character string representing the parameters passed to the DLL function. Each character in the string represents one of the following data types:

| Character | Data Type |
|-----------|-----------|
| u | WORD |
| U | DWORD |
| i | short int |
| I | int |
| s | PSTR |
| S | LPSTR |

**See Also**
ExecProgram

**Example**
Create a macro that will call the MessageBeep() Windows API function and assign the macro to a button:

```
[CONFIG]
   RegisterRoutine("USER", "MessageBeep", "I")
   CreateButton("BTN_BEEP", "Bee&p", "MeesageBeep(0)")
```

# SaveMark

**Purpose**
You use the SaveMark() macro to assign a text string to the current topic. You can then call the GotoMark() macro to return to the topic. You can also use the IfThen() and IfThenElse() macros to conditionally execute a macro based on the presence or absence of a particular text marker.

**Syntax**
```
SaveMark("MarkerText")
```

*"MarkerText"*
    Text marker for the current topic.

**See Also**
DeleteMark, GotoMark, IfThen, IfThenElse, IsMark, Not

# Search

**Purpose**
The Search() macro displays the WINHELP "Search" dialog box shown in Figure 8-9. Executing this macro is equivalent to the user pressing WINHELP's [Search] button. You should not use this macro when a secondary window has the focus.

**Syntax**
```
Search()
```

**See Also**
About, Annotate, BookmarkDefine, BookmarkMore, CopyDialog, FileOpen, History, PrinterSetup

# SetContents

**Purpose**
You use the SetContents() to the change the topic and help file used by WINHELP as the Contents topic.

**Syntax**
```
SetContents("HelpFile", ContextNumber)
```

*"HelpFile"*
 Filename for the new help file.

*ContextNumber*
 Context number for a topic.

**See Also**
Contents, JumpContents

# SetHelpOnFile

**Purpose**
You use the SetHelpOnFile() to change the file used by WINHELP when the user selects the [Help][How to Use Help] menu item or you execute the HelpOn() or JumpHelpOn() macro.

**Syntax**
```
SetHelpOnFile("HelpFile")
```

**See Also**
HelpOn, JumpHelpOn

## UncheckItem (UI)

### Purpose

The DeleteItem() macro removes a check mark from a menu item check by an earlier call to the CheckItem() macro.

### Syntax

```
UncheckItem("ItemId")
UI("ItemId")
```

*"ItemId"*

The ID for the menu item to uncheck. This should be the *"ItemId"* parameter you used with an earlier call to the InsertItem() or AppendItem() macro.

### See Also

AppendItem, ChangeItemBinding, CheckItem, DeleteItem, DisableItem, EnableItem, InsertItem

# RICH TEXT FORMAT REFERENCE

All the topic files in a help project must be Rich Text Format (RTF) files. The following is a reference guide for formatting codes as they apply to RTF files compiled by the Help Compiler. See the *Microsoft Word for Windows Technical Reference* or the RTF specification published in the March 1987 issue of the *Microsoft Systems Journal* for a complete description of the specifications regarding RTF files.

## General RTF Syntax

RTF text is composed of text groupings enclosed with curly braces, { . . . }. The entire RTF text file is considered a text grouping and must be entirely enclosed within curly braces. This means the RTF text file must begin with a '{' character and end with a '}'. Your RTF text may also contain text groupings within the RTF text file grouping. Any formatting specified within a text grouping does not affect the formatting outside of that text grouping.

Control words are used to control the formatting of the text. A control word has the following general format:

```
\stringXXX
```

A backslash character, '\', designates the start of a control word. The 'string' portion is the alphabetic string for the control word and the 'XXX' is a numeric parameter between -31,767 and 31,767. Not all control words require a numerical parameter.

The '\' symbol also serves as the RTF equivalent of a C language escape character. For example, if you need to use the '\', '{', or '}' characters displayed in the help text, you precede them with a '\' character. This prevents the Help Compiler from interpreting the character as either the start of a control word or part of a text grouping.

Line breaks within an RTF file are not significant since WINHELP reformats the text according to the placement of paragraph markers. You may place line breaks anywhere you wish to make the RTF text more readable.

## Rich Text Format Signature and Version

The \rtf1 control word is the RTF file signature. The numerical '1' instructs the Help Compiler that the RTF text corresponds to the RTF standard version 1. The current Help Compiler does not recognize standards later than 1. This control word must be included in all Help Compiler RTF files.

## Character Sets

Table 8-1 lists the control words for the character sets supported by the Help Compiler.

| CONTROL WORD | CHARACTER SET |
|---|---|
| \ansi | ANSI |
| \mac | Apple Macintosh |
| \pc | IBM PC (OEM character set) |
| \pca | IBM PC (Used by IBM PS/2) |
| \Windows | Windows |

**Table 8-1 Character set control words**

The character set the RTF file requires should be listed immediately following the RTF signature control word. Your .RTF text for topic files should use the \ansi character set.

## Font Tables

A text grouping with the \fonttbl control word designates a font table grouping. All RTF text files must contain a font table. Within the font table text grouping you list a font index followed by the font family and the font name. You can list as many fonts as you like provided each listing is separated by a semicolon. For example, the following font table defines the font zero name as 'Helv', font one as 'Courier', and font two as 'Symbol' (these correspond to the 'Swiss', 'Modern', and 'Tech' font families):

```
{\fonttbl{\f0\fswiss Helv;}{\f1\fmodern Courier;}{\f2\ftech Symbol}}
```

The text in the RTF file can then be formatted in the different fonts using the \f0, \f1, or \f2 control word. Table 8-2 is a list of the different font family control words supported by the Help Compiler. Use the \fsNum control word to designate the size of the text in half-point units.

| CONTROL WORD | FONT FAMILY |
|---|---|
| \fdecor | Decorative fonts such as Old English and ITC Zapf Chancery |
| \fmodern | Fixed spaced serif and sans serif fonts such as Courier, Elite, and Pica |
| \fnil | Unknown or default font |
| \froman | Proportionally spaced serif fonts such as Tms Rmn and Palatino |
| \fscript | Script fonts such as Script and Cursive |
| \fswiss | Proportionally spaced sans serif fonts such as Swiss and Helv |
| \ftech | Technical, symbolic, or mathematical fonts such as Symbol |

**Table 8-2 Font family control words**

## Color Tables

RTF files have the option of containing a color table. The color table is a list of RGB values that can be referenced in the text to control the foreground and background color of the displayed characters.

For example, consider the following color table:

```
{\colortbl;\red0\green0\blue0;\red255\green255\blue255;\red255\green0\b
lue0;\red0\green255\blue0;\red0\green0\blue255;}
```

The above color table defines the following color indexes:

0  Black

1  White

2  Red

3  Green

4  Blue

These color indexes are later used in the text with the \cf and \cb control words which designate the foreground and background colors for the text, respectively. For example, consider the following which displays the first sentence in the default colors and the second sentence in blue on white:

```
This text is in the default colors. {\cf4\cb1 This text is in blue on
a white background}
```

## Footnotes

Footnotes consist of a footnote reference in the main text followed by the footnote text using the \footnote control word in a text grouping. For example, the following uses the '#' character as the footnote reference:

```
#{\footnote This is the footnote text}
```

Different footnotes in an RTF topic file have different meanings to the Help Compiler. Table 8-3 is a list of how the Help Compiler interprets the footnote text for various footnote references:

| FOOTNOTE REFERENCE | FOOTNOTE TEXT |
|---|---|
| Asterisk (*) | Build Tag |
| Pound Sign (#) | Context String |
| Plus Sign (+) | Brawse Sequence |
| Dollar Sign ($) | Topic Title |
| Letter 'K' | Keyword List |
| Exclamation Point (!) | Help Macro (BC++ 3.1 only) |
| Any other letter | Alternate Keyword List |

**Table 8-3 Footnote references used by the Help Compiler**

## Special Control Words

The Help Compiler uses several RTF control words differently than a normal word processor. For example, the \page control word designates a page break for a document based RTF reader whereas the Help Compiler interprets a page break at the end of a topic. Table 8-4 is a list of the control words that are interpreted differently by a document based RTF reader and the Help Compiler:

| CONTROL WORD | DOCUMENT READER | HELP COMPILER |
|---|---|---|
| \keep | Keep paragraph intact | Do not wrap text |
| \page | Page break | End of topic |
| \strike | Strikethrough text | Text hyper-link hotspot |
| \ul | Single underline | Context string for a hyper-link popup topic |
| \uldb | Double underline | Text hyperlink hotspot |
| \v | Hidden text | Context string for a hyper-link jump-to-topic |

**Table 8-4 Special control words**

## Paragraph and Character Formatting Control Words

Table 8-5 is a list of control words that are used to control the formatting of paragraphs such as the setting of tab positions and indents. Some of the control words accept a numerical parameter in twips. There are 1440 twips per inch. Note that border control locations must precede any border pattern control words. Table 8-6 is a list of character formatting control words.

| CONTROL WORD | MEANING |
| --- | --- |
| \box | Box border |
| \brdrb | Bottom border |
| \brdrdb | Double border |
| \brdrr | Right border |
| \brdrs | Single-line border (default border pattern) |
| \brdrsh | Shadowed border |
| \brdrt | Top border |
| \brdrth | Thick border |
| \brsp*Num* | Space between border and text or picture |
| \fi*Num* | First-line indent (default is zero) |
| \li*Num* | Left indent (default is zero) |
| \line | Line break, but no paragraph break |
| \par | End of a paragraph |
| \pard | Paragraph default settings |
| \ql | Left-aligned text (default) |
| \qr | Right-aligned text |
| \qj | Justified text |
| \qc | Centered text |
| \ri*Num* | Right indent (default is zero) |
| \sa*Num* | Space after a paragraph (default is zero) |
| \sb*Num* | Space before a paragraph (default is zero) |
| \sl*Num* | Space between lines (default is the tallest letter). Negative values indicate an absolute value even if the value is smaller than the tallest letter. Positive values indicate to use the size only if it is larger than the tallest letter |
| \tqc | Centered tab |
| \tqr | Right-aligned tab |
| \tqdec | Decimal-aligned tab |
| \tx*Num* | Set tab position |

**Table 8-5 Paragraph formatting control words**

Table 8-6 lists the control words for text formatting, such as boldface and italics.

| CONTROL WORD | MEANING |
| --- | --- |
| \~ | Nonbreaking space character |
| \- | Nonbreaking hyphen character |
| \'*xx* | Character value in hexadecimal notation |
| \b | Bold |
| \i | Italic |
| \f*Index* | Font index from the font table (see \fonttbl) |
| \fs*Num* | Font size in half-point units |
| \plain | Default character attributes |
| \tab | Tab character |

**Table 8-6 Character control words**

# RESOURCE
# UTILITY
# REFERENCE

# 9

Both BC++ Version 3.0 and Version 3.1 come with two different resource compilers: Microsoft's Resource Compiler (RC.EXE) and Borland's Resource Workshop (WORKSHOP.EXE). The RC resource compiler is the same resource compiler shipped with Microsoft's Software Developer's Kit (SDK) and is licensed for use by Borland with BC++. The DOS IDE uses RC to compile resource script files and bind binary resource (.RES) files to a Windows application or Dynamic Link Library (DLL). WORKSHOP is a standalone resource editor. Like the RC script compiler, it will also compile a .RC file into a .RES file. Additionally, WORKSHOP can edit an existing .RES file as well as directly edit the resources in an .EXE or .DLL file.

Additionally, BC++ Version 3.1 comes with three other resource utilities: BR.EXE, BRCC.EXE, and RLINK.EXE. The BRCC utility compiles resource scripts and the RLINK utility binds the resulting resource to an application or DLL. The BR utility is a call compatible with Microsoft's RC and calls either the BRCC or RLINK utility as appropriate.

Also included with both versions of BC++ is a custom control library called Borland Windows Custom Controls (BWCC). This is a DLL that contains custom control resources created by Borland. You can use these resources in your application to create resources with the Borland look.

This chapter is a detailed reference for the RC and WORKSHOP utilities and the BWCC custom control library. This chapter also covers the creation of custom controls that can be used by the WORKSHOP resource editor.

## WINDOWS RESOURCES

Windows will allow the user to run multiple instances of the same application provided the application does not require multiple data segments. This means the applications you create should use either the small or medium memory model and cannot contain any far data declared directly in the source code; however, in lieu of far data, Windows applications can place virtually all of their static data into different Windows resources, such as RCDATA and User Defined resources. Other types of resources include menus, string tables, accelerators, dialog templates, icons, cursors, text fonts, and bitmaps. These resources are then available to all instances of the application.

You can fully define some of these resources, such as a menu, using only script. Other resources, such as cursors and bitmaps, are more easily defined and stored in a .CUR or .BMP file with the filename referenced in the resource script. Table 9-1 summarizes the different resources, the type of resource (i.e., whether you define it in script format or reference a binary file containing the data), and a brief description.

| SCRIPT STATEMENT | TYPE | DESCRIPTION |
| --- | --- | --- |
| ACCELERATORS | Script | Assigns a WM_COMMAND message identifier to a keystroke. |
| BITMAP | .BMP File | Bitmap resource. |
| DIALOG | Script | Defines a dialog box template used by Windows to create a dialog box. |
| CURSOR | .CUR File | Cursor resource. |
| FONT | .FNT File | Font resource. (Note that font resources are not used directly by Windows applications, but are instead used to create a special type of Dynamic Link Library with a .FON filename extension.) |
| ICON | .ICO File | Icon resource. |
| MENU | Script | Defines a menu structure and hot-keys. |
| RCDATA | Script | Contains any static data required by the Windows application. |
| STRINGTABLE | Script | An unnamed resource that contains most of the text strings used by the Windows application. |
| VERSIONINFO | Script | Creates a version information resource for use by the file installation library. This resource is only available in BC++ Version 3.1. |
| user-defined | Script or File | Same as RCDATA except that you can also define the data in a binary file. |

**Table 9-1 Windows resource types**

# RC.EXE COMMAND LINE OPTIONS

The Project Manager in the BC++ IDE automatically calls Microsoft's RC.EXE compiler to compile resource scripts listed in the project file. RC uses the following syntax for compiling script files:

```
RC [options] script [executable]
```

This will compile the resource script and bind the resource information to the existing executable application or DLL. For example, the following will compile the TEST.RC script into a TEST.RES file and then bind TEST.RES to TEST.EXE:

```
rc test.rc test.exe
```

If you do not specify an .EXE file, RC will automatically bind the resource to an executable file with the same name. For example, the following is identical to the previous example:

```
rc test.rc
```

You can instruct RC to only compile the resource script into a .RES file and not bind it to an executable file by using the -r command line option. The BC++ Project Manager does this whenever it executes RC to compile a script file. The Project Manager also uses RC.EXE to bind the resulting binary resource file to the application executable or DLL. The syntax for this usage of RC is as follows:

```
RC [options] resfile [executable]
```

For example, the following will bind TEST.RES to TEST.EXE:

```
rc test.res test.exe
```

Note that the TEST.EXE parameter is optional. If you leave out the .EXE parameter, RC will bind the .RES file specified to an .EXE file with the same base name. For example, the following is identical to the previous example:

```
rc test.res
```

The *options* parameters control the operation of the RC utility. Options are not case sensitive. Note that not all the options, such as -L and -M, actually apply to resources, but instead control how the resulting executable will operate in the Windows environment. The following are the options that can be used with RC.EXE:

| | |
|---|---|
| -? | Displays the help screen for RC. |
| -30 | Compile/bind a resource file that will work in either Windows Version 3.0 or 3.1. This is the default option for BC.EXE. |
| -31 | Compile/bind a resource file that will only work with Windows 3.1 or later. This is the default option for RC.EXE. |
| -D | Defines a macro definition. |
| -E | Creates a DLL that uses global memory above the EMS bank line instead of below the line. |
| -FE *name* | Renames the resulting .EXE file. |
| -FO *name* | Renames the resulting .RES file. |
| -H | Displays the help screen for RC. |
| -I *path* | Specifies a default directory path. |
| -K | The RC utility normally rearranges segments into contiguous blocks for faster loading. The -K option disables this feature. |
| -L | Same as -LIM32 below. |
| -LIM32 | Instructs Windows to use the LIM 3.2 expanded memory specification. |
| -M | Same as -MULTINST below. |
| -MULTINST | Instructs Windows to provide each instance of the application with a unique block of EMS memory. Each instance will share the same EMS memory if this option is not used. |
| -P | Creates a private DLL that can only be used by one application. |

657

| | |
|---|---|
| -R | Creates a binary resource (.RES) file from a script file without binding the resources to an executable or DLL. |
| -T | Disables operation of the application in the real mode. The resulting application will only be loaded by Windows if it is running in either the standard or enhanced mode. |
| -V | Verbose listing mode that displays resource names as they are compiled. |
| -X | Instructs the resource compiler to ignore the INCLUDE environmental variable. |

Note that Turbo C++ for Windows (TCW) cannot call RC to compile resource script files. It will, however, bind a binary resource file to a Windows application or DLL provided it is in the same directory as your project and the base filename is the same as the project name. If you are using TCW, you should use WORKSHOP to either compile a resource script or create your resources directly in a .RES file. Borland C++ for Windows (BCW) contains an integrated resource compiler that will compile script files.

# WORKSHOP.EXE COMMAND LINE OPTIONS

The WORKSHOP Resource Editor uses the following command line syntax:

    WORKSHOP [options]

The following are the valid command line options for WORKSHOP:

| | |
|---|---|
| -fx *exefile* | Duplicates the changes to the current resource in an executable file. This is useful if you want the changes saved to either a script or .RES file, but also want to test the changes in the executable file without having to rebuild the project. |
| -fo *resfile* | Duplicates changes in a .RES file. This is useful if you are working with a script file and need the changes saved in a .RES file, such as when you are working with the Windows IDE in TCW. |
| -i *path* | Specifies an include path WORKSHOP should use when searching for header files. |
| -x | Instructs WORKSHOP to ignore any include path specified in the [Preferences] section. This option is normally used in combination with the -i *path* option. |

# RESOURCE SCRIPT REFERENCE

The following section lists the statements you can use as resource scripts compiled by either RC or WORKSHOP. Note that the block statement scripts can either be C or

PASCAL style block statements. PASCAL style block statements use the BEGIN and END statements, whereas the C style block statements use the '{' and '}' characters. This reference section uses C style block statements.

Each statement in the resource script reference is listed as either *Mult-line* or *Binary*. A *Binary* resource is one in which the resource information is actually contained in a file and the filename is only referenced in the resource script. For example, a BITMAP resource statement in the script references a filename that contains the actual bitmap image. A *Mult-line* resource is a type of resource in which the resource information is defined in the script. *Mult-line* is an abbreviation for "Multiple-Line."

Many of the resource script statements use the *Load Option* and *Memory Option* parameters. These refer to the following:

*Load Option*

PRELOAD—Load the resource when the application is loaded.

LOADONCALL—Load the resource when required.

*Memory Option*

FIXED/MOVEABLE—FIXED means the resource is not moved in memory once it is loaded. MOVEABLE means it can be moved to different locations in memory by Windows as required.

[NON]DISCARDABLE—DISCARDABLE means the resource can be discarded and subsequently reloaded from the disk when required. This only applies to MOVEABLE resources. The NONDISCARDABLE attribute means it must stay in memory. A FIXED attribute implies NONDISCARDABLE.

[IM]PURE—A PURE attribute means the resource is not modified after loading. An IMPURE attribute means the resource may be modified. The IMPURE attribute should not be used with the DISCARDABLE attribute.

The above attributes are controlled using the [Resource][Memory Options] menu item in the WORKSHOP application for all resource types.

Each reference listing demonstrates how to use the reference in an example Windows application. Because Windows applications are by nature rather involved, the lines of code or script that apply to the referenced resource are listed in bold to make it easier to for you to locate the relevant code or script.

## Resource Script Preprocessor Directives

Resource script file compilers support the following preprocessor directives:

`#define macro` *`string`*

Defines *macro as string*.

`#elif(`*`expression`*`)`

Designates an optional portion to another conditional compilation block and compiles the conditional block if *expression* is nonzero.

`#else`
Designates an optional portion to a conditional compilation block.

`#endif`
Designates the end of a conditional compilation block.

`#if(expression)`
Starts a conditional compilation block if *expression* is nonzero.

`#ifdef macro`
Starts a conditional compilation block if *macro* is defined.

`#ifndef macro`
Starts a conditional compilation block if *macro* is not defined.

`#include <filename>` *or* `#include "filename"`
Includes *filename* in the script compilation.

`#undef macro`
Removes the definition for *macro*.

These preprocessor directives operate identically to their C and C++ counterparts in BC++. Note that the resource compilers also predefined a macro called RC_INVOKED. This is useful for creating common header files for the resource compiler and your C or C++ source code. For example, you could create one header file for your application and include the C prototype declarations inside a conditional compilation block as follows:

```
#include <windows.h>

#define IDM_FILES
#define IDM_HELP

#ifndef RC_INVOKED
/* If this header file is being used by a resource script compiler,
   then this section will be ignored. */

struct MY_STRUCT
{
    int x, y;
}

void Prototype(struct *MY_STRUCT);

#endif
```

## Differences Between WORKSHOP's Script Compiler and RC

Both Microsoft's RC.EXE used by the IDE's Project Manager and the resource script compiler available in WORKSHOP.EXE will compile the same resource script with the following exceptions:

- RC requires the macros defined in the WINDOWS.H include file. The macros are predefined in the WORKSHOP editor.

- WORKSHOP allows binary resources to be listed in a text format within the script file as a multi-line resource using the raw data format.

- WORKSHOP evaluates numerical expressions in any field of the resource script. For example, 2+5-3 would evaluate to a numerical 4 in WORKSHOP, whereas the expression would generate an error in RC.

- WORKSHOP allows you to enter raw data as a hexadecimal string. For example, 'ff 34 2a 61' is an acceptable raw data format in WORKSHOP only.

- WORKSHOP permits the RCDATA resource to be entered either directly in the script or as a file. RC only permits RCDATA resources to be entered directly.

- RC permits parameterized #define directives. For example, the following is permitted in the script by the RC resource compiler:

```
#define m(x) MENUITEM x

MyMenu MENU
{
    m(&Bacon)
    m(&Eggs)
}
```

The above will generate an error in the WORKSHOP script compiler.

## ACCELERATORS                    Keyboard Accelerator Resource

- Mult-line            Binary

### Purpose
The ACCELERATORS statement defines an accelerator table. This table is used by the TranslateAccelerator() function to generate WM_COMMAND messages whenever the user presses a keystroke defined in the table. Accelerators are normally used to provide keyboard alternatives to mouse actions, add alternative "hot-keys" to menu items, or execute some other action that has no mouse or menu item equivalent.

### Script Syntax
```
name ACCELERATORS
{
    key, idvalue, [type] [modifier] [NOINVERT]
    . . .
}
```

*name*
> Name of the resource.

*key*

| | |
|---|---|
| "C" | Keyboard character. |
| "^C" | Same as above with the CONTROL accelerator option listed below. |
| *num* | ASCII numerical value or VK_*xxx* macro definition. |

*idvalue*
> Numerical value of *wParam* for the WM_COMMAND message.

*type*

| | |
|---|---|
| ASCII | The *key* field represents an ASCII keyboard character (default). |
| VIRTKEY | The *key* field is a numerical value for a virtual key macro identifier. |

*modifier*
> The accelerator is activated only when the listed combination of modifier keys are held down while the keyboard character or virtual key is pressed. You can use any combination or none of the following modifiers:

| | |
|---|---|
| ALT | The (Alt) key is held down. |
| CONTROL | The (Ctrl) key is held down. |
| SHIFT | Either the right or left (Shift) key is held down. |
| NOINVERT | Windows will normally highlight, or flash, the menu item with the same numerical value as the *idvalue* field. This option instructs Windows not to flash any corresponding menu items. |

## Description

Menu items are normally selected through a series of mouse selections or keypresses. Accelerators provide an alternative method for executing menu items. You define an accelerator to a normal ASCII text character or as one of the virtual characters listed in Table 9-2.

With the accelerator keys defined in a named resource, your application then loads the accelerators using the LoadAccelerators() function. You application's message loop will have to call the TranslateAccelerator() function to translate the user's keystrokes into WM_COMMAND messages as follows:

```
/* Enter the message loop */
while(GetMessage(&msg, 0, 0, 0))
{
    /* If the message is a keystroke listed on the accelerator
       table, then translate the accelerator and do not dispatch
       the keystroke. */
    if(!TranslateAccelerator(hWnd, hAccTable, &msg))
    {
        TranslateMessage(&msg);
        DispatchMessage(&msg);
    }
}
```

Note that because modal Dialog Boxes, i.e., Dialog Boxes created using the DialogBox() or DialogBoxIndirect() function, use their own internal message loop, the TranslateAccelerator() function in your application's message loop is not called and keystrokes are not translated into command messages.

Windows normally operates on an IBM compatible, but it is designed so that the same Windows application can run on many different machines. Not all machines use keyboards that are IBM compatible, but they usually have similar keys. Because of this, Windows references the function and paging control keys as virtual keys. Virtual keys allow you to reference keystrokes without having to worry about the actual numerical value sent by the keyboard to the system. Windows translates the operating system keystrokes into virtual keystrokes at run time. Table 9-2 lists the virtual keys defined in WINDOWS.H and the equivalent keystrokes on an IBM-compatible keyboard. Not all virtual keys have equivalent keystrokes on an IBM compatible. These virtual keys are listed with a '(none)' indicating there is no IBM-compatible equivalent. Virtual keys with an 'N/A' do not apply to accelerators.

| VIRTUAL KEY | IBM KEY | VIRTUAL KEY | IBM KEY |
|---|---|---|---|
| VK_ADD | Grey Plus | VK_BACK | Backspace |
| VK_CANCEL | Ctrl Break | VK_CAPITAL | (none) |
| VK_CLEAR | Keypad 5 | VK_CONTROL | N/A |
| VK_DECIMAL | Keypad. | VK_DELETE | Delete |
| VK_DIVIDE | Grey Divide | VK_DOWN | Down Arrow |
| VK_END | End | VK_EXECUTE | (none) |
| VK_ESCAPE | Esc | VK_F1 | F1 |
| VK_F2 | F2 | VK_F3 | F3 |
| VK_F4 | F4 | VK_F5 | F5 |
| VK_F6 | F6 | VK_F7 | F7 |
| VK_F8 | F8 | VK_F9 | F9 |
| VK_F10 | F10 | VK_F11 | F11 |
| VK_F12 | F12 | VK_F13 | (none) |
| VK_F14 | (none) | VK_F15 | (none) |
| VK_F16 | (none) | VK_HELP | (none) |
| VK_HOME | Home | VK_INSERT | Insert |
| VK_LEFT | Left Arrow | VK_LBUTTON | N/A |
| VK_MBUTTON | N/A | VK_MENU | (none) |
| VK_MULTIPLY | Grey Multiply | VK_NEXT | Page Down |
| VK_NUMPAD0 | Grey 0 | VK_NUMPAD1 | Grey 1 |
| VK_NUMPAD2 | Grey 2 | VK_NUMPAD3 | Grey 3 |

*Table 9-2 (continued)*

| | | | |
|---|---|---|---|
| VK_NUMPAD4 | (Grey 4) | VK_NUMPAD5 | (Grey 5) |
| VK_NUMPAD6 | (Grey 6) | VK_NUMPAD7 | (Grey 7) |
| VK_NUMPAD8 | (Grey 8) | VK_NUMPAD9 | (Grey 8) |
| VK_NUMLOCK | (Num Lock) | VK_PAUSE | (Pause) |
| VK_PRINT | (none) | VK_PRIOR | (Page Up) |
| VK_RBUTTON | N/A | VK_RETURN | (Enter) |
| VK_RIGHT | (Right Arrow) | VK_SELECT | (none) |
| VK_SEPARATOR | (none) | VK_SHIFT | N/A |
| VK_SNAPSHOT | N/A | VK_SPACE | (Space) |
| VK_SUBTRACT | (Grey Minus) | VK_TAB | (Tab) |
| VK_UP | (Arrow Up) | | |

**Table 9-2 Virtual keys defined in WINDOWS.H and the equivalent keys on an IBM-compatible keyboard**

An Accelerator does not necessarily have to correspond to a menu item. You can use them whenever you would like a WM_COMMAND message generated whenever a particular keystroke combination is pressed.

Figure 9-1 shows the accelerator editor available in WORKSHOP. The fields in the resource script correspond to the window fields listed in Table 9-3.

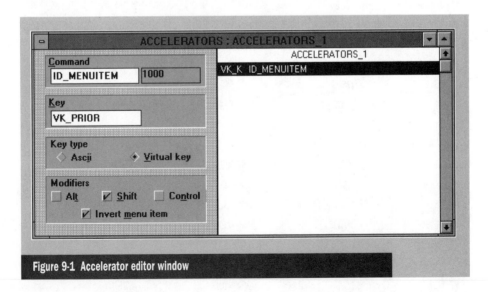

**Figure 9-1 Accelerator editor window**

| WORKSHOP FIELD | SCRIPT FIELD |
|---|---|
| Command | *idvalue* field |
| Key | *key* field |
| Ascii | ASCII type option |
| Virtual key | VIRTKEY type option |
| Alt | ALT modifier option |
| Shift | SHIFT modifier option |
| Control | CONTROL modifier option |
| Invert Menu item | Omit NOINVERT option |

**Table 9-3 WORKSHOP accelerator editor menu items and their corresponding script fields**

# RELATED WINDOW FUNCTIONS

`HANDLE LoadAccelerators(HANDLE, LPSTR);`

Loads an accelerator resource.

`int TranslateAccelerator(HWND, HANDLE, LPMSG);`

Placed in a message loop to screen for accelerator keystrokes and translate them to WM_COMMAND messages.

### Example

Write a Windows application that uses accelerators to define the (Esc) key as the IDM_EXIT menu item. The following application uses the LoadAccelerators() and TranslateAccelerator() functions as discussed in the Description section.

**acc\hello.h**

```
#include <windows.h>

/* Define the menu item macros */
#define IDM_EXIT     2000
```

**acc\hello.rc**

```
#include "hello.h"

; The application's main menu
MainMenu MENU
{
    MENUITEM "E&xit",  IDM_EXIT
}

; The accelerator table
AccTable ACCELERATORS
{
    VK_ESCAPE, IDM_EXIT, VIRTKEY
}
```

**acc\hello.c**

```c
#include "hello.h"

char AppTitle[] = "Hello, Windows!";
HANDLE hThisInstance;

/* We know not all the variables are used, so we may as well disable
   the warning message. */
#pragma warn -par

/* Define the application window's message processing function */
long FAR PASCAL WndProc( HWND hWnd, unsigned msg, WORD wParam,
                         LONG lParam)
{
    RECT rect;
    PAINTSTRUCT ps;
    HDC hDC;

    switch(msg)
    {
        /* Is it a menu command? */
        case WM_COMMAND:
            switch(wParam)
            {
                case IDM_EXIT:
                    /* Leave the application by destroying the
                       main window */
                    DestroyWindow(hWnd);
                    break;
            }
            break;

        /* Paint the window */
        case WM_PAINT:
            hDC = BeginPaint(hWnd, &ps);

            /* Display the application title in the center of
               the window */
            GetClientRect(hWnd, &rect);
            DrawText(hDC, AppTitle, sizeof(AppTitle) - 1, &rect,
                    DT_SINGLELINE | DT_VCENTER | DT_CENTER);

            EndPaint(hWnd, &ps);
            break;

        /* Time to quit! */
        case WM_DESTROY:
            PostQuitMessage(0);
            break;

        /* All other messages go here. */
        default:
            return(DefWindowProc(hWnd, msg, wParam, lParam));
    }
    return(0);
}
```

```
int PASCAL WinMain(HANDLE hInstance, HANDLE hPrevInstance,
                   LPSTR lpCmdLine, int nCmdShow)
{
   int xDim, yDim;
   HWND hWnd;
   MSG msg;
   HANDLE hAccTable;

   /* Make the instance handle globally available */
   hThisInstance = hInstance;

   /* Register the application window class */
   if(!hPrevInstance)
   {
        WNDCLASS wc;

   wc.style            = CS_HREDRAW | CS_VREDRAW;
   wc.lpfnWndProc      = WndProc;
   wc.cbClsExtra       = 0;
   wc.cbWndExtra       = 0;
   wc.hInstance        = hInstance;
   wc.hIcon            = LoadIcon(NULL, IDI_HAND);
   wc.hCursor          = LoadCursor(NULL, IDC_ARROW);
   wc.hbrBackground    = GetStockObject(WHITE_BRUSH);
   wc.lpszMenuName     = "MainMenu";
   wc.lpszClassName    = AppTitle;

   if(!RegisterClass(&wc))
       return(FALSE);
   }

   /* Load the accelerator table resource */
   hAccTable = LoadAccelerators(hInstance, "AccTable");

   /* Get the screen dimensions */
   xDim = GetSystemMetrics(SM_CXSCREEN);
   yDim = GetSystemMetrics(SM_CYSCREEN);

   hWnd = CreateWindow(AppTitle, AppTitle, WS_OVERLAPPEDWINDOW,
          xDim / 4, yDim / 4, xDim / 2, yDim / 2,
          NULL, NULL, hInstance, NULL);

   if(hWnd == NULL)
     return(FALSE);

   /* Display the window */
   ShowWindow(hWnd, nCmdShow);

   /* Enter the message loop */
   while(GetMessage(&msg, 0, 0, 0))
   {
     /* If the message is a keystroke listed on the accelerator
        table, then translate the accelerator and do not dispatch
        the keystroke. */
     if(!TranslateAccelerator(hWnd, hAccTable, &msg))
     {
```

```
        TranslateMessage(&msg);
        DispatchMessage(&msg);
    }
}

/* Exit the application */
return(O);
}
```

# BITMAP

Mult-line   ▪ Binary

### Purpose
The BITMAP statement includes a bitmap (.BMP) file as a named resource available to the application. The bitmaps can then be displayed in the application in either a window or dialog box.

### Script Syntax
*name* BITMAP [*Load Option*] [*Memory Option*] *filename*

*name*
> Name of the bitmap resource.

*filename*
> The name of the bitmap (.BMP) file.

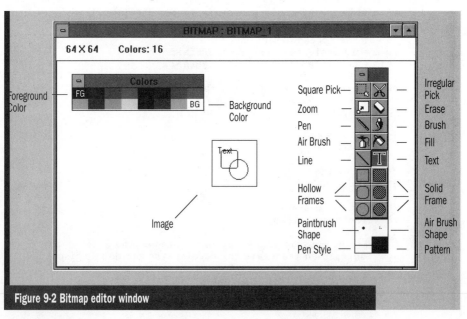

**Figure 9-2 Bitmap editor window**

## Description

When you first open the WORKSHOP editor for bitmaps, as shown in Figure 9-2, you have the choice of either script or binary format. The script format places the bitmap in the text of the script as raw hexadecimal data. Note that bitmap script format cannot be compiled by the RC script compiler used by the BC++ Project Manager. The binary format saves the bitmap as a normal .BMP file and references the file in the script text.

You choose the foreground painting color by clicking the left mouse button on one of the colors in the *Colors* window. Clicking a color with the right mouse button sets the background color. Double clicking on a particular color with either the left or the right button allows you to redefine the color.

The tools window lets you move portions of the image using either the square or irregular shaped pick, zoom or erase the image, draw with a pen, brush, air brush, or fill color, and draw straight lines, as well as hollow and solid rectangles, rounded rectangles, and circles. Bitmaps can be created by any paint program that supports the .BMP format. This includes the PBRUSH Windows application and the bitmap editor in WORKSHOP.

## Related Window Functions

```
HBITMAP LoadBitmap(HANDLE, LPSTR);
```
Returns a handle to a bitmap resource.

```
HANDLE SelectObject(HDC, HANDLE);
```
Selects a bitmap in the memory display context.

## Example

Modify the "Hello, Windows!" application to display a bitmap resource in the upper-lefthand corner of the main application window. The following are the required modifications to the "Hello, Windows!" application used in the ACCELERATOR statement example:

**bitmap\hello.rc**

```
#include "hello.h"

; The application's main menu
MainMenu MENU
{
    MENUITEM "E&xit",  IDM_EXIT
}

; The accelerator table
AccTable ACCELERATORS
{
    VK_ESCAPE, IDM_EXIT, VIRTKEY
}

HelloBMP BITMAP PRELOAD MOVEABLE hello.bmp
```

**bitmap\hello.c**

. . .

```
        HDC hDC, hMemDC;
        HBITMAP hOldBitmap;

. . .

        /* Paint the window */
        case WM_PAINT:
            hDC = BeginPaint(hWnd, &ps);

            /* Display the application title in the center of
               the window */
            GetClientRect(hWnd, &rect);
            DrawText(hDC, AppTitle, sizeof(AppTitle) - 1, &rect,
                     DT_SINGLELINE | DT_VCENTER | DT_CENTER);

            /* Create a memory DC and select the bitmap */
            hMemDC = CreateCompatibleDC(hDC);
            hOldBitmap = SelectObject(hMemDC, hHelloBMP);

            /* Copy the bitmap onto the window */
            BitBlt(hDC, 0, 0, 64, 64, hMemDC, 0, 0, SRCCOPY);

            /* Delete the memory display context */
            SelectObject(hMemDC, hOldBitmap);
            DeleteDC(hMemDC);

        EndPaint(hWnd, &ps);
        break;

. . .

    /* Load the accelerator table resource */
    hAccTable = LoadAccelerators(hInstance, "AccTable");

    /* Load the bitmap resource */
    hHelloBMP = LoadBitmap(hInstance, "HelloBMP");

    /* Get the screen dimensions */
    xDim = GetSystemMetrics(SM_CXSCREEN);
    yDim = GetSystemMetrics(SM_CYSCREEN);

. . .
```

In the above application for processing a WM_PAINT message, a memory display context is created and the bitmap resource is selected. The BitBlt() function is then used to copy the bitmap from the memory display context to the window's display context.

# CURSOR

**Cursor Resource**

Multi-line   ■  Binary

## Purpose
The CURSOR statement includes a mouse cursor (.CUR) file as a named resource available to the application.

## Script Syntax

*name* CURSOR [*Load Option*] [*Memory Option*] *filename*

*name*
    Name of the cursor resource.

*filename*
    The name of the cursor (.CUR) file.

## Description

You can define different mouse cursors for an application as a resource using the CURSOR statement in the resource script. The LoadCursor() function is used in the application to retrieve a handle to the cursor resource.

Figure 9-3 shows the cursor editor available in WORKSHOP. When the cursor window is opened, you have the choice of either script or binary format. The script format places the cursor in the text of the script as raw hexadecimal data. This format cannot be compiled by the RC script compiler used by the BC++ Project Manager. The binary format saves the cursor as a normal .CUR file and references the file in the script text.

The tools available in the cursor editor are the same as with the bitmap editor (see the BITMAP statement). The pixel mapping for the cursor consists of four color components: black, white, transparent, and inverted. The cursor editor displays the black and white portions of the cursor drawing in black and white. The transparent and inverted portions are displayed in blue and yellow, respectively. Clicking the left mouse button on one of these four color components selects that component as the drawing tool's foreground color. Clicking the left button on a component selects it as the tool's background color.

A cursor also has a point known as the "Hot Spot." This is the pixel on the cursor map that references the cursor's location when the cursor is moved or clicked. You set the cursor's hot-spot by selecting the [Cursor][Set hot spot] menu item.

## Related Window Functions

HCURSOR LoadCursor(HANDLE, LPSTR);
    Returns a handle to a cursor resource.

HCURSOR SetCursor(HANDLE);
    Temporarily changes the cursor shape. Note that if the cursor is not captured using the SetCapture() function, Windows will set the default cursor shape when the cursor is moved.

SetClassWord(HWND, int, int);
    Used to change the default cursor shape when the cursor is positioned over a window.

## Example

Modify the "Hello, Windows!" application to display the 'H' cursor when the cursor is positioned over the application window. The following are the required modifications to the "Hello, Windows!" application used in the ACCELERATOR statement example:

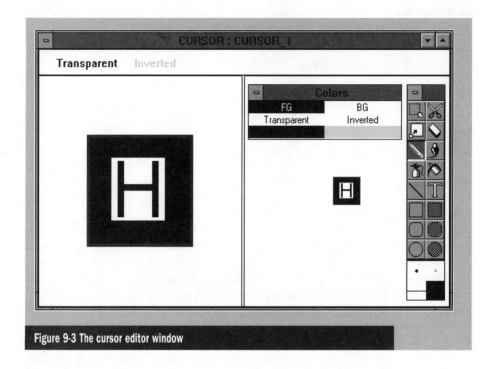

**Figure 9-3 The cursor editor window**

**cursor\hello.h**

```
#include <windows.h>

/* Define the menu item macros */
#define IDM_EXIT      2000
#define IDM_HCURSOR   3000
```

**cursor\hello.rc**

```
#include "hello.h"

; Cursor resource
hCursor CURSOR PRELOAD MOVEABLE hello.cur

; The application's main menu
MainMenu  MENU
{
   MENUITEM  "E&xit",      IDM_EXIT
   MENUITEM  "'&H' Cursor", IDM_HCURSOR
}

; The accelerator table
AccTable ACCELERATORS
{
   VK_ESCAPE, IDM_EXIT, VIRTKEY
}
```

**cursor\hello.c**

```
    . . .

    HCURSOR hCursor;

    . . .

        case WM_COMMAND:
            switch(wParam)
            {
                case IDM_HCURSOR:
                    SetClassWord(hWnd, GCW_HCURSOR, hCursor);
                    break;

                case IDM_EXIT:

    . . .

    /* Load the accelerator table resource */
    hAccTable = LoadAccelerators(hInstance, "AccTable");

    /* Load the cursor resource */
    hCursor = LoadCursor(hInstance, "hCursor");

    . . .
```

When the ['H' cursor] menu item is selected, the SetClassWord() function is called to change the shape of the cursor to the H-shaped cursor defined in the HELLO.CUR cursor file.

# DIALOG                                                  Dialog Box Resource

▪ Mult-line          Binary

## Purpose
The DIALOG statement starts the definition of a dialog box resource.

## Script Syntax
```
name DIALOG [Load Option] [Memory Option] xPos, yPos, width, height
[STYLE DialogStyle]
[CAPTION "title"]
[MENU MenuName]
[CLASS "WindowClass"]
[FONT size, "FontName"]
{
    [CHECKBOX text, id, xPos, yPos, width, height, [ControlStyle]]
    [CONTROL text, id, WindowClass, ControlStyle, xPos, yPos, width,
        height]
    [COMBOBOX id, xPos, yPos, width, height [ControlStyle]]
    [CTEXT text, id, xPos, yPos, width, height, [ControlStyle]]
    [DEFPUSHBUTTON text, id, xPos, yPos, width, height, [ControlStyle]]
```

```
[EDITTEXT id, xPos, yPos, width, height, [ControlStyle]]
[GROUPBOX text, id, xPos, yPos, width, height [ControlStyle]]
[ICON IconName, id, xPos, yPos, width, height, [ControlStyle]]
[LISTBOX id, xPos, yPos, width, height, [ControlStyle]]
[LTEXT text, id, xPos, yPos, width, height, [ControlStyle]]
[PUSHBUTTON text, id, xPos, yPos, width, height, [ControlStyle]]
[RADIOBUTTON text, id, xPos, yPos, width, height, [ControlStyle]]
[RTEXT text, id, xPos, yPos, width, height, [ControlStyle]]
[SCROLLBAR id, xPos, yPos, width, height, [ControlStyle]]
 . . .
}
```

*name*

The name of the dialog resource.

*xPos, yPos*

This is the position of the upper-lefthand corner of the dialog box relative to the parent window in dialog units. For control windows, this is the position relative to the dialog box client area in dialog units. See the Description section for an explanation of dialog units.

*width, height*

These parameters define the dimension of the dialog box or control window in dialog units.

STYLE *DialogStyle*

The window style for the dialog box. The default style is WS_POPUP | WS_CAPTION if this statement is not used. The style value can be any valid combination of styles used with the CreateWindow() function.

CAPTION *"title"*

The title for the dialog box. The default title is a NULL string. For most controls, a letter preceded by an '&' character will be displayed as an underlined character and used as an accelerator key. Use '&&' to actually display the '&' character.

MENU *MenuName*

The resource name for the dialog box's menu. The dialog box will not have a menu if this statement is missing.

CLASS *"WindowClass"*

The window class for the dialog box. The standard dialog window class is used if this statement is missing. If a custom window class is used, the procedure processing window messages must call the DefDlgProc() function instead of the DefWindowProc() function. Also, the *cbWndExtra* field of the window class must be set to DLGWINDOWEXTRA. If you are using Borland Windows Custom Controls (BWCC), then you should use the "BorDlg" window class with this statement.

FONT *size*, *"FontName"*

The *size* parameter is the point size for the text displayed in the dialog box. The *FontName* is the name of the font to be used by the dialog box. The default font and size are the system font. The desired font must be loaded before displaying the dialog box. This is done by either the user having the font loaded as part of the WIN.INI file or your application loading the font using the LoadFont() function.

### Description

The dialog box resource defines the size and characteristics of a dialog box created using either the CreateDialog() or DialogBox() function. All the control windows listed in the body of the DIALOG statement are automatically created and displayed in the order listed in the script. Figure 9-4 shows the window for defining the attributes of the dialog box window in the WORKSHOP editor.

Figure 9-4 Dialog box editor

## Dialog Box Size and Position

The size and position of the dialog box within the dialog box editor will be the position of the dialog box values stored for the position and width parameters in the resource script text. These values are in dialog units. Dialog units are based on a measure called the *dialog base* unit. This unit of measure varies depending on the size of the user's system font. This method for sizing and positioning a dialog box and the various controls enables the dialog box to be displayed proportional to the resolution of the user's screen resolution. The horizontal and vertical value of the dialog unit is calculated using the GetDialogBaseUnit() function. This function returns the height and width of the system font in pixels as the high and low word of the returned value, respectively. The pixel width of the horizontal dialog unit is 1/4 the value of the pixel width for the system font. The vertical pixel height of a dialog unit is 1/8 the height of the system font. For example, the exact size of a dialog box can be calculated as follows:

```
DlgPixelWidth = (LOWORD(GetDialogBaseUnits()) / 4) * width;
DlgPixelHeight = (HIWORD(GetDialogBaseUnits()) / 8) * height;
```

The position of the dialog box can also be calculated in a similar fashion if required as well as the size and position of the dialog box's control windows.

## Dialog Box Attributes

The attributes for the dialog box are edited in WORKSHOP by double-clicking the dialog box's caption. This will display the "Window style" window shown in Figure 9-5 for changing the dialog box's attributes.

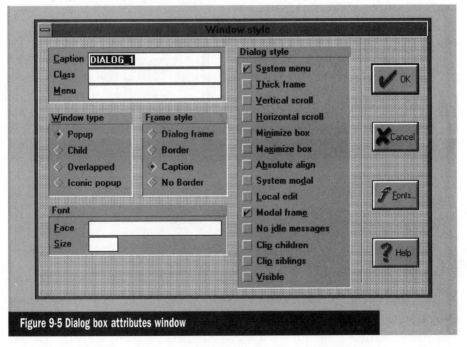

**Figure 9-5 Dialog box attributes window**

This window allows you to change the default STYLE, CAPTION, MENU, CLASS, and FONT attributes for the window. See Table 9-4 for a listing of the Window type, Frame style, and Dialog style sections corresponding to the following window style parameters defined in WINDOWS.H. You should refer to your Windows programming reference manuals or look up the "Windows Style" topic for the CreateWindow() function in the BC++ on-line help for an explanation of windows style attributes.

| ITEM | STYLE ATTRIBUTE |
| --- | --- |
| Window type | |
| Popup | WS_POPUP |
| Child | WS_CHILD |
| Overlapped | WS_OVERLAPPED |
| Iconic popup | WS_ICONICPOPUP |
| Frame style | |
| Dialog frame | DS_DLGFRAME |
| Border | WS_BORDER |
| Caption | WS_CAPTION |
| No Border | (none) |
| Dialog style | |
| System menu | WS_SYSMENU |
| Thick frame | WS_THICKFRAME |
| Vertical scroll | WS_VSCROLL |
| Horizontal scroll | WS_HSCROLL |
| Minimize box | WS_MINIMIZEBOX |
| Maximize box | WS_MAXIMIZEBOX |
| Absolute align | DS_ABSALIGN |
| System modal | DS_SYSMODAL |
| Local edit | DS_LOCALEDIT |
| Modal frame | DS_MODALFRAME |
| No idle messages | DS_NOIDLEMSG |
| Clip children | WS_CLIPCHILDREN |
| Clip siblings | WS_CLIPSIBLINGS |
| Visible | WS_VISIBLE |

**Table 9-4 WORKSHOP menu items and their corresponding style parameters**

## Windows Dialog Box Control Statements

A dialog box control is the same as any window you create using the CreateWindow() function except that it is created automatically whenever the main dialog box window is created. This is why the CONTROL statement uses many of the same parameters as the CreateWindow() function. The parameters for a CONTROL statement are passed by the function creating the dialog box directly to the CreateWindow() function. For ex-

677

ample, the following is the relationship between the CONTROL statement and the CreateWindow() function:

```
HWND CreateWindow(WindowClass, text, ControlStyle, xPos, yPos,
                  width, height, hDlg, id, hInstance, lpParam);

CONTROL text, id, WindowClass, ControlStyle, xPos, yPos, width, height
```

Each of the parameters of the CreateWindow() function shown in bold face correspond to a field in the CONTROL statement. The *hDlg*, *hInstance*, and *lpParam* parameters are supplied by the function creating the dialog box. Note that the position and size parameters are translated from dialog units to client coordinates at run time.

Other dialog box control statements are translated by the script compiler into a CONTROL statement. Table 9-5 relates the specific control statements to their equivalent CONTROL statement class and style. Note that the WORKSHOP editor writes the script for dialog box controls as a CONTROL statement if the control is created in the editor.

CHECKBOX text, id, xPos, yPos, width, height, ControlStyle
    CONTROL *text, id,* "BUTTON", BS_CHECKBOX | *ControlStyle, xPos, yPos, width, height*

COMBOBOX id, xPos, yPos, width, height ControlStyle
    CONTROL "", *id,* "COMBOBOX", CBS_SIMPLE | *ControlStyle, xPos, yPos, width, height*

CTEXT text, id, xPos, yPos, width, height, ControlStyle
    CONTROL *text, id,* "STATIC", SS_CENTER | *ControlStyle, xPos, yPos, width, height*

DEFPUSHBUTTON text, id, xPos, yPos, width, height, ControlStyle
    CONTROL *text, id,* "BUTTON", BS_DEFPUSHBUTTON | *ControlStyle, xPos, yPos, width, height*

EDITTEXT id, xPos, yPos, width, height, ControlStyle
    CONTROL "", *id,* "EDIT", ES_LEFT | *ControlStyle, xPos, yPos, width, height*

GROUPBOX text, id, xPos, yPos, width, height ControlStyle
    CONTROL *text, id,* "BUTTON", BS_GROUPBOX | *ControlStyle, xPos, yPos, width, height*

ICON IconName, id, xPos, yPos, width, height, ControlStyle
    CONTROL "*IconName*", *id,* "STATIC", SS_ICON | *ControlStyle, xPos, yPos, width, height*

LISTBOX id, xPos, yPos, width, height, ControlStyle
    CONTROL "", *id,* "LISTBOX", LBS_NOTIFY | *ControlStyle, xPos, yPos, width, height*

LTEXT text, id, xPos, yPos, width, height, ControlStyle

    CONTROL *text, id,* "STATIC", SS_LEFT | *ControlStyle, xPos, yPos, width, height*

PUSHBUTTON text, id, xPos, yPos, width, height, ControlStyle

    CONTROL *text, id,* "BUTTON", BS_PUSHBUTTON | *ControlStyle, xPos, yPos, width, height*

RADIOBUTTON text, id, xPos, yPos, width, height, ControlStyle

    CONTROL *text, id,* "BUTTON", BS_RADIOBUTTON | *ControlStyle, xPos, yPos, width, height*

RTEXT text, id, xPos, yPos, width, height, ControlStyle

    CONTROL *text, id,* "STATIC", SS_RIGHT | *ControlStyle, xPos, yPos, width, height*

SCROLLBAR id, xPos, yPos, width, height, ControlStyle

    CONTROL "", *id,* "SCROLLBAR", *ControlStyle, xPos, yPos, width, height*

**Table 9-5 Specific control window statements as they relate to CONTROL statements**

See the description for the CreateWindow() function in the IDE's or TCW's on-line help for information on the different styles available for each control window class.

## Borland Windows Custom Control Statements

The Borland Windows Custom Control (BWCC) statements use four different window classes, "BorBtn," "BorRadio," "BorShade," and "BorStatic." Each of these classes is derived from the Windows control equivalent and uses the same style parameters. The Borland specific style option macros, such as BBS_BITMAP and BBS_OWNERDRAW, are not defined in WINDOWS.H. The following Borland specific header file can be used both in a resource script and in your application's source code to define these macros:

**bwccdef.h**

```
#ifdef RC_INVOKED

#define BSS_GROUP            1L
#define BSS_HDIP             2L
#define BSS_VDIP             3L
#define BSS_HBUMP            4L
#define BSS_VBUMP            5L
#define BBS_OWNERDRAW        0x1000L
#define BBS_PARENTNOTIFY     0x2000L
#define BBS_DLGPAINT         0x4000L
#define BBS_BITMAP           0x8000L

#else
#include <bwcc.h>
#endif
```

The RC_INVOKED macro is only defined during compilation of a resource script and not while compiling C or C++ source code. This means the above header file will only define the macros when compiled by RC. When the file is compiled using BC++, then the BWCC.H header file is included instead. The BWCC.H file also contains the function prototypes and message macros used by BWCC in addition to the style macros. Note that if you are using the WORKSHOP script compiler, you will not need to use the above header files as they are already predefined in WORKSHOP.

See the Borland Windows Custom Controls Reference for details on the Borland specific styles.

### Related Window Functions
```
HWND CreateDialog(HANDLE, LPSTR, HWND, FARPROC);
```
Creates a modeless dialog box.

```
int DialogBox(HANDLE, LPSTR, HWND, FARPROC);
```
Creates a modal dialog box.

### Example
Modify the "Hello, Windows!" application to include an "About" dialog box.


# FONT                                          Text Font Resource

Mult-line   ▪ Binary

### Purpose
The FONT statement includes a font typeface (.FNT) file as a named resource in a font resource (.FON) file.

### Script Syntax
*number* FONT [*Load Option*] [*Memory Option*] *filename*

*number*
Unique number for the font resource.

*filename*
The name of the font (.FNT) file.

### Description
Font resources cannot be used directly as an application resource. Instead, a font typeface (.FNT) file is created using the Font editor in WORKSHOP shown in Figure 9-6.

Next, the .FNT file is compiled into a resource script file using the FONT script statement. The *name* parameter should be a numerical value. The resource script file is then used to create a Dynamic Link Library with a .DEF file containing descriptions of the font resources. The Description statements in the .DEF file must have one of the following formats:

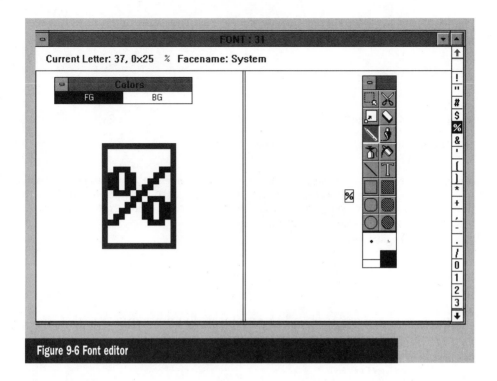

**Figure 9-6 Font editor**

*Raster Font*
```
Description 'FONTRES AspectRatio, LogPixelsX, LogPixelsY: Comment'
```

*Vector Font*
```
Description 'FONTRES CONTINUOUSSCALING: Comment'
```

*Device Screen Font*
```
Description 'FONTRES DISPLAY: Comment'
```

*Device Specific Font*
```
Description 'FONTRES DEVICESPECIFIC DeviceType: Comment'
```

Note that the Font Editor in WORKSHOP will only create *Raster Font* .FNT files.

The information *AspectRatio*, *LogPixelsX*, and *LogPixelsY* parameters contain for these types of font files is used by Windows to match the font with a device having similar characteristics. The *LogPixelsX* and *LogPixelsY* parameters are the number of pixels per inch in the horizontal and vertical directions, respectively. The *AspectRatio* parameter is calculated as follows and rounded to the nearest integer:

```
LogPixelsX
LogPixelsY      * 100
```

For example, consider the following description statement:

```
Description 'FONTRES 133,96,72 : My Fonts'
```

681

The *LogPixelsX* is 96 and the *LogPixelsY* is 72. The *AspectRatio* value of 133 is calculated as follows:

```
96
72        * 100 = 133.33333333
```

## Related Window Functions

```
int AddFontResource(LPSTR lpFilename);
```
   Loads a .FON file.

```
HFONT CreateFont(int nHeight, int nWidth, int nEscapement, int nOrientation,
    int nWeight, BYTE cItalic, BYTE cUnderline, BYTE cStrikeOut, BYTE
    cCharSet, BYTE cOutputPrecision, BYTE cClipPrecision, BYTE cQuality,
    BYTE cPitchAndFamily, LPSTR lpFacename);
```
   Creates a logical font.

```
BOOL RemoveFontResource(LPSTR lpFilename);
```
   Removes a .FON file resource from the system.

## Example
Create a MYFONT.FON file from a MYFIX.FNT and MYPROP.FNT font file.

**font\myfont.rc**
```
100 FONT MyFix.FNT
101 FONT MyProp.FNT
```

**font\myfont.c**
```
#include <windows.h>

#pragma warn -par
int FAR PASCAL LibMain(HANDLE hInstance, WORD wData, WORD wHeap,
    LPSTR lpCmdLine)
{
  if(wHeap != 0)
     UnlockData(0);
  return(1);
}
```

**font\myfont.def**
```
LIBRARY MyFont

Description 'FONTRES 133,96,72 : My Fonts'

STUB 'WINSTUB.EXE'
DATA NONE
```

The linker will generate a file called MYFONT.DLL, which is then renamed MYFONT.FON. The MYFONT.FON file can then be listed in the [fonts] section of the user's WIN.INI file or loaded at run time using the AddFontResource() function.

# ICON

Mult-line   ▪   Binary

## Purpose

An ICON statement instructs the script compiler to include an icon (.ICO) file as an application resource.

## Script Syntax

```
name ICON [Load Option] [Memory Option] filename
```

*name*
> Unique name for the icon resource.

*filename*
> The name of the icon (.ICO) file.

## Description

An icon is a specialized form of a bitmap that usually, but not always, represents a minimized window. You create a .ICO file using the Icon editor in WORKSHOP shown in Figure 9-7.

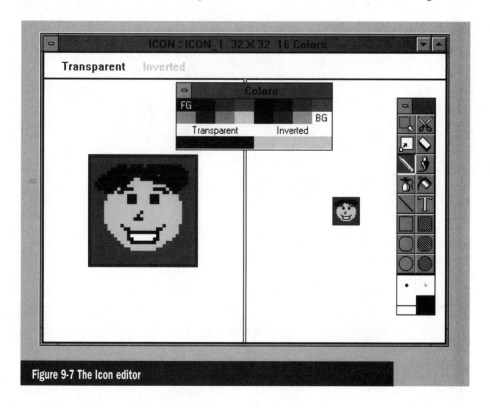

Figure 9-7 The Icon editor

Note that even though the Icon Editor will create a 256 color icon, Windows will only display the icon in 16 colors.

### Related Window Functions
```
HICON LoadIcon(HANDLE hInstance, LPSTR lpIconName);
```
Retrieve the handle for an icon resource.

### Example
Modify the "Hello, Windows!" application to include an icon for the application window.

**icon\hello.rc**
```
#include "hello.h"

HelloIcon ICON LOADONCALL DISCARDABLE Hello.ICO

; The application's main menu
MainMenu  MENU
{
. . .
```

**icon\hello.c**
```
. . .
    if(!hPrevInstance)
    {
       WNDCLASS wc;

       wc.style           = CS_HREDRAW | CS_VREDRAW;
       wc.lpfnWndProc     = WndProc;
       wc.cbClsExtra      = 0;
       wc.cbWndExtra      = 0;
       wc.hInstance       = hInstance;
       wc.hIcon           = LoadIcon(hInstance, "HelloIcon");
       wc.hCursor         = LoadCursor(NULL, IDC_ARROW);
       wc.hbrBackground   = GetStockObject(WHITE_BRUSH);
       wc.lpszMenuName    = "MainMenu";
       wc.lpszClassName   = AppTitle;

       if(!RegisterClass(&wc))
           return(FALSE);
    }
. . .
```

The above changes will display the HELLO.ICO icon when the "Hello, Windows!" application window is minimized.

# MENU                                        Menu Resource

- Mult-line      Binary

### Purpose
The MENU script statement compiles a menu resource.

### Script Syntax

```
name MENU [Load Option] [Memory Option]
{
    MENUITEM text, ID, [CHECKED] [GRAYED] [HELP] [INACTIVE]
        [MENUBARBREAK] [MENUBREAK]
    MENUITEM SEPARATOR
    POPUP text, [CHECKED] [GRAYED] [INACTIVE] [MENUBARBREAK] [MENUBREAK]
    {
        . . .
    }
```

*name*

Unique name for the menu resource.

*text*

The menu item name for either the MENUITEM or POPUP statement. Placing an '&' symbol immediately before a character will display that character as an underline and Windows will use it for keyboard access. Use '&&' to display an actual '&' character. The '\t' escape character will insert a tab and should be used to align columns. The '\a' escape character will right-justify the text after the character to the far right side of the menu.

*ID*

The numerical value Windows should use for the *wParam* parameter of the WM_COMMAND message when the menu item is selected.

CHECKED

The menu item or popup menu is initially displayed with a check mark. This option does not apply to top-level menu items on the menu bar.

GRAYED

The menu item or popup menu is initially inactive and displayed in a lightened shade.

HELP

The menu item is displayed with a vertical bar to the left of the text.

INACTIVE

The menu item or popup menu is displayed normally, but cannot be selected.

MENUBREAK

Places the menu item on a new line. Places popup menus in a new column with no vertical dividing line.

MENUBARBREAK

Same as MENUBREAK for menu items. For popup menus, it places the popup menu in a new column with a vertical dividing line.

MENUITEM SEPERATOR

Creates an inactive menu item that is displayed as a horizontal bar.

POPUP

A popup menu item followed by the definition of the popup menu.

## Description

The MENU statement starts the definition of a menu resource. Menus can be created in the WORKSHOP Menu editor shown in Figure 9-8, although it is generally easier to create menus as a resource script.

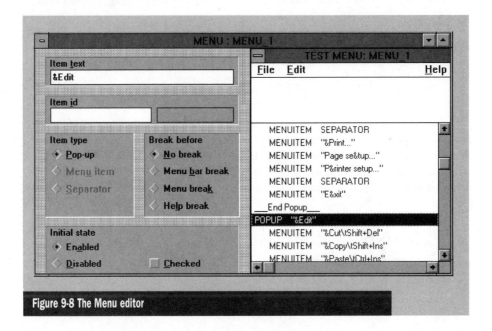

**Figure 9-8 The Menu editor**

Menu items and popup menus are displayed identically, but are different operationally. When a menu item is selected, Windows generates a WM_COMMAND message and sends the window owning the menu with the w*Param* portion of the message set to the *ID* for the menu item. Popup menus do not generate WM_COMMAND messages, but instead display another menu when selected.

Note that top-level menu items and top-level popup menus are displayed in the menu bar for the window.

## Related Window Functions

`HMENU LoadMenu(HANDLE hInstance, LPSTR lpMenuName);`

Retrieves the handle to a named menu resource.

## Example

Modify the "Hello, Windows!" application to place the [Exit] menu item in a popup menu called [Files].

Figure 9-9 "Hello, Windows!" menu

**menu\hello.rc**

```
#include "hello.h"

; The application's main menu
MainMenu MENU
{
  POPUP "&Files"
  {
    MENUITEM "E&xit",  IDM_EXIT
  }
}
```

Figure 9-9 shows the resulting menu as it appears when selected in the "Hello, Windows!" application.

# RCDATA AND *user-defined*                   User-Defined Resource

▪ Mult-line    ▪ Binary

### Purpose

The RCDATA statement and generic *user-defined* resource definition statements create raw data resources for any static data required by the application. The *user-defined* resource type is functionally identical to the RCDATA resource except that it allows the raw resource data to be stored in a file rather than explicitly listed in the script.

### Script Syntax

```
name RCDATA [Load Option] [Memory Option]
{
  . . .
}
```

```
name user-defined [Load Option] [Memory Option] [filename]

name user-defined [Load Option] [Memory Option]
{
    . . .
}
```

*name*
> Name of the resource.

*user-defined*
> Name of a resource type.

*filename*
> Name of the raw data file for the *user-defined* resource.

## Description

Because Windows operates best when an application is compiled using a memory model with near data, the amount of static data actually compiled into the application is normally limited to 64K. Much of your application's static data, however, can be stored in the form of either an RCDATA statement, which requires the raw static data to be listed in the text script, or as a *user-defined* resource type, which can either be listed in the script text or stored in a file. The raw data in the file is then added as an application resource just as the script compiler would add an icon or bitmap resource. The name for the resource type assigned to a *user-defined* parameter has no significance and can be called anything that will make the script more readable.

Note that strings stored in a raw data format must have the NULL terminator explicitly appended to the end of the string.

## Related Window Functions

`HANDLE FindResource(HANDLE hInstance, LPSTR lpName, LPSTR lpType);`
> Returns a resource handle for a named resource that can be used with the LoadResource() function.

`HANDLE LoadResource(HANDLE hInstance, HANDLE hResInfo);`
> Loads a resource or, if it is already loaded, returns the handle to the resource.

`LPSTR LockResource(HANDLE hResData);`
> Locks the global memory associated with a resource handle returned by the LoadResource() function. The LPSTR value returned is a far pointer to the data in the associated resource.

## Example

Modify the "Hello, Windows!" application to store the text string displayed in the window as an RCDATA resource.

**rcdata\hello.h**

```
#include <windows.h>

/* Define the menu item macros */
#define IDM_EXIT        2000
#define APP_TITLE       3000
```

**rcdata\hello.rc**

```
#include "hello.h"

APP_TITLE RCDATA LOADONCALL DISCARDABLE
{
    "Hello, Windows!\0"
}
```

**rcdata\hello.c**

```
#include "hello.h"

LPSTR AppTitle;
. . .
    /* Locate the resource and retrieve the handle */
    hTextLoc = FindResource(hInstance, MAKEINTRESOURCE(APP_TITLE),
                            RT_RCDATA);

    /* Load the resource into memory */
    hTextRes = LoadResource(hInstance, hTextLoc);

    /* Get the pointer to the resource data */
    if((AppTitle = LockResource(hTextRes)) == NULL)
        return(NULL);

. . .

    /* Remove the lock on the resource */
    UnlockResource(hTextRes);

    /* Free the memory used by the resource */
    FreeResource(hTextRes);

. . .
```

In the above modifications, the "Hello, Windows!" string is stored as an RCDATA type with a numerical resource identifier defined by the APP_TITLE macro. The MAKEINTRESOURCE() macro converts the integer into a format useable by the FindResource() function, which is an LPSTR with a selector of zero. After a handle to the resource is retrieved, it is loaded into memory by the LoadResource() function and locked with the LockResource() function. A call to UnlockResource() and FreeResource() is made after the resource is no longer required.

689

# STRINGTABLE                                       String Table Resource

- Mult-line          Binary

## Purpose

The STRINGTABLE statement creates a string table application resource. A string table resource is best suited for replacing the static character arrays normally found in an application, because as a resource they will not take up valuable local memory.

## Script Syntax

```
STRINGTABLE [Load Option] [Memory Option]
{
    ID, "string"
    . . .
}
```

*ID*
  Numerical ID for the string.

*"string"*
  The text for the string.

## Description

Because Windows operates best when an application is compiled using a memory model with near data, the amount of static strings actually compiled into the application is normally limited to 64K. All of your application's strings, however, can be stored in a string table resource, thereby freeing room for more static memory.

Strings table are easily entered either as resource script or in the WORKSHOP String editor shown in Figure 9-10.

Note that there is only one string resource table in an application. The resource script compiler will combine multiple STRINGTABLE resource statements into a common string table.

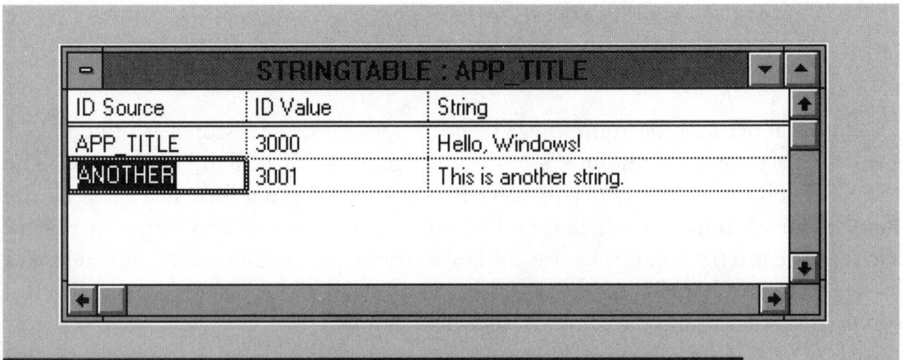

**Figure 9-10 String editor**

Unlike the RCDATA and *user-defined* formats, the strings in a STRINGTABLE resource have NULL terminators appended automatically.

### Related Window Functions
```
int LoadString(HANDLE hInstance, WORD wID, LPSTR lpBuffer);
```
Loads a string resource.

### Example
Modify the "Hello, Windows!" application to use a string resource for the application title.

**strtable\hello.h**
```
#include <windows.h>

/* Define the menu item macros */
#define IDM_EXIT      2000
#define APP_TITLE     3000
```

**strtable\hello.rc**
```
#include "hello.h"

STRINGTABLE
{
  APP_TITLE "Hello, Windows!"
}
```

**strtable\hello.c**
```
. . .
    /* Load the APP_TITLE string resource */
    LoadString(hInstance, APP_TITLE, AppTitle, sizeof(AppTitle));
. . .
```

# VERSIONINFO                                    Version Information

▪ Mult-line      Binary

### Purpose
The VERSIONINFO resource places version information into an application, Dynamic Link Library (DLL), Driver, or Font library file that is readable by installation applications that use the functions in the Windows VER.DLL library and the DOS VER*x*.LIB libraries. Note that these libraries are not included with the initial release of BC++ 3.1. However, all Windows 3.1 end users have VER.DLL in their Windows directory.

This resource type is specific to Windows 3.1 or later. Only the resource compilers and Resource Workshop shipped with BC++ 3.1 will compile a VERSIONINFO resource.

### Script Syntax
```
VersionID VERSIONINFO [Load Option] [Memory Option]
FILEVERSION FileVersion
PRODUCTVERSION ProdVersion
```

```
FILEFLAGSMASK FileFlagMask
FILEFLAGS FileFlags
FILEOS FileOperSys
FILETYPE FileType
FILESUBTYPE FileSubType
{
  BLOCK "VarFileInfo"                          a VarFileInfo block is optional
  {
    VALUE "Translation",
      LanguageID, CharSetID[,]
      [LanguageID, CharSetID]
      [. . .]
  }
  BLOCK "StringFileInfo"
  {
    BLOCK "Language/CharSet"
    {
      VALUE "CompanyName", "CompanyString"
      VALUE "FileDescription", "FileDescString"
      VALUE "FileVersion", "FileVerString"
      VALUE "InternalName", "InternalNameString"
      VALUE "OriginalFilename", "FilenameString"
      VALUE "ProductName", "ProdNameString"
      VALUE "ProductVersion", "ProdVerString"
      [VALUE "Comments", "CommentString"]        optional
      [VALUE "LegalCopyright", "CopyrightString"] optional
      [VALUE "LegalTrademarks", "TrademarkString"] optional
      [VALUE "PrivateBuild", "PrivBuildString"]   optional
      [VALUE "SpecialBuild", "SpecialBuildString"] optional
    }
  }
}
```

*VersionID*

Resource identifier. This should always be VS_VERSION_INFO.

*FileVersion*

File version number. This should be four 16-bit identifiers separated by commas as follows:

```
xx, yy, ww, zz
```

The resource compiler will combine these four numbers into a 64-bit identifier. The VerQueryValue() function places these values in the *dwFileVersionMS* and *dwFileVersionLS* members of the VS_FIXEDFILEINFO structure. The VerInstallFile() function will return a VIF_SRCOLD flag if an installing application attempts to overwrite a preexisting file with an older file version.

*ProdVersion*

Product version number. This should be four 16-bit identifiers separated by commas as follows:

```
xx, yy, ww, zz
```

The resource compiler will combine these four numbers into a 64-bit identifier. The VerQueryValue() function places these values in the *dwProductVersionMS* and *dwProductVersionLS* members of the VS_FIXEDFILEINFO structure.

### FileFlagMask

Mask of the allowable file types. A value of 0x3F allows all file types. The following is a list of allowable file types defined in Windows 3.1:

| Value | Attribute |
|---|---|
| VS_FF_DEBUG | The file contains debugging information. |
| VS_FF_INFOINFERRED | The file contains dynamically created version resource information. You should not use this file type with a VERSIONINFO resource definition. |
| VS_FF_PATCHED | The file is a modified version of a file with the same version number. |
| VS_FF_PRERELEASE | The file is still in testing and is not intended for commercial distribution. |
| VS_FF_PRIVATEBUILD | The resource contains comments in the *PrivBuildString* parameter of the *StringFileInfo* block on how you built the file. |
| VS_FF_SPECIALBUILD | The resource contains comments in the *SpecialBuildString* parameter of the *StringFileInfo* block on how the file differs from the standard version. |

### FileFlags

File attributes. This should be a logically OR'ed combination of the VS_FF_ types listed with above for the *FileFlagsMask* parameter. The VerInstallFile() function will return a VIF_MISMATCH flag if an installing application attempts to replace a preexisting file with a new file that does not have a matching *FileFlags* attribute.

### FileOperSys

Intended operating system for the file. This value should be one of the following:

| Value | Intended Operating System |
|---|---|
| VOS_DOS | DOS (Windows 3.0 or 32-bit Windows) |
| VOS_DOS_WINDOWS16 | Window 3.0 or later under DOS |
| VOS_DOS_WINDOWS32 | 32-bit Windows under DOS only |
| VOS_NT | Windows NT only |
| VOS_NT_WINDOWS32 | 32-bit Windows under Windows NT only |

| VOS_OS216 | 16-bit OS/2 |
|-----------|-------------|
| VOS_OS232 | 32-bit OS/2 |
| VOS_OS216_PM16 | 16-bit Presentation Manager under 16-bit OS/2 |
| VOS_OS232_PM32 | 32-bit Presentation Manager under 32-bit OS/2 |
| VOS__PM16 | 16-bit Presentation Manager |
| VOS__PM32 | 32-bit Presentation Manager |
| VOS_WINDOWS16 | Windows 3.0 or later (either DOS or Windows NT) |
| VOS_WINDOWS32 | 32-bit Windows (either DOS or Windows NT) |
| VOS_UNKNOWN | Operating system unknown to Windows |

The VerInstallFile() function will return a VIF_DIFFTYPE flag if an installing application attempts to replace a preexisting file with a new file that does not have a matching *FileOperSys*.

*FileType*
General information on the type of file. This should be one of the following values:

| Value | Type |
|-------|------|
| VFT_APP | Application |
| VFT_DLL | Dynamic Link Library |
| VFT_DRV | Device Driver (requires a sub-filetype) |
| VFT_FONT | Font (requires a sub-filetype) |
| VFT_STATIC_LIB | Static Library |
| VFT_VXD | Virtual Device |
| VFT_UNKOWN | The type is unknown to Windows |

The VerInstallFile() function will return a VIF_DIFFTYPE flag if an installing application attempts to replace a preexisting file with a new file that does not have a matching *FileType*.

*FileSubType*
Type of driver or font file. This should be one of the following if the *FileType* parameter is either VFT_DRV or VFT_FONT:

| Value | Sub-Type |
|-------|----------|
| VFT2_DRV_COMM | Communications driver |
| VFT2_DRV_DISPLAY | Display driver |

694

| | |
|---|---|
| VFT2_DRV_INSTALLABLE | Installable driver |
| VFT2_DRV_KEYBOARD | Keyboard driver |
| VFT2_DRV_LANGUAGE | Language driver |
| VFT2_DRV_MOUSE | Mouse driver |
| VFT2_DRV_NETWORK | Network driver |
| VFT2_DRV_PRINTER | Printer driver |
| VFT2_DRV_SOUND | Sound driver |
| VFT2_DRV_SYSTEM | System driver |
| VFT2_FONT_RASTER | Raster font |
| VFT2_FONT_TRUETYPE | TrueType font |
| VFT2_FONT_VECTOR | Vector font |
| VFT2_UNKNOWN | The sub-type is unknown to Windows |

The VerInstallFile() function will return a VIF_DIFFTYPE flag if an installing application attempts to replace a preexisting file with a new file that does not have a matching *FileSubType*.

*LanguageID*

A numerical value representing the language definition blocks available in the resource. This should be one of the following per language block:

| Language | Decimal Value | Hex Value |
|---|---|---|
| Albanian | 1052 | 0x041C |
| Arabic | 1025 | 0x0401 |
| Bahasa | 1057 | 0x0421 |
| Bulgarian | 1026 | 0x0402 |
| Catalan | 1027 | 0x0403 |
| Chinese (Simplified) | 2052 | 0x0804 |
| Chinese (Traditional) | 1028 | 0x0404 |
| Croato-Serbian (Latin) | 1050 | 0x041A |
| Czech | 1029 | 0x0405 |
| Danish | 1030 | 0x0406 |
| Dutch | 1043 | 0x0413 |
| Dutch (Belgian) | 2067 | 0x0813 |
| English (U.K.) | 2057 | 0x0809 |
| English (U.S.) | 1033 | 0x0409 |
| Finnish | 1035 | 0x040B |

| Language | Decimal Value | Hex Value |
| --- | --- | --- |
| French | 1036 | 0x040C |
| French (Belgian) | 2060 | 0x080C |
| French (Canadian) | 3084 | 0x0C0C |
| French (Swiss) | 4108 | 0x100C |
| German | 1031 | 0x0407 |
| German (Swiss) | 2055 | 0x0807 |
| Greek | 1032 | 0x0408 |
| Hebrew | 1037 | 0x040D |
| Hungarian | 1038 | 0x040E |
| Icelandic | 1039 | 0x040F |
| Italian | 1040 | 0x0410 |
| Italian (Swiss) | 2064 | 0x0810 |
| Japanese | 1041 | 0x0411 |
| Korean | 1042 | 0x0412 |
| Norwegian - Bokmål | 1044 | 0x0414 |
| Norwegian - Nynorsk | 2068 | 0x0814 |
| Polish | 1045 | 0x0415 |
| Portuguese | 2070 | 0x0816 |
| Portuguese (Brazilian) | 1046 | 0x0416 |
| Rhaeto-Romanic | 1047 | 0x0417 |
| Romanian | 1048 | 0x0418 |
| Russian | 1049 | 0x0419 |
| Serbo-Croatian (Cyrillic) | 2074 | 0x081A |
| Slovak | 1051 | 0x041B |
| Spanish (Castilian) | 1034 | 0x040A |
| Spanish (Mexican) | 2058 | 0x080A |
| Swedish | 1053 | 0x041D |
| Thai | 1054 | 0x041E |
| Turkish | 1055 | 0x041F |
| Urdu | 1056 | 0x0420 |

The resource should have a separate *StringFileInfo* block for each *LanguageID* listed.

*CharSetID*

Numerical value representing the character set for the language block. This should be one of the following per language block:

| Character Set | Decimal Value | Hex Value |
|---|---|---|
| 7-bit ASCII | 0 | 0 |
| Unicode | 1200 | 0x04B0 |
| Windows, Arabic | 1256 | 0x04E8 |
| Windows, Cyrillic | 1251 | 0x04E3 |
| Windows, Japan (Shift - JIS X-0208) | 932 | 0x03A4 |
| Windows, Greek | 1253 | 0x04E5 |
| Windows, Hebrew | 1255 | 0x04E7 |
| Windows, Korea (Shift - KSC 5601) | 949 | 0x03B5 |
| Windows, Latin-2 (Eastern European) | 1250 | 0x04E2 |
| Windows, Multilingual | 1252 | 0x04E4 |
| Windows, Taiwan (GB5) | 950 | 0x03B6 |
| Windows, Turkish | 1254 | 0x04E6 |

Each *LanguageID* entry should have a corresponding *CharSetID* parameter.

*"Language/CharSet"*

32-bit numerical string value representing the language and character set for the *StringFileInfo* block.

*CompanyString*

Contains the name of your company.

*FileDescString*

Text description of the file presented to the end user such as "Brand-X 23pt Courier Font", "Portuguese Language Driver\000", or "Fractal Dynamic Link Library\000".

*FileVerString*

Text string of the file version presented to the end user such as "3.1\000" or "5.1a\000".

*InternalNameString*

Internally used name for the file if it exists. If the file does not have an internal name, this should be the same as the *FilenameString* without the filename extension.

*FilenameString*

Name of the file. The VerFindFile() function uses name when looking for a file. This ensures that the function finds the proper file even if it has been renamed by the user after a previous installation.

*ProdNameString*

Name of the product presented to the user such as "Microsoft Windows\000".

*ProdVerString*

Text representation of the product version number such as "3.10\000" or "5.1a\000".

*CommentString*

Contains any comments you'd like to add about the file.

*CopyrightString*

Copyright string such as "Copyright © 1992, The Yankee Programmer\000".

*TrademarkString*

String listing all registered trademarks such as "Windows® is a trademark of Microsoft Corp. \ni386® is a trademark of Intel Corp.\000"

*PrivBuildString*

Text comments on how the file was built. You should only define this string in file versions that have a *FileFlags* parameter with the VS_FF_PRIVATEBUILD attribute.

*SpecialBuildString*

Text comments on how this file differs from the standard version of the file. You should only define this string in file versions that have a *FileFlags* parameter with the VS_FF_SPECIALBUILD attribute.

## Description

Installation applications, such as Microsoft's "Setup Toolkit," need information on the characteristics of a file, such as the version number, language, or an intended operating system, in order for them to correctly install a file. They also need text information that they can present in a dialog box so that the user can make an intelligent on decision installation choices.

The VERSIONINFO resource allows you to attach this information to an application or any other type of file that contains resource information. Installation applications then use the GetFileVersionInfo() function to load the VERSIONINFO resource into memory and the VeryQueryValue() function to retrieve specific information from the resource, such as the file version number and copyright string.

Borland did not ship BC++ with the Windows VER.DLL or the VER*x*.LIB files. However, Borland did include the VER.H header file, and end users with Windows 3.1 have VER.DLL in their Windows directory that they can use. Note that any installation application you write that depends on the end user's VER.DLL file will likely fail if the user has installed a later version of Windows.

## Related Window Functions

```
BOOL WINAPI GetFileVersionInfo(LPCSTR lpstrFilename, DWORD dwHandle,
DWORD dwLen, void FAR* lpData);
```

Load the *lpData* buffer with the VERSIONINFO resource data.

```
DWORD WINAPI GetFileVersionInfoSize(LPCSTR lpstrFilename, DWORD FAR
    *lpdwHandle);
```
Determine the buffer size needed to hold the data for a VERSIONINFO resource.

```
UINT WINAPI VerFindFile(UINT uFlags, LPCSTR szFileName, LPCSTR szWinDir,
    LPCSTR szAppDir, LPSTR szCurDir, UINT FAR* lpuCurDirLen, LPSTR
    szDestDir, UINT FAR* lpuDestDirLen);
```
Determine if the end user has installed a previous version of a given file.

```
DWORD WINAPI VerInstallFile(UINT uFlags, LPCSTR szSrcFileName, LPCSTR
    szDestFileName, LPCSTR szSrcDir, LPCSTR szDestDir, LPCSTR
    szCurDir, LPSTR szTmpFile, UINT FAR* lpuTmpFileLen);
```
Install a newer version of a given file or force the installation of an older file or a file using a different language.

```
UINT WINAPI VerLanguageName(UINT wLang, LPSTR szLang, UINT nSize);
```
Translates a language identifier into a language string that you can present to a user. For example, the VerLangaugeName() function will fill the *szLang* buffer with "Polish" if you call this function with a *wLang* parameter of 0x0415.

```
BOOL WINAPI VerQueryValue(const void FAR* pBlock, LPCSTR lpSubBlock,
    void FAR* FAR* lplpBuffer, UINT FAR* lpuLen);
```
Retrieves specific information from a VERSIONINFO resource loaded into a buffer by the GetFileVersionInfo() function.

### Example
Write a VERSIONINFO resource for a typical application:

**verinfo\myapp.rc**
```
    VS_VERSION_INFO VERSIONINFO LOADONCALL MOVEABLE
    FILEVERSION 3, 10, 0, 425      /* File Version 3.1.0.425 */
    PRODUCTVERSION 3, 10, 0, 425   /* Product version 3.1.0.425 */
    FILEFLAGSMASK 0x3F             /* All file attributes are allowable */
    FILEFLAGS VS_FF_SPECIALBUILD | /* Contains a "SpecialBuild" string */
          VS_FF_PRIVATEBUILD   /* Contains a "PrivateBuild" string */

    FILEOS VOS__WINDOWS16          /* 16-bit Windows Operating System */
    FILETYPE VFT_APP               /* The file is an application */
    {
      BLOCK "StringFileInfo"       /* String information block */
      {
        BLOCK "040904E4"           /* String information block for
                                      the U.S. English language and
                                      translation using the Multilingual
                                      character set */
        {
          VALUE "CompanyName", "My Company Inc.\000"
          VALUE "FileDescription", "My application file\000"
          VALUE "FileVersion", "3.10.425\000"
          VALUE "InternalName", "MYAPP\000"
          VALUE "LegalCopyright",
             "Copyright' 1991-1992, My Company Inc.\000"
          VALUE "LegalTrademarks",
             "Windows" is a trademark of Microsoft Corporation.\000"
```

```
        VALUE "OriginalFilename", "MYAPP.EXE\000"
        VALUE "ProductName", "My Product\000"
        VALUE "ProductVersion", "3.10.425\000"
        VALUE "PrivateBuild", "Large memory model\000"
        VALUE "SpecialBuild", "Modified Gadget() function\000"
    }
  }
}
```

# BORLAND WINDOWS CUSTOM CONTROLS (BWCC)

BC++ Version 3.0 comes with a Dynamic Link Library called BWCC.DLL that contains several custom control resources that you can use in your applications. These custom controls allow you to easily create dialog boxes with Borland's "chiseled steel" that you find in Turbo C++ for Windows (TCW), Borland C++ for Windows (BCW), and the Resource Workshop (WORKSHOP). In summary, the BWCC.DLL contains the following resources:

- Eight predefined bitmapped push-buttons that automatically display correctly on VGA, EGA, and monochrome systems: OK, Cancel, Abort, Retry, Ignore, Yes, No, and Help.

- Four predefined static bitmaps for VGA, EGA, and monochrome systems: Hand, Question Mark, Exclamation Point, and *i*.

- Easy integration of your own customized static bitmaps and bitmapped push-buttons.

- A call-compatible MessageBox() function that displays a Borland style dialog box.

- Gray group boxes that appear "Chiseled" out of the dialog steel.

- Vertical and horizontal "Dips" for dividing dialog box sections.

- Vertical and horizontal "Bumps" for dividing gray panel sections.

This section covers each of these topics followed by a reference section containing the details of each control available in BWCC.DLL.

## Using the BWCC Dynamic Link Library

There are several requirements for using the BWCC Dynamic Link Library:

1. Your dialog boxes should use the "BorDlg" window class. This is done by adding the CLASS statement to the dialog box definition as follows:

```
name DIALOG . . .
. . .
CLASS "BorDlg"
. . .
{
. . .
}
```

For example, consider the dialog boxes displayed in Figure 9-11.

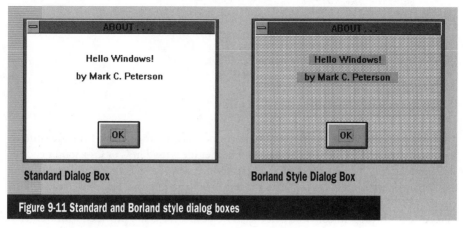

**Figure 9-11 Standard and Borland style dialog boxes**

The dialog box on the left uses the standard Windows dialog box and static controls as defined in the following resource script:

**bwcc\standard.dlg**
```
demo DIALOG 18, 18, 142, 92
CAPTION "ABOUT . . ."
STYLE DS_MODALFRAME | WS_POPUP | WS_CAPTION | WS_SYSMENU
{
    CONTROL "OK", 101, "BUTTON",
            BS_DEFPUSHBUTTON | WS_CHILD | WS_VISIBLE | WS_TABSTOP,
            54, 64, 32, 20
    CONTROL "by Mark C. Peterson", -1, "STATIC",
            SS_CENTER | WS_CHILD | WS_VISIBLE | WS_GROUP,
            32, 27, 77, 8
    CONTROL "Hello Windows!", -1, "STATIC",
            SS_CENTER | WS_CHILD | WS_VISIBLE | WS_GROUP,
            41, 14, 59, 8
}
```

The dialog box on the right side of Figure 9-11 is exactly the same as the above resource script except that it contains the CLASS "BorDlg" statement as follows:

```
demo DIALOG 18, 18, 142, 92
CAPTION "ABOUT . . ."
CLASS "BorDlg"
```

If you are working in the WORKSHOP editor, you can use a Borland style dialog box by selecting the [Resources][Edit as text] menu item and enter the above CLASS statement. Another method is to double-click the dialog box's caption or border to pull up the "Window Style" dialog box and enter "BorDlg" in the [Class] field.

2. If you are compiling a script resource, you need to include the following header file:

```
#ifdef RC_INVOKED

#define BSS_GROUP           1L
```

```
#define BSS_HDIP              2L
#define BSS_VDIP              3L
#define BSS_HBUMP             4L
#define BSS_VBUMP             5L
#define BBS_OWNERDRAW         0x1000L
#define BBS_PARENTNOTIFY      0x2000L
#define BBS_DLGPAINT          0x4000L
#define BBS_BITMAP            0x8000L

#else
#include <bwcc.h>
#endif
```

This will ensure that the Borland style option macros are defined if you are compiling a script resource in the IDE. If the above header file is used in C or C++ source code, it will automatically include the BWCC.H header file, which also contains macros defining the Borland specific messages as well as the style macro definitions. The above header file is not required if you are compiling a resource script in WORKSHOP, as these macro definitions are already predefined. Note that the above header file is not provided with BC++.

3.  You must place the BWCC.LIB file in your project list if you are using the BC++, BCW, or TCW IDE. If you are performing an external link, the BWCC.LIB file must be linked before linking the IMPORT.LIB library. This is because BWCC.LIB contains entries referencing four functions located in BWCC.DLL:

```
CreateDialog();
CreateDialogParam();
DialogBox();
DialogBoxParam();
```

Linking BWCC.LIB before IMPORT.LIB ensures your application is linked to the dialog box creation functions in BWCC.DLL rather than the standard Windows equivalent functions with the same name. Note that there is no support for the indirect creation of Borland-style dialog boxes. For example, you cannot create a Borland-style dialog box using the CreateDialogIndirect() or the DialogBoxIndirect() functions.

Note that if your application uses Borland Custom Controls, but does not contain a call to one of the functions listed above, you should call the BWCCGetVersion() function somewhere in your application. This links a function in the BWCC.LIB library that ensures that Windows will load the BWCC.DLL file on startup. An alternative method is to explicitly load the BWCC.DLL using Windows' LoadModule() function before using a BWCC control.

4.  Because your application is linked with functions in the BWCC Dynamic Link Library, Windows will automatically load BWCC.DLL when it loads your application. This means the BWCC.DLL *must* be located on the user's system in a directory that can be found by Windows. Windows will search for the BWCC.DLL in the following order:

- The same directory as your application (preferred).
- The Windows startup or system directory.
- Any directory in the user's PATH statement.
- Any directory in the list of directories mapped in a network.

Because the end user will probably have other applications that use the BWCC.DLL, some of which may require a later or earlier version, it is best to install the BWCC.DLL file in the same directory as your application to prevent overwriting any other version on the user's system.

The "No Nonsense License Statement" for the BC++ compiler package concerning distribution of proprietary supporting files, such as the BWCC.DLL file, states that "you may distribute these support files in combination with these programs, provided you do not use, give away or sell the supporting

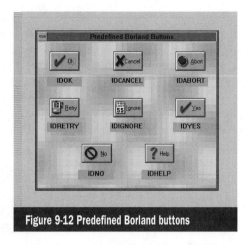

**Figure 9-12 Predefined Borland buttons**

files separately, and all copies or your programs bear a valid copyright notice." This means you are licensed to distribute BWCC.DLL only with your application and only if you first copyright your application and display your copyright notice in the application.

## Using Predefined Bitmapped Push-buttons in BWCC

The BWCC control library contains the eight predefined bitmapped push-buttons shown in Figure 9-12.

Your existing code can easily be modified to use these predefined bitmapped buttons by changing the window class field in the resource script from "BUTTON" to the "BorBtn" window class and using one of the control IDs listed in Figure 9-12. For example, to change the "OK" push-button used in the previous dialog box script to a bitmapped "OK" push-button with a green check mark, we rewrite the CONTROL statement in the resource script as follows:

```
CONTROL "OK", IDOK, "BorBtn",
        BS_DEFPUSHBUTTON | WS_CHILD | WS_VISIBLE | WS_TABSTOP,
        54, 64, 32, 20
```

The resulting dialog box is shown in Figure 9-13.

The IDOK macro is predefined in WORKSHOP and it is also defined in WINDOWS.H. All the macros listed in Figure 9-12 are defined in WINDOWS.H with the exception of the IDHELP macro. This macro should be defined as follows if you are compiling the resource script from the DOS IDE:

```
#define IDHELP      998
```

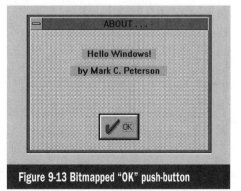

**Figure 9-13 Bitmapped "OK" push-button**

Also note that the *text* field for bitmapped push-buttons is ignored by the "BorBtn" control. If you are editing an existing dialog box in WORKSHOP and want to change an existing push-button to a bitmapped push-button, then select the [**Resources**][Edit as **text**] and enter the above changes to the script text. If you are originating a control in a dialog box using WORKSHOP, either select the Borland push-button displayed on the righthand side of the "Tools" window or select the [Control][**Custom**] menu item. This will display a list of the BWCC custom controls for you to choose from. After selecting either the "Default Pushbutton" or "Pushbutton," you then select the [Control][Style][Control **id**] menu item and enter "IDOK."

## Displaying "Chiseled" Recessed Gray Panels

The gray panels in the Borland style dialog box are defined in a dialog box template using the "BorShade" custom control window class with the BSS_GROUP style. For example, the previous dialog box can be defined with the static control windows in a recessed background by adding the following control:

```
CONTROL "", -1, "BorShade",
    BSS_GROUP | WS_CHILD | WS_VISIBLE,
    29, 9, 84, 32
```

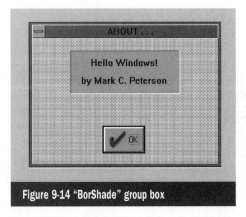

Figure 9-14 "BorShade" group box

As shown in Figure 9-14, the background color of the added group box control window blends with the color of the two static controls so that it appears as if the static controls are drawn on the recessed area.

## Using 'dips' and 'bumps'

There are four other styles for the "BorShade" control window, BSS_H-BUMP, BSS_HDIP, BSS_V–BUMP, and BSS_VDIP, which create the appearance of dips and bumps in the Borland-style dialog box in either the horizontal or vertical direction. The bitmaps for the "dips" are designed to blend in with the main area of the Borland-style dialog box and are normally used as dividers between the passive area of the dialog box, where the settings are made or information is displayed, and the active area, where the push-buttons are located that either accept or cancel the new settings or dismiss the dialog box. The bitmaps for the "bumps" are designed to be used within the gray panel area of a "BorShade" group box to subdivide different sections. For example, consider the following control window additions:

```
CONTROL "", -1, "BorShade",
    BSS_HBUMP | WS_CHILD | WS_VISIBLE,
    29, 24, 84, 2
CONTROL "", -1, "BorShade",
```

```
BSS_HDIP | WS_CHILD | WS_VISIBLE,
0, 53, 142, 2
```

The resulting dialog box is shown in Figure 9-15.

Adding a horizontal 'dip' separates the active area, such as the area containing push-buttons for activating or dismissing the dialog box, from the passive area with group box shade and other static information. The horizontal 'bump' is used in the group shade box to separate the application title from the author.

Note that the 'dip' control windows look best when they are sized the same as the dialog box. The 'bump' control windows look best when they are sized to either the same height or width of the group shade depending on their orientation.

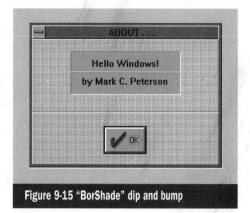

**Figure 9-15 "BorShade" dip and bump**

## Borland-style Check Boxes and Radio Buttons

Unlike the standard Windows "BUTTON" window class that is used to create the standard check boxes and radio buttons, the "BorBtn" does not support these control styles. Instead, the "BorCheck" window class is used for check boxes and the "BorRadio" window class is used for radio buttons. The bitmaps used for these two classes are designed to match the look of the Borland-style dialog box, as shown in Figure 9-16.

**Figure 9-16 Borland-style check boxes and radio buttons**

The following is the resource script used to create the dialog box in Figure 9-16:

**bwcc\checkbox.dlg**

```
DIALOG_1 DIALOG 18, 18, 158, 141
CAPTION "DIALOG_1"
CLASS "BorDlg"
STYLE DS_MODALFRAME | WS_POPUP | WS_CAPTION | WS_SYSMENU
{
   CONTROL "Auto Save", 101, "BorCheck",
        BS_AUTOCHECKBOX | WS_CHILD | WS_VISIBLE | WS_TABSTOP,
        11, 30, 64, 10
   CONTROL "Create Backups", 102, "BorCheck",
        BS_AUTOCHECKBOX | WS_CHILD | WS_VISIBLE | WS_TABSTOP,
```

```
                11, 50, 64, 10
CONTROL "Insert", 104, "BorRadio",
        BS_AUTORADIOBUTTON | WS_CHILD | WS_VISIBLE,
        86, 30, 64, 10
CONTROL "Overwrite", 105, "BorRadio",
        BS_AUTORADIOBUTTON | WS_CHILD | WS_VISIBLE,
        86, 50, 64, 10
CONTROL "Strikethrough", 106, "BorRadio",
        BS_AUTORADIOBUTTON | WS_CHILD | WS_VISIBLE,
        86, 70, 64, 10
CONTROL "", -1, "BorShade",
        BSS_GROUP | WS_CHILD | WS_VISIBLE,
        8, 8, 144, 77
CONTROL "", -1, "BorShade",
        BSS_VBUMP | WS_CHILD | WS_VISIBLE,
        79, 8, 2, 77
CONTROL "Check Boxes", -1, "STATIC",
        SS_CENTER | WS_CHILD | WS_VISIBLE | WS_GROUP,
        18, 14, 49, 8
CONTROL "Radio Buttons", -1, "STATIC",
        SS_CENTER | WS_CHILD | WS_VISIBLE | WS_GROUP,
        91, 14, 49, 8
CONTROL "Button", IDOK, "BorBtn",
        BS_DEFPUSHBUTTON | WS_CHILD | WS_VISIBLE | WS_TABSTOP,
        14, 109, 32, 20
CONTROL "Button", IDCANCEL, "BorBtn",
        WS_CHILD | WS_VISIBLE | WS_TABSTOP,
        62, 109, 32, 20
CONTROL "Button", IDHELP, "BorBtn",
        WS_CHILD | WS_VISIBLE | WS_TABSTOP,
        110, 109, 32, 20
CONTROL "", -1, "BorShade",
        BSS_HDIP | WS_CHILD | WS_VISIBLE,
        0, 97, 158, 2
}
```

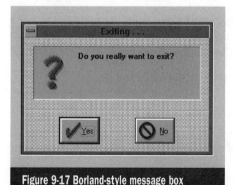

**Figure 9-17 Borland-style message box created by the BWCCMessageBox() function**

## Borland-style Message Boxes

The BWCC Dynamic Link Library contains a function called BWCCMessageBox() that operates exactly like the standard Message-Box() function used in Windows except that the dialog box is displayed in the Borland style. Also, instead of the standard icons and push-buttons, the BWCCMessageBox() functions use the bitmapped push-buttons and a custom set of icons. For example, consider the following change to the "Hello, Windows!" application:

```
#include <bwcc.h>
. . .

                    case IDM_EXIT:
                         /* Prompt the user using the Borland style
                            message box */
                         if(BWCCMessageBox(hWnd,
                           "Do you really want to exit?",
                           "Exiting . . .",
                           MB_ICONQUESTION | MB_YESNO) == IDYES)
                    {
                             /* Exit the application by destroying the
                                main window */
                             DestroyWindow(hWnd);
                    }
                         break;
```

The above code displays the message box shown in Figure 9-17 just before the user exits.

The bitmapped push-buttons shown in Figure 9-17 are the same bitmapped push-buttons as the predefined bitmapped push-buttons shown previously in Figure 9-12. Other predefined bitmapped push-buttons are used when you designate the MB_ABORTRETRYIGNORE, MB_OK, MB_OKCANCEL, MB_RETRYCANCEL, and MB_YESNOCANCEL message box flags.

Note that the question mark icon in Figure 9-17 is not the same as the question mark icon normally used in message boxes. Borland-style message boxes use a different set of icons. Figure 9-18 shows the custom icons used with the BWCCMessageBox() function.

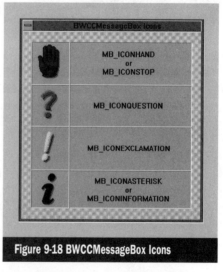

**Figure 9-18 BWCCMessageBox Icons**

## Using Your Own Bitmaps for Bitmapped Push-buttons

A push-button has three display states: unpushed without the focus, unpushed with the focus, and pushed. The predefined bitmapped push-buttons use two sets of three resource bitmaps for each of the predefined bitmap push-buttons available in BWCC to display the three states of the push-button. One set of bitmaps is for when Windows is running in a VGA display mode and the second set is for when it is in the EGA or monochrome display mode. For example, Figure 9-19 shows the six bitmap resources in BWCC for the IDOK bitmapped push-button.

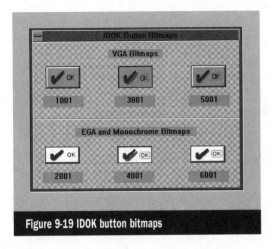

**Figure 9-19 IDOK button bitmaps**

Of the VGA bitmaps, the resource bitmap named "1001" is for when the IDOK button is unpushed and does not have the focus, "3001" is for when the push-button is pushed, and "5001" is for when the push-button is not pushed and has the focus. The bitmaps for the three corresponding states used for EGA and monchrome display modes are named "2001," "4001," and "6001," respectively.

The "BorBtn" control window determines which bitmap to display based on the ID for the control window using the following formulas:

VGA display mode bitmaps
  (Control ID) + 1000 = Unpushed bitmap (without the focus)
  (Control ID) + 3000 = Pushed bitmap
  (Control ID) + 5000 = Unpushed bitmap (with the focus)


EGA and monochrome bitmaps
  (Control ID) + 2000 = Unpushed bitmap (without the focus)
  (Control ID) + 4000 = Pushed bitmap
  (Control ID) + 6000 = Unpushed bitmap (with the focus)

The following control ID macros for the different predefined bitmaps are defined in WINDOWS.H:

```
#define IDOK        1
#define IDCANCEL    2
#define IDABORT     3
#define IDRETRY     4
#define IDIGNORE    5
#define IDYES       6
#define IDNO        7
#define IDHELP    998
```

This means if the ID for the "BorBtn" control evaluates to the number 998, i.e., you use the IDHELP macro, then the "BorBtn" control will automatically use the bitmap resources named "1998," "3998," and "5998" for VGA displays and "2998," "4998," and "6998" for EGA and monochrome displays.

You can create your own sets of bitmaps and have them automatically displayed by the "BorBtn" control class by coordinating the control ID for the push-button with the names for the desired sets of bitmaps. Consider the following control ID macro definition:

```
#define ID_MYBUTTON    100
```

The "BorBtn" control will then automatically use the bitmap resources named "1100," "3100," and "5100" on VGA systems and "2100," "4100," and "6100" on EGA and monochrome systems. If the BWCC.DLL cannot find the bitmap resources with these names in your application, then it will display the default Borland-style push-button. You could include bitmaps that are stored as files for use by BWCC when displaying "BorBtn" controls with the ID_MYBUTTON by including the following in the resource script:

```
; VGA bitmaps
1100 BITMAP vnofocus.bmp       ; Unpushed without the focus
3100 BITMAP vpushed.bmp        ; Pushed
5100 BITMAP vwfocus.bmp        ; Unpushed with the focus

; EGA and monochrome bitmaps
2100 BITMAP enofocus.bmp       ; Unpushed without the focus
4100 BITMAP epushed.bmp        ; Pushed
6100 BITMAP ewfocus.bmp        ; Unpushed with the focus
```

If the bitmaps are already an integral part of the resource file, you could also use the WORKSHOP editor to rename the bitmap resources to the appropriate number using the [Resource][Rename] menu item.

The following considerations are recommend when designing bitmaps for Borland-style push-buttons:

■ Start with the push-button template bitmap resources located in BWCC.DLL. These bitmaps are used by the "BorBtn" window class when it cannot find a bitmap resource that matches the control ID. You can retrieve these bitmaps by opening the BWCC.DLL file with WORKSHOP and saving the following bitmaps as separate files using the [Resource][Save Resource as] menu item:

1999  Unpushed VGA bitmap with or without the focus

2999  Unpushed EGA/monochrome bitmap with or without the focus

3999  Pushed VGA bitmap

4999  Pushed EGA/monochrome bitmap

You can then edit the saved bitmaps without affecting the normal push-button bitmaps.

■ Place small drawings, or *glyphs*, to the left side of the push-button bitmaps and create a shadow for the glyph.

■ Use normal 8-point Helvetica text, not bold or italic.

■ Box in the text on the pushed bitmap and the unpushed bitmap with the focus using a dotted line pattern.

■ Offset the button's text and glyph shadow down and to the right for the pushed bitmap so that it appears to move with the push-button.

Note that there are also methods for dynamically setting the push-button bitmaps at run time either by using the BBS_OWNERDRAW button style or by sending the BBM_SETBITS message. See the "BorBtn" BWCC class reference later in this chapter for details on using these methods.

## Static Bitmaps

The "BorBtn" window class has the BBS_BITMAP style that defines the push-button control as a static bitmap. "BorBtn" controls with the BBS_BITMAP style are exactly the same as normal bitmapped push-buttons except they are static, i.e., they cannot be pushed or receive the focus. This means the push-button always displays the bitmap for the unpushed state without the focus. Static bitmaps are normally used to automatically display bitmaps as opposed to manually loading a bitmap and painting it to a window in your application code.

As with normal bitmapped push-buttons, the bitmap displayed is based on the ID for the control as follows:

VGA display mode bitmaps = (Control ID) + 1000

EGA and monochrome bitmaps = (Control ID) + 2000

For example, the resource names for the BWCCMessageBox() function icons in the BWCC.DLL file are 1901, 1902, 1903, and 1904 for the VGA bitmaps and 2901, 2901, 2903, and 2904 for the EGA/monochrome bitmaps. This means using a control ID of 901, 902, 903, or 904 for a static bitmap control will display the Hand, Question Mark, Exclamation, or Information icon, respectively. These control IDs were used with static bitmaps to create the icons shown in Figure 9-18 as follows:

```
CONTROL "Button", 901, "BorBtn",
     BBS_BITMAP | WS_CHILD | WS_VISIBLE,
     13, 12, 26, 33
CONTROL "Button", 902, "BorBtn",
     BBS_BITMAP | WS_CHILD | WS_VISIBLE,
     13, 51, 26, 33
CONTROL "Button", 903, "BorBtn",
     BBS_BITMAP | WS_CHILD | WS_VISIBLE,
     13, 90, 26, 33
CONTROL "Button", 904, "BorBtn",
     BBS_BITMAP | WS_CHILD | WS_VISIBLE,
     13, 129, 26, 33
```

By coordinating the naming of your bitmap resources with the ID of the static bitmap controls windows, you can have the "BorBtn" automatically display your own custom bitmaps. Also, as with the normal bitmapped push-buttons, you can set the bitmaps at run time either by using the BBS_OWNERDRAW button style or by sending the BBM_SETBITS message.

## Borland Windows Custom Controls Reference

The following reference section covers each of the window classes available in the BWCC.DLL Dynamic Link Library. The "Inherited Styles" and "Inherited Messages" sections list the window styles and messages inherited from the standard Windows equivalent function. Refer to the documentation on the CreateWindow() function for details on these styles. The "Borland Styles" and "Borland Messages" list the styles and messages unique to BWCC controls. See the preceding tutorial section for a detailed discussion of the BWCC controls and example usage.

# BorBtn                                          Window Control Class

## Purpose
Used to display either active or static bitmapped push-buttons.

## Inherited Styles
`BS_DEFPUSH-BUTTON`
`BS_PUSH-BUTTON`

## Unique Styles
`BBS_BITMAP`
> Creates a static push-button for displaying a bitmap.

`BBS_OWNERDRAW`
> Equivalent to the BS_OWNERDRAW button style for standard push-buttons. Sends a WM_DRAWITEM message when the state of the push-button changes or needs painting.

`BBS_PARENTNOTIFY`
> Enables the generation of BBN_SETFOCUS, BBN_SETFOCUSMOUSE, BBN_GO-TATAB, and BBN_GOTABTAB messages.

## Inherited Messages
`BN_CLICKED`
`BM_GETSTATE`
`BM_SETSTATE`
`BM_SETSTYLE`
`WM_DRAWITEM`      *for BBS_OWNERDRAW style only*

## Unique Messages
`BBN_GOTABTAB`
> Notification message sent by the control to the parent window when the push-button receives the focus due to a back tab (a (Shift)-(Tab) keystroke) and the push-button was created with the BBS_PARENTNOTIFY style.

`BBN_GOTATAB`
> Notification message sent by the control to the parent window when the push-button receives the focus due to a forward tab (a ªTabº keystroke) and the push-button was created with the BBS_PARENTNOTIFY style.

**BM_SETBITS**

Used to send a contiguous array of three bitmap handles for the push-button to use as the pushed, unpushed, and unpushed with the focus states. The first handle is the bitmap for the unpushed state without the focus, the second for the pushed state, and the third for the unpushed state with the focus.

**BBN_SETFOCUS**

Notification message sent by the control to the parent window when the push-button gains the focus and the push-button was created with the BBS_PARENTNOTIFY style.

**BBN_SETFOCUSMOUSE**

Notification message sent by the control to the parent window when the push-button receives the focus due to a mouse click event and the push-button was created with the BBS_PARENTNOTIFY style.

# BorCheck                                              Window Control Class

## Purpose
Used to create a Borland-style checkbox.

## Inherited Styles
BS_AUTOCHECKBOX
BS_CHECKBOX
BS_LEFTTEXT

## Unique Styles
**BBS_DLGPAINT**

For internal use only by BWCC.

**BBS_OWNERDRAW**

Equivalent to the BS_OWNERDRAW button style for standard push-buttons. Sends a WM_DRAWITEM message when the state of the push-button changes or needs painting.

**BBS_PARENTNOTIFY**

Enables the generation of BBN_SETFOCUS, BBN_SETFOCUSMOUSE, BBN_GOTATAB, and BBN_GOTABTAB messages.

## Inherited Messages
BM_GETCHECK
BM_SETCHECK
BM_GETSTATE
BM_SETSTATE
BN_CLICKED

**Unique Messages**
Same as the "BorBtn" window class.

# BorDlg                                            Window Control Class

**Purpose**
Used to create a fast, Borland-style dialog box.

**Inherited Styles**
All normal dialog box styles.

**Unique Styles**
None

**Inherited Messages**
All standard dialog box messages.

**Unique Messages**
None

# BorRadio                                          Window Control Class

**Purpose**
Used to create a Borland-style radio button.

**Inherited Styles**
BS_AUTORADIOBUTTON
BS_LEFTTEXT
BS_RADIOBUTTON

**Unique Styles**
Same as for the "BorCheck" window class.

**Inherited Messages**
Same as for the "BorCheck" window class.

**Unique Messages**
Same as for the "BorBtn" window class.

## BorShade

### Purpose

Used to create a Borland-style gray panel group box as well as dips or bumps oriented in either the horizontal or vertical direction.

### Inherited Styles

None

### Unique Styles

BSS_GROUP

Creates a gray panel group box.

BSS_HBUMP

Creates a horizontal bump.

BSS_HDIP

Creates a horizontal dip.

BSS_VBUMP

Creates a vertical bump.

BSS_VDIP

Creates a vertical dip.

### Inherited Messages

None

### Unique Messages

None

## BWCCDefDlgProc    Default BWCC Dialog Function
## BWCCDefMDIChildProc    Default BWCC MDI Function
## BWCCDefWindowProc    Default BWCC Window Function

### Purpose

The BWCCDefDlgProc() is used when creating a subclass of the "BorDlg" window class. The BWCCDefWindowProc() and BWCCDefMDIChildProc() functions are used when creating windows with the Borland-style look.

### Syntax

```
LONG FAR PASCAL BWCCDefDlgProc(HWND hWnd, WORD message, WORD wParam,
LONG lParam);
```

```
LONG FAR PASCAL BWCCDefWindowProc(HWND hWnd, WORD message, WORD wParam,
LONG lParam);
LONG FAR PASCAL BWCCDefMDIChildProc(HWND hWnd, WORD message, WORD
wParam, LONG lParam);
```

HWND *hWnd*
> The handle to the window.

WORD *message*
> The message number.

WORD *wParam*
> The 16-bit parameter associated with the message.

LONG *lParam*
> The 32-bit parameter associated with the message.

## Return
LONG
> The return value is the result of the processing for the message.

## Description
The message processing function for a dialog box window that is based on the "BorDlg" window class should call this function instead of the DefDlgProc() for standard dialog boxes for any unprocessed messages. Additionally, the procedure should pass the following messages to BWCCDefDlgProc() even if the message is processed:

```
WM_CTLCOLOR
WM_NCCREATE
WM_CREATE
WM_NCDESTROY
WM_SETFONT
WM_PAINT
WM_ERASEBKGND
```

The BWCCDefDlgProc() function implements a "turbo painting" algorithm for Borland-style controls that eliminates any unnecessary static control windows, maintains a private list of dialog controls, and also preforms the painting of the controls, which results in a faster, more responsive dialog box.

The name of any window class that uses the BWCCDefDlgProc() function must begin with "BorDlg . . .," such as "BorDlg_MyClass." Window class names may not have any leading underscores and cannot use the "BorDlg" itself. Note that the case of a window class name is not significant.

You would use the BWCCDefWindowProc() and BWCCDefMDIChildProc() functions to replace the DefWindowProc() and DefMDIChildProc() functions for standard windows when creating windows with the Borland style. The messages listed above for the BWCCDefDlgProc() function should also be passed to the BWCCDefWindowProc() and BWCCDefMIDChildProc() functions.

Note that there is not a BWCC specific function for the Windows DefFrameProc() function.

# BWCCGetVersion

## Purpose

The BWCCGetVersion() function returns the version of the version number for the BWCC.DLL. This function should be called if your application uses BWCC controls and does not use any other function in the BWCC.LIB library or a dialog box.

## Syntax

```
WORD FAR PASCAL BWCCGetVersion(void);
```

## Return

WORD

The version number with the high byte as the major version and the low byte as the minor version.

## Description

The BWCC.H header file contains the definition for the BWCCVERSION macro returned by this function. This is the same header file used to compile the BWCC.DLL file. You can use the BWCCGetVersion() function to ensure the version of BWCC on the user's system is the same as or a higher version than that used to create your application.


# BWCCGetPattern

## Purpose

The BWCCGetPattern() function is used to retrieve the background brush for the "BorDlg" window.

## Syntax

```
HBRUSH FAR PASCAL BWCCGetPattern(void);
```

## Return

HBRUSH

A handle to the brush used to paint the background of the "BorDlg" window class. Because this brush is used by the "BorDlg" window class, it should not be deleted by your application.

## Description

The brush used to paint the background of the Borland-style dialog boxes is retrieved using the BWCCGetPattern() function. Once the handle to the brush is obtained, your application should call the UnrealizeObject() and SetBrushOrg() functions to align the brush pattern with the position in the window before selecting it to a device context.

# BWCCMessageBox                    Borland-Style Message Box

## Purpose

The BWCCMessageBox() function is a function that is call compatible with the standard MessageBox() function in Windows, but instead displays a message box in the Borland style with custom icon bitmaps and bitmapped push-buttons.

## Syntax

```
int FAR PASCAL BWCCMessageBox(HWND hWndParent, LPSTR lpText, LPSTR
    lpCaption, WORD wType);
```

HWND *hWndParent*

    The handle to the parent window for the message box. Set this parameter to NULL to use the desktop window as the parent.

LPSTR *lpText*

    The text displayed in the message box.

LPSTR *lpCaption*

    The title for the message box. Setting this parameter to NULL uses "Error!" as the title in BWCC.DLL Versions 1.01 and higher.

WORD *wType*

    The attributes for the message box. This should be a bitwise OR of any combination of the following:

| | |
|---|---|
| MB_ABORTRETRYIGNORE | A message box with the "Abort," "Retry," and "Ignore" bitmapped push-buttons. |
| MB_APPMODAL | The message box is an application modal dialog box (default). |
| MB_DEFBUTTON1 | The first button is the default push-button (default). |
| MB_DEFBUTTON2 | The second button is the default push-button. |
| MB_DEFBUTTON3 | The third button is the default push-button. |
| MB_ICONASTERISK | Places the information 'i' icon in the message box. Same as MB_ICONINFORMATION. |
| MB_ICONEXCLAMATION | Places the exclamation-point icon in the message box. |
| MB_ICONHAND | Places the hand icon in the messages box. Same as MB_ICONSTOP. |

| MB_ICONINFORMATION | Places the information 'i' icon in the message box. Same as MB_ICONAS-TERISK. |
| MB_ICONQUESTION | Places the question mark icon in the message box. |
| MB_ICONSTOP | Places the hand icon in the messages box. Same as MB_ICONHAND. |
| MB_RETRYCANCEL | A message box with the "Retry" and "Cancel" push-buttons. |
| MB_SYSTEMMODAL | All processing in Windows is halted while the message box is displayed. |
| MB_TASKMODAL | All processing for a task is halted while the message box is displayed. This is the same as MB_APPMODAL for Windows Version 3.x and lower. |
| MB_YESNO | A message box with the "Yes" and "No" push-buttons. |
| MB_YESNOCANCEL | A message box with the "Yes," "No," and "Cancel" push-buttons. |

Note that not all combinations are allowable, such as using message-box types defining different sets of push-buttons.

### Return
`int`

The push-button in the message box that was pressed which corresponds to one of the following:

| IDABORT | The "Abort" push-button |
| IDCANCEL | The "Cancel" push-button |
| IDIGNORE | The "Ignore" push-button |
| IDNO | The "No" push-button |
| IDOK | The "OK" push-button |
| IDRETRY | The "Retry" push-button |
| IDYES | The "Yes" push-button |

### Description
The BWCCMessageBox() function operates identically to the Windows MessageBox() function except that the message box is displayed in Borland style, uses different icons, and also uses bitmapped push-buttons. Figures 9-12 and 9-18 in the tutorial section show the different bitmapped push-buttons and icon bitmaps used with the BWCCMessageBox() function.

## Object Windows and Borland Custom Controls

Each of the BWCC controls has a corresponding C++ object class in the Object Windows Library (OWL). The following reference lists the OWL C++ classes, the corresponding include file, and the member functions. The C++ object class after the colon in the heading is the BWCC control's base class. The include file is listed immediately following the heading followed by the public and protected function members.

As with non-OWL BWCC controls, the "BORDLG" window class should be used with dialog boxes. If the application does not use a dialog box, then it should make a call to the BWCCGetVersion() function to ensure the BWCC.DLL file is loaded by Windows with the application. The BWCC.LIB library must be in the project list or, for external linking, it must be linked before linking IMPORT.LIB. The BWCC.DLL must be distributed with the resulting application.

Note that all BWCC specific OWL classes must be used in either a "BorDlg" class dialog box or a TBWindow. There is no OWL class for the "BorDlg".

## TBButton : TButton                    Bitmapped Push-Button

BBUTTON.H

### Public
```
TBButton(PTWindowsObject AParent, int AnId, LPSTR AText, int x, int y,
    int w, int h, BOOL IsDefault, PTModule AModule=NULL);
```
Places a bitmapped push-button on the *AParent* window located at client coordinates *x* and *y* with *w* and *h* for the width and height. If *IsDefault* is TRUE, the BS_DEFPUSH-BUTTON style is used. The *AnId* parameter is the control ID for the control window. The *AText* parameter is the text placed on the push-button and is ignored if the *AnId* parameter corresponds to an existing set of push-button bitmap resources.

```
TBButton(PTWindowsObject, AParent, int ResourceId, PTModule
    AModule=NULL);
```
Creates a TBButton object using the parameters for a "BorBtn" control identified by *ResourceId* on the *AParent* TDialog window.

```
static PTStreamable build();
```
Calls the TBButton(StreamableInit) constructor before reading a stream.

### Protected
```
TBButton(StreamableInit);
```
Creates a TBButton stream using TButton's stream constructor.

```
virtual LPSTR GetClassName();
```
Returns "BORBTN."

### Default Attributes
WS_CHILD | WS_VISIBLE | WS_GROUP | WS_TABSTOP | [BS_PUSHBUTTON/BS_DEFPUSHBUTTON]

## TBCheckBox : TCheckBox                              Borland-Style Checkbox

BCHKBOX.H

### Public
```
TBCheckBox(PTWindowsObject AParent, int AnId, LPSTR ATitle, int x, int
     y, int w, int h, PTGroupBox AGroup, PTModule AModule=NULL);
```
Places a Borland-style checkbox on the *AParent* window located at client coordinates *x* and *y* with *w* and *h* for the width and height. The *AnId* parameter is the control ID for the control window. The *AGroup* parameter should be set to a pointer to a group box or NULL. The *ATitle* parameter is the text associated with the checkbox.

```
TBCheckBox(PTWindowsObject AParent, int ResourceId, PTGroupBox AGroup,
     PTModule AModule=NULL);
```
Creates a TBCheckBox object using the parameters for a "BorCheck" control identified by *ResourceId* on the *AParent* TDialog window.

```
static PTStreamable build();
```
Calls the TBCheckBox(StreamableInit) constructor before reading a stream.

### Protected
```
TBCheckBox(StreamableInit);
```
Creates a TBCheckbox stream using the TCheckBox stream constructor.

```
virtual LPSTR GetClassName();
```
Returns "BORCHECK".

### Default Attributes
WS_CHILD | WS_VISIBLE | WS_TABSTOP | BS_AUTOCHECKBOX

## TBDivider : TControl                              Borland Style Dips and Bumps

BDIVIDER.H

### Public
```
TBDivider(PTWindowsObject AParent, int AnId, LPSTR ATitle, int x, int y,
     int w, int h, BOOL IsVertical, BOOL IsBump, PTModule AModule=NULL);
```
Places a vertical or horizontal 'Dip' or 'Bump' on the *AParent* window located at client coordinates *x* and *y* with *w* and *h* for the width and height. The *IsBump* parameter creates a 'Bump' if set to TRUE or a 'Dip' if set to FALSE. The *IsVertical* parameter controls the orientation of the 'Dip' or 'Bump' and should be set to TRUE for a vertical

orientation or FALSE for a horizontal orientation. The *h* parameter should be set to 2 for horizontal TBDivider controls. For vertical TBDivider controls, set the 'w' parameter to 2. The *AnId* parameter is the control ID for the window. The *ATitle* parameter is not used by the resulting window.

```
TBDivider(PTWindowsObject AParent, int ResourceId, PTModule
AModule=NULL);
```
Creates a TBDivider object using the parameters for a "BorShade" control identified by *ResourceId* on the *AParent* TDialog window.

```
static PTStreamable build();
```
Calls the TBDivider(StreamableInit) constructor before reading a stream.

**Protected**
```
TBDivider(StreamableInit);
```
Creates a TBDivider stream using the TControl stream constructor.

```
virtual LPSTR GetClassName();
```
Returns "BORSHADE."

**Default Attributes**
WS_CHILD I WS_VISIBLE I WS_TABSTOP I WS_GROUP

# TBGroupBox : TGroupBox    Borland Shaded Group Box

BGRPBOX.H

**Public**
```
TBGroupBox(PTWindowsObject AParent, int AnId, LPSTR ATitle, int x, int
y, int w, int h, PTModule AModule=NULL);
```
Places a Borland-style gray panel on the *AParent* window located at client coordinates *x* and *y* with *w* and *h* for the width and height. The *AnId* is the control ID for the control window. The *ATitle* parameter is the text associated with the group box.

```
TBGroupBox(PTWindowsObject AParent, int ResourceId, PTModule
AModule=NULL);
```
Creates a TBGroupBox object using the parameters for a "BorShade" control identified by *ResourceId* on the *AParent* TDialog window.

```
static PTStreamable build();
```
Calls the TBGroupBox(StreamableInit) constructor prior to reading a stream.

**Protected**
```
TBGroupBox(StreamableInit);
```
Creates a TBGroupBox stream using the TGroupBox stream constructor.

```
virtual LPSTR GetClassName();
```
Returns "BORSHADE".

**Default Attributes**
WS_CHILD I WS_VISIBLE I WS_GROUP I BS_GROUPBOX

# TBRadioButton : TRadioButton  Borland-Style Auto Radio Button

BRADIO.H

### Public
```
TBRadioButton(PTWindowsObject AParent, int AnId, LPSTR AText, int x, int
     y, int w, int h, PTGroupBox AGroup, PTModule AModule=NULL);
```
Places a Borland-style radio button on the *AParent* window located at client coordinates *x* and *y* with *w* and *h* for the width and height. The *AnId* is the control ID for the control window. The *AGroup* parameter should be set to a pointer to a group box or NULL. The *AText* parameter is the text associated with the radio button.

```
TBRadioButton(PTWindowsObject AParent, int ResourceId, PTGroupBox
     AGroup, PTModule AModule=NULL);
```
Creates a TBRadioButton object using the parameters for a "BorRadio" control identified by *ResourceId* on the *AParent* TDialog window.

```
static PTStreamable build();
```
Calls the TBRadioButton(StreamableInit) constructor before reading a stream.

### Protected
```
TBRadioButton(StreamableInit);
```
Creates a TBRadioButton stream using the TRadioButton stream constructor.

```
virtual LPSTR GetClassName();
```
Returns "BORRADIO".

### Default Attributes
WS_CHILD I WS_VISIBLE I BS_AUTORADIOBUTTON

# TBStatic : TStatic                     Borland-Style Static

BSTATIC.H

### Public
```
TBStatic(PTWindowsObject AParent, int AnId, LPSTR AText, int x, int y,
     int w, int h, WORD ATextLen, PTModule AModule=NULL);
```
Places a left text static control on the *AParent* window located at client coordinates *x* and *y* with *w* and *h* for the width and height. The *AnId* is the control ID for the control window. The *AText* parameter is the text displayed in the static window. The *ATextLen* parameter is the maximum length of the text string.

```
TBStatic(PTWindowsObject AParent, int ResourceId, WORD ATextLen,
    PTModule AModule=NULL);
```
Creates a TBStatic object using the parameters for a "Static" control identified by *ResourceId* on the *AParent* TDialog window.

```
static PTStreamable build();
```
Calls the TB(StreamableInit) constructor before reading a stream.

**Protected**
```
TBStatic(StreamableInit);
```
Creates a TBStatic stream using the TStatic constructor.

```
virtual LPSTR GetClassName();
```
Returns "BORSTATIC."

**Default Attributes**
WS_CHILD I WS_VISIBLE I WS_GROUP I SS_LEFT


# TBStaticBmp : TControl                                   Static Bitmap

BSTATBMP.H

**Public**
```
TBStaticBmp(PTWindowsObject AParent, int AnId, LPSTR ATitle, int x, int
    y, int w, int h, PTModule AModule=NULL);
```
Places a static bitmap on the *AParent* window located at client coordinates $x$ and $y$ with $w$ and $h$ for the width and height. The *AnId* is the control ID for the control window and should correspond to a bitmap resource with a name of (1000+AnId) for a VGA bitmap or (2000+AnId) for an EGA/monochrome bitmap. The *ATitle* parameter is not used in the resulting control window unless the WS_CAPTION style attribute is used.

```
TBStaticBmp(PTWindowsObject AParent, int ResourceId, PTModule
    AModule=NULL);
```
Creates a TBStaticBmp object using the parameters for a "BorBtn" control identified by *ResourceId* on the *AParent* TDialog window.

```
static PTStreamable build();
```
Calls the TBStaticBmp(StreamableInit) constructor before reading a stream.

**Protected**
```
TBStaticBmp(StreamableInit);
```
Creates a TBStaticBmp stream using the TControl stream constructor.

```
virtual LPSTR GetClassName();
```
Returns "BORBTN".

**Default Attributes**

WS_CHILD | WS_VISIBLE | WS_GROUP | WS_TABSTOP

## TBWindow : TWindow    Borland-Style Window

BWINDOW.H

### Public

```
TBWindow(PTBWindowsObject AParent, LPSTR ATitle, PTModule AModule=NULL);
```
   Creates a window class identical to TWindow except it uses the Borland-style background brush.

```
static PTStreamable build();
```
   Calls the TBWindow(StreamableInit) constructor before reading a stream.

```
virtual void GetWindowClass(WNDCLASS &AWndClass);
```
   Fills the *AWndClass* structure with a WNDCLASS structure identical to the TWindow classes except for a different background brush.

### Protected

```
TBWindow(StreamableInit);
```
   This is a NULL inline function called by the input and output stream operators.

```
virtual LPSTR GetClassName();
```
   Returns "TBWindow".

### Default Attributes

WS_VISIBLE | WS_OVERLAPPEDWINDOW    *if 'AParent' set to NULL*
WS_VISIBLE    *if the window has a parent*

# INTERFACING A CUSTOM CONTROL LIBRARY WITH RESOURCE WORKSHOP

There are provisions in WORKSHOP for loading custom control Dynamic Link Libraries that you write yourself. The following reference section provides some details on the functions WORKSHOP expects to find in your DLL. The subject of writing custom controls requires a book in itself, however, so no explicit examples are given. Note that the function prototypes and structure definitions are located in the CUSTCNTL.H include file supplied with BC++. All functions that are callable from WORKSHOP must be exported using the *_export* keyword or listed in the EXPORTS section of the module definition (.DEF) file.

   The examples used with these functions come from the BITBTN.C example file provided with BC++. The BITBTN.C is a source code file for a DLL for a bitmapped push-button control similar to the "BorBtn" control class. The contents of the BITBTN.C file are Copyright (C) 1991 by Borland International. Portions of BITBTN.C are reprinted here with the permission of Borland International.

# CTLCLASSLIST                                        Structure

## Purpose
CTLCLASSLIST is a structure returned by the ListClasses() function that contains a list of the control classes available in the DLL.

## Definition
```
typedef struct
{
  short       nClasses;
  RWCTLCLASS  Classes[];
} CTLCLASSLIST, FAR *LPCTLCLASSLIST;
```

`short nClasses`
   The number of control classes in the DLL.

`RWCTLCLASS Classes[]`
   An array of RWCTLCLASS structures containing the name and function pointers associated with a control class.

## Description
WORKSHOP calls the DLL's ListClasses() function to retrieve the CTLCLASSLIST structure. Each window control class registered by the DLL should have a RWCTLCLASS structure entry in the *Classes* array.

## See Also
ListClasses       DLL Function
RWCTLCLASS       Structure

## Example
The CTLCLASSLIST structure is dynamically allocated by BITBTN.C, then the structure is filled with the appropriate information and returned by the ListClasses() function.

```
HANDLE FAR PASCAL ListClasses(LPSTR szAppName,
      WORD wVersion, LPFNLOADRES fnLoad, LPFNEDITRES fnEdit)
{
      HANDLE hClasses = GlobalAlloc(GMEM_SHARE | GMEM_ZEROINIT,
          sizeof(int) + sizeof(RWCTLCLASS));

      LoadResRW = fnLoad;

      if ( hClasses )
      {
          LPCTLCLASSLIST      Classes = (LPCTLCLASSLIST)
                              GlobalLock(hClasses);

          Classes->nClasses = 1;
          Classes->Classes[0].fnRWInfo      = BitBtnInfo;
          Classes->Classes[0].fnRWStyle     = BitBtnStyle;
          Classes->Classes[0].fnFlags       = BitBtnFlag;
```

```
        lstrcpy(Classes->Classes[0].szClass, "BitButton");
        GlobalUnlock(hClasses);
    }

    return hClasses;
}
```

# ListClasses                                          DLL Function

## Purpose

The ListClasses() function is called by WORKSHOP when the [Options][Install control library] menu item is selected from the DIALOG editor. WORKSHOP uses this function to both initialize the DLL for use by WORKSHOP and also retrieve information on the classes in the DLL. This function must be included in all Custom Control DLLs.

## Syntax

```
HANDLE FAR _export PASCAL ListClasses(LPSTR szAppClass, WORD
    wVersion,  LPFNLOADRES fnLoad, LPFNEDITRES fnEdit);
```

LPSTR *szAppClass*

Title of the application calling the Custom Control DLL.

WORD *wVersion*

Version number of the application calling the DLL. The high byte of the word contains the major version number and the low byte contains the minor version number. For example, a value of 0x0203 is Version 2.03.

LPFNLOADRES *fnLoad*

Far pointer to a function that can be used by the DLL to retrieve a binary version of any resource in the project that is currently being edited by WORKSHOP. The function operates in similar fashion to the Windows LoadResource() function. See LPFNLOADRES for more detailed information.

LPFNEDITRES *fnEdit*

Far pointer to a function that can request WORKSHOP to call the editor for a particular resource. See LPFNEDITRES for more information.

## Returns

HANDLE

Global memory handle to a CTLCLASSLIST structure. The DLL should not free the global memory for this handle once it is passed to WORKSHOP. WORKSHOP will free the memory associated with the handle when it is no longer needed.

## Description

WORKSHOP has to know what control classes are available in your DLL. It determines this by calling the ListClasses() function in your DLL. WORKSHOP expects the DLL to return a global memory handle that contains the CTLCLASSLIST structure, which provides details on the number of control classes, their names, and the function addresses WORKSHOP can call to retrieve more detailed information, set the style, or convert the binary flags information into a text string.

### See Also

LPFNEDITRES          WORKSHOP Function
LPFNLOADRES          WORKSHOP Function

### Example

The ListClasses() function in BITBTN.C saves the *fnLoad* parameter for the LPFNLOADERS and returns a handle to global memory containing a CTLCLASSLIST structure.

```
HANDLE FAR PASCAL ListClasses(LPSTR szAppName,
    WORD wVersion, LPFNLOADRES fnLoad, LPFNEDITRES fnEdit)
{
    HANDLE hClasses = GlobalAlloc(GMEM_SHARE | GMEM_ZEROINIT,
        sizeof(int) + sizeof(RWCTLCLASS));

    LoadResRW = fnLoad;

    if ( hClasses )
    {
        LPCTLCLASSLIST      Classes = (LPCTLCLASSLIST)
                            GlobalLock(hClasses);

        Classes->nClasses = 1;
        Classes->Classes[0].fnRWInfo      = BitBtnInfo;
        Classes->Classes[0].fnRWStyle     = BitBtnStyle;
        Classes->Classes[0].fnFlags       = BitBtnFlag;
        lstrcpy(Classes->Classes[0].szClass, "BitButton");
        GlobalUnlock(hClasses);
    }

    return hClasses;
}
```

# LPFNEDITRES                                    WORKSHOP Function Pointer

### Purpose

The LPFNEDITRES function pointer is passed to a DLL when the ListClasses() function is called by WORKSHOP. This function is called by the DLL whenever it needs to execute the resource editor for a particular resource.

### Syntax

```
BOOL (FAR PASCAL *LPFNEDITRES)( LPSTR szType, LPSTR szId);
```

LPSTR *szType*
    The name of the resource type, i.e., BITMAP, DIALOG, etc.

LPSTR *szId*
    Resource name.

### Returns
BOOL
    Returns a nonzero value if successful. Otherwise, the function returns FALSE.

### Description
The LPFNEDITRES function pointer makes any of the resource editors in WORK-SHOP available to the DLL. You simply pass the function the type and resource name for the desired resource and WORKSHOP will execute the appropriate editor.

### See Also
ListClasses        DLL Function
LPFNLOADRES    WORKSHOP Function

### Example
The LPFNEDITRES pointer passed to the ListClasses() function is not used in BITBTN.C.

# LPFNFLAGS                                              **DLL Function**

### Purpose
The LPFNFLAGS function pointer for a control refers to the function in your DLL that converts the flag bits representing a control window's style to a text expression.

### Syntax
```
WORD (FAR PASCAL *LPFNFLAGS) (DWORD dwFlags, LPSTR lpBuff,
    WORD wBuffLength);
```

DWORD Flags
    Parameter containing the binary information that is to be converted to a string. This value corresponds to the *dwStyle* member of the RWCTLTYPE and RWCTLSTYLE structures for the control.

LPSTR lpBuff
    Character array in WORKSHOP that will receive the text expression.

WORD wBuffLength
    Size of the character array in WORKSHOP.

### Returns
WORD

The libraries instance handle if the operation was successful. Otherwise, it should return a FALSE.

## Description

WORKSHOP has provisions for editing controls either visually or as resource script using the [Resource][Edit as text] menu item. WORKSHOP could convert the binary style information in the *dwFlags* parameter to a number, but this would not be very informative to the user. Instead, it calls the function pointed to by LPFNFLAGS and gives your DLL an opportunity to convert the number to a more meaningful expression. Normally your DLL should convert each bit in the *dwFlags* parameter to the corresponding macro definition and write the result as a logically OR'ed expression to the *lpBuff* character array.

## See Also

ListClasses       DLL Function Pointer
LPFNIDTOSTR  WORKSHOP Function Pointer
RWCTLCLASS   Structure
RWCTLINFO     Structure
RWCTLTYPE     Structure
LPFNSTYLE      DLL Function Pointer

## Example

The BitBtnFlag() function is used in BITBTN.C to convert the binary *Style* parameter to the macro string equivalent. A pointer to the BitBtnFlag() function is passed to WORKSHOP via the RWCTLCLASS structure returned by ListClasses().

```
WORD FAR PASCAL BitBtnFlag(DWORD Style, LPSTR Buff,
    WORD BuffLength)
{
    lstrcpy(Buff, (Style & 0xF) == BS_DEFPUSHBUTTON ?
        "BS_DEFPUSHBUTTON" : "BS_PUSHBUTTON");
    return 0;
}


    . . .


HANDLE FAR PASCAL ListClasses(LPSTR szAppName,
    WORD wVersion, LPFNLOADRES fnLoad, LPFNEDITRES fnEdit)
{
    HANDLE hClasses = GlobalAlloc(GMEM_SHARE | GMEM_ZEROINIT,
        sizeof(int) + sizeof(RWCTLCLASS));

    LoadResRW = fnLoad;

    if ( hClasses )
    {
        LPCTLCLASSLIST    Classes = (LPCTLCLASSLIST)
    GlobalLock(hClasses);
```

```
              Classes->nClasses = 1;
              Classes->Classes[0].fnRWInfo      = BitBtnInfo;
              Classes->Classes[0].fnRWStyle     = BitBtnStyle;
              Classes->Classes[0].fnFlags       = BitBtnFlag;
              lstrcpy(Classes->Classes[0].szClass, "BitButton");
              GlobalUnlock(hClasses);
        }

        return hClasses;
  }
```

# LPFNIDTOSTR                                    **WORKSHOP Function Pointer**

## Purpose
The LPFNIDTOSTR function pointer is used by the DLL to convert a control ID to a text string.

## Syntax
```
WORD (FAR PASCAL *LPFNIDTOSTR)(WORD wCtlID, LPSTR szStrBuff,
      WORD wStrLen);
```

WORD *wCtlID*
> The numerical ID to be converted to a string.

LPSTR *szStrBuff*
> The buffer that will receive the string for the converted ID.

WORD *wStrLen*
> The size of the *szStrBuff* character array.

## Returns
WORD
> The number of characters written to *wStrLen* including the terminating '\0'.

## Description
When WORKSHOP calls the style function in your DLL for a control, it provides the numerical ID for the control, but not the text ID. Your DLL can call the LPFNIDTOSTR function in WORKSHOP to convert the numerical ID to the equivalent macro string definition at the start of the style function and display it in the style dialog box for the control. This function can also be used to update the text ID display if the user prefers to enter a numerical ID.

## See Also
ListClasses          DLL Function Pointer
LPFNSTRTOID    WORKSHOP Function Pointer

RWCTLCLASS     Structure
RWCTLINFO      Structure
RWCTLTYPE      Structure
LPFNSTYLE      DLL Function Pointer

## Example

WORKSHOP calls the BitBtnStyleDlg() function for a control when the [Control][Style] menu item is selected. It is passed a handle to global memory containing a LPCTLSTYLE structure pointer. The string for the control ID is passed to WORKSHOP's LPIDTOSTR function to convert the numerical ID for the control to a string and display it in the dialog box.

```
DWORD FAR PASCAL BitBtnStyleDlg(HWND hWnd, WORD wMessage,
    WORD wParam, DWORD lParam)
{
. . .
    case WM_INITDIALOG:
    {
        HANDLE  hRec        = LOWORD(lParam);
        LPPARAMREC Rec      = (LPPARAMREC) GlobalLock(hRec);
        LPCTLSTYLE Style    = (LPCTLSTYLE)
                              GlobalLock(Rec->CtlStyle);
        char S[81];

        // Save hRec for future use in other messages.
        SetProp(hWnd, "Prop", hRec);

        // SetCaption
        SetDlgItemText(hWnd, ID_CAPTION, Style->szTitle);

        // Set control id
        (*Rec->IdToStr)(Style->wId, S, sizeof(S));
        SetDlgItemText(hWnd, ID_CONTROLID, S);
```

# LPFNINFO                                    DLL Function Pointer

## Purpose

LPFNINFO is a pointer to a function in the DLL that returns information relating the different styles available for the control, the default sizes, the bitmap WORKSHOP should use in the Toolbox window, the menu name for the control, etc.

## Syntax
```
HANDLE (FAR PASCAL *LPFNINFO)(void);
```

## Returns
```
HANDLE
```

Global memory handle containing the RWCTLINFO structure. The DLL should not free the global memory for this handle once it is passed to WORKSHOP. WORK-SHOP will free the memory associated with the handle when it is no longer needed.

## Description
WORKSHOP needs to know certain information about a control class. Each control class has a unique information function that can be called by WORKSHOP to retrieve this information. The pointer is passed to WORKSHOP with the RWCTLCLASS returned by the ListClasses() function.

## See Also
| | |
|---|---|
| LPFNFLAGS | DLL Function Pointer |
| ListClasses | DLL Function Pointer |
| RWCTLCLASS | Structure |
| RWCTLINFO | Structure |
| RWCTLTYPE | Structure |
| LPFNSTYLE | DLL Function Pointer |

## Example
The BitBtnInfo() function in BITBTN.C returns information to WORKSHOP on the style available for the "BitButton" class. The function pointer to the BitBtnInfo() function is originally passed to WORKSHOP via the RWCTLCLASS structure returned by the ListClasses() function.

```
HANDLE FAR PASCAL BitBtnInfo(void)
{
        HANDLE     hInfo = GlobalAlloc(GMEM_SHARE | GMEM_ZEROINIT,
                        sizeof(RWCTLINFO));

        if ( hInfo )
        {
                LPRWCTLINFO Info = (LPRWCTLINFO) GlobalLock(hInfo);

                Info->wVersion   = 0x0100;      // Version 1.00
                Info->wCtlTypes = 2;            // 2 types
                lstrcpy(Info->szClass, "BitButton");
                lstrcpy(Info->szTitle, "Button");

                // Normal (un-default) push button type
                Info->Type[0].wWidth = 63 | 0x8000;
                Info->Type[0].wHeight = 39 | 0x8000;
                lstrcpy(Info->Type[0].szDescr, "Push Button");
                Info->Type[0].dwStyle = BS_PUSHBUTTON | WS_TABSTOP;
                Info->Type[0].hToolBit  = LoadBitmap(hInstance,
                        MAKEINTRESOURCE(BT_UNDEFBITS));
                Info->Type[0].hDropCurs= LoadCursor(hInstance,
                        MAKEINTRESOURCE(CR_UNDEFCURS));

                // Default push button type
                Info->Type[1].wWidth  = 63 | 0x8000;
                Info->Type[1].wHeight = 39 | 0x8000;
```

```
                    lstrcpy(Info->Type[1].szDescr, "Default Push Button");
                    Info->Type[1].dwStyle  = BS_DEFPUSHBUTTON| WS_TABSTOP;
                    Info->Type[1].hToolBit = LoadBitmap(hInstance,
                            MAKEINTRESOURCE(BT_DEFBITS));
                    Info->Type[1].hDropCurs= LoadCursor(hInstance,
                            MAKEINTRESOURCE(CR_DEFCURS));

                    GlobalUnlock(hInfo);
            }

            return hInfo;
    }

    HANDLE FAR PASCAL ListClasses(LPSTR szAppName,
            WORD wVersion, LPFNLOADRES fnLoad, LPFNEDITRES fnEdit)
    {
            HANDLE hClasses = GlobalAlloc(GMEM_SHARE | GMEM_ZEROINIT,
                    sizeof(int) + sizeof(RWCTLCLASS));

            LoadResRW = fnLoad;

            if ( hClasses )
            {
                    LPCTLCLASSLIST   Classes = (LPCTLCLASSLIST)
                    GlobalLock(hClasses);

                    Classes->nClasses = 1;
                    Classes->Classes[0].fnRWInfo   = BitBtnInfo;
                    Classes->Classes[0].fnRWStyle  = BitBtnStyle;
                    Classes->Classes[0].fnFlags    = BitBtnFlag;
                    lstrcpy(Classes->Classes[0].szClass, "BitButton");
                    GlobalUnlock(hClasses);
            }

            return hClasses;
    }
```

# LPFNLOADRES                                    **WORKSHOP Function Pointer**

### Purpose

The LPFNLOADRES function pointer is passed to a DLL when the ListClasses() function is called by WORKSHOP. This function is called by the DLL whenever it needs the binary information for the resource currently available in WORKSHOP.

### Syntax

```
HANDLE (FAR PASCAL *LPFNLOADRES)( LPSTR szType, LPSTR szId);
```

LPSTR *szType*

> The name of the resource type, i.e., BITMAP, DIALOG, etc.

LPSTR *szId*

> Resource name.

## Returns

HANDLE

Global memory handle for the requested binary information. The DLL is expected to free the memory associated with the handle when it is no longer needed.

## Description

The function pointed to by LPFNLOADRES operates in a similar fashion to Windows' LoadResource() function in that it makes the binary information contained in a resource available to the DLL.

## See Also

| | |
|---|---|
| ListClasses | DLL Function |
| LPFNEDITRES | WORKSHOP Function Pointer |

## Example

In this example from BITBTN.C, the LoadBitmap() function must retrieve the bitmap associated with the push-button. It calls the LPFNLOADRES function pointer as it would the LoadResource() function in Windows. The GlobalLock() function is used to obtain a far pointer to the bitmap resource.

```
static HBITMAP LoadBitmapRW(LPSTR szTitle)
{
        HBITMAP hRet = NULL;
        HANDLE  hRes = LoadResRW(RT_BITMAP, szTitle);

        if ( hRes )
        {
                LPBITMAPINFOHEADER pBits = (LPBITMAPINFOHEADER)
        GlobalLock(hRes);
```

# LPFNSTRTOID                        WORKSHOP Function Pointer

## Purpose

The LPFNSTRTOID function pointer calls a WORKSHOP function, which will convert a character string to a numerical ID. The pointer to this function is supplied by WORKSHOP when it calls the LPFNSTYLE function for a control.

## Syntax

DWORD (FAR PASCAL *LPFNSTRTOID)(LPSTR String);

LPSTR *String*

A NULL terminated character string that is to be converted to a numerical ID.

**Returns**

DWORD

The HIWORD of the return value contains the numerical ID for the string. The return is zero if the string does not correspond to a valid string.

**Description**

When WORKSHOP calls the style function for one of your DLL controls and the user enters a new string ID, you should call the function pointed to by the LPFNSTRTOID parameter passed to the style function. This function will search the list of defined macros for a match to the string entered by the user and return the corresponding ID.

Note that the usage of the LPFNSTRTOID pointer in the BITBTN.C example control supplied with BC++ Version 3.0 is incorrect as it uses the low word of the return value instead of the high word.

**See Also**

| | |
|---|---|
| ListClasses | DLL Function Pointer |
| LPFNIDTOSTR | WORKSHOP Function Pointer |
| RWCTLCLASS | Structure |
| RWCTLINFO | Structure |
| RWCTLTYPE | Structure |
| LPFNSTYLE | DLL Function Pointer |

**Example**

WORKSHOP calls the BitBtnStyleDlg() function for a control when the [Control][Style] menu item is selected. Just before the style dialog box terminates, the text ID for the control is retrieved for the style dialog box and converted to a numeric by the LPFNIDTOSTR function in WORKSHOP.

```
DWORD FAR PASCAL BitBtnStyleDlg(HWND hWnd, WORD wMessage,
    WORD wParam, DWORD lParam)
{
. . .
        case WM_COMMAND:
        {
                switch( wParam )
                {
                . . .
                        case IDOK:
                        . . .
                        // Get control id
                        GetDlgItemText(hWnd, ID_CONTROLID, S,
                                sizeof(S));
                        Style->wId = (HIWORD((*Rec->StrToId)(S));
                        . . .
```

# LPFNSTYLE

## Purpose
The LPFNSTYLE function pointer for a control is called by WORKSHOP whenever the user selects the [Control][Style] menu item or double-clicks the control window in the dialog editor display. The DLL is expected to display a dialog box, which allows the user to modify the control window style.

## Syntax
```
BOOL (FAR PASCAL *LPFNSTYLE) (HWND hWnd, HANDLE hCntlStyle,
    LPFNSTRTOID lpfnSID, LPFNIDTOSTR lpfnIDS);
```

HWND *hWnd*
> Window handle to the Dialog editor window in WORKSHOP.

HANDLE *hCntlStyle*
> Global memory handle to the RWCTLSTYLE structure for the control.

LPFNSTRTOID *lpfnSID*
> Function pointer that can be called by the DLL to convert a string to an numerical ID.

LPFNIDTOSTR *lpfnIDS*
> Function pointer that can be called by the DLL to convert the control's ID to a string.

## Returns
BOOL
> The DLL should return a value of TRUE if the user changed the control's style information. The DLL should return FALSE if the style change was cancelled or there was an error.

## Description
WORKSHOP has no way of knowing what the style bits for your custom control represent. Instead, WORKSHOP calls the control's fnRWStyle() function pointer in the RWCTLCLASS structure returned by the DLL's ListClasses() function. This function in your DLL is expected to display a dialog box that displays the information in the RWCTLSTYLE structure passed via the *hCntlStyle* global memory handle and to allow the user to modify the style bits, caption, and control ID for the control. The modified information should be stored in the RWCTLSTYLE structure before returning.

The DLL is expected to call the *lpfnSID* function pointer to obtain the text string corresponding to the control ID. If the user changes the string, the DLL should call the *lpfnIDS* function pointer to convert the string to a numerical ID. The DLL should also modify the RWCTLSTYLE structure as necessary.

## See Also
ListClasses     DLL Function Pointer
LPFNFLAGS     DLL Function Pointer

LPFNINFO     DLL Function Pointer
RWCTLCLASS   Structure
RWCTLSTYLE   Structure

## Example

WORKSHOP calls the LPFNSTYLE function pointer for a control when the [Control][Style] menu item is selected in WORKSHOP. In BITBTN.C, the dialog box for the "BitButton" control class is called. The message processing function for the dialog box modifies the characteristics for the control by modifying the global memory associated with the *hCtlStyle* handle. The function pointer to the BitBtnStyle() function is originally passed to WORKSHOP via the RWCTLCLASS structure returned by the ListClasses() function.

```
BOOL FAR PASCAL BitBtnStyle(HWND hWnd, HANDLE hCtlStyle,
  LPFNSTRTOID StrToId, LPFNIDTOSTR IdToStr)
{
  BOOL   result  = FALSE;
  HANDLE hRec     = GlobalAlloc(GMEM_SHARE, sizeof(PARAMREC));

  if ( hRec )
  {
        LPPARAMREC       Rec    = (LPPARAMREC) GlobalLock(hRec);
        HWND             hFocus = GetFocus();

        // Setup the parameter record
        Rec->IdToStr = IdToStr;
        Rec->StrToId = StrToId;
        Rec->CtlStyle = hCtlStyle;
        GlobalUnlock(hRec);

        // Invoke the dialog box
        result = DialogBoxParam(hInstance,
                MAKEINTRESOURCE(ID_BUTTONSTYLE),
                hWnd, (FARPROC) BitBtnStyleDlg, (DWORD) hRec);

        // Restore focused window since Windows does not do it
        if ( hFocus )
                SetFocus(hFocus);

        GlobalFree(hRec);
  }

  return result;
}

. . .

HANDLE FAR PASCAL ListClasses(LPSTR szAppName,
        WORD wVersion, LPFNLOADRES fnLoad, LPFNEDITRES fnEdit)
{
        HANDLE hClasses = GlobalAlloc(GMEM_SHARE | GMEM_ZEROINIT,
                sizeof(int) + sizeof(RWCTLCLASS));

        LoadResRW = fnLoad;

        if ( hClasses )
        {
```

```
            LPCTLCLASSLIST   Classes = (LPCTLCLASSLIST)
    GlobalLock(hClasses);

            Classes->nClasses              = 1;
            Classes->Classes[0].fnRWInfo   = BitBtnInfo;
            Classes->Classes[0].fnRWStyle  = BitBtnStyle;
            Classes->Classes[0].fnFlags    = BitBtnFlag;
            lstrcpy(Classes->Classes[0].szClass, "BitButton");
            GlobalUnlock(hClasses);
        }

        return hClasses;
    }
```

# RWCTLCLASS                                          Structure

## Purpose
The RWCTLCLASS structure is part of the information structure returned by the
DLL's ListClasses() function. It contains the function address information for the DLL's
Info(), Style(), and Flags() functions.

## Definition
```
typedef struct
{
  LPFNINFO  fnRWInfo;
  LPFNSTYLE fnRWStyle;
  LPFNFLAGS fnFlags;
  char   szClass[ CTLCLASS];
} RWCTLCLASS, FAR *LPRWCTLCLASS;
```

LPFNINFO *fnRWInfo*
> Far pointer to the DLL's Info() function for a custom control class.

LPFNSTYLE *fnRWStyle*
> Far pointer to the DLL's Style() function for a custom control class.

LPFNFLAGS *fnFlags*
> Far pointer to the DLL's Flags() function for a custom control class.

char *szClass[CTLCLASS]*
> A 20-character array containing the name of the custom control class.

## Description
The RWCTLCLASS structure contains the function information for an individual cus-
tom control class. The function pointers in the structure will be called as needed by
WORKSHOP. The *szClass* parameter is the name of the window class registered by the
DLL for the control.

## See Also

## Example

The RWCTLCLASS structure is dynamically allocated by BITBTN.C, then the structure is filled with the appropriate information and returned by the ListClasses() function as part of the CTLCLASSLIST structure.

```
HANDLE FAR PASCAL ListClasses(LPSTR szAppName,
     WORD wVersion, LPFNLOADRES fnLoad, LPFNEDITRES fnEdit)
{
     HANDLE hClasses = GlobalAlloc(GMEM_SHARE | GMEM_ZEROINIT,
          sizeof(int) + sizeof(RWCTLCLASS));

     LoadResRW = fnLoad;

     if ( hClasses )
     {
          LPCTLCLASSLIST    Classes = (LPCTLCLASSLIST)
GlobalLock(hClasses);

          Classes->nClasses = 1;
          Classes->Classes[0].fnRWInfo    = BitBtnInfo;
          Classes->Classes[0].fnRWStyle   = BitBtnStyle;
          Classes->Classes[0].fnFlags     = BitBtnFlag;
          lstrcpy(Classes->Classes[0].szClass, "BitButton");
          GlobalUnlock(hClasses);
     }

     return hClasses;
}
```

# RWCTLINFO                                                    Structure

## Purpose

The RWCTLINFO structure is returned by a control's LPFNINFO function to inform WORKSHOP of the different styles available for a window class via an array of RWCTLTYPE structures.

## Definition

```
typedef struct
{
  WORD wVersion;
```

```
  WORD wCtlTypes;
  char szClass[CTLCLASS];
  char szTitle[CTLTITLE];
  char szReserved[10];
  RWCTLTYPE  Type[CTLTYPES];
} RWCTLINFO;
```

WORD *wVersion*

   The version number assigned to the window control class.

WORD *wCtlTypes*

   The number of control style types that share this window control class.

char *szClass*[CTLCLASS]

   A 20-character array for storing the name of the window class registered by the DLL.

char *szTitle*[CTLTITLE]

   A 94-character array window class title.

char *szReserved*[10]

   A 10-character array reserved for future use.

RWCTLTYPE *Type*[CTLTYPES]

   An array of 12 RWCTLTYPE structures for the different control style types that share this window control class.

## Description

The ListClasses() function in the DLL returns a list of the window control classes available in the DLL. Each of these control classes must have a corresponding RWCTLINFO structure that is returned when WORKSHOP calls the LPFNINFO function pointer associated with the window control class. You can have up to 12 different control style types that share a given window class.

## See Also

| | |
|---|---|
| ListClasses | DLL Function Pointer |
| LPFNINFO | DLL Function Pointer |
| RWCTLCLASS | Structure |
| RWCTLINFO | Structure |
| RWCTLTYPE | Structure |

# RWCTLSTYLE                                   Structure

## Purpose

The RWCTLSTYLE structure contains the information regarding the characteristics for a specific control window in a dialog box.

**Definition**

```
typedef struct {
  WORD  wX;
  WORD  wY;
  WORD  wCx;
  WORD  wCy;
  WORD  wId;
  DWORD dwStyle;
  char  szClass[CTLCLASS];
  char  szTitle[CTLTITLE];
  BYTE  CtlDataSize;
  BYTE  CtlData[ CTLDATALENGTH];
} RWCTLSTYLE;
```

WORD *wX*

The width of the control window.

WORD *wY*

The height of the control window.

WORD *wCx*

The horizontal position of the control in the dialog box in dialog units.

WORD *wCy*

The vertical position of the control in the dialog box in dialog units.

WORD *wId*

The numerical ID for the control. Use the LPFNIDTOSTR function pointer to convert the ID to the string macro definition for the ID and the LPFNSTRTOID pointer to convert a string to a numerical ID.

DWORD *dwStyle*

The style bits for the control window.

char *szClass*[CTLCLASS]

The name of the window class for the control.

char *szTitle*[CTLTITLE]

The title or caption for the control.

BYTE *CtlDataSize*

The size of the data stored in the *CtlData* array.

BYTE *CtlData*[ CTLDATALENGTH]

An array of 255 bytes that is passed to the control via a far pointer in the *lParam* of the WM_CREATE message. This message is generated by Windows when it creates the control window at run time.

## Description

WORKSHOP has no way of knowing what the style bits for your custom control represent. Instead, WORKSHOP calls the control's fnRWStyle() function pointer in the RWCTLCLASS structure returned by the DLL's ListClasses() function. This function in your DLL is expected to display a dialog box that displays the information in the RWCTLSTYLE structure passed via the *hCntlStyle* global memory handle and to allow the user to modify the style bits, caption, and control ID for the control. The modified information should be stored in the RWCTLSTYLE structure before returning.

## See Also

ListClasses        DLL Function Pointer
LPFNFLAGS     DLL Function Pointer
LPFNSTYLE      DLL Function Pointer

# RWCTLTYPE                                              Structure

## Purpose

The RWCTLTYPE structure contains the information regarding the default characteristics for a given control style type, the control's menu name, the bitmap WORKSHOP should display in the "Tools" window, and the cursor WORKSHOP should use when placing the control in a dialog box.

## Definition

```
typedef struct
{
    WORD   wType;
    WORD   wWidth;
    WORD   wHeight;
    DWORD  dwStyle;
    char   szDescr[CTLDESCR];
    HBITMAP hToolBit;
    HCURSOR hDropCurs;
}   RWCTLTYPE;
```

WORD *wType*
     The control's type style.

WORD *wWidth*
     The default width of the control window.

WORD *wHeight*
     The default height for the control window.

**DWORD** *dwStyle*

The default style for the control window.

**char** *szDescr*[CTLDESCR]

A 22-character array for storing the title WORKSHOP should use in the [Control][Custom] menu item.

**HBITMAP** *hToolBit*

A handle to a 24x24 pixel bitmap WORKSHOP should display in the "Tools" window. WORKSHOP will invert the bitmap when it is selected by the user. Set this field to 0 if you do not want the control displayed in the "Tools" window. WORK-SHOP will release the bitmap when it is no longer required and it should therefore not be released by the DLL.

**HCURSOR** *hDropCursor*

A handle to a cursor WORKSHOP should use the mouse cursor when the user selects the control from the "Tools" window. WORKSHOP will use the cross-hair cursor if this field is set to 0.

## Description

The RWCTLTYPE structure is passed to WORKSHOP in the *Type* field of the RWCTLINFO structure, which is returned when WORKSHOP calls the LPFNINFO function pointer for a window control class. For example, the "BitBtn" window class in BWCC has two control style types: Bitmapped Pushbuttons and Static Bitmaps. Each control style type has a separate bitmap in the "Tools" window and a separate entry in the [Control][Custom] menu item, as well as different default characteristics, so they each have a unique RWCTLTYPE structure for the "BitBtn" window class.

## See Also

| | |
|---|---|
| ListClasses | DLL Function Pointer |
| LPFNINFO | DLL Function Pointer |
| RWCTLCLASS | Structure |
| RWCTLINFO | Structure |

# FRACTAL
# DLL AND
# APPLICATION

# 10

Throughout the preceding chapters, we have looked in turn at the compiler, linker, assembler, and other major tools needed for developing significant DOS and Windows applications. In this chapter, we will design and develop a full-fledged, interesting Windows application that draws a variety of fractals. Although we cannot cover all the details of Windows programming in one chapter, this extensive example will help you see the elements involved in the construction and use of a Dynamic Link Library, FRACTDLL.DLL, and a Windows application, WFRACTAL.EXE, written to fully utilize the capabilities of the C++ compiler, assembler, and linker. The process of building and testing the program will also help you see how you can use the tools in the preceding chapters in an actual programming project.

The WFRACTAL application serves as a front-end user interface for the FRACTDLL. All the fractal calculation algorithms, and even the list of supported fractals, are in FRACTDLL. On startup, the WFRACTAL application queries FRACTDLL for the list of fractal types it supports and their characteristics. WFRACTAL uses this information to create its menus. This disassociation between the application engine, FRACTDLL, and the front end, WFRACTAL, has several benefits for creating projects. First, it allows a programmer to focus on the two distinctly different tasks of writing a user interface and developing the actual application engine. Second, it allows easy upgrading of the application engine without having to modify the front end. For example, this version of FRACTDLL only supports a limited number of fractal types. As designed, it is relatively simple to add more fractal types to FRACTDLL without having to make any changes to WFRACTAL. Third, it allows you to write multiple front-end applications based on the same application engine. For example, you could develop a multi-tiered product package, with demonstration, beginner's, and advanced applications, all of which use the same application engine and different front ends.

Another important reason for writing the engine of a Windows application as a DLL is that it places no restrictions on the language used to write the front end. The FRACTDLL can be used by a Windows application written in C, C++, Pascal, or even Visual Basic. For example, the book *Visual Basic How-To*, by Robert Arnson, et. al, contains a Windows application written in Visual Basic that uses the FRACTDLL described in this chapter. This powerful programming feature allows you to create Windows projects using a wide variety of language platforms.

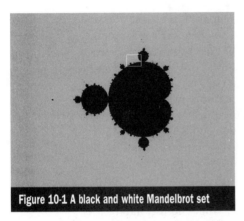

Figure 10-1 A black and white Mandelbrot set

## FRACTAL BASICS

This next section is a brief discussion that provides some background knowledge on fractals. Those readers who are interested in more in-depth descriptions should refer to *The Waite Group's Fractal Creations* by Tim Wegner and myself.

Most people are familiar with the integral dimensions of Euclidean geometry. For example, you know that a number line, which depicts one-dimensional space, marks off the numbers on either side of zero into infinity. The two-dimensional Cartesian plane uses two number lines: the original one-dimensional number line in the horizontal direction and a second number line oriented vertically. Three-dimensional space uses a third number line that marks off units of depth. One, two, and three dimensions are fine for describing the normal geometric shapes like line segments, squares, and cubes. For example, to map all the points in a square, all you need are two dimensions. To map all the points in a cube, you need to use three dimensions, because a cube is a three-dimensional object. Some objects, however, such as the Mandelbrot set shown in Figure 10-1, are too big to fit in just two dimensions and yet too small to fill three-dimensional space. These objects do not exist in either two- or three-dimensional space, but instead exist somewhere in-between. In other words, they are 2.25 or 2.354 dimensional.

When we diagram a mathematical object that does not have an integral dimension on a two-dimensional Cartesian plane, we see this fractional component of the dimension as infinite detail in scale. For example, on normal two-dimensional objects, if you zoom into, i.e., magnify, different areas of the perimeter, no matter

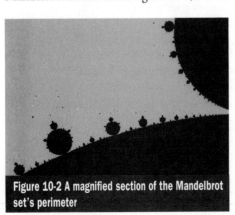

Figure 10-2 A magnified section of the Mandelbrot set's perimeter

how intricate the drawing, you eventually reach a point where the object breaks down into your basic points, line segments, and curves. This is not true with the Mandelbrot set. As shown in Figure 10-2, if you magnify an area of the perimeter, instead of getting simpler, the drawing becomes more complex. Regardless of how far you zoom into an area of the Mandelbrot set's perimeter, the drawing is always more complex and never breaks down into simple two-dimensional components. Any object which has an infinite detail in scale cannot be fully drawn using integral dimensions. Because these objects have fractional components to their dimension, they are referred to as *fractals*.

## Generating the Mandelbrot Fractal

Generating a fractal usually involves successively iterating an equation and determining when the result has either fallen into a periodic loop or has exceeded some other predetermined condition. For example, to generate the Mandelbrot set shown in Figures 10-1 and 10-2, you use the following equation:

$$z' = z^2 - c$$

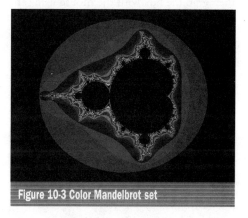

Figure 10-3 Color Mandelbrot set

Note that $z$ and $c$ are complex numbers with both a real and an imaginary component. The real component corresponds to the x-axis on the Cartesian plane, whereas the imaginary component corresponds to the y-axis. To generate the Mandelbrot set, you relate your drawing to coordinates on the Cartesian plane. For most fractals you scale the x-axis to from -2.0 to +2.0 and the y-axis to between 1.5 and -1.5. You then successively examine each point in the drawing using the coordinate location on the Cartesian plane as one of the parameters in the fractal formula. For example, to generate the Mandelbrot set, you use the Cartesian coordinate of the point as the value for $c$ and set the initial value of $z$ to 0. You then calculate '$z2 - c$' to determine a new value for $z$ and then calculate again. If the point falls into a periodic loop, then it is definitely in the Mandelbrot set and is shown in black. If you calculate a certain number of iterations (which is 20,000 for Figures 10-1 and 10-2), and the location of $z$ was never farther away than 2 units from the origin, then you assume the point is part of the set and also show it in black.

The most interesting depictions of fractals, however, result when you assign

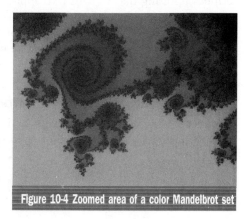

Figure 10-4 Zoomed area of a color Mandelbrot set

749

a color value to the number of iterations you calculate before the location of $z$ is 2 units greater than the origin, as shown in Figure 10-3.

When you depict the number of iterations, the areas near the perimeter of the Mandelbrot set form intricately beautiful patterns, as shown in Figure 10-4.

The WFRACTAL application depicts a color Mandelbrot set when you select the [Fractal][Mandelbrot] menu item. You can zoom into different sections of the Mandelbrot set, or any other fractal, by holding down the left mouse button, sizing the box shown in the window, and releasing the button when the box is the desired size. You then grab the box with the mouse using the left mouse button, move it to the area you want to view, and double-click the left mouse button. If you need to resize the box, press (Esc) before you double-click and create a new box.

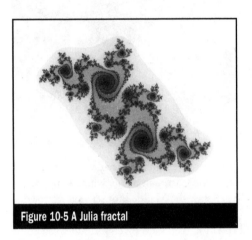

**Figure 10-5 A Julia fractal**

## Julia Fractals

There are many other types of fractals. For example, the Julia set shown in Figure 10-5 uses the same formula as the Mandelbrot set, except that instead of using the drawing coordinate as the value of $c$, you keep the value of $c$ constant and use the drawing coordinate as the initial value of $z$. If you compare the zoomed section of the Mandelbrot set shown in Figure 10-4 with the Julia set in Figure 10-5, you'll notice that the Julia set has the same general pattern as that shown in Figure 10-4. This is because Figure 10-5 used a value of $c$ from one of the coordinate points in Figure 10-4. There is a mathematical and geometric relationship between points in the Mandelbrot set and those in the various Julia sets. You can examine this relationship using the WFRACTAL application by selecting the [Fractal][At Point] menu item and clicking the mouse on the desired point. WFRACTAL will then generate the Julia set associated with that point on the Mandelbrot set.

Note that the [Fractal][Julia] menu item draws the Julia set using the coordinate (0.3, 0.6) for the value of $c$.

## The Mandelbrot Sine and Lambda Sine Fractals

Another of the many different fractal types is the Mandelbrot Sine fractal. This fractal, shown in Figure 10-6, uses the following formula:

```
z' = c * sine(z)
```

Like the normal Mandelbrot fractal, you use the drawing coordinate as the initial value of $c$ and start with an initial value of 0 for $z$. Instead of stopping the iterations when the location of $z$ is more than 2 units from the origin, for the Mandelbrot Sine, you stop iterating when the real portion of $z$ exceeds 32. WFRACTAL will draw the Sine Mandelbrot set when you select the [Fractals][Mandelbrot Sine] menu item.

There are also Julia sets associated with each point on the Mandelbrot Sine fractal. The WFRACTAL application

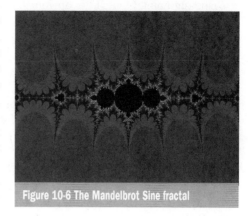

Figure 10-6 The Mandelbrot Sine fractal

depicts a point you select after choosing the [Fractal][At Point] menu item. These Julia sets are sometimes referred to as Lambda Sine fractals. The [Fractal][Lambda Sine] menu item draws the Julia set associated with the point (1.0, 0.4) on the Mandelbrot Sine fractal.

## The Newton Fractal

The Newton fractal shown in Figure 10-7 is a fractal that is generated while trying to determine the correct answers for using Newton's method where $n$ is the number 4. The following is the iteration equation for doing this:

$$z' = \frac{(n-1)z^n + 1}{nz^{(n-1)}} \quad --> \quad z' = \frac{3z^4 + 1}{4z^3}$$

For this fractal drawing, you stop the iterations when the value of $z$ is close to one of the values for the correct answer. A quick method for determining this is to see how close the value of $z^4$ is to -1.

## THE FRACTAL DLL

WFRACTAL itself is a front-end application for the FRACTDLL. The FRACTDLL library actually performs all the calculations for the drawings using one of three different types of math:

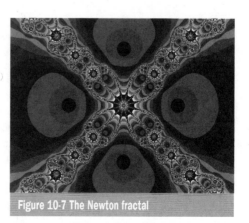

Figure 10-7 The Newton fractal

| | |
|---|---|
| Floating-point | This option uses Borland's C++ floating-point emulation library or a floating-point coprocessor if one is present at run time. |
| QFLOAT | Quick floating-point uses a fast floating-point format that takes advantage of the 32-bit integer math capabilities of an 80386. This option is only available if the computer is an 80386 or better. The math format is always faster than normal floating-point on machines that do not have a math coprocessor. |
| Fixed 16-bit | Uses FIXED math. This is the fastest math format, though it is not available for all fractal types. Like the QFLOAT math format, it requires the user's machine to be an 80386 or better. |

The Fractal DLL maintains a list of supported fractal types. An application that uses the Fractal DLL first determines the number of fractal types supported by the DLL by calling the NumberFractals() function. The application then determines the name of each fractal by calling the FractalName() function with an index to the desired fractal type. Information about a fractal type can be determined by the shell application using the following function:

| | |
|---|---|
| FractalParamOne | Describes how parameter one is used in fractal generation. |
| FractalParamTwo | Describes how parameter two is used in fractal generation. |
| FractalDefaults | Returns the recommended default parameters associated with a fractal and other important information, such as supported math types, symmetry, and any associated fractal type. |

A front-end program, such as WFRACTAL, requests the DLL to initialize the generation of a fractal by calling the CreateFractal() function. This function allocates and initializes the global and local memory needed by the DLL to generate a fractal. The CreateFractal() function allocates moveable global memory. The memory must be locked by calling the ActivateFractal() function before the fractal handle can be used. The memory is unlocked using the IdleFractal() function. Note that more than one fractal can be created and active at one time depending on the memory available on the computer at run time.

The color of each point in the fractal drawing is determined using the FractalPoint() function. This function is passed the handle to an active fractal and the pixel coordinate to be calculated. FractalPoint() then returns the number of the associated color. The color index normally refers to the number of iterations required to exceed some specific parameter. Generally, the higher the color value, the longer it took for the Fractal DLL's calculations to exceed this threshold. The color index values should be totaled and control of the computer returned to Windows after the total exceeds some predetermined level. For example, the WFRACTAL application returns control of the computer back to Windows after the Fractal DLL has performed 2000 iterations, i.e., when the total of all the calculated colors exceeds 2000. A programmer could simply calculate 'x' number of pixels, however, some points in the fractal take much longer to calculate than others. The totaling method ensures that Windows regains control of the computer at regular intervals.

Some fractal types, such as the Mandelbrot set, have other fractals associated with each point in the drawing. The AssocFractDefaults() function is used to determine the settings for the parameters which will generate the fractal associated with a specific point on a fractal.

## Custom Math Libraries

The Fractal DLL can use type double numbers to perform all fractal calculations. In addition, it can also use a custom floating-point format and a fixed point format via the QFLOAT and FIXED <16> object classes. Both the QFLOAT and FIXED <16> classes require a 32-bit microprocessor, such as the DX or SX version of an 80386 or 80486.

The QFLOAT object class is a faster implementation of floating-point numbers than the emulated floating-point library that comes with BC++. It takes advantage of the 80386 32-bit processing capabilities and performs high-speed calculations up to six times faster than emulated floating-point. Type QFLOAT numbers have the same range as type long double numbers, $10^{+/-4932}$, and an accuracy of nine significant digits. They perform calculations somewhat more slowly than when the equivalent floating-point instructions are executed on a coprocessor and are best utilized when floating-point performance is required on 80386, 80386SX, and 80486SX machines that are not equipped with a coprocessor. The Windows Fractal application uses QFLOAT numbers to generate the Newton fractal if there is no coprocessor available at run time.

The FIXED<16> object class used by the Fractal DLL is faster than both the QFLOAT object class and coprocessor floating-point. Like the QFLOAT object class, the FIXED<16> object class utilizes 32-bit processing, however, unlike the QFLOAT class, the FIXED<16> object class performs calculations with the binary exponent fixed at $2^{-16}$. Fixing the exponent to one value has several advantages. First, the number can be represented by storing only the 32-bit signed mantissa. This allows the compiler to generate functions that return FIXED<16> numbers in the DX and AX registers rather than through memory. Secondly, addition and subtraction calculations are performed using type integer mathematics, which is many times faster than the floating-point equivalent executed on a coprocessor. Thirdly, multiplication and division require roughly the same amount of time as floating-point multiplication and division on a coprocessor. Overall, FIXED<16> calculations are always faster than floating-point on any machine. The disadvantage of these types of calculations is their limited range. FIXED<16> numbers have a range of 32767.9999 to 0.00001, or four decimal places.

## Quick Floating-Point

The quick floating-point format is a faster version of floating-point numbers than the type double number format normally used in C applications. The type double format is shown in Figure 10-8. Figures 10-9 and 10-10 show the numbers -1 and 2.5 are stored as doubles.

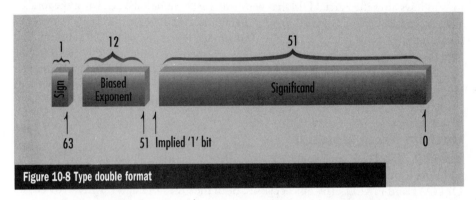

Figure 10-8 Type double format

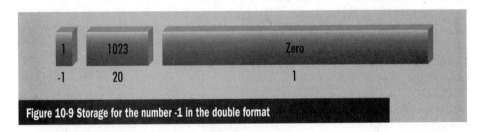

Figure 10-9 Storage for the number -1 in the double format

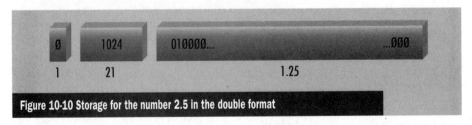

Figure 10-10 Storage for the number 2.5 in the double format

Type double numbers are stored with one bit representing the sign of the number, a 12-bit biased exponent, and a 51-bit significand. If you were to convert this number format into a number you could enter into a calculator, you'd use the following formula:

$$(-1)^{\text{Sign}} * 2^{(\text{Exp - 1023})} * \left(\frac{\text{Significand}}{2^{51}}\right) + 1$$

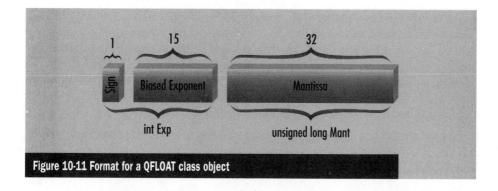

**Figure 10-11 Format for a QFLOAT class object**

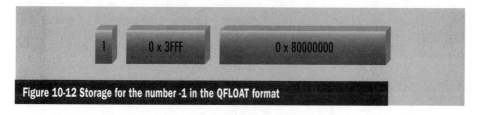

**Figure 10-12 Storage for the number -1 in the QFLOAT format**

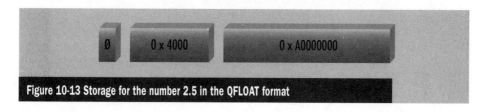

**Figure 10-13 Storage for the number 2.5 in the QFLOAT format**

The following demonstrates how the storage values shown in Figures 10-2 and 10-3 are used to determine the value of the stored number:

$$(-1)^1 * 2^{(1023 - 1023)} * \left( \frac{0}{2^{51}} + 1 \right) = -1 * 2^0 * 1 = 1$$

$$(-1)^0 * 2^{(1024 - 1023)} * \left( \frac{2^{49}}{2^{51}} + 1 \right) = 1 * 2^1 * 1.25 = 2.5$$

The double format, however, is rather awkward to handle on a 32-bit machine. The significand has to be separated from the exponent via bitshifting and the implied 'one' bit must be added before any type of math can be performed on the number. The reverse of this decoding process must be performed to store the number in memory as a type double. This decoding and encoding process takes a significant amount of processing time.

The QFLOAT format, however, stores a 32-bit mantissa instead of a significand. The size of the mantissa enables the CPU to load the mantissa into a register using one instruction and the explicit 'one' bit enables usage of the mantissa immediately after loading, as shown in Figure 10-11. The biased exponent is a full 31 bits with the remaining bit used to indicate the sign of the number. Figures 10-12 and 10-13 show the same numbers, -1 and 2.5, stored in the type QFLOAT format.

The format is defined in C++ without any class function members as follows:

```
class QFLOAT
{
  int Exp;
  unsigned long Mant;
};
```

As with the double format, the bit representing the sign is the most significant bit. The exponent is also biased like the type double; however, the QFLOAT format uses a bias of $2^{14}$-1 ( 0x3FFF or 16,383) instead of $2^{11}$-1 (0x3FF or 1023). Decoding the format uses a formula similar to the type double:

$$(-1)^{Sign} * 2^{(Exp - 0x3FFF)} * \left( \frac{Mantissa}{2^{31}} \right)$$

$$(-1)^1 * 2^{(0x3FFF - 0x3FFF)} * \left( \frac{0x80000000}{2^{31}} \right) = -1 * 2^0 * 1 = -1$$

$$(-1)^0 * 2^{(0x4000 - 0x3FFF)} * \left( \frac{0xA0000000}{2^{31}} \right) = 1 * 2 * 1.25 = 2.5$$

Operator functions must be defined to allow the QFLOAT object class to be used in the same way as any other type of number. The QFLOAT.CPP file defines a few base level functions for conversion, addition, multiplication, division, and comparison. The majority of the operator functions are defined as inline functions for speed.

The QFLOAT.H header file contains the QFLOAT object class definition inline function members for the QFLOAT class.

**qfloat.h**

```
/* QFLOAT.H

   This module defines the operators for the QFLOAT math type. This
   is used to calculate fractals requiring a large dynamic range,
   such as the Newton fractal, on machines which do not have floating-
   point coprocessors. The range of the QFLOAT format is the same as
   the 'long double' type used in C. To increase the speed, however,
   the precision is trucated to 12 significant digits instead of 24
   for a 'long double' type or the 15 significant digits for the
   'double' type.
*/
```

```
extern unsigned Overflow;
extern double QfloatDouble;

class QFLOAT
{
   /*The QFLOAT object class stores numbers as a signed biased
      expontent and a 32-bit unsigned mantissa. These correspond
      to the 'int' and 'unsigned long' types, respectively.
   */
   int Exp;
   unsigned long Mant;

public:
   QFLOAT() { }

   /* Use the operator=(double) function for constructin a QFLOAT
      using a double number.
   */
   QFLOAT(double Number) { operator=(Number); }

   /* The Double() function converts back to a type double. An
      explicit function is used for the conversion rather than a
      type cast to avoid ambiguities.
   */
   double Double();

// Assignment operators
   /* This is no more than the default copy constructor supplied
      by C++.
   */
   QFLOAT& operator=(QFLOAT& Operand)
   {
      Exp = Operand.Exp;
      Mant = Operand.Mant;
      return(*this);
   }

   /* The lower-level function for converting from a type double
      to a QFLOAT is defined in QFLOAT.CPP.
   */
   QFLOAT& operator=(double Operand);

   // Unary Operators
   int operator!()
   {
      /* If the mantissa is 0, then the number is 0. */
      return(!Mant);
   }

   // List of friends
   friend QFLOAT operator-(QFLOAT a);
   friend QFLOAT operator+(QFLOAT a, QFLOAT b);
   friend QFLOAT operator-(QFLOAT& a, QFLOAT& b);
   friend QFLOAT operator*(QFLOAT a, QFLOAT b);
   friend QFLOAT operator/(QFLOAT a, QFLOAT b);
   friend QFLOAT Distance(QFLOAT a, QFLOAT& b);
   friend QFLOAT Twice(QFLOAT a);
};
```

```
inline QFLOAT operator-(QFLOAT& a, QFLOAT& b)
{
   /* Subtraction is the same as adding a negative number, so
      we'll define it that way.
   */
   return(a + (-b));
}

inline QFLOAT operator-(QFLOAT a)
{
   /* The sign bit is the most siginificant bit of the exponent.
      We can change the sign of a QFLOAT by toggling the sign bit.
   */
   a.Exp ^= 0x8000;
   return(a);
}

// Compound operators
/* We'll use the binary operator functions to calculate the
   equivalent compound operator.
*/
inline QFLOAT& operator+=(QFLOAT& a, QFLOAT& b)
{
   a = a + b;
   return(a);
}

inline QFLOAT& operator-=(QFLOAT& a, QFLOAT& b)
{
   a = a - b;
   return(a);
}

inline QFLOAT& operator*=(QFLOAT& a, QFLOAT& b)
{
   a = a * b;
   return(a);
}

inline QFLOAT& operator/=(QFLOAT& a, QFLOAT& b)
{
   a = a / b;
   return(a);
}

/* This function is needed for template compatibility */
inline double Double(QFLOAT a) { return(a.Double()); }

/* The Distance() function calculates the absolute value of 'a - b'
*/
inline QFLOAT Distance(QFLOAT a, QFLOAT& b)
{
   a -= b;

   /* If the exponent is negative, then the number is negative. */
   if(a.Exp < 0)
      a = -a;
```

```
    return(a);
}

/* The Compare(x, y) function returns the following:
   < 0        if x < y
   == 0       if x == y
   > 0        if x > y
*/

int Compare(QFLOAT x, QFLOAT y);

// Logical operators
/* We'll define the logical operators using the Compare() function.
*/
inline int operator<=(QFLOAT& a, QFLOAT& b)
{
    return(Compare(a, b) <= 0);
}

inline int operator>=(QFLOAT& a, QFLOAT& b)
{
    return(Compare(a, b) >= 0);
}

inline int operator< (QFLOAT& a, QFLOAT& b)
{
    return(Compare(a, b) < 0);
}

inline int operator> (QFLOAT& a, QFLOAT& b)
{
    return(Compare(a, b) > 0);
}

inline int operator!=(QFLOAT& a, QFLOAT& b)
{
    return(Compare(a, b) != 0);
}

inline int operator==(QFLOAT& a, QFLOAT& b)
{
    return(Compare(a, b) == 0);
}

/* The Twice() function performs a quick muliplication by two.
   This is done by simply incrementing the exponent.
*/
inline QFLOAT Twice(QFLOAT x)
{
    x.Exp++;

    /* We need to make sure we didn't overflow */
    if(_FLAGS & (1 << 11))
      Overflow = 1;

    return(x);
}
```

The QFLOAT.CPP file contains the out-of-line member functions required by the QFLOAT object class.

**qfloat.cpp**

```
/* QFLOAT.CPP

    This file contains the lower-level assembly language routines
    used by the QFLOAT object class.
*/

#pragma inline

#include "qfloat.h"

double QfloatDouble;

/* The IDE assembler does not recognize some of the 80386 specific
   instructions, such as 'shld' and 'cdg', so we'll just disable
   that warning message.
*/
#pragma option -w-asm

int Compare(QFLOAT x, QFLOAT y)
{
    int Ans;

    asm {
    .386
            xor   si, si            // Clear the 'si' and 'di' registers
            xor   di, di
            mov   ax, x.Exp         // Load the 'x' exponent and mantissa
            mov   edx, x.Mant
            mov   bx, y.Exp         // Load the 'y' exponent and mantissa
            mov   ecx, y.Mant
            or    ax, ax            // Is the 'x' exponent positive?
            jns   AtLeastOnePos

            or    bx, bx            // Is the 'y' exponent positive?
            jns   AtLeastOnePos

            mov   si, 1             // Both exponents are negative.
            and   ah, 7fh           // Make them both positive and
            and   bh, 7fh           //    flag a reversal in the 'si'
                                    //    register
    }
    AtLeastOnePos: asm {
            cmp   ax, bx            // Is the 'x' exponent less than
            jle   Cmp1              //    or equal to the 'y' exponent

            mov   di, 1             // No, flag 'x' as greater and exit
            jmp   ChkRev
    }
    Cmp1: asm {
            je    Cmp2              // Were the exponents equal?

            mov   di, -1            // No, then 'x' must be less than 'y'
            jmp   ChkRev
    }
```

```
Cmp2: asm {
        cmp   edx, ecx        // The exponents are equal, so check
        jbe   Cmp3            //   the mantissas

        mov   di, 1           // The 'x' mantissa is greater than 'y'
        jmp   ChkRev
}
Cmp3: asm {
        je    ChkRev          // Were the mantissas equal?
        mov   di, -1          // No, 'x' must be less than 'y'
}
ChkRev: asm {
        or    si, si          // Should we reverse the result?
        jz    ExitCmp
        neg   di              // Yes!
}
ExitCmp: asm {
        mov   Ans, di
        .8086
}
return(Ans);
}


QFLOAT& QFLOAT::operator=(double x)
{
  QFLOAT Ans;

    asm {
    .386
        /* Load the exponent and the top section of the mantissa */
        mov   si, WORD PTR [x+6]

        /* Load the entire double number into the edx and eax
           register. */
    mov   edx, DWORD PTR [x+4]
    mov   eax, DWORD PTR [x]

    mov   ebx, edx            // Check to see if its 0
    shl   ebx, 1             // First get rid of the sign bit
    or    ebx, eax           // Or all the bits into ebx
    jnz   Non0              // Jump if it isn't 0

    xor   si, si             // It was 0, so clear the
    xor   edx, edx          //   si and edx registers.
    jmp   StoreAns
}
NonZero: asm {
        /* Save the sign bit of the number in the carry bit of the
           flag register. Save it on the stack for a bit, get rid of
           the top section of the mantissa, and then retrieve the
           sign bit. */
        shl   si, 1
        pushf
        shr   si, 4
        popf
        rcr   si, 1

        /* Change from a 1023 biased exponent to a bias of 16,383 */
        add   si, (1 SHL 14) - (1 SHL 10)
```

761

```
        /* Convert from a 51-bit mantissa with an implied one bit
           to a 32-bit mantissa with an explicit 1 bit. */
        shld edx, eax, 12
        stc
        rcr  edx, 1
    }
StoreAns: asm {
        mov  Ans.Exp, si
        mov  Ans.Mant, edx
    .8086
    }
    *this = Ans;
    return(*this);
}

double QFLOAT::Double()
{
    QFLOAT x = *this;
    double Ans;

    asm {
    .386
        /* Convert from a 16,383 biased exponent to a 1023 bias */
        sub  WORD PTR x.Exp, (1 SHL 14) - (1 SHL 10)
        jo   Overflow           // Did we overflow?

        mov  bx, x.Exp

        /* Are there any bits left at the top? */
        and  bx, 0111100000000000b
        jz   InRangeOfDouble    // Jump if we're within range
    }
Overflow: asm {
        mov  Overflow, 1        // Flag an overflow
        xor  eax, eax           // Store a 0
        xor  edx, edx
        jmp  StoreAns
    }
InRangeOfDouble: asm {
        /* Place the sign bit as bit 5 and the the exponent as bits
           0 through 4 of the bx register. */
        mov  bx, x.Exp
        mov  ax, bx
        shl  bx, 5
        shl  ax, 1
        rcr  bx, 1
        shr  bx, 4

        /* Put the mantissa into edx and get rid of the one bit */
        mov  edx, x.Mant
        shl  edx, 1

        /* Put the bottom part of the mantissa into eax and the
           exponent and sign bits with the top section of the
           mantissa in the edx register. */
        xor  eax, eax
        shrd eax, edx, 12
        shrd edx, ebx, 12
    }
```

```
    StoreAns:  asm {
        mov   DWORD PTR Ans+4, edx
        mov   DWORD PTR Ans, eax
    .8086
    }
    return(Ans);
}


QFLOAT operator+(QFLOAT x, QFLOAT y)
{
    QFLOAT Ans;

    asm {
    .386
        /* Load 'x' into the si and eax registers */
        mov   si, x.Exp
        mov   eax, x.Mant

        /* Load 'y' into the di and edx register */
        mov   di, y.Exp
        mov   edx, y.Mant

      /* If the sign bits are different, then set up for
         subtraction. */
        mov   cx, si
        xor   cx, di
        js    Subtract

        /* We can only add the mantissas if they are the same relative
           magnitude. Jump to where we actually add the mantissas
           if the exponents are already the same magnitude. */
        jz    SameMag

        cmp   si, di            // Is 'x' greater than 'y'?
        jg    XisGreater

        xchg  si, di            // 'y' is greater, so swap the two
        xchg  eax, edx
    }
    XisGreater:  asm {
        /* What is the difference in magnitude between 'x' and 'y'? */
        mov   cx, si
        sub   cx, di

        /* If the difference in magnitude between 'x' and 'y' is 31
           or more, then this addition operation is insignificant.
           We'll just return the greater number. */
        cmp   cx, 32
        jge   StoreAns

        /* Shift the mantissa of the greater number to the same order
           of magnitude as 'x' */
        shr   edx, cl
    }
    SameMag:  asm {
        /* We can add the mantissas now that we're sure both mantissas
           are the same relative magnitude. */
        add   eax, edx
```

```
            /* If there was a carry, we have to adjust the exponent */
            jnc   StoreAns
            rcr   eax, 1
            add   si, 1

            /* Did we overflow? Not likely, but still possible! */
            jno   StoreAns
   }
     Overflow: asm {
            mov   Overflow, 1
   }
     ZeroAns: asm {
            xor   si, si              // Store a 0 as the answer
            xor   edx, edx
            jmp   StoreAns
   }
     Subtract: asm {
            /* The signs of 'x' and 'y' were different, so we'll have to
               subtract the mantissas instead of adding them.  First
               toggle the sign bit of 'y' so that it matches 'x' and
               compare relative magnitudes of each.  */
            xor   di, 8000h
            mov   cx, si
            sub   cx, di
            jnz   DifferentMag

            /* The magnitudes are the same.  If the mantissas are also the
               same, then the answer is 0. */
            cmp   eax, edx
            jg    SubtractNumbers
            je    ZeroAns

            /* The 'x' mantissa is less then the 'y' mantissa, so toggle
               the sign of the answer and swap the two mantissas. */
            xor   si, 8000h
            xchg  eax, edx
            jmp   SubtractNumbers
   }
  DifferentMag: asm {
            /* 'x' and 'y' have different relative magnitudes.  Is the 'x'
               exponent less than 'y' as indicated by a negative value
               in the cx register? */
            or    cx, cx
            jns   NoSwap

            /* 'x' is less than 'y'.  We need to swap the two numbers and
               mantissas as well as toggle the sign of the answer.  Negate
               the cx register to make it a positive difference in
               magnitude. */
            xchg  si, di
            xchg  eax, edx
            xor   si, 8000h
            neg   cx
   }
     NoSwap: asm {
            /* If the difference in magnitude is more than 31, then the
               subtraction operation is insignificant.  Just store the
               number with the larger magnitude as the asnwer. */
            cmp   cx, 32
            jge   StoreAns
```

```
            /* Shift the mantissa of the smaller number to match the
               magnitude of the larger number. */
            shr   edx, cl
   }
      SubtractNumbers: asm {
            /* Subtract the two mantissas */
            sub   eax, edx

            /* We need to determine the new position of the one bit. */
            bsr   ecx, eax
            neg   cx
            add   cx, 31

            /* Shift the one bit to the most significant bit position and
               adjust the exponent.  Note that if the 1 bit was in the
               most significant position, cx is 0 and this code section
               does nothing. */
            shl   eax, cl
            sub   si, cx
            jo Overflow              // Did we overflow?
      }
      StoreAns: asm {
            mov   Ans.Exp, si
            mov   Ans.Mant, eax
      .8086
      }
   return(Ans);
}


QFLOAT operator*(QFLOAT x, QFLOAT y)
{
      QFLOAT Ans;

      asm {
      .386
            /* Move the 'x' and 'y' exponents and signs into the ax and bx
               register */
            mov   ax, x.Exp
            mov   bx, y.Exp

            /* Set the most significant bit of the ch register with
               the sign bit for 'y' */
            xor   ch, ch
            shl   bh, 1
            rcr   ch, 1
            shr   bh, 1

            /* Calculate the sign of the answer in leave it in the ax
               register. */
            xor   ah, ch

            /* Calculate the exponent of the answer */
            sub   bx, (1 SHL 14) - 2
            add   ax, bx

            /* Make sure we didn't overflow */
            jno   NoOverflow
      }
```

```
    Overflow:  asm {
        /* If we did overflow, was one of the numbers 0?  If it
           was, then the answer is also 0. */
        or    WORD PTR [x.Mant+2], 0
        jz    ZeroAns
        or    WORD PTR [y.Mant+2], 0
        jz    ZeroAns

        mov   Overflow, 1
    }
    ZeroAns:  asm {
        /* Either 'x' or 'y' is 0, so store 0 as the answer. */
        xor   edx, edx
        mov   Ans.Exp, dx
        jmp   StoreMant
    }
    NoOverflow:  asm {
        /* So far, so good. We still need to make sure one of the
           numbers isn't 0. */
        mov  Ans.Exp, ax

        mov   eax, x.Mant
        mov   edx, y.Mant

        /* Is the 'x' mantissa 0? */
        or    eax, eax
        jz    ZeroAns

        /* Is the 'y' mantissa 0? */
        or    edx, edx
        jz    ZeroAns

        /* Neither mantissa is 0, so that means neither number is
           0. We can go ahead and multiply. */
        mul   edx

        /* Is the one bit in the most significant position as
           indicated by a negative edx register? */
        or    edx, edx
        js    StoreMant

        /* If edx was positive, we need to shift the result over by
           one bit and adjust the exponent. */
        shld  edx, eax, 1
        sub   WORD PTR Ans.Exp, 1

        /* Check for an overflow just in case */
        jo  Overflow
    }
    StoreMant:  asm {
        mov   Ans.Mant, edx
    .8086
    }
    return(Ans);
}

QFLOAT operator/(QFLOAT x, QFLOAT y)
{
```

```
QFLOAT Ans;

asm {
.386
    /* Calculate the sign of the answer just as we did in the
       multiply operator. */
    mov    ax, x.Exp
    mov    bx, y.Exp
    xor    ch, ch
    shl    bh, 1
    rcr    ch, 1
    shr    bh, 1
    xor    ah, ch

    /* Because we are dividing this time, we subtract the exponents
       instead of adding them. */
    sub    bx, (1 SHL 14) - 2
    sub    ax, bx
    jno    NoOverflow        // Always check for an overflow.
}
Overflow: asm {
    mov    Overflow, 1
}
ZeroAns:  asm {
    xor    eax, eax
    mov    Ans.Exp, ax
    jmp    StoreMant
}
NoOverflow: asm {
    mov    Ans.Exp, ax

    /* Clear the eax register. */
    xor    eax, eax

    mov    edx, x.Mant
    mov    ecx, y.Mant

    /* If 'x' is 0, then the answer is 0. */
    or     edx, edx
    jz ZeroAns

    /* If 'y' is 0, then we have an overflow. */
    or     ecx, ecx
    jz     Overflow

    /* We need to make sure edx is smaller than ecx.  If we were
       to divide under those conditions, the result would not
       fit in the eax register and the processor would generate a
       divide by 0 interupt. */
    cmp    edx, ecx
    jb     Divide

    /* The edx register was larger than ecx, so shift the whole 64
       bits down by 1 and adjust the exponent of the answer. */
    shr    edx, 1
    rcr    eax, 1
    add    WORD PTR Ans.Exp, 1
    jo     Overflow             // Make sure we didn't overflow
```

767

```
    }
  Divide:  asm {
  /* We divide edx:eax, which is the 'x' mantissa shifted to the
     left by 32 bits, by the 'y' mantissa in the ecx register.
     The processor places the result in the eax register. */
     div   ecx
  }
  StoreMant: asm {
     mov   Ans.Mant, eax
  .8086
  }
  return(Ans);
}
```

## Fixed Point

Unlike the type double and QFLOAT formats, the FIXED format does not use an exponent that can change. Instead, it uses an implied exponent that is fixed at different values depending on the object class. FIXED template class numbers are stored as type long integers which are scaled to this implied exponent. For example, the FIXED<16>

**Figure 10-14 Storage format for the FIXED<16> object class**

object class stores numbers as long integers scaled to $2^{16}$. The FIXED<16> object class reserves 16 bits of the type long for the fractional component of the number, 15 bits for the integer portion, and 1 bit for the sign of the number, as shown in Figure 10-14.

The advantage of this math format of the double and the QFLOAT types is that numbers with fractional components can be manipulated using the CPU's high speed integer math capabilities. As an example for comparison, it takes approximately 30 clock cycles to perform a floating-point addition on an 80387 coprocessor. The same addition operation using register addition on the CPU takes as little as 2 clock cycles. Additionally, FIXED template class objects only use 4 bytes for storage as compared with 8 and 6 for the double and QFLOAT formats.

The FIXED template class is best defined using the C++ template capabilities of BC++ Version 3.0. The following application defines a simplified FIXED template class with only a type double constructor and a member function that returns the number in a double format:

**fixed30.cpp**
```
template <int BITSHIFT> struct FIXED
{
    long x;

    FIXED(double Number)
    {
        x = (long)(Number * (1L << BITSHIFT));
```

```
        }
        double Double()
        {
            return(((double)x) / (1L << BITSHIFT));
        }
};

FIXED<26> One(1.0), Two(2.0);
FIXED<16> Three(3.0), Four(4.0);

#include <iostream.h>

void main(void)
{
   cout << "One = "   << One.Double()   << "\n";
   cout << "Two = "   << Two.Double()   << "\n";
   cout << "Three = " << Three.Double() << "\n";
   cout << "Four = "  << Four.Double()  << "\n";
}
```

The problem with using templates is that Version 2.0 of BC++ does not support them. To get around this, template classes can be translated into code compatible with BC++ 2.0 by using macro definitions. First, the FIXED class in the above application is redefined without using the template keyword and saved as FIXED.H.

**fixed.h**
```
   struct FIXED
   {
       long x;

       FIXED(double Number)
       {
           x = (long)(Number * (1L << BITSHIFT));
       }
       double Double()
       {
           return(((double)x) / (1L << BITSHIFT));
       }
   };
```

The application can then be written to include the FIXED.H file two times. The first #include directive is executed with the BITSHIFT and FIXED macros defined as 26 and FIXED26. The macros are redefined to 16 and FIXED16 before the second #include. This process creates exactly the same object class as the FIXED<26> and FIXED<16> classes in the first application, as shown below:

**fixed20.cpp**
```
   #define BITSHIFT 26
   #define FIXED    FIXED26
   #include "fixed.h"

   #undef BITSHIFT
   #undef FIXED
```

```
#define BITSHIFT  16
#define FIXED     FIXED16
#include "fixed.h"

FIXED26 One(1.0), Two(2.0);
FIXED16 Three(3.0), Four(4.0);

#include <iostream.h>

void main(void)
{
    cout << "One   = " << One.Double()   << "\n";
    cout << "Two   = " << Two.Double()    << "\n";
    cout << "Three = " << Three.Double() << "\n";
    cout << "Four  = " << Four.Double()  << "\n";
}
```

The FIXED.H file used by the Fractal DLL contains BC++ Version 2.0 compatible code for defining the FIXED template classes.

### fixed.h

```
/* FIXED.H

    This header file assumes that FIXED is declared as some other
    class name, such as FIXED26, using a #define directive. The
    BITSHIFT macro should be defined as some integer. For the
    FIXED<26> class, this would be 26.
*/

#include "fmath.h"

struct FIXED
{
    /* Most of the math operations can be handled in the same way as
        the compiler normally handles a type long, so we'll store the
        number as a type long called 'x'.
    */
    long x;

// Constructors
        FIXED() { }                 // NULL constructor

    /* If we construct a FIXED template class using a type long, then
        we'll assume the number has already been properly bitshifted.
    */
    FIXED(long& Num) { x = Num; }

    /* Type double numbers are converted to a type FIXED template
        class by multiplying by 2**BITSHIFT. This places the binary
        equivalent of the decimal point in the BITSHIFT position of
        the 32-bit number.
    */
        FIXED(double Num)
    {
        x = (long)(Num * (1L << BITSHIFT));
    }
```

```
    // Assignment operators
FIXED& operator=(FIXED& Operand)
{
    x = Operand.x;
    return(*this);
}

/* Convert type doubles before assigning them to 'x' */
    FIXED& operator=(double Operand)
  {
    x = (long)(Operand * (1L << BITSHIFT));
    return(*this);
  }

  // Compound assignment operators
    FIXED& operator+=(FIXED& a)
  {
  /* Type FIXED template class objects are added and subtracted
     in the same way as type long integers. We just need to make
     sure the operation does not cause an overflow.
  */
    x += a.x;
    if(_FLAGS & (1 << 11))   // Check the overflow flag
    Overflow = 1;            // Flag our overflow variable
    return(*this);
  }
    FIXED& operator-=(FIXED& a)
  {
    x -= a.x;
    if(_FLAGS & (1 << 11))   // Check for overflow flag
    Overflow = 1;            // Flag our overflow variable
    return(*this);
  }

  /* For multiplication and division, we need to call our lower-level
     routines.
  */
  FIXED& operator*=(FIXED& a)
  {
    x = Multiply(x, a.x, BITSHIFT);
    return(*this);
  }
  FIXED& operator/=(FIXED& a)
  {
    x = Divide(x, a.x, BITSHIFT);
    return(*this);
  }

  // Unary Operators
  /* Treat negation and the NOT operator exactly as we would a type
     long.
  */
  FIXED& operator-()
  {
    x = -x;
    return(*this);
  }
  int operator!()
  {
```

```
   return(!x);
}

double Double();
};

// Binary operators
/* Unlike the compound operators, the binary operators need to re
   turn a temporary object to function correctly.
*/
inline FIXED operator+(FIXED a, FIXED& b)
{
   a.x += b.x;
   if(_FLAGS & (1 << 11))     // Check for overflow flag
   Overflow = 1;              // Flag our overflow variable
   return(a);
}

inline FIXED operator-(FIXED a, FIXED& b)
{
   a.x -= b.x;
   if(_FLAGS & (1 << 11))     // Check for overflow flag
   Overflow = 1;              // Flag our overflow variable
   return(a);
}

inline FIXED operator*(FIXED a, FIXED& b)
{
   a *= b;
   return(a);
}

inline FIXED operator/(FIXED a, FIXED& b)
{
   a /= b;
   return(a);
}

// Distance function
/* The distance function returns the absolute value of 'a - b' */
   inline FIXED Distance(FIXED a, FIXED& b)
{
   a.x -= b.x;
   if(_FLAGS & (1 << 11))     // Check for overflow flag
   Overflow = 1;              // Flag our overflow variable
   if(a.x < 0)
   a.x = -a.x;
   return(a);
}

/* The Twice() function performs a quick multiplication by two. */
inline FIXED Twice(FIXED a)
{
   a.x <<= 1;
   if(_FLAGS & (1 << 11))     // Check for overflow flag
   Overflow = 1;              // Flag our overflow variable
   return(a);
}
```

```
inline void SinCos(FIXED& Angle, FIXED& Sin, FIXED& Cos)
{
   SinCos(Angle.x, BITSHIFT);
   Sin.x = fSinAns;
   Cos.x = fCosAns;
}

inline void SinhCosh(FIXED& Angle, FIXED& hSin, FIXED& hCos)
{
   SinhCosh(Angle.x, BITSHIFT);
   hSin.x = fSinhAns;
   hCos.x = fCoshAns;
}

// Logical operators
/* The logical operators for the FIXED template classes are exactly
   the same as the type long logicals, so just compare the 'x'
   values.
*/
inline int operator<=(FIXED& a, FIXED& b) { return(a.x <= b.x); }
inline int operator>=(FIXED& a, FIXED& b) { return(a.x >= b.x); }
inline int operator< (FIXED& a, FIXED& b) { return(a.x <  b.x); }
inline int operator> (FIXED& a, FIXED& b) { return(a.x >  b.x); }
inline int operator!=(FIXED& a, FIXED& b) { return(a.x != b.x); }
inline int operator==(FIXED& a, FIXED& b) { return(a.x == b.x); }

inline double Double(FIXED& a)
{
   return(((double)a.x) / (1L << BITSHIFT));
}
```

All the object classes defined using the FIXED template class use the Multiply() and Divide() functions defined in FMATH.CPP. Additionally, the SinCos() and SinhCosh() functions for both the FIXED template class and type double numbers are defined in the FMATH.CPP file.

The SinCos() function for the FIXED template class calculates a simultaneous sine and cosine of a number. Likewise the SinhCosh() function calculates a simultaneous hyperbolic sine and cosine. These values are required by the Fractal DLL to determine the sine or cosine of a complex number. Calculating both the sine and cosine or hyperbolic sine and cosine simultaneously is much faster than calculating the values separately.

Both functions use a technique that reduces a number down to a specific range through the application of various trigonometric identities. For example, the SinCos() function reduces the value of 'x' to less than 45 degrees and keeps track of the number's original octant. Both the sine and the cosine of the reduced number is then calculated using a single series expansion. For example, consider the following Taylor's series for calculating a sine and a cosine:

$$\sin(x) = \frac{x}{1!} - \frac{x^3}{3!} + \frac{x^5}{5!} - \frac{x^7}{7!} + - \ldots + (-1)^n \frac{x^{2n+1}}{(2n+1)!} + \ldots$$

$$\cos(x) = 1 - \frac{x^2}{2} + \frac{x^4}{4} - \frac{x^6}{6} + - \ldots + (-1)^n \frac{x^{2n}}{(2n)!} + \ldots$$

Both the sine and cosine series are identical, except the sine calculation uses odd powers of 'x' and factorials, whereas the cosine calculation uses even powers of 'x' and factorials. The SinCos() function successively calculates both the odd and even powers and factorials required by both series and sums the odd and even terms separately in sine and cosine registers. The terms of the series are calculated until the value of the term is less than the TrigLimit variable. The calculated value is then corrected for the original octant of 'x'.

The SinhCosh() function for the FIXED template classes performs the calculations using the following formulas:

$$\sinh(x) = \frac{e^x - e^x}{2} \qquad\qquad \cosh(x) = \frac{e^x + e^x}{2}$$

Time is saved in this function by only calculating ev once and then using this value to derive the sinh(x) and the cosh(x). First, the SinhCosh() function reduces the value of 'x' to between 0 and the natural log of 2. It then uses the Taylor series to calculate ex as follows:

$$e^x = 1 + \frac{x}{1!} + \frac{x^2}{2!} + \frac{x^3}{3!} + \frac{x^4}{4!} + \frac{x^5}{5!} + \frac{x^6}{6!} + \ldots + \frac{x^n}{n!} + \ldots$$

The value of $e^{-v}$ is calculated by calculating $\frac{1}{e^v}$. The values of $e^x$ and $e^{-x}$ are then bitshifted to the left and right to obtain the real values and the sinh(x) and cosh(x) calculated.

The FMATH.CPP file also contains the functions SinCos() and SinhCosh() for double numbers. The SinCos() function takes advantage of the fsincos instruction available on 80387 or better coprocessors. The SinhCosh() for doubles first calculates the value of $e^x$ and then determines the values for the sinh(x) and cosh(x) using the formulas above.

The following FMATH.H header file contains the prototype and variable declarations for the functions and variables in FMATH.CPP:

**fmath.h**

```
//          Global variables for the FIXED routines
extern      unsigned Overflow;
extern      double FixedDouble;
extern      long fSinAns, fCosAns;
extern      long fSinhAns, fCoshAns;
extern      double dSinAns, dCosAns, dSinhAns, dCoshAns;

//          Routines shared by all FIXED template classes
long        Multiply(long x, long y, unsigned Bitshift);
long        Divide(long x, long y, unsigned Bitshift);
void        SinCos(long x, unsigned Bitshift);
void        SinhCosh(long x, unsigned Bitshift);
void        SinCos(double x);
void        SinhCosh(double x);
```

The following FMATH.CPP file contains the functions and variables that are common to all the FIXED template classes:

**fmath.cpp**

```
/*    FMATH.CPP
      The Multiply() and Divide() functions are used by the different
      FIXED template classes.
*/

#pragma inline
/*    The '#pragma inline' directive tells the compiler right at the
      start of the source code that it needs to generate assembly
      language instructions and pass the result to an external
      assembler.
*/

#include <math.h>
#include "fmath.h"

unsigned Overflow;
double FixedDouble;

/* InvPi33 = 1/Pi in the FIXED<33> format */
static unsigned long InvPi33    = 0xA2F9836EL;

/* Ln2Fixed32 = ln(2) in the FIXED<32> format */
static unsigned long Ln2Fixed32 = 0xB17217F7L;


/*    The IDE assembler does not recognize some of the 80386 specific
      instructions, such as 'shld' and 'cdg', so we'll just disable
      that warning message.
*/
#pragma option -w-asm

long Multiply(long x, long y, unsigned Bitshift)
{
   long Ans;

    asm {
    .386
       mov   eax, x             // Load the 'x' parameter

       /* Perform signed multiplication by 'y'. The processor will
          leave the 64-bit result in the edx:eax registers. */
       imul  DWORD PTR y

       /* Shift 'Bitshift' bits from the edx register into the eax
          register. */
       mov   cx, Bitshift
       shrd  eax, edx, cl

       /* If there is anything left in the edx register after
          shifting by 'Bitshift', then we may have overflowed. */
       sar   edx, cl
       jz    Exit
```

```
                  /* If the edx register bits are all set to one, then this
                     just means the answer was negative. We can quickly verify
                     this by incrementing and then checking to see if the result
                     is 0. */
                  inc    edx
                  jz     Exit

                  /* The edx register was neither 0 or -1 so it
                     must be an overflow. */
                  mov    Overflow, 1           // Flag an overflow
                  xor    eax, eax              // Load -1 as the result
                  dec    eax
                  }
                  Exit: asm {
                  mov    Ans, eax              // Return the answer
                  .8086
              }
          return(Ans);
      }

long Divide(long x, long y, unsigned Bitshift)
{
    long Ans;

         asm {
         .386
              mov    eax, x            // Load 'x' into 'eax'
              mov    ebx, y            // Load 'y' into 'ebx'

              mov    edi, ebx          // Compute the sign of the answer
              xor    edi, eax

              or     eax, eax          // Is 'x' negative?
              jns    PositiveX

              neg    eax               // Make 'x' positive
         }
         PositiveX: asm {
              or     ebx, ebx          // Is 'y' negative?
              jns    PositiveY

              neg    ebx               // Make 'y' positive
         }
         PositiveY: asm {
              mov    cx, Bitshift      // Left shift 'x' by 'Bitshift'
              cdq                      // First clear the 'edx' register
              shld   edx, eax, cl      // Shift 'Bitshift' bits into 'edx'
              shl    eax, cl           // Left shift 'eax' by 'Bitshift'

              cmp    edx, ebx          // Is the high word still larger
                                       // than 'y'?
              jae    Overflow

              /* Perform an unsigned division by 'y' */
              div    ebx               // Divide by 'y'

              /* If the result is negative, we overflowed. */
```

```
          or      eax, eax
          jns     ChkSign
      }
Overflow: asm {
          mov     Overflow, 1        // Flag an overflow and set up
          xor     eax, eax           // to return -1
          dec     eax
          jmp     Exit
      }
ChkSign:  asm {
          or      edi, edi           // What did we compute to be the
          jns     Exit               // sign of the answer?

          neg     eax                // Answer should be negative.
      }
Exit: asm {
          mov     Ans, eax
      .8086
      }
      return(Ans);
}
```

/* The SinCos386 function calculates a simultaneous sine and cosine
   for a FIXED class number. The algorithm was originally written
   to reduce the angle to less than 90 degrees, but thanks to the
   work of Chris J Lusby Taylor, the angle is now reduced to less
   than 45 degrees, which enables faster calculation times.
*/

/* Define a few macros as 80386 register so that the code is more
   readable.
*/
```
#define Term       eax
#define Number     ebx
#define Factorial  ecx
#define Sine       esi
#define Cosine     edi
```

/* The 'TrigLimit' variable determines the accuracy of the
   trig calculations. The calculated numbers will always have
   an accuracy of at least on bit higher than the value of
   'TrigLimit'. The 'fSinAns' and 'fCosAns' variables will
   hold the results of the SinCos() function.
*/
```
long fSinAns, fCosAns;

void SinCos(long x, unsigned Bitshift)
{
    long One, TrigLimit;
    int Octant = 0;

    asm {
    .386
    /* Load the absolute value of 'x' into the 'eax' register */
        mov eax, x
        or  eax, eax
        jns AnglePositive
```

```
    neg  eax
    mov  WORD PTR Octant, 8
}
AnglePositive: asm {
/* Convert 'x' to a varient of the FIXED format. The regular
   FIXED formats store numbers relative to some multiple of 2.
   For the SinCos() function, we store numbers in a format
   relative to 1/2 * 1/Pi * (2**32). In other words, the angle
   is stored as a 32-bit fraction of 1/2 Pi radians.

   The original algorithm only reduced the angle to less than
   90 degrees. Thanks to the work of Chris Lusby Taylor, the
   algorithm operates much more quickly with the angle reduced
   to less than 45 degrees!
*/
    mul  DWORD PTR InvPi33
    mov  cx, Bitshift
    shrd eax, edx, cl
    shr  edx, cl
    and  dx, 3
    shl  dx, 1

/* Set the value of TrigLimit */
    xor  ebx, ebx
    stc
    rcr  ebx, cl
    shr  ebx, 1
    mov  DWORD PTR TrigLimit, ebx

/* Is the angle less than or greater than 45 degrees? */
    or   eax, eax
    jns  LessThan45Degrees

    inc  dx
    neg  eax
}

/* With the angle now less than 45 degrees and greater than 0,
   we can enter a high-speed loop to calculate the Taylor series.
*/
LessThan45Degrees: asm {
/* Store the value of 'eax' in the 'Number' and 'Sine' registers.
*/
    mov  Number, eax
    mov  Sine, Number

/* Update the Octant */
    add  Octant, dx

/* Remember that we are storing numbers in a format as 32-bit
   fractions of 1/2 Pi. This means the variable 'InvPi33' is
   actually the number 1 in this storage format. The following
   code stores the value of 1 in the 'Factorial', 'One', and
   'Cosine' registers.
*/
    mov  Factorial, DWORD PTR InvPi33
    mov  One, Factorial
    mov  Cosine, Factorial
}
```

```
/* The following section of code implements the Taylor series
   for calculating the sin(x) and cos(x). The 'Factorial'
   register is incremented by 'One' before each ratio. If
   this results in a carry, then the storage format for
   the 'Factorial', 'One', and 'Number' registers are reduced
   by a factor of 2. This change in format has no effect on the
   format of the 'Term' register because a ratio is always
   unit-less. The 'Term' register remains as a 32-bit fraction
   of 1/2 Pi throughout the calculation loop.
*/
LoopIntSinCos:  asm {
/* Increment the 'Factorial' register. */
    add   Factorial, One
    jnc   Ratio_1

/* Reduce the format of 'Factorial', 'Number', and 'One' by a
   factor of 2.
*/
    rcr   Factorial, 1
    shr   Number, 1
    shr   DWORD PTR One, 1
}
Ratio_1:  asm {
/* Ratio the 'Term' register */
    mul   Number
    div   Factorial

/* Subtract the term from the 'Cosine' register */
    sub   Cosine, Term

/* Exit the loop if the 'Term' register is less than our
   accuracy limit.
*/
    cmp   Term, DWORD PTR TrigLimit
    jbe   ExitLoop

    add   Factorial, One
    jnc   Ratio_2

    rcr   Factorial, 1
    shr   Number, 1
    shr   DWORD PTR One, 1
}
Ratio_2:  asm {
    mul   Number
    div   Factorial

/* Subtract the 'Term' from the 'Sine' register. */
    sub   Sine, Term
    cmp   Term, DWORD PTR TrigLimit
    jbe   ExitLoop

    add   Factorial, One
    jnc   Ratio_3

    rcr   Factorial, 1
    shr   Number, 1
    shr   DWORD PTR One, 1
}
```

779

```
Ratio_3: asm {
   mul   Number
   div   Factorial

/* Add the 'Term' to the 'Cosine' register. */
   add   Cosine, Term
   cmp   Term, DWORD PTR TrigLimit
   jbe   ExitLoop

   add   Factorial, One
   jnc   Ratio_4

   rcr   Factorial, 1
   shr   Number, 1
   shr   DWORD PTR One, 1
}
Ratio_4: asm {
   mul   Number
   div   Factorial

/* Add the 'Term' to the 'Sine' register. */
   add   Sine, Term
   cmp   Term, DWORD PTR TrigLimit
   jnbe  LoopIntSinCos
}
ExitLoop: asm {
   xor   eax, eax
   mov   ecx, eax

/* If 'Cosine' is equal to 'InvPi33', then the result
   is actually the value one.
*/
   cmp   Cosine, DWORD PTR InvPi33
   jb    CosDivide

/* Store a value of one and skip the division. */
   inc   ecx
   jmp   StoreCos
}
CosDivide: asm {
/* Convert 'Cosine' from a 32-bit fraction of 1/2 Pi to a
   FIXED<32> format.
*/
   mov   edx, Cosine
   div   DWORD PTR InvPi33
}
StoreCos: asm {
   mov   Cosine, eax
   xor   eax, eax
   mov   ebx, eax

/* Is the value of 'Sine' actually one? */
   cmp   Sine, DWORD PTR InvPi33
   jb    SinDivide

/* Store a value of one and skip the division. */
   inc   ebx
   jmp   StoreSin
}
```

```
SinDivide:  asm {
/* Convert 'Sine' from a 32-bit fraction of 1/2 Pi to a
   FIXED<32> format.
*/
    mov   edx, Sine
    div   DWORD PTR InvPi33
}
StoreSin:  asm {
/* The values of sin(x) and cos(x) are now in the 'ecx:Sine'
   and 'ebx:Cosine' registers. Take into account the original
   octant of 'x' by either exchanging or negating each value
   as appropriate.
*/
    mov   Sine, eax
    mov   ax, Octant
    inc   al
    test  al, 2
    jz    ChkNegCos

    xchg  ebx, ecx
    xchg  Sine, Cosine
}
ChkNegCos:  asm {
    inc   al
    test  al, 4
    jz    ChkNegSin

    not   Cosine
    not   ecx
    add   Cosine, 1
    adc   ecx, 0
}
ChkNegSin:  asm {
    inc   al
    inc   al
    test  al, 8
    jz    CorrectOctant

    not   Sine
    not   ebx
    add   Sine, 1
    adc   ebx, 0
}
CorrectOctant:  asm {
/* We've corrected for the original octant. Now we convert the
   values from a 64-bit FIXED<32> format to the format re
   quired by the calling object class and store the results in
   'fCosAns' and 'fSinAns'.
*/
    mov   edx, ecx
    mov   cx, 32
    sub   cx, Bitshift
    shrd  Cosine, edx, cl
    adc   Cosine, 0          // Round-off

    mov   DWORD PTR fCosAns, Cosine
    shrd  Sine, ebx, cl
    adc   Sine, 0            // Round-off
```

781

```
    mov   DWORD PTR fSinAns, Sine
.8086
}
}
```

```
/* The 'fSinhAns' and 'fCoshAns' variables will contain the
   results from the SinhCosh() function.
*/
long fSinhAns, fCoshAns;
```

```
/* Define a few more register macros to keep the code readable.
*/
#define e2x    esi
#define One    edi
#define e2Negx edi
```

```
void SinhCosh(long x, unsigned Bitshift)
{
    int Sign = 0, PwrTwo;
    long TrigLimit;
```

```
asm {
.386
/* Load the absolute value of 'x' into the eax register and
   keep track of the original sign of 'x'. We'll calculate us
   ing a positive value for 'x' and negate the 'SinhAns' after
   wards if 'x' was negative.
*/
    mov   cx, 32
    sub   cx, WORD PTR Bitshift

    mov   eax, x
    or    eax, eax
    jz    zero
    jns   CalcExp

    neg   eax
    inc   WORD PTR Sign
}
CalcExp: asm {
/* First we need to calculated the exp(x). We start by moving
   the binary equivalent of the decimal point to the 32nd bit
   position. All the calculations are performed in a FIXED<32>
   format using one 32-bit register to hold the whole numbers
   and another to hold the fraction.
*/
    cdq
    shld  edx, eax, cl
    shl   eax, cl

/* Set the value of TrigLimit */
    xor   ebx, ebx
    stc
    rcl   ebx, cl
    mov   DWORD PTR TrigLimit, ebx

/* Determine how many multiples of ln(2) there are in 'x'. */
    div   DWORD PTR Ln2Fixed32
```

```
/* If there are more than 32 multiples of ln(2), then
   the answer won't fit in the FIXED format.
*/
    cmp   ax, 32
    jnae  StorePwrTwo
}
HypOverflow: asm {
/* If we end up here, we overflowed somewhere during the
   calculation. Flag the overflow and clear the 'fSinhAns'
   and the 'fCoshAns' variables.
*/
    mov   WORD PTR Overflow, 1
    xor   eax, eax
    mov   DWORD PTR fSinhAns, eax
    mov   DWORD PTR fCoshAns, eax
    jmp   Exit
}
zero: asm {
/* The value of 'x' is 0. The means the hyperbolic cosine
   is equal to 1 and the hyperbolic sine is 0.
*/
    xor   eax, eax
    mov   DWORD PTR fSinhAns, eax
    stc
    rcr   eax, cl
    mov   DWORD PTR fCoshAns, eax
    jmp   Exit
}
StorePwrTwo: asm {
/* Save the multiples of ln(2). */
    mov   WORD PTR PwrTwo, ax

/* Is there a remainder from the division? */
    or    edx, edx
    jnz   TaylorSeries

/* No remainder. This means the answer to the exp(x) is a
   multiple of 2. Calculating mulitples of 2 is much faster
   using bitshifts rather than muliplication. Store 1
   in the 'e2x' register and bitshift to the left and right
   by the PwrTwo to calculate exp(x) and exp(-x).
*/
    xor   e2x, e2x
    inc   e2x              // 'e2x' contains 1
    xor   e2Negx, e2Negx   // 'e2Negx' contains 0
    mov   cx, ax           // 'cx' contains the PwrTwo
    shrd  e2Negx, e2x, cl
    shl   e2x, cl


    mov   edx, e2x
    xor   eax, eax

/* Now the 'edx:eax' register holds the exp(x) and the 'e2Negx'
   register contains the exp(-x).
*/
    jmp   CalcHyp
}
```

```
/* Now we calculate the exp(x % ln(2)), i.e., the exponential
   for the remainder from our earlier division.
*/
    mov   Number, edx
    mov   e2x, edx
    mov   Term, edx

/* Store the number 1 in the FIXED<31> format in both the 'One'
   and 'Factorial' registers.
*/
    xor   One, One
    stc
    rcr   One, 1
    mov   Factorial, One

/* Convert the 'Number' register from the FIXED<32> format to
   the FIXED<31> format. Then it will be in the same format as
   the 'One' and 'Factorial' registers and we can ratio
   without any intermediate bitshifts.
*/
    shr   Number, 1
}
TaylorLoop: asm {
/* Increment the 'Factorial' register.  If there is a carry,
   then convert 'Factorial', 'One', and 'Number' to the next
   smaller FIXED format.
*/
    add   Factorial, One
    jnc   Ratio

    rcr   Factorial, 1
    shr   One, 1
    shr   Number, 1
}
Ratio: asm {
    mul   Number
    div   Factorial
    add   e2x, Term

/* Is the 'Term' register less than our accuracy limit? */
    cmp   Term, DWORD PTR TrigLimit
    jnbe  TaylorLoop

/* The 'e2x'register contains the exp(x % ln(2))-1.  Now calcu-
   late 1/exp(x % ln(2)) and place it in the 'e2Negx' register.
   Don't forget to add the number 1!
*/
    xor   eax, eax
    xor   edx, edx
    stc
    rcr   edx, 1
    mov   ebx, e2x
    stc
    rcr   ebx, 1
    div   ebx
    mov   e2Negx, eax
```

```
/* We also need to add 1 to the value in the 'e2x'. After that,
   we can bitshift by the 'PwrTwo' and have a genuine exp(x)
   in the 'edx:eax' registers in the FIXED<32> format.
*/
    mov   cx, WORD PTR PwrTwo
    mov   eax, e2x
    xor   edx, edx
    inc   edx
    shld  edx, eax, cl
    shl   eax, cl

/* Bitshifting the 'e2Negx' register to the right will give us
   the value for exp(-x) in the FIXED<32> format.
*/
    shr   e2Negx, cl
}
CalcHyp: asm {
/* With the value of exp(x) in the 'edx:eax' register and the
   value of exp(-x) in the 'e2Negx' register, we can calculate
   the values for sinh(x) and the cosh(x). First, save the
   value of exp(x) in the 'esi:ebx' register.
*/
    mov   esi, edx
    mov   ebx, eax

/* Load the bitshifting required to convert the FIXED<32> for
   mat to the format required by the calling object class.
*/
    mov   cx, 32
    sub   cx, WORD PTR Bitshift

/* Toss in an extra division by two */
    inc   cl

/* Calculate the cosh(x) */
    add   eax, e2Negx
    adc   edx, 0
    shrd  eax, edx, cl

/* Round-off */
    adc   eax, 0

/* Did we overflow? This would be indicated by a nonzero value
   in the 'edx' register after shifting.
*/
    shr   edx, cl
    jz    CheckForNegCosh
}
OtherHypOverflow: asm {
/* The first Overflow code section is too distant for a rela
   tive jump and BC++ only allows SHORT jumps for inline assem-
   bly language. We'll just duplicate another overflow code
   section here.
*/
    mov   WORD PTR Overflow, 1
    xor   eax, eax
```

```
        mov   DWORD PTR fSinhAns, eax
        mov   DWORD PTR fCoshAns, eax
        jmp   Exit
    }
    CheckForNegCosh: asm {
    /* The cosh(x) is always positive. If the result in the 'eax'
       register has the sine bit set, then we overflowed.
    */
        or    eax, eax
        js    OtherHypOverflow

    /* Store the result in the 'fCoshAns' variable */
        mov   DWORD PTR fCoshAns, eax

    /* Now calculate sinh(x) */
        sub   ebx, e2Negx
        sbb   esi, 0
        shrd  ebx, esi, cl

    /* Round-off */
        adc   ebx, 0

    /* The |sinh(x)| is always less than the cosh(x). So if the
       cosh(x) calculation didn't overflow, we don't have to check
       for an overflow after the sinh(x) calculation. If the
       original sign of 'x' was negative, we need to negate the
       value of our calculated sinh(x), store the result, and then
       we're finished!
    */
        cmp   WORD PTR Sign, 0
        je    StoreSinhAns

        neg   ebx
    }
    StoreSinhAns: asm {
        mov   DWORD PTR fSinhAns, ebx
    }
    Exit:
}


double dSinAns, dCosAns;
extern int Coprocessor;

void SinCos(double x)
{
    /* Is there an 80387 on the system? */
    if(Coprocessor >= 387)
    {
        asm {
        .386
        .387
            fld   QWORD PTR x
            fsincos
            fstp  QWORD PTR dCosAns
            fstp  QWORD PTR dSinAns
        .8087
        .8086
```

```
            }
        }
        else
        {
            dSinAns = sin(x);
            dCosAns = cos(x);
        }
}

double dSinhAns, dCoshAns;
#undef One
void SinhCosh(double x)
{
    unsigned Control;
    static double PointFive = 0.5, One = 1.0, Two = 2.0;

    asm {
        fstcw WORD PTR Control
        push  Control
        or    Control, 0000110000000000b
        fldcw Control

        fldln2                  // ln(2)
        fdivr QWORD PTR x       // x/ln(2)

        cmp   BYTE PTR x+7, 0
        jns   XisPositive

        fchs                    // x = |x|
    }
    XisPositive: asm {
        fld   st                // x/ln(2), x/ln(2)
        frndint                 // int = integer(|x|/ln(2)), x/ln(2)
        fxch                    // x/ln(2), int
        fsub  st, st(1)         // rem < 1.0, int
        fdiv  QWORD PTR Two     // rem/2 < 0.5, int
        f2xm1                   // (2**rem/2)-1, int
        fadd  QWORD PTR One     // 2**rem/2, int
        fmul  st, st            // 2**rem, int
        fscale                  // e**|x|, int
        fstp  st(1)             // e**|x|

        cmp   BYTE PTR x+7, 0
        jns   ExitFexp

        fdivr QWORD PTR One     // e**x
    }
    ExitFexp: asm {
        fld   st                // e**x, e**x
        fdivr QWORD PTR PointFive // e**-x/2, e**x
        fld   st                // e**-x/2, e**-x/2, e**x
        fxch  st(2)             // e**x, e**-x/2, e**-x/2
        fdiv  QWORD PTR Two     // e**x/2, e**-x/2, e**-x/2
        fadd  st(2), st         // e**x/2, e**-x/2, cosh(x)
        fsubr                   // sinh(x), cosh(x)

        fstp  QWORD PTR dSinhAns
        fstp  QWORD PTR dCoshAns
```

787

```
        pop  Control
        fldcw Control          // Restore control word
    }
}
```

## The ZNUM Template Class

The Fractal DLL uses another BC++ Version 2.0 compatible template class called ZNUM which defines the algorithms for complex mathematics. A simple ZNUM template class written using the 'template' keyword available in BC++ Version 3.0 would look like this:

**znum.cpp**

```
#include <iostream.h>

template <int BITSHIFT> struct FIXED
{
    long x;

    FIXED(double Number)
    {
        x = (long)(Number * (1L << BITSHIFT));
    }
    double Double()
    {
        return(((double)x) / (1L << BITSHIFT));
    }
};

template <class NUMBER> struct ZNUM
{
    NUMBER Real;
    NUMBER Imag;

    ZNUM(double r, double i)
    {
        Real = r;
        Imag = i;
    }
};

ZNUM<double>        dPureReal(1.0, 0.0),    dPureImag(0.0, 1.0);
ZNUM<FIXED <16> >   fPureReal(1.0, 0.0),    fPureImag(0.0, 1.0);
ZNUM<class QFLOAT>  qPureReal(1.0, 0.0),    qPureImag(0.0, 1.0);
```

In the above code, the ZNUM template was used to create three different complex number formats: type double, FIXED<16>, and QFLOAT. The Fractal DLL uses all three formats. Again, however, to maintain compatibility with Version 2.0 of BC++, the code is written using macros to define both NUMBER and ZNUM and compiled into modules called ZDOUBLE, ZFIXED16, and ZQFLOAT.

All three modules use the following ZNUM.H and ZNUM.TP file:

**znum.h**

```
/* This header file and the associated ZNUM.CPP file perform
   triple duty. The same source code is used as a template to com
   pile three different applications modules called ZDOUBLE.OBJ,
   ZFIXED.OBJ, and ZQFLOAT.OBJ. This is done by compiling with
   the NUMBER macro set to either FIXED, QFLOAT, or double. The
   ZNUM macro is then set to either ZFIXED, ZQFLOAT, or ZDOUBLE,
   respectively.
*/

/* The ZNUM template class is functionally equivalent to the
   complex class, that is, a number with a real and an imaginary
   component.
*/
struct ZNUM
{
    NUMBER Real, Imag;

    // Define the constructors
    ZNUM(NUMBER x, NUMBER y)
    {
        Real = x;
        Imag = y;
    }
    ZNUM() { }

    /* The Modulus function computes the absolute distance of the
       complex number from the origin. Note that this function
       returns the modulus squared. You will need to calculate a
       square root of the result to get the actual modulus. Square
       root calculations are very time consuming and for most
       purposes the squared return can be used as is.
    */
    NUMBER Modulus();
    ZNUM& operator+=(ZNUM& a)
    {
        Real += a.Real;
        Imag += a.Imag;
        return(*this);
    }
};

/* Addition and subtraction of complex numbers are accomplished
   by simply adding and subtracting the real and imaginary components.
*/
inline ZNUM operator+(ZNUM x, ZNUM& y)
{
    x.Real += y.Real;
    x.Imag += y.Imag;
    return(x);
}

inline ZNUM operator-(ZNUM x, ZNUM& y)
{
    x.Real -= y.Real;
    x.Imag -= y.Imag;
    return(x);
}
```

```
/* Define the operators involving real numbers */
inline ZNUM operator+(ZNUM x, NUMBER y)
{
   x.Real += y;
   return(x);
}

inline ZNUM operator+(NUMBER y, ZNUM x)
{
   x.Real += y;
   return(x);
}

inline ZNUM operator-(ZNUM x, NUMBER y)
{
   x.Real -= y;
   return(x);
}

inline ZNUM operator-(NUMBER y, ZNUM x)
{
   x.Real = y - x.Real;
   x.Imag = -x.Imag;
   return(x);
}

inline ZNUM operator*(ZNUM x, NUMBER y)
{
   x.Real *= y;
   x.Imag *= y;
   return(x);
}

inline ZNUM operator*(NUMBER y, ZNUM x)
{
   x.Real *= y;
   x.Imag *= y;
   return(x);
}

inline ZNUM operator/(ZNUM x, NUMBER y)
{
   x.Real /= y;
   x.Imag /= y;
   return(x);
}

/* The remaining functions are defined in the ZNUM.TP template. */
extern ZNUM operator*(ZNUM& x, ZNUM& y);
extern ZNUM operator/(ZNUM& x, ZNUM& y);

/* Declare a square function.  Squaring a number can be defined
   more efficiently using dedicated routines.
*/
extern NUMBER Sqr(ZNUM* z);
extern ZNUM sin(ZNUM& z);
```

**znum.tp**

```
ZNUM operator*(ZNUM& x, ZNUM& y)
{
    ZNUM Ans;

    /* Multiplying complex numbers is performed like this where
       'i' is an imaginary number.
       (a + ib) * (c + id) = (ac + (i*i)bd) + iad + ibc
                           = (ac - bd) + i(ad + bc)
    */

    Ans.Real = (x.Real * y.Real) - (x.Imag * y.Imag);
    Ans.Imag = (x.Real * y.Imag) + (x.Imag * y.Real);
    return(Ans);
}


NUMBER ZNUM::Modulus()
{
    NUMBER Mod = Real * Real;
    Mod += Imag * Imag;
    return(Mod);
}

/* The Sqr() function performs double duty. It both squares the
   value of 'z' and returns the modulus of the original value
   of 'z'.
*/
NUMBER Sqr(ZNUM* z)
{
    NUMBER RealSqr, ImagSqr;

    /* The mathematics behind this function is as follows:
       (a + ib) * (a + ib)   = (aa + (i*i)bb) + iab + iab
                             = (aa - bb) + 2i(ab)
    */

    ImagSqr = z->Imag * z->Imag;
    RealSqr = z->Real * z->Real;
    z->Imag = Twice(z->Imag * z->Real);
    z->Real = RealSqr - ImagSqr;

    /* Calculate the modulus */
    RealSqr += ImagSqr;
    return(RealSqr);
}

ZNUM operator/(ZNUM& x, ZNUM& y)
{
    ZNUM Ans;

    /* Division of complex numbers is performed this way:

        a + ib   (a + ib) * (c - id)
        ------ = -------------------
        c + id   (c + id) * (c - id)
```

$$= \frac{(ac + bd) + i(ad - bc)}{cc + dd}$$

Note that 'cc + dd' is the modulus squared, which we can obtain from the Modulus() function.
*/

```
Ans.Real = (x.Real * y.Real) + (x.Imag * y.Imag);
Ans.Imag = (x.Real * y.Imag) - (x.Imag * y.Real);

NUMBER Modulus = y.Modulus();
Ans.Real /= Modulus;
Ans.Imag /= Modulus;
return(Ans);
}


/* Only defined for double and FIXED math */
#ifndef TYPE_Q_MATH

#include "math.h"

ZNUM sin(ZNUM& x)
{
  ZNUM Ans;
  NUMBER Sine, Cosine, HypSine, HypCosine;

  // Calculate a simultaneous sine and cosine
  SinCos(x.Real, Sine, Cosine);

  // Calculate a simultaneous hyperbolic sine and cosine
  SinhCosh(x.Imag, HypSine, HypCosine);

  Ans.Real = Sine * HypCosine;
  Ans.Imag = Cosine * HypSine;
  return(Ans);
}

#endif
```

The ZDOUBLE.H file defines the NUMBER and ZNUM macros as double and ZDOUBLE. It also defines a few inline functions that are unique to type double complex operations.

**zdouble.h**

```
#ifndef ZDOUBLE_H
#define ZDOUBLE_H

#ifdef NUMBER
  #undef NUMBER
  #undef ZNUM
#endif

#define TYPE_D_MATH
#define NUMBER     double
#define ZNUM       ZDOUBLE
```

```
extern unsigned Overflow;

inline double Double(double& x) { return(x); }

inline double Distance(double a, double& b)
{
   a -= b;
   if(a < 0)
      a = -a;
   return(a);
}

#include "fmath.h"
#include "znum.h"

inline void SinCos(double& x, double& Sin, double& Cos)
{
   SinCos(x);
   Sin = dSinAns;
   Cos = dCosAns;
}

inline void SinhCosh(double& x, double& hSin, double& hCos)
{
   SinhCosh(x);
   hSin = dSinhAns;
   hCos = dCoshAns;
}

#endif
```

The ZDOUBLE.CPP file uses ZDOUBLE.H to define the NUMBER and ZNUM macros for type double complex numbers and then includes the ZNUM.TP template file.

**zdouble.cpp**
```
#define NUMBER double
#define ZNUM   ZDOUBLE

#define Twice(x) ((x) * 2.0)

#include "zdouble.h"
#include "znum.tp"
```

The ZQFLOAT.H header file defines NUMBER and ZNUM as the macros QFLOAT and ZQFLOAT.

**zqfloat.h**
```
#ifndef ZQFLOAT_H
#define ZQFLOAT_H

#ifdef NUMBER
   #undef NUMBER
   #undef ZNUM
#endif
```

```
#define NUMBER QFLOAT
#define ZNUM  ZQFLOAT

#include "qfloat.h"
#include "znum.h"

#endif
```

The ZQFLOAT.CPP file ZQFLOAT.H defines the NUMBER and ZNUM macros and then includes the ZNUM.TP template to create the ZQFLOAT object definitions.

**zqfloat.cpp**
```
#define TYPE_Q_MATH
#define NUMBER QFLOAT
#define ZNUM  ZQFLOAT

#include "qfloat.h"
#include "znum.h"
#include "znum.tp"
```

The ZFIXED16.H file defines BITSHIFT and FIXED macros as 16 and FIXED16. It also defines the NUMBER and ZNUM macros as FIXED16 and ZFIXED 16.

**zfixed16.h**
```
#ifndef ZFIXED16_H
#define ZFIXED16_H

#define BITSHIFT   16
#define FIXED      FIXED16

#ifdef NUMBER
       #undef NUMBER
       #undef ZNUM
#endif

#define NUMBER     FIXED16
#define ZNUM       ZFIXED16

#include "fixed.h"
#include "znum.h"

#endif
```

The ZFIXED16.CPP file declares similar macros to the FIXED16.H file and includes the ZNUM.TP file to actually create the FIXED16 object classes.

**zfixed16.cpp**
```
#define TYPE_F_MATH
#define BITSHIFT   16
#define FIXED      FIXED16
#define NUMBER     FIXED16
#define ZNUM       ZFIXED16

#include "fixed.h"
#include "znum.h"
#include "znum.tp"
```

## The FRACTAL Class Template

The Fractal DLL only uses one file, called FRACTAL.TP, for the fractal algorithms. Like the FIXED and ZNUM templates, this file is written in BC++ Version 2.0 compatible code, i.e., without the template keyword. Instead, each of the source files, DFRACTAL.CPP, FFRACTAL.CPP, and QFRACTAL.CPP, defines the class names in FRACTAL.TP to a name unique to that source file. For example, the JULIA object class in FRACTAL.TP is defined as D_JULIA in DFRACTAL.CPP, F_JULIA in FFRACTAL.CPP, and Q_JULIA in QFRACTAL.CPP.

All the fractal classes are derived from one common object class called _FRACTAL. The _FRACTAL base class allows the Fractal DLL to treat all the fractals as one common class of objects regardless of fractal type or math format. The Fractal DLL calls a function defined as NEW_FRACTAL() in the FRACTAL.TP file to actually create a fractal. This function is defined as D_NEW(), F_NEW(), and Q_NEW() in each of the three fractal source files created using FRACTAL.TP.

**fractal.h**

```
#ifndef FRACTAL_H
#define FRACTAL_H

#ifdef __DLL__
    #ifdef FIXED
        #undef FIXED
        #define FIXED WFIXED
    #endif
    #include <windows.h>
    #ifdef FIXED
        #undef FIXED
        #define FIXED FIXED16
    #endif
#else
    #include <dos.h>
#endif

struct DPOINT
{
    double x, y;
};

struct PARAM
{
    DPOINT p1, p2;
};

struct _FRACTAL
{
    PARAM Param;
    _FRACTAL far *Handle;
    BOOL IdleFlag;
    unsigned xdots, ydots;

    /* This is called to calculate the number of iterations associ-
        ated with a point */
    #pragma argsused
```

```
virtual unsigned long CalcPoint(unsigned x, unsigned y)
{
    return(0L);
}

/* The Valid() function informs the NEW_FRACTAL() function
   if the constructors were successful.
*/
_FRACTAL()
{
    Handle = this;
}
virtual BOOL Valid() { return(TRUE); }

/* Let the compiler know there are destructors associated with
   the derived classes.
*/
virtual ~_FRACTAL() { }

#pragma argsused
virtual PARAM AssocParam(unsigned x, unsigned y)
{
    return(Param);
}

#ifdef __DLL__
        /* These functions and data members are only required in
           the Windows version of the fractal application.  */
    virtual void Idle() { }
    virtual BOOL Activate() { return(TRUE); }
#endif
};

enum {
    NO_FRACTAL = -1,
    JULIA_NUM,
    MANDELBROT_NUM,
    NEWTON_NUM,
    SIN_JULIA_NUM,
    SIN_MAND_NUM,
    NUM_FRACTALS
};

_FRACTAL *D_NEW(unsigned FractNum, unsigned xdots, unsigned
        ydots, double Left, double Right, double Top, double
        Bottom, unsigned long maxit, double p1x, double p1y,
        double p2x, double p2y);

_FRACTAL *F_NEW(unsigned FractNum, unsigned xdots, unsigned
        ydots, double Left, double Right, double Top, double
        Bottom, unsigned long maxit, double p1x, double p1y,
        double p2x, double p2y);

_FRACTAL *Q_NEW(unsigned FractNum, unsigned xdots, unsigned
        ydots, double Left, double Right, double Top, double
        Bottom, unsigned long maxit, double p1x, double p1y,
        double p2x, double p2y);

#endif
```

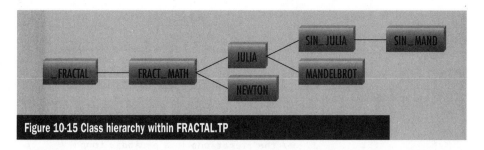

Figure 10-15 Class hierarchy within FRACTAL.TP

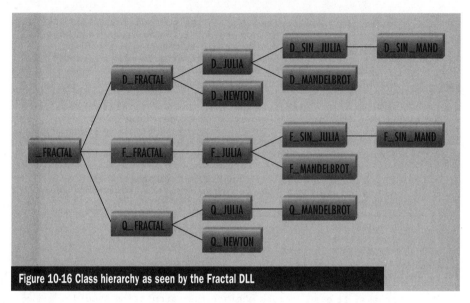

Figure 10-16 Class hierarchy as seen by the Fractal DLL

All the fractals in FRACTAL.TP are derived from a template base class called FRACT_MATH. This class is defined as D_FRACTAL, F_FRACTAL, and Q_FRACTAL in the DFRACTAL.CPP, FFRACTAL.CPP, and QFRACTAL.CPP source files. Figure 10-15 shows the class hierarchy within the FRACTAL.TP file. Figure 10-16 shows the overall hierarchy as seen by the Fractal DLL. Note that not all the fractal types are supported by every math format.

**fractal.tp**

```
#include "fractal.h"

class FRACT_MATH : public _FRACTAL
{
    HANDLE hxdots, hydots;
    NUMBER DeltaX, DeltaY;

protected:
    NUMBER *xdot, *ydot;  // Number array

    /* Should we always look for a periodic loop? */
```

797

```
    BOOL AlwaysCheckPeriod;

    ZNUM
        z,              // The current iteration point
        Saved,          // The point saved for periodicity checking
        Point;          // The calculation point

    unsigned long
        CheckEvery,     // Flags when to save a new iteration point
        ThisPeriod,     // Used to guess the current periodicity
        LastPeriod;     // Used to verify that we've actually caught
                        // the iterations in a periodic loop

    /* This inline algorithm defines the periodicity checking
       method. The routine returns FALSE if the iterations are
       not in a periodic loop or peridicity checking is disabled.
       The routine returns TRUE if the iterations are in a periodic loop.
    */
    int PeriodicityCheck();

    /* This virtual function performs any initialization required
       by a fractal for each new point calculation
    */
    virtual int Initialize()       { return(TRUE); }
    virtual unsigned long Iterate() { return(OL);  }

    /* Declare our own Idle() and Activate() procedures to lock
       and unlock the global memory used by the 'xdot' and 'ydot'
       NUMBER arrays.
    */
    void Idle();
    BOOL Activate();
    ~FRACT_MATH();

public:
    /* The constructor allocates and initializes the xdot and ydot
       arrays. It also decides whether the calculation should
       always look for a periodic loop.
    */
    FRACT_MATH(unsigned xdots, unsigned ydots, double Left,
        double Right, double Top, double Bottom, unsigned long maxit,
        double p1x, double p1y, double p2x, double p2y);

    BOOL Valid()
{
    return(!Overflow && (xdot != NULL) && (ydot != NULL));
}
    unsigned long maxit;    // The maximum iteration level
    BOOL CheckingPeriodicity;

    /* The DistLimit variable defines how close a point needs
       to be to satisfy the periodicity checking algorithm
    */
    NUMBER DistLimit;

    unsigned long CalcPoint(unsigned x, unsigned y);
};

static NUMBER Four = 4.0;
```

```
FRACT_MATH::FRACT_MATH(unsigned xdots, unsigned ydots, double
   Left, double Right, double Top, double Bottom, unsigned long
   maxit, double p1x, double p1y, double p2x, double p2y)
{
   _FRACTAL::xdots = xdots;
   _FRACTAL::ydots = ydots;

   Param.p1.x = p1x;
   Param.p1.y = p1y;
   Param.p2.x = p2x;
   Param.p2.y = p2y;

   hxdots = GlobalAlloc(GMEM_MOVEABLE, ((long)sizeof(NUMBER)) *
   xdots);
   hydots = GlobalAlloc(GMEM_MOVEABLE, ((long)sizeof(NUMBER)) *
   ydots);

   if((hxdots != NULL) && (hydots != NULL))
   {
      xdot = (NUMBER*)GlobalLock(hxdots);
      ydot = (NUMBER*)GlobalLock(hydots);
   }

   Overflow = 0;
   if(!Valid())
      return;

   IdleFlag = FALSE;
   FRACT_MATH::maxit = maxit;

   double dDeltaX = ((Right - Left) / xdots);
   double dDeltaY = ((Bottom - Top) / ydots);

   xdot[0] = Left + (dDeltaX / 2);
   ydot[0] = Top + (dDeltaY / 2);

   DeltaX = dDeltaX;
   DeltaY = dDeltaY;

   for(unsigned n = 1; n < xdots; n++)
      xdot[n] = xdot[n-1] + DeltaX;
   for(n = 1; n < ydots; n++)
      ydot[n] = ydot[n-1] + DeltaY;

   DistLimit = DeltaX;
   CheckingPeriodicity = FALSE;

   /* It's generally faster to always look for a period loop if
      the maximum iteration level is more than 2000.  For lower
      values it's faster to look only if the last iteration level
      reached the maximum iteration level */
   IF (MAXIT) > 2000
      AlwaysCheckPeriod = TRUE;
   else
      AlwaysCheckPeriod = FALSE;
   }

   FRACT_MATH::~FRACT_MATH()
   {
```

```
      GlobalFree(hxdots);
      GlobalFree(hydots);
   }

   int FRACT_MATH::PeriodicityCheck()
   {
      if(!CheckingPeriodicity)
         return(FALSE);

      /* How close are we to the last point we saved? */
         if((Distance(z.Real, Saved.Real) < DistLimit) &&
         (Distance(z.Imag, Saved.Imag) < DistLimit))
         return(TRUE);
      else
      {
         /* Increase the maximum peroid level we'll look for in
            the iterations. Is it time to save a new point? */
         if(ThisPeriod++ == CheckEvery)
         {
            CheckEvery <<= 2;    // Double the period level
            ThisPeriod = 1;      // Reset periodicity to 1
            Saved = z;           // Save a new reference point
         }
      }
      return(FALSE);
   }

   #ifdef __DLL__

   void FRACT_MATH::Idle()
   {
      if(IdleFlag == FALSE)
      {
         GlobalUnlock(hxdots);
         GlobalUnlock(hydots);
         IdleFlag = TRUE;
      }
   }

   BOOL FRACT_MATH::Activate()
   {
      if(IdleFlag == TRUE)
      {
         xdot = (NUMBER*)GlobalLock(hxdots);
         ydot = (NUMBER*)GlobalLock(hydots);
         IdleFlag = FALSE;
      }
      return((xdot != NULL) && (ydot != NULL));
   }

   #endif

   unsigned long FRACT_MATH::CalcPoint(unsigned x, unsigned y)
   {
      unsigned long Color;

      Point.Real = xdot[x];
      Point.Imag = ydot[y];
```

```
        if(Initialize() == FALSE)
            return(0);

        if(CheckingPeriodicity == TRUE)
        {
        /* Initialize periodicity checking */
        Saved = z;              // Start with the current point
        CheckEvery = 3;
        ThisPeriod = 1;
    }

    /* Perform the iterations */
    Color = Iterate();

    if(!AlwaysCheckPeriod)
    {
        /* Set up to look for periodicity on the next calculation only
           this calculation. */
        if(Color == maxit)
            CheckingPeriodicity = TRUE;
        else
            CheckingPeriodicity = FALSE;
    }

    return(Color);
}


/************** Julia Fractal Definition **************/

/* All iterative style fractals are derived from the FRACT_MATH
   object class.
*/

struct JULIA : FRACT_MATH
{
    ZNUM c;
    JULIA(unsigned xdots, unsigned ydots, double Left, double
            Right, double Top, double Bottom, unsigned long maxit,
            double p1x, double p1y);

    int Initialize();
    unsigned long Iterate();
};

int JULIA::Initialize()
{
    z = Point;
    return(TRUE);
}

JULIA::JULIA(unsigned xdots, unsigned ydots, double Left,
        double Right, double Top, double Bottom, unsigned long
        maxit, double p1x, double p1y) : FRACT_MATH(xdots, ydots,
        Left, Right, Top, Bottom, maxit, p1x, p1y, 0.0, 0.0)
{
    c.Real = p1x;
    c.Imag = p1y;
}
```

```
unsigned long JULIA::Iterate()
{
    unsigned long n;

    Overflow = 0;
    for(n = 1; n < maxit; n++)
    {
        /* Check to see if 'z' has exceeded a modulus of 2.  To save
           on calculation time, we won't bother extracting the square
           root, but instead ensure the modulus squared is less than 4.
        */

        NUMBER Modulus = Sqr(&z);
        if(Modulus >= Four)
            break;

        /* The value of 'z' was squared by the Sqr() function. */
        z += c;

        /* If the math routines resulted in an overflow, we'll break
           out of the loop here and return the number of iterations.
        */
        if(Overflow)
            break;

        /* If we're caught in a periodic loop, we may as well quit now
           and save on calculation time.
        */
            if(PeriodicityCheck() == TRUE)
            return(maxit);
    }
    return(n);
}

/************* Mandelbrot Fractal Definition *************/

/* The Mandelbrot fractal is the same as the Julia fractal except
   the value of 'c' is always set to the initial point.
*/
struct MANDELBROT : JULIA
{
    MANDELBROT(unsigned xdots, unsigned ydots, double Left,
        double Right, double Top, double Bottom, unsigned long maxit);
    int Initialize()
    {
        c = z = Point;
        return(TRUE);
    }
    PARAM AssocParam(unsigned x, unsigned y);
};

PARAM MANDELBROT::AssocParam(unsigned x, unsigned y)
{
    PARAM NewParam;

    NewParam.p1.x = Double(xdot[x]);
    NewParam.p1.y = Double(ydot[y]);
    NewParam.p2.x = NewParam.p2.y = 0.0;
```

```
      return(NewParam);
}


MANDELBROT::MANDELBROT(unsigned xdots, unsigned ydots, double Left,
      double Right, double Top, double Bottom, unsigned long maxit) :
      JULIA(xdots, ydots, Left, Right, Top, Bottom, maxit, 0.0, 0.0)
      { }

/* The NEWTON fractal is only defined for type double and QFLOAT
   math.
*/
#ifndef TYPE_F_MATH

/************** Newton Fractal Definition **************/
static NUMBER One = 1.0, Three = 3.0, Threshold = .001;

struct NEWTON : FRACT_MATH
{
    ZNUM old;

    int Initialize();
    unsigned long Iterate();
    NEWTON(unsigned xdots, unsigned ydots, double Left, double Right,
           double Top, double Bottom, unsigned long maxit);
};

NEWTON::NEWTON(unsigned xdots, unsigned ydots, double Left,
      double Right, double Top, double Bottom, unsigned long maxit) :
      FRACT_MATH(xdots, ydots, Left, Right, Top, Bottom, maxit,
      0.0, 0.0, 0.0, 0.0)
      { }

int NEWTON::Initialize()
{
    z = Point;
    return(TRUE);
}

unsigned long NEWTON::Iterate() {
    ZNUM zSqr, zCube, Temp;

    /*
          (3 * z**4) + 1
      z = -------------
            4 * z**3
    */

    for(unsigned long n = 0; n < maxit; n++)
    {
        /* Calculate z**2 */
        zSqr = z * z;

        /* Calculate z**3 */
        zCube = zSqr * z;

        /* Calculate z**4 */
        z = zCube * z;
```

```
        /* See if (z**4 - root) is close to 0 */
        Temp = z;
        Temp.Real -= One;
        if(Temp.Modulus() < Threshold)
            break;

        /* Finish calculating the remainder of the formula */
        z.Real *= Three;
        z.Imag *= Three;
        z.Real += One;
        zCube.Real *= Four;
        zCube.Imag *= Four;
        z = z / zCube;
    }
    return(n);
}

#endif

/* These fractal type are only defined for type double and FIXED
   numbers
*/
#ifndef TYPE_Q_MATH

/************** Sine Julia Fractal Definition **************/

/* All iterative style fractals are derived from the FRACT_MATH
   object class.
*/

struct SIN_JULIA : JULIA
{
    /* The constructor is the same as the JULIA constructor */
    SIN_JULIA(unsigned xdots, unsigned ydots, double Left,
        double Right, double Top, double Bottom, unsigned long maxit,
        double p1x, double p1y) : JULIA(xdots, ydots, Left,
        Right, Top, Bottom, maxit, p1x, p1y) { }

    unsigned long Iterate();
};

unsigned long SIN_JULIA::Iterate()
{
    unsigned long n;
    static NUMBER ThirtyTwo = 32.0, O = 0.0;

    Overflow = 0;
    for(n = 1; n < maxit; n++)
    {
        NUMBER Dist;

        Dist = z.Imag;
        if(Dist < O)
            Dist = -Dist;
        if(Dist >= ThirtyTwo)
            break;
```

```
      else
      {
         z = c * sin(z);

         if(Overflow != 0)
            break;
         else if(PeriodicityCheck() == TRUE)
            return(maxit);
      }
   }
   return(n);
}


/************** Mandelbrot Fractal Definition **************/

/* The Mandelbrot fractal is the same as the Julia fractal except
   the value of 'c' is always set to the initial point.
*/
struct SIN_MAND : SIN_JULIA
{
   SIN_MAND(unsigned xdots, unsigned ydots, double Left,
      double Right, double Top, double Bottom, unsigned long maxit)
      : SIN_JULIA(xdots, ydots, Left, Right, Top, Bottom, maxit, 0.0,
      0.0) { }

   int Initialize()
   {
      c = z = Point;
      return(TRUE);
   }
   PARAM AssocParam(unsigned x, unsigned y);
};

PARAM SIN_MAND::AssocParam(unsigned x, unsigned y)
{
   PARAM NewParam;

   NewParam.p1.x = Double(xdot[x]);
   NewParam.p1.y = Double(ydot[y]);
   NewParam.p2.x = NewParam.p2.y = 0.0;
   return(NewParam);
}

#endif

/************** NEW_FRACTAL Definition **************/
#pragma argsused

_FRACTAL *NEW_FRACT(unsigned FractNum, unsigned xdots,
      unsigned ydots, double Left, double Right, double Top,
      double Bottom, unsigned long maxit, double p1x, double p1y,
      double p2x, double p2y)
{
   _FRACTAL *Fractal;

   switch(FractNum)
   {
```

```
        case JULIA_NUM:
            Fractal = new JULIA(xdots, ydots, Left, Right, Top, Bottom,
                            maxit, p1x, p1y);
            break;

        case MANDELBROT_NUM:
            Fractal = new MANDELBROT(xdots, ydots, Left, Right, Top,
Bottom,
                            maxit);
            break;

/* Exclude in the FFRACTAL.CPP module */
#ifndef TYPE_F_MATH
        case NEWTON_NUM:
            Fractal = new NEWTON(xdots, ydots, Left, Right, Top, Bottom,
                            maxit);
            break;
#endif

/* Exclude for the QFRACTAL.CPP module */
#ifndef TYPE_Q_MATH
        case SIN_JULIA_NUM:
            Fractal = new SIN_JULIA(xdots, ydots, Left, Right, Top,
                            Bottom, maxit, p1x, p1y);
            break;

        case SIN_MAND_NUM:
            Fractal = new SIN_MAND(xdots, ydots, Left, Right, Top,
                            Bottom, maxit);
            break;
#endif
        default:
        return(NULL);
    }

    if(Fractal != NULL)
    {
        if(Fractal->Valid())
            return(Fractal);
        else
            delete Fractal;
    }
    return(NULL);
}
```

The DFRACTAL.CPP file contains the macro definitions for creating type double fractal object classes using the FRACTAL.TP template file.

**dfractal.cpp**

```
        /* Load the math type header */
        #include "zdouble.h"

        /* Define the template math macro */
        #define TYPE_D_MATH
```

```
#define SIN_JULIA          D_SIN_JULIA
#define SIN_MAND           D_SIN_MAND
#define JULIA              D_JULIA
#define MANDELBROT         D_MANDELBROT
#define NEWTON             D_NEWTON
#define FRACT_MATH         D_FRACTAL
#define NEW_FRACT          D_NEW

/* Compile the fractal template */
#include "fractal.tp"
```

The FFRACTAL.CPP file contains the macro definitions for creating type FIXED<16> fractal object classes using the FRACTAL.TP template file.

**ffractal.cpp**

```
/* Load the math type header */
#include "zfixed16.h"

/* Define the template macros */
#define TYPE_F_MATH
#define SIN_JULIA          F_SIN_JULIA
#define SIN_MAND           F_SIN_MAND
#define JULIA              F_JULIA
#define MANDELBROT         F_MANDELBROT
#define NEWTON             F_NEWTON
#define FRACT_MATH         F_FRACTAL
#define NEW_FRACT          F_NEW

#define DEBUG

/* Compile the fractal template */
#include "fractal.tp"
```

The QFRACTAL.CPP file contains the macro definitions for creating type QFLOAT fractal object classes using the FRACTAL.TP template file.

**qfractal.cpp**

```
/* Load the math type header */
#include "zqfloat.h"

/* Define the template math macro */
#define TYPE_Q_MATH
#define SIN_JULIA          Q_SIN_JULIA
#define SIN_MAND           Q_SIN_MAND
#define JULIA              Q_JULIA
#define MANDELBROT         Q_MANDELBROT
#define NEWTON             Q_NEWTON
#define FRACT_MATH         Q_FRACTAL
#define NEW_FRACT          Q_NEW

/* Compile the fractal template */
#include "fractal.tp"
```

807

## The FRACTDLL.CPP Source Code

When Windows loads an application which was linked with the Fractal DLL, it first loads and initializes the Fractal DLL immediately before starting the application. The initialization code, located in LibMain(), merely locks the data segment associated with the DLL and places the names for the fractal types and default settings for each onto the global atom table. The FractalDLL terminates after the last application using the DLL.

The FRACTDLL.H file compiles differently depending on whether the compiler is compiling an application or the DLL. If the compiler is building the FRACTDLL file, then the EXPORT macro is defined as _export_ and the FRACTAL macro is defined as a far pointer to a FRACTAL object class. When the compiler is building a Windows application, on the other hand, the EXPORT keyword is defined as a NULL macro and FRACTAL is defined as a void far pointer. This enables the DLL and all applications which are linked with the DLL to use the same header file, which means any changes to the header file will force a rebuild of both the FRACTDLL and the Windows application.

**fractdll.h**

```
#ifndef FRACTDLL_H
#define FRACTDLL_H

/* Stamp this header file as Fractal DLL Version 1.00 */
#define DLL_VERSION 100

#ifdef __DLL__
    #include "fractal.h"
    #define EXPORT _export
    typedef class _FRACTAL FAR *FRACTAL;
#else
    #include <windows.h>
    #define EXPORT
    typedef void FAR *FRACTAL;
#endif

typedef enum { D_MATH = 1, F_MATH = 2, Q_MATH = 4 } MATHTYPE;
typedef enum { NO_SYMMETRY, ORIGIN, X_AXIS, XY_AXIS } SYMMETRY;

/* The following is a list of functions that can be called from the
   DLL. Name mangling of the function names is suspended by
   declaring them as linkage functions to the "C" language.
*/
extern "C" {
    BOOL FAR PASCAL EXPORT IdleFractal(FRACTAL Fractal);
    BOOL FAR PASCAL EXPORT ActivateFractal(FRACTAL Fractal);
    unsigned FAR PASCAL EXPORT FractalDLLVersion();
    unsigned FAR PASCAL EXPORT NumberFractals();
    ATOM FAR PASCAL EXPORT FractalName(unsigned FractNum);
    ATOM FAR PASCAL EXPORT AssocFractDefaults(FRACTAL Fractal,
        unsigned x, unsigned y);
    ATOM FAR PASCAL EXPORT FractalParamOne(unsigned FractNum);
    ATOM FAR PASCAL EXPORT FractalParamTwo(unsigned FractNum);
    ATOM FAR PASCAL EXPORT FractalDefaults(unsigned FractNum);
    FRACTAL FAR PASCAL EXPORT CreateFractal(unsigned FractNum,
```

```
            unsigned xdots, unsigned ydots, MATHTYPE MathType,
            double Left, double Right, double Top, double Bottom,
            unsigned long maxit, double p1x, double p1y, double p2x,
            double p2y);
        unsigned long FAR PASCAL EXPORT FractalPoint(
            FRACTAL Fractal, unsigned x, unsigned y);
        BOOL FAR PASCAL EXPORT DestroyFractal(FRACTAL Fractal);
    }

    #endif
```

The FRACTDLL.CPP file contains the DLL initialization code and termination code as well as all the export function definitions. Note that the export functions must be declared as *extern "C"* so as to prevent the compiler from mangling the function names. This enables the DLL to be used by Windows applications written in C, C++, Pascal, or Visual Basic.

### fractdll.cpp

```
    #include "fractdll.h"

    /* We need the STDIO.H include file for the sprintf() function
       prototype. */
    #include <stdio.h>

    /* Define an object class to help manage a list of global atoms. */

    struct GLOBAL_ATOM
    {
       ATOM Atom;

       GLOBAL_ATOM() { Atom = NULL; }
       void operator=(char *Str)
       {
          Atom = GlobalAddAtom(Str);
       }
        ~GLOBAL_ATOM();
    };

    GLOBAL_ATOM TempAtom;

    /* Delete the atom when object is deleted. */
    GLOBAL_ATOM::~GLOBAL_ATOM()
    {
       if(Atom != NULL)
          GlobalDeleteAtom(Atom);
    }

    struct FRACT_ATOM
    {
       GLOBAL_ATOM Name, p1, p2, Default;
    };

    struct FRACT_DEF
    {
       char *Str;
```

```
    FRACT_DEF(unsigned MathType, double Left, double Top,
        double Bottom, double Right, unsigned long maxit,
        double p1x, double p1y, double p2x, double p2y,
        SYMMETRY Symmetry, int AssocFractal);
    ~FRACT_DEF() { delete(Str); }
};

FRACT_DEF::FRACT_DEF(unsigned MathType, double Left, double Right,
        double Top, double Bottom, unsigned long maxit,
        double p1x, double p1y, double p2x, double p2y,
        SYMMETRY Symmetry, int AssocFractal)
{
    char DefStr[] = "%d, %g, %g, %g, %g, %ld, %g, %g, %g, %g, %d, %d";
    char Scratch[240];

    /* Print the defaults in a character string format */
    sprintf(Scratch, DefStr, MathType, Left, Right, Top, Bottom,
        maxit, p1x, p1y, p2x, p2y, Symmetry, AssocFractal);

    /* Allocate the free storage space and copy. */
    Str = new char[lstrlen(Scratch) + 1];
    lstrcpy(Str, Scratch);
}

FRACT_ATOM FractAtom[NUM_FRACTALS];
int Coprocessor = 0;

#pragma argsused
int FAR PASCAL LibMain(HANDLE hInstance, WORD wDataSegment,
                       WORD wHeapSize, LPSTR lpszCmdLine)
{
    MATHTYPE TypeFQ, TypeF, TypeQ;

    /* Only allow type D_MATH on 16-bit machines */
    DWORD Flags = GetWinFlags();
    if((Flags & WF_CPU086) || (Flags & WF_CPU186) ||
       (Flags & WF_CPU286))
    {
        TypeF = TypeQ = TypeFQ = D_MATH;
    }
    else
    {
        TypeFQ = D_MATH | F_MATH | Q_MATH;
        TypeF  = D_MATH | F_MATH;
        TypeQ  = D_MATH | Q_MATH;
        if(Flags & WF_80x87)
            Coprocessor = 387;
    }
                        /******* Julia Set Atoms *******/
    FractAtom[JULIA_NUM].Name = "&Julia";
    FractAtom[JULIA_NUM].p1   = "Value of 'c' in '(z*z) + c'";
    FRACT_DEF JuliaDef(TypeFQ, -2.0, 2.0, 1.5, -1.5, 150L, 0.3, 0.6,
        0.0, 0.0, ORIGIN, NO_FRACTAL);
    FractAtom[JULIA_NUM].Default = JuliaDef.Str;

                        /******* Mandelbrot Set Atoms *******/
    FractAtom[MANDELBROT_NUM].Name = "&Mandelbrot";
    FRACT_DEF MandelDef(TypeFQ, -2.0, 2.0, 1.5, -1.5, 150L, 0.0,
        0.0, 0.0, 0.0, X_AXIS, JULIA_NUM);
```

```
    FractAtom[MANDELBROT_NUM].Default = MandelDef.Str;

            /******* Newton Atoms *******/
    FractAtom[NEWTON_NUM].Name = "&Newton";
    FRACT_DEF NewtonDef(TypeQ, -2.0, 2.0, 1.5, -1.5, 150L, 0.0,
        0.0, 0.0, 0.0, XY_AXIS, NO_FRACTAL);
    FractAtom[NEWTON_NUM].Default = NewtonDef.Str;

            /******* Sine Julia *******/
    FractAtom[SIN_JULIA_NUM].Name = "&Lambda Sine";
    FRACT_DEF SinJuliaDef(TypeF, -8.0, 8.0, -6.0, 6.0, 150L, 1.0,
        0.4, 0.0, 0.0, ORIGIN, NO_FRACTAL);
    FractAtom[SIN_JULIA_NUM].Default = SinJuliaDef.Str;

            /******* Sine Mandelbort *******/
    FractAtom[SIN_MAND_NUM].Name = "Mandelbrot &Sine";
    FRACT_DEF SinMandDef(TypeF, -8.0, 8.0, -6.0, 6.0, 150L, 0.0,
        0.0, 0.0, 0.0, XY_AXIS, SIN_JULIA_NUM);
    FractAtom[SIN_MAND_NUM].Default = SinMandDef.Str;

  if(wHeapSize != 0)
     UnlockData(0);
  return(TRUE);
}

#pragma argsused
int FAR PASCAL WEP(int bSystemExit)
{
  return(1);
}

extern "C" {

ATOM FAR PASCAL _export FractalDefaults(unsigned FractNum)
{
  if(FractNum < NUM_FRACTALS)
    return(FractAtom[FractNum].Default.Atom);
  return(NULL);
}

unsigned FAR PASCAL _export FractalDLLVersion()
{
  return(DLL_VERSION);
}

unsigned FAR PASCAL _export NumberFractals()
{
  return(NUM_FRACTALS);
}

ATOM FAR PASCAL _export FractalName(unsigned FractNum)
{
  if(FractNum < NUM_FRACTALS)
    return(FractAtom[FractNum].Name.Atom);
  return(NULL);
}

ATOM FAR PASCAL _export FractalParamOne(unsigned FractNum)
{
```

```
   if(FractNum < NUM_FRACTALS)
      return(FractAtom[FractNum].p1.Atom);
   return(NULL);
}

ATOM FAR PASCAL _export FractalParamTwo(unsigned FractNum)
{
   if(FractNum < NUM_FRACTALS)
      return(FractAtom[FractNum].p2.Atom);
   return(NULL);
}

ATOM FAR PASCAL _export AssocFractDefaults(FRACTAL Fractal,
   unsigned x, unsigned y)
{
   PARAM Param;
   BOOL Reactivated = FALSE;

   if(Fractal != NULL)
   {
      if(Fractal == Fractal->Handle)
      {
         if(Fractal->IdleFlag != TRUE)
         {
             /* Try activating the fractal */
             if(Fractal->Activate() == FALSE)
             return(NULL);
             else
                 Reactivated = TRUE;
         }
         char Str[100];

         Param = Fractal->AssocParam(x, y);
         sprintf(Str, "%g, %g, %g, %g",     Param.p1.x, Param.p1.y,
                                            Param.p2.x, Param.p2.y);
         TempAtom = Str;
         if(Reactivated == TRUE)
           Fractal->Idle();
         return(TempAtom.Atom);
      }
   }
   return(NULL);
}

BOOL FAR PASCAL _export ActivateFractal(FRACTAL Fractal)
{

   if(Fractal != NULL)
   {
      if(Fractal == Fractal->Handle)
         return(Fractal->Activate());
   }
   return(FALSE);
}

BOOL FAR PASCAL _export IdleFractal(FRACTAL Fractal)
{
   if(Fractal != NULL)
   {
```

```
      if(Fractal == Fractal->Handle)
      {
         Fractal->Idle();
         return(TRUE);
      }
   }
   return(FALSE);
}


unsigned long FAR PASCAL _export FractalPoint(FRACTAL Fractal,
         unsigned x, unsigned y)
{
   if(Fractal != NULL)
   {
      if(Fractal->IdleFlag == FALSE)
      {
         if(Fractal == Fractal->Handle)
            return(Fractal->CalcPoint(x, y));
      }
   }
   return(0L);
}


FRACTAL FAR PASCAL _export CreateFractal(unsigned FractNum,
         unsigned xdots, unsigned ydots, MATHTYPE MathType,
         double Left, double Right, double Top, double Bottom,
         unsigned long maxit, double p1x, double p1y, double p2x,
         double p2y)
{
   FRACTAL Fractal;

   /* Make sure the fractal type requested is a valid type */
   if(FractNum >= NUM_FRACTALS)
      return(NULL);

   /* The QFLOAT and FIXED29 math types both require a 386 class
      machine or better.  Return an error if the user is requesting
      either of these math types. */

   if(MathType != D_MATH)
   {
      DWORD Flags = GetWinFlags();
      if((Flags & WF_CPU086) || (Flags & WF_CPU186) ||
        (Flags & WF_CPU286))
         return(NULL);
   }

   switch(MathType)
   {
      case D_MATH:
         Fractal = D_NEW(FractNum, xdots, ydots, Left, Right, Top,
                        Bottom, maxit, p1x, p1y, p2x, p2y);
         break;

      case F_MATH:
         Fractal = F_NEW(FractNum, xdots, ydots, Left, Right, Top,
                        Bottom, maxit, p1x, p1y, p2x, p2y);
         break;
```

813

```
    case Q_MATH:
      Fractal = Q_NEW(FractNum, xdots, ydots, Left, Right, Top,
                       Bottom, maxit, p1x, p1y, p2x, p2y);
      break;

    default:
      return(NULL);
  }

  if(Fractal == NULL)
    return(NULL);

  /*Idle the fractal just in case it takes awhile before it is
    put to use. */
  Fractal->Idle();

  return(Fractal);
}

BOOL FAR PASCAL _export DestroyFractal(FRACTAL Fractal)
{
  if(Fractal != NULL)
  {
    if(Fractal == Fractal->Handle)
    {
      if(Fractal->IdleFlag == FALSE)
        Fractal->Idle();

      /* If it's a valid pointer, delete the fractal object. */
      if(Fractal != NULL)
      {
        delete Fractal;
        return(TRUE);
      }
    }
  }
  return(FALSE);
}

}
```

## Building the Fractal DLL

The Fractal DLL is normally built using a .PRJ from the DOS IDE. Note that because Turbo C++ for Windows does not support calling an external assembler, which is required to compile the inline 80386 instructions, you cannot use it to build FRACTDLL.DLL. The following FRACTDLL.MAK file was created using PRJ2MAK and is the .MAK file equivalent of the .PRJ file.

The PRJ2MAK utility places all the .PRJ compiler options in a file called FRACTDLL.CFG, which is created automatically by MAKE if it does not exist or is out of date with the .MAK file. Note that all warning messages are enabled in the .PRJ file. However, the PRJ2MAK utility incorrectly disables many of the warning options.

**fractdll.mak**

```
.AUTODEPEND

#              *Translator Definitions*
CC = bcc +FRACTDLL.CFG
TASM = TASM
TLIB = tlib
TLINK = tlink
LIBPATH = C:\BORLANDC\LIB
INCLUDEPATH = C:\BORLANDC\INCLUDE

#              *Implicit Rules*
.c.obj:
  $(CC) -c {$< }

.cpp.obj:
  $(CC) -c {$< }

#              *List Macros*
Link_Exclude =      \
fractdll.res

Link_Include = \
 dfractal.obj \
 fractdll.obj \
 fractdll.def \
 ffractal.obj \
 fmath.obj \
 qfloat.obj \
 qfractal.obj \
 zdouble.obj  \
 zfixed16.obj \
 zqfloat.obj

#              *Explicit Rules*
fractdll.dll: fractdll.cfg $(Link_Include) $(Link_Exclude)
  $(TLINK) /v/x/c/P-/Twd/L$(LIBPATH) @&&|
c0dc.obj+
dfractal.obj+
fractdll.obj+
ffractal.obj+
fmath.obj+
qfloat.obj+
qfractal.obj+
zdouble.obj+
zfixed16.obj+
zqfloat.obj
fractdll.dll
              # no map file
mathwc.lib+
import.lib+
cwc.lib
fractdll.def
|
  RC fractdll.res fractdll.dll
```

```
        IMPLIB FRACTDLL.LIB FRACTDLL.DLL
#                *Individual File Dependencies*
dfractal.obj: fractdll.cfg dfractal.cpp

fractdll.obj: fractdll.cfg fractdll.cpp

fractdll.res: fractdll.cfg fractdll.rc
        RC -R -I$(INCLUDEPATH) -FO fractdll.res FRACTDLL.RC

ffractal.obj: fractdll.cfg ffractal.cpp

fmath.obj: fractdll.cfg fmath.cpp

qfloat.obj: fractdll.cfg qfloat.cpp

qfractal.obj: fractdll.cfg qfractal.cpp

zdouble.obj: fractdll.cfg zdouble.cpp

zfixed16.obj: fractdll.cfg zfixed16.cpp

zqfloat.obj: fractdll.cfg zqfloat.cpp
#                *Compiler Configuration File*
fractdll.cfg: fractdll.mak
copy &&|
-R
-mc!
-v
-G
-O
-Og
-Oe
-Om
-Ov
-Ol
-Ob
-Op
-Oi
-Z
-k-
-r-
-d
-WDE
-vi
-H=FRACTDLL.SYM
-w-ret
-w-nci
-w-inl
-w-par
-w-cpt
-w-dup
-w-pia
-w-ill
-w-sus
-w-ext
```

```
-w-ias
-w-ibc
-w-pre
-w-nst
-I$(INCLUDEPATH)
-L$(LIBPATH)
-P.C
| fractdll.cfg
```

# THE WFRACTAL FRONT-END APPLICATION

The WFRACTAL application is written to use the Fractal DLL. Because WFRACTAL was linked with the library file generated by the IMPLIB utility, Windows automatically loads the Fractal DLL before starting the WinMain() function in WFRACTAL. If more than one application is started that uses the DLL, Windows increases the lock count on the DLL as each application initializes and decreases the lock count as each application terminates. Windows only removes the DLL from memory after the last application using the DLL terminates.

The front-end application itself is very simple. Like any Windows application, it first registers the window class for its main window and then creates the window. During the creation of the windows, i.e., while processing the WM_CREATE message, the application modifies the 'Fractal' menu item to include a list of all the fractal types supported by the Fractal DLL. The actual generation and display of the fractal image is controlled by an object class called DRAWING. The DRAWING object class also creates the bitmap which contains the image, updates the window's client area during painting requests from Windows, and performs almost all the function calls to the Fractal DLL.

## Background Processing

The background processing needed to generate the fractal without interfering with other tasks running under Windows is accomplished using the following message loop:

```
while(Done == FALSE)
{
   while(PeekMessage(&msg, NULL, NULL, NULL, PM_REMOVE))
   {
      if(msg.message == WM_QUIT)
      {
         Done = TRUE;
         break;
      }
      else
      {
         TranslateMessage(&msg);
         DispatchMessage(&msg);
      }
   }
   if(!Done)
   {
      if((DrawingFractal == TRUE) && (Zoom.Active == FALSE))
         CurrentDrawing->DrawFractal(hWnd);
      else
```

```
            WaitMessage();
        }
    }
```

The message loop uses the PeekMessage() and WaitMessage() functions rather than the traditional GetMessage() function. Whereas the GetMessage() function will only return when there is a message to process, the PeekMessage() function returns even if there is no message in the queue. The call to PeekMessage() allows Windows to perform its multitasking, thereby giving other applications running concurrently with the WFRACTAL application a portion of the computer's processing time. After PeekMessage() returns and any messages are processed, generation of the fractal image continues. If the application is not drawing a fractal, then the WaitMessage() function is called. The combination of the WaitMessage() and the PeekMessage() functions is equivalent to a GetMessage() function call.

The following WFRACTAL.H header file is used by both the C++ compiler and the resource compiler. The first section contains the macro definitions common to both the C++ source code and the resource script. The section after the #ifndef RC_INVOKED directive contains the C++ specific header information. This section is skipped over when compiled by the resource compiler because the RC_INVOKED macro is a predefined macro in both Microsoft's resource compiler and the WORK-SHOP script compiler. However, this section is compiled with the .CPP files because the RC_INVOKED macro is not a predefined macro in BC++.

**wfractal.h**

```
    #ifndef WFRACTAL_H
    #define IDI_FILENAME      3500
    #define IDI_XDIM          3600
    #define IDI_YDIM          3700
    #define IDI_256           3256
    #define IDI_16            3016
    #define IDI_MONO          3002
    #define IDI_SAVE          103
    #define IDI_CANCEL        104
    #define SAVE_DLG          "SAVE_DLG"
    #define WFRACTAL_H

    #define IDM_EXIT          1000
    #define IDM_FRACTAL       2000
    #define IDM_ABOUT         3000
    #define ID_OK             4000
    #define IDM_FIXED         5000
    #define IDM_QFLOAT        6000
    #define IDM_FLOAT         7000
    #define IDM_ATPOINT       8000

    /* Tell the resource compiler not to bother trying to make
       sense of the C++ declarations.
    */
    #ifndef RC_INVOKED

    #include "fractdll.h"
    #include "palette.h"
```

```
class DRAWING
{
    HBITMAP hBitmap,          // The current memory bitmap
    hOldBitmap;               // The bitmap that came with the hDC
    HDC hDC;                  // Handle to the memory device context
    unsigned

                    x,        // The current 'x' position
                    y;        // The current 'y' position
    RECT Rect;                // General-purpose variable

    /* These variables hold the default values returned by the
       DLL for a particular fractal. */
    unsigned long maxit;
    double Left, Right, Top, Bottom;
    double p1x, p1y, p2x, p2y;
    SYMMETRY Symmetry;

    /* This SetPixel() function calls the Windows SetPixel()
       unction */
    void SetPixel(unsigned x, unsigned y, unsigned char c)
    {
        /* Call Windows' SetPixel() function */
        ::SetPixel(hDC, x, y, PALETTEINDEX((int)c));
    }

    /* We use these functions internally */
    void SetPixel(unsigned char c);
    void DeleteFractal(HWND hWnd);
    void InvalidateRect(HWND hWnd);
    void SetDefaults(HWND hWnd, WORD FractNum);
public:
    MATHTYPE AvailMathTypes;
    POINT Dim,                // Bitmap and window client area dimensions
         Limit;               // Limits how much of the image we actually
                              // calculate.
    FRACTAL Fractal;          // Handle returned by the DLL
    int AtPointFractal;

    DRAWING(HWND hWnd, unsigned xDim, unsigned yDim);
    ~DRAWING();

    /* This function makes sure everything went well during
       construction of the DRAWING object. */
    Valid() { return((hDC != NULL) && (hBitmap != NULL)); }

    /* The Display() function is used to process the WM_PAINT
       message. */
    void Display(HDC hDestDC, RECT Rect);

    /* The DrawFractal() function is called by the message loop
       after processing messages so as to continue drawing the
       fractal */
    void DrawFractal(HWND hWnd);

    /* This function actually starts the ball rolling */
    void CreateFractal(HWND hWnd, WORD FractNum);
    void ZoomFractal(HWND hWnd);
    void FractalAtPoint(HWND hWnd, POINT Point);
};
```

```
extern  DRAWING* CurrentDrawing;
extern  unsigned NumFract, FractNum, PollingFreq;
extern  BOOL TimeToQuit, DrawingFractal;
extern  MATHTYPE MathType;
extern  PC_PALETTE Palette;
extern  HANDLE hThisInstance;

void SetMath(HWND hWnd, WORD wParam);
long FAR PASCAL MainWndProc(HWND hWnd, unsigned msg, unsigned wParam,
                LONG lParam);

void About(HWND hWnd);

#endif
#endif
```

The WFRACTAL.CPP file contains the function definitions that are not associated with an object class. These include the MainWndProc(), which is used for processing messages sent by Windows to the main application window, and WinMain(), which contains the application initialization code and message loop.

**wfractal.cpp**
```
#include "wfractal.h"
#include "zoom.h"
#include "atpoint.h"

DRAWING* CurrentDrawing;
unsigned NumFract, NumColors = 256;
unsigned PollingFreq = 200;
BOOL TimeToQuit = FALSE, DrawingFractal = FALSE;
MATHTYPE MathType = F_MATH;
unsigned MathSelect = IDM_FIXED;
PC_PALETTE Palette;
unsigned FractNum = 0, LastFractNum = 0;
HANDLE hThisInstance;

void SetMath(HWND hWnd, WORD wParam)
{
    HMENU hMenu = GetMenu(hWnd);
    CheckMenuItem(hMenu, MathSelect, MF_UNCHECKED);
    CheckMenuItem(hMenu, wParam, MF_CHECKED);
    MathSelect = wParam;
    switch(wParam)
    {
        case IDM_FIXED:
            MathType = F_MATH;
            break;

        case IDM_QFLOAT:
            MathType = Q_MATH;
            break;

        case IDM_FLOAT:
            MathType = D_MATH;
    }
}
```

```
BOOL CreateFractalMenu(HWND hWnd)
{
   NumFract = NumberFractals();

   /* Add the fractal popup menu to the main menu */
   HMENU hWndMenu = GetMenu(hWnd);
   HMENU hFractMenu = GetSubMenu(hWndMenu, 2);

   /* Add each available fractal to the menu */
   for(unsigned n = 0; n < NumFract; n++)
   {
      char Name[40];

      ATOM FractAtom = FractalName(n);
      if(FractAtom == NULL)
         return(FALSE);
      GlobalGetAtomName(FractAtom, Name, sizeof(Name));
      InsertMenu(hFractMenu, n, MF_ENABLED | MF_STRING |
                 MF_BYPOSITION, IDM_FRACTAL + n, Name);
   }
   CheckMenuItem(hFractMenu, FractNum, MF_CHECKED |
                 MF_BYPOSITION);
   return(TRUE);
}

void UpdateFractMenu(HWND hWnd)
{
   WORD Flags = MF_DISABLED | MF_GRAYED;

   HMENU hWndMenu = GetMenu(hWnd);
   if(CurrentDrawing->AtPointFractal >= 0)
      Flags = MF_ENABLED;

   EnableMenuItem(hWndMenu, IDM_ATPOINT, Flags);

   HMENU hFractMenu = GetSubMenu(hWndMenu, 2);
   CheckMenuItem(hFractMenu, LastFractNum, MF_UNCHECKED |
                 MF_BYPOSITION);
   CheckMenuItem(hFractMenu, FractNum, MF_CHECKED |
                 MF_BYPOSITION);
   LastFractNum = FractNum;

   if((CurrentDrawing->AvailMathTypes & F_MATH) == 0)
      EnableMenuItem(hWndMenu, IDM_FIXED, MF_DISABLED | MF_GRAYED);
   else
      EnableMenuItem(hWndMenu, IDM_FIXED, MF_ENABLED);

   if((CurrentDrawing->AvailMathTypes & Q_MATH) == 0)
      EnableMenuItem(hWndMenu, IDM_QFLOAT, MF_DISABLED | MF_GRAYED);
   else
      EnableMenuItem(hWndMenu, IDM_QFLOAT, MF_ENABLED);
}

long FAR PASCAL MainWndProc(HWND hWnd, unsigned msg, unsigned wParam,
      LONG lParam)
{
   PAINTSTRUCT ps;

   switch(msg)
   {
   case WM_CREATE:
      if(CreateFractalMenu(hWnd) == TRUE)
         {
```

```
        RECT Rect;

        GetClientRect(hWnd, &Rect);
        CurrentDrawing = new DRAWING(hWnd, Rect.right,
                               Rect.bottom);
        if(CurrentDrawing->Valid() == FALSE)
        {
            delete(CurrentDrawing);
            CurrentDrawing = NULL;
        }
        SetMath(hWnd, IDM_FIXED);
        UpdateFractMenu(hWnd);
    }
    break;

case WM_COMMAND:
    switch(wParam)
    {
        case IDM_ABOUT:
            About(hWnd);
            break;

        case IDM_EXIT:
            DestroyWindow(hWnd);
            break;

        case IDM_FIXED:
        case IDM_QFLOAT:
        case IDM_FLOAT:
            SetMath(hWnd, wParam);
            DrawingFractal = FALSE;
            CurrentDrawing->CreateFractal(hWnd, FractNum);
            break;

        case IDM_ATPOINT:
            AtPoint.Start(hWnd);
            break;

        default:
            FractNum = wParam - IDM_FRACTAL;
            if(FractNum < NumFract)
            {
                CurrentDrawing->CreateFractal(hWnd, FractNum);
                UpdateFractMenu(hWnd);
            }
            break;
        }
        break;

case WM_LBUTTONDOWN:
    if(Zoom.Active)
        Zoom.StartMoving(hWnd, lParam);
    else if(!AtPoint.Active)
        Zoom.StartSizing(hWnd, lParam);
    break;

case WM_LBUTTONUP:
    /* Were we moving the zoom box? */
```

```
    if(Zoom.Moving)
        Zoom.StopMoving(hWnd, lParam);

    /* Were we setting the size of the zoom box? */
    else if(Zoom.Sizing)
        Zoom.StopSizing(hWnd, lParam);

    /* Are we looking for an associated fractal? */
    else if(AtPoint.Active)
    {
        AtPoint.Execute(hWnd, lParam);
        UpdateFractMenu(hWnd);
    }
    break;

case WM_LBUTTONDBLCLK:
    if(Zoom.Active)
    {
    if(Zoom.Execute(hWnd, lParam) == TRUE)
        CurrentDrawing->ZoomFractal(hWnd);
    }
    break;

case WM_CHAR:
    /* The only character keystroke we care point is the
       <Esc> key. */
    if(wParam == VK_ESCAPE)
    {
        /* Should we cancel a zoom request? */
        if(Zoom.Active)
          Zoom.Escape(hWnd);

        /* Should we cancel an at point fractal request? */
        else if(AtPoint.Active)
          AtPoint.Escape();

        /* See if the user wants to exit the application. */
        else
        {
        int Ans = MessageBox(hWnd,
          "You've hit the <Esc> key.\nDo you really want to \
exit?",
            "Exiting. . .", MB_OKCANCEL | MB_ICONQUESTION);
            if(Ans == IDOK)
                DestroyWindow(hWnd);
        }
        }
    break;

case WM_MOUSEMOVE:
    if(Zoom.Moving)
        Zoom.Move(hWnd, lParam);
    else if(Zoom.Sizing)
        Zoom.Size(hWnd, lParam);
    break;

case WM_PAINT:
    HDC hDC = BeginPaint(hWnd, &ps);
```

```
        if(CurrentDrawing != NULL)
            CurrentDrawing->Display(hDC, ps.rcPaint);
        EndPaint(hWnd, &ps);
        break;

    case WM_DESTROY:
        delete(CurrentDrawing);
        PostQuitMessage(0);
        break;

    default:
        return(DefWindowProc(hWnd, msg, wParam, lParam));
    }
    return(NULL);
}

#pragma argsused
int PASCAL WinMain(HANDLE hInstance, HANDLE hPrevInstance,
    LPSTR lpCmdLine, int nCmdShow)
{
    POINT Dim;
    MSG msg;

    if(!hPrevInstance)
    {
        WNDCLASS wc;

        wc.lpszClassName = "MainWindow";
        wc.lpszMenuName  = "MainMenu";
        wc.lpfnWndProc   = MainWndProc;
        wc.style         = CS_DBLCLKS;
        wc.hInstance     = hInstance;
        wc.hIcon         = LoadIcon(hInstance, "Fractal");
        wc.hCursor       = LoadCursor(NULL, IDC_ARROW);
        wc.hbrBackground = GetStockObject(BLACK_BRUSH);
        wc.cbClsExtra    = 0;
        wc.cbWndExtra    = 0;

    if(!RegisterClass(&wc))
        return(FALSE);
    }

    hThisInstance = hInstance;

    /* Base the size and position of the window on the screen
       dimensions.
    */
    Dim.x = GetSystemMetrics(SM_CXSCREEN);
    Dim.y = GetSystemMetrics(SM_CYSCREEN);

    HWND hWnd = CreateWindow(
        "MainWindow",
        "Demo Application for Fractal DLL",
        WS_OVERLAPPED | WS_CAPTION | WS_SYSMENU | WS_MINIMIZEBOX,
        Dim.x / 4,
        Dim.y / 4,
        Dim.x / 2,
        Dim.y / 2,
```

```
            NULL,
            NULL,
            hInstance,
            NULL
    );

    if(hWnd == NULL)
        return(FALSE);

    /* Display the window */
    ShowWindow(hWnd, nCmdShow);

    /* Display the introduction */
    About(hWnd);

    if( CurrentDrawing == NULL)
        return(FALSE);

    /* Match the displayed palette to the drawing palette */
    HDC hWndDC = GetDC(hWnd);
    Palette.SetPalette(hWndDC);
    RealizePalette(hWndDC);
    ReleaseDC(hWnd, hWndDC);

    /* Enter the message loop */
    BOOL Done = FALSE;
    while(Done == FALSE)
    {
        while(PeekMessage(&msg, NULL, NULL, NULL, PM_REMOVE))
        {
            if(msg.message == WM_QUIT)
            {
                Done = TRUE;
                break;
            }
            else
            {
                TranslateMessage(&msg);
                DispatchMessage(&msg);
            }
        }
        if(!Done)
        {
            if((DrawingFractal == TRUE) && (Zoom.Active == FALSE))
                CurrentDrawing->DrawFractal(hWnd);
            else
                WaitMessage();
        }
    }

    /* Exit the application */
    return(msg.wParam);
}
```

The DRAWING.CPP file contains the member functions for the DRAWING object class defined in WFRACTAL.H. This object class performs most of the function calls to the Fractal DLL for creating and generating a fractal drawing.

**drawing.cpp**

```
#include "wfractal.h"
#include "zoom.h"

/* We need to include STDIO.H to use the sscanf() function */
#include <stdio.h>

void DRAWING::InvalidateRect(HWND hWnd)
{
    /* We need to update the upper-left portion of the screen for
       all symmetries.
    */
    ::InvalidateRect(hWnd, &Rect, FALSE);

    switch(Symmetry)
    {
        RECT SymRect;

        case XY_AXIS:
            SymRect.top = Rect.top;
            SymRect.left = Dim.x - Rect.right;
            SymRect.bottom = Dim.y - Rect.top;
            SymRect.right = Dim.x - Rect.left;
            ::InvalidateRect(hWnd, &SymRect, FALSE);

            /* Update the lower righthand section of the screen */
            SymRect.top = Dim.y - Rect.bottom;
            SymRect.left = Dim.x - Rect.right;
            SymRect.bottom = Dim.y - Rect.top;
            SymRect.right = Dim.x - Rect.left;
            ::InvalidateRect(hWnd, &SymRect, FALSE);

            /* Fall through to X_AXIS Symmetry */

        case X_AXIS:
            /* Update the bottom section of the screen */
            SymRect.top = Dim.y - Rect.bottom;
            SymRect.left = Rect.left;
            SymRect.bottom = Dim.y - Rect.top;
            SymRect.right = Rect.right;
            ::InvalidateRect(hWnd, &SymRect, FALSE);
            break;

        case ORIGIN:
            /* Update the lower right-hand section of the screen */
            SymRect.top = Dim.y - Rect.bottom;
            SymRect.left = Dim.x - Rect.right;
            SymRect.bottom = Dim.y - Rect.top;
            SymRect.right = Dim.x - Rect.left;
            ::InvalidateRect(hWnd, &SymRect, FALSE);
            break;

        case NO_SYMMETRY:
        default:
            break;
    }
}
```

```
void DRAWING::SetPixel(unsigned char c)
{
   SetPixel(x, y, c);
   switch(Symmetry)
   {
      case XY_AXIS:
         SetPixel(Dim.x - x - 1, Dim.y - y - 1, c);
         SetPixel(Dim.x - x - 1, y, c);
         SetPixel(x, Dim.y - y - 1, c);
         break;

      case X_AXIS:
         /* The bottom half is a mirror image of the top half. */
         SetPixel(x, Dim.y - y - 1, c);
         break;

      case ORIGIN:
         /* The bottom half is the reverse of the top half. */
         SetPixel(Dim.x - x - 1, Dim.y - y - 1, c);
         break;

      case NO_SYMMETRY:
      default:
         break;
   }
}


DRAWING::DRAWING(HWND hWnd, unsigned xDim, unsigned yDim)
{
   /* Save the screen dimmensions */
   DRAWING::Dim.x = xDim;
   DRAWING::Dim.y = yDim;
   Fractal = NULL;
   x = y = 0;

   /* Get the device context for the window */
   HDC hWndDC = GetDC(hWnd);

   /* Create a memory device context that matches the machines
      display.
   */
   hDC = CreateCompatibleDC(hWndDC);
   ReleaseDC(hWnd, hWndDC);

   /* Create a memory bitmap that matches the display */
   if(hDC)
   {
      switch(Palette.Colors())
      {
         case 256:   // 256 color VGA display or true color
            hBitmap = CreateBitmap(Dim.x, Dim.y, 1, 8, NULL);
            break;

         case 16:    // 16 color EGA display
            hBitmap = CreateBitmap(Dim.x, Dim.y, 4, 1, NULL);
            break;
```

```
            case 4:      // 4 color CGA display
               hBitmap = CreateBitmap(Dim.x, Dim.y, 1, 2, NULL);
               break;

            case 2:      // Monochrome
               hBitmap = CreateBitmap(Dim.x, Dim.y, 1, 1, NULL);
      }

      if(hBitmap)
      {
         /* Tell the device context to use the memory bitmap and
            save currently used by the device context.
         */
         hOldBitmap = SelectObject(hDC, hBitmap);
         Palette.SetPalette(hDC);

         /* Set all the pixels to black */
            PatBlt(hDC, 0, 0, Dim.x, Dim.y, BLACKNESS);
      }
   }
   SetDefaults(hWnd, FractNum);
}

DRAWING::~DRAWING()
{
   if(Fractal != NULL)
      DeleteFractal(NULL);

   /* Select the original bitmap before deleting the current
      bitmap and then delete the memory device context.
   */
   SelectObject(hDC, hOldBitmap);
   DeleteObject(hBitmap);
   DeleteDC(hDC);
}

void DRAWING::DrawFractal(HWND hWnd)
{
   unsigned char Color;
   unsigned n = 0;

   /* Activate the fractal */
   if(!ActivateFractal(Fractal))
      return;

   if(Fractal == NULL)
      return;

   /* Save the values of 'x' and 'y' before we get started */
   Rect.top = y;
   Rect.left = x;

   /* Calculate the number of iterations called for by the
      'PollingFreq' variable and then check for system messages.
   */
   while(n < PollingFreq)
   {
      /* Get the pixel color for the fractal */
```

```
        Color = (unsigned char)FractalPoint(Fractal, x, y);

        /* Monitor the total number of iterations calculated */
        n += Color;

        /* Display the inside of the fractal in blue */
        if(Color == maxit)
            Color = 1;
        if(Color > Palette.Colors())
            Color &= Palette.Colors() - 1;
        SetPixel(Color);

        /* Check on the limit of 'x' and 'y' */
        if(++x == Limit.x)
        {
          x = 0;
          if(++y == Limit.y)
          {
            /* We've finished the drawing! */
            DrawingFractal = FALSE;
            break;
          }
        }
    }
  }

  /* Display what we've done thus far */
  Rect.bottom = y + 1;
  if(y == Rect.top)
    Rect.right = x;
  else
  {
    Rect.left = 0;
    Rect.right = Dim.x;
  }
  InvalidateRect(hWnd);

  /* Time to check on the system messages.  Idle the fractal
     memory resourses while the computer is released to process
     system messages.
  */
  IdleFractal(Fractal);
}

void DRAWING::Display(HDC hDestDC, RECT Rect)
{
  BitBlt(hDestDC, Rect.left, Rect.top, Rect.right - Rect.left + 1,
      Rect.bottom - Rect.top + 1, hDC, Rect.left, Rect.top, SRCCOPY);
}

void DRAWING::SetDefaults(HWND hWnd, WORD FractNum)
{
  char DefStr[] = "%d, %lg, %lg, %lg, %lg, %ld, %lg, %lg, %lg, \
%lg, %d, %d";
  char Scratch[240];

  ::FractNum = FractNum;

  /* Get the default characteristics of the fractal */
```

829

```
      ATOM DefAtom = FractalDefaults(FractNum);
      GlobalGetAtomName(DefAtom, Scratch, sizeof(Scratch));
      sscanf(Scratch, DefStr, &AvailMathTypes, &Left, &Right, &Top,
         &Bottom, &maxit, &p1x, &p1y, &p2x, &p2y, &Symmetry,
         &AtPointFractal);

      switch(Symmetry)
      {
         case XY_AXIS:
            Limit.x = Dim.x / 2;
            Limit.y = Dim.y / 2;
            break;

         case X_AXIS:
         case ORIGIN:
            Limit.x = Dim.x;
            Limit.y = Dim.y / 2;
            break;

         case NO_SYMMETRY:
         default:
            Limit = Dim;
      }

      if((MathType & AvailMathTypes) == 0)
      {
         SetMath(hWnd, IDM_FLOAT);
         MessageBox(hWnd, "The current math type is not supported by \
this fractal type. Floating-point math has been set.", "Note. . .",
            MB_OK | MB_ICONASTERISK);
      }
}

void DRAWING::CreateFractal(HWND hWnd, WORD FractNum)
{
   if(Fractal != NULL)
      DeleteFractal(hWnd);

   SetDefaults(hWnd, FractNum);

   /* Call the DLL CreateFractal() function */
   Fractal = ::CreateFractal(FractNum, Dim.x, Dim.y, MathType, Left,
            Right, Top, Bottom, maxit, p1x, p1y, p2x, p2y);

   /* If everything went correctly, draw the fractal */
   if(Fractal != NULL)
      DrawingFractal = TRUE;
}

void DRAWING::FractalAtPoint(HWND hWnd, POINT Point)
{
   char Scratch[100];

   if(Fractal == NULL)
      return;

   /* Grab the associated fractal parameters before we delete the
```

```
    fractal */
ATOM Atom = AssocFractDefaults(Fractal, Point.x, Point.y);
DeleteFractal(hWnd);

/* Get the normal defaults */
SetDefaults(hWnd, AtPointFractal);

/* Set the associated parameters */
GlobalGetAtomName(Atom, Scratch, sizeof(Scratch));
sscanf(Scratch, "%lg, %lg, %lg, %lg", &p1x, &p1y, &p2x, &p2y);

/* Call the DLL CreateFractal() function */
Fractal = ::CreateFractal(FractNum, Dim.x, Dim.y, MathType, Left,
         Right, Top, Bottom, maxit, p1x, p1y, p2x, p2y);

/* If everything went correctly, draw the fractal */
if(Fractal != NULL)
    DrawingFractal = TRUE;
}

void DRAWING::ZoomFractal(HWND hWnd)
{
    if(Fractal != NULL)
        DeleteFractal(hWnd);

    /* Determine the scale of the currrent drawing */
    double xScale = (Right - Left) / Dim.x;
    double yScale = (Top - Bottom) / Dim.y;
    if(xScale < 0) xScale = -xScale;
    if(yScale < 0) yScale = -yScale;

    /* Translate the origin of 'Zoom' from the upper lefthand corner
       to the center of the screen and flip the y-axis. */
    Zoom.Center.x -= Dim.x / 2;
    Zoom.Center.y = -(Zoom.Center.y - (Dim.y / 2));

    /* Calculate a new center */
    double dxCenter = (Left + Right) / 2;
    double dyCenter = (Top + Bottom) / 2;
    dxCenter += xScale * Zoom.Center.x;
    dyCenter += yScale * Zoom.Center.y;

    /* Calculate the extent */
    Left   = dxCenter - (xScale * Zoom.Dim.x);
    Right  = dxCenter + (xScale * Zoom.Dim.x);
    Top    = dyCenter + (yScale * Zoom.Dim.y);
    Bottom = dyCenter - (yScale * Zoom.Dim.y);

    /* Disable symmetry */
    Limit = Dim;
    Symmetry = NO_SYMMETRY;

    /* Call the DLL CreateFractal() function */
    Fractal = ::CreateFractal(FractNum, Dim.x, Dim.y, MathType, Left,
             Right, Top, Bottom, maxit, p1x, p1y, p2x, p2y);

    /* If everything went correctly, draw the fractal */
    if(Fractal != NULL)
       DrawingFractal = TRUE;
```

```
}

void DRAWING::DeleteFractal(HWND hWnd)
{
    /* Reset the current coordinates to the upper left-hand corner */
    x = y = 0;

    /* Tell the DLL we're no longer generating this fractal */
    if(Fractal != NULL)
    {
        DestroyFractal(Fractal);
        Fractal = NULL;
    }

    /* Clear the old drawing out of the bitmap */
    PatBlt(hDC, 0, 0, Dim.x, Dim.y, BLACKNESS);

    if(hWnd != NULL)
    {
        Rect.top = Rect.left = 0;
        Rect.right = Dim.x;
        Rect.bottom = Dim.y;

        /* Erase the window display with the background color */
        ::InvalidateRect(hWnd, &Rect, TRUE);
    }

    /* Toggle off the 'DrawingFractal' flag. Now the message loop
       will call the WaitMessage() function and not hog a good chunk
       of the computer processing time.
    */
    DrawingFractal = FALSE;
}
```

The INTRO.CPP file contains the About() function definition for calling the introductory dialog box and the AboutDlgProc() function for processing messages for the dialog box window.

**intro.cpp**

```
#include "wfractal.h"

#pragma argsused
BOOL FAR PASCAL AboutDlgProc(HWND hDlg, unsigned msg, WORD wParam,
    LONG lParam)
{
    switch(msg)
    {
        case WM_INITDIALOG:
            HWND hButton = GetDlgItem(hDlg, ID_OK);
            SetFocus(hButton);
            break;

        case WM_COMMAND:
            EndDialog(hDlg, 0);
            break;

        default:
```

```
                return(FALSE);
        }
        return(TRUE);
}

void About(HWND hWnd)
{
    HANDLE hInstance = GetWindowWord(hWnd, GWW_HINSTANCE);
    DialogBox(hInstance, "ABOUT", hWnd, (FARPROC)AboutDlgProc);
}
```

The WFRACTAL.RC and WFRACTAL.DLG files contain the resource script for defining the menu and dialog box used in the application. The WFRACTAL.RC file also contains resource declarations for the WFRACTAL.ICO icon and ATPOINT.CUR cursor files.

### wfractal.rc

```
#include "wfractal.h"
#include <windows.h>
#include "about.dlg"

Fractal ICON DISCARDABLE PRELOAD WINFRACT.ICO

MainMenu MENU
{
  POPUP "&File"
  {
     MENUITEM "E&xit",    IDM_EXIT
     MENUITEM SEPARATOR
     MENUITEM "&About",   IDM_ABOUT
  }
  POPUP "&Math"
  {
  MENUITEM "&Fixed Point",         IDM_FIXED, CHECKED
  MENUITEM "&Quick Float",         IDM_QFLOAT
  MENUITEM "F&loating Point",      IDM_FLOAT
  }

  POPUP "F&ractal"
  {
     MENUITEM SEPARATOR
     MENUITEM "&At Point",        IDM_ATPOINT, GRAYED, INACTIVE
  }
}

ATPOINT_CUR CURSOR atpoint.cur
```

### about.dlg

```
ABOUT DIALOG DISCARDABLE LOADONCALL PURE MOVEABLE 24, 18, 108, 75
STYLE WS_POPUP | WS_CAPTION | WS_SYSMENU | 0x80L
CAPTION "About Fractal DLL . . . ."
BEGIN
   CONTROL "Fractal DLL" 101, "STATIC", WS_CHILD | WS_VISIBLE | 0x1L,
32, 9, 45, 12
   CONTROL "(C) 1991 Mark Peterson" 102, "STATIC", WS_CHILD |
WS_VISIBLE | 0x1L, 10, 25, 89, 12
```

```
    CONTROL "All Rights Reserved" 103, "STATIC", WS_CHILD |
WS_VISIBLE | Ox1L, 15, 37, 78, 11
    CONTROL "OK" 104, "BUTTON", WS_CHILD | WS_VISIBLE | WS_TABSTOP,
38, 55, 32, 12
    CONTROL "FRACTAL" 105, "STATIC", WS_CHILD | WS_VISIBLE | Ox3L, 10,
4, 17, 17
END
```

The PALETTE.H file contains the PC_PALETTE object class definition for automatically creating a Windows palette at run time.

**palette.h**
```
#ifndef PALETTE_H
#define PALETTE_H

/* The PC_PALETTE class creates a palette compatible with the hardware
   available at run-time. */
class PC_PALETTE
{
   HANDLE hPalMemory;
   HPALETTE hPalette;
   int NumColors;

public:
   PC_PALETTE();
   ~PC_PALETTE()
   {
      if(hPalette)
         DeleteObject(hPalette);
      if(hPalMemory)
         GlobalFree(hPalMemory);
   }
   HPALETTE Handle() { return(hPalette); }
   Colors() { return(NumColors); }
   HPALETTE SetPalette(HDC hDC)
   {
      if(hPalette)
         return(SelectPalette(hDC, hPalette, TRUE));
      return(NULL);
   }
};

#endif
```

The PALETTE.CPP file contains the constructor function for the PC_PALETTE class, which automatically creates a DIB palette using the default Windows palette.

**palette.cpp**
```
#include "wfractal.h"

PC_PALETTE::PC_PALETTE()
{
   hPalette = NULL;
   hPalMemory = NULL;

   /* Get the display characteristics */
   HDC hDC = GetDC(NULL);
   int PalSize = GetDeviceCaps (hDC, SIZEPALETTE);
```

834

```
    int RasterCaps = GetDeviceCaps (hDC, RASTERCAPS);
    RasterCaps = (RasterCaps & RC_PALETTE) ? TRUE : FALSE;
    if(RasterCaps)
        NumColors = GetDeviceCaps(hDC, SIZEPALETTE);
    else
        NumColors = GetDeviceCaps(hDC, NUMCOLORS);
    ReleaseDC(NULL, hDC);

    if((NumColors < 0) || (NumColors > 256))
        NumColors = 256;

    PalSize = sizeof(LOGPALETTE) + (sizeof(PALETTEENTRY) * NumColors);
    hPalMemory = GlobalAlloc(GMEM_MOVEABLE, PalSize);
    LPLOGPALETTE pLogPal = (LPLOGPALETTE)GlobalLock(hPalMemory);
    if(pLogPal == NULL)
        return;

    pLogPal->palVersion    = 0x300;
    pLogPal->palNumEntries = NumColors;
    for(unsigned n = 0; n < NumColors; n++)
    {
        pLogPal->palPalEntry[n].peRed   = n;
        pLogPal->palPalEntry[n].peGreen = 0;
        pLogPal->palPalEntry[n].peBlue  = 0;
        pLogPal->palPalEntry[n].peFlags = PC_EXPLICIT;
    }

    /* Swap the blue and red colors */
    if(NumColors < 0 || NumColors > 4)
    {
        pLogPal->palPalEntry[1].peRed = 4;
        pLogPal->palPalEntry[4].peRed = 1;
    }

    hPalette = CreatePalette(pLogPal);
    GlobalUnlock(hPalMemory);
}
```

The ZOOM.H file contains the ZOOM object class definition for controlling the user interface during fractal zoom operations.

**zoom.h**
```
#ifndef ZOOM_H
#define ZOOM_H

/* The ZOOM structure is used to size and move the zoom box. */
struct ZOOM
{
    BOOL Active, Moving, Sizing;
    POINT Center, Dim, InitPos;
    HBRUSH hBrush;
    HPEN hPen;
    RECT Rect;

    ZOOM();
    void StartMoving(HWND hWnd, LONG lParam);
    void Move(HWND hWnd, LONG lParam);
    void StopMoving(HWND hWnd, LONG lParam);
    void StartSizing(HWND hWnd, LONG lParam);
```

835

```
    void Size(HWND hWnd, LONG lParam);
    void StopSizing(HWND hWnd, LONG lParam);
    void Escape(HWND hWnd);
    void XorBox(HWND hWnd);
    BOOL Execute(HWND hWnd, LONG lParam);
};

extern  ZOOM Zoom;

#endif
```

The ZOOM.CPP file contains the member function definitions for the ZOOM object class. It automatically creates the required pen and brush objects when constructed. The destructor deletes the painting objects.

**zoom.cpp**

```
    #include "wfractal.h"
    #include "zoom.h"

    ZOOM Zoom;

    ZOOM::ZOOM()
    {
        Sizing = Moving = Active = FALSE;
        hBrush = GetStockObject(BLACK_BRUSH);
        hPen = GetStockObject(WHITE_PEN);
    }

    inline unsigned iabs(int x)
    {
        if(x < 0)
            return(-x);
        return(x);
    }

    void ZOOM::XorBox(HWND hWnd)
    {
        HDC hDC;
        HANDLE hOldBrush, hOldPen;
        int OldMode;

        hDC = GetDC(hWnd);

        hOldBrush = SelectObject(hDC, hBrush);
        hOldPen = SelectObject(hDC, hPen);
        OldMode = SetROP2(hDC, R2_XORPEN);

        Rectangle(hDC, Center.x - Dim.x, Center.y - Dim.y,
                    Center.x + Dim.x, Center.y + Dim.y);

        SelectObject(hDC, hOldBrush);
        SelectObject(hDC, hOldPen);
        SetROP2(hDC, OldMode);

        ReleaseDC(hWnd, hDC);
    }
```

```
void ZOOM::StartSizing(HWND hWnd, LONG lParam)
{
   GetClientRect(hWnd, &Rect);
   Center = MAKEPOINT(lParam);
   Dim.x = Dim.y = 2;
   XorBox(hWnd);
   Active = Sizing = TRUE;
   SetCapture(hWnd);
}

void ZOOM::Size(HWND hWnd, LONG lParam)
{
   POINT NewDim, NewPoint;
   unsigned ScaledY;
   unsigned xdots = CurrentDrawing->Dim.x;
   unsigned ydots = CurrentDrawing->Dim.y;

   NewPoint = MAKEPOINT(lParam);
   NewDim.x = iabs(Center.x - NewPoint.x);
   NewDim.y = iabs(Center.y - NewPoint.y);
   ScaledY = (unsigned)(((long)NewDim.y) * xdots / ydots);
   if(NewDim.x  < ScaledY)
      NewDim.x  = ScaledY;
   else
      NewDim.y  = (unsigned)(((long)NewDim.x) * ydots / xdots);

   if(NewDim.x   < 2)
      NewDim.x   = 2;
   if(NewDim.y   < 2)
      NewDim.y   = 2;

   if((NewDim.x != Dim.x) || (NewDim.y != Dim.y))
   {
      XorBox(hWnd);
      Dim = NewDim;
      XorBox(hWnd);
   }
}

void ZOOM::StopSizing(HWND hWnd, LONG lParam)
{
   Sizing = FALSE;
   ReleaseCapture();
   POINT p = MAKEPOINT(lParam);
   if((p.x < Rect.left)  || (p.y < Rect.top) ||
   (p.x > Rect.right)    || (p.y > Rect.bottom))
   Escape(hWnd);
}

void ZOOM::Escape(HWND hWnd)
{
   Active = Sizing = Moving = FALSE;
   XorBox(hWnd);
}

void ZOOM::StartMoving(HWND hWnd, LONG lParam)
{
```

```
   POINT Dist;

   InitPos = MAKEPOINT(lParam);
   Dist.x = iabs(InitPos.x - Center.x);
   Dist.y = iabs(InitPos.y - Center.y);
   if((Dist.x < Dim.x) && (Dist.y < Dim.y))
   {
      Moving = TRUE;
      SetCapture(hWnd);
   }
}

void ZOOM::Move(HWND hWnd, LONG lParam)
{
   POINT NewPos;

   XorBox(hWnd);
   NewPos = MAKEPOINT(lParam);
   Center.x += NewPos.x - InitPos.x;
   Center.y += NewPos.y - InitPos.y;
   XorBox(hWnd);
   InitPos = NewPos;
}


void ZOOM::StopMoving(HWND hWnd, LONG lParam)
{
   Moving = FALSE;
   ReleaseCapture();
   POINT p = MAKEPOINT(lParam);
   if((p.x < Rect.left) || (p.y < Rect.top) ||
      (p.x > Rect.right) || (p.y > Rect.bottom))
      Escape(hWnd);
}

BOOL ZOOM::Execute(HWND hWnd, LONG lParam)
{
   RECT Rect;

   Rect.left   = Center.x - Dim.x;
   Rect.top    = Center.y - Dim.y;
   Rect.right  = Center.x + Dim.x;
   Rect.bottom = Center.y + Dim.y;
   POINT p = MAKEPOINT(lParam);
   if((p.x >= Rect.left) && (p.y >= Rect.top) &&
      (p.x <= Rect.right) && (p.y <= Rect.bottom))
   {
      Escape(hWnd);
      return(TRUE);
   }
   return(FALSE);
}
```

The ATPOINT.H file contains the AT_POINT object class definition for controlling the user interface when the [Fractal][At point] menu item is selected.

**atpoint.h**
```
#ifndef ATPOINT_H
#define ATPOINT_H
```

```
struct AT_POINT
{
  BOOL Active;
  HCURSOR hOldCursor, hCross;

  AT_POINT()
  {
    Active = FALSE;
  }
  void Start(HWND hWnd);
  void Execute(HWND hWnd, DWORD Point);
  void Escape();
};

extern AT_POINT AtPoint;

#endif
```

The ATPOINT.CPP file contains the member function definitions for the AT_POINT object class.

**atpoint.cpp**
```
#include "wfractal.h"
#include "atpoint.h"

AT_POINT AtPoint;

void AT_POINT::Start(HWND hWnd)
{
  if(!Active)
  {
    SetCapture(hWnd);
    hCross = LoadCursor(hThisInstance, "ATPOINT_CUR");
    hOldCursor = SetCursor(hCross);
    Active = TRUE;
  }
}

void AT_POINT::Execute(HWND hWnd, DWORD Point)
{
  RECT Rect;

  GetClientRect(hWnd, &Rect);
  POINT p = MAKEPOINT(Point);
  if((p.x >= Rect.left)    && (p.y >= Rect.top) &&
     (p.x < Rect.right)    && (p.y < Rect.bottom))
     CurrentDrawing->FractalAtPoint(hWnd, MAKEPOINT(Point));
  Escape();
}

void AT_POINT::Escape()
{
    SetCursor(hOldCursor);
    ReleaseCapture();
    Active = FALSE;
}
```

TLINK uses the following WFRACTAL.DEF file for setting the initial size of the local heap and the size of the stack.

**wfractal.def**

```
NAME            WFRACTAL

Description     'Demonstration Program for Fractal DLL'

EXETYPE         WINDOWS

STUB            'WINSTUB.EXE'

CODE    PRELOAD MOVEABLE DISCARDABLE

DATA    PRELOAD MOVEABLE

HEAPSIZE        2048
STACKSIZE       10240
```

The following WFRACTAL.MAK file was created from the WFRACTAL.PRJ file using the PRJ2MAK utility. Note that as with the FRACTDLL.MAK file created by the PRJ2MAK utility, many of the warning messages are disabled in the option list for the WFRACTAL.CFG file. These options are actually enabled in the .PRJ file.

**wfractal.mak**

```
.AUTODEPEND

#               *Translator Definitions*
CC = bcc +WFRACTAL.CFG
TASM = TASM
TLIB = tlib
TLINK = tlink
LIBPATH = C:\BORLANDC\LIB
INCLUDEPATH = C:\BORLANDC\INCLUDE;C:\BORLANDC\CLASSLIB\INCLUDE

#               *Implicit Rules*
.c.obj:
  $(CC) -c {$< }

.cpp.obj:
  $(CC) -c {$< }

#               *List Macros*
Link_Exclude =    \
  wfractal.res

Link_Include = \
  atpoint.obj \
  drawing.obj \
  {$(LIBPATH)}fractdll.lib \
  intro.obj \
  palette.obj \
  wfractal.obj \
  wfractal.def \
  zoom.obj
```

```
#                 *Explicit Rules*
wfractal.exe: wfractal.cfg $(Link_Include) $(Link_Exclude)
  $(TLINK) /v/x/c/P-/Vt/Twe/L$(LIBPATH) @&&|
cOws.obj+
atpoint.obj+
drawing.obj+
intro.obj+
palette.obj+
wfractal.obj+
zoom.obj
wfractal
                # no map file
fractdll.lib+
mathws.lib+
import.lib+
cws.lib
wfractal.def
|
  RC wfractal.res wfractal.exe


#                 *Individual File Dependencies*
atpoint.obj: wfractal.cfg atpoint.cpp

drawing.obj: wfractal.cfg drawing.cpp

intro.obj: wfractal.cfg intro.cpp

palette.obj: wfractal.cfg palette.cpp

wfractal.obj: wfractal.cfg wfractal.cpp

wfractal.res: wfractal.cfg wfractal.rc wfractal.h about.dlg
        RC -R -I$(INCLUDEPATH) -FO wfractal.res WFRACTAL.RC

zoom.obj: wfractal.cfg zoom.cpp

#                 *Compiler Configuration File*
wfractal.cfg: wfractal.mak
   copy &&|
-R
-v
-y
-r-
-d
-WS
-vi
-H=WFRACTAL.SYM
-w-ret
-w-nci
-w-inl
-w-par
-w-cpt
-w-dup
-w-pia
-w-ill
-w-sus
-w-ext
```

```
-w-ias
-w-ibc
-w-pre
-w-nst
-I$(INCLUDEPATH)
-L$(LIBPATH)
| wfractal.cfg
```

## Export Function Reference

The majority of the code in FRACTDLL.CPP contains the _export functions which interface with the calling application. The following is a detailed explanation of each export function.

# ActivateFractal

### Purpose

The ActivateFractal() function locks the memory resources associated with a newly created fractal or one that was made idle by a call to the IdleFractal() function.

### Prototype

```
BOOL FAR PASCAL ActivateFractal(FRACTAL Fractal);
```

### Description

When a fractal is created, the Fractal DLL allocates large memory arrays containing the complex numbers associated with each point in a fractal drawing. These arrays are unlocked when a fractal is first created or whenever a call is made to IdleFractal(). The ActivateFractal() function locks the fractals-associated memory arrays.

A fractal should be activated whenever your program is actively drawing a fractal. You should call IdleFractal() before your application returns control to Windows.

Any number of fractals can be active at one time up to the limit of the computer's available memory space.

### Parameters

FRACTAL Fractal

The handle to a fractal created by the CreateFractal() function.

### Returns

Returns TRUE if the memory resources are locked. Returns FALSE if the Fractal DLL is unable to lock the fractals memory, the fractal handle is invalid, or the fractal was not idle.

### Example Usage

```
void DRAWING::DrawFractal(HWND hWnd)
{
    unsigned char Color;
```

```
unsigned n = 0;

/* Activate the fractal */
if(!ActivateFractal(Fractal))
    return;

if(Fractal == NULL)
    return;

/* Save the values of 'x' and 'y' before we get started */
Rect.top = y;
Rect.left = x;

/* Calculate the number of iterations called for by the
    'PollingFreq' variable and then check for system messages.
*/
while(n < PollingFreq)
{
    /* Get the pixel color for the fractal */
    Color = (unsigned char)FractalPoint(Fractal, x++, y);

    /* Monitor the total number of iterations calculated */
    n += Color;

    /* Display the inside of the fractal in blue */
    if(Color == maxit)
        Color = 1;
    if(Color > Palette.Colors())
        Color &= Palette.Colors() - 1;
    SetPixel(Color);

    /* Check on the limit of 'x' and 'y' */
    if(x == Limit.x)
  {
        x = 0;
        y++;
        if(y == Limit.y)
        {
          /* We've finished the drawing! */
          DrawingFractal = FALSE;
          break;
        }
  }
}

/* Display what we've done thus far */
Rect.bottom = y + 1;
if(y == Rect.top)
    Rect.right = x;
else
{
    Rect.left = 0;
    Rect.right = Dim.x;
}
InvalidateRect(hWnd);

/* Time to check on the system messages.  Idle the fractal
    memory resources while the computer is released to process
```

```
      system messages.
   */
   IdleFractal(Fractal);
}
```

# AssocFractDefaults

## Purpose
The AssocFractDefaults() function is used to determine the appropriate p1x, p1y, p2x, and p2y parameters needed to generate a fractal associated with a specific point on a fractal.

## Prototype
```
ATOM FAR PASCAL AssocFractDefaults(FRACTAL Fractal, unsigned x, unsigned y);
```

## Description
Some fractals, such as the Mandelbrot set, have other fractals associated with different points on the fractal. For example, every point on the Mandelbrot set is associated with a different Julia set. The AssocFractal parameter returned by the FractalDefaults() function specifies the associated fractal type. The AssocFractDefaults() function is called to determine the appropriate p1x, p1y, p2x, and p2y parameters needed to generate the fractal.

## Parameters
```
FRACTAL Fractal
```
The handle to a fractal created by the CreateFractal() function.

```
unsigned x, unsigned y
```
Specifies the pixel coordinates the AssocFractDefaults() function should use to determine the associated fractal parameters.

## Returns
Returns a NULL if the Fractal handle is invalid or there is no fractal associated with the fractal point. Otherwise the function generates a handle to a string on the Global Atom table containing the values of the p1x, p1y, p2x, p2y parameters for the associated fractal. Use the sscanf() function to extract the double values from the string.

## Example Usage
```
    void DRAWING::FractalAtPoint(HWND hWnd, POINT Point)
    {
      char Scratch[100];

      if(Fractal == NULL)
         return;

      /* Grab the associated fractal parameters before we delete the
         fractal */
      ATOM Atom = AssocFractDefaults(Fractal, Point.x, Point.y);
      DeleteFractal(hWnd);
```

```
/* Get the normal defaults */
SetDefaults(hWnd, AtPointFractal);

/* Set the associated parameters */
GlobalGetAtomName(Atom, Scratch, sizeof(Scratch));
sscanf(Scratch, "%lg, %lg, %lg, %lg", &p1x, &p1y, &p2x, &p2y);

/* Call the DLL CreateFractal() function */
Fractal = ::CreateFractal(FractNum, Dim.x, Dim.y, MathType, Left,
        Right, Top, Bottom, maxit, p1x, p1y, p2x, p2y);

/* If everything went correctly, draw the fractal */
if(Fractal != NULL)
    DrawingFractal = TRUE;
}
```

# CreateFractal

### Purpose
Use the CreateFractal() function to tell the Fractal DLL the type of fractal you'd like to generate.

### Prototype
```
FRACTAL FAR PASCAL CreateFractal(unsigned FractNum, unsigned xdots,
        unsigned ydots, MATHTYPE MathType, double Left, double Right,
        double Top, double Bottom, unsigned long maxit, double p1x, double
        p1y, double p2x, double p2y);
```

### Description
The CreateFractal function informs the Fractal DLL about the type of fractal you'd like to generate, the size, the type of math to use, and other miscellaneous information. This function must be called before calls are made to FractalPoint() to obtain the coloration of the fractal points.

The fractal is idle after it is created. Use the ActivateFractal() to lock the fractal memory before calling FractalPoint() to determine the color of each point in the fractal.

### Parameters
unsigned FractNum
    The identification number associated with a fractal type. Use FractalName() to identify the name associated with the fractal.

unsigned xdots, unsigned ydots
    The xdots and ydots parameters specify the size of the fractal. They should be the same size as the target image. The Fractal DLL uses this information to allocate memory for two number arrays. These number arrays are used to provide high-speed lookup of the coordinates to associate with a given point.

MATHTYPE MathTyp
    The Fractal DLL supports three different math formats, normally type double, QFLOAT, and FIXED<16>. These correspond to the D_MATH, Q_MATH, and

F_MATH enumerations, respectively. The MathType parameter requests the Fractal DLL to generate the fractal using the given math type. Note that not all math types are supported for the different fractals. For example, the CreateFractal() function will return a NULL handle if an attempt is made to generate a Newton fractal type using the F_MATH. Use the FractalDefaults() function to obtain the math type recommended by the Fractal DLL.

### double Left, double Right, double Top, double Bottom

These four parameters provide the Fractal DLL with the coordinate information needed to build the two number arrays. The Left and Right parameters specify the range of the fractal along the x-axis of the Cartesian plane. The Top and Bottom parameters specify the domain along the y-axis. The FRACTDLL uses these values to relate the screen coordinates to coordinates on the Cartesian plane. For example, values of -2.0, 2.0, 1.5, and -1.5 for Left, Right, Top, and Bottom mean that the pixel at screen coordinate (0, 0) corresponds to the Cartesian coordinate (-2.0, 1.5). Use the FractalDefaults() function to obtain a set of parameters that will result in a good image.

### unsigned long maxit

Normally, the return value of the FractalPoint() is the number of iterations performed before an iteration calculation exceeded some predetermined value. This predetermined value will never be exceeded for some points. The maxit parameter tells the Fractal DLL the maximum number of iterations it should calculate before forcing a return from a FractalPoint() function call.

### double p1x, double p1y, double p2x, double p2y

The meaning of these parameters varies for different fractal types and they are not always used. Call the FractParamOne() function to obtain descriptive text on how the Fractal DLL uses p1x and p2y for a given fractal type. The FractParamTwo() function returns text on the usage of the p2x and p2y parameters. Use the FractDefaults() function to get the recommended values from the Fractal DLL.

## Returns

The value returned by CreateFractal is a 16-bit handle to a fractal. This handle is then used in other Fractal DLL functions to reference a fractal being generated. CreateFractal() returns NULL if the Fractal DLL cannot generate the requested fractal. This could be due to insufficient memory, an invalid fractal type, or if a math type other than D_MATH was requested on an XT or AT class machine.

## Example Usage

The following code calls CreateFractal() using the default values returned by FractalDefaults():

```
#include "fractdll.h"
    MATHTYPE MathType;
    double Left, Right, Top, Bottom;
    unsigned long maxit;
    double p1x, p1y, p2x, p2y;
    SYMMETRY Symmetry;
```

```
FRACTAL CallFractCreate(unsigned FractNum)
{
    FRACTAL Fractal;
    ATOM DefAtom;
    char DefStr[] = "%d, %lg, %lg, %lg, %lg, %ld, %lg, %lg, %lg, \
%lg, %d";
    char Scratch[240];

    /* Get the default characteristics of the fractal */
    DefAtom = FractalDefaults(FractNum);
    GlobalGetAtomName(DefAtom, Scratch, sizeof(Scratch));

    /* Scan the string for default values */
    sscanf(Scratch, DefStr, &MathType, &Left, &Right, &Top, &Bottom,
            &maxit, &p1x, &p1y, &p2x, &p2y, &Symmetry, &AssocFractal);

    /* Call the DLL CreateFractal() function */
    Fractal = CreateFractal(FractNum, Dim.x, Dim.y, MathType, Left,
            Right, Top, Bottom, maxit, p1x, p1y, p2x, p2y);
    return(Fractal);
}
```

# DestroyFractal

## Purpose
Use to release the memory resources allocated by the Fractal DLL to generate a specific fractal.

## Prototype
```
BOOL FAR PASCAL DestroyFractal(FRACTAL Fractal);
```

## Description
The Fractal DLL allocates local and global memory to contain information related to the generation of a fractal. The DestroyFractal() function frees this memory.

## Parameters
FRACTAL Fractal
    The handle of the fractal used to destroy. This must be a handle previously returned by a call to the CreateFractal() function.

## Returns
Returns TRUE if the fractal is destroyed. The return value is FALSE if the Fractal parameter is not a valid handle.

## Example Usage
```
    #include "fractdll.h"

    FRACTAL Fractal;
```

847

```
. . .
    /* Create a fractal */
    Fractal = CreateFractal(FractNum, Dim.x, Dim.y, MathType, Left,
                Right, Top, Bottom, maxit, p1x, p1y, p2x, p2y);

. . .
    /* Generate the fractal drawing here */
. . .

    /* Tell the Fractal DLL you're finished */
    DestroyFractal(Fractal);
```

# FractalDLLVersion

### Purpose
Use to determine the user's Fractal DLL version at run time.

### Prototype
`unsigned FAR PASCAL FractalDLLVersion();`

### Description
The FRACTDLL.H header file is used to build FRACTDLL.DLL and should also be used to build any application that uses the DLL. This header file contains the macro DLL_VERSION, which is defined as the version number for the DLL. The FractalDLLVersion() function returns the value of this macro. The return value of the FractDLLVersion() function would normally be used to ensure that Windows did not load an obsolete version of the DLL.

### Parameters
None

### Returns
Returns the version number of the Fractal DLL times 100. For example, Version 1.00 of the Fractal DLL returns a value of 100.

### Example Usage
The ValidateDLLVersion() function displays a warning message and returns FALSE if the Fractal DLL version loaded by Windows is older than the required version.

```
#include "fractdll.h"

BOOL ValidateDLLVersion(unsigned ReqVer)
{
    unsigned VerNum = FractalDLLVersion();

    if(VerNum < ReqVer)
    {
        char MsgStr[120];
```

```
        wsprintf(MsgStr, "You're using Fractal DLL Version %d.%.2d. \
This application requires Version %d.%.2d or better.", VerNum /
        100, VerNum % 100, ReqVer / 100, ReqVer % 100);
        MessageBox(GetFocus(), MsgStr, "Obsolete Version"!,
                MB_ICONEXCLAMATION | MB_OK);
        return(FALSE);
    }
    return(TRUE);
}
```

# FractalDefaults

### Purpose

The FractalDefaults() function is used to obtain the default parameters associated with a fractal.

### Prototype

`ATOM FAR PASCAL FractalDefaults(unsigned FractNum);`

### Description

The FractalDefaults() function returns a string containing the default settings recommended by the DLL to generate a fractal type. It also provides information on the type of symmetry associated with the fractal and any other fractal type that is associated with the points in a drawing.

### Parameters

`unsigned FractNum`
 An index to the Fractal DLL's list of available fractal types.

### Returns

Returns a handle to a string on the Global Atom table containing the default information. The string has the following format:

```
        MATHTYPE AvailMathTypes, double Left, double Right, double Top,
        double Bottom, unsigned long maxit, double p1x, double p1y, double
        p2x, double p2y, unsigned Symmetry, int AtPointFractal
```

The AvailMathTypes parameter contains the composite number of the math types that can be used to generate the fractal. If the machine at run time does not have an 80386 or better microprocessor, then only the double math type will be available. Note that type double math is always available for all fractal types and all machines. Use a bitwise AND to determine if a math type is available. For example, the following determines if the FIXED math format is available:

```
        if(AvailMathTypes & F_MATH)
        {
          . . .
```

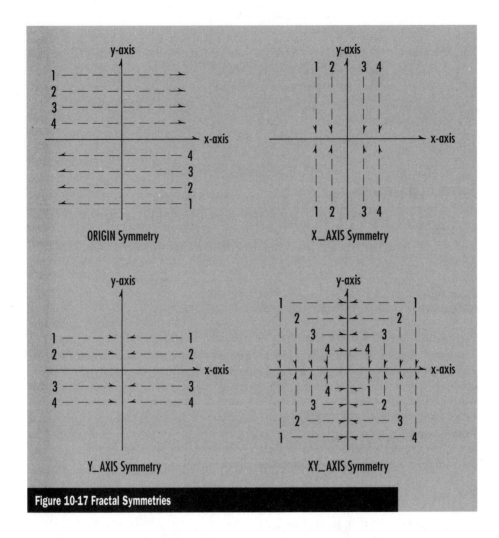

Figure 10-17 Fractal Symmetries

The Left, Right, Top, and Bottom parameters are the coordinates that usually provide an overall view of the fractal.

The maxit parameter is the recommended maximum iteration level.

The p1x, p1y, p2x, p2y parameters are the recommended default parameters that should be used with CreateFractal(). Note that with some fractals, such as the Julia set, changing these parameters will produce an entirely different fractal. Use the FractalParamOne() and FractalParamTwo() functions to determine how these parameters are used to generate the fractal.

The Symmetry parameter describes the symmetrical characteristics of the fractal. This information can be used to help speed the generation of the drawing. The different types of symmetry are as follows:

ORIGIN    The fractal is symmetrical about the origin. With this type of symmetry, the bottom half of the image is upside-down and leftside-right in comparison to the top half of the image if the origin is in the center of the drawing. All Julia fractals have a symmetry about the origin.

X_AXIS    The fractal is symmetrical about the x-axis. This means the bottom half is a mirror image of the top half if the origin is in the center of the drawing. Mandelbrot fractals are an example of a fractal with a symmetry about the origin.

Y_AXIS    The fractal is symmetrical about the y-axis. This means the right half is a mirror image of the left half if the origin is in the center of the screen. None of the fractals currently supported by this library have y-axis symmettry.

XY_AXIS   The fractal is symmetrical about both the x- and y-axes. This means the upper-lefthand quarter of the image can be used to generate the remaining three quarters. The forth-degree Newton fractal displayed by this library has a symmetry about the x- and y-axis.

Figure 10-17 shows diagrams of each type of symmetry.

The AtPointFractal parameter specifies another fractal type that is associated with each point in the fractal. This value is set to -1 if there is no associated fractal.

### Example Usage

```
void DRAWING::SetDefaults(HWND hWnd, WORD FractNum)
{
  char DefStr[] = "%d, %lg, %lg, %lg, %lg, %ld, %lg, %lg, %lg, \
%lg, %d, %d";
  char Scratch[240];

  /* Get the default characteristics of the fractal */
  ATOM DefAtom = FractalDefaults(FractNum);
  GlobalGetAtomName(DefAtom, Scratch, sizeof(Scratch));
  sscanf(Scratch, DefStr, &AvailMathTypes, &Left, &Right, &Top,
    &Bottom, &maxit, &p1x, &p1y, &p2x, &p2y, &Symmetry,
    &AtPointFractal);
}
```

# FractalName

### Purpose

Determine the fractal type text name associated with a fractal number.

### Prototype

```
ATOM FAR PASCAL FractalName(unsigned FractNum);
```

## Description

The Fractal DLL contains a list of available fractal types. The NumberFractals() function is used to determine the number of fractals in the list. The FractalName() function is used to determine the name of the fractal type associated with an index.

## Parameters

`unsigned FractNum`

An index to the Fractal DLL's list of available fractal types.

## Returns

Returns NULL if the FractNum parameter is an invalid index; otherwise, it returns a handle to a string on the Global Atom table.

## Example Usage

The following example shows how to create a menu of fractal types using the NumberFractals() and FractalName() functions:

```
BOOL CreateFractalMenu(HWND hWnd)
{
  NumFract = NumberFractals();

  /* Add the fractal popup menu to the main menu */
  HMENU hWndMenu = GetMenu(hWnd);
  HMENU hFractMenu = GetSubMenu(hWndMenu, 2);

  /* Add each available fractal to the menu */
  for(unsigned n = 0; n < NumFract; n++)
  {
    char Name[40];

    ATOM FractAtom = FractalName(n);
    if(FractAtom == NULL)
        return(FALSE);
    GlobalGetAtomName(FractAtom, Name, sizeof(Name));
    InsertMenu(hFractMenu, n, MF_ENABLED | MF_STRING |
              MF_BYPOSITION, IDM_FRACTAL + n, Name);
  }
  CheckMenuItem(hFractMenu, FractNum, MF_CHECKED |
                                      MF_BYPOSITION);
  return(TRUE);
}
```

# FractalParamOne, FractalParamTwo

## Purpose

These two functions, FractalParamOne() and FractalParamTwo(), are used to obtain a text description of how the p1x, p1y, p2x, and p2y parameters are used by the Fractal DLL to generate a given fractal type.

## Prototype
```
ATOM FAR PASCAL FractalParamOne(unsigned FractNum);
ATOM FAR PASCAL FractalParamTwo(unsigned FractNum);
```

## Description
The p1x, p1y, p2x, and p2y parameters are used for different purposes for different fractal types. They are not used at all for some fractals. The FractalParamOne() returns a text description for how the p1x and p1y parameters are used in a specific fractal type. The FractalParamTwo() function returns information on the p2x and p2y parameters.

## Parameters
```
unsigned FractNum
```
An index to the Fractal DLL's list of available fractal types.

## Returns
Returns NULL if the index to the fractal type is invalid or the parameter is not used in the fractal generation; otherwise, the two functions return a handle to a string on the Global Atom table.

# FractalPoint

## Purpose
The FractalPoint() function returns the number of iterations associated with a pixel coordinate. This is generally used as the fractal's color.

## Prototype
```
unsigned long FAR PASCAL FractalPoint(FRACTAL Fractal, unsigned x,
unsigned y);
```

## Description
After a fractal is created using the CreateFractal() function and activated using the ActivateFractal() function, the color associated with each point in the fractal drawing is determined using the FractalPoint() function.

## Returns
Returns the number of iterations associated with the pixel coordinate on the fractal. The function returns zero if the handle is invalid or the fractal is idle.

## Example Usage
See the example for the ActivateFractal() function.

# IdleFractal

### Purpose
Unlocks the memory associated with a fractal created by the Fractal DLL.

### Prototype
`BOOL FAR PASCAL IdleFractal(FRACTAL Fractal);`

### Description
The Fractal DLL allocates significant amounts of moveable global memory for each fractal created by the CreateFractal() function. This memory must be locked by a call to the ActivateFractal() function before using a fractal handle. The fractal should be unlocked with a call to the IdleFractal() function before returning control of the computer back to Windows. This enables Windows to efficiently manage the limited memory resources available on the user's computer.

### Parameters
`FRACTAL Fractal`
      The handle of the fractal used to destroy. This must be a handle previously returned by a call to the CreateFractal() function.

### Returns
Returns TRUE if the fractal was previously active. Returns FALSE if the fractal was already idle or the fractal handle is invalid.

### Example Usage
See the example for the ActivateFractal() function.

# NumberFractals

### Purpose
The NumberFractals() function returns the number of fractal types supported by the Fractal DLL.

### Prototype
`unsigned FAR PASCAL NumberFractals();`

### Description
The Fractal DLL contains a list of available fractal types. The NumberFractals() function is used to determine the number of fractals in the list. The FractalName() function is used to determine the name of the fractal type associated with an index.

**Parameters**

None

**Returns**

Returns the number of fractal types supported by the Fractal DLL.

**Example Usage**

See the example for the FractalName() function.

# INDEX

Books have a substantial influence on the destruction of the forests of the Earth. For example, it takes 17 trees to produce one ton of paper. A first printing of 30,000 copies of a typical 480 page book consumes 108,000 pounds of paper which will require 918 trees!

Waite Group Press™ is against the clear-cutting of forests and supports reforestation of the Pacific Northwest of the United States and Canada, where most of this paper comes from. As a publisher with several hundred thousand books sold each year, we feel an obligation to give back to the planet. We will therefore support and contribute a percentage of our proceeds to organizations which seek to preserve the forests of planet Earth.

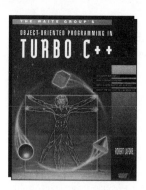

# Save Yourself Time and Trouble with
## The Waite Group's
# Companion Disk for
# *Borland C++ Develop er's Bible*

**H**ave we got a bargain and a time saver for you! Thanks to the magic of compression technology, we've managed to cram 3.4 megabytes of material related to the *Borland C++ Developer's Bible* onto one floppy disk.

**A**ll the C and C++ program listings in the book are included on your choice of 3.5- or 5.25-inch disk formats. The programs are organized in directories and named to match the book's listings. Each program has been pretested and debugged by the author; just load each listing into your compiler and go to it! You can use the program as it is, modify it, or use it to build your own programs. And, as you can see from the program listings in the book, there are plenty of useful programs to choose from. Short program examples will demonstrate how to write professional programs and optimize them using Borland C++'s compilers, the IDE, Make utility, Linker, Turbo Assembler, Turbo Debugger, Profiler, Help compiler, and Resource Utilities. Included is the fascinating, professional-quality Windows fractal generating program that ties all the demonstration programs together. Find all the complete C and C++ programs, assembly routines, macros, library files, and custom functions found in the book.

**S**pend quality time computing, not typing! Only $19.95, plus applicable taxes and shipping fees. To order see the postage-paid order card or extra order form in this book.

# Disk Order Form

Filling out this order form may save your fingers, move you up the corporate ladder, or give you time for a social life. Spend a little time ordering the *Borland C++ Developer's Bible* companion disk and save a lot of typing time. All the program listings contained in this book are on the disk. They're organized to follow the book, pretested and debugged.

**To order by phone call 800-368-9369 or 415-924-2576 (FAX)**
or send to Waite Group Press, 200 Tamal Plaza, Corte Madera, CA 94925

Name

Company

Address
Street Address Only, No P.O. Box

City          State    ZIP          —

Daytime Phone

## Quantity and Type

| Name | Item # | Quantity | Price |
|------|--------|----------|-------|
| The Waite Group's *Borland C++ Developer's Bible* companion disk | WGP-CD13 | ☐ | x $19.95 = |

Sales Tax—California addresses add 7.25% sales tax.

Shipping—Add $5 USA, $10 Canada, or $30 Foreign for shipping and handling. Standard shipping is UPS Ground. Allow 3 to 4 weeks. Prices subject to change. Purchase orders subject to credit approval, and verbal purchase orders will not be accepted.

| | |
|---|---|
| Sales Tax | |
| Shipping | |
| Total Due | |

**Disk Type:** ☐ 5.25-inch  ☐ 3.5-inch

## Method of Payment

Checks or money orders, payable to The Waite Group. To pay by credit card, complete the following:

☐ Visa   ☐ Mastercard   Card Number

Cardholder's Name _____   Exp. Date

Cardholder's Signature _____

Phone Number _____

# —Notes—

# —Notes—

# —Notes—

*Function Jump Table,*
*continued on inside back cover*

# Disk Order Form

Filling out this order form may save your fingers, move you up the corporate ladder, or give you time for a social life. Spend a little time ordering the *Borland C++ Developer's Bible* companion disk and save a lot of typing time. All the program listings contained in this book are on the disk. They're organized to follow the book, pretested and debugged.

## To order by phone call 800-368-9369 or 415-924-2576 (FAX)
### or send to Waite Group Press, 200 Tamal Plaza, Corte Madera, CA 94925

Name

Company

Address
Street Address Only, No P.O. Box

City                    State        ZIP          –

Daytime Phone

## Quantity and Type

| Name | Item # | Quantity | Price |
|------|--------|----------|-------|
| The Waite Group's *Borland C++ Developer's Bible* companion disk | WGP-CD13 | ☐ | x $19.95 = |

Sales Tax—California addresses add 7.25% sales tax.

Shipping—Add $5 USA, $10 Canada, or $30 Foreign for shipping and handling. Standard shipping is UPS Ground. Allow 3 to 4 weeks. Prices subject to change. Purchase orders subject to credit approval, and verbal purchase orders will not be accepted.

**Sales Tax**

**Shipping**

**Total Due**

**Disk Type:** ☐ 5.25-inch  ☐ 3.5-inch

## Method of Payment

Checks or money orders, payable to The Waite Group. To pay by credit card, complete the following:

☐ Visa  ☐ Mastercard     Card Number

Cardholder's Name _____     Exp. Date

Cardholder's Signature _____

Phone Number _____

FOLD HERE

DATE DUE